35° 30'

Spinalonga
(Leper Colony)

Y. NIKOLAOS

GULF of
MERABELLO

SITIA BAY

SITIA

S I T I A

Sfaka

Tourtoula

Stomios

Zakros

THRIFTI
4839'

Stavrokhori

KHANDRA

Ziros

IERAPETRA

nos

35°

25   30   MILES

30   KILOMETERS

26°

R.L. WILLIAMS

CRETE

A CASE STUDY OF AN
UNDERDEVELOPED AREA

CRETE

A CASE STUDY OF
AN UNDERDEVELOPED
AREA

BY LELAND G. ALLBAUGH

FIELD DIRECTOR, CRETE SURVEY

THE ROCKEFELLER FOUNDATION

WITH THE EDITORIAL ASSISTANCE OF

GEORGE SOULE

PRINCETON, NEW JERSEY

PRINCETON UNIVERSITY PRESS

1953

DEDICATION

This book is respectfully dedicated
to those thousands of faithful government, missionary, philanthropic,
and business representatives from the United States,
who, in spite of personal and family sacrifices,
have been or are living in foreign countries
and making lasting contributions to a better understanding
among the peoples of different cultures

FOREWORD

PUBLIC and private organizations in many lands face an urgent current problem: What is to be done about underdeveloped countries the world over? The question is being asked by leaders of the countries themselves. It is being asked by the highly industrialized nations who, in the Atlantic Charter, stated their desire to encourage the spread of industrial development. Where underdeveloped areas are emerging from colonial dependence, they have the double task of establishing their statehood and of securing for their people a higher level of living.

These problems are not unrelated. Nor are they posed in a national vacuum, the sole concern of each country chiefly involved. On the contrary, what happens in areas now underdeveloped is a matter of lively interest to nations already industrialized. They want to help. If their purposes are malevolent, their "helping" will be in terms of their own benefit without regard to injuries done the victim. But even where motives are benevolent, haste and lack of sensitivity may cause irreparable damage. It is imperative that the problems of underdeveloped countries be clearly understood before overt moves are made to assist them.

This is no simple task. "Underdeveloped" may describe the information available about a country as well as its industrial status. There may be few reliable facts to go on. Data, readily accessible in more highly developed countries, may be wholly lacking, or, while apparently available, highly inaccurate.

How, then, can a sound approach be made to this problem? If the people in countries with low levels of living are not to be let alone— either by their leaders or by the outside world—what is an intelligent method of procedure? Two basic truths must undergird the answer. The first is that every culture has its own values—values not to be arbitrarily smothered by the imposition of an alien culture no matter how superior the latter may seem to its proponents. The second is that the life of a people is a rounded entity, its parts so interrelated that abrupt change at one point may have destructive repercussions at many others. And this applies not only to the economic, the political, the social life of a country but also to its spiritual well-being.

With these basic beliefs then in mind, The Rockefeller Foundation undertook a survey of the Island of Crete. This study, begun in 1948, was made at the invitation of the Greek Government to the Interna-

tional Health Division of The Rockefeller Foundation. The cooperation of the Greek Government was generously available throughout.[1] The purpose was to see if the level of living in Crete could
be raised. It was found that there were any number of ways in which
this could be done. Two general methods of approach would be possible: by revolutionary moves initiated and carried out from the top
down; by evolutionary processes set in motion at the grass-roots,
geared to the real desires, capacities, and local needs of the people
themselves. The first method would be quicker, more spectacular, less
apt to stick, more likely to destroy important values caught in the
overriding process. The second would be harder, more demanding of
ingenuity and patience, probably much more enduring.

The Foundation conceived of the project as an experiment in fact-
finding. What should be known about any underdeveloped area before
moves toward its industrialization are made? How much of such
necessary information can be obtained?

There are several ways of finding out about a country. All official
reports may be read: reports by the country itself, reports by outsiders—by United Nations agencies, by private organizations, by
governmental bodies of other nations. All these steps were taken in
launching the study of Crete. Then the country may be visited,
viewed at firsthand through conferences with officials and with various private individuals who live on the spot. This too was done. On
a more professional basis, a series of interviews may be arranged
with specialists in various fields of interest and their views tabulated.
This also was carried through.

Valuable as these approaches are, however, they do not necessarily
furnish a realistic cross section of the life of the people whose level
of living is the prime concern of the inquiry. To get at basic data,
to discover what life is like at the grass-roots, requires some other
method. To meet this need a survey on a sampling basis was planned
—a scientifically selected house-to-house canvass carried out by specially trained Greek interviewers. The results were richly revealing,
and a method may have been set for scientific, factual exploration in
other underdeveloped areas in advance of industrial planning for
their futures.

Evolution to higher levels of living cannot be a speedy matter even
though the need is urgent. Urgency of action must be balanced by

[1] A copy of the letter from the Greek Government inviting The Rockefeller Foundation to conduct the survey will be found in Appendix 1 C6.

democratic procedures and cultural acceptance. Even in Europe and
the United States, the industrial revolution grew from small beginnings. One-man forges made iron utensils, wagon parts, horseshoes,
before there was a steel mill. Before machine tools were even thought
of, people tinkered with simple machinery at crossroads shops. Is it
sensible to reverse the process, to build a modern steel mill in a region
where farmers still lack wagons, roads, metal utensils? Such a venture is likely to be either economically inefficient, if its market is
confined to the locality, or, if its product is exported, a device for
extracting profits for foreign investors. Either way it may be little
more than an enclave in a culture which benefits little from the investment.

This does not mean, however, that each country must go through
the same kind of economic development experienced by the United
States and other industrialized nations. The process may be short-
ened. Isolated areas may never build railroads but may move directly
from crude transportation to the use of trucks and planes. Farming
may change from hand labor or oxen to tractor power without ever
using horse-drawn equipment. But human skills must be developed
along with new techniques. To make good use of modern technology,
a people must be prepared for it. Such preparation takes time. It
requires not only widespread basic education but the employment of
practical reason in the solution of day-to-day problems. It requires,
in addition, a large body of men and women trained in modern science, in technology, in business organization.

A nontechnical culture, moreover, may cherish values that have
little to do with more efficient production and distribution of material
goods. These values may be disrupted by the introduction of alien,
unfamiliar elements. Handicraft skills may be cherished for their
aesthetic or ceremonial meaning. Family organization may be based
upon a household economy. Religious tenets may interpose barriers
to more efficient use of land or animals. In short, the question may
be raised as to whether a people will be happier if their ancient cul-
ture-patterns are broken up for the purpose of providing them with
more of the things considered essential in a Western society. And,
entirely aside from this broader question of the desirability of modern technology, nonmaterial values may interpose thorny obstacles
to its economic use.

Underdeveloped nations need, and most of them want, capital investment from abroad. Yet experience has led them to fear and resent
financial imperialism. This fear is aggravated by propaganda which

attributes the international economic activity of the Western nations to a desire to extend the profits and power of their wealthy minorities. What safeguards for both parties are needed in any given case? How is foreign investment to be extended on terms that will give reasonable assurance that the investment will be productive and safe from political interference, and still not compromise the independence and welfare of the recipient? If available private capital is to find the opportunities in underdeveloped areas attractive and if these areas are to receive maximum benefit, more will be needed than the uncoordinated private investment of the past. And if a series of blunders as well as futile expenditures of energy and money are to be avoided, more detailed and better-coordinated information will be required than exists in many of the regions seeking development.

The Crete Survey defined two principal groups of problems: physical and social. For the consideration of these it tried to marshal inclusive and balanced data. Those directing the survey found this to be an extremely complicated assignment. Fortunately, the problems of health were familiar terrain—Dr. McIntosh's survey reflects the years of experience of the International Health Division in getting at the essentials of public health situations in many countries. For the economic and social survey, Dr. Allbaugh was obliged to develop special methods, thereby, it is believed, breaking new ground in the matter of such surveys in underdeveloped countries. The Rockefeller Foundation acknowledges its debt to Dr. Allbaugh, to Dr. McIntosh, and to their colleagues for the skill, care, and integrity with which they carried out the difficult task of this survey.

With the problems of the physical and social life of the Cretan people high-lighted by the findings of the survey, various possible lines of action emerged. In the belief that both these facts and these recommendations have significance not only for Crete but for underdeveloped areas in other parts of the world, this book is made available to the public.

In view of the number of United Nations and United States agencies that have been working in Greece and Crete, The Rockefeller Foundation has not considered it necessary to implement the recommendations contained in this report.

CHESTER I. BARNARD
President

The Rockefeller Foundation
June 16, 1952

ACKNOWLEDGMENTS

THIS book is the joint effort of many people. It would not have been possible without the encouragement and assistance of Dr. Joseph H. Willits, Director, and Dr. Norman S. Buchanan, Associate Director, for the Social Sciences of The Rockefeller Foundation. The very adequate statements on the survey methodology in Appendix 1 and Chapter 1 were prepared by Dr. Raymond J. Jessen and Mr. Norman V. Strand, who had technical responsibility for all phases of the Sample Survey of Crete, including the statistical analysis of the data obtained. Without their assistance this distinctive feature of the Crete Survey would not have been possible. A large proportion of the tables in Appendix 5 were prepared under their direction at the Statistical Laboratory at the Iowa State College. Chapters 2 and 3 were the joint effort of Dr. Willits, Mrs. Julia M. H. Carson, and the senior author. A very great debt of gratitude is due Mrs. Carson for editorial assistance in the final organization of the book.

The discussions of levels of living and community facilities in Chapter 5 and part of Chapter 8 are based on a report prepared in 1949 for The Rockefeller Foundation by Dr. E. Jean Learned Mickey, consumption economist. The educational section of Chapter 8 is based on a report prepared in 1949 for The Rockefeller Foundation by Dr. Ralph H. Woods, President of Murray State Teachers College. The basic analysis for Chapter 6, "Food and Nutrition," was made by Dr. Calla Van Syckle, consumption economist, Michigan State College, assisted by Miss Helen N. Sdrin, nutritionist, Athens, and Dr. J. R. Trémolières, medical nutritionist, Paris; this statement was prepared by Miss Thelma J. Norris, nutrition officer, FAO, Washington, assisted by Miss Andromache Tsongas, nutrition consultant for FAO to the Greek Government, and the senior author. A large share of Chapter 7, "Health," is based on the detailed report, "Public Health Survey of Crete, Greece," prepared by Dr. W. A. McIntosh, International Health Division, The Rockefeller Foundation. Dr. Paul M. Densen, Department of Biostatistics, University of Pittsburgh, and Dr. V. G. Valaoras, United Nations, assisted in the development and analysis of the statistical material for this chapter. The discussion of water geology and possible solutions to the water problems in Crete are based on the report prepared for The Rockefeller Foundation in 1949 by Mr. Irving B. Crosby, consulting water geologist and engineer.

Special thanks are also due Dr. V. G. Valaoras, Mr. C. S. Stephanides, Mr. George Coutsoumaris, and Miss Helen N. Sdrin, all native Greeks, and one-time employees of the Greek Government, who also understand America, for their frequent and critical reading of certain chapters in the manuscript.

Acknowledgments are gratefully made to the officials of the various ministries in the Greek Government at the national, island, and local levels, who made this survey possible and who gave valuable assistance. Special mention is made of Prime Minister Th. Sophoulis (now deceased), S. Venizelos, and C. Tsaldaris for the groundwork laid in preparation for the survey, and of ex-Governor General A. Chompidis and C. A. Doxiadis, Ministry of Coordination, and their staffs for their assistance. A special word of thanks is due the 765 household heads, 346 farmers, and 128 housewives who so willingly cooperated in supplying information and data of a very personal and confidential nature. The seven volunteer nurses and twelve university-trained students should be commended for their persistence, tact, and accurate interview work. Thanks are also due to the Royal Greek Embassy Information Service in Washington, D.C. for making available a generous selection of photographs, several of which have been reproduced in this book.

While this survey was made possible through the joint efforts of the International Health Division, the Social Sciences, and the Natural Sciences of The Rockefeller Foundation, special credit is due Dr. George K. Strode and Dr. Joseph H. Willits for its initiation and Dr. Andrew J. Warren for his counsel and general supervision of the project. A more complete list of the persons working on this project and their major responsibilities, together with those who have reviewed certain portions of the manuscript and made many helpful suggestions, will be found in Appendix 3.

However, the senior author accepts full responsibility for any errors of judgment in the content of the survey, in its conduct, in the selection of data, and for the conclusions presented herewith. This book is written with the hope that, in spite of its many important gaps, the findings will be useful in themselves and stimulate others to further research on additional underdeveloped areas.

LELAND G. ALLBAUGH

CONTENTS

MAPS, FIGURES, AND PLATES

COLORED MAPS

FIGURES

TABLES

PART I

SUMMARY STATEMENT

CHAPTER 1

THE SURVEY

THE SURVEY OF CRETE was pointed toward two objectives: first, toward answering the question whether it was possible and practicable to raise the levels of living; second, toward discovering ways by which the knowledge and skills of industrialized countries might best serve and least injure an underdeveloped area such as Crete.

An attempt to find the answers to these questions is difficult in a country like Crete because accurate basic data are limited. Outside students, therefore, are dependent on miscellaneous sources such as interviews, newspaper accounts, government reports, and statements by tourists. The result often does not reach deeper than impressions, episodes, and personal opinions. It is small wonder that outsiders on short missions so rarely get below the surface of the societies they study. There is no substitute for long immersion in another culture if adequate knowledge is to be acquired. But long immersion was not possible in the survey of Crete. To offset the limitations of conventional sources of information, sample communities were selected. And in those communities, sample households were selected—one out of every one hundred and fifty on the island.

Teams of Greek interviewers were trained to visit these homes and obtain information on composition of the household, dietary patterns, food consumption, equipment and supplies, home industry, household income, mortality, morbidity, health, education, employment, land and capital resources, indebtedness, crop and livestock production, agricultural problems, community facilities, marketing procedures and problems, and social customs. This method was used to reach isolated communities and to probe below the surface for data about the farms and homes of Crete. It is believed that a more nearly representative picture of Cretan life and problems was thus obtained. The methods used in this survey are described later in the chapter and are presented in detail in Appendix 1.

Throughout the survey two thoughts were kept firmly in the foreground—first, that the only enduring help is self-help. What Greeks and Cretans do for Crete will be vastly more important and more lasting than anything outsiders may do. The survey focused on finding ways by which the efforts of Cretans and Greeks might be further aroused and invigorated.

In the second place, it was constantly borne in mind that in such a survey the foremost concern must be human beings, their values, and their way of life. It was clearly realized, also, that the life of the people of Crete is an integrated whole and not a set of independent fragments. The values, the customs, the mores, the institutions, the relations of that life and that culture are what history has made them. They are the stabilizers of Cretan society. Changes introduced should be gradual—not rapid—so as not to uproot these moorings of Cretan life. Nor was it forgotten that societies which provincial Westerners may call "primitive" have their own contributions to make. From the culture of Crete and Greece, Western civilization has derived some of its most cherished lessons.

Several considerations prompted the selection of Crete for a case study to check general impressions of a given area, supplement available governmental statistics, and provide a cross-sectional view of a whole culture. As an island community, not too great in extent or in variety of conditions, it offered a subject that might more readily be brought into focus than a larger or more varied region. It was recognized that, as an actual or potential economic factor in the world, Crete had none of the importance of a Brazil, a Turkey, or a Mexico. But as the subject of a study to illuminate the general health, social, and economic problems of an area, it offered unusual advantages. Further, it seemed to have problems of natural, human, and capital resources which made it typical of a large part of the Mediterranean Basin. And finally, its economy was almost untouched by modern technology.

Impressive, also, were the independence, the cooperative attitude, and the pride in their own history of the Cretan people. This pride seemed to be attached less to a particular state or government than to a linguistic group with its own tenaciously preserved culture and religion, its own myths and historic splendors extending back to the most remote times. According to legend, Crete was the birthplace of Zeus, father of the gods. Factual history records that it was on the Island of Crete, some three thousand years before Christ, that the Minoan civilization arose, precursor of the brilliant age of ancient Greece. Excavations of archaeologists have discovered the remains of a high level of civilization at Knossos, where the king's palace stood. The disk of Phaestos, made of baked clay with engraved characters running in a spiral from the edge to the center, is one of the world's oldest known examples of writing.

The Minoan regime was followed by the invasion from the North of the Dorians—a tribe of the Greeks or Hellenes. Thereafter Crete remained, not a part of the Greek nation, for there was no single nation, but a part of Hellenic culture. This situation continued until the Greek world was conquered by the Romans about 67 B.C. St. Paul landed on Crete during the Roman period and planted the seed which led later to the conversion of the country to Christianity. In A.D. 330 the Roman Empire split and Constantine established the Eastern or Byzantine Empire, with a capital at Constantinople. It was Christian and largely Greek in composition. Most Greeks, and especially Cretans, think of the period of the Byzantine Empire as the height of their power and well-being. Many regard it as a political unit which might be reconstituted with great benefit to them.

Crete remained part of the Byzantine Empire for approximately 500 years. In A.D. 832 the Arabs (Saracens) invaded and conquered the island. Frequent revolts against the conquerors punctuated the Saracen rule for more than a century. In A.D. 961, Byzantine forces renewed the old connection which endured for more than two centuries longer. Finally, the rising power of Venice penetrated the Eastern Mediterranean and, as was natural for a maritime power, Venice coveted the island and conquered it. Venetian rule lasted from 1204 to 1669.

For almost 700 years after the Venetian conquest Crete was governed—and exploited—by foreign invaders. Periodically throughout these seven centuries the Cretans rose in futile revolt against them. No less than fourteen insurrections against Venice took place. The Turks attacked the city of Iraklion in 1648 and took it after a siege lasting twenty-one years. For the next seventy-five years they struggled to subdue the island. Turkish rule was interrupted by a revolution in 1821; the Egyptians then invaded and took over for a few years but had to quell a revolt in 1833. Crete was restored to Turkey in 1840; in 1841 rebellion broke out. Intermittent trouble continued until in 1897 Crete was separated from Turkey and placed under an international commission. The Greek mainland had by then achieved its own independence, and in 1913 Crete was at last, after many centuries of struggle, reunited with Greece, under the modern kingdom.

Crete contributed to Greece the great liberal leader, E. Venizelos, who achieved a world-wide reputation for his internal reforms. It is not so widely realized, however, that Venizelos represented the ideal of extending Greek rule to a territory including much of ancient Byzantium.

In the 1930's the liberal democratic regime in Greece was succeeded by the dictatorship of Metaxas, fascist in spirit and friendly to the Germans. Crete of course participated in the Greek resistance to Italian invasion, and then in 1941 the island itself was invaded and occupied by Germany. During the occupation, it was an important foothold of the underground movement against the Axis, and Cretans aided many of the British soldiers who made their way back from the Greek mainland after their unsuccessful expedition.

A number of surveys of the economic potentialities of regions have been made by both governmental and private agencies. Though adding much to knowledge of the problems of underdeveloped countries and offering suggestions for solving them, they have not exhausted the possibilities of useful work of this kind. Some have centered about a single phase of the culture in question such as agriculture or industry. Some have been undertaken hastily for the immediate purpose of providing a guide for practical action in the near future and are by no means cross-sectional studies of whole cultures. Some are the work of one or two experts with such assistance as might be provided by existing statistics or local advisers.[1]

Further, action as well as studies have helped prepare the ground for efforts to raise living standards. The experience and success of philanthropic and missionary organizations in providing funds and personnel to assist groups throughout the world pointed the way.

[1] Among the more notable studies have been: (1) Food and Agriculture Organization, *Report of the FAO Mission for Greece.* Washington, 1947. (2) International Agricultural Collaboration, *Report of the United States-Lebanon Agricultural Mission.* Washington, Office of Foreign Agricultural Relations, U.S.D.A., 1948. (3) Harvey S. Perloff, *Puerto Rico's Economic Future: A Study in Planned Development.* University of Chicago Press, 1950. 435 pp. (4) Lydia J. Roberts and Rosa L. Stefani, *Patterns of Living in Puerto Rican Families.* Chicago, Photopress, Inc., 1949. (5) Max Weston Thornburg, Graham Spry, and George Soule, *Turkey, an Economic Appraisal.* New York, Twentieth Century Fund, 1949. 324 pp. (6) Nathan Laselle Whetten, *Rural Mexico.* University of Chicago Press, 1948. 671 pp. (7) George Wythe, Royce A. Wright, and Harold M. Midkiff, *Brazil: An Expanding Economy.* New York, Twentieth Century Fund, 1949. 412 pp. (8) Simon G. Hanson, *Economic Development in Latin America.* Washington, Inter-American Affairs Press, 1951. 531 pp. (9) Lowry Nelson, *Rural Cuba.* Minneapolis, University of Minnesota Press, 1950. 285 pp. (10) T. Lynn Smith and Alexander Marchant, *Brazil: Portrait of Half a Continent.* New York, The Dryden Press, 1951. 466 pp. (11) Carl C. Taylor, *Rural Life in Argentina.* Baton Rouge, Louisiana State University Press, 1948. 464 pp.

The Near East Foundation, many church missions, The Rockefeller Foundation, and other groups have conducted studies and carried on projects and programs in most of the countries of the world—all with the major objective of improving the lot of mankind.

More recently, private business concerns, carrying on business in other countries, have instituted welfare programs for their native employees: the United Fruit Company in Central America, Stettinius Associates in Liberia, the International Basic Economy Corporation in South America, and others. Their pioneer efforts have resulted in both successes and mistakes which are relevant to future programs.

Governmental aid to foreign countries—especially the Latin Americas—to increase production of critical items during World War II also showed that cooperative effort toward a common goal could obtain results. The method of sending experienced technicians to work with and train native personnel was successfully demonstrated. In spite of great differences in cultural background and human desires, resulting in varying rates and degrees of acceptance of new ideas, changes have taken place.

To aid in determining what specific categories of information were to be the aim of the Crete Survey, consideration was given to the basic economic causes of low living levels—low output per man—existing anywhere in the world. In general there appeared to be four: limited natural resources, scarcity of capital, low productivity of labor, and lack of management or entrepreneurial ability, both private and governmental.

The first of these—limited natural resources—may result from such causes as climate, soils unsuitable for agricultural production, lack of minerals and oil for fuel and power, and large numbers of people relative to "effective" land resources.

Evidence of the second basic cause—scarcity of capital—appears in the lack of industrial plants and factories, transportation and communication facilities, housing, and facilities for health, education, banking and credit. Scarce capital may result from any of four causes: lack of security for saving and investment due to chronic inflation and political instability, incomes so low they must be used largely for food and subsistence, a non-saving (profligate) group of property owners, and failure to use funds of investors for the most productive types of development.

The third—low labor productivity—may be occasioned by the lack of facilities for education, especially for vocational education, by unwillingness to develop new skills, or by lack of contact with other skilled workers. Amount of output is also affected by the degree of priority placed upon leisure, recreation, and other cultural factors.

And finally, the fourth—lack of management or entrepreneurial ability—may result from a basic unwillingness to take risks, from lack of contact with managers and entrepreneurs within the country or outside it, from lack of willingness to permit outside management and entrepreneurs to come into the country to establish businesses, or from government regulations which force outside groups to conform to local standards, however inefficient. Other unfavorable circumstances within the country may include immobility between social classes; lack of educational facilities or their cost; and government regulations which prevent free entry into and effective operation of business.

In the organization of the Crete Survey three main stages of work were involved: preliminary reconnaissance; a sampling survey[2] to discover at firsthand the conditions, attitudes, and problems of the people; study and interpretation of the results, supplemented by data already available from other sources.

After examining background information in the United States Public Health Service, the Office of Foreign Agricultural Relations, the State Department, the Food and Agriculture Organization (FAO), and the United Nations Relief and Rehabilitation Administration (UNRRA), representatives of The Rockefeller Foundation arrived in Greece on May 3, 1948. There they conferred with officials of the Greek Government, the United States Embassy, the American Mission for Aid to Greece, the World Health Organization, and the Near East Foundation.

Except for occasional visits to Athens, they then spent the period from May 19 to November 15, 1948, on the island of Crete. A ten-day reconnaissance survey of the island provided an over-all view of social and economic conditions. In the various communities, problems and requests for aid were presented orally and in writing by individuals and groups. Many local problems and promotional schemes

[2] Although technically composed of several sampling surveys—household, farm, community, and diet—the term "sampling survey" (or "sample survey") is used throughout to cover all four.

were brought forward. But the major projects suggested were of the large governmental type rather than those which might be undertaken locally or by the people themselves. Not until individual conferences and data from individual householders became available were the projects which might benefit most from research and technical assistance discovered or confirmed.

With the cooperation of a representative of the Greek Ministry of Hygiene, a public health investigation was undertaken by the "specialist interview" type of survey. Government officials at island, nome (county), community, and municipal levels, public health officials, doctors, nurses, institutional, hospital, and clinic officials and workers were interviewed. As a basis for obtaining an island-wide conception of public health problems, interviews and conferences were held in 36 of the 44 communities and municipalities selected for the sample survey. Brief contacts were made in many others. For a period of two months a medical statistician from the United States Veterans Administration assisted in collecting and analyzing medical and vital statistics. The results of this survey are summarized in Chapter 7, and the details are presented in a separate unpublished report prepared by Dr. W. A. McIntosh.[3]

Early contacts indicated that lack of water was a major problem in Crete. The Natural Sciences division of the Foundation enlisted a consulting engineering geologist to make a reconnaissance investigation of the water resources of Crete to determine the possibility of improving water supplies, through locating underground resources which could be developed without detailed studies of the geological structure. Twenty-eight of the 44 sample communities were visited. The Greek Ministry of National Economy assisted in this survey, and separate reports are on file.[4] The major conclusions are contained in the various chapters which follow.

The survey of general economic and social problems utilized both the "specialist-interview" and the sample-survey methods. The former method provided most of the information on government, industry, and trade, and supplementary data for other phases of the economy. The sample survey provided most of the data and information on vital statistics, living levels, wages and incomes, indebtedness, agri-

[3] A typed copy of this detailed report is on file in a designated depository library (see Appendix 4).

[4] Mimeographed copies of this report are on file in selected depository libraries (see Appendix 4).

culture, transportation, education, home industry, business houses, land resources, marketing, and community facilities. Data on food habits, diets, and nutritional levels were supplied by seven-day-diet records from a subsample group of survey households with supplementary information from the larger sample.

The data of the sample surveys were obtained in such a manner that they would represent all households, almost all farms, and all communities of Crete. Scientific methods of sampling were used to achieve this objective. The sample is not necessarily a completely accurate representation of the whole island, but for most of the characteristics observed the sampling error is small. Data obtained from a carefully devised and executed sampling survey are certain to be superior to general impressions and even, in some cases, to government statistics. The sampling survey is therefore one of the distinctive features of the Crete study. (See Appendix 1 for details of method and quality check, and Appendix 2 for content of schedules.)

By design, only persons residing in households were included in the survey. Those in institutions, such as prisons, asylums, and orphanages were omitted. Inquiry about agricultural production was confined to that portion under the management of householders operating farms of less than 250 acres. Agricultural production from the public domain, from farms over 250 acres, or by religious organizations was omitted—not a relatively large amount.

The main units observed during the course of the sample surveys may be briefly described. The community in Crete consists of one or more villages, usually two or three, all under a single president. The municipality may include one or more villages in addition to the major town or city. Municipalities are nome capitals, demes or towns of 10,000 population or more, or towns having a court of first instance. All land in Crete is in some community or municipality. Another unit figuring in the survey was the household. The concept of household was similar to that used by the United States Bureau of the Census with slight modifications. In most cases it meant the family but it also included unrelated persons living with the family and regarded as members of the household. The definition of a farm, however, was somewhat different from that commonly used in the United States. The individual stated whether or not he was operating a farm. If he said he was, then information pertaining to that farm was obtained on a special questionnaire. This was done in order to make the term more comparable with that used in Greek statistics. Additional information on agricultural activities was obtained from what may be regarded as "sub-farms." A sub-farm was defined as a place not regarded as a farm by the householder yet a place on which he carried out some agricultural enterprises (garden, cereals, a small number of goats, chickens, etc.). Although few details were obtained from sub-farms, nevertheless their aggregate agricultural production was estimated.

The samples consisted of 40 communities and 4 municipalities out of a total of 546 communities and 4 municipalities (1940 census), and of 765 occupied dwelling units out of a total of about 115,000 occupied dwelling units. Also included were 346 farms from a total of 51,900 farms, 271 sub-farms out of a total of 40,350 sub-farms, and 128 households providing information on their diets and household inventories to represent 115,000 households. Both the communities and the occupied dwelling units selected for the sample were designated by those in charge of the survey or by rules which they formulated in the headquarters office. Figure 1 shows the location and relative size of the sample communities and municipalities.

Information was obtained from all the communities and municipalities specified in the sampling plan; gross coverage of households specified in the plan was 95.8 per cent complete,[5] a high percentage even for the United States.

All these data were obtained from specific respondents, designated in advance for the investigators. For the information covering communities and municipalities, the designated respondents were the community presidents and the municipality mayors and their assistants, usually including the secretary, priest, physician, and schoolteachers. The information on households was usually obtained from the heads. If this was impossible or impracticable, then it was obtained from the spouse of the head or some other person who appeared to be able to provide accurate answers. For the farm information the farm operator himself was usually interviewed. The

[5] "Incompleteness" in eliciting replies was due to three main causes: (1) to the respondent's refusing to give information, (2) to the relevant respondent's not being home or available, and (3) to special subsampling techniques that were adopted in the field. Of the households, three, or 0.4 per cent, were not reached because of refusals; nine, or 1.2 per cent, because the respondent was not home; thirteen, or 1.9 per cent, because subsequent subsampling excluded the households in question from the investigation; and three, or 0.4 per cent, for miscellaneous reasons. No substitutes for the specified communities, households, or farms were allowed in this survey for any reason.

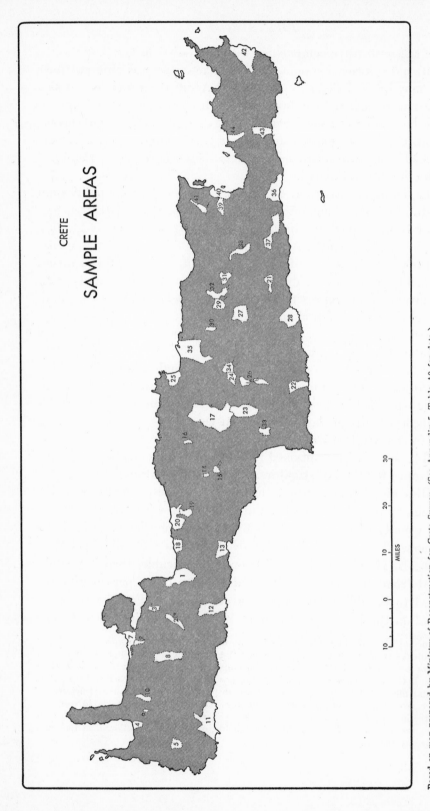

CRETE

SAMPLE AREAS

MILES

Based on map prepared by Ministry of Reconstruction for Crete Survey. (See Appendix 5, Table A9 for data.)

FIGURE 1. Location and size of sample communities, Crete, 1948

(See Appendix 5, Table A9, for numbered list of community names)

Interviewing a household in Yeoryioupolis, Khania nome

Volunteer nurse, Greek Red Cross, weighing food for the seven-day diet survey

Olive, carob, oak, and cypress groves are scattered on rocky, barren mountains, as in this scene in Lasithi nome

The western Mesara Plain beyond Minoan ruins, seen from the acropolis at Phaestos. This is the largest of the alluvial intermount and coastal plains scattered over the island

information covering the diet was obtained from housewives, partly by interview and partly by day-to-day record-keeping.

Twelve male investigators were trained to carry out the field work of the general sample survey. All but three were under twenty-five years of age. Before going to the field, they were given thorough training for five days in Khania, including a number of actual interviews. Seven young women, who were volunteer Greek Red Cross nurses, received similar training and performed the field work on the seven-day diet phase of the survey, visiting each of the 128 families once a day for a seven-day period.

Several different questionnaires were constructed for the general sample survey, one each for the community, the household, and the farm. In addition, a recording form was prepared for the diet study. All questions on the questionnaire were written in English as well as in Greek, requiring the translation only of replies using Greek words. Since a large proportion of the answers were stated in Arabic figures, the necessary translations were entered on the questionnaire itself. This greatly reduced the chance for copy-errors and the amount of time required. In editing the questionnaires, omitted entries for income of the household and value of the farm were supplied by estimated values so that these particular items would be "complete." Only 5 per cent of the cases required this treatment. The few missing data for other items were not supplied.

The accuracy of data from any investigation whether based on a sample or a complete census depends ultimately on the accuracy of the observations themselves—which in the surveys of Crete were data obtained by questioning people about their households, farms, and communities. There is evidence that data of this sort can contain errors—in some cases serious errors—attributable to such causes as misunderstanding of what is wanted, inability of the memory to recall accurately, or deliberate falsification. Possibilities of error of this sort were recognized in the planning of the surveys and a number of measures were taken to detect such errors by obtaining information on the same subject in different ways either from the same source or from different sources. Unfortunately time and resources did not permit an exhaustive investigation of these possible errors. What was actually done and the findings on these matters are discussed in Appendix 1.

In developing the survey schedules and supplementary background information, advisers were provided by the Greek Government from the Ministries of Agriculture, Reconstruction, Public Works, Hygiene, and Education. They also assisted in the selection and training of the interviewers.

The processing of the sample survey data was relatively simple, since the sample of households was deliberately chosen so that totals for the whole of Crete could be estimated merely by multiplying the figures from the sample by 150. Similar results were possible for the communities and municipalities on the island.

The information so obtained was then compared with other data from numerous sources. Economic statistics, whenever available, geographical, historical, and other materials were utilized. Actual observation and contact with the problems in the field were also extremely helpful. But most useful of all in the interpretation of the problems in Crete were the opinions obtained in the sample survey from the farmers, housewives, and community officials as to their major problems and the possible solutions. In addition to providing original data on economic and social problems through the sample survey, it is believed that the Cretans interviewed in the survey broadened their view of their own problems. The respondents were making judgments as to the relative importance of these problems and considering possible procedures for their solution. Thus much groundwork was laid for any action program which might follow.

CHAPTER 2

CRETE AND ITS PROBLEMS

THE CRETANS have a potential need for almost everything. Economic Cooperation Administration reports indicate that Greece, before World War II, had the lowest per capita national income of any country in Europe. Since then the successive devastations of war, enemy occupation, and guerrilla activity have further lowered the level of living. The Greek standard of living has been supported by heavy importations of food from abroad, financed by friendly governments. The Cretans live and work under severe physical handicaps, and under social handicaps that are equally serious and much more difficult to alter.[1]

In comparison with most of Europe and with the United States, Crete has meager natural resources, abundant though untrained human resources, and extremely limited capital resources. Natural resources include cavernous limestone mountains, largely denuded of forests; scarce water supplies during droughty summers in spite of torrential rains in the winters; soils lacking in humus, nitrogen, and phosphorus but rich in potassium and calcium carbonate; unknown mineral resources; and limited supplies of fish. The island has a relatively young and growing population—30 per cent illiterate, lacking in technical skills and in vocational training, practicing self-sufficient household industry and farming to a high degree. Relative to its human resources, the paucity of Crete's capital resources is evident in all fields of endeavor. Nevertheless, a listing of such capital resources as do exist places the country in an entirely different category from such other underdeveloped areas as India with its severe population problem, the more undeveloped regions of Africa and South America, and the industrializing areas of Mexico, Brazil, Venezuela, and Argentina.[2] In Crete, capital formation has taken place, but natural resources are lacking for any great industrial expansion.

The chief physical problems of the island concern (a) the supply

[1] More detailed discussions of the conditions and problems will be found in Part II under the eight chapter headings: Resources, The Cretan Family, Food and Nutrition, Health, Community Facilities and Living Level Comparisons, Government Organization and Its Impact on the Economy, Agriculture, and Industry and Commerce.

[2] A more complete discussion of what the author considers to be the four categories of underdeveloped areas will be found in the latter part of Chapter 8.

of water, (b) agricultural production, and (c) health. Basic is the lack of water—for power, irrigation, sanitation, and even for everyday household use. Crete has what geographers call the "Mediterranean" type of climate. This means seven months of moderate moisture and five summer months during which rainfall is very severely limited. In all it totals much less annually than in the eastern United States. On the southeast coast of the island, rainfall is scarcely more than in the semi-arid Great Plains. Some land was found to be irrigated by 83 per cent of the farmers, but the total land irrigated (some 30,000 acres) amounted to only 5 per cent of the land in farms; and even on these acres only a little more than half was irrigated sufficiently.

The base of Crete is her land, and the level of living is largely determined by its produce. Whatever intelligently serves the processes of agriculture serves the fundamental life of the island. The survey revealed that little change has occurred in the work and life of most Cretan farmers since Biblical times. It also showed how numerous were the problems confronted by the farmers of Crete and how many of them called for skills and experience which they did not possess and which were not then effectively available to them. The survey disclosed further that there was not available to Cretan farmers the sort of help which technical knowledge and experience were giving to the farmers of the United States and many other countries.

Eighty per cent of the estimated 475,800 population in 1948 were rural. These people, more than 375,000 in number, subsisted on a total of about 628,000 acres of land in cultivation, plus 52,000 acres of infertile or grazing land. Except for nomadic grazing, the land capable of producing any kind of yield, vegetable or animal, is equivalent to less than two acres per person, even excluding the people in towns. Mountains, largely devoid of trees, cover the rest of the land.

The largest plain on the island suitable for cultivation, the Mesara, is only twenty-three miles long by six wide. Outside of this, most of the farmers live in narrow valleys, or on the coastal plains in the north, which combined comprise less than 3 per cent of the land area of the island. In Europe, only Poland, Norway, and Switzerland have as high a density of agricultural population per square mile of "arable equivalent agricultural land"—485 to the square mile. And these other nations have more moisture and more forests.

Centuries of political and economic instability have taught the

Cretan farmer to plan and operate his farm for security and self-sufficiency. With very few exceptions the farms are small, owner-operated, and free from land mortgages. The value of home production of food and clothing equals half the total income. With small farms and limited production, a majority of the farmers belong to one or more cooperatives as a means of improving their market outlets, or to facilitate purchases of supplies and equipment. Ninety-six per cent of the farmers own all or part of their land. The average farm, though under ten acres, is made up of thirteen lots scattered throughout the community—a result of the practice of dividing land among children by bequest in such a way that each may have some of the best.

In 1948, farm operators on the average used tools and equipment valued at about $32—usually nothing more than a plow, a sickle, and a hoe. More than half the farms had less than $20 worth. In addition, the average farmer had a donkey, an ox or a work cow, and harness. Two-thirds of the farmers had saddles, two-fifths wooden plows, and about one-fifth had sprayers, wooden harrows, and steel plows. There were thirty-seven tractors on the island owned and operated by the government for their schools or for hire to farmers through the agricultural bank. Three tractors in Iraklion were privately owned.

The production of olives is the most important enterprise in Crete. Olive oil yields per tree were found to be higher in Crete than for all Greece, Italy, or Turkey. But the dacus fly greatly reduces the yield. To control the dacus fly the government spent in Crete $160,000 in 1947 and $80,000 in 1948. And yet the full life cycle of the dacus fly is not known, nor, according to some authorities, is the actual effectiveness of control measures currently being used.

Ninety-seven per cent of the farmers and many town families were found to have olive trees. Estimates indicated that 13 million olive trees were growing on the island. Olives furnish food, light, and heat as well as cash income to the family. They are the basis of much of the industrial production of Crete. They furnished about one-sixth (in weight) of island exports and over one-third—pre-war and post-war—of the value of island receipts in the balance of payments. Olives grow on good land, on land unsuited to crops other than forests or carobs, or on land used for grazing sheep and goats.

Except for olives and table grapes, crop yields in Crete were found to be exceedingly low in comparison with the yields of nearby countries. Most yields were also low in comparison with the possibilities as revealed by experimental or demonstrational results. Of the farmers who had heard of new and more profitable varieties, less than a third had actually planted them.

Nine-tenths of the farmers in the survey listed fertilizer as their main farm problem. The continuing use of 6-8-8 fertilizer containing nitrogen, phosphorus, and potassium in these ratios on soils already possessing an abundant supply of potassium was merely one example of the need for technical study and practical assistance.

Barren mountains and flooding torrents in the winter indicate the consequence of deforestation in Crete. Fuel and lumber were found to be scarce and high-priced. The forests with which the mountains of ancient Crete were covered and which produced a more even run-off of water have been destroyed by conquerors, by charcoal burners, and by herds of goats and sheep.

As for the food and nutrition situation in Crete, the survey found no noticeable evidence of widespread malnutrition, though more foods of animal origin would improve the diets. For some forty centuries the basic foods have been olives, cereal grains, pulses, wild greens and herbs, fruits, goat meat and milk, game, and fish in limited quantities. Bread was served with every meal. All barley used was grown on the island but about half the wheat consumed was imported, including that used for flour and macaroni. Rice was also popular, all of it imported. Ninety-two per cent of the families used open fireplaces for cooking. Private ovens were owned by only two-fifths of the families; public ovens were available in all the cities. There was almost no refrigeration. Most of the people appeared to have an understanding of the relative importance of various foods in the diet and made good use of the foods that were available. Sound practices included: the use of whole grains in bread, the use of wild herbs and greens, full utilization of slaughtered animals, the widespread practice of boiling milk, and large amounts of time spent in the sun.

On the whole, the Cretans are a vigorous people. The island's crude death rate (11.9 in 1938) was not dissimilar from that of the United States (10.7 in 1938) and England (11.6 in 1938). A great health victory has been won in the demonstration that malaria—the scourge of Greeks for centuries—can be controlled. Families interviewed in the survey were still reporting malaria (probably relapses) as one of their major health problems—along with tuberculosis, typhoid, pneumonia, trachoma, dysentery, and oriental sore.

While doctors, dentists, nurses, pharmacists, and trained midwives were found to receive adequate training, the numbers available were limited, especially in rural areas. Public health services consisted of a few understaffed health centers in the major cities. The central organization, in spite of much paper planning, was failing to utilize the local lay leaders and professional personnel effectively or to coordinate the auxiliary services working on health problems. Nor was public health education well developed. The few seacoast municipalities which had sewerage systems were directing them into the coastal waters which were thereby polluted. More than four-fifths of the rural communities had no provision for sewage disposal. But during the three years preceding the survey, one-third of the communities had made some type of sanitary improvement—public latrines, pumps, pipe lines, or water reservoirs.

Nor do such physical problems as those discussed above furnish the only handicaps under which the Cretans live and work. Problems of social organization also bulk large. Before discussing these limitations, however, it is appropriate to mention some of the positive aspects of social conditions in Crete. Fortunately there are solid assets on which to build. With few exceptions the land is not held in large estates; the problems of agricultural Crete are the problems of owners of small holdings, with reduced efficiency due to land fragmentation. Over 95 per cent had no real estate mortgages against their property. The visitor to Crete has a sense of quality in the human material. One feels this quality also in the little mountain villages to which have fled the men who have resisted the invader over the centuries. There is a pride in the history and culture of Greece and especially of Crete whose Minoan society constituted Europe's first great civilization four thousand years ago.

Households usually consist of three to five members. Over four-fifths of the families live in rural communities. Since custom requires that parents never be left to live alone unless the son is in the army or works in a distant community, there are many households in which three generations live together. The family is probably the strongest influence in the Cretans' culture. Family goals are home and land ownership and financial security. Some make great sacrifices to educate their children. The accumulation of large dowries (in terms of actual clothing and home furnishings) preoccupies the women. The men spend their leisure in coffee houses. Particularly in the rural communities, Cretan women worked harder than Cretan men. Managing a Cretan home seemed frequently to require caring for children, cooking, cleaning, spinning, weaving blankets and clothing fabrics, sewing, embroidering, making garments, and helping with farming activities which had a symbolic significance when performed by women. Women also did the laundry, usually near the community water supply, carried water needed for household purposes, and served the men at meals.

Cretan houses are mostly one-story structures, consisting of two or three rooms with high ceilings and shuttered windows. Most windows are unglazed and screens are not used. Native stone is the building material; in rural communities the floor is frequently earth. Animals are apt to be sheltered in the house or an adjoining room. Charcoal, wood, and olive by-products are used for fuel. Four-fifths of the houses were heated by fireplaces in cold weather. Only 2 per cent of the rural and less than one-half of the city households had running water in the home.

While Cretan housewives had few conveniences in their homes, they possessed the essential dishes, tableware, bed and table linens, and kitchen utensils. Trestle beds, sturdy kitchen chairs, and dining tables were found in most homes. Most homes had some type of decoration on the painted or whitewashed walls. A few houses had window draperies.

Though in towns ordinary European dress is the rule, in the country, where most of the people live, the Cretan national costume prevails. The man wears a pair of short, baggy trousers, bound tightly around the waist by a cloth girdle wound several times about the body. On his feet are knee boots, black or brown, as a protection against thorns and winter snows. He wears a blue double-breasted waistcoat and a jacket. On his head is a tightly wound black kerchief embroidered with black silk. When made of the best wool and silk and properly embroidered, the costume may cost hundreds of dollars; hence as a rule it is made of cotton for ordinary wear. He will probably have a large moustache; usually only priests and mourners wear beards. Women dress more in the European manner, though with a black kerchief or shawl on the head.

Part of being a Greek is being a member of the Greek Orthodox Church. The clergy, many lacking higher education, exert an important influence in their parishes. There are about twice as many priests as doctors and a third as many priests as teachers. The church is closely associated with the history of the country and with the present state. Greek nationalism is nourished by the church; patriotism and loyalty to the church are almost indistinguishable. The majority of Cretans are, as a matter of course, communicants, but services may be poorly attended. The many religious festivals and ceremonials, however, play a leading role in the life of the village. They offer holidays on which group activity and aesthetic expression contribute an essential element to the local life.

Crete has powerful social liabilities. They can best be understood when viewed against the background of war—and the threat of war. Of the last 1,000 years of its history, the island has been occupied by invaders during all but 50 years. The first airborne attack in World War II was centered on Crete. In a sixth of the villages one-fourth of the buildings were damaged. In five towns all buildings were completely destroyed. War and revolution have been the usual, not the exceptional, thing in Cretan history. This fact has many social consequences, apart from the production of valorous soldiers. It has produced a highly centralized government—without a strong democratic tradition. The Governor-General of Crete, the nomarchs of the four nomes, the mayors of each city, the presidents of the little village communities, and the schoolteachers—even in elementary schools— were found by the survey to be appointed, paid, and removed by Athens. Most of the taxes were collected and disbursed from Athens. There is no common legislative body for Crete. Its government is carried on chiefly by appointees of the ministries in Athens. It was learned that if a businessman wished to import goods he had to obtain a license from Athens, a procedure often entailing a personal visit to the mainland with, perhaps, no answer received for months. If one asked why a road remained in bad repair, one was told that Athens had not acted.

This practice of centralizing government in Athens was found to be linked with both political patronage and unemployment relief. More than that, however, it seemed to accord with the mental habit of the people who for centuries have been accustomed to ideas and leadership handed down from above, who expect things to be done for (or to) them by a remote central authority. The idea that it is desirable, or even possible, to improve their daily life through changes they might introduce locally seems not to be a prominent part of the customary pattern of Cretan thought. The avid concern of the Cretans with politics must also be interpreted in the light of their history. In a sense they are intensely independent, but they have not had much experience in running their own affairs without overlordship from some remote center of power. They have experienced ancient empire and feudalism. They have been ruled from Constantinople by the Byzantine emperors, from Italy by the Romans and Venetians, and more recently from Turkey by the Turks. After their liberation and annexation to Greece, they were governed for a part of the time by a Greek dictatorship. It is scarcely to be wondered at that when Cretans think of political change they are likely to imagine world-shaking events rather than improvements that they themselves might bring about within their villages, and that they regard government as something that brings benefits or injuries from afar rather than as an expansion of their local initiative.

War filled Greece with refugees who totalled 10 per cent of her population in 1948. War and its aftermath have not only left their mark on the political system of Greece, they have crippled its economic structure. The economy of Greece is not a self-contained economy. Greece must buy many products from abroad, especially cereals, which cannot be produced adequately at home. The exports from Greece—olives and olive oil, grapes and raisins, and other fruits— are luxury products which have gone chiefly to four countries. The demand for these products is highly elastic. The demand of Greece for cereals and other products is inelastic—her people must have these products to live. Greece—and, therefore, Crete—is sensitively dependent on international trade and the delicate balance of monetary and exchange relations that underlie such trade. Greece is also dependent on capital with which to develop industries and give employment, for the farms of Greece produce an excess of population which must find employment elsewhere.

These are essential foundations of the Greek economy which war and its aftermath have undermined. The dominant feature has been a roaring inflation; the drachma that was 5 to the dollar in 1915 had depreciated to 125 to the dollar by 1939, and was 15,000[3] to the dollar in 1950. Taxes were heavy and the budget was seriously unbalanced. ECA reports indicate that taxation (chiefly indirect) and inflation had reduced real wages and the salaries of civil servants to

[3] With exchange certificate; 5,000 without exchange certificate.

one-half of their pre-war amount. Public finance was in a precarious state; the tax structure was in need of serious re-examination.

The annihilation of the currency has had many results. There has been a dissipation of the funds of private owners. There has been an exhaustion of bank deposits and a fairly complete breakdown of the credit system. Both private and state credit have been shaken to the foundations. Bank deposits were stated in the interim report of ECA for 1948 to have been but 10 per cent of what they were pre-war. At the time of the survey very little saving was taking place. There had been a severe decline in the volume of credit extended by banks; the credit supply was wholly inadequate. Interest rates on commercial loans were extremely high. What capital there was tended to seek more secure investment outside the country.

As a further consequence of this disorganization of the monetary and exchange system, domestic prices were far above the international level. The ECA report for 1948 indicated that the prices of imports had tripled, whereas the prices of exports had only doubled. Exports, therefore, were handicapped, and the domestic production cost of articles using some outside materials was affected. There was lack of goods for sale. These price differentials constituted a serious blow to economic equilibrium. Private initiative—always an important factor in economic development—was deterred from making its contribution.

In general, these highly technical problems were beyond the powers of the inhabitants of Crete. They were tasks for the experts of the Greek Government, the Greek Central Bank (Bank of Greece), international agencies, and friendly governments interested in Greece —working together. The importance of these problems was realized by these agencies. They could hope for success in the efforts to terminate inflation, stabilize currencies, adopt sound fiscal and budgetary policies, and diminish exchange controls only if guerrilla war was not resumed and if serious threat of international strife remained away from the Aegean.

This is the background against which the more specific social problems of Cretan society must be examined. The abatement of war is the task of governments and international agencies. Adaptation to the consequences of war must be dealt with at more humble levels. We turn now to a consideration of some of these more specific problems.

If health measures decrease the toll of disease and increase the vigor of the Cretan farmer, if his supply of water is slowly increased, if he is aided in his production problems so that output expands, and if conditions more favorable to international trade are restored, then the problems of markets for his excess crops and adequate means of transport to those markets follow. It has been pointed out that Crete buys from abroad more than one-half the cereals she consumes. She must pay for these and other needed products by finding suitable markets for her olives, olive oil, grapes, raisins, and other fruits. Great Britain, Germany, and the United States were the principal markets before the war. Great Britain, with her austerity policy on food, has been turning to empire countries which have greatly expanded production of similar products. Germany has not yet recovered sufficiently to provide a significant market. Political difficulties have prevented exchange of Cretan products for cereals with the close neighbors to the north. Surplus production of fruit and raisins in the United States has been curtailing demand. Moreover, United States importers have reported Cretan products to be of uncertain quality and to arrive in poor condition. As world supplies of fruit, fats, and oils become more plentiful, the problem of securing markets becomes more acute. The disorganization of world markets, if continued, and any serious economic recession in buyer countries will add to the difficulty in finding markets for Crete's luxury products.[4] The Secretary-General of the Governor-General in Crete properly stated that finding market outlets was the most important problem on which outside help could be used in Crete.

Seventy per cent of the farmers of Crete were found to belong to some kind of cooperative—to buy goods, to sell produce, or to obtain credit. A law of 1929 brought these cooperatives into formal existence and placed them under the supervision of the Ministry of Agriculture. The cooperative movement is one means of reaching and aiding the small farmer on the business side of his task. About half of the farmers belonged to an agricultural credit cooperative at the time of the survey, one-fourth to an agricultural cooperative. Smaller cooperatives existed for olive oil, for grapes, for irrigation, for drainage, and for other miscellaneous matters. Much the most important were the Agricultural Credit Cooperatives which supervised the granting of loans to their members through the Agricultural Bank for the purchase of seeds, fertilizers, agricultural imple-

---

[4] On the other hand, if supplies of vegetable oils from the Far East should be diverted from Europe, additional demand for olive oil might be expected.

ments, etc. The Agricultural Bank had empowered the union of these cooperatives to take delivery, store in the union warehouses, transport, and distribute agricultural supplies, against a commission (⅙ cent per pound) to the union for supplies handled. These credit cooperatives also collected, stored, processed, and sold the products offered by their members at a price fixed by an official body. These operations were financed by the Agricultural Bank at relatively reasonable interest rates (7 to 8½ per cent) and enabled the farmer to obtain funds at harvest time without dumping his produce at flooded market prices.

The survey showed further that Crete was not able to realize on its agricultural production because of the inadequacy and cost of transportation. There were no railroads in Crete in 1948. There were only 860 miles of surfaced road, and these were very rough for perishable products. Most of the remaining "roads" were mere mountain trails on which the donkey with a basket on either side was the agent of land transport. Coastwise transport was irregular, undependable, and costly. Duties in Cretan ports were high and discouraged coastwise transportation of products.

Broadly speaking, education is high in the scale of values among the Cretans. Even though Greece was one of the first nations to install free, compulsory education, three-sevenths of the women and one-seventh of the men over twenty-one were found to have received no formal education at all or to have had less than one year in school. Only 3 per cent of the women and 7 per cent of the men had completed the gymnasium or high school. Two per cent of the adult population had attended a college or a university, four times as many men as women attending.

The school system was found to consist of a six-year compulsory elementary school, a six-year secondary school, and limited opportunities for two to six years of higher education. Numerous courses, many hours in school, and emphasis on the classics characterized the curriculum. Partly on account of war destruction, the schools were inadequately supplied with desks, blackboards, chairs, books, and even teachers. School lunches were provided to over three-fifths of the children—without cost to those unable to pay.

The Greek system of elementary and secondary education was

found to be substantially uniform throughout Greece. It was managed by the central government at Athens and was held to make for pride in history and a sense of unity in Greece. During the twenty years preceding the survey, real progress had been made in increasing literacy.

CHAPTER 3

POSSIBLE LINES OF ACTION

THAT it is technically possible to effect improvement with respect to each of Crete's chief physical problems—water supply, agricultural production, and health—is the considered conclusion of the survey. The main difficulty is not that technical knowledge does not exist and could not be helpfully used. The problem lies in how to proceed effectively in the social context that is Crete. How—with the limitations of income, of trained and dedicated personnel—may help be effectively delivered?

Though the basic condition of low rainfall cannot be altered, the supply of *available* water can be increased if proper authorities, backed by technically competent men, make it their business to do so. The reconnaissance made by the water geologists for the survey indicates that the supply of water can be substantially increased and that avoidance of waste of water is possible throughout the island. The following steps were recommended by the survey:

(1) A thoroughgoing study should be made of the ground water geology of Crete. Such a study would outline the basic elements in the problem of water supply[1] and conservation and indicate the practical action appropriate in particular situations. It is believed that such a survey would indicate many more sources of underground water. Unless, however, such a ground water survey could be based upon a detailed investigation of the geologic structure, the new sources of water would be largely confined to ground water in the alluvium and in the metamorphic and other insoluble rocks. Large subterranean streams exist in the soluble limestone, but detailed knowledge of the geologic structure would be required to tap these. Such streams have, however, been successfully tapped under similar conditions, but where the structure of the rock was better known—in Haiti, for example.

(2) The services of a "water engineer" should be available over a period of years to advise and help villages and cities find better ways

[1] A detailed study of the geology of Crete with emphasis on the geologic structure does not exist but should be made since such knowledge is basic to many other purposes besides water supply. In the judgment of the survey's consulting geologist such a survey might be completed in two years with four young Greek geologists working under the direction of a consulting geologist experienced in the problems of limestone, provided full cooperation was had from the geologists of the Greek Government.

of obtaining, conserving, and using water. What is needed is help of
a small-scale nature at innumerable points. Help given should be
adapted to the scale of life and work of the people—not the reverse.
Large dams—the favorite proposal of many who would apply, ready-
made, the techniques of highly industrialized countries—are not indicated for Crete. Geological formations are not suitable, only one
such feasible site having been observed by the survey staff. Moreover,
social developments are not geared to use such giant mechanisms. Illustrations of the types of problems[2] on which villages and cities need
the services of a "water engineer" follow: (a) augmenting the supply of available water—by deepening village wells, proper construction of small dams near springs or in streams, proper construction
(and plans for use) of canals, development in irrigation projects of
supplementary uses for water at "off times," construction of large
underground cisterns to store winter rains for later use (as was done
by the Minoans and recently by the Germans during the occupation), development of underground cutoffs to bring the underflow
of dry streams to the surface; (b) exploring the possibilities of small
water power projects in springs, streams, and canals; (c) developing
simple measures to insure sanitary community water supplies; (d)
assisting municipal engineers in developing more effective water
systems.

Such services by a competent "water engineer" could pay rich
dividends to the Cretan people. Inventiveness of mind and ability to
win cooperation would be as important in such a man as technical
competence. How to get things done with unskilled labor, local materials, limited funds, and governmental ineffectiveness would be as
important as deciding what should be done. Such a man would need
the sympathetic backing and cooperation of the Greek Government,
and the services should be financed—soon, if not initially—by the
Greek Government, local as well as national. He should have the
backing of a first-class water geologist—presumably the one who
made the survey. One or more Greek engineers should be associated
with him—if he should come from outside Greece.

By such methods the limitations imposed on Cretan levels of living by lack of water could be greatly ameliorated but, of course, not
completely removed. The restrictions on domestic supplies could generally be removed. As to irrigation, great improvement could be made

[2] The problem of reforestation and its influence on the runoff of water is discussed
in the next section.

These native dress costumes are seen only on special occasions

The typical mixture of native and western costumes is shown by this family and
their neighbors in Ay. Ioannis, Rethimnon nome

Much of Crete's capital investment is in houses, schools, churches, and public buildings, as shown in this sample community of Monasteraki, Rethimnon nome

In front of a coffee house

in some cases, moderate improvement in other cases, and little improvement in still others. As to the possibilities of hydroelectric power, the opportunities for improvement are few.

In regard to agricultural production, the survey found various possibilities for constructive work. Studies of the varied problems of olive production should serve not only Crete and Greece but the entire Mediterranean Basin. Such studies could include varieties, irrigation, fertilizers, pruning methods, the dacus fly, and the causes of alternate-year short-crop production. The most important opportunity lies in the study of the dacus fly. According to Greek and Italian authorities, the problem of the dacus fly has not been attacked by modern research methods anywhere in the Mediterranean area. Such a study should be made by a competent entomologist. A phytopathological laboratory in Iraklion was found to be available for reactivation. The director of the Bureau of Phytopathology in the Ministry of Agriculture expressed his interest in having an American entomologist as a consultant and adviser in its reactivation and in the training and development of Greek personnel. Malaria entomologists in the Ministry of Hygiene were interested in cooperating on a study of joint control methods for the mosquito and the dacus fly.

The study of soils and of fertilizer use constitutes a further opportunity. The possibility of alternative crops such as rice, cotton, and soy beans should also be explored. Further, the services of an agronomist versed in soil science and fertilizers could be of great value—if the right type of man were continuingly available. And here it may be appropriate to note that research results were not getting through effectively to the farmers at the time of the survey. Individual efficiency and well-being awaited increased emphasis on education as contrasted with regulation. Though Cretan farmers recognized some of their more important problems and many knew what should be done about them, something more appeared to be necessary to stimulate action.

Returning, meanwhile, to the various over-all problems of agricultural production in Crete, the question of reforestation should be considered. Those who would impose ready-made plans without regard to human beings and their established ways of life would simply recommend an extensive program of reforestation, imposed and carried out by the government. The problem is not so simple. Over the centuries, the lives of many Cretans have been built upon the use of the mountains for grazing herds of sheep and goats. No arbitrary and revolutionary change in this situation is practicable or even desirable. But the problem of the most effective use of the rough lands of high elevation—and these constitute about one-third of the surface of Crete—is one which should receive the attention of technical men and of the leaders of Greece and Crete. How to adjust the needs and rights of the present users of the mountains with the demands of a better future is a problem that can be solved only by intensive study, sympathetic cooperation, patient educational efforts, and modest experimental steps. The provision for a larger acreage of forage crops for grazing herds was suggested for certain areas. For others a modest experiment in reforestation might be indicated. But the starting point is in a thorough study of the best use of Crete's rough land. Until that study is made by a competent man, no one can indicate where beginnings should be made. A plant ecologist, well trained in grass and forest production, together with a livestock specialist, experienced in the utilization of rough land, might form a team, with Greek associates. The team might best be attached either to the Ministry of Agriculture or to an existing private agency.

Until more irrigation is provided, no great changes in land use seem possible. A certain proportion of the fallow lands could be used for winter forage crops and to prevent erosion. Over a period of years, a considered acreage of low-yielding grazing land could be used to grow higher-income and higher-yielding food-producing crops of olives, almonds, walnuts, and carobs. Improved breeds of sheep and goats for milk production would increase animal products from present numbers of livestock. But any large increase in animal products with which to improve the diets of Cretans awaits both increased water supplies for summer forage feeds and increased incomes with which people can purchase more animal products. Interim improvement, before meat and milk can be increased, might be made by increasing consumption of fish to supply protein and riboflavin, and pulses to provide riboflavin, calcium, and high-quality vegetable protein.

More definite recommendations respecting changes in dietary habits, food-consumption levels, and food production should await basic studies. These would include additional seasonal studies of food consumption, metabolism studies, clinical studies, and biochemical examinations of population samples. Although a small percentage of the families had a calorie intake below that usually considered near minimum levels, the diets and food-consumption levels of the Cretan households were surprisingly good. On the whole, their food pattern and food habits were extremely well adapted to their natural and economic resources as well as their needs.

These instances in olive production, in soils and fertilizers, and in rough land utilization are but illustrations of the opportunities for the intelligent aiding of the Cretan farmer in his efforts to gain production from the land. Throughout these studies, the goal should be not to "do things" for the Cretan farmers but to stress opportunities for him to initiate for himself, singly or in cooperation with others.

Turning to matters of health, it appears from the survey findings that the major needs are for preventive services: holding the line on malaria, improving sanitation, and using present funds more effectively. The building of expensive tuberculosis sanitariums with high overhead and few persons benefited is not entitled to as high a priority as are preventive sanitary measures in a country whose economic base is extremely limited.

As irrigation projects increase, the advice of a competent sanitary engineer as adviser to the Ministry of Hygiene and Public Works in Crete would be invaluable. In view of the importance of health problems generally, a public health administrator from outside might well serve in an advisory capacity to the island public health services and to the Ministry of Hygiene. The purpose of such an arrangement would be to obtain more from funds spent and to teach administrators how to develop responsibility in others. Such an official could study the costs and probable benefits from the solution of other public health problems. To measure the effects of efforts to improve health and to learn more definitely about the relative importance of problems, improvement in the methods of collecting health statistics is also recommended. A consultant from outside who could occasionally assist officials in the Ministry of Hygiene on such problems would be desirable.

Certainly the physical basis of life in Crete is potentially capable of substantial improvement through such measures as the survey has revealed. The knowledge and the personnel for effecting such improvement exist outside Greece if not in Greece itself. But the physical foundations are merely the beginning. Even more important to the improvement of life in Crete is change in certain limiting factors that are social and human in nature. These limitations are more numerous and more difficult. They include such social problems as marketing and transportation, local responsibility and initiative in respect to local government, education, and limited industrial expansion.

The study of the processes of marketing and of transportation of products from the Cretan farm to their ultimate market is as important for Crete as the study of the life cycle of the dacus fly. At present each person in the process of distribution of Cretan products is preoccupied with one step and no one is looking at the process as a whole. A marketing specialist acquainted with trade outlets for Cretan products, who would work with exporters and agricultural cooperatives, could perform a needed service. He would work on such problems as the following: (a) standardization, grading, and packaging of products; (b) processing of perishable products to prevent market gluts; (c) refrigeration; (d) transportation; (e) market outlets; (f) agricultural credit; (g) organization and functions of cooperatives; (h) process of obtaining effective governmental cooperation (e.g. import and export licenses); and (i) training of Greek personnel.

The cooperatives should receive special attention from such a person. They represent one of the instrumentalities through which greater local responsibility and initiative might develop. It would be fruitful if leaders, especially younger leaders, could be aided with travel grants to study the functions, organization, and management of cooperatives in other countries whose problems are not dissimilar to Crete's. The marketing specialist, suggested above, should be a man sensitive to the possibilities of cooperative work.

Improved production in agriculture could give only limited aid to the Cretan level of living, if effective means of transport to markets were not available at reasonable cost. Improvement in transport can come only slowly. Fortunately Greek road engineers are competent. Improvement of the physical facilities for transport waits upon such social factors as peace, advance in the economy, and the development of local responsibility, initiative, and funds. A survey and recommendation by an outside consulting road engineer, attached to the Ministry of Public Works, would help to define and kindle interest in practical possibilities. Such assistance was being supplied by ECA at the time of the survey. Similar attention might be given to the possibilities of coastwise shipping.

But the stimulus to basic improvement in transport should come out of more local responsibility and initiative. There is an abundance of local materials for road-making. The male inhabitants of Crete were found to have much idle time, the farmers in the sample reporting an average of only 160 eight-hour days worked a year. Local materials and under-employed local farmers and other workers need to be teamed up in the interest of better roads. The means whereby this result might be aided from Athens and locally will be discussed in the next section.

It has already been noted that the history of Greece has produced a highly centralized type of government with concentration of power, funds, and initiative in Athens. Whether the handicaps of over-centralization, over-staffing, incompetence, and inefficiences can be remedied would appear to depend upon the ability of competent political leaders in all active parties to reorganize the government, clarify functions, assign responsibilities, and develop a large number of conscientious, hard-working, competent civil servants. Closer contact with the people by officials at all levels of government and out-of-school education for both youths and adults are greatly needed. Budgets at all levels need revision to meet the financial realities in Greece. Taxing methods and credit facilities need study to encourage the formation and use of capital in productive enterprises. Improvements in the general economic situation are vitally dependent on political stability and personal security.

At the time of the survey, local initiative in Crete seemed to be largely paralyzed. A strengthening of the spirit and opportunity for self-help is vital. Such a growth cannot occur unless local responsibility and initiative are systematically encouraged. The Greek Government was recognizing this and was believed to be ready to consider a program for decentralizing responsibility, power, and resources for those functions essentially local in nature. The process of achieving this change of direction in a democratic way must be slow, for the habits of years cannot be altered overnight without sacrificing human values. Greater local competence and participation cannot be quickly developed. Three steps are suggested:

(1) A readiness of the central government of Greece to use Crete as a laboratory of decentralization for those governmental functions which are essentially local in nature. There are many ways of achieving this end and many voluntary agencies which can be used in the

process. Such efforts—if soundly conceived—will result in a strengthening, not a weakening, of the ties between Crete and Athens.

(2) A well-thought-out analysis of the problem should be made as the basis for the selection of specific steps with which to begin. A student of local government and administration, working in cooperation with the Greek central government officials and Greek local authorities and agencies, might well be the person to make such a study. Included in the range of subjects might be the following, among others:

A study of government functions with a view to ascertaining those which, immediately or ultimately, might appropriately be decentralized.

An analysis of governmental instrumentalities needed to implement these changes.

Methods of developing more community responsibility or participation in building, financing, and maintaining roads.

Ways of increasing local participation in the public school system.

Ways of developing local tax revenue for community purposes with local authority to decide on its use.

Possibilities of local elections for community officials.

Methods of utilizing community groups for educational discussion of local issues. Along with the selection of such problems as these, on which a beginning might be made, should go recognition of the value of gradualness in carrying forward policies of appropriate decentralization.

(3) Some individual or agency to serve as a continuing catalytic agent for aiding local initiative is desirable. Perhaps such a person should make the study. It is probable that beginning efforts should center on more responsibility for roads, for education, for the election of certain local officials, and more funds subject to local control.

In any listing of social problems, education stands high in importance for Cretans. An increase in the supply of people with essential specialized knowledge and skills is a necessary part of any program for improvement in Crete's living levels. Outsiders need to speak with reserve about the educational system of any country other than their own, and must make suggestions only with great caution. This is especially true after a brief survey. However, the findings of the survey seem to make it clear that the system of education does need to be supplemented in ways that will give training in the knowledge and skills essential for dealing with the practical problems of living. Certain examples follow:

(1) Training of specialists in health, agriculture, marketing, sanitary engineering, local government, taxation, and vocational and extension education. This could be done by having young Cretans work in Crete with specialists from abroad or by travel grants for practical studies abroad.

(2) Training of more men competent to serve the farm agent (county agent) function and make effective the knowledge of better varieties and modern agricultural methods to farmers.

(3) Utilization of cooperatives, coffee houses, and other such media for purposes of education in problems of production and distribution.

(4) Discussion of these problems with the leaders of the church.

Throughout it should be borne in mind that any change in emphasis in Crete's educational system must be achieved through the central government, specifically the Higher Educational Council of the Ministry of Education in Athens in cooperation with the local authorities.

Finally, the improvement of the living level of Crete will involve a gradual expansion of industrial production—although not so much as to affect the fundamentally agricultural character of the island's economy. Industrial expansion should evolve out of the island's natural resources and agricultural production and its large supply of under-employed workers. The proposal—encountered in the course of the survey—for an iron and steel industry in Crete is wide of the mark. Lack of power, fuel, known natural resources, and technological skills make any such development unsound at this time. Small industries connected directly with needed materials or the processing of agricultural production represent possible lines of development. Processing plants for fruits, olives, and vegetables, refrigeration for fruits and fish, and increased production of tile, brick, and crushed rock for buildings represent more promising possibilities. Relevant to these and other undertakings requiring power would be the development of lignite mines, two of which the Germans opened and then destroyed before leaving. Such developments are worthy of study in order to determine what is feasible and what conditions are necessary to development. Such an expansion of small industry is essential to any program for raising living levels in Crete and furnishing opportunity to the surplus population[3] from her farms.

The restoration of tourist trade could also be of economic importance to Crete. The island's climate, location, and people combine with the restored evidences of the first great European civilization—the Minoan—to make Crete a suitable object of interest to tourists from many lands. Such visitors could help to augment Greece's supply of foreign exchange.

In conclusion, then, it is obvious from the Crete Survey that the levels of living in Crete are capable of slow but substantial improvement. To achieve this, certain conditions are essential:

The people of Crete and the government of Greece shall agree with the objective and shall pledge cooperation.

The prime responsibility for a self-help program shall rest on the Cretan people themselves.

The knowledge and skills now available in the world shall be made effectively available to Crete.

Any or all of the following lines of practical action are possible:

(1) Any of the many institutions and agencies interested in Crete may take up any of the data or recommendations in this survey which are of interest to them. That some general interest may ensue from this survey is the reason, as previously stated, for making the results public. It is hoped that the people of Crete, the Greek Government, the United Nations, representatives of the United States Government, and other interested groups may find something relevant to their interests. As a by-product, those interested in similar unindustrialized countries may find the analysis of problems useful.

(2) Private agencies and individuals interested in Crete may also find opportunities that are of interest. Any such private agency might proceed in either of two ways. It could assume limited responsibility only—choosing a single task at a time. Such an agency could choose out of the long list of opportunities presented above the one that seemed most promising or suitable for it to undertake. It might choose, for example, the study and control of the dacus fly, or a

---

[3] The pressure of population on resources is not discussed at length in this survey since the present population of Crete is less than that of earlier centuries. The expansion of income through the restoration of peace and through such steps as are herein suggested can be adequate to serve the present population. But the problem will need to be studied in the future.

study of water resources and of the means of increasing available water supply, the continuance of malaria control, a study of local government and the means of decentralizing functions that are local in nature, or a survey of markets and market outlets for Cretan products. There is much to be said for such a limited-liability, "rifle-shot" approach, especially if a number of agencies with projects selected in accordance with their individual interests participated in close coordination with each other and the government.

(3) It is also possible for any agencies interested in Crete to select one or two or even three communities, and center their efforts to serve Cretans by making well-rounded demonstrations at these points. This method also has the advantage of modesty of effort and expense.

(4) It is also possible for an agency to proceed on a more ambitious scale and perhaps more fundamentally. Such an approach would assume the view that life in Crete, as in any community, is an inseparable whole and that the maintenance of the "balance" of Cretan life is primary. This means being prepared to work now on water supply, now on the dacus fly, now on health, now on problems of marketing or local government, and now on education or population—always with carefully thought-out coordination and sequence. Such an approach would be possible only if the agency responsible were ready to commit itself to continuity of effort over a substantial period of time. A team of two persons—possibly three, with one as captain—could be the nucleus of the effort. An ideal team might include a public health man, an agricultural scientist, a specialist on social problems of the farm-agent or community-organization type. These men would work as those in the Near East Foundation and the International Health Division of The Rockefeller Foundation have worked for several decades in many countries of the world. Through the backing of their sponsoring organizations, these field men would be able to call in, from time to time, more specialized skill and knowledge.

If such an integrated attack were undertaken by some agency, those in charge of this survey hope that certain precepts which observation in Crete and experiences in other countries have suggested as wise would be followed:

a. A respectful attitude should be maintained toward the values and motives of the people and the country concerned.

b. The aim should not be to impose industrialized Western culture or to make others over in the American or any other image.

c. Work should be done at the grass roots—where people live and work—not just from the top down.

d. The media through which to work should be chosen most carefully.

e. The accepted ways of life and living of another people should not—cannot—be changed in a hurry.

f. The rate of change should be adapted to the human and financial ability to absorb and sustain.

g. The responsibility and most of the cost should be kept on Crete and the Greek nation since only self-help endures.

h. Money is necessary, but money alone—or too much money—from outside would only weaken.

i. Continuity and integrated effort should be given the highest priority.

An effort, organized on some such lines as these and continued modestly over time, could help Cretans to help themselves to an expanding life. Such an effort might also have special significance for Mediterranean countries. Further, it could furnish an example of integrated effort that would have meaning for all those who wish to aid unindustrialized countries with Western knowledge and skills.

PART II

A DETAILED STUDY OF THE ELEMENTS

OF CRETAN LIVING LEVELS

CHAPTER 4

RESOURCES

As STATED EARLIER, in comparison with most of Europe or the United States, Crete has meager natural resources, abundant though untrained human resources, and extremely limited capital resources.

A. NATURAL RESOURCES

The natural resources of Crete consist of cavernous limestone mountains, denuded of forests; scarce water supplies during droughty summers in spite of torrential winter rains; soils lacking in humus, nitrogen, and phosphorus but rich in potassium and calcium carbonate; unknown mineral resources; and limited supplies of fish. Less than one-third of the land was in agricultural production. Crete is quite typical of much of the area adjoining the Mediterranean Sea.

1. Location, Area, and Topography[1]

Crete is in the Aegean Sea 160 miles south of Athens, 200 miles north of Africa, 325 miles south of the Dardanelles, 450 miles northwest of Port Said on the Suez Canal, and 550 miles from Lebanon (see Crete, inset map).[2]

The island lies in an east-west orientation (between 23°30′ and 26°20′ E. longitude and between 34°54′40″ and 35°41′34″ N. latitude), is 160 miles long, and varies in width from 7 to 35 miles. It has an area of approximately 3,200 square miles or 2,050,000 acres.[3]

The northern coastline of Crete is very irregular, with deep indentations forming the gulfs of Kisamos, Khania, Iraklion, Mallia, and Merabello. To the east of the Gulf of Khania a rocky peninsula, Akrotiri, shelters Suda Bay, the only well-protected harbor for large vessels afforded by the island. This harbor is 8.5 square miles in area and is considered the best in the Eastern Mediterranean. The

[1] This and a portion of the following section are drawn largely from: (1) British Army Air Forces, *Maps of Crete*, Greece Sheet, G-19 Khania, and G-20 Iraklion. Scale, 1:250,000, Reprint. Athens, 1944. (2) Office of Foreign Agricultural Relations, *Agricultural Geography of Europe and the Near East*, Misc. Pub. 665, Maps. Washington, United States Department of Agriculture, 1948.

[2] Three fold-out color maps are included in this book—a general map of the island, called "Crete map," at the front, a Soils map facing page 286, and a Land Use map at the back. Reference is also made, as here, to the small inset maps such as "Crete inset map," "Land Use inset map," and "Soils inset map."

[3] Ministry of Reconstruction. Measurements provided for Crete Survey. Khania, 1948.

southern coast is less irregular and possesses no natural harbors; in many parts the mountains form a virtual wall along the sea (see Crete map).

Crete has four principal ranges of mountains.[4] The Levka or White Mountains overhanging the southwest coast, with two spurs ranging off to the northern coast, have their highest point at Pakhnes, 8,661 feet. The smaller Psiloritis, Idhi, or Ida Range lies in the center of the island with the highest point in Crete at Stavros, 8,878 feet. East of the Idhi Range are the Lasithi or Dhikti Mountains with the highest point at Dhikti, 7,047 feet. At the extreme east lie the mountains of Sitia with the highest point at Thrifti, 4,839 feet. The Kophinos or Asterousia Mountains with a summit of 4,039 feet separate the large central Mesara Plain from the southern coast.[5]

Approximately 10 per cent of the island has an elevation of less than 300 feet; 35 per cent 300 to 1,300 feet; 30 per cent 1,300 to 2,600 feet; and 25 per cent 2,600 feet or more (see Appendix 5, Table A8).

The level upland inter-mountain basins in Crete furnish excellent pasture during the summer months. Among the more important are Nida in the Idhi Mountains at an elevation of 5,000 feet, the Askifos and the Omalos in the White Mountains, and the Lasithi Plain near Mt. Dhikti—the latter two over 3,000 feet and each drained through subterranean limestone sinkholes. The Lasithi Plain, a large area with a number of villages, has a highly developed agriculture. The smaller inter-mountain basin of Ziros on the eastern end of the island is also well developed agriculturally.

Such high mountains on a narrow island imply steep slopes and deep, narrow ravines bordered by precipitous cliffs. While small areas for cultivation are found in the narrow valleys, *intensively* cultivated crops are found chiefly, in addition to the Lasithi Plain, on the narrow coastal plains bordering each of the gulfs on the Aegean Sea. These northern coastal plains comprise less than 3 per cent of the land area and have alluvial and diluvial types of soil.

The Mesara Plain, the largest (140 square miles) on the island, lies between Mt. Idhi and the Kophinos Range and extends west to

[4] United States Army Air Forces, *World Aeronautical Chart for Crete*. Aeronautical Chart Service, Nos. 424 and 425. Scale 1:1,000,000. Revised May 1949. Washington. This map also served as the latest source for the mountain peak elevations set forth in this paragraph.

[5] Unless otherwise qualified, the term Mesara Plain will refer to the whole Mesara-Monofatsi Plain or valley.

the coast at Mesara Bay near Tymbakion. Smaller plains are found near Kastelli-Pedhiadhos and Arkalokhori southeast of Iraklion, and above Ierapetra on the narrow neck between Merabello Gulf and the Liberian Sea.

There are four principal rivers. Draining the Mesara Plain are the Yeropotamos and the Anapodharis, which reach the sea west and east respectively of the Kophinos Range. The Platinias River flows northward from the Levka Mountains to the Gulf of Khania. The Milopotamos (ancient Oaxes) flows northward from Idhi to the sea east of Rethimnon. All but the Platinias are in the central portion of the island and drain from the Idhi Range. The location of these rivers and their drainage areas is shown on the color maps of Crete.

The watershed basins in which the four principal rivers are located cover one-fifth of the island, contain the major cereal and citrus fruit areas, and are also important in olive production. The twenty-two major watershed basins cover about one-half of the land area, with the remainder drained by more than 60 small, short, seasonal streams originating in the mountains and flowing directly to the sea.

2. Climate and Rainfall

Crete's temperature, though moderated by the sea, is varied. On the plains in summer, midday temperatures are high, ranging from 80° to 100°, and the nights cool at 60° to 75°; even in winter freezing temperatures are rare. Mountain winters, on the other hand, are severe. On the coastal plains, the mean temperature for the period from April to September is about 74° and from October to March about 60°. For monthly average temperatures at six stations, see Appendix 5, Table A4. More recent (1945-1948) temperature readings for Khania show little change from those for the pre-war period.

The island's prevailing winds are the strong steppe winds blowing from the north across the Aegean Sea with such force as to prevent tree growth in many exposed places on the north coast. These are the steadiest winds and in many areas furnish power for irrigation pumping. On the other hand, the hot dry sirocco from Africa in the spring can do much damage if it coincides with the critical developmental stage of cereal or fruit crops, especially in southern coastal areas.

Crete is characterized by a rainy season (October through March) and dryness throughout the remainder of the year. About seven-eighths of the annual rainfall comes during the rainy season. Except for the high mountainous areas, the average annual precipitation varies from 27.8 inches at Khania on the northwest coast to 18.0 inches at Sitia on the northeast coast and 8.1 inches at Ierapetra on the southeast coast. The heavy rainfall (44.2 inches) at Anoyia far up the northern slope of Mt. Idhi and the even heavier rainfall on the Levka Mountains reach little land under cultivation and largely fall as snow during the winter months. The relatively heavy rainfall at 25.6 inches at Mesara in the south central area is explained by the fact that the station is located at the foot of the south slope of Mt. Idhi. With scanty rainfall and subtropical temperatures at Ierapetra, the need for irrigation in the production of early crops is clear. (See Table 1 and Land Use inset map.) The scanty rainfall from May through August at all stations is evident from the data in Appendix 5, Tables A3, A4, and A5.

TABLE 1. Average rainfall (in inches) in "dry" and "rainy" seasons, Crete, five stations, 1894-1929, and Mesara, 1936-1939

Period	Khania	Anoyia	Iraklion	Sitia	Ierapetra	Mesara
Dry season (April-September)	3.25	6.15	3.24	1.67	0.92	1.68
Rainy season (October-March)	24.58	38.09	17.05	16.29	7.22	23.87
Annual total	27.83	44.24	20.29	17.96	8.14	25.55

Source: Ministry of Air. Meteorological Service, Athens. Data provided by courtesy of Russell H. Gist, ECA.

Somewhat incomplete data for the immediate pre-war period indicate that Crete had a less than normal amount of precipitation during 1933-1935, with most stations reporting one-third to two-thirds the average amount of rainfall in 1933. More recent post-war data for Khania show little change from the long-time average precipitation.

At the Khania station, precipitation was recorded on 66 per cent of the days during the three winter months (December, January, February) of 1945 to 1948. In contrast, rainfall was recorded on only 5 per cent of the days during June, July, and August in 1945 to 1948.[6] The few rains during the summer help reduce the number of copper sulphate sprays required to control vine diseases.

The wide variation in rainfall over the island and during the year affects the seasonality and types of crops as well as irrigation needs. From half to three-quarters of the farmers stated that the rainfall was insufficient for their main crops of grapes, olives, and cereals. Farmers suggested that there is even insufficient rainfall for fall-sown cereal grains, which mature in late spring. Some land was irrigated by 83 per cent of the farmers. Only half of these believed they had sufficient water on all or a part of their irrigated land. The investigation shows a total of 30,000 acres of land irrigated in Crete, of which 59 per cent was irrigated sufficiently. But the total land irrigated was only 5 per cent of the land in farms, or equivalent to about one-third of the rich unirrigated Mesara Plain.

3. Water Resources and Geological Formations

The water resources of Crete, though numerous and varied, are not plentiful. In Khania and western Rethimnon nomes, there are two permanent rivers, a few large springs, many smaller springs, and ground water in alluvial coastal plains, valley fillings, and alluvium-floored intermount basins. The only fresh-water lake on the island, Lake Kournas on the northern coast 11 miles west of Rethimnon, covers 160 acres or about two-thirds of a square kilometer.

Central Crete has three permanent rivers, many large springs, and excellent opportunities for successful wells. The nome of Lasithi in eastern Crete is a relatively dry region but has one small permanent river and several springs and ground water supplies in alluvium-floored intermount basins and in dry-stream-bed underflows.

The highly seasonal character of the rains and the scarcity of adequate streams, together with the cavernous limestone rock formations throughout the island except in the extreme west, make storage dams generally impractical. There are thus very few opportunities for the development of hydroelectric power. As stated by the water geologist who made a study of the ground water resources for the Crete study: "The idea is prevalent in Crete that dams are needed in many places. Actually there are very few if any places where conditions are suitable for a dam with a satisfactory reservoir. This is due to the following facts: the reservoir basins are generally small

---

[6] D. Droussolakis, "Rainfall and Temperature Data for Khania Station." Unpublished data. Khania Meteorological Station, February 1949.

and the life of the reservoir would be short due to its filling with debris washed from the barren mountains. Many of the possible dam sites are unfavorable due to the presence of cavernous limestones. Although in some cases it might be possible to make the foundations of a dam on cavernous limestone tight, it would be extremely expensive and would make the development cost out of proportion to its benefits. In general there is very little opportunity for developing hydroelectric power, but possibilities which would not be considered in the United States may be justified in Crete where the power shortage is very severe."

Small dams were used to divert water from small spring-fed streams to provide irrigation, mill power, and village water supplies. One-fifth of the sample communities had such water facilities, which served one or more of their villages. In some cases, hydroelectric development of mill power would give greater efficiency with a small surplus of electric power.

For village and domestic uses, water was supplied by many small springs, shallow dug wells in alluvial soils along the coastal plains, or large cisterns which filled during the rainy season. Wells and springs were about equally common as sources of household water supply. Together they provided 72 per cent of the households with water, at the time of the survey.

Only one village in the sample was without any source of water— except as carried from a neighboring village over the mountain. But many villages reported an inadequate supply of water even for essential cooking and drinking purposes during the dry season.

Since a large-scale geological map of Crete was not available, the geology of Crete was known only in a general way (see Soils inset map). According to the reconnaissance survey:[7]

"The rocks of Crete include folded metamorphic rocks overlain unconformably by limestone and other sedimentaries of different facies and ages. Igneous rocks intrude both the metamorphic and sedimentary rocks. The whole mass has been cut by numerous faults and great slices of rock have been thrust over other rocks of different age and characteristics, producing complex geologic relations. The resulting geologic structure controls the movement of underground water in the rocks of Crete. . . .

[7] Irving B. Crosby, "Reconnaissance Report on Ground Water Resources of Crete for The Rockefeller Foundation." Unpublished manuscript. New York, February 1949, pp. 3, 5.

"The hard pure limestones, of whatever age, are honeycombed with solution channels and the drainage is largely subterranean. On them has been produced typical karst topography with numerous enclosed basins whose drainage is entirely subterranean. These are known as uvalas or poldjes in Europe but are similar to the large sinks in the limestone country of the southern United States. Two important valleys of this type in the White Mountains are the Askifos Valley and the Omalos Valley. In the Psiloritis Range the Nidha Valley is of this type. The largest of all these enclosed valleys is the Lasithi Plain in the Lasithi Mountains. The Ziros Valley south of Sitia in the eastern mountains is another good example of a completely enclosed valley drained by a sink hole.

"Many alluvial floored mountain valleys, of which the drainage is at least partly by surface streams, exist. Special mention should be made here of the Pedhiadhos Plain south of Kastelli-Pedhiadhos (Iraklion nome) which has a great depth of alluvium. The small Khandra Plain south of Sitia appears to be of this type also.

"The greatest development of alluvium is in the coastal plains. These extend intermittently along the north coast of the island as long narrow strips of alluvial plain from a fraction of a kilometer to several kilometers in width. The more important ones are the Kisamos Coastal Plain, the coastal plain west of Khania, that east of Rethimnon and the one beginning east of Iraklion and extending east of Mallia. The principal coastal plain on the south shore of the island is that in the vicinity of Ierapetra. The alluvial deposits of these coastal plains all contain important aquifers.

"The Mesara Plain, the most important plain in Crete, is an alluvial plain in an elongated basin of structural origin. It lies between a faulted mass on the north and the faulted mass of the Asterousia or Kophinos Mountains on the south. On the north side of the valley strata of Tertiary limestone dip steeply towards the valley. On the south side the impervious basement rocks rise above the floor of the valley presenting a barrier to the southward movement of water. This has produced conditions especially favorable to the accumulation of ground water.

"Earthquakes attest that earth movements have not died. Movement continues slowly and sometimes by jumps. The island was tilted in the sixth century A.D., the west end being raised 26 feet and the east end depressed."

Two earthquakes in the last one hundred years were exceedingly destructive in Iraklion; considerable damage was caused as recently as 1931. Other towns on the north coast are also affected by earthquakes. In contrast, seismic shocks on the southern part of the island are rarely destructive.[8] Since earth tremors are not uncommon in Crete, they must be considered in planning dams or other types of construction affected by them.

4. *Soil Types and Soil Fertility*

The soils of Crete have been divided into two main groups and ten soil types by K. Nevros and I. Zyorykin of Athens in their bulletin *The Soils of the Isle of Crete.*[9] (See Soils map and Appendix 5, Tables A84, A85, and A86.)

About 85 per cent of the soils in Crete are on "limestone, containing calcium carbonate and saturated with bases" and only 15 per cent on "rock formations not containing calcium carbonate and not saturated with bases." Over half the soils of Crete are "red soils and pebble-mixed soils, originating from erosion and decomposition of limestone rock formations" on limestone containing calcium carbonate.

The best soils for cultivation on the island comprise about 130,000 acres or less than 7 per cent of the total area of Crete. More than two-thirds of these better soil types are located in the Mesara Plain, where lack of water is a serious problem.

Although most of the soils in Crete are situated on limestone or decomposed from limestone rock, about one-third of the samples in Khania, Rethimnon, and Lasithi nomes showed acidity (a lack of calcium carbonate) by test.[10] On the other hand, half of these soil samples in Khania and Rethimnon, four-fifths in Iraklion, and one-third in Lasithi nome showed 10 per cent or more calcium carbonate by test. This high percentage of calcium carbonate is thought by some to diminish the availability of phosphorus to plants. Only 10 per cent of these soil samples in Khania, Rethimnon, and Iraklion and 25 per cent in Lasithi nome contained between 0.1 and 1.9 per cent of calcium carbonate, which is considered within the best range

[8] George Aronis, "Preliminary Survey for Irrigation and Water Supply Projects in Crete." Unpublished manuscript in Greek with English translation. Athens, Ministry of National Economy, 1949, p. 4.

[9] K. Nevros and I. Zyorykin. *The Soils of the Isle of Crete*, Soil Research Bulletin, vol. 1/bd. vi, no. 4/5. Athens, 1939, p. 292.

[10] N. Kavelopoulos, "Analysis of 9000 Soil Samples in Greece." Unpublished manuscript. Athens, Institute of Chemistry and Agriculture, pre-war.

for legume plant growth.[11] Soils with these small amounts of calcium carbonate or neutral soils have phosphorus present in quite readily available forms for plant growth.

The analyses of several hundred soil samples from 327 villages in Crete showed that most of the soils—72 to 97 per cent—were "rich" in potassium and only 1 per cent were classified as "very poor." Soils badly deficient in potassium were common in Khania nome.[12]

In phosphorus content, more than half of the soils in all nomes were classified as "poor" or "very poor." Only 15 to 24 per cent were in the "rich" category. Even in these "rich" soils of Crete, the high calcium content might make much of the phosphorus unavailable to plants. For this reason, it is necessary to conduct field trials on these several soil types with varying percentages of calcium carbonate content to determine the effect of varying rates of fertilizers under varying moisture conditions for each crop.

These conclusions are supported by experiments on the mainland which were summarized by P. D. Caldis in "Soil Fertility," Appendix D of the *Report of the FAO Mission for Greece,*[13] in the following: "These experiments [in Greece] have amply demonstrated that the Greek soils [similar to Crete] in general are low in nitrogen and phosphorus but with few exceptions they have ample supplies of potash."

The very small acreages of legumes (most of which were used for food for humans and beasts) and limited quantities of animal manures necessitated the use of commercial nitrogen fertilizers to provide this element for plant growth. Next to the shortage of water, the lack of fertilizers was chiefly responsible for low yields of crops in Crete. The small acreages of forage and green-manure crops, together with high summer temperatures in the plains areas, kept soil humus at a low level.

In summary, the survey found that some of the best soils on the island lacked water for irrigation; soils which were suitable for cultivation were limited in acreage, and a large percentage of them lacked nitrogen, phosphorus, and the proper percentage of calcium carbonate for good crop production.

11 In some soils, low availability of phosphorus is found as a 2.0 per cent content of calcium carbonate is approached.

12 *ibid.*

13 P. D. Caldis, *Report of the FAO Mission for Greece.* Washington, March 1947, Appendix D.

5. Minerals

While the island is reputed to be rich in minerals—iron, lead, talc, manganese, lignite, sulphur, copper, and zinc—the evidence was little more than reports of prospects and crude surveys. Only the talc mine in the Katharos mountain area has been explored for possible commercial exploitation, and lack of roads has prevented any development. Gypsum occurs in many parts of the island, some being mined and a small amount exported. Small lime kilns are common throughout Crete. The Germans utilized two lignite mines (Kandanos and Vourvoulitis-Armiri) during their occupation, but blew the mine openings as they retreated. (See Soils inset map.)

One report on mineral resources was presented by Mr. John Nanadakis, who was reputed to have three unworked mines as prospects under lease, near Palaiokhora, Meskla, and Kastelli-Kisamos. These were alleged to contain gem stones, gold, silver, copper, tungsten, platinum, magnetite, emery, graphite, and possibly tin and apatite. Indications of petroleum were reputedly found in the Palyrinia mine district west of Kastelli-Kisamos.

A second statement on the mineral resources of Crete was presented through the Iraklion Chamber of Commerce by G. Antoniou, mining engineer, and J. Miliarakis, chemist.[14] They indicated 20 appearances of iron ore, 12 of copper, 10 of gypsum, and 3 to 6 each of manganese, talc, lignite, lead, and zinc. One appearance of chromite was also reported.

6. Forests

Although Crete is reported to have been covered with dense cypress forests in ancient times, there were no large forest areas on the island at the time of the survey. Small forests of pines, cypress, and oak scattered over the island covered only about 2 per cent (41,000 acres) of the land.[15] (See Land Use map.)

Half the forest land was located in Khania nome, mostly on the southern slopes of the White Mountains. Of this, one-half was in maquis (evergreen broadleaves) and the remainder in pine (halep) or a thin mixture of the two with pastures. About one-fifth of the

[14] Iraklion Chamber of Commerce and Industry, "Reports of Chromatourgia Co., Ltd., and Joseph Miliarakis, Chemist." Memorandum to Rockefeller Institute Committee. Khania, May 7, 1948.

[15] Panos Anagnostopoulos, "Some Agricultural Statistics of Crete." Unpublished manuscript based on Ministry of Agriculture data. Khania, August 1948.

total forest area was in oaks and conifers on the eastern and southern slopes of Mt. Ida. The remaining forests were about equally divided between pines and maquis scattered over Lasithi and eastern Iraklion nomes.

Each district was characterized by specific tree growth. The nome of Khania had many small chestnut forests; Rethimnon had forests of carob and oak trees; while rocky Lasithi had almonds and carobs. Chestnut trees, which grow best in non-calcareous soils, were found on the metamorphic rock formations of the west end near Elos. Cypress and olive trees prefer calcareous soils. However, the extensive olive groves (estimated at 150,000 to 250,000 acres and occupying 7 to 12 per cent of the land) were widely scattered over the island up to an elevation of 1,900-2,600 feet.

About 20,000 acres, or one-half of the forest lands, were owned by individuals, two-fifths by the communities, and the remaining one-tenth by the monasteries. In addition to these forest lands, individual householders included an average of 0.3 acre in their farm holdings. For all of Crete this would mean approximately 17,000 acres of farm forests. A large share was in small acreages scattered over the communities. For those who had forest lands (6 per cent of the community households), the average was 5.5 acres.[16]

Some of the longer run effects of continuing deforestation upon the agricultural resources of Crete were suggested by the consulting geologist in his report on the ground water resources: "The deforestation and consequent removal of soil from the mountains of hard relatively pure limestones has caused an almost irreparable injury. In the areas of impure limestones, shales and metamorphic rocks the injury is less serious. The formation of a foot of soil by the decomposition of a relatively pure limestone takes many tens of thousands or hundreds of thousands of years. Only the impurities in the rock are available for the production of soil and they may be removed by erosion almost as fast as produced. In the case of shales, soil formation may be only a matter of decades. With the schists, conditions are intermediate but thousands of years may be necessary to produce a foot of soil.

16 These estimates are based on an analysis of data secured from the 1948 Sample Survey of Crete, Form B, Farm Schedule. Since a major portion of this book is based on data secured from the Household, Farm, Community, Seven-day Diet, or Household Equipment schedules used in the Sample Survey of Crete, further references for such data will not be cited, except to indicate sources under each table presented. References for data from sources other than the Sample Survey will be indicated.

"In contrast, reforestation would help hold the remaining soil on the mountain slopes, tend to slowly produce more soil and to reduce the quantity of detritus spread on arable lowlands. Reforestation would also tend to reduce the winter run-off which is largely wasted and would hold more water in the ground, increase the dry season flow and prolong the dry season life of streams and springs."[17]

Attempts at reforestation have met and will continue to meet severe resistance from nomadic sheep and goat farmers until some provision for greater forage removes the necessity for reducing the size of their flocks and herds. For this reason, the Governor-General of Crete, a native of the nomadic grazing community of Khora Sfakion, suggested that the efforts of the survey should be concentrated on the crop production phase of the economy, rather than on the reforestation problem.

In view of this recommendation, and the need for concentrating limited funds and personnel upon problems which might provide more immediate economic returns, this problem of reforestation was left for later study. Another reason for postponement is the need for careful study of the applicability to the Cretan culture and economy of any solutions to the forestry problem achieved by neighboring countries.

7. Fisheries

Similarly, the fisheries problem received only incidental treatment in this survey due to lack of time for obtaining qualified personnel. A constant shortage of fish on the Khania market was found during the period May to November 1948, even at high prices. Dynamiting for fish was reported all along the coastline—even though the practice was recognized as destructive. The penalties for dynamiting were so severe that gendarmes were not anxious to catch any person in the act; consequently it went on unabated. Boats, netting, and fishing equipment were reported to be in poor condition, and replacement costs were extremely high.

Fishing cooperatives were quite active in Crete, providing the means of operating vessels, purchasing equipment and supplies, and marketing the catch. There were eleven fishing cooperatives in Crete; four each in Lasithi and Khania nomes, two in Iraklion, and one in Rethimnon. The larger number of cooperatives at each end of the island was due to the fact that the major catches of fish were found

[17] Irving B. Crosby, *op. cit.*, p. 11.

Scarcity of water, even for household use, is a major problem

A community laundry in Iraklion nome

A street-side market in Iraklion

Market-day fair at Voukolies

Three stages of dacus-fly damage on the three olives of a single branch

DDT airspray control is used in this section of the Mesara Plain

Donkey-pump well in Rethimnon nome

Cross-country travel by a family in Iraklion nome

there. The most common catch consisted of small fish, but the big run of the two seasons consisted of the tunny on their seasonal migrations to and from the Black Sea. This run of tunny was around the eastern end of the island, making the principal fishing grounds off the southeast coast. But much fishing was also done in the channel between Crete and the Peloponnesus.

While a survey of the fishing banks surrounding the island was not made, discussions with interested Greeks and Americans in Athens indicated the problem to be more complex than expected for an island. In the first place, the off-shore coastline of Crete was reported to be very precipitous and the off-shore waters too deep for good fish production or fishing. Second, the fish runs near Crete were said to be off the southeast coast of the island, where good harbor facilities were lacking, or far up in the Aegean Sea off the coast of the mainland. Since prices on the Athens fish market were even higher than in Crete, fish from the upper Aegean were sold on the mainland. Third, there were neither refrigerated fishing boats nor refrigerated storage space for fish at the ports in Crete so that the markets fluctuated wildly, depending on the catch. And finally, the sudden rough seas of the Aegean caused many boats to stay out at sea so long after a fish catch that without refrigeration the fish spoiled, requiring a second catch and greatly increasing the cost.

Whether these reports reflected the true fishing possibilities around Crete, and whether they justified the current scarcity of fish in relation to both the demand and the need for more animal protein food, will not be known until some research studies by the Hydrobiological Institute at Athens have been made. Recent issues of the *Battle for Survival*, weekly bulletin,[18] indicated that a research vessel *Alkyoni*, modernized with UNRRA and ECA aid, had made its maiden test cruise and was starting on a longer research study. Hydrobiological studies in the waters adjacent to Crete may be delayed for many months because the large demand for fish in Athens will give it priority over Crete in such surveys.

8. Land Use and Land Ownership

Two-thirds of the land area in Crete is made up of mountains, rivers, and torrents, according to an estimate by Dr. Panos Anagnostopoulos, Greek Agricultural Adviser, and later confirmed by data

[18] Ministry of Coordination, *Battle for Survival*, no. 46. Athens, July 20, 1949, p. 14.

from the Ministry of Coordination. (See Figure 2 and Table 46.) Only one-third of the land area was in forests, grazing, and crop production, although nomadic grazing, fuel wood, essential oils, chestnuts, honey, etc., were also furnished by the mountain areas.

LAND USE

Based on data for 1948 supplied by Ministry of Coordination and Ministry of Agriculture, Athens. (See Table 46, Chapter 10 for data.)

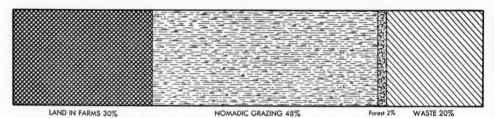

LAND IN FARMS 30%   NOMADIC GRAZING 48%   Forest 2%   WASTE 20%

Total Area 2,050,000 Acres

FIGURE 2. Land use in Crete, 1948

The land problem in Crete was found to be not one of tenancy, but of small and inefficient farms owned by the cultivators. After 1917 the few relatively large private holdings, as well as those of church and monastery, were reduced in size by redistribution to farmers. One-half of the church lands were made available for distribution to Asia Minor refugees and veterans of World War I. Private estates were reduced to a limit of 50 acres (200 stremma) for each member of the family except for special cases of war heroes and descendants of leaders in wars of liberation.

Although data for all land on the island were incomplete and inaccurate, estimates by the nome agriculturists indicated that 81 per cent of the land was privately owned, 12 per cent state owned, 4 per cent owned by the communities, 2 per cent by churches and monasteries, and 1 per cent by veterans' organizations.[19]

The custom of dividing land among the children upon the death of the owner tended to reduce the size of farms and to scatter the land in each holding.

B. HUMAN RESOURCES

Crete was found to have a relatively young and growing population—30 per cent illiterate, lacking in technical skills and vocational

[19] S. G. Boultadakis, C. Lelakis, C. Kafatos, George Kavouras, "Land Ownership in Crete." Unpublished data. Khania, 1949.

training, and practicing self-sufficient household industry and farming to a high degree. One-third of the population was in the labor force, of which three-fifths were in agriculture and only one-sixth in industry, commerce, and transportation.

1. *Population*

At the time of the survey, Crete had its largest population since the fourth century but less than half the estimated population of 1,200,000 inhabitants during the reign of the Sea Kings about 1550 B.C. The island had an estimated population of 475,800 people in 1948 as compared to 386,427 in 1928—an increase of 23 per cent in the 20-year period. According to the data available at the Ministry of National Economy, the population increased 58 per cent during the preceding 48 years and 70 per cent during the preceding 67 years.

With only 30 per cent of its land in farms and a high percentage of its population engaged in agriculture, Crete showed one of the highest densities of agricultural population (485) per square mile of "arable equivalent" agricultural land in Europe.[20]

Crete had only one-half to two-thirds as much tillage land per inhabitant as Yugoslavia, Bulgaria, Rumania, Hungary, and France, and less than a fourth as much as the United States. In grain resources per inhabitant it had one-half to one-fourth as much as these countries. For a country in which two-fifths of the diet was made up of cereals, this relationship was important.[21]

Pre-war and post-war vital statistics for Crete indicated that pressure on the land due to the upward trend in population would continue to increase. In 1948 Crete showed an excess of births over deaths of 15.5 per 1,000 population, one-fourth greater than the 1930-1938 average of 12.2. Infant mortality rates were lower and births per marriage were higher in the post-war period than during the 1930's. The pre-war birth rate in Crete was 40 to 65 per cent higher than in the United States, England, and France. The pre-war death rate was 25 per cent less than for France and only 10 per cent higher than for the United States and England. In 1947 and 1948

[20] Office of Foreign Agricultural Relations. *Agricultural Geography of Europe and the Near East*, Misc. Pub. 665. Washington, United States Department of Agriculture, 1948, p. 22.

[21] International Institute of Agriculture. *International Yearbook of Statistics, 1941-42 to 1945-46.* Bureau of the FAO, Rome, 1947. vol. 1, pp. 3-43 and vol. 3 for selected countries.

crude birth rates and death rates were about the same for the United States and Crete at 24-26 and 10-11 per 1,000 population respectively.[22] The effect on Crete's birth and death rates of the island's younger age distribution, in comparison with the distribution in the industrialized countries, should be kept in mind. Higher death rates and lower birth rates might be expected in the industrialized countries, with their older age distributions.

Crude birth rates, death rates, excess of births over deaths, infant mortality, and crude fertility rates were all lower for Crete than for Greece in the pre-war period.[23] The decline in the death rate for Crete in the post-war period is similar to that in Italy and France, according to Dr. J. R. Trémolières of Paris. Except for some understatement of deaths, the improvement accords with expectations, since during the war the more susceptible individuals of all age groups suffered death in many occupied countries.

TABLE 2. Vital statistics for Greece and Crete, pre-war and post-war[a]

	1938 Greece	1938 Crete	1946-1948[b] Crete
Marriage rate	6.5	6.8	6.3
Birth rate (crude)	26.1	24.1	26.1
Death rate (crude)	13.3	11.9	10.6
Excess births/deaths	12.8	12.2	15.5
Infant mortality rate	99.4	91.1	72-85

a All figures show annual rate per 1,000 population, except infant mortality, which shows deaths under one year per 1,000 live births.
b Data for 1946-1948 adjusted by V. G. Valaoras.
Source: Ministry of National Economy. *L'Annuaire Statistique de la Grèce*, 1938. vol. x, p. 76, Athens, 1939. Data reported by V. G. Valaoras. Survey of Crete, Form C, Community.

Although the sample survey data on vital statistics for Crete were taken from official records in the sample communities and four municipalities, a specialist in Greek population problems[24] believes they

[22] Statistical Office of the United Nations, in collaboration with Department of Social Affairs, *Demographic Yearbook*, 1948, Tables 14, 20, 24, 28. New York, United Nations, 1949.
[23] V. G. Valaoras, "Some Vital Statistics on Crete and Greece." Unpublished manuscript. New York, March 1948. Also his "Some Effects of Famine on the Population of Greece," *Milbank Memorial Quarterly*, 27(3), July 1946, pp. 215-234.
[24] Dr. V. G. Valaoras, Social Affairs Officer, Population Division, United Nations, since 1947, and formerly a professor in the Department of Biostatistics, Athens

should be adjusted for under-registration, place of registration, and
seasonality of data for 1948. The sample survey data indicated a
crude birth rate of 24.6 for 1946-1948; this has been adjusted to
26.1 births per 1,000 population, the same rate as shown by the data
for 1946 and 1947. The crude death rate of 8.8 per 1,000 population
in Crete has been increased by 20 per cent to 10.6, leaving the excess
of births over deaths at 15.5 or about the same as the sample survey
showed. Infant mortality rates for 1946 and 1947 seemed unreason-
ably low so that an estimate of 72 to 85 infant deaths under one year
per 1,000 live births has been used, an increase of 0 to 20 per cent
over the 1948 data. (For more detailed data see Appendix 5, Table
A16.)

Birth rates in the four nome capitals were 50 per cent higher than
in the rural communities, according to the official records. Although
ordinarily rural birth rates are higher than urban, the recorded
data for Crete may be explained by births being registered where
they occur. Even though relatively few maternity cases may go from
the villages to hospitals in the cities, it was known that some expectant mothers went to urban relatives in order to be near doctors.
Moreover, under-registration of births and deaths was probably more
frequent in rural areas.

The average age at death from January 1946 to August 1948
was 48.2 years. Average age at death for rural people was 50.4 years
but only 41.2 for persons in the four municipalities, or a difference
of 9 years. For females the difference was even greater, averaging
11 years.

The post-war increase in the rate of population growth promised
to intensify further the present pressure of the population upon the
limited resources of agricultural land, unless additional irrigation
projects were developed or unless the birth rate fell. Contraceptives
apparently were not widely used. According to common report, their
use was opposed by the clergy, and in any case low income deterred
their purchase. The fact that they were for sale at the local pharmacies suggested that there might be a market among certain higher
income groups.

School of Hygiene. The adjustments to the data in the ensuing sentences in the text
are an "informed guess" in the best sense of that phrase. They seem "reasonable"
in relation to pre-war figures for Crete and those published for some other Mediterranean areas.

2. Geographical Distribution[25]

Because of climate, soil, and harbor facilities, a majority of the people lived along the northern coastline. Less than one-fourth of the population (about 110,000 people), including 50,000 inhabitants of the rich Mesara Plain, lived on the southern half of the island. All the large towns, except Ierapetra, were on the north coast (see Figure 3).

Approximately one-third (150,000) of the population lived in 77 coastal communities where the principal villages had an elevation of less than 328 feet (100 meters). These principal villages were used as a measure of the elevation of the community, since a large share of the population resided there. Of the nine towns with more than 3,000 people, all except Kritsa, Anoyia, and Neapolis were found in these coastal communities at a low altitude. (See Appendix 5, Tables A8 and A9.)

Wars, malaria, and availability of land have helped to determine the location of more than half of the principal villages, which have an elevation of 1,000 feet or more on an island where the rigors of mountain winters are in sharp contrast to above-zero temperatures in coastal areas. But only a fourth of the island population was found in these higher communities.

In 1940, one-fourth of the island population lived in 11 municipalities and communities having more than 2,500 population each. Slightly less than one-fifth of the population lived in three nome capitals of 10,000 population or more. (For details see Appendix 5, Tables A10 and A14.)

According to the 1940 census, almost half the communities of the island contained less than 500 population. Only 2 per cent of the communities had 2,500 or more population and about 15 per cent had 1,000 or more population.

3. Age, Sex, Height, and Weight

As previously pointed out, the population of Crete has a younger age distribution than the United States. In 1940, Mexico had a still younger age distribution with 51 per cent of its population under 20 years of age in comparison with Crete's 41 per cent and the United States' 34 per cent. These differences are clearly indicated

[25] Ministry of National Economy, *Population de la Grèce*, no. 1153-29. October 16, 1940.

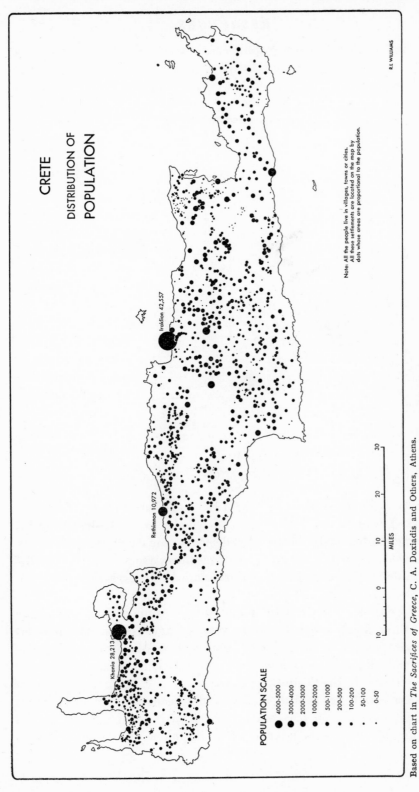

CRETE

DISTRIBUTION OF
POPULATION

R.I. WILLIAMS

Note: All the people live in villages, towns or cities.
All these settlements are located on the map by
dots whose areas are proportional to the population.

Iraklion 42,557

Rethimnon 10,972

Khania 28,213

POPULATION SCALE

4000-5000
3000-4000
2000-3000
1000-2000
500-1000
200-500
100-200
50-100
0-50

10   0   10   20   30
MILES

Based on chart in *The Sacrifices of Greece*, C. A. Doxiadis and Others, Athens.

FIGURE 3. Crete: Distribution of population, 1940

by the shape of the demographic charts in Figure 4, which show, by sex, the percentage of the total population in various five-year age groups. These charts also present evidence of the effect of wars and economic depressions upon the age distribution of the population.

The effect of heavy death losses in World War I upon the male, in comparison with the female, population in Crete is evident in the group 40 to 54 years old in the 1940 census and in the 50-to-64 group for 1948. Similarly the effect of World War II on the 30-to-39

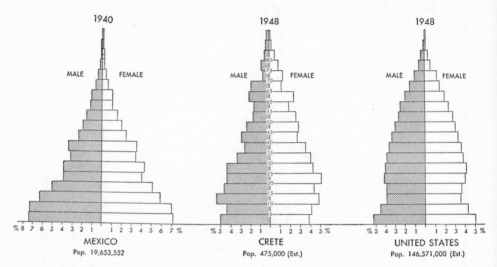

Based on data in Appendix 5, Tables A12 and A13.

FIGURE 4. Demographic comparison of Crete, Mexico, and the United States

group in Crete is shown in the 1948 age distribution chart. The marked reduction in both males and females in the 10-to-19 groups for the United States in the 1948 demographic chart is generally ex-plained by the reduced birth rates resulting from the economic de-pression of the early 1930's. (For detailed figures, see Appendix 5, Tables A11, A12, A13.)

More than one-half of the population were under 30 years of age and three-fourths were under 45 years of age. Of the male popula-tion, 39 per cent were under 20 years of age; of the female popula-tion only 34 per cent. The female population had slightly higher percentages in the 20-to-65 groups.

Less than 8 per cent of the household heads were under 30 years of age and only 29 per cent under 40 years of age. Since custom required that parents never be left to live alone unless the son was in the army or worked in a distant community, there were many households in which three generations lived together. Although the 60-to-69 group comprised only 12 per cent of the adult population, it included 21 per cent of the household heads. Ten per cent of the household heads were 70 or older. In general 10 per cent of household heads were found in each of the eight 5-year age groups from 30 through 69.

For all ages over 18, the males averaged 5 feet 5.6 inches in height, 3 inches taller than the females, who averaged 5 feet 2.6 inches. The adult males averaged 142 pounds in weight, 18 pounds heavier than the adult females.

4. *Levels of Education*

In 1948, 30 per cent of the population eight years old and over said they could not read or write. On a comparable basis, 43 per cent were illiterate in 1928.

This indicates a considerable increase in literacy in Crete during the past two decades, especially among females, whose illiteracy rate declined from 59 per cent to 40 per cent in the 20-year period. For the male population, the decline in illiteracy was from 26 to 18 per cent.

Of the adult population 21 years or older, three-sevenths of the women and one-seventh of the men had received no formal education, or less than one year in school. Only 3 per cent of the females and 7 per cent of the males had completed the gymnasium or high school. In the rural areas, only 1 per cent of the females and 4 per cent of the males had completed high school. Only 2 per cent of the adult population had attended college or university, four times as many males as females attending.

In a country like Crete, the education of the household head is also an important factor in determining the human resources. One-fourth of the household heads had received no formal education, and less than half had completed the fourth grade. Only 4 per cent had finished high school, roughly equivalent to the twelfth grade in the United States, though with more concentration on classical studies, history, and routine learning. Two per cent of the household heads had taken some advanced work toward higher degrees. Five times as many heads of households in cities as in rural communities had finished high school and taken college work. Evidently the cities had absorbed the better trained group and also had provided better opportunities for higher education.

5. *Industries and Occupations*

In 1948, about 59 per cent of the labor force in Crete were engaged in agriculture, forestry, and fishing; 18 per cent in industry and transportation; 6 per cent in trade; 12 per cent in government service; and 5 per cent in other professions and services. After 1928, the decline in the percentage of the population gainfully employed in agriculture, forestry, and fisheries was offset by the increase in the percentage engaged in government work. Since government workers were probably included with "other professions" in 1928, this separate listing overemphasizes the increase in their proportion since then—probably by a fourth or a third. (See Figure 5 and

OCCUPATIONS 1948

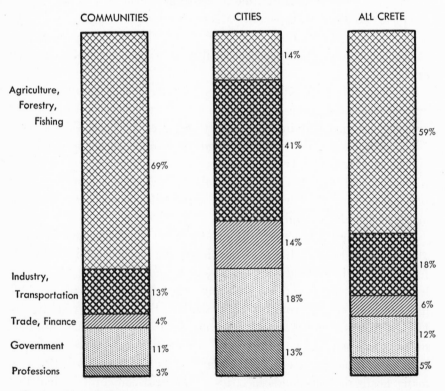

Based on data in Table 3.

FIGURE 5. Industry distribution of gainfully employed population, 1948

Table 3 below. For further details, see Appendix 5, Tables A22 to A25.)

In the rural communities, about nine-tenths of the population were engaged in agriculture, manufacturing, and government. In the cities, two-fifths of the gainfully employed population were engaged in industry and transportation, one-sixth in government, and about one-seventh in each of the remaining three categories: agriculture and fisheries, trade and finance, and professions and other classes.

TABLE 3. Percentage of gainfully employed population in various industries, Crete, 1948 and 1928

Industry class	1948			1928
	Commu- nities	Cities	All Crete	All Crete
Agriculture, forestry, and fisheries	69	14	59	69
Industry, mining, and transportation	13	41	18	16
Trade, finance, insurance, and repair	4	14	6	7
Government	11	18	12	*
Professions and other classes	3	13	5	8
Total	100	100	100	100

* Government employees probably included in "Professions and other classes" in 1928.

Source: Sample Survey of Crete, Form A, Household, 1948 and Ministry of National Economy, *Population de la Grèce*, 1928.

The sample survey indicated that on September 1, 1948, 35 per cent or about one-third of the population were employed—the same ratio as in 1928. The labor force, as defined in this survey and in the United States Census, does not include members of families (e.g. women and children under 14 years of age) working in the fields and in the home without pay.

Of all persons gainfully employed (in the labor force) in 1948, more than half were occupied in agriculture as farmers (31 per cent), farm laborers (12 per cent), or unpaid farm workers over 14 years of age (13 per cent); one-sixth were craftsmen, operatives, foremen, and kindred workers; and one-seventh were service workers. Only 2 per cent were listed as professional workers and 4 per cent as proprietors, managers, and officials. About 5 per cent were non-farm laborers, only 1 per cent were occupied as domestic service workers, and 1 per cent were listed as unemployed but seeking work. (See Appendix 5, Table A22.)

6. *Labor and Management Skills and Capacities*

The proportion of a population engaged in the production of goods for sale increases with the growth of a market economy and technological advance; it therefore provides some indication of the standard of living. In the more industrialized countries, more than two-fifths of the population are found in the labor force (40 per cent in the United States). In Crete the percentage was 35, though this figure did not include women and small children who worked on the family farm.

In summary, of the total population of Crete, about one-third were in the labor force, one-third in (own) housework, and over one-fourth in school or under school age. The remaining 5 per cent were unable to work or attend school, or were unreported.

The number of days worked was relatively small, especially in agriculture. On the average, the farm operators worked at least part of 201 days annually, and only 133 full days. The farm family put in an additional 152 days, of which 92 were full days. The majority of farmers spent eight hours in the field, and the average for all farms was the same. Cretan farmers worked one-half to two-thirds as many hours annually as Minnesota and Illinois farmers with their diversified agriculture. Other members of the Cretan family worked more hours on the farm than family members in the Illinois cash-grain area but only one-half as many as were worked on the Minnesota general livestock farms, which were included in a supervised farm accounting route.

Since such a large proportion of the population—65 per cent of the household heads—were engaged in producing food directly for domestic consumption or for exchange for clothing and other types of food, relatively little manpower and management capacity remained with which to produce other goods or services. The fact that the natural resources of Crete are niggardly, requiring an unusual amount of effort and skill in cultivation, reduces the total output and living levels of the population, in comparison with those of other more productive areas.

The low level of education, the lack of vocational schools, the centralization of advanced learning, of government, and of industry in Athens and Salonika, and the higher living levels in larger cities tended to drive labor and management skills from such areas as Crete. Even on the island itself, educational and other community facilities in the four larger cities tended to drain the more rural areas.

History, customs, and cultural patterns were found to affect the skills and capacities of people. Centuries of conquerors, wars, and revolutions had affected human initiative and developed Cretan attitudes toward capital formation, long-time investments, population trends, and living standards that seem strange to a Western democracy which has fought a war on its own soil only twice in the past century and a half. Since 1913, the modern Cretan has not known ten successive years of peace or freedom from political crises. Such conditions tend to destroy the social conscience of individuals and imply that self-sufficiency, self-defense, and movable capital assets will be highly prized.

C. CAPITAL RESOURCES

In Crete the paucity of capital resources relative to human resources was evident in all fields of endeavor.

1. Location and Extent[26]

Unfortunately, accurate physical data were not available on most of Crete's real capital resources. Inflation made any monetary estimates of doubtful validity. However, some rough summary estimates are presented which will suggest the general character of the capital resources for possible comparison with those in other underdeveloped and undeveloped areas.

The agricultural capital resources of Crete included 628,000 acres of land in 52,000 farms and 40,000 sub-farms estimated by the owners to be worth $386,000,000 in 1948. In addition, they had machinery, equipment, and tools worth $2,000,000 and livestock and animal power valued at $30,000,000. Included in this land value were about 13 million olive trees, 3.6 million fruit trees, 100 million grape vines, and irrigation facilities for 30,000 acres of land. Summer shelter houses, pumps and windmills, etc., valued at $1,250,000, were included in the land value.

Since the dwellings were located in villages and not on the farming land, the 268,000 rooms for living quarters, 26,000 rooms for stable

[26] References for estimated "Capital Resources" are given in the later detailed discussions.

space, and 62,000 rooms for home storage were valued separately at $1,000 per room (double pre-war), or approximately $350,000,000. To this might be added $450 for the value of clothing, linens, blankets, and household equipment in each of the 115,000 households for an estimated total of $50,000,000 at the inflated prices of 1948.

The above capital resources had a total estimated value of $818,-000,000. To this should be added the value of those items mentioned below for which estimates were not available.

The capital resources of Crete included 41,000 acres of forest lands and a small but unknown number of fishing boats, together with their fishing equipment and other fishing facilities. There were 165 quarries and 10 gypsum mines in operation. Various other mines in operation were of unknown extent and feasibility and involved no investment in capital equipment.

In manufacturing and industry, the capital resources included 200 factories of various sizes and plants for processing food, fiber, fuel, and building material, most of them employing less than 11 persons and utilizing relatively little power and equipment. In addition, there were 2,400 olive crushers, 2,600 olive presses, and 136 grape pressers and distillators scattered over the island. There were 42,000 hand looms in the households of Crete.

Capital resources in commerce and trade included 860 miles of asphalt, macadam, and stone roads, available for use by 950 trucks, autos, and busses, and 60,000 mules and donkeys.

There were two airports suitable for twin-engine planes but without hangar accommodations. Harbor facilities included two harbors for ocean-going vessels and six harbors for smaller vessels and coastwise caïques. There were 12,000 business houses and service stores and 302 cooperative marketing and purchasing associations.

Adequate warehousing space of unknown amount was available at all points except Iraklion and Suda Bay harbors. Additional storage tanks for olive oil were said to be needed in Iraklion and Lasithi nomes.

Communication facilities included 300 telephones, 400 radios, and 80 post office, telegraph, and cable stations. A radio station had recently been erected near Khania.

Banking facilities were available in 8 towns from 28 branches of 7 banks located in Athens. In addition, there were 427 cooperative credit associations.

Six towns and 30 villages distributed water to individual homes through a central water system. The other main sources of water supply for family use included 2,500 springs, 10,000 wells, and 4,700 cisterns.

Nome and municipal public buildings for the four nome capitals and the island capital at Khania were in use and crowded. Other towns and larger community villages provided municipal or community office space as needed by building or renting, or by using the local coffee house. All types of state and municipal hospitals had a total capacity of 1,000 beds. An additional 400 beds were estimated to be in private hospital clinics.

Community health centers were found in the major towns on the island with a few private clinics in addition at Khania and Iraklion.

There were 813 elementary, 28 secondary, and 5 private schools in Crete, most in disrepair and in need of equipment and supplies. There were, in addition, two government agricultural experiment stations and two agricultural schools.

Many town and village churches and country chapels were scattered over the island. Though these were well built, they were not elaborate and had no expensive appointments.

For recreation, there were a few clubs in the two large cities, one stadium at Khania, and a half-dozen summer camps for children scattered over the island—without permanent buildings or equipment since the war. Small parks of less than two city blocks in area were found in only three of the nome capitals. Beach facilities were available for bathing but these were without accommodations.

Archaeological items of unknown value, but of interest to tourists, included the Iraklion Museum and its treasures from the Minoan civilization; the excavations at Knossos, Mallia, Phaestos, and Gortyna; the Venetian walls and moats; and Mt. Ida, Yuktas, and other spots famous in mythology.

Some capital has enhanced the value of human resources by investment in education and technical skills. In Crete, there were 300 doctors, 75 dentists, 60 trained nurses, 75 trained midwives, 25 veterinarians, 1,500 schoolteachers, 50 bankers, 200 lawyers, 300 engineers, 580 priests, 50 druggist-pharmacists, and perhaps 500-1,000 professional government workers. In addition there were the skilled workers in the factories and processing plants, and the clerks and typists in government and private offices.

Granting the incompleteness of the data, the long list of capital resources in Crete places it in an entirely different category of "underdeveloped" areas from India with its severe population problem, or more primitive areas, such as Africa, the South Pacific Islands, or a large proportion of comparable rural areas of Mexico and the South Americas. Capital formation has taken place in Crete. Has the economy become ossified at a "subsistence" living level? Is the lack of natural resources the basic factor here? What are the real causes of economic stagnation at this level? Can they be remedied? These questions will be discussed in later parts of the book.

2. *Losses during the War*[27]

The first great airborne attack in World War II was centered on Crete. The island suffered serious property damage. An official bulletin shows that in one-sixth of the villages of Crete one-fourth of the property was largely destroyed.[28] Regardless of the figures, the war damage in Crete was very substantial. In five towns of less than 2,500 population and in one of 3,500 inhabitants, all buildings were completely destroyed. About one-third of the buildings were destroyed in the cities of Khania and Iraklion and 30 per cent in 96 settlements of Khania nome. In 225 villages of Crete, 23 per cent of the buildings were estimated to be 50 per cent or more destroyed and 3 per cent partially destroyed.[29] Of the families surveyed, one-fourth were living in houses which had been damaged during the war; one-fourth of these had been damaged more than 50 per cent. In 1948, as a result of war destruction, about 200 families were still living in caves in the outskirts of Iraklion and still others were scattered in various communities. (For details see Appendix 5, Tables A19 and A20.)

Estimated war damage in terms of buildings alone was approximately $10 million. At present prices the cost of reconstruction would be three times as great. In addition, roads, harbors, airports, and telephone and telegraph lines were seriously damaged. Automobiles, trucks, engines, machinery, and equipment were damaged or removed. In a country where dowries play such an important role in the economic and social system, the destruction and looting of a large share of the handwoven linens, woolens, clothing, and personal

[27] C. A. Doxiadis, *Such Was the War in Greece.* Athens, Department of Reconstruction, bul. no. 9, 1947. Also his *The Sacrifices of Greece,* illustrated. Athens, Department of Reconstruction, 1947.

[28] C. A. Doxiadis, *Destruction of Towns and Villages.* Athens, Department of Reconstruction, bul. no. 11, 1947, p. 46.

[29] *ibid.*

effects in the majority of homes have placed an added burden upon the economy in the post-war period.

The loss of human lives was also great in Crete due to the war. Although losses for Crete are not known, government estimates are available for all Greece. Since Crete, recognized by all Greeks as furnishing some of their most courageous men in war, put up a valiant resistance during occupation, it is fair to assume that the loss of life among Cretans was at least proportional to that for all Greece. The Greeks proudly but sadly point out that deaths directly due to war in Greece were about 2 per cent of the total population. In comparison, the losses in Great Britain were less than 1 per cent and in the United States about 0.5 per cent of the total population. An additional 3.5 per cent of the Greek population died of starvation during the war. Since the majority of these deaths from starvation occurred in the large cities, Crete suffered relatively less than the mainland.

Despite the civil war on the Greek mainland after liberation, a considerable proportion of the war-damaged houses in Crete had been reconstructed during the three years preceding the survey. Funds were made available through the Ministry of Reconstruction and a small proportion of the houses were built under contract. New buildings are free of taxes for ten years. On the whole, individual householders took the responsibility of rebuilding their homes, with some financial aid from the government. Perhaps three-fourths of the destroyed houses in villages had been partially replaced by some type of permanent shelter. Even Anoyia, a town of 3,500 people, which was completely destroyed except for four rooms, had rebuilt by the summer of 1948 for all but 500 of its population. In the cities, especially Khania, large residential areas near the port had not been rebuilt.

Roads were being improved, harbors had been partially cleared, and communications rebuilt; but the large repairs, although planned with ECA assistance, were yet to be made in 1948. To the extent that this is possible before the Marshall Plan ends, the people of Crete will return to their pre-war level of economy. This should greatly assist in building morale and increasing the desire for further improvements.

D. Governmental Organization: A Resource

In a country with a highly centralized government, limited natural resources, scarce foreign exchange, a large stake in foreign trade, and dependence in local communities upon outside aid (government or foreign groups), the governmental administration exerts important influences both upon the development and the use of natural, human, and capital resources. How well it functions in carrying out the desires of its people and at the same time developing their long-run social responsibilities and opportunities will have an important bearing upon resource use and present and future living levels. Since the structure of the Greek Government will be discussed in detail in Chapter 9, only a summary of the more important aspects affecting resource development and use will be presented here.

The Greek Government consists of three branches: legislative, executive, and judicial. The legislative branch is elected by proportional representation for four-year terms. The Prime Minister and Cabinet of fifteen Ministers determine policies and make decisions within the framework of legislation passed by Parliament. In 1948, the government's regional representative in Crete was the Governor-General[30] nominated by the Council of Ministers in Athens and appointed by the King. Nome and municipal presidents were still appointed (since 1936) from Athens. Even the rural community schoolteachers were "hired and fired" by the Ministry of Education in Athens.

The Greek Government, at the time of the survey, was highly centralized at the capital. Many business transactions, including negotiations for import and export licenses, required much time; usually the person who was interested in obtaining the permit found it necessary to be present in Athens in order to secure due consideration in the maze of papers required. In some cases a week or more of constant follow-up wasted the time and energy of persons who might have made larger contributions to social well-being in other ways. Similarly, the enforcement of regulations and decrees together with "paper work" kept government officials so busy that they were unable to perform more useful functions. Educational programs dealing with agricultural practices which would increase the economic output of the island were hindered by these chores.

Priorities on business loans as well as on import and export licenses

[30] Reports in 1950 indicate that this position has been dispensed with.

were reported to be given to business groups in or near Athens. High customs duties were levied for revenue to meet government expenses, and import controls were exercised with little regard for the relative amount of domestic production of the items imported.

Continuing guerrilla warfare, uncertainties as to a third world war, and wide differences in political philosophies leading to serious tensions between various political parties were all contributory to an unstable government with frequent reorganizations.

In Crete, however, there were few "bandits" or revolutionaries—an estimated 300 in May 1948, and only 35 six months later. In 1948, the people of Crete overwhelmingly belonged to the Venizelist Liberal Party, which was somewhat left of center. Twenty of the twenty-one members of Parliament belonged to this Liberal Party. In 1950, however, only seven of the sixteen members were Venizelist Liberals, while six belonged to the Plastiras-Tsouderos Party and three to the Popular (Royalist) Party. As yet, women cannot become members of Parliament, although they were granted the right to hold municipal and community offices by a law enacted on April 29, 1950. By this law, women were accorded the right to vote at age 25, although men may vote at age 21, at which both sexes become legally of age.

E. Summary of Problems Concerning Resources

The quantity and quality of the natural, human, capital, and government resources of a country are major factors in determining the present state of its development and the possibilities for improvement in the living levels of its population. In Crete there was lack of power, fuel, water, and mineral resources. Only limited areas were suitable for cultivation. There was need for conservation, for reforestation, and for the development of land, water, and fisheries. In the field of education, a functional program will be required if new skills and initiative are to be developed.

Commerce and trade were closely controlled by licenses through the central government. Favoritism and inefficiency were reasons commonly given for the wasted time and effort required to transact business or to start a new enterprise. A large number of splintered parties with strong party followings, constantly jockeying for position and power in the government ministries, resulted in political instability. This, in turn, had its unfortunate impact upon the monetary stability of the country.

The majority of the capital resources of Crete were contained in land improvement—orchards, vineyards, etc., in archaeological sites, houses, household equipment, service industries, and the religious, educational, and health facilities of the 550 communities. While productive working capital and equipment, credit facilities, and productive human resource capital—education, training, and skills—were large in comparison with some undeveloped areas, they were extremely meager in comparison with the more industrialized countries. The recent war and subsequent occupation destroyed much of the working capital and equipment in addition to the roads, harbors, buildings, and communications. Extensive replacement will be required before even pre-war levels of living can be reached.

CHAPTER 5

THE CRETAN FAMILY

As ALREADY NOTED, Crete is predominantly rural, with over 80 per cent of its population away from urban centers in 1948. Here life moved at a slower pace and in much the old manner. In 1948, about three-quarters of the men who were heads of households were residing in the same community in which they were born.[1]

A. COMMUNITY AND URBAN HOUSEHOLDS

Rural farm as well as rural non-farm families lived in the communities—two-fifths of the island inhabitants in villages with a population of less than 500. The farm families did not live on their farm land and were not separated by considerable distances from other families as farm families usually are in the United States. Instead, they resided in a village from which they went out to their various lots in the surrounding area. Though they might have close neighbors in their village, they might be quite isolated from the outside world; often their village was without a road, being accessible only on muleback or on foot.

At the time of the survey the community household[2] averaged about 4.2 members. They resided, typically, in whitewashed stone houses with roofs of clay, tile, or a combination of the two materials. In most cases (81 per cent), the heads of families were men ranging in age from 20 to 95 years with a median age of about 47 years. Certain households frequently included others than immediate dependents, as can be seen from Table 4 below. (For details see Appendix 5, Table A26.)

Of all the rural households, 90 per cent lived in single-family structures[3] while 9 per cent lived in structures housing two households.

[1] A large part of this chapter is based on a report prepared in 1949 by Mrs. E. Jean Learned Mickey for The Rockefeller Foundation from the Sample Survey of Crete. Information for all Cretan households was obtained through sampling 765 of them—617 in rural villages of the communities and 148 in municipalities.

[2] For survey purposes, "Household" in most cases meant the family, but when persons not related were living with the family they were usually regarded as members of the household (p. 2, Instructions for Interviewers). More than one family could be living in the same room or set of rooms, but if they kept separate accounts, had separate heads, "and other distinguishing characteristics" they were regarded as separate households (Instructions for Interviewers, p. 9).

[3] A single structure might house a number of households. This was distinguished

TABLE 4. Composition of households in communities and cities, Crete, 1948

Relation to head	Communities		Cities	
	Per cent of H.H.[a] having	Per cent of persons	Per cent of H.H.[a] having	Per cent of persons
Head	100	24	100	24
Spouse	72	17	66	17
Children	74	49	73	46
Parents	10	3	9	2
Brother or sister	6	2	6	3
Others	17	5	22	8

[a] H.H. is abbreviation for households.
Source: Sample Survey of Crete, Form A, Household.

This compares with an estimated 68 per cent and 28 per cent, respectively, for city households.

Besides the households which had farms, 37 per cent of the community household heads not classified as farmers were partly engaged in some kind of agricultural activity. Among the rural household heads in the labor force in 1948, 77 per cent were engaged in primary industries—agriculture, forestry, fishing, or agriculture and some other occupation.

In comparison with community households, the average number of inhabitants in city households was a little smaller—3.9 as compared with 4.2 in the communities. Only a few of these city households had farms, but 28 per cent of household heads who were not farmers engaged in some kind of agricultural activity. Only 13 per cent of the city household heads relied on agriculture, forestry, or fishing for a livelihood. Household heads, 76 per cent men and 24 per cent women, ranged in age from 15 to 95 years with a median age of about 52 years. Only 17 per cent were born in the city where they were residing. As in the communities, approximately one-fourth had not completed one school year.

B. FAMILY GOALS

The Cretans place a very high value on family ties; the family is probably the strongest influence in their culture. This feeling ex-

in the survey from the "dwelling unit" which was coexistent with the household. For example, "if it has been determined that two distinct households occupy one room, then within that one room there are two dwelling units" (*ibid.*, p. 3).

tends beyond the immediate household; the Cretans are clannish, and occasionally resort to feuds like the traditional Kentucky mountaineer. The parents have a very strong feeling of protection for children but also much of the patriarchal and matriarchal attitude. Children are to be seen and not heard. They do not argue with parents. They work together closely and their recreation is walking together or family gatherings. Marriage, baptism, and christening are very important events in the family circle. Chastity is usual among unmarried women and girls; high social approval is placed upon it. Responsibility for the care of parents in their old age rests with the children, with whom the parents sometimes reside.

Family goals give home ownership and land ownership a high priority in Crete. Some families make great sacrifices to educate their children. In general the survey found that the desires for food, education, leisure, and health took precedence over additional shelter, recreation, and "gadgets." But above these individual and family desires were found the broader and more basic goals of security from outside political interference and of freedom of culture, speech, and religion. Centuries of foreign domination and two world wars have served only to deepen convictions on the importance of these more fundamental goals.

While the crude marriage rate was low, 6.3 per 1,000 of the population as compared with 15.0 per 1,000 in the United States (1946-1947), divorce rates were still lower—14 per 1,000 marriages against 252 per 1,000 in the United States. The pre-war marriage rate of 6.8 in Crete was also lower than the average of 10.6 for the United States in 1934-1939.

The tendency was for women to marry younger than men. The legal age for marriage was 16 for females and 18 for males. Only 2 per cent of the bridegrooms at the time of marriage were under twenty years, while one-seventh of the brides were in their teens. The ages 20-24 included one-half of the brides but only one-third of the grooms. In other words, two-thirds of the bridegrooms were over 24 at the time of marriage. This was as might be expected, since custom required that all girls in the family marry in age sequence and take the marriage vows before any of their brothers. This assured larger dowries for the sisters and caused the young men to wait until they were older and in a better economic position to support a family. Men were also deterred from early marriage because they were subject to two years of compulsory military training at the age of 21.

Over the years a girl's dowry was assembled in anticipation of her marriage. This showed up on the inventories of households with unmarried daughters who were approaching the usual marrying age of about 20-25 years. In some homes almost from the time a girl was born, sheets, blankets, table linens, etc., were woven and made up into the finished products. Other equipment was acquired, too. When such collections were not dissipated during times of necessity—a war, for instance—the accumulations might become very large.

C. Customs and Leisure-Time Activities

Property transfers by inheritance have been largely responsible for the small and scattered land holdings found in Crete. Since property is transferred to all members of the family, even where no will exists, holdings are subdivided and then subdivided again.

If a will is made, the testator is required by law to bequeath each of his children at least one-half of the share which that heir would receive without any will. The father may disinherit any child who has "tried to kill or do bodily harm" to the testator, the child's own mother (but not the stepmother), or any other children of the testator. Similarly, any child leading an "infamous and dissipated life in spite of the advice of his parent" may be disinherited. In both cases, such occurrences must be mentioned in the will.

If there is no will, the wife receives one-fourth of the estate and the remaining three-fourths are divided equally among the children, regardless of sex. If there are no children, however, the wife receives one-half of the estate, with the remainder going to relatives of the deceased.

Since the land in each community varies widely in quality, topography, nearness to the village, access to water and markets, and productivity of fruit and olive trees, each parcel of land is divided among the heirs according to their share. This may apply to houses also, as indicated by one respondent's statement, "This house is the property of six brothers."

In their leisure time men frequented the coffee houses, where they might talk, listen, play cards, sip the black Turkish coffee from their small cups, or just sit. Estimates from the survey indicate that in rural communities each man averaged nine hours per week in the coffee house, while men in the municipalities averaged as much as 12 hours per week. Politics, local and national, was a favorite and often exciting topic at the coffee shop table. From habit many of the men would take from their pockets a tasseled string of large "conversation" beads. These they would nonchalantly finger throughout the discussions—whether actively engaged in conversation or not. To them, these beads, frequently made of amber and quite expensive, were more practical and in the long run less costly than cigarettes and matches, or paper and pencil for "doodling," commonly used by Americans to release nervous energy.

There was a variety of newspapers from both Crete and the Greek mainland. Almost two-fifths of the men and one-ninth of the women read newspapers in Crete. In both communities and cities three times as many men as women read the papers. In the cities the percentage of men and women reading newspapers was twice as high as in the rural villages.

The patriotism of the Cretan extended to his church. Part of being a Greek was being a member of the Greek Orthodox Church. The clergy, often lacking in formal education, exerted great influence in their parishes. In Crete the survey showed about twice as many priests as doctors and about one-third as many priests as teachers.

The priest performs all marriages in Crete. The local priest must petition the local bishop for his authorization. The bishop's office also enters in divorce proceedings. A divorce moves into the courts only after the bishop's efforts to effect a reconciliation have failed.

One gets the impression that Cretan women work harder than the men—particularly in the communities. Managing a Cretan home frequently requires caring for children, cooking, cleaning, spinning, weaving blankets and clothing fabrics, sewing, embroidering, making garments, and helping with some farming activities which have a symbolic significance when performed by women. Women also do the laundry, usually near the community water supply. The community laundry or watering place might well be called the "women's coffee house," for it is here that they exchange news, views, and gossip. The women, assisted by the children, carry the water from the community spring, well, or other source. At meals, traditionally, the men are served by the women, who eat afterwards.

Recreation for women or for families as a whole is rare and shows little variety. One-third of the families in the survey stated that they had no recreation; one-sixth attended a festival or family party once a year; another sixth enjoyed, on the average, two or three such festivities annually. Only the remaining third were able to take the time or had the occasion for more frequent celebrations. A few of the city families who enjoyed American movies—mostly wild Westerns of a decade ago, with Greek titles added—attended once a month. Reasons for the deprivation on the part of those who did not participate in any form of recreation may be gathered from such comments as the following: "We are in mourning, so we have none"; "We have no father or brother"; "We have no recreation now that we have a soldier"; "Cretans do not dance when their men are at war." Daily walks in the evening or family walks on Sunday are a favorite pastime in the cities. These evening walks fill the streets in the cities with people, often in a carnival spirit not unlike that in any midwestern American town on a Saturday night.

Cretan communities have none of the organized clubs or "societies" so common in America. Only one-fifth of the communities and municipalities listed any such organizations, and these were such church groups as "Sunday Schools," "Missionary Society," "Religious Union of Crete," and a "Club for Distributing Christian Literature." The number of these suggests that they are found only in the municipalities and the communities with the larger villages.

D. The Family Income

The "living" produced in Crete necessarily consisted of much that makes up a "living" elsewhere: food, shelter, clothing, leisure time, religion, medical and governmental services, etc.—though some of these were in very small amounts. In comparison with most of the households in industrialized countries, a relatively smaller proportion of these goods and services were purchased with cash income by the Cretan households. The larger share of these items was provided by the housewife and other family members engaged in direct production of goods in the home or derived from owned houses and household equipment or from community services.

1. Cash Income

By American standards most Cretans are poor. Getting even a mean living from a none-too-fertile soil, with little equipment and with few modern compensations for the usual risks of nature, is hard work. The standards of the rural households in Crete were, in many respects, comparable to those of the self-sustaining farmers on the so-called "sub-marginal" land in the United States, as in parts of the Southern Appalachians or Ozarks.

Sale of farm products—crop, animal, or both—was found to be the main source of cash income for a number of Cretan families. Of the 52,000 households whose heads were farmers or farm managers, 57 per cent had annual *cash* incomes of less than $250, and 95 per cent had less than $750.[4]

Other household heads were employed as farm laborers. Prevailing wages for men in this occupation ranged from about $1.00 to $3.50 per day, 95 per cent receiving from $1.50 to $3.00. An average of prevailing daily wage rates for men residing in both cities and communities was $1.88. Women averaged less pay than men for a day's work. Wages for women ranged from $.50 to $2.50 per day, with 87 per cent receiving from $1.00 to $2.00, the average daily wage rate for all women hired being $1.11. The average annual cash income of farm laborers was $201 per household, indicating that they worked relatively few days during the year for wages—perhaps an average of 110 to 150 days annually. This low cash income resulted from the highly seasonal character of the farm work in Crete and the small number of days of outside labor required by the majority of farmers hiring such labor. The fact that these farm-labor households produced an average of only $85 worth of home-produced goods suggests a great deal of underemployment in these households. On the other hand the cash income of $201 is only $73 less than that for the farm operators. Although these figures seem small, about one-tenth of those classified as farmers in the United States had an estimated "value of products sold or used by farm households" of less than $250 each in 1945.

4 Throughout this report—for convenience and because of the wide variation in the value of the drachma from month to month during 1947 and 1948—the monetary quantities in all tables will actually be expressed in ten thousand drachmas (0000 omitted), but dollars will be used in the table heading and discussion. Ten thousand (10,000) drachmas will be considered as the equivalent of one dollar, although the official rates varied from 5,000 to 10,030 (with exchange certificate prices included) drachmas during 1947-1948 and the "free market" rates varied from 9,000 to 14,000 drachmas. The official rate in 1947-1948 was 5,000 drachmas, to which exchange certificate prices were added after October 1947, at prices ranging from 3,000 drachmas at that time to a high of 5,030 in November 1948, and averaging 4,654 for the calendar year 1948. For the period July, August, and September, 1948, when the schedules were taken, this exchange rate (including exchange certificate prices) averaged 10,007.

Farmers, farm managers, combinations of farmer and some other occupation, farm laborers—these constituted an estimated 77 per cent of household heads in the communities and 13 per cent in the cities. Other occupations provided a source of cash income for other households.

a. *Cash income by occupations.* Average cash income was largest in the professional occupations, being $1,035. Even this was not high by U.S. standards. Figure 6 shows the various occupations in order of the size of cash income received per household in 1947. Seven of the ten groups averaged less than $500 per year. Households of white-collar workers and craftsmen, as a whole, averaged higher cash incomes than those of laborers (both farm and non-farm). (See Figure 6 and Appendix 5, Tables A28 to A32.)

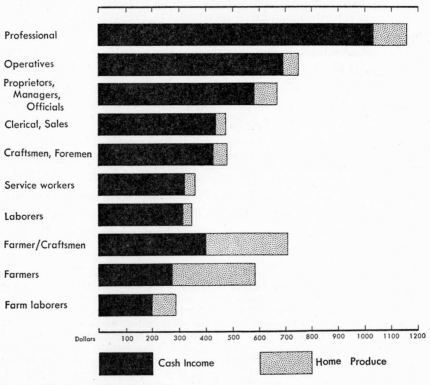

AVERAGE ANNUAL HOUSEHOLD INCOME 1947

Based on data in Appendix 5, Table A28.

FIGURE 6. Average annual cash and total household incomes, by occupation of household head, 1947

No household derived what ordinarily would be considered in the United States as a high money income from any occupation. Among all community household heads, except "operatives and kindred workers," at least 50 per cent were earning less than $500 cash per year per household, regardless of occupation. Except for the professional people, at least 50 per cent—and in some cases many more —of the city households in various occupation groups were receiving less than $750 per year. This is the more significant when one considers the inflated prices of goods which families had to buy. (For details see Tables 37, 38, and 39 in Chapter 9.)

An analysis of cash income by households shows relatively more rural households in the lower income brackets—almost two-thirds receiving less than $250 cash annually. About one-third of city families fall in the same class (Table 5).

TABLE 5. Percentage of households having less than the specified cash incomes in communities, cities, and all Crete, 1947

Percentage of households	Communities	Cities	All Crete
10	$ 12	$ 60	$ 20
20	50	120	50
30	80	240	100
40	120	360	150
50	180	480	200
60	204	600	300
70	300	630	360
80	400	840	480
90	600	1,200	720
100	2,520	2,400	2,520

Source: Sample Survey of Crete, Form A, Household.

Before more comparisons are made, however, the other sources of income should be taken into account. The differences between urban and rural households are reduced when an estimated value of the family's production of clothing and food during the year is added to the cash income. (For comparisons see Figure 6 and Appendix 5, Tables A27 and A28.)

2. Total Income[5]

Annual money income may or may not indicate what a household uses or has available for use. Where goods purchased with money income are supplemented by household production, gifts, and community services, total real income can exceed money income appreciably, particularly in an economy like that of Crete. Where there is less specialization of marketing functions and productive services, the family is necessarily more self-sufficient. When we note total income (money income, plus the estimated value of home produce at local market prices), the importance of the latter becomes evident, especially among farmers, farm managers, and farm laborers. (See Appendix 5, Table A28.)

TABLE 6. Home produce as a percentage of total income, Crete, 1947

Income class	Communities	Cities	All Crete
(dollars)		(percentage)	
0-249	47	9	41
250-499	49	6	39
500-749	46	9	39
750 and over	42	5	32
All income groups	45	8	36

Source: Sample Survey of Crete, Form A, Household.

Tables 6 and 7 also illustrate this point. In community households home production was relatively more important at all income levels than in city households. For income groups receiving less than $750, almost half the total income of community households was produced directly by family members. Such an important contribution to value of goods available for use eliminates the urban-rural contrasts implied when only money-income data are used. When total-income averages are taken, the difference between households in the rural villages and municipalities is not large in quantity of goods consumed, though it illustrates a variance in types of production.

[5] Total income includes cash income and the value of home produce, which is the respondent's estimate of "value of your family's production of clothing and food during the year in terms of money." Both types of items are apt to be valued at "home or farm prices" in the rural areas, as there is considerable exchange between families directly, at the local fair, or on market day. In the cities, this figure for home produce may include a larger share at local retail prices or local village prices.

TABLE 7. Average total income per household, Crete, 1947

Type of income	Communities	Cities	All Crete
Cash	$ 249	$ 544	$ 306
Home produce	204	37	172
Total	453	581	478

Source: Sample Survey of Crete, Form A, Household.

Even though average cash incomes of city households exceeded those of community households, total incomes differed less because of the differences in value of home-produced goods.

a. *Household production.* In the Crete Survey there is a positive relationship between size of total income and the average number of persons per household. It is possible that this may be explained, in part, by the larger number of persons whose labor may contribute to cash income and/or home production (Table 8).

Such a statement of this relationship must be used with caution in refuting the argument that there may be too many people trying to make a living from small pieces of land—some who might well be shifted into other occupations. The desire of farmers to educate most of their children for other opportunities so that the land may be passed on without further division is well founded. The larger in-

TABLE 8. Average number of persons per household in specified total income groups, Crete, 1948

Income group	Average number of persons per household			Total income per person
	Communities	Cities	All Crete	
(dollars)		(number)		(dollars)
0-249	3.2	3.0	3.2	37
250-499	4.2	3.8	4.1	89
500-749	4.6	4.2	4.5	133
750-999	5.5	4.9	5.4	158
1,000-1,249	5.4	5.3	5.4	195
1,250-1,499	6.5	2.5	5.5	277
1,500 and over	5.6	5.3	5.5	387
Average	4.2	3.9	4.1	116[a]

a Cash income per person is $74.
Source: Sample Survey of Crete, Form A, Household.

comes of the larger families may come from many sources and do not imply that additional labor used on land, alone, would yield higher economic returns than if used on land together with other alternative opportunities.

The percentage of household heads who were women was higher in the lower income groups, decreasing as income increased. The lower wages of women may partly, though by no means entirely, explain this relationship between size of income and sex of household head. When the head was a woman, moreover, the number of household members contributing to income was smaller.

As would be expected, handicrafts were practiced in relatively more community than city households. Three-fifths of the rural families practiced spinning and two-fifths weaving. Furniture making, leather working, silver smithing, stone carving, stone sculpturing, and the making of handbags or dolls were also practiced in some homes.

Eight per cent of the community households did not engage in any agricultural activity, even as a means of supplementing family income. Fifty-five per cent of the community households had farms, and an additional 37 per cent of them were classified as sub-farm households. Although not properly classified as operating farms, these sub-farm households engaged in some form of agricultural activity. In the communities, 16 per cent of them raised crops only, 13 per cent animals only, and 71 per cent both crops and animals. The animals most frequently found in farm and sub-farm households were sheep, goats, donkeys, swine, and poultry. Households having poultry and rabbits slaughtered more of these for home use than other animals that might be used for meat. However, animals slaughtered annually for home use were not numerous enough to contribute much meat to a family's yearly food supply.

About 30 per cent of city households carried on agricultural activity. A few were classified as farmers, but about one-fourth also engaged in agriculture on "sub-farms." Of these, 32 per cent raised only crops, 41 per cent only animals, and 27 per cent a combination of crops and animals. More goats and poultry than other animals were owned by the city households. As in the communities, more rabbits than other meat animals were slaughtered per household for home use, though again not in large numbers.

Processing of food is another form of household production—for the most part, taking place relatively more in community than in city households. The survey indicates this in the production of hondros (a mixture of crushed wheat and milk, salted, cooked, and dried), tsikoudia (a distilled liquor), butter, cheese; the canning and bottling of food; the preservation of meat; and the drying of various fruits. Over half the community households, in 1948, made hondros, tsikoudia, and dried fruits. Raisins and figs were the fruits most frequently dried in both city and community households which engaged in this kind of production.

Many of the food products prepared at home were kept for home use only. However, some families also marketed all or part of such processed items. In most cases, food processing supplemented family income through direct production of food for family uses; in others the sale of products added to the cash income.

Besides these important sources—cash and household production —the services from an owned home and durable goods, plus certain community services, also contributed to the level of family living.

b. *Use value of durable goods owned.* About 89 per cent of the community households owned their own homes and only 3 per cent rented, the remainder living in rent-free houses belonging to relatives or unsettled estates. In the cities 62 per cent owned their homes but almost a third rented houses.

For these home-owning households, the annual use value of a house was an important part of their real income, since cash income was not used to pay rent and might be allocated elsewhere. Rental rates were under government control and varied from $3 to $10 per month for most houses. Post-war estimates of the value for such dwellings indicated a figure of about $1,000 per room as compared to $500 pre-war. The typical two- to three-room structure would, then, average about $2,000 to $3,000 in value.

c. *Other goods owned by Cretan families.* Cretan households were not equipped with the appliances and conveniences of a house in a modern urban center. Most families cooked their meals and heated their houses with fireplaces or braziers. Very few houses, especially in the rural communities, had electricity or running water. Household furnishings, including linen and bedding (in some cases large supplies), utensils, and clothing, along with the houses, made up most of the goods owned and used by Cretan families.

Though no precise comparisons between households can be made on the basis of monetary value of goods owned, if a household owned an average number of every household item listed in the inventory, the value probably would not exceed $450, according to a rough estimate made by a Greek home economist who visited many of the sample households. Obviously, differences in quality were not taken into account. Effects of the war were evident in the inventories of families who contributed blankets and other supplies to the war effort, or used up items which could not be replaced because of wartime scarcities. Other families were forced to sell some items to meet family emergencies. Although inventories were taken three years after the close of the war, many families probably had less than average pre-war amounts of household furnishings and supplies.

E. Clothing

In Crete the clothing was a mixture of native costumes and Western dress. In most cases, chief emphasis was placed on durability. Garments made in the home of homespun fabrics would wear for years or even a lifetime. Although supplies were quite limited, the majority of families had sufficient clothing to permit each member one or more changes of the most essential items.

1. Native Costume

Women often dressed in black with a shawl over their heads. Walking along the dusty roads, they might hold the shawl across the mouth and nose. The traditional costume of young girls in the country, seldom seen now, consisted of "black blouses braided with gold, reddish snoods with gold embroidery, silver necklaces, and strings of gold coins."[6]

If dressed up in complete native costume, men might be seen wearing knee-high boots, dark trousers, and long red-lined cloaks over a blue, heavily braided vest. For everyday wear the boots were common, with riding breeches or the baggy Turkish trousers, but the rest of the costume (particularly the vest) was much less commonly seen. The complete outfit was expensive—probably costing as much as $300 in 1948. Around the waist men wear an "immense cummerbund whose countless folds serve more than a purely decorative purpose as they afford an admirable and much needed protection to the liver and kidneys in a climate where the temperature is subject to violent changes in the course of a few hours; and the small black turbans with a pendant, satanic fringe level with the eyebrows—all

[6] E. Wilson, "Greek Diary." *New Yorker*, 21:81-96. November 17, 1944.

combine to produce an effect of elegant ferocity which is still further enhanced by the immense mustaches lovingly cultivated by all those of an age to do so."[7]

This picturesque costume was giving way to modern Western dress. Boots were still common, but leather belts were replacing the wide cummerbund. Sudden daily changes in temperature necessitated the addition of a wool undershirt, even in the summertime, if the cummerbund was abandoned. The high boots were a necessary protection against the rocks and thorny bushes on the mountainside. In the cities, low shoes were more comfortable and less expensive. In addition they carried a certain prestige value by being novel yet socially acceptable.

Even since the war, the color and style of women's clothing had undergone some change. There appeared to be less black and more bright colors. Black is traditional and was especially common during the war and the early post-war period when so many families were mourning the loss of a relative. Clothing sent for relief aid may have had some influence; apparently brighter colors were being chosen when purchases were made.

But ready-made dresses were not available; the purchases were of yard goods. Since few sewing machines were available, most of the dresses were sewed by hand, and dressmaking was a trade for many women in the cities. Clothing of sheer materials was seldom worn.

While relief shipments of shoes to Crete added variety, they had not caused much change in the style of shoes worn by the women and girls. At least the high-heeled "party" shoes sent by some well-meaning donors from the Western world have had little effect—other than to cause wonder as to how they might be made into something useful. Anyone having seen the Cretan dance with its extremely high tempo and "heavy" steps can understand why such shoes would be unserviceable even at the festivals. But many low-heeled shoes suitable for walking or working in the fields have been received by the Cretan womenfolk from their American friends and relatives. Wooden-soled huaraches were quite commonly worn. Shoes were a part of the social pattern for the women and children of Crete—contrary to the situation in large segments of the population in many countries with a similar climate. Of course many children went barefooted during the summer for comfort as well as economy.

[7] Osbert Lancaster, "The Island Greeks." *Atlantic Monthly*, 182:59-64, 1948.

2. Clothing Supplies

Since clothing supplies were included in the household inventory lists compiled during the seven-day diet survey, some general observations are of interest.

Most households (80 to 100 per cent) had on hand supplies of men's underwear, shirts, stockings, boots, shoes, and trousers. In general the same was true for boys' clothing. Only 8 per cent of the households reported such items as pajamas, hats, ties, scarfs, gloves, slippers, raincoats, and umbrellas. Not being a customary accessory for the well-dressed Cretan, neckties are worn primarily to impress visitors. Three-fourths of the city men had complete suits and shoes in comparison with two-fifths of the rural men. More rural men had boots, cape-shawls, and waist-belts than city men. (For details see Appendix 5, Table A39.)

Girls appear to have been best supplied with shoes, handkerchiefs, slips, and dresses, and with only slightly fewer blouses, sweaters, coats, and skirts. Judging from the inventories, one would say that households were best supplied with the following articles of women's clothing: jackets, stockings, shoes, handkerchiefs, kerchiefs, brassières, dresses, and aprons. (For details see Appendix 5, Table A40.)

No doubt the war had a great effect on clothing supplies as well as on household furnishings and equipment. Though similar information on pre-war inventories was not available for the sample families, from present stocks one can infer with considerable confidence that the clothing supplies of families were below par when the survey was made.

F. Cretan Houses and Furnishings

The Cretan house, typically, was a one-family structure with thick stone walls and clay or tile roofs, high ceilings, and shuttered windows. Most windows were unglazed, and screens were not used. In the rural areas these unpretentious dwellings appeared in clusters in small villages.

1. Construction

The construction of Cretan houses today is of the same materials as in centuries past. Ninety-five per cent of the walls in the community houses and 88 per cent in the city houses were made of native stone; the rest were of brick or stone in combination with other materials.

Over half the roofs in the communities were made of clay (43 per cent) or a combination of clay and tile (14 per cent) ; a quarter of them were of tile. Most of the others were of concrete or a combination of tile and concrete. In the cities more of the roofs were made of tile (56 per cent), concrete (11 per cent), or a combination of concrete and tile (6 per cent). Clay alone was used for 13 per cent, and various combinations of these materials for 14 per cent of the roofs.

Earth was a frequently used material for floors in Crete—either alone or in combination with something else. Earth, earth and wood, earth and concrete, or a combination of the three made up the floors in 87 per cent of the houses. A few were made solely of wood or concrete. In the cities there was a significant number of earth and earth-combination floors, though other materials—wood, concrete, stone— were used in over half the floors of city dwellings. (For further details see Appendix 5, Tables A41 to A47.)

The earth floor was prepared by pounding the earth until it was very hard. Sometimes this was accomplished not simply by laborious pounding but by inviting friends over to a dance—making a new floor at the same time.

2. Size and Condition

A large number of houses in Crete were one- or two-story structures. In the communities 64 per cent of the dwellings had only a "general floor" (one story) and 36 per cent a "first floor"—or what we would call two stories. In the cities, it is estimated that 70 per cent of the houses had one story, 28 per cent two stories, and 2 per cent three stories.

Two-thirds of the dwellings had three rooms or less. Fewer community than city households were living in one room. However, if rooms used only for living quarters are included, the urban-rural differences are less. In the cities almost one-fourth of the households had more than three rooms, while in communities only 9 per cent had more than three.

More important than the actual number of rooms is the use to which they are put and their "adequacy" in meeting family needs— size, furnishings, facilities, and the general condition of the rooms. These must be considered in relation to family size, age of members, sex composition, occupation, and the various activities carried on in the home by its members.

The average number of square meters of floor space per dwelling unit was actually greater in the rural areas: 56 in communities as compared to 39 in the cities. This allowed an average of 13 square meters per person in communities and 10 per person in the cities. But when living quarters only are considered, the average per dwelling was 39 in community households and 37 in the cities—or about nine square meters per person in each.

The amount of *dry* floor space per dwelling and per person is probably more indicative of welfare than mere total area available. Of course, the dry area is difficult to determine as its amount would vary with the seasons. Because of the number of clay roofs and earth floors, particularly in the communities, one might expect dampness during the rainy season. At any rate, this seemed an important reason in the minds of some families for dissatisfaction with their housing accommodations. After answering the question, "Are you satisfied with your housing accommodation?" some who said "No" gave reasons such as: "in winter the roof leaks and water runs in"; "the house is damp"; "the clay roof leaks in winter"; "water comes in in the winter"; "in winter water comes up from the floor." It is impossible to say how widespread is this problem of dampness. However, in noting comments on the schedules, one is impressed that needed roof repairs and dampness are often mentioned. In a radius of a hundred yards in one municipality, four roofs made of clay collapsed during heavy rains in February 1949.

In communities, storage space was provided in one-half the homes; 41 per cent of the families had one room and 10 per cent more than one. In comparison, 92 per cent of the city homes had no rooms used exclusively for storage purposes, and only 7 per cent had one room for that purpose. The amount of storage space was also larger in the communities—42 per cent of the households having more than 10 square meters of floor space as compared to 4 per cent in the cities. The rural houses required more storage space because of more self-sustaining households and the absence of retail merchants.

Most Cretan dwellings in 1948 were not satisfactory to their inhabitants. Of all the families, 26 per cent said they were satisfied, while 74 per cent indicated dissatisfaction. On the whole, more city families seemed to be satisfied (39 per cent) with their housing accommodation than rural families (22 per cent).

3. Housing of Animals

Four-fifths of the rural and one-fourth of the city households had livestock on hand. In both communities and cities, less than half of the households had separate shelters for their animals. In rural areas 14 per cent reported no shelter—stabling animals in the yard. The rest of the community households sheltered their animals in rooms connected with the house (25 per cent), under the main room (11 per cent), in the same room with the family (8 per cent), or with the neighbors (1 per cent).

Only 2 per cent of the city households had no shelters for their animals. In 32 per cent of the city households, the animals were sheltered in rooms connected with the house; in 14 per cent they were co-sheltered with the families; and in 11 per cent, under the main room.

4. *Furnishings and Facilities*

Cretan households, particularly in the communities, so used their small yards that they might often be considered almost a part of the dwelling unit. Besides providing a place for children to play, for the family to sit, and as an approach to the house, the yard or the court also served as storage space for wood and farm equipment and a place to stable or tether animals.

a. *Conveniences*. In the communities four-fifths of the families used a fireplace to heat their houses in cold weather, though a few used braziers or stoves. Most of these burned wood for fuel, while some used charcoal, and a few olive by-products.

In contrast, four-fifths of the city households used the brazier for heating, and only a few depended on the fireplace. Also charcoal was more often burned as fuel in the city than in the country because it was cheaper to transport and store and was also more convenient. About 8 per cent of the families—rural and urban—did not heat their homes.

City families were more often dependent upon community ovens than were those living in the communities. Less than a tenth of the city households had their own ovens, while in the rural areas almost half of the families had ovens. Many small villages did not have a community oven.

Cretan housewives had few "conveniences" in their houses. Of the community households in which meals were prepared, 97 per cent cooked on the open fireplace. In city homes, 70 per cent relied on fireplaces; 13 and 17 per cent on braziers and kerosene stoves, respectively.

Nearly all rural families carried water from springs, wells, or other sources. Almost two-thirds of these lived far enough from the source of supply so that it took more than ten minutes to fetch the water. For 15 per cent of the families, 30 to 90 minutes were required. More city homes had running water. The city families that did not have this convenience lived, on the average, a shorter distance from the source; for approximately 80 per cent, five minutes or less were required to fetch water.

b. *Decorations.* Inside the house, walls were painted or white-washed. This was a customary annual pre-Easter job in each household. One very common article of household equipment was a white-washing brush. When available, fresh flowers might be used to brighten the interior.

In some homes numerous photographs, pictures, and wall hangings decorated the walls. More rural than city homes were barren of such adornment, though over half of the rural homes had from one to nine pictures or hangings.

There were few glass windows to admit light during inclement weather. In communities, most of the windows had shutters (67 per cent) or a combination of glass and shutters (15 per cent), and these were thrown open to admit light and air. Some dwellings had no windows at all. Draperies were seldom seen adorning the windows of a rural home. Families who used them had, on an average, two draped or curtained windows.

In the cities more of the houses had glass or a combination of glass and shutters for their windows. Though approximately half of the families interviewed had no drapes in 1948, those who did have drapes used them on an average of more than three windows.

How essential windows and draperies were to the Cretan family is difficult to say. During the interview a few indicated that they would like to put more windows in their houses. As for draperies, the figures collected for 1948 may or may not approximate the pre-war number. During hostilities some families converted washable curtain fabrics into underclothing or other garments.

Mirrors were a rather common part of house furnishings. Community households averaged one and city homes more than one. A few boasted several.

c. *Furniture.* Few houses were found to be entirely without chairs, though community homes averaged fewer than city homes. Except for a few of the higher income households with special living room furniture, chairs were of the sturdy kitchen type—similar to the hickory chairs with woven bark seats of pioneer days. These Cretan chairs were quite comfortable, otherwise they would have been less popular at the coffee house—where extra chairs were available for foot rests, arm rests, or for hanging the cane or coat.

In Crete, boards placed across a trestle composed the beds of many families. Even trestle beds, on an average, were few in number. Families having no beds (8 per cent in the communities) presumably slept on the floor. Though the number of inhabitants per dwelling varied considerably, against an average of 4.1 persons per household in the communities, there were only 1.8 beds available. The ratio was a little higher in cities, where an average of 3.9 persons per household had an average of 2.6 beds. (For more details on furnishings and household supplies see Appendix 5, Tables A35, A36, A37, and A38.)

5. *Attitudes toward Housing*

Reasons for dissatisfaction were as varied as the people making them. For example, a 70-year-old woman said she was not satisfied with her dwelling but was not thinking of doing anything about it— "What use could it be to me, since I am expecting death?" Another said, ". . . because it is small, I would like a new and larger one so that we would not be obliged to cook, sleep, and store everything in the same room." One woman wants "a lavatory; also at least one room which I can offer as a living room to a stranger." And a discouraged couple said, "Since we were married, every year we think of building a new floor, but each year our funds worsen." Some families mentioned the desire for "healthier" quarters. Apparently high ceilings are considered desirable in Crete. One householder believed "the air hinders us very much because the house has a northern aspect; it also has low ceilings and so it is unhealthy." The natives of Kandanos severely criticized the Ministry of Reconstruction for building separate houses out in the fields rather than in the formerly tightly packed villages. Their objection was that the new houses were inconveniently located for water supplies. This scattering of houses forced some change in the customs in a mountainous area, where fierce family and clan feuds were common.

All in all, the desire to enlarge the dwelling, increase the facilities, and make repairs seemed to predominate. The Cretan's dissatisfaction with his dwelling was more a dissatisfaction with its condition than with the kind or style of home he had. Nor was there any reason why he should feel otherwise. The native materials which have been used for centuries can still be employed to construct adequate, attractive houses. In the architect's proposed rebuilding plans to make the new Khania a model city, "the houses themselves are conceived in the spirit of native materials and native skills; simple construction, familiar to every Greek artisan, local stone and lime mortar used as it (sic) has been for centuries with a great feeling for handsomeness. The heavy walls are native insulation against the Cretan sun. The small beams are cut from the arid pine or rejuvenated olive that cover the hills. Even seaweed is used to build up flat roofs just as the laborers used it in the days of the labyrinth. The simple lines of the houses will make new Canea (Khania) look modern as a world's fair, but they are as traditional as a temple. . . ."[8]

For some families the problem was to rebuild what was destroyed during the war. As might be expected, more city houses were damaged than rural houses. A little less than half (46 per cent) of city homes in the sample were damaged, 78 per cent of these being less than 50 per cent damaged, and 22 per cent, more than 50 per cent damaged. In the communities, 82 per cent of the dwellings escaped damage. Of the remaining 18 per cent, only 27 per cent were damaged more than 50 per cent. It should be remembered that houses completely demolished, or partially destroyed and not then lived in, had no opportunity to be included in the survey. Consequently the above figures understate the war damage to Cretan homes. A survey by the Ministry of Reconstruction in Crete indicated that about 23 per cent of all buildings in 225 settlements were damaged more than 50 per cent.[9]

For other families, expansion of space and facilities—particularly sanitary facilities—and the making of needed repairs should have priority. However, it is to be hoped that throughout the island, as in the proposed new Khania, "all that is beautiful, indigenous and particularly Cretan will be kept, as it should be. Reconstruction is not revolution, it is rebirth."[10]

[8] Unsigned article, "The Future of a Greek Town." *House and Garden*, 87:63-5, 1945.

[9] C. A. Doxiadis, *Destruction of Towns and Villages*. Athens, Department of Reconstruction, bul. no. 11, 1947, p. 46.

[10] Unsigned article, "The Future of a Greek Town." *House and Garden*, 87:63-5, 1945.

G. Summary

The Cretan household included, roughly, four persons. Over four-fifths of the families lived in rural communities. Three-fourths of the male household heads were born in the same communities in which they resided at the time of the survey.

Two-thirds of all household heads were engaged in agriculture, while nearly four-fifths of those in the communities were so occupied. The average cash income for all households in 1947 was estimated to be $306; $249 for rural households and $544 for city families. The professional group had the highest average cash income, $1,035; the farm-labor group (other than domestic service) the lowest average cash income, $201.

Household production contributed an important part ($172) to the average total income ($478) in most Cretan homes—particularly in the communities. Some goods and services were purchased with cash income which the family received chiefly from the sale of farm products or from the labor of its members—but in addition to this, much that the family consumed was produced in the home for direct consumption. The most important sources of such income were: food produced for home use, including animals slaughtered; food processing, canning, bottling, and drying; and services of family members in the form of spinning, weaving, and other crafts. Further sources of real income, not estimated, were the services from owned homes, and from such durable goods as the family had, in addition to certain community services—roads, schools, health facilities, etc., which will be discussed in later chapters. (See Chapters 7 and 8.)

Sudden temperature changes and rigorous winters in the mountains necessitated heavy woolen clothing, underwear, and boots or heavy shoes. While clothes were not plentiful, most families had the "bare necessities," but city families had the larger supplies of complete suits for men and dresses for women. Boots, trousers, jackets, and the waist-belt were still commonly worn by half or more of the rural men. Leather belts and woolen undershirts were replacing the cummerbund for men, and colored dresses were taking the place of the traditional black for women. Durability was most important. Homespun clothing was common and ready-made dresses were rare.

For the most part, Cretans lived in whitewashed stone houses with clay or tile roofs. A majority of the dwellings had two or three rooms, and averaged 9 square meters of floor space per person. The small number of rooms did not assure what United States standards would define as adequate privacy, but this was less serious at the moment than the leaky roofs, damp floors, the need for post-war reconstruction, and the making of neglected "maintenance" repairs.

CHAPTER 6

FOOD AND NUTRITION

PRE-WAR LEVELS of food consumption in Crete and Greece—estimated by the United States Department of Agriculture at 2,300-2,499 calories daily per capita—were, together with those of Albania and Portugal, the lowest in Europe during the period 1933-1937 (Figure 7). Data from the recent Crete Survey indicate that with certain adjustments for wines consumed and for seasonal differences, the 1948 level of food consumption of about 2,550 calories was slightly above the upper limit of the pre-war range. Since it is generally con-

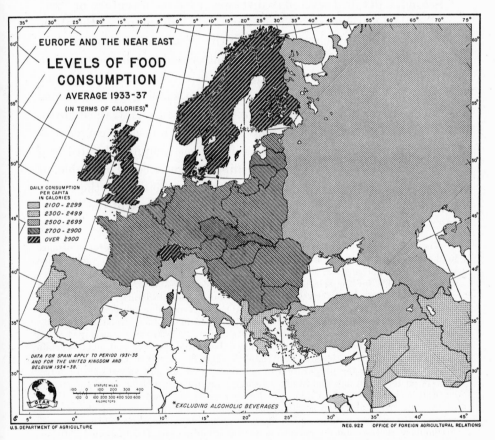

FIGURE 7. Levels of food consumption in Crete, Europe, and Near East, pre-war

ceded that more food per person is available and consumed in Crete than in all Greece, these data seem reasonable.[1]

A. Dietary Survey Method Used

In studying the food habits and food consumption levels of the Cretan families, three types of information were sought. First, an estimate of annual food consumption was obtained from each of the 765 households selected by recognized random sampling procedures. (For detailed methodology see Appendix 1.) Information was elicited not only on food consumed but on its production and purchase, as well as on methods of cooking, preserving, and storing. (See Appendix 2, Form A.)

Second, a detailed seven-day diet survey by the inventory or "record" method was made of 128 or a one-sixth sub-sample of the above random-selected households. The quantity of all foods consumed during one week of the fall season—September and October—was carefully determined by weighing all foods in the household at the beginning and end of the week, in addition to keeping a daily record of foods consumed. (See Appendix 2, Form Ia.) A trained investigator visited each of these households daily for seven consecutive days. The nutrient content of these foods was computed by utilizing tables of values for foods in the Mediterranean Area, if available, or other data. Menus, food purchases, and food habits of these sub-sample families were studied in more detail than those of the remaining sample households.

[1] The authors wish to express their indebtedness to various individuals for assistance in the development of the material in this chapter. (See Appendix 3 for detailed responsibilities.) Dr. R. J. Jessen, N. V. Strand, and J. C. Dodson, statisticians, were responsible for the selection of the households, phrasing of questions, training and supervision of interviewers, and supervision of the statistical analysis of the data. Miss A. Tsongas, Nutrition Officer, FAO, was responsible for general planning of the food and nutrition phase in Crete and assisted in the final preparation of this chapter; Dr. J. R. Trémolières, medical nutritionist, Paris, France, developed plans for the nutrition information in the general household survey, and made certain analyses and critical reviews of this chapter; Miss Helen Sdrin, Greek nutritionist, was responsible for the preparation of schedules, training and supervision of interviewers on the seven-day diet study, editing of schedules, provision of historical and cultural background of the Cretans, and assistance in the analysis and interpretation of the data. Dr. Calla Van Syckle, consumption economist, was responsible for developing the general outline of the analysis of the data, the basic tables, and such preliminary analysis and interpretation as time would permit. Dr. E. Jean L. Mickey, consumption economist, summarized the 765-family income and diet data. Miss Thelma J. Norris, Nutrition Officer, FAO, developed the final outline for this chapter and prepared much of the text.

Third, "food balance sheet" data showing per capita food consumption for Greece in the pre-war and post-war periods were compared with consumption data—annual and seasonal—from the Cretan sample families. Allowing for differences in food production, supplies, exports, and imports between Crete and Greece, an estimate of the average daily food consumption per capita in Crete was determined for 1948. Although comparison with a "food balance sheet" for Crete was preferred, loss of island pre-war records of commodity imports and exports, and the relatively unreliable production and importation data since the end of World War II made this procedure inadvisable.

General knowledge of the types of food, seasonality, and relative importance was also used in making final judgment of the adequacy of the Cretan diet. In addition, a reconnaissance survey was made of 200 school children in the city of Khania by a medical nutritionist, Dr. J. R. Trémolières of Paris, France. His observations did not disclose any noticeable evidence of widespread malnutrition in Crete.

Since the detailed survey covered only one week in the fall, the data on the annual food consumption by 765 sample survey families, and the Food Balance Sheet Estimates for Greece for 1948-1949 have been used also in making estimates of annual food consumption and tentative judgments as to the nutrients which, in 1948, were least satisfactory in comparison with the National Research Council Recommended Dietary Allowances.

In interpreting the discussion which follows on food and nutrition, the following limitations of this survey should be kept in mind: (1) major dependence upon an autumn diet study, when certain foods are relatively more plentiful, especially in the mountainous areas; (2) lack of specific data on the nutrient content of the foods grown in Crete; and (3) lack of clinical studies of the people of Crete to determine their food needs in relation to health status. However, the results of the survey are the best available data for Crete and so far as known now are the best in the Mediterranean Basin for presenting a general picture of the food habits and relative nutrient intake levels of various groups of food.

B. Food Pattern, Food Habits, and Attitudes Towards Food

Olives, cereal grains, pulses, wild greens and herbs, and fruits, together with limited quantities of goat meat and milk, game, and fish have remained the basic Cretan foods for forty centuries. Evidences of this include the agricultural products, storage facilities, equipment, and art work found in the Minoan ruins. Additional indications of the food patterns of the past and the changes which have taken place are found in the writings of Homer and others down through the centuries. Except for the addition of citrus fruit and tomatoes during the past millennium, and of apples, grapes, wine, pomegranates, and sheep during the Doric era almost three millenniums ago, the basic foods for the modern Cretan diet are probably much the same as during the Minoan period about 2000 B.C.

The survey showed that no meal was complete without bread. Even diabetics attempted to reduce other sources of carbohydrates enough to permit at least a small amount of bread in the diet. Bread was also symbolic. As a housewife completed the shaping of a new loaf she might cross herself; she might imprint the sign of the cross on the bottom of the loaf. Breads were important in church ceremonies and in commemorating important events or crises in the family. For example, loaves and rolls might be taken to the church for a time after the death of a relative—later to be distributed to the poor.

Olives and olive oil contributed heavily to the energy intake. To the foreign visitor, food seemed literally to be "swimming" in oil. In addition to being used freely as a cooking fat and as an oil for salads, it was added to soups and cooked vegetables.

Methods of food preparation were relatively simple and in most instances probably preserved the nutritive value of food rather well.

1. Types of Foods Used

The Cretan diet consisted chiefly of foods of vegetable origin, with cereals, vegetables, fruits, and olive oil predominating. Pulses and nuts were eaten in appreciable quantities—especially during the winter—and potatoes were used quite extensively. On the other hand, meat, fish, milk, eggs, and sweets were consumed in relatively small amounts. Butter was seldom used. Slightly more cheese per person was consumed in Crete than in the United States. (For details as to kinds and quantities of food consumed during the Seven-day Diet Survey see Appendix 5, Table A51.)

The foods which were distributed on ration during 1948 at the time of the survey were: sugar, wheat flour, rice, powdered milk, pulses during certain seasons, tinned or powdered milk for special groups such as children, nursing mothers, and pregnant women during the last four months of pregnancy. The daily milk and raisin bun served to school children during the school year provided 560 calories and 26 grams of protein, of which 17 grams were animal protein. Indigent families (defined by law as those with per capita incomes up to $2.50 monthly) received rations of sugar, maize, and soya flour free of charge. According to Ministry of Welfare reports, about 15 per cent of the population in Crete was listed as indigent in April 1948, although community officials reported that 31 per cent of the elementary school children came from indigent families. The seven-day diet data, upon which most of the following discussion was based, included all food consumed in the households, regardless of source.

2. Methods of Preparation

The methods of food preparation were simple, and the cooking equipment used was primitive and very limited. Ninety-two per cent of the families used the open fireplace as the main cooking device. Only two-fifths of the families, most of whom lived in the rural areas, owned private ovens. However, public ovens were available in all cities and in many villages and communities. Foods requiring baking or roasting could be left at the public oven with the baker for a small fee. The main methods of cooking were stewing and boiling. In the case of meat, the survey indicated that these two methods were the principal ones used by 99 per cent of the households. The tendency to use one-dish meals might be due to the type of cooking equipment available, as well as to the scarcity of fuel. Of the many families interviewed, approximately one-half cooked only once a day. Home refrigeration or even commercial refrigeration was almost nonexistent on the island.

There was no special equipment for food preservation. Preserving was practiced more in the rural communities than in the municipalities. Simple methods, such as sun drying, were used.

Hondros[2] was prepared by three-fifths of all families interviewed, but twice as often among rural as city families.

The frequent use of braising and boiling and the commendable habit of dipping bread into the sauce saved nutrients, particularly minerals and vitamins.

The lack of fuel and adequate cooking space, the public oven arrangement, the habit of cooking once a day, and the extensive use

[2] Hondros is crushed wheat and milk (sweet or sour), salted and cooked together, then spread out in thin sheets and dried in the sun. It may be kept for long periods.

of nonsolid fat (olive oil) explain the tendency to serve food cold or lukewarm.

3. Meal Patterns

The day of the Cretan, who is most often a rural person, is long. The meals are spread over a period of many hours. The number of meals averages 3.7 with as many as six meals being served in a few households each day.

Typical meals were found to vary somewhat in the communities and the municipalities, depending upon the working hours, place and proximity of the work, and the income. In the rural areas, breakfast was usually eaten between 6 and 7 o'clock in the morning; midmorning lunch between 9 and 10 a.m.; dinner from noon to 1 p.m.; midafternoon snack from 4 to 4:30 p.m.; and supper between 6 and 8 p.m. In the cities, dinner was usually served between 1 and 3 p.m. and supper after 8 p.m. More variation in the time for each meal for various families and communities was found in Crete than would be true in most areas of the United States. Below are some of the more typical meals served in Crete.

Breakfast: Bread with tea or coffee; sometimes supplemented by milk, cheese, or olives.

Midmorning: Bread with tea, coffee, or wine; occasionally supplemented by milk, cheese, or olives as in the breakfast, or by food left over from the previous day. For the rural people who went to the fields early in the morning, this might be the main breakfast, their early breakfast being only a cup of coffee or tea.

Noonday meal, workday: (1) A main course consisting of one of the following: vegetable, alone or with cereal; pulses, alone or with vegetable or cereal; fish, alone or with pulses, vegetable, or cereal. (2) Bread and wine. (3) To the above, about half of the families might add fruit, cheese, nuts, olives.

Midafternoon: One of the following: fruit; bread; bread with fruit; olives; or cheese. Sweets were served more frequently at this meal than any other, alone or as a supplement to some other item.

Supper: (1) One of the following: leftovers from previous meal; fresh vegetables, alone or in combination with cereal; leftovers with meat, fish, eggs, or fresh vegetables. (2) Bread and wine. (3) Fruit or cheese.

Sunday noon meal: The Sunday noon meal was more elaborate. In addition to bread and wine, and meat, alone or with pulses, two-thirds of the families in the municipalities and half of the families in the communities served a fresh vegetable or cereal. Fish in place of meat was used by a small percentage of the families. About 44 per cent of the families did not supplement the main dish with other foods. Fruit was the main supplement when one was used. Forty-four per cent of the families in municipalities and 38 per cent in the communities used fruit as an additional course in the Sunday noon meal.

Cretans do not serve desserts—except fresh fruit in season—as a formal course at the end of the meal, as is done in the United States. Cake is seldom served and pie almost never. Canned fruit is not in favor with Cretans, since some kind of fresh fruit is available somewhere on the island every month of the year.

4. Social and Religious Influences on Food Patterns

In the Greek Orthodox religion, there are many fast periods and frequent fast days. The fast periods may be as long as 42 days for the pre-Easter fast season, 40 days before Christmas and 15 days during the first half of August. Fasting on Wednesdays and Fridays is carried out by some, but this may be a mere abstention from meat. The Greek Orthodox fast is a strict one and means abstaining from all foods of animal origin, including fish, cheese, eggs, and butter. On some of the important fast days, like Good Friday, no olive oil or fats are used by some people. The "non-blood" foods such as roe, shrimp, snails, etc., are allowed during the fast periods. The degree of keeping fasts varies from family to family and by age groups. Children frequently are not expected to observe long fasts or strict fasts, whereas the older people may fast during all of the periods.

The following (in decreasing order of importance) were named as foods eaten during fasts: (1) fresh vegetables, including tomatoes and potatoes, (2) pulses, (3) olives, (4) bread, rice, macaroni, etc., (5) fish roe, shrimps, squid, (6) honey, halvas,[3] must syrups,[4] (7) fresh fruit, (8) tea and sugar, (9) sesame emulsion, and (10) hondros.

The frequent feast days are occasions for great festivities and

[3] Confection made from sesame (decorticated) sweetened with honey.

[4] Must syrup or petimezi is a syrup, about the color and consistency of light molasses, made from grape juice.

special and elaborate foods. "Name" days, Christmas, Easter, and other holidays are special occasions. In 1948, twenty-two such holidays were observed by government services and banks in Khania; 14 of these were ordinarily observed by shopkeepers and other businesses. (See Appendix 5, Table A21.) On "name" days some very rich sweet is served to the visitors. This may be a spoonful of preserved fruit or a baked sweet. Other foods to go with wine, ouzo, or tsikoudia are usually served. Foods such as shortbreads, fritters or doughnuts, cakes, and macaroons are associated with Christmas and the New Year. At Easter, milk buns are popular. They are made from white flour, milk, sugar, eggs, and butter.

The custom of serving to any visitor, as a symbol of friendliness, a spoonful of preserved fruit (raisins, cherries, small whole lemon or orange) is carried out throughout the year. Some families offer almonds dipped in honey, or serve ouzo, tsikoudia, or some other alcoholic beverage. Coffee may be available in the house and, in many families, is used only for visitors. It is considered essential to have something in the house at all times in case visitors arrive.

For government officials, both national and foreign, representatives of foreign organizations and distinguished guests, the households of the village or community may pool their food and serve sumptuous meals of seven or more courses. Except for the final course of fruit, each course of the meal includes scarce meat, poultry or game, or fish served in various types of dishes. Families will go on short rations for weeks afterwards in order to show their hospitality. Among the Cretans these feasts for visitors enable them to show the products of the community. Since they have so little livestock and their fields are so scattered, this is a means of showing to the visitor that they have done much with their resources. And at the same time they are giving expression to their heartfelt pride in their community. These "banquets" are evidence of a deep-seated tradition of hospitality which is far in excess of Western standards.

5. *Attitudes toward Food and Its Importance*

The Cretan people have many commendable attitudes toward foods. The superstitions that it is a sin to have crumbs fall on the ground and good luck to spill wine show the importance given to an item normally in short supply as compared to wine which is in abundance.

Two-thirds of the families indicated an awareness that children should have special foods. Milk, butter, meat, rice, and eggs were, in this order of importance, the foods considered most necessary to help children grow.

The short supply of rice and its use by the medical profession for the treatment of gastro-intestinal diseases of children may explain the important place given to this food. The stress placed on milk for children may have resulted from the extensive child-feeding programs —milk rations and school feeding—conducted in previous years and at the time of the survey.

Only one out of six families said their diets were satisfactory. One family reported, "We are hungry most of the time." To a degree this skimpiness has been characteristic of the Greek diet since before the time of Christ. The Persians, who were great eaters, often remarked, "Greeks leave off eating while hungry." Plato's meals were reported to be so simple that some persons maliciously observed, "Those who dine with Plato will be in excellent health next morning." This may explain in part why Cretans are slim-waisted, erect, and able to withstand hunger during war and revolutions.

Foods considered necessary to improve the family diet, according to householders interviewed, were, in order of priority, meat, rice, fish, macaroni and pastes, butter, and cheese. Meat alone or with cereal was mentioned as a "favorite food" of 72 per cent of the families questioned. There was no mention of a special fondness for sweets.

These attitudes of the Cretan people could lend themselves very well to an all-round educational and action program aimed at improving their diets. For instance, preserved milk, both tinned (evaporated) and dried, had been used by 98 per cent of the families. Seventy per cent of all families liked tinned milk whereas only 35 per cent liked powdered milk.

Community officials reported to interviewers that "the tinned milk was 'excellent,'" "generally liked," and "consumed with pleasure." One-fourth of the communities did not like tinned meat; one respondent stated, "Canned meats are not good for the organisms." One group stated that they "liked it without the fat." This distaste for animal fats was also evident in very low-income households which refused to accept bacon grease and other animal fats as gifts. In a fourth of the communities canned fish was not liked, and in several others people expressed a dislike for "mashed fish" or fish paste. As one community president said, "We mistrust the good effect on health" of canned fish. As might be expected, the distaste for canned meats was especially marked in the villages having sheep and goats, where fresh meats of strong flavor were preferred.

C. Food Consumption Levels and Source of Supply

In spite of wide differences in types of diet according to the season, there was practically no difference in the daily calorie consumption, whether computed from the seven-day diet or from the adjusted estimate based upon knowledge of the seasonal availability of various foods and utilization of data from the 765 family estimates of annual food consumption. Since the latter is subject to errors due to memory bias, omission of certain food items in the list of inquiry, and nondietary uses made of food items, major dependence has been placed on the seven-day diet data. It seems reasonable that the adjusted estimate should show less potatoes, fresh vegetables, and fruits, and more eggs, milk, cheese, pulses, nuts, and olives than the fall season diet survey (Table 9). The large adjustment in alcoholic beverages is justified by observation and an expressed feeling by the respondents that the visiting Americans might be expected to frown upon heavy wine consumption where food was short.

In comparison with the seven-day diet, the "adjusted" estimate showed a decrease of one-third in potatoes and fruits, one-fifth in fresh vegetables, and one-tenth in fish. The increases were 50 per cent for milk, 20 per cent each for eggs, cheese, and pulses, and 10 per cent for nuts. Olives, cereals, sugar, meat, and oils and fats remained the same for both sets of estimates.

1. Cereals and Cereal Products

The consumption of cereals and cereal products was high—according to the survey, 5.4 pounds per capita per week, as compared to 3.8 pounds in the United States. The main cereals used were wheat and barley. The barley was all grown on the island, but slightly more than one-half of all cereals used for food was imported as wheat, flour, or macaroni. More than half of the cereal consumption on the island was in the form of bread, rolls, and rusks made from wheat. Bread made from a mixture of wheat and barley or entirely of barley was used where barley was grown locally. Rusks made from a wheat and barley mixture were eaten extensively, particularly in the rural areas. The extraction rate of the flour used was high, from 85 to 100 per cent. Commercial pastes, such as macaroni, and homemade pastes, including hondros, were common items in the diet.

TABLE 9. Annual consumption by major food groups, Crete and Greece, 1948 seven-day diet, "adjusted" estimate, householders' annual estimate, and Greek food balance estimates for 1948-1949

	Crete			Greece
		Adjusted	Householder	
	7-day diet	annual	annual	Food balance
	Fall	estimate	estimate	sheet estimate
Food Groups	1948	1948	1947	1948-1949
	(pounds per capita per year)			
Cereals	281	282[a]	366	348
Potatoes	130	85	139	68
Sugar, honey, etc.	12	12	—	20
Pulses and nuts	44	51	60	33
Vegetables, fruits, olives	387	291	273[b]	265
Meat, fish, eggs	63	61	44[c]	51
Milk and cheese[d]	56	76	98	77
Oils and fats	68	68	100[e]	33
Wine, beer and spirits	22	85	115	83
Total pounds annually	1,063	1,011	—	978
Energy, calories per day	2,547	2,554	3,362[f]	2,443

[a] Difference from seven-day diet caused by rounding off figures in okes (2.8219 pounds).

[b] Survey (Form A) omitted listing of some vegetables and fruits, making this an underestimate. Certain fruits and vegetables, such as tomatoes and grapes, were in season and consumed at a higher than annual rate; others, especially citrus fruits and greens, were out of season.

[c] Fish omitted in survey.

[d] Milk and cheese on a whole-milk basis, including dried and evaporated milk.

[e] Olive oil estimates on annual basis probably include oil for lamps and other uses.

[f] Total calories computed include sugar category and fish at same rate as in the "adjusted" estimate.

Sources: Sample Survey of Crete, Form Ia, Seven-day Diet; Form A, Household. A. Tsongas, "Food Balance Sheet for Greece, 1948-49." Unpublished data. FAO and Greek Government. Washington, 1950.

Rice is a popular cereal among the people of Crete. During the survey the consumption level was quite low, as the commodity was in short supply and expensive. All the rice was imported.

2. Starchy Roots and Tubers

The only food of this group that appeared in the diet was potato, which was eaten in fair amounts. During the autumn when the survey was made, the rate was 2.5 pounds per capita per week as compared to 2.7 pounds in the United States. The annual average consumption

of potatoes, all of which were grown in Crete, was probably somewhat less than this because of seasonal fluctuations in supply. The
average consumption level of potatoes among the rural families was
almost twice that of the families living in the municipalities.

3. Sugars and Syrups

The consumption of sugars, syrups, and other sweets was found
to be low—less than 4 ounces per capita per week, as compared to
32 ounces in the United States. The sugar was all imported. The
syrups were chiefly local honey and "must" made from grapes. The
sugar was used mainly in the making of confections, sweet pastries,
and fruit preserves for special occasions, and in Turkish coffee.

4. Pulses, Nuts, and Seeds

"Pulses are the poor man's meat" is a common Greek saying.
Numerous varieties of pulses and nuts are grown locally and used
extensively. Sesame seeds are also eaten. The amount of all these
items consumed during the survey was 0.8 pound or about 13 ounces
per capita per week. This was more than twice as much of these
items as were eaten in the United States. The main pulses were
white beans, broad beans, lentils, fava beans, split peas, and chick
peas. There were some imports of pulses. Of the nuts, the chestnut
was consumed in the greatest amounts during the survey. Almonds,
walnuts, and peanuts were also common.

The average annual consumption of this food group, particularly
the pulses, is undoubtedly higher than the consumption during the
survey. The dietary pattern included pulses mainly during the winter
months, chiefly because of the long cooking time required, and the
joint use of the heat for warmth in the home. The consumption of
pulses during early fall was particularly low because of the abundance of fresh green vegetables.

5. Vegetables

Many kinds of vegetables are used, predominantly green vegetables, including many dark green leafy vegetables such as dande-
lions, radikia, mustard greens, spinach, and many unspecified wild
"mountain greens." Cabbages, green beans, and small squashes are
also consumed in considerable amounts. Root vegetables used during
the survey were chiefly onions and radishes. Many other vegetables
are eaten, including eggplant, cauliflower, okra, leek, peppers, and

celery. Beets and carrots are not liked by the Cretans. The consumption of preserved vegetables—bottled, canned, and dried—was negligible.

A feature of the diet was the very high level of consumption of vegetables, with an average of 2.3 pounds per capita per week during the survey. One-half of the vegetables were of the green and yellow type, as classified by nutritionists.

6. Citrus Fruit and Tomatoes

During the survey the consumption of tomatoes was very high, averaging 1.8 pounds per capita per week. On the other hand, the consumption of citrus fruits, chiefly lemons, was low. All the tomatoes and citrus fruits were obtained locally, and there was, of course, a marked seasonal variation in the consumption. At the time of the survey, tomatoes were available at the peak of supply and served twice a day in many homes. Tomato paste is used widely in the cooking of vegetables and main dishes when fresh tomatoes are not available. The citrus fruit season begins in the late fall and continues until early summer. From November through May, oranges and tangerines are available in abundance in the coastal areas and in more limited quantities for the mountain villages.

7. Other Fresh Fruit

During the time of the survey the main fresh fruit was grapes, the average consumption of grapes alone being 3.1 pounds per capita per week. Considerably more were consumed in the rural districts than in the municipalities. Grapes were in peak supply during the survey, thus accounting for the high consumption. The average consumption of all other fruits was about one pound per week per capita, consumption being more than twice as high in the communities as in the municipalities. Other fresh fruits consumed included apples, melons, and pomegranates, together with lesser quantities of figs, peaches, pears, quinces, and prickly pears. Plums, cherries, and apricots were also used seasonally in May and June. Olives are used throughout the year in large quantities—usually as ripe olives, although some green olives are eaten also. Some dried fruits, mostly raisins and figs, are eaten, but other preserved fruits—canned or bottled—are not available. The average annual consumption of fruit was estimated to be about 20 per cent lower than during the week of the survey when grapes were in season.

The total consumption of fruits and vegetables during the fall diet survey in Crete was 8.3 pounds per capita per week—about the same rate as in the United States throughout the year. But relatively more fruit and less green and yellow vegetables were consumed in Crete.

8. *Meat, Poultry, Fish, and Eggs*

Most of the meat is goat and kid, with lamb and mutton next in importance. Beef and pork are eaten in small amounts. The average consumption of meat and meat products was only 7.5 ounces per capita per week. The offals—liver, brain, kidney, lungs, and tripe— are all eaten. The eyes of the fish are considered a special delicacy. The Cretans enjoy picking bits of meat from the head of a roasted animal, just as Americans lunch by picking bits of the meat from the carcass bones of a recently carved roasted turkey.

The use of preserved and processed meat and meat products— canned meats, sausage, bacon, etc.—was very limited. Most of the meat was obtained from local sources so that the consumption level during the survey was probably representative of the average consumption throughout the year. The consumption of poultry and game was very low—less than two ounces per capita per week.

Most of the snails were consumed in the communities, where the average level was 1.7 ounces per person per week as compared with 1.0 ounce in the municipalities.

During the survey the chief fish eaten was cod, salted and dried. Other preserved fish used included herrings, sardines, and cuttle fish. The average consumption of fish, both fresh and processed, was about 6 ounces per capita per week. The level of consumption was about the same in the municipalities and in the communities. There was, however, almost three times as much fresh fish eaten in the municipalities as in the communities. This included smelts, mullet, sea bream, and octopus. The consumption of fresh fish was probably higher at this season than the average throughout the year. The fall period is one of the two major fresh fish seasons.

The total amount of meat, poultry, game, snails, and fish consumed per capita in Crete was only 30 per cent of the per capita quantity in the United States.

Very few eggs were eaten. During the survey the consumption was a little more than one egg per person per week. In the United States, the average consumption per person was one egg per day, or five to six times as many as were consumed per person in Crete.

9. Milk and Milk Products

Most of the milk consumed is goat milk, although some sheep milk is used. A considerable amount of milk is employed to make cheese, both hard and soft varieties. Most of the cheese is produced from sheep's milk in the spring as flocks are moved to mountain pastures. The consumption of fresh fluid milk was 6 ounces per person per week (approximately three-fourths of a cup of milk per week) with the average level slightly higher in the communities than in the municipalities. It is probable that the average annual consumption was about one-third higher than during the survey, as the peak of supply is late fall and spring. This would increase fresh fluid milk consumption to slightly more than one cup per person per week.

Consumption of evaporated milk, which was imported, was slightly higher in the municipalities than in the communities. A small amount of imported dried milk was consumed, but only in the communities. Consumption of cheese in the municipalities was considerably higher than in the communities. The total consumption of milk and milk products in fluid milk equivalent was less than one-third of a cup daily per person, or about one-half cup if correction is made for the low fall seasonal consumption. In the United States, the average consumption of milk equivalent was three cups, or six times as much per person daily.

10. Oils and Fats

Consumption of oils and fats was very high, chiefly olive oil. The large amount of olive oil used was in fact an outstanding feature of the Cretan diet, being relatively higher than for Greece as a whole. Small quantities of butter and very small quantities of margarine were consumed. They were all obtained from local sources with certain vitamins being added to "vitam" and other margarines of olive oil base. The level of consumption during the week of the survey was probably representative of the average consumption over the entire year. The average consumption level of oils and fats, without pork fat, was 1.3 pounds per capita per week, almost 50 per cent higher than in the United States as a whole. There are certain areas in the United States where fat intake is as high or higher than in Crete.

Surveys made in Tennessee[5] and in North Carolina[6] show that the fat intake per adult constitutes 30 to 40 per cent of the total calories, as compared to 29 per cent in Crete. The high percentage of visible fats (vegetable oils) in the Cretan diet is somewhat deceiving when compared with the still greater consumption of "hidden fats" (animal fats) in the diets of many groups in the southern United States.

D. Nutrient Sources and Nutrient Content of the Diet

The importance of cereals, olive oil, fruits, and vegetables in providing the principal nutrients to the Cretan diet is shown in Figure 8. According to the seven-day diet survey, cereals were 30 per cent (by weight) of the total diet, and furnished two-fifths of the calories and iron; one-half of the protein, thiamine, and niacin; one-third of the riboflavin; and one-sixth of the calcium in the diet of the Cretans. In contrast, vegetables and fruits comprised 46 per cent, by weight, of the diet and furnished 8 to 14 per cent of the calories, protein, thiamine, and niacin. However, they provided four-fifths of the ascorbic acid and vitamin A; one-fourth of the calcium and riboflavin; and one-fifth of the iron.

Pulses, nuts, milk, cheese, meat, fish, and eggs comprised 10 per cent of the weight of food consumed and provided one-seventh of the energy; about one-fifth of the thiamine, vitamin A, and niacin; one-third of the riboflavin and iron; two-fifths of the protein; and more than one-half of the calcium in the diet. Oils and fats were 7 per cent of the food consumed and supplied 29 per cent of the calories. Sugar and beverages supplied 3 per cent of the energy from about 4 per cent of the foods by weight. The percentages of the various nutrients supplied by each food group are shown in detail in Appendix 5, Table A49.

1. Calories

The average daily per capita calorie consumption during the 1948 fall season was 2,547[7] and was approximately the same during the

[5] John B. Youmans, White Patton, and Ruth Kern, "Surveys of the Nutrition of Populations (Rural Middle Tennessee)." *American Journal of Public Health*, 33, 1:62, January 1943.

[6] D. F. Milam, "A Nutrition Survey of a Small North Carolina Community." *American Journal of Public Health*, 32, 4:406, April 1942.

[7] These 128 families containing 502 persons showed a consumption of 2,879 calories per day per nutrition unit (453.6 energy consumption-units), as compared to 2,547 calories per day per person equivalent (512.7 person-equivalents).

SOURCES OF NUTRIENTS
1948

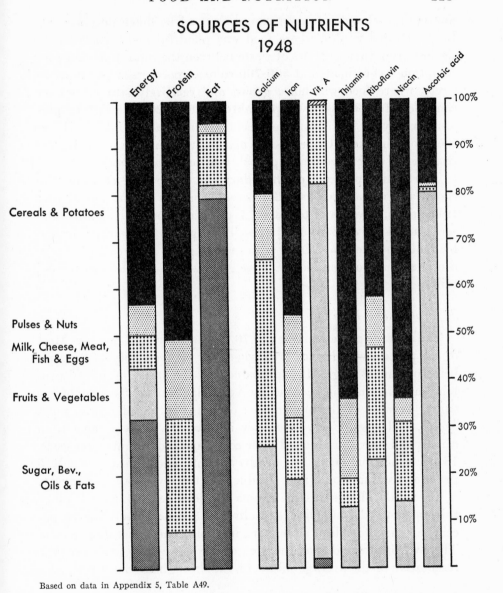

Based on data in Appendix 5, Table A49.

FIGURE 8. Sources of nutrients for seven-day diet families, 1948

year as a whole. The figure most nearly comparable for the United
States was the estimate of 3,129 calories per person per day purchased at the retail level in 1948-1949. However, it should not be
inferred from these figures that calorie intake in Crete was only
81 per cent of that in the United States. The factor of waste between

the retail level and actual consumption must be taken into account. In the United States, where food was plentiful and incomes high, the loss from various types of waste between the retail level and consumption was estimated at 500-700 calories per person per day.[8] In Crete, where food was home grown and relatively scarce, and incomes low, food wastage was probably less than 200 calories per person per day, or less than 8 per cent of total calorie intake. Hence the calorie intake in Crete was not markedly lower than in the United States; the difference would probably be less than 10 per cent.

Thirty-nine per cent of the calories in Crete were derived from cereals and cereal products, 29 per cent from oils and fats, 4 per cent from fruits, olives, and tomatoes, 7 per cent from pulses, nuts, and seeds, and 4 per cent from potatoes. Throughout the year it is probable that the percentage from pulses was slightly higher and the percentage from potatoes, lower. (See Appendix 5, Table A49 for details.)

2. Protein and Fats

The average protein intake was 70.7 grams per head per day. Most of the protein was derived from vegetable sources, only 17.3 grams being of animal origin. It is probable that the intake of animal protein was somewhat higher over the year than during the week of the survey because of the higher level of consumption of pulses, milk, cheese, and eggs. Forty-seven per cent of the protein came from cereals and cereal products, 17 per cent from pulses, nuts, and seeds, 18 per cent from meat, fish, poultry, game, and snails, and only 5 per cent from milk and milk products in the seven-day diet survey.

The intake of fats was 107 grams per head per day. Almost all of this was derived from olives and olive oil (78 per cent). Eleven per cent came from foods of animal origin—milk, cheese, meat, eggs, etc. The level of intake during the week of the survey was probably representative of the average intake of fat throughout the entire year.

3. Calcium and Iron

The average intake of calcium was 0.46 grams per head per day. The chief sources of the calcium in the diet were milk and milk products (27 per cent), cereals (17 per cent), pulses, nuts, and seeds (14 per cent). The average annual consumption might have been

[8] John Donald Black, and Maxine Enlow Kiefer, *Future Food and Agricultural Policy*. McGraw-Hill, 1948, p. 8.

considerably higher than this because of the higher consumption of pulses and milk, and for other reasons discussed later under "adequacy of the diet."

The average intake of iron was 20.1 milligrams per head per day. The chief sources of iron in the diet were cereals and cereal products (41 per cent), pulses, nuts, and seeds (22 per cent), and fruit (13 per cent). The intake level throughout the year was probably similar to the level during the week of the survey, the decrease in iron due to the lower average consumption of fruit throughout the year than during the survey week being offset by the higher consumption of pulses.

4. The Vitamins

The average intake level of vitamin A was 3,853 I.U. (International Units). Only 17 per cent of this was obtained preformed from animal foods. The chief source of vitamin A in the diet was the carotene from tomatoes (36 per cent) and green vegetables (38 per cent). Due to the large amounts of greens of various kinds eaten during the rainy winter and spring months in all but the higher mountain regions, the level of intake of vitamin A throughout the year probably averaged about the same as, or higher than, during the period of the survey—even though tomatoes were eaten in large quantities only for approximately six months of the year.

The average per capita intake of thiamine (vitamin B_1) was 1.65 mg. per day, niacin 19.6 mg., and riboflavin (vitamin B_2) 0.98 mg. Approximately 55 per cent of the thiamine and niacin and 35 per cent of the riboflavin were obtained from cereals and cereal products. The other chief sources of thiamine were pulses (17 per cent) and potatoes (10 per cent). The thiamine intake during the survey was probably representative of the average for the year, because of the higher consumption of pulses replacing the lower consumption of potatoes. Apart from cereals, the chief source of niacin in the diet was meat, fish, and eggs (10 per cent). Fourteen per cent of the riboflavin was obtained from this group of foods, 11 per cent from pulses and nuts, and 10 per cent from milk and milk products.

The average intake of ascorbic acid was 90 milligrams per head per day. Thirty-eight per cent of this came from fresh vegetables, 33 per cent from tomatoes, and 18 per cent from potatoes. The average annual intake was possibly a little lower than during the week of the survey, but the difference would not be great because of the replace-

ment of tomatoes by citrus fruits. The probable lower intake of potatoes would, however, have some effect, and so the yearly intake may
have averaged nearer 80 milligrams than 90.

E. Adequacy of the Diet

The adequacy of the diet has been assessed in the first place by comparing the nutrient intake levels with the National Research Council
Recommended Dietary Allowances.[9] The average daily per capita dietary allowance was derived from the NRC scale according to age, sex,
and activity composition of the group surveyed, and the nutrient
intake per head per day was compared with this.

In order to reduce misinterpretations of these recommended allowances in comparison with the Crete data, the following statement
from the National Research Council circular may be helpful:

"The Quantitative Level of the Recommendations—The general
principle is followed here as previously of recommending allowances
sufficiently liberal to be 'suitable for maintenance of good nutritional
status.'

"The quantitative data in the accompanying table are intended to
represent exactly what is implied in a literal interpretation of the
words *recommended dietary allowances.* Hence, in contrast to some
previously promulgated standards, the data in the accompanying
table are rather to be understood as representing levels of nutrient
intakes which the Food and Nutrition Board recommends as normally desirable goals or objectives.

"The recommendations are not called 'requirements' because they
are intended to represent not merely the literal (minimal) requirements of average individuals, but levels enough higher to cover substantially all individual variations in the requirements of normal
people.

"The figures here recommended are, therefore, generally higher
than average requirements but generally lower than the doses used
to meet needs created by pathological states or certain environmental
conditions or in compensating for an earlier period of depletion.

"The Board recognizes a responsibility to explain as clearly as it
can (even at the cost of some near-repetition) just how the levels of
nutrient intake which it *recommends* are related to the lesser quanti-

[9] National Research Council, *Recommended Dietary Allowances, Revised 1948,*
Reprint and Circular Series, no. 129. Washington, October 1948. pp. 16-17.

ties which are essential to avoid manifest nutritional deficiencies. Studies on man, as well as more complete experience with animals, clearly indicate substantial improvements in growth and function when the intakes of certain nutrients are increased above the level which is just sufficient to prevent obvious deficiency symptoms. The level above which lesions or symptoms are not commonly observed is merely one point on a long curve relating intake to function. The allowance of a margin of intake above the critical level for each nutrient is, therefore, designed to permit additional benefits as well as to cover individual variations. No fixed formula for computing the margin between 'minimal requirements' and 'recommended allowances' would be equally logical for all nutrients or for all population groups. There is now much evidence from long-term animal experimentation that, aside from individual variations of need, the margins between optimal intake and minimal requirements are wider for some nutrients than for others. . . .

"The usual undiscriminating view is that, if the diet furnishes enough of any given factor to meet functional need, any further amount supplied by the food is normally a matter very nearly of indifference, significant only as a sort of insurance against some emergency. This may be true for most of the essential food factors. Of a few nutrients, however, there is evidence from long-term (animal) experimentation that one may, in the course of a lifetime, derive increased benefit from increased intake up to levels very considerably above those of ordinarily accepted adequacy. (Ascorbic acid, vitamin A, and calcium are perhaps the best-established cases of this kind.) Conversely, it may be true of some other nutrient factors that surplus intakes should be held within bounds if undesirable consequences are to be avoided. The outstanding and undisputed example of the latter is the energy value of calories of the diet, of which any considerable surplus intake tends to induce overweight."[10]

In the following discussion it is important, therefore, to recognize that these "NRC recommended dietary allowances" with which the average nutrient intakes of households in Crete are compared are higher than average needs in order to "cover substantially all individual variations in the requirements of normal people." The size of this safety factor, between allowances and needs—"estimated to be approximately 30 per cent in most categories"—will be discussed for each of the nutrients where possible deficiencies are suggested by

10 *ibid.*, pp. 5-6.

a comparison of average nutrient intake with recommended dietary allowances.[11]

For the group as a whole, it was found that for calories the intake was slightly less than the allowance, for vitamin A approximately 80 per cent of the allowance, for riboflavin, 60 per cent, and for calcium 50 per cent of the recommended allowances.[12] The average intake level of all other nutrients was greater than the allowances. In the municipalities, the intake of vitamin A in the diet was more satisfactory when compared with the suggested allowances than it was in the communities. On the other hand, the riboflavin intake in the communities was slightly more satisfactory when compared with the allowances than was true in the municipalities.

Only 4 per cent of the families had intake levels of all nine nutrients which were 80 per cent or more of the National Research Council recommended dietary allowances. On the other hand all of the families had 80 per cent or more of the recommended allowance for at least one of the nine nutrients. However, such summary statements do not take into account the relative degree to which intake levels are below the NRC allowances. For example, an extremely low intake for one nutrient in a family might be more serious than moderately low intakes for four or five nutrients.

The averages mask the situation in the individual households. It was found that there was a considerable range in the adequacy of intake of each nutrient when compared with this standard. The median intake (middle family when arranged according to intake) for calories was approximately 111 per cent of the recommended allowances with a range from 31 to 216 per cent. Protein and ascorbic acid median intakes were of the same order in percentage while thiamine, niacin, and iron had median intakes of 50 per cent or more above the allowances. In contrast the median intake for calcium was only one-third and for vitamin A and riboflavin three-fifths of the allowances set forth. (See Appendix 5, Table A50.)

1. *Calories*

The average intake of 2,547 calories for the group was approximately 100 calories, or 4 per cent, below the NRC recommended allowances. (See Table 10.) The intake of the highest income group in the communities exceeded the recommended allowances by ap-

---

[11] *ibid.*, p. 23.
[12] See later discussion for a more adequate statement on calcium and vitamin A.

Table 10. Nutrient intake and NRC recommended dietary allowance per person per day, 128 subsample families, Crete, Fall 1948. (Calories and eight essential nutrients.)

Nutrient intake	Crete seven-day diet Household survey consumption	National Research Council Recommended dietary allowance
Energy, calories	2,547	2,648
Protein grams	70.7[a]	65.1
Animal protein, grams	(17.3)[a]	—
Fat, grams	107.1	—
Calcium, grams	0.46[b]	1.05[c]
Iron, milligrams	20.1	11.6
Vitamin A, I.U.	3,853[a]	4,564
Preformed vitamin A, I.U.	(733)	—
Thiamine (vitamin B_1), milligrams	1.65	1.27
Riboflavin, milligrams	0.98	1.63
Niacin, milligrams	19.6	12.7
Ascorbic acid, milligrams	90.0[d]	71.0

[a] Indicates the items for which the daily per capita consumption on the adjusted annual basis would be larger than the one given here.

[b] The figure given is for 7-day fall diet, without inclusion of calcium in water consumed. Including the calcium estimated in six glasses of water consumed daily the figure is 0.69. In addition, the amount of milk consumed daily on an annual basis would be greater and further increase the amount of calcium intake.

[c] This NRC–RDA figure is considered overgenerous by many nutritionists.

[d] The estimated daily annual adjusted figure is less than the fall survey and is 80.0.

Source: Sample Survey of Crete, Form Ia, Form I, Seven-day Diet Record, Form A, Household. National Research Council Recommended Dietary Allowances, computations based on assigned levels of activity suggested by Miss Helen Sdrin, Ministry of Education, Athens.

proximately 200 calories, while in the lowest income group there was a deficiency of approximately 240 calories. In the municipalities the average intake met the recommendations, but in the communities the intake was approximately 130 calories below. Due to seasonal differences in the degree of activity of rural people, this suggested deficit of 130 calories in the communities may be slightly exaggerated, when considered on an annual basis—as much as 75 calories or about one-half. This is caused by a too-liberal allowance—on an annual basis—for adult males in the communities; two-thirds being classified under severe activity in the fall season study and given an allowance of 4,500 calories daily. Even with the great amount of daily walking over stony and hilly terrain, the small number of days worked by

the Cretan farmer (160 to 200 days annually—see Chapter 10) suggests that on a yearly basis the daily allowances for calories in the
communities might be about 3 per cent less than indicated in the
seven-day diet study. The effect of this activity differentiation is
discussed here since it has significance only in relation to the recommended allowances for calories—no other nutrient being affected by
the degree of activity.

The recommended dietary allowances of 2,648 calories determined
by the NRC methods relate to American people living in the American climate. The calorie requirements of the group surveyed in Crete,
calculated according to the system recommended by the Committee
on Calorie Requirements convened by FAO,[13] is approximately 2,300
calories. Using this standard, which conforms more with the conditions prevailing in Crete than does the American standard, it is seen
that on the average the diet of even the lowest income group was
adequate from the point of view of total energy value.

2. *Protein*

The total protein intake was adequate in quantity, although the
amount of animal protein obtained was slightly less than the generally recommended one-third of the total. In the lower income
groups, there were indications that some increase in the consumption
of animal protein might be desirable—though not essential.

3. *Calcium*

Comparison of the intake of calcium (from foods alone) with the
NRC recommended allowances would indicate that this nutrient was
obtained in the least satisfactory amounts of any in the Cretan diet.
For the group as a whole, the difference was 50 per cent, and for the
higher income group, about 45 per cent. The distribution of calcium
intake in the various families showed that only 13 per cent of households obtained 80 per cent or more of the allowances while 70 per
cent had less than one-half of the recommended allowances.

However, possible inaccuracies of the nutrient intake figures and
the conditions relating to the standard must be considered when assessing these figures. While the food composition data were derived

[13] Committee on Calorie Requirements, *Calorie Requirements*. Food and Agriculture
Organization of the United Nations, Washington, June 1950. These requirements
are computed for the population under consideration by utilizing a "reference man
or woman" whose daily calorie needs are related to age, body size, environmental
temperature, and activity.

from figures in published tables of the best known authoritative source (The Combined Working Party Special Report D2), the composition of locally grown varieties of foods in Crete, such as vegetables, etc., may differ significantly from that of the foods upon which these tables were based. The calcium content of wild herbs, wild greens, and snails may be greater in an area of limestone soils because of variety adaptation through time.[14] Cretans also eat the bones of small fish, which may not be fully accounted for in the summarized data.

Water is another important source of calcium in the Cretan diet. The soils of Crete contain much limestone, and water analyses[15] indicate an average of 0.15 grams of calcium carbonate per 1,000 grams (about one quart). A person drinking six glasses of water daily (1,500 grams) would increase his calcium intake by 0.23 grams —from 0.46 to 0.69 grams—or 50 per cent above food intake, alone.[16] This low calcium intake during the fall also results from the seasonally low consumption of fluid milk in comparison with an adjusted annual estimate. The utilization of the available calcium is probably very high, since the mild climate permits exposure of the body to sunshine for a large part of the year—particularly in the case of children—and such increased vitamin D production assists in calcium utilization.

The calcium allowance set forth in the NRC tables has been considered overgenerous by some. In a recent article, Dr. Maynard cites a study in Canada by Pett, who found that 50 per cent of the adults were in calcium balance on an intake which was only 40 per cent of the presently recommended allowances.[17]

In view of the food habits, possible differences in food composition, the large amount of calcium in the water, the increased fluid milk consumption on an annual basis, and the extremely large safety factor in the NRC recommended dietary allowance, the purported calcium

[14] For further discussion see Leonard A. Maynard, "Soils and Health." *Journal of the American Medical Association.* July 1, 1950, vol. 143, pp. 807-812.

[15] Helen N. Sdrin, "Report of a Greek Chemist on Analyses of the Water in Crete." Unpublished manuscript. Athens, 1949.

[16] Another possible addition to the calcium intake is suggested in a recent note in *The Lancet*: "Calcium (from water) is actually deposited on vegetables during cooking, thereby making more calcium available for consumption—an increase of about 20 per cent for cauliflower and 80 per cent for potatoes." D. H. Donald, *The Lancet*, no. II of vol. II, 1950, no. 6619, vol. CCLIX, p. 76.

[17] Leonard A. Maynard, "Evaluation of Dietary Survey Methods." *Federation Proceedings.* vol. 9, no. 3, September 1950. Symposium on Nutritional Appraisal of Human Subjects. Atlantic City, April 20, 1950.

deficiency would seem to disappear completely or be limited to a very few families who were not able to include any appreciable amounts of dairy products, snails, or pulses in their diets.

4. *Vitamin A*

While the average intake level of vitamin A was only 20 per cent below the NRC allowance, the large percentage (more than four-fifths) of vitamin A derived from carotene in the diet rather than from preformed vitamin A indicates that the intake level might be less satisfactory than these figures suggest. Knowledge of human requirements of vitamin A is perhaps less extensive than for the other major nutrients, but a recent British study confirms the fact that the recommended allowances are not excessive. Hume and Krebs, after taking into account the large losses of vitamin A from most foods through human metabolism, recommend a daily allowance of 2,500 I.U. of vitamin A or 7,500 I.U. of carotene alone. Only on the basis of carotene being "less than half" that for preformed vitamin A, can these recommendations be brought roughly within the latest NRC allowance of 5,000 I.U. Both sets of recommendations suggest that a large percentage of the households surveyed may not have a satisfactory vitamin A intake—especially in the fall season.[18]

However, consideration must be given to the fact that this dry fall-season diet did not include as many greens as would be found in most Cretan household diets during the rainy season. Since the Cretans are especially fond of cooked greens—tame or wild, hot or cold—their annual diets would tend to be less deficient in vitamin A than this fall-season diet indicates. Also the large liver reserves— 500,000 I.U. in the British experiment—can be drawn on over a long period of time, 400 days in the above study. This suggests that any such seasonal deficiencies may not be serious, if these reserves can be rebuilt during the seasons which follow.

While 25 per cent of the households surveyed reached the vitamin A allowance figure, 31 per cent had an intake level of less than half that suggested figure. For this latter segment of the population at least, the situation appeared extremely unsatisfactory. While 60 per cent of the highest income group had 80 per cent or more of the

18 E. M. Hume, and H. A. Krebs, "Vitamin A Requirement of Human Adults," Medical Research Council Special Report Series no. 264. His Majesty's Stationery Office, London, 1949. 145 pp.

recommended figure, only 32 per cent of the lowest income group reached that level.

5. Riboflavin

In all but a few households the intake of riboflavin was below the recommended allowance. Only 21 per cent of the households reached 80 per cent of the allowance, and 33 per cent of the households were obtaining less than half that amount. In the highest income class in the communities, 50 per cent of the families were obtaining 80 per cent or more of the allowances, and in the lowest class only 14 per cent. Since the consumption of cereals, pulses, and nuts was of the same order amongst these various area and income classes, the low and varying levels of riboflavin consumption were primarily related to the consumption of animal products—meat, eggs, milk, and cheese.

6. Thiamine and Ascorbic Acid

In assessing the adequacy of the intake of these B and C vitamins, the fact that the nutrient content of the diet has been calculated without making allowance for any losses due to cooking must be taken into consideration. Approximately one-third of the ascorbic acid was obtained from tomatoes and citrus fruits eaten fresh, approximately two-thirds from potatoes and green vegetables which were cooked before eating. If there was a 50 per cent loss of ascorbic acid from cooking vegetables, the average intake level would be approximately 60 milligrams per head per day, which is still quite an adequate level. The loss of thiamine due to cooking may be of the order of 15 per cent. A deduction from the intake figure to allow for this loss still leaves an adequate intake when compared with the recommended dietary allowances.

7. Niacin and Iron

This seven-day diet study indicated quite adequate levels of niacin and of iron nutrients in the diets of all groups of the Cretan population. With respect to iron, the percentage of households showing adequate intake was higher than in the case of any other nutrient. Niacin was not adequate in as high a percentage of families in the cities as in the rural communities.

8. *Summary*

The above comparison between actual consumption and recommended dietary allowances of the NRC or FAO is indicative only of possible inadequacies of the diet. To determine the adequacy of the diet, good criteria for evaluating the nutritional status of the population would be necessary. A clinical examination, by a medical nutritionist on the survey staff, of 200 children 6 to 16 years of age from the lowest income group in Khania did not show any significant sign of avitaminosis (vitamin deficiency). Nor did Cretan physicians feel that avitaminoses were important health problems.

On the other hand, indications of malnutrition among the children living in the caves near Iraklion and in certain mountain villages were observed by other staff members. Although 3 per cent of the survey families received less than 1,600 calories per person per day, this might reflect the abnormalities of the consumption of a particular week and/or failure to get a record of total actual food intake in these certain families. In any case, the dietary survey, limited clinical examination, and personal observations of staff members all suggested that any serious nutritional problems in Crete were probably limited to a relatively small number of households, living under conditions of very low income and little home production of food. Since Crete has no very large cities, the conditions for extreme malnutrition were not present—and to this extent the survey was not typical for the large city communities, such as Athens and Salonika, where most of the starvation occurred during the war and occupation period.

F. FACTORS AFFECTING THE ADEQUACY OF THE DIET

In Crete, where agriculture is such an important segment of the total economy, the quantity and types of food produced have an important bearing on both the amount of food and quality of the diet for the whole population. Moreover, there were differences in food consumption between rural and urban (semi-urban) groups and differences between income groups within the rural communities. The small number of detailed diet records for city families precluded any study of the effect of differences in incomes within that group.

1. *Diet in Relation to Food Production*

With limited acreages of agricultural land and a large number of people per acre in Crete, the use of land for the production of those crops which will produce the largest amount of food nutrients per acre, directly or through exchange of commodities, is especially important. Under the conditions existing on the island, the growing of energy-producing foods takes precedence over other types, at least up to some point above minimum calorie requirements. A comparison of the amount of food produced per acre (in terms of calories and grams of protein) from various crops may throw some light on the relationship between food production and the diet of the Cretan people. It should furnish some background for later suggestions as to means of improving the food supply or the level of incomes with which to improve other segments of living levels.

Although recent long-time yields of all crops in terms of the major food nutrients and net returns are needed to arrive at final conclusions as to the highest yielding crops in terms of food nutrients or cash income, an example of a possible procedure for analysis is presented here. The 1947 average yields from an acre of land in wheat, barley, pulses, olive oil, potatoes, tomatoes, and oranges are used for illustrative purposes. Meat, dairy products, vegetables, and fruits are omitted only because satisfactory yield data were not available. The percentage contribution to calorie and protein intake made by each food crop in comparison with the calorie and protein yield per acre and the gross value per acre at average local market prices in 1947 is shown in Table 11.

In 1947, olives and potatoes produced the largest number of calories per acre, 50 to 100 per cent more per acre than any other main crop. Pulses and tomatoes produced the most protein nutrients per acre, 50 to 100 per cent more than any other crop. The highest gross value of product per acre was from tomatoes, oranges, and potatoes, with three to nine times as much gross income per acre as in the case of the remaining crops. These facts, together with the climatic, soil, and water resource differences on the island, suggest reasons for the present diversity of crops in Crete.

The data in Table 11 indicate that in general there is close agreement between food habits and food production of olive oil and wheat. But the high yields of calories and proteins from barley and pulses would seem to justify a greater consumption of them if food habits could be changed. However, long-time averages for both production and prices would be necessary before any such suggestion would be valid. Based on farmer estimates of normal yields (past five years), barley produced 1.1 million calories per acre, only 10 per cent more

TABLE 11. Calorie and protein intake, contribution, production per acre, and gross product value per acre of selected food crops, Crete, 1947

Food items	Contribution[a] to intake of		1947 production per acre		1947 gross value of product per acre
	Calories	Protein	Calories	Protein	
	(percentage)		(thousands)	(kilograms)	(dollars)
Wheat	30.0	37.0	767	27.6	44
Barley	4.0	5.0	986	32.7	46
Pulses	7.0	17.0	950	77.2	44
Olive oil	29.0	0	1,710	0	68
Potatoes	4.0	4.0	1,344	32.6	135
Oranges	0.3	0.1	634	10.6	138
Tomatoes	0.8	2.3	636	52.4	380
All others	24.9	34.6	—	—	—
Total	100.0	100.0	—	—	—

a The proportion used here is the same as in the seven-day diet survey, merely as an example. The annual figures would be somewhat higher for pulses, considerably higher for oranges, and perhaps one-third less for tomatoes. The cereals and potatoes figures would remain about the same. The calories for olive oil include other vegetable oils, butter, and lard, which are about 10 per cent of this figure.

Source: Sample Survey of Crete, Form Ia, Seven-day Diet and Form B, Farm; Farm Price Estimates by Nome Agriculturists, Crete, 1948.

than wheat, and 37.7 kilograms of protein per acre, or about the same as for wheat, over a period of years. Palatability is also a factor in their consumption. These comparative data explain why relatively more barley is already grown in Crete than in other areas of Greece. Since the normal yield of pulses has been about 1.3 million calories and 90 kilograms of protein per acre, according to yield estimates of farmers, further investigation is needed to explain why larger acreages of pulses are not grown.

For economic reasons, which are evident in the gross value of product per acre, oranges are produced in spite of the lower yield of calories and proteins per acre. The average gross value of oranges per acre in 1947 was almost twice as great as for the cereal crops and about the same as for potatoes. Oranges, tomatoes, and potatoes require irrigation, and this and other cash-out-of-pocket costs must be deducted in order to determine the relative net cash return from the various crops. Oranges also require protection from strong coastal winds and frost or freeze damage. But in the main, olives, oranges, and tomatoes are produced both for home use and for sale in order to purchase sugar, rice, and other imported foods or other goods and services.

In general, the Cretan people have developed a pattern of food consumption which fits their agricultural production, and in turn have developed an agricultural production program which is fitted to the land and climate resources. While some improvements may be possible, these will be discussed in the chapter on agriculture.

2. Diet in Relation to Place of Residence

Except for calories, the National Research Council recommended dietary allowances for the various nutrients for both rural and city households are essentially the same. Consequently, direct comparisons between the two groups, except for calories, suggest the relative adequacy of the diet between rural and urban households.

Even though the diets of households in the communities contained 100 calories more per person per day than the city households, they lacked 130 calories of attaining the NRC recommended allowances, while the calorie intake of the city group was almost the same as the allowance. This seeming discrepancy is due to the greater activity of rural men and women, requiring larger dietary allowances.

In brief, the diets of the community group contained more protein, iron, thiamine, niacin, and riboflavin when compared with the city group or with their recommended allowances (See Table 12). The calcium and ascorbic acid content of the diets were very similar. The greatest difference occurred in the vitamin A intake, with much less deficiency suggested for the city group. But all these differences were small when compared with the differences between income groups.

3. Diet in Relation to Income

Although the small number of city households in the diet survey precluded any study of the effect of income upon their diets, it is believed that the analysis for the rural households was quite indicative for all households, especially since they made up such a large percentage of the total households in Crete.

The calorie value of the diet and also the intake of each of the other nutrients showed a progressive increase from the lowest to the highest of the three income groups in the communities (see Table 13). The income groups were determined by the amount of income per person in the household, and included 199 equivalent persons in

TABLE 12. Nutrient intake in relation to place of residence, Crete, Fall 1948 (calories and eight essential nutrients)[a]

Nutrient	Place of residence	
	Communities	Cities
Energy, calories	2,565	2,459
Protein, grams	71.3	67.9
Animal protein, grams	(17.1)	(18.5)
Fat, grams	108.8	99.2
Calcium, grams[b]	0.46	0.45
Iron, milligrams	20.6	17.4
Vitamin A, I.U.	3,733	4,417
Preformed vitamin A, I.U.	(743)	(681)
Thiamine, milligrams	1.70	1.46
Riboflavin, milligrams	1.00	0.88
Niacin, milligrams	20.8	13.5
Ascorbic acid, milligrams	89.0	94.0

[a] Except for calories, these data may be compared with the NRC-RDA set forth in the second column of Table 14. The computed NRC-RDA calorie allowance for community families is 2,695 and for municipality families, 2,474 calories.

[b] In addition to this calculated amount of calcium intake from food, there is estimated to be an additional calcium intake of 50 per cent through the drinking water.

Source: Sample Survey of Crete, Form Ia and Form I, Seven-day Diet Record.

the lowest income group ($0-99 total income per person), 149 in the middle group ($100-199), and 75 persons in the highest income group ($200-299). The average calorie intake for the lowest income group was 2,393, as compared to 2,544 calories for the middle income group, and 3,065 calories for the highest income group. The difference in calories, protein, calcium, riboflavin, and niacin between the highest and the middle income groups was greater than the difference between the lowest and the middle income groups. As between the lowest and the highest income groups, the greatest differences were noted in the intake of animal protein (80 per cent) and riboflavin (50 per cent). For the remaining nutrients the difference was about 20 to 30 per cent. The highest income group consumed more than twice as much milk, meat, game, and poultry, and three times as much cheese as the lowest income group. The lower level of vitamin A, riboflavin, calcium, and animal protein consumption in the lower income groups would seem to be due chiefly to a lack of income to provide sufficient food of animal origin from which such nutrients are derived.

TABLE 13. Nutrient intake for three rural income groups,[a] Crete, Fall 1948
(calories and eight essential nutrients)

Nutrient	Rural income group		
	$0-99	$100-199	$200 & over
Energy, calories	2,393	2,544	3,065
Protein, grams[b]	65.2	72.7	84.8
Animal protein, grams[b]	(14.4)	(16.3)	(25.2)
Fat, grams	103.6	102.0	135.7
Calcium, grams[c]	0.43	0.44	0.55
Iron, milligrams	18.8	21.5	23.8
Vitamin A, I.U.[b]	3,461	3,879	4,164
Preformed vitamin A, I.U.	(435)	(885)	(1,283)
Thiamine, milligrams	1.51	1.78	2.03
Riboflavin, milligrams	0.85	1.06	1.30
Niacin, milligrams	18.7	21.6	24.7
Ascorbic acid, milligrams[d]	84.0	92.0	98.0

a Rural income groups based on income per person in the household.

b Indicates that the daily per capita consumption on an adjusted annual basis would be larger for all groups.

c This figure is for seven-day diet only—without calcium in water included. An increase of 50 per cent or more in this figure might be expected. See discussion under adequacy of diet for details.

d An adjusted annual figure would be smaller—perhaps 10 to 15 per cent less.

Source: Sample Survey of Crete, Form Ia and Form I, Seven-day Diet Record.

4. Percentage of Budget Spent on Food

On the average, Cretan families spent a large percentage of their incomes for food—this being the largest single item in the expenditure pattern. In all areas of the world (and Crete is no exception) outlays for food account for a larger proportion of total expenditures among low income than among high income groups. Table 14 presents evidence of this in Crete.

As incomes increase, the food bill may get larger in an absolute sense, but it becomes smaller relative to other expenditures. Also, where incomes are higher there may be a greater variety in the diet. In Crete, families in the highest income group served meat almost twice as frequently on Sunday as did those in the lowest income bracket. They also tended to serve more often those food items which supplement the main food combinations. This explains, in part at least, the superior nutritive value of diets frequently found among higher income families.

TABLE 14. Percentage of cash income spent for food in households classified according to total income, Crete, 1947

Income Class	Communities	Municipalities	All Crete
(dollars)		(percentage)	
0-249	83	91	85
250-499	73	83	77
500-749	71	82	75
750 and over	66	74	69
All classes	70	79	73

Source: Sample Survey of Crete, Form A, Household.

In spite of the narrow income range used in Table 14 and the fact that average incomes were low, the average consumption of all food nutrients increased as income level per capita increased. Though the same nutrients had a low level of intake relative to the NRC recommended allowances in all four income groups, they appeared less serious at the higher income levels.

G. COMPARISON OF FOOD CONSUMPTION IN CRETE, GREECE, AND THE UNITED STATES

The total weight of food consumed per person in Crete in 1948 was 926 pounds, or 4 per cent more than the 895 pounds per person for Greece as a whole in 1948-1949. This figure for Crete was only three-fifths as much as the apparent average consumption per person in the United States during 1948-1949 (Table 15).

As compared to Greece, Crete consumed a fifth less cereals and only three-fifths as much sugar. But consumption of oils and fats per capita in Crete was double the average for all Greece. From observation, Athenians on the survey staff commented on the greater consumption of olive oil in Crete, even before survey results were available. Pulses and nuts were a half greater, potatoes and animal protein foods (meat, fish, and eggs) were a fifth larger, and vegetables and fruits a tenth more in Crete than Greece. Dairy products were about the same. These large differences cannot be explained by the different time periods covered by the data; they indicate differences in dietary patterns.

The major differences from food consumption patterns in the United States are found in the lesser amounts of sugar, dairy products, meats, and vegetables and fruits consumed in Crete. Cereals, pulses and nuts, and oils are the items consumed in greater quantities by the Cretan families.

TABLE 15. Annual consumption (pounds per capita per year) in major food categories in Crete, Greece, and United States, 1948

Food Group	Crete 1948	Greece 1948-1949	United States 1948-1949
		(pounds)	
Cereals	282	348	172
Potatoes	85	68	108
Sugar, honey, etc.	12	20	103
Pulses and nuts	51	33	15
Vegetables and fruits	291	265	447
Meat, fish, and eggs	61	51	222
Dairy products	76	77	420
Oils and fats	68	33	45
Total	926	895	1,532

Note: Alcoholic beverages have been omitted.

Source: *Crete*: Adjusted estimates based on Sample Survey of Crete, Form Ia, Seven-day Diet, and Form A, Household. *Greece: Food Balance Sheets for Greece, 1948-1949*, prepared by Greek Ministry of Coordination and Ministry of Agriculture, under direction Miss A. Tsongas, FAO. *United States: Food Balance Sheets*, 1950 Supplement. FAO. Washington, April 1950.

1. *Sources of Calories Consumed*

Cereals, oils, and fats were the chief sources of energy in all three countries studied; they supplied roughly two-fifths, two-thirds, and three-fourths of the calories in the United States, Crete, and Greece respectively. In Crete, vegetables and fruits provided 11 per cent of the calories and in neither Crete nor Greece did any remaining food category provide more than 7 per cent of the calories. In the United States, the meat, fish, and egg group provided 19 per cent, sugar 15 per cent, and dairy products 14 per cent of the calories. These higher percentages in other food groups resulted in a much lower percentage contribution from cereals in the United States. (For further details see Table 16 below.)

With reference to the above data, it should be noted that the method used in arriving at the total food consumption per person (calories per person per day) in Crete differed from that used in Greece and the United States. A seasonal sample household survey method

TABLE 16. Sources of calories consumed, by percentages,
Crete, Greece, and United States, 1948

Food Group	Crete Fall 1948	Greece Fiscal 1948-1949	United States 1948-1949
	(percentage of calories)		
Cereals	39	61	25
Potatoes	4	2	3
Sugar and honey	2	4	15
Pulses and nuts	7	6	3
Vegetables and fruits	11	5	6
Meat, fish and eggs	4	3	19
Dairy products	3	4	14
Oils and fats	29	15	15
Wine, beer, and spirits	1	*	*
Total	100	100	100
Total calories per person per day	2,547	2,477	3,129

* Not given.

Source: *Crete*: Sample Survey of Crete; Form Ia, Seven-day Diet. *Greece: Food Balance Sheets for Greece, 1948-1949*. Ministry of Coordination and Ministry of Agriculture, Athens. *United States: Food Balance Sheets*, 1950 Supplement. FAO. Washington, April 1950.

was used in Crete; the quantities of food for consumption were taken at retail level in Greece and the United States. As previously pointed out, the household survey method would show relatively little loss from food wastage in comparison with the rather large losses between the retail level and actual consumption in the United States. Even though similar methods were used in Greece and the United States, low incomes and more direct marketing methods in Greece would result in very much lower losses from food wastage. Earlier statements on adjusting the seasonal data for Crete to an annual basis also suggest that certain food groups would be affected more than others. Nevertheless, with full consideration for all these points, the data in Table 16 indicate in a rough way the major differences in the sources of calories by food groups among the countries studied.

2. Sources of Protein Consumed

One of the outstanding differences between the diets of the Mediterranean peoples and of Americans is the small amount of animal protein consumed by Mediterraneans. Cretans obtained one-fourth of their protein from animal products and Greeks less than one-fifth, while Americans received about two-thirds of an even larger total amount of protein from meat and animal products. Crete differed from both Greece and the United States in the high proportion (25 per cent) of protein in the diet from pulses, nuts, vegetables, and fruits. (For further comparisons see Table 17 below.)

TABLE 17. Sources of protein in the diet, by percentages,
Crete, Greece, and United States, 1948

Food Group	Crete Fall, 1948	Greece 1948-1949	United States 1948-1949
	(percentage of protein)		
Cereals	47	65	21
Potatoes	4	2	2
Sugar, etc.	0	0	0
Pulses and nuts	17	10	5
Vegetables and fruits	8	4	6
Meat, fish and eggs	19	11	40
Dairy products	5	8	26
Oils and fats	*	*	*
Total protein	100	100	100
Animal protein	24	19	66
Vegetable protein	76	81	34

* Less than 0.5 per cent.
Source: *Crete*: Sample Survey of Crete, Form Ia, Seven-day Diet. *Greece: Food Balance Sheet for Greece, 1948-1949*. Ministry of Agriculture and Ministry of Coordination. Athens. *United States: Food Balance Sheets*, 1950 Supplement. FAO. Washington, April 1950.

The consumption of proteins per capita per day in Crete was 70.7 grams according to the seven-day diet survey, or about three-fourths that of the United States and about the same as for Greece.

H. SUMMARY

The annual food consumption level was obtained from data secured by a seven-day diet survey of sample families, and was modified by other available information on production and consumption for Crete and Greece. The quantitative seasonal diet variation needs further study to ascertain with greater accuracy the average annual consumption level of the whole island and various regional and economic sub-groups.

The dietary pattern and food habits in Crete were dictated to a considerable extent by the supply of water, fuel, and household equipment. Most families cooked only once a day and, except for the main meal, menus differed according to the different ways of eating bread: bread with olives, bread with tea, bread with wine, bread with tomatoes or fruits, bread with cheese, or hondros, which also contains cereals. Most of the people had an understanding of the relative importance of various foods in the diet and made good use of the foods that were available and within their budgetary limitations. The use of whole grain cereals in bread, the use of wild herbs and greens, the full utilization of slaughtered animals, the widespread practice of boiling milk, and the large amount of time spent in the sun are all examples of habits developed by a people who have adapted their food habits to the available resources. The percentage of income spent on food was very high: 70 to 90 per cent.

In general, the diet in Crete is as described by Homer centuries ago. This diet in 1948 consisted of: (a) cereals, supplying 39 per cent of the calories and 47 per cent of the protein consumed; (b) olive oil, furnishing 29 per cent of the calories; (c) vegetables, fruits, and pulses, supplying 18 per cent of the calories and 25 per cent of the protein; and (d) small amounts of dairy products (one-sixth that of the United States) and meat, fish, and eggs (one-third of the United States, 1948-1949). These levels reflect a relatively low consumption of foods of animal origin.

The average intake of all nutrients studied, with the exception of calcium, riboflavin, and vitamin A, reached the level of the recommended dietary allowances of the National Research Council. With certain seasonal and other adjustments made, calcium and vitamin A deficiencies became relatively unimportant. A comparison with the NRC allowances alone does not indicate an actual deficiency state with regard to these three nutrients.[19] An increased consumption of milk and milk products would raise the intake level of each of these nutrients. In view of the trend of higher income groups to have more of the protective foods, particularly those of animal origin, and the fact that these higher income groups set a food pattern which the

[19] A recent study in Mexico shows a fairly good nutritional status with a diet much lower than the one observed in Crete. See B. K. Anderson, G. Scarous, G. C. Payne, "A Study of the Nutritional Status and Food Habits of Adonis Indians in the Mezquital Valley of Mexico." *American Journal of Public Health*, vol. 36, no. 8, p. 883, 903. 1946.

lower income groups tend to follow, when their incomes are increased, a rise in per capita incomes would produce a ready outlet for increased production of these foods.

Apparently income is the factor which exercises the greatest influence on levels of nutrition. The daily consumption by high income families was approximately 500 calories and 20 grams of protein more than that of the low income group. They consumed mainly more animal products: cheese, meat, eggs, and milk. In the cities, consumption was a little higher than in rural areas in animal products and sweets, and lower in bread, olive oil, and fruits. In general, food production per acre, calculated in terms of energy and protein, was in accordance with the high consumption of wheat and olive oil, but would justify a still higher consumption of pulses.

By making a careful study of the yield per acre in terms of nutrients, and knowing the present food habits, food patterns, and trends in food consumption of the higher income groups, agriculturists can encourage production and trade of the most adequate foods for Crete. Since income appears to be one of the main factors influencing the adequacy of the diet, the major requirement for improving the diet is to devise means of raising the economic level of the people of Crete so that they may purchase the higher priced protective foods (foods of animal origin). It is also necessary to establish an agricultural and food program which will provide the supply of these foods to meet the rising demand. Some problems involved in accomplishing this will be discussed later in Chapter 10.

A final assessment of the adequacy of the diets can be made only by comparing the nutrient intakes with the nutritional status of the people. Further detailed investigations are needed to ascertain whether the suggested lack of riboflavin and vitamin A is a definite deficiency among the population of Crete, the degree of deficiency, and its incidence. These studies would include additional seasonal surveys of food consumption, metabolism and clinical studies, and biochemical examinations of samples of the population.

In brief, the data from this study suggested that the food and nutrition problems in Crete were primarily economic: (1) the provision of exchange funds for the importation of cereals, sugar, etc., (2) a general improvement in incomes to enable a larger proportion of the population to purchase additional foods, especially those of animal origin, and (3) the development of more effective methods of food distribution to certain vulnerable groups and communities.

CHAPTER 7

HEALTH

WESTERN CULTURE places great emphasis upon the individual and his ability to contribute to society. By these standards health, as measured by mortality and morbidity, is an important and contributing factor to the relative levels of living of a country. On the other hand, the availability of health facilities and services, together with food, shelter, clothing, and the per capita income with which to provide and utilize them, suggests the extent to which living levels contribute to the health of the population.[1]

A. MORTALITY

The types of health problems and their relative seriousness in a country are suggested by the mortality rates, as indicated by crude death rates from various causes, differences in rural-urban death rates, average age at death, and infant mortality rates.

1. Crude Death Rates

Although Greece and the Mediterranean countries are usually considered as areas of medium high death rates (14.0 to 18.0 per 1,000 inhabitants), death rates on the Island of Crete have been below this level continuously since before 1930 (with the possible exception of the war years of 1941 through 1943). Except for the Jews in Palestine and the Island of Cyprus after 1938, no other important area in the Mediterranean basin has had as low a death rate as the Island of Crete, according to data compiled by the United Nations in their Demographic Yearbook for 1948. It was 11.3 to 13.7 pre-war, and about 10.6 in 1946-1948.

---

[1] In addition to data from the Sample Survey of Crete, this chapter has utilized material from a manuscript, "Public Health Survey in Crete, Greece" by Dr. W. A. McIntosh, a member of the survey team. His manuscript has been translated into Greek and issued for limited distribution by the Greek Government. The authors accept all responsibility for any errors or misinterpretations resulting from their use of Dr. McIntosh's material. Since birth rates were discussed in Chapter 4 under population, the section on natality has been omitted here.

For additional health surveys in foreign countries see Bhore Committee. *Report of the Health Survey and Development Committee (India)*, vols. I, II, III, IV. Manager of Publications, Delhi, Government of India Press, Calcutta, 1946. 228 pp., 532 pp., 351 pp., 90 pp. High Commissioner for Hygiene and Public Health. *Commission for the Study of the Reorganization of the Health Care Services (Italy)*, vols. I and II. Alto commissariato per l'igiene e la sanità pubblica, Rome, 1949. 79 pp., 271 pp.

2. Rural-Urban Death Rates

The survey data obtained by interview from registrars in the sample communities and municipalities of Crete showed death rates of 11.0 for the municipalities and 8.5 for the rural areas in 1946-1948. Data collected by Dr. McIntosh for three rural towns, only recently classified as municipalities, indicated these rural-urban communities also had death rates of less than 8.0 during 1946-1948. A higher death rate in the more urban areas is consistent with findings in other countries.[2] However, some of the difference between rural and urban death rates in Crete may be due to larger under-registration in rural areas and the effect of the place-of-occurrence registration in cities.

According to Whetten, "Numerous studies in other countries seem to suggest that the greater comparative lack of medical facilities in the country districts is more than counterbalanced by the relatively greater problems of sanitation, lack of fresh air, indoor work, and contagious infection that are usually associated with congested urban living."[3] In Crete, much of the rural population lives at higher altitudes and enjoys isolation from port facilities and attendant dangers from malaria and epidemic diseases of the Mediterranean area.

3. Average Age at Death and Life Expectancy

The average age at death in Crete was 48 years in 1948, as compared to 40 years in 1938. If the spread of seven to eight years between average age at death and life expectancy was the same in 1948 as it was ten years before, the life expectancy at birth in Crete would have been about 55-56 years in 1948. In the United States the average age at death is 58 years and life expectancy at birth is 67 years —a difference of nine years. Because of the younger population in Crete, this difference between average age at death and life expectancy is probably one year less.

In 1935, almost two-fifths of the deaths were of persons over 64 years of age, one-fifth under one year, and about one-third under five years of age. For the same year in the United States, corresponding ratios were two-fifths, one-eleventh, and one-ninth respectively.[4]

In Crete the average age at death in 1948 was only one-half year

2 P. A. Sorokin, C. C. Zimmerman, and C. J. Galpin, *Systematic Source Book in Rural Sociology*, Minneapolis, 1932. vol. iii, ch. xix, pp. 121-122.

3 Nathan Laselle Whetten, *Rural Mexico*, University of Chicago Press, 1948, p. 332. Also see reference above, Sorokin et al., p. 135.

4 Bureau of Census, U.S. Department of Commerce, *Mortality Statistics, 1935*. Government Printing Office, Washington, 1937. Table 7, pp. 200-201.

higher for females than males. In rural communities as compared to municipalities, males averaged 7.5 and females 11.0 years older at death during 1946-1948. If, as in total death rates, a number of births and infant deaths among rural families occurred in a municipality, this fact would affect considerably the statistics of average age at death in the cities.

4. Infant Mortality

Infant mortality rates (infant deaths under one year of age per 1,000 live births) in Crete averaged 99 for the 7-year period 1932-1939. This was relatively low in comparison with Greece as a whole (116) and the neighboring countries of Egypt (165), Bulgaria (148), Yugoslavia (146), Cyprus (133), Moslem Palestine (155), Spain (120), and slightly lower than Italy (109) but considerably above France (70) and the Jewish sector of Palestine (70).[5] In 1948, the infant mortality rate in Crete, according to official community statistics, was 72, although the fact that the figures for 1946 and 1947 were only 42 and 40 respectively indicates that considerable under-registration of deaths must have taken place in those years. Dr. Valaoras estimated the infant mortality rate in Crete for 1948 at 72 to 85 per 1,000 live births. Even in the municipalities where registrars are located and where births are recorded when they occur, rather than according to the residence of parents, the rates were only 58, 75, and 49 for the years 1946, 1947, and 1948, according to the official statistics.

Unless one has been in war areas and observed destruction of buildings, personal property, and records, it is difficult to understand the length of time required to return to pre-war completeness and accuracy in government data. For this reason many of the statistics dependent on community records in 1941 to 1946 inclusive are apt to be incomplete or rough estimates. However, the contact of an interviewer with the officials of each sample community did increase the completeness of coverage for these sample communities as compared to the usual government reporting.

Of the infant deaths occurring in four nome capitals and two other large towns, about one-fourth occurred within the first two weeks, and more than one-third within the first 30 days. In the United

[5] Statistical Office of the United Nations, *Statistical Yearbook, 1948*. United Nations, New York, 1949. Table 4, pp. 42-45.

States two-thirds of all infant deaths in 1947 occurred within the first two weeks and 71 per cent within the first month.[6]

During 1935, one-fifth of the total deaths in Crete were of infants under one year of age and an additional 30 per cent were of one to four years of age. Thus one-half of all deaths occurring were of children under five years of age. By 1946, deaths in this age group had declined to two-fifths of all deaths in the municipalities, with one-sixth under one year and one-fourth from one to four years of age. In Mexico, a neighboring country of the United States, comparable figures for 1939-1943 indicated that almost three-fourths of total deaths were of children under five years of age, including one-fourth under one year and almost one-half from one to four years of age.

5. *Fetal Deaths*

Thirty per cent of the household heads indicated that a fetal death, defined in the survey as "having had a baby born dead," had occurred in their family life. Of these households, one-fourth indicated this had occurred twice, one-twelfth three times, and 5 per cent from four to seven times.

B. CAUSES OF DEATH

According to the data secured from the catalogues of deaths in the sample communities and municipalities, the major cause of death (except senility) during 1946, 1947, and 1948 was pneumonia (15 per cent). Violent and accidental deaths and cardio-vascular diseases were next in importance with 11 and 10 per cent respectively. Cancer, tuberculosis, and cerebral hemorrhage each caused slightly less than 5 per cent of the deaths. Among the other major causes were dysentery, diarrhea, enteritis, and typhoid—a group hereafter called "intestinal infections"[7] which accounted for an additional 3 per cent of the deaths.

In percentages of the total deaths and also deaths per 100,000 population, marked declines were shown in deaths due to malaria, influenza, congenital debility, and intestinal infections during the years from 1933-1937 to 1946-1948. Small declines were shown in pneumonia, tuberculosis, and cerebral hemorrhages. But increases in death due to cardio-vascular diseases and cancer were especially noticeable. (See Figure 9 and Table 18.)

[6] National Office of Vital Statistics, Public Health Service, Federal Security Agency, *Vital Statistics of the United States*, 1947, Part II. Government Printing Office, Washington, 1949. Table 30, p. 631.

[7] These same diseases are designated as "filth-borne diseases" by Dr. McIntosh in his report.

CAUSE OF DEATH

CRETE   UNITED STATES   MEXICO

1933-37   1946-48   1940   1946-47   1940   1946-48

Pneumonia, Influenza

Accident, Violence

Heart trouble

Cancer, Tumors

Tuberculosis

Cerebral hemorrhage

Congenital

Dysentery

Typhoid, Paratyphoid

Malaria

Other causes

SCALE   100 DEATHS

During the decade, the deaths per 100,000 population declined about one-sixth in Crete, according to best estimates from the data obtained, including a 20 per cent allowance for under-registration of all deaths. The three-year average of 879 deaths per 100,000 population (8.8 deaths per 1,000) obtained by the Sample Survey in Crete may be more nearly accurate than seems possible at first glance, in view of the very heavy death losses during the war and occupation period, when the most vulnerable of each age group may have succumbed. However, Dr. V. G. Valaoras estimated that a figure of 1,055 per 100,000 (10.6 per 1,000) was a more reasonable one, in view of the past history. Except for the United Kingdom and Bulgaria, data for all the war-torn countries indicate a decline in post-war death rates of 2.0 or more per 1,000 in Europe and the Balkans. For this reason the Crete data may be understated in the order of 10 per cent rather than 20 per cent. But this would not affect the general picture as to causes of death nor comparisons with pre-war data or other countries.

The death rate in Crete differed little from the rate in the United States in the post-war period and was only 13 per cent higher during the 1933-1937 period. But there were wide differences between Crete and the United States as to the specific causes of death. Pneumonia, influenza, and intestinal infections caused three to four times as many total deaths per 100,000 population in Crete as in the United States. Deaths due to tuberculosis and violent accidents were also 40 per cent greater in Crete. On the other hand, the death rates for cardio-vascular diseases, cancer, and nephritis were one-third to one-fourth less in Crete than in the United States, and cerebral hemorrhages about one-half as large in proportion to the population. These latter diseases are more characteristic of old age and might be expected to be more prevalent in the United States, which has an older age population, demographically. The mortality rate for diseases of the intestinal tract in Crete was about the same in 1946-1948 as for the United States in 1930, while the mortality rate from typhoid on the island in 1946-1948 was similar to the 1920 rate for this country.

Because Mexico, especially North Pacific Mexico, has climatic conditions somewhat similar to those in Crete, the comparison between mortality in the two countries is of interest. There is a wide difference in the number and causes of deaths. In all Mexico almost twice as many persons died per 100,000 population as in Crete in

TABLE 18. Causes of death per 100,000 population in Crete, United States, and Mexico, pre-war and post-war

Cause of Death	Crete		United States		Mexico	
	1933-37	1946-48[a]	1940	1946-47	1940	1946-48
Pneumonia & influenza	248	163	70	44	373	316
Accident, poison, violence	33[b]	116	84	87	119	102
Cardio-vascular (heart)	65	105	292	314	54	70
Cancer and other tumors	36	51	120	131	23	25
Tuberculosis	66	49	46	35	56	52
Cerebral hemorrhage	53	48	91	91	19	16
Congenital disabilities (malformation & premature)	57	29	35	42	79	92
Dysentery, enteritis, diarr.	75	27	10	6	534	316
Typhoid & paratyphoid	17[b]	7	1	*	31	—
Malaria	15[b]	1	1	*	119	22
Other causes	591	459	324	253	875	774
Total	1,256	1,055	1,074	1,003	2,282	1,785

* Less than 0.5 per 100,000 population.

a Crete survey data has been increased by 20 per cent to cover under-registration and bring data in line with V. G. Valaoras' estimate of a death rate of 10-11, giving a total of 1,055 per 100,000 population.

b Data for 1938 only available.

Sources: Ministry of National Economy, *Statistiques des Causes de Décès*, 1938. Data supplied by Dr. V. G. Valaoras, New York, 1948. Sample Survey of Crete, Form C, Community. U.S. Bureau of Census, *Statistical Abstract of the United States*, 1949. Washington, 1949, Table 80, p. 73. Nathan Laselle Whetten. *Rural Mexico*. University of Chicago Press, 1948, Table 70, p. 338. Pan American Sanitary Bureau. "Death Rates per 100,000 Population by Selected Causes, Mexico, 1946 and 1947." Unpublished manuscript. Washington, May, 1950. Data from official Mexican reports and computations by the Pan American Sanitary Bureau.

the pre-war period, and 70 per cent more in the post-war period 1946-1948. Even North Pacific Mexico, which has a seacoast and climate quite similar to Crete, had a 40 per cent higher pre-war death rate than Crete.[8] There was probably somewhat less difference after the war. Especially noticeable is the higher percentage of deaths due to dysentery, diarrhea, and enteritis in Mexico—almost one-fourth for the whole country and one-fifth for North Pacific Mexico in comparison with less than three per cent for Crete.[9] Malaria, whooping cough, and tuberculosis were also much more frequent causes of death in North Pacific Mexico. While deaths due to pneumonia were

8 Nathan Laselle Whetten, *op. cit.* Appendix A, Table 36, p. 610.
9 *ibid.*, Table 69, p. 334.

slightly higher in North Pacific Mexico, they were more than twice as high in all Mexico as in Crete. Deaths due to cancer, cardio-vascular diseases, and cerebral hemorrhage were more frequent in Crete than in Mexico. This is as might be expected, since the Mexican population is of a much younger age than the population in Crete. Mexico has a higher birth rate, higher infant mortality rate, higher death rate, a lower life expectancy at birth, and a lower average age at death, than Crete.

Since the climate, soil, sanitation, and conditions favoring malaria are similar in Crete and Mexico, it would seem that the Cretans have had much greater success in adjusting themselves to their habitat. Centuries of Western civilization and currently higher educational levels in Crete probably have been important contributing factors in the making of these adjustments.

In Cretan municipalities, tuberculosis caused 12 per cent of the deaths. One reason for the high rate in these cities is the inclusion of a large tuberculosis sanitarium in one of them, which admits advanced cases—more than half of whom die within a 30-month period after admission.

According to the data collected for 1946-1948 in the municipalities by Dr. McIntosh, almost 30 per cent of the infant deaths occurring under one year of age were caused by malnutrition and by diseases peculiar to the first year of life. Almost half of these deaths were caused by undernourishment.[10] An additional 29 per cent of infant deaths were caused by respiratory diseases, mainly pneumonia. Enteritis, dysentery, and other gastro-intestinal diseases caused 21 per cent of the infant deaths, while parasitic and other infectious diseases caused about 8 per cent of the deaths.

Comparable data for the United States in 1947 indicated 55 per cent of the infant deaths occurring under one year were due to diseases peculiar to the first year, 11 per cent to pneumonia and influenza, less than 5 per cent to diarrhea and enteritis, and 3 per cent to parasitic and infectious diseases.[11] These data suggest that the causes of infant mortality in the United States are primarily peculiar

[10] While the original report included "scorbutus" as an important cause of infant deaths, Dr. V. G. Valaoras questioned its inclusion because of the high vitamin C content of the Cretan diet, including the widespread use of large amounts of lemon juice in soups and on foods.

[11] National Office of Vital Statistics, Public Health Service, Federal Security Agency, *Vital Statistics of the United States*, 1947, Part ii. Government Printing Office, Washington, 1949. Table 30, p. 631.

to the first year of life and are not so susceptible to environmental control. In contrast, the situation is quite different in Crete, as indicated in the preceding paragraph, and would seem to offer a great opportunity for preventive work.

In Crete, as in Mexico and in certain sections of the United States, there are people who look upon death as caused by some unknown spirit or "evil eye," or as a punishment.[12] One interviewer reported, "They were triplets who died 40 days later from the evil eye!" This fear of the "evil eye" is reported to affect other phases of Cretan life; some shepherds seldom count their flocks or report the correct number to any interrogators, fearful that they may soon lose some.

C. MORBIDITY

Seven per cent of the population of Crete, or about 30,000 people, were ill—unable to carry on their usual activities—during a twenty-four-hour period in the late summer of 1948, or had been ill for one week during the previous twelve months. The economic loss from such illnesses may be great, especially in an agricultural area where seasonal planting and harvesting are important.

What, then, are the major causes of the prevalent illnesses, according to the statements from householders?[13]

In Crete, colds, influenza, and grippe were three times as prevalent as malaria, the next most common disease. Economically, malaria probably has been more important than any other disease because of its greater prevalence during the work season. Dysentery, diarrhea, and typhoid, infectious diseases of the intestinal tract, ranked next in prevalence, and they, too, were common during the six months' summer and fall work season. Measles, whooping cough, and trachoma had about the same prevalence, but the continuing effects of trachoma make it relatively more important economically and socially. Tuberculosis and oriental sore ranked next in prevalence. Of these, tuberculosis has a more lasting effect on the economy of the family, and also on the economy of the government, if any cure is attempted through hospitalization. Tuberculosis occurred at about the same rate in Crete in the post-war period as in the United States

[12] See Nathan Laselle Whetten, *op. cit.*, p. 340.

[13] To some readers the statements made in the following paragraph and a later section on "dysentery" may seem to have little medical significance. The discussion is included because it summarizes what the people of Crete believe to be their major illnesses. It should serve as useful background for determining the type of educational program needed.

before the war; the rate in the United States is strikingly lower for malaria and typhoid.

Perhaps further discussion of the more important diseases and a brief statement of others not set forth above will give a broader understanding of the health problem in Crete.

1. More Prevalent Diseases

a. *Droplet-borne diseases.* Influenza and colds are prevalent in Crete—most cases occurring during the winter rainy months. In the survey, the rate for these was three times as great as the next most prevalent disease, malaria. While pneumonia did not show up as one of the more important prevalent illnesses, it did appear as the one most likely to be fatal—with the highest percentage cause of death in Crete in both 1946-1948 and 1933-1937. Perhaps it was included under colds until it became sufficiently serious to prove fatal.

Whooping cough is one of the more frequent causes of illness, being rated sixth according to the survey. According to the nomiatroi (nome doctors), mumps is also a common disease, but it is not included among the more prevalent diseases listed by community officials. Meningitis and pleurisy were found, and diphtheria was not uncommon.

b. *Malaria.* Before the general use of DDT, Greece as a whole, in epidemic years, had an incidence of malaria as high as 30 per cent. The average yearly incidence was estimated at one to two million cases in a population of over six million.[14] About thirty million man-days per year were estimated by malariologists to be lost in Greece because of malaria. In certain years the quantity of quinine imported into Greece was reported as up to 5 per cent of the world's production. As this indicates, malaria was a very disabling condition in Greece from both the public health and the economic standpoints.

Crete was also considered highly malarious. But the mortality from malaria in Crete was only 15 per 100,000 population, as against 40 per 100,000 for all Greece.

According to a study of Dr. M. C. Balfour[15] in 1930-1933, the splenic index of malaria in six villages of Crete varied from 7 per

---

[14] League of Nations Health Organization, Malaria Commission, "Note sur le voyage d'étude de Prof. M. Ciuca en Grèce pour la lutte antipaludique." C.H.: Malaria, 154, 1931.

[15] M. C. Balfour, "Malaria Studies in Greece, Measurements of Malaria, 1930-1933." *American Journal of Tropical Medicine*, vol. 15. Also in *Collected Papers of the International Health Division*, The Rockefeller Foundation. 12:5, 1935.

cent in Kandanos, with an elevation above 1,312 feet (400 meters), to 100 per cent for the seaside village of Yeoryioupolis, both in the nome of Khania. In 1948, ten villages in Khania nome were examined for malaria and showed a splenic index varying only from zero to 10 per cent, with all but one less than 7 per cent.[16] Interestingly enough, the sample survey for 1948 also showed Yeoryioupolis as the highest among the 44 communities in percentage of households stating they had had a case of malaria in the past twelve months.

The seasonal distribution of malaria cases, which revealed wide variation, showed in general a rise beginning in May and reaching a peak early in June; these cases in all probability were due mostly to relapses. There was a decline in the curves in the latter part of June and early July. Thereafter a rise reached its maximum in August and was maintained through August, September, and October. All three common types of malaria, widespread throughout Greece, were found in Crete. One of these types, *P. falciparum*, predominates in epidemic years; this form is short-lived and disappears when the epidemic interval subsides. The other two forms, *P. vivax* and *P. malariae*, become relatively important in the endemic or inter-epidemic periods. Of anopheline mosquitoes found in Crete, an important type, *A. superpictus*, breeds in torrents, streams, irrigation channels, and other moving water. The mosquitoes of the maculipennis group breed in marshes or ponds and are adaptable to smaller, more stagnant bodies of water. Another species, *A. sacharovi* (*A. elutus*), bites man freely and is a dangerous carrier of malaria; as it tolerates more salt than the other types, its distribution tends to be coastal and along the coast it is the predominating carrier. Malaria in the central mountainous parts of the island is transmitted solely by the type *A. superpictus*, which breeds in mountain streams.[17]

With the introduction of DDT, the incidence of malaria in Greece has been greatly reduced—from one or two million to 50,000 cases annually. Some 65,000 blood smears were taken in 1947-1948 and of these 13,000 were examined in the laboratory, with only 31 positive for malaria.

Prior to DDT spraying, 90 to 100 villages situated in the malaria

[16] The 1948 splenic index in Khania nome varied from 0 to 10 per cent for 10 villages examined—0, one village; 1.3 per cent, one village; 2 per cent, two villages; 4 per cent, four villages; 6 per cent, one village; and 10 per cent, one village.

[17] The types of anopheline mosquitoes reported in Crete were the following: *A. superpictus; A. maculipennis* (syn. *typicus*); *A. messeae; A. melanoon subalpinus; A. sacharovi* (*A. elutus*); *A. claviger; A. algeriensis;* and *A. hyrcanus.*

region of Crete were involved. While physicians admit that cases occur, they are in general agreement that there has been a marked reduction. Anopheline mosquitoes have been reduced too, although they have not been completely eradicated.

Contrary to very optimistic reports by the malariologists, the people and the community officials still reported malaria as their second most prevalent disease with a rate of 53 per 1,000 population. Perhaps this represented relapses; perhaps it was faulty diagnosis, being merely a hangover from the days when there was much malaria. In any case it represents what the local people thought and suggests a need for further check-up surveys and an educational program on this phase of the health problem. (See Appendix 5, Table A53.)

In spite of the many recent attempts to stamp out malaria through drainage projects and anti-malaria control campaigns, one-fifth of the households indicated some member as having had malaria in the last 12 months. On the average these households reported 1.7 cases per family. Since 5.3 per cent of the population were indicated as having had malaria during the past 2½ years, these figures seem consistent. About half (47 per cent) of the population indicated they had had malaria at least once during their lifetimes. Dr. Valaoras felt that memory bias had understated this situation; his judgment indicated that the correct figure was between 80 and 90 per cent, since almost every person over 10 years of age and some of those below that age had had malaria at some time.

Among the sample communities and municipalities, there was a wide difference in the percentage of households having had at least one case of malaria in the twelve months preceding the survey. The four municipalities at approximate sea level—16 to 80 feet (5 to 25 meters) elevation—and 23 communities with elevations above 985 feet (300 meters) reported about 13 per cent of the households having had a malaria case during the previous year. The 14 rural communities of less than 985 feet in elevation reported 31 per cent of the households having had malaria, or more than twice the above rate. The highest percentage of households with malaria cases (average of 60 per cent) was found in the three communities with many nearby springs and without road facilities. Even though at an average elevation of 1,080 feet, most of their crop land was at much lower elevations. These communities could be reached only by long and difficult mule-back rides. Probably the lack of communication as well as the water supply near the lower agricultural land were important

factors in causing the incidence of malaria to be four times as high
here as in other villages of high elevation. The percentage of households with malaria was almost twice as high in the rural communities
as in the four municipalities.

Some doctors objected to the malaria campaign because of the
possible reduction in the number of their patients. One farmer objected because he "had a nagging wife who got malaria relapses two
or three times a year and did not want her to get over it, since that
was God's way of punishing her for nagging him." But in general
the malaria control campaign was well received by professional and
lay people. Many times the people expressed their appreciation for
the riddance (though temporary in some instances) of household
pests—lice, fleas, and flies—more earnestly and vociferously than
for the riddance of the mosquitoes.

c. *Dysentery*. Dysentery was the third most prevalent cause of
illness in the period 1946-1948. Cretan physicians and experts
agreed that amoebic dysentery[18] was prevalent; bacillary dysentery
was thought also to occur, but its extent was not known.

One-third of the household heads stated that they did not know
the cause of dysentery in children, one-fourth thought fruit and diet
were the cause; one-tenth, unclean food; one-eleventh, water; and
one-eighth each said colds or colds and diet. An especially noticeable
difference between the rural and urban group was the higher percentage of rural people (four times higher than the rate among city
people) who thought dysentery was caused by water and colds. In
contrast, 60 per cent more of the city people reported that dysentery
was caused by unclean food. In view of the tendency to look upon all
digestive disturbances as either dysentery, diarrhea, or enteritis, this
may be somewhat indicative of the unprotected water supplies in
rural areas in contrast to greater possibilities for food contamination in the cities. Only 30 per cent of rural households stated they
did not know the cause, while almost half of the city families so
stated (Table 19). The opinion of parents on dysentery and its
causes is of course without much medical significance except perhaps

[18] "The Microbiologist in Iraklion stated that amoebic dysentery is not so prevalent
as commonly supposed; his laboratory findings indicate that it may be confused
clinically with other types of dysentery. The Athens Medical Association is of the
same opinion. Many dyspepsias and other gastro-enteric disorders are confused with
amoebic dysenteries. Rural physicians are not in a position to distinguish the true
nature and mostly favor the idea of attributing these to the amoeba."—Dr. W. A.
McIntosh.

as an index of their degree of sophistication about hygiene. Many conditions resembling dysentery may result from causes other than the specific micro-organisms peculiar to that disease. Without careful examination, it is difficult to know the exact nature of such illnesses.

TABLE 19. Opinions of household heads concerning causes of dysentery in children, Crete, 1948

Cause of Dysentery	Community	City	Island
		(percentage)	
Do not know cause	30	47	32
Diet and fruit	24	23	24
Unclean food	9	15	10
Water	9	2	8
Diet and colds	13	9	13
Colds	15	4	13

Source: Sample Survey of Crete, Form A, Household.

While one-third of the household heads or wives stated they did not know the cause of dysentery, only one-fourth of them admitted they did not know the remedy for it. Among the families interviewed, 34 different remedies or combinations of remedies were used. Since their replies provide some insight into the customs of the people, they are presented in Table 20 below.

For dysentery among children, almost one-third of the households used a doctor (and treatment); one-fourth used some kind of tea with or without other types of treatment—one-seventh using regular tea only. One-eighth of the families modified the diet by using rice, rice water, pulse water, or other dietary changes in combination with other treatments. Practical treatments along with rubbings, cuppings, and poultices in various combinations were used by 6 per cent of the households for dysentery.

Wild herb tea was used by five times as many rural families as city families and practical treatments by twice as many. In contrast, twice as many city families used diet changes to correct dysentery.

d. *Typhoid and paratyphoid.* While typhoid fever was not fourth among the diseases, it is an infectious disease of the intestinal tract and for that reason will be treated here. Typhoid fever is especially prevalent during the dry season. One-tenth of the physicians inter-

TABLE 20. Percentage of households using certain remedies for dysentery in children, Crete, 1948

Type of Remedy	Community	City	Island
	(percentage)		
Do not know remedy	26	26	26
Doctor & treatments	30	32	30
Regular tea	15	15	15
" ", etc.ᵃ	5	2	5
Wild herb tea, etc.ᵃ	5	1	4
Camomile tea, etc.ᵃ	2	1	2
Rice or rice water	4	9	5
Diet, etc.ᵃ	5	11	6
Pulse water	1	—	1
Practical treatments	7	3	6
Total	100	100	100

[a] "Etc." includes various combinations of such treatments as poultices, rubbings, and cuppings.
Source: Sample Survey of Crete, Form A, Household.

viewed by Dr. McIntosh placed the prevalence of typhoid fever as "high," while 50 per cent rated it as "rare."

In contrast, 70 per cent of these doctors were of the opinion that the prevalence of diarrhea and enteritis for children under two years was "high" and the remaining 30 per cent said "medium." No one rated this as "low." Prevalence of amoebic dysentery was adjudged "high" by 20 per cent of the doctors, as "medium" by 30 per cent, and as "low" by 50 per cent.

The favorable conditions for the spread of diarrhea, dysentery, typhoid, and other intestinal infections are found in unprotected water supplies, absence of sanitary provisions for disposal of human excreta, exposure of food to flies, and other unhygienic practices. Unfortunately flies, which were multitudinous and omnipresent, prior to DDT spraying, were adapting themselves to the insecticide and becoming common again.

e. *Trachoma.* Trachoma was introduced from Africa many years ago, and more recent infections have occurred. When in 1923 the exchange of population with Turkey occurred, the incidence of trachoma among returning Greeks was said to be as high as 70 per cent. In 1939, 5.6 per cent of the school children in the municipality of Khania had the disease, and in neighboring villages 20 per cent. In

Lasithi nome, trachoma infection rates were 25 to 30 per cent in the major towns and were reported up to 50 per cent in some villages. In Rethimnon the rates were 5 to 10 per cent.

In the post-war period, the nomiatros of Rethimnon regarded the incidence of trachoma as negligible, while the medical director of trachoma services in Lasithi estimated it at 5 to 20 per cent. In the Iraklion area, it was estimated to be 15 per cent for adults and 8 per cent for children. In Khania a survey of primary school children (excluding 500 school children known to be already infected) showed 4.2 per cent of the children in the city and 12 per cent of the children in 10 nearby villages infected. These data from clinical examinations of 16,000 children under 14 years of age and 18,000 people over 14 years of age suggest that the figure of 1 per cent secured from the survey data, even though obtained through interviews with doctors and community officials, was an understatement for trachoma.

Dr. McIntosh states, "Trachoma victims are very unfortunate and unhappy people—even more so than those who have tuberculosis. This is so because of the 'non-acceptance' factor involved—excluded from schools, from places of occupation and from travel. In addition, these people suffer the hardships of blindness. Indeed, trachomatous patients are often destined to become dependent or are forced to become beggars." This kind of stigma on the disease probably influenced the replies to the questionnaire.

f. *Tuberculosis.* Since tuberculosis is not a reportable disease in Greece, official morbidity data are not available. However, both mortality and morbidity data obtained in the sample survey indicate that it is one of the ten most prevalent diseases in Crete. Because of the stigma attached to tuberculosis, the sample data probably constitute an understatement of the actual situation. Both Dr. J. R. Trémolières and Dr. V. G. Valaoras felt that this was the case and suggested the possibility that some cases of tuberculosis were reported as malaria.

Private doctors belonging to the National Organization for Christian Help have estimated the percentage of tuberculosis cases in adults to be as high as 7 per cent. A mass X-ray of the urban population by UNRRA, representing 40 per cent of the total population of Greece, showed 3 per cent with clinical evidence of tuberculosis. Before the war, death rates from tuberculosis were more than twice as high in urban as in rural areas. Thus clinical incidence in rural areas might be expected to be somewhat less than 3 per cent.

In 1936 and 1937, total deaths from tuberculosis in Crete averaged 303, which might be increased to 380, if there was an estimated 25 per cent under-registration. This total would increase the mortality to about 80 persons (instead of 66 as shown in Table 18) per 100,000 population and about 6.7 per cent of all deaths in that pre-war period.

Late in 1948, a Danish tuberculosis vaccination (BCG) team carried out tuberculin skin tests on children in some selected urban and rural elementary and gymnasium schools. While some of these schools were located in sample communities, there was no attempt to choose them on a scientific sampling basis. Time and accessibility were prime considerations in this preliminary test to discover the evidence of positive and negative readings as a basis for further planning. Among the approximately 17,000 children whose first tests were read, about one-sixth were positive (5 mm)[19] to 10 units of tuberculin. In Khania the negative group was given a second test of 100 units of tuberculin, and it was found that one-fifth were positive to both strengths (10 and 100 units) of the tuberculin test. Of 900 other children tested with histoplasmin in the four nomes, there were no positive reactors (more than 5 mm).

The diagnostic clinic services for tuberculosis reported 885 positive cases for 1947, of which 434 or almost half were "far advanced" and about one-fourth each were "moderate" and "minimum" cases. In 1948, the total number of cases had declined by one-fourth from that of the previous year, the proportion of "far advanced" cases declining to 40 per cent of the total, while the "minimum" increased to 35 per cent of the total cases. The change in total numbers may reflect a post-war accumulation in 1947, while the change in proportions between "far advanced" and "minimum" cases may logically be attributed to more intensive case finding as the post-war period lengthened.

The tuberculosis sanitariums appeared to be used as isolation wards for "far advanced" cases, rather than as curative hospitals. An indication of this was the 48 per cent death-admissions ratio at the Khania sanitarium. Perhaps more long-run benefits might be obtained by utilizing a larger share of the hospital facilities for

---

[19] This refers to the diameter of the *inflamed* area at the site of tuberculin inoculation. If more than 5 mm in diameter, the test is read as "positive." If less, "negative." A "positive" reading is believed to indicate that the person has been sensitized to tuberculosis by previous infection.

"minimum" and "moderate" cases. At least, certain hospitals near the larger towns might be so utilized. Increased emphasis on case-finding in order to hospitalize these early cases and to prevent exposure to other individuals would be in line with present-day approaches to the problem. It would also be more economical for the government.

In a recent study made by Dr. V. G. Valaoras as to the correlation of the mortality rate of malaria with that of various other diseases, a high correlation was found with pulmonary tuberculosis, pneumonia, puerperal infection, and general mortality.[20]

Tuberculosis of the pulmonary type was the most prevalent form in Crete. The general practice of consuming boiled milk in Crete has in all probability been a factor in limiting the dissemination of bovine tuberculosis.

g. *Sandfly-borne diseases.* Oriental sore was the most common of the sandfly-borne diseases, according to reports, with a prevalence of 3.5 per 1,000 population. The frequency of the oriental sore scars, similar to a smallpox vaccination scar but located on the cheeks, nose, and forehead of the former victims, is mute evidence of its prevalence in the past. All age groups are susceptible. The vector is a sandfly which is found in cracks of walls or rocks. The use of DDT spraying to destroy sandflies raises hopes that the prevalence of oriental sore, as well as kala-azar, may be reduced. Kala-azar, a disease of infancy, which, at the time of the survey, was localized to a few areas on the periphery of Khania, was also believed to have been reduced by the destruction of stray dogs, which are supposed to be a reservoir for the disease.

2. Less Prevalent Diseases

a. *Leprosy.* Crete has one of the higher leprosy rates in Greece. Her leprosarium contained over 10 per cent of the approximate 2,000 lepers in Greece although her total population was only 6 per cent of the nation.

In Eastern Crete leprosy was a serious problem in 61 villages. These constituted more than half of the 119 towns or villages in Crete in which leprosy had occurred at some time in the past. Iraklion had only four of these villages, while Khania and Rethimnon had 24 and 30, respectively. At the time of the survey, the nomiatros

[20] V. G. Valaoras, *Malaria and Public Health.* "Practika," Academy of Athens. 19:288. 1944.

of Lasithi and the physician in charge of the leprosarium at Spina
Longa had surveyed two villages with a population of 1,650 people
and disclosed 12 lepers. A few of these patients had become recon-
ciled to their fate, but a strong popular protest was made for the
others, especially since some of the lepers were children. It was necessary to make arrests and confine the lepers to prison while provision
was made for their removal. The police are obligated to apprehend
lepers wherever found in Crete and to conduct them back to Spina
Longa.

b. *Miscellaneous communicable diseases.* The island has been free
from rabies for a number of years, but recently infection was introduced which gave rise to a widespread outbreak among animals.
While anthrax was not considered a significant public health problem in Crete, it had been contracted by women in Greece when carding
wool; the gastro-intestinal type, due to improper cooking of meat,
was also found. Species of flies were found which are known to trans-
mit anthrax to man and animals. Four cases of anthrax were reported in 1946 and three in 1947. Various forms of brucellosis have
been diagnosed in cattle, swine, and goats, but brucellosis would not
appear to be a problem among human beings in Crete, owing, probably, to the almost universal practice of boiling milk. Eight cases
were reported in 1946 and ten in 1947. Cooley's anemia occurred
and, as it is characterized by anemia and splenomegaly, it must be
considered in the differential diagnosis of malaria and kala-azar.
Rheumatic fever was not uncommon. Dermatological diseases such
as ringworm, favus, scabies, and impetigo were found to be common
in Crete.

From time to time foot-and-mouth disease had resulted in an
alarming loss of livestock, particularly in the summer months, but
no human cases had been reported. Glanders occurred in horses,
mules, and donkeys, as well as occasionally in man; goats that live
in close contact with human beings contract tuberculosis; many of
the cattle of Crete had Texas fever. Leptospirosis had been recognized on several occasions in Greece, and it is probable that its true
incidence might have been masked by confusing it with blackwater
fever or epidemic jaundice. Tetanus also occurred; in 1946, 23 cases
and eight deaths occurred and, in 1947, 17 cases and three deaths.
Paralytic poliomyelitis would appear to be absent or very rare in
Crete, and scarlet fever presumably also had a low incidence.

While venereal diseases were not reportable, the community survey data indicated about 1,000 cases in both 1947 and 1948, or a prevalence of about 2.1 persons per 1,000 population. This was about one-third of the reported cases in the United States, and the understatement for the United States was probably very much greater than for Crete. The reported prevalence of venereal diseases was six times as high in the cities as in the rural areas of Crete.

In the summer of 1948, only 13 patients were found in the two VD hospitals, which provide for 48 beds. Data from the hospital records showed a marked decline (from 178 to 84) in the number of syphilis cases from 1946 to 1948, while gonorrhea cases fluctuated between 260 and 340 annually during the three years. There were seven times as many cases in Iraklion, where an army training camp was located, as in Khania.

3. Diseases That May be Introduced into Crete

While louse-borne and flea-borne typhus fever and boutonneuse fever have occurred at times in Greece, no cases, it would appear, have been reported from Crete. The vectors of these diseases, however, were present. Indeed, it was known that the common dog tick occurred in great numbers—at times sheep, goats, cows, pigs, and donkeys being literally covered with these parasites. The tick which is thought to be responsible for tick paralysis in man was also found in Crete. It was not known whether louse-borne or tick-borne relapsing fever occurred in Crete, but isolated cases had been reported in Greece.

Plague had not been reported during recent years in Crete, but rats and fleas existed in considerable numbers in the ports. While cholera was absent from Crete, a vaccination program was carried out in 1947, because of the island's proximity to Egypt, where an outbreak occurred. Although the *Aedes aegypti* mosquito had been widespread in former years, yellow fever had not occurred at any time in Crete. Crete's last epidemic of dengue was in 1928. Its clinical features were unusually severe. While it is probable that only a small portion of the population is immune, the extensive use of DDT in the suppression of malaria may prove to be an effective barrier against the reappearance of this disease, as well as providing additional protection against the possible introduction of yellow fever.

Owing to the fact that a fresh-water snail which acts as the intermediate host of a serious worm disease (schistosomiasis) is found in Crete, there is a potential danger that this disease could become indigenous if infected people from endemic areas such as Egypt were to migrate to Crete. The culicine mosquitoes, vectors of filariasis, a diseased state due to worms (*Wuchereria bancrofti*) which attack the human blood, occur in Crete. It is conceivable that this disease could be introduced if infected persons were to come to Crete from areas such as Turkey, Yugoslavia, Libya, and Egypt, where the disease is known to exist.

4. *Deformities*

Deformities were reported by interviewers only in noticeable cases, such as club foot, crossed eyes, and missing limbs. In some cases all members of the family were not seen, so that the estimate is undoubtedly an understatement. About 3 per cent (4 per cent in the cities) of the household members had such noticeable deformities. In 83 cities of the United States where examinations were made in a public health survey and such items as missing toes and other deformities which would not be seen by an interviewer were included, 1.9 per cent had deformities, or about half as many as reported in Crete.

D. MEDICAL SERVICES

The doctor's degree in medicine, graduation from the University Dental School, and diplomas in nursing, pharmacy, and midwifery were prerequisite for obtaining a license from the Ministry of Hygiene to practice these professions or skills in Crete. The Medical School offered a full course and required internship training. Certified medical specialists limited their practice entirely to their restricted fields of medicine. A physician was not permitted to be his own pharmacist, except where none existed; partnerships between doctors and dentists with pharmacists were not permissible. In areas where there were no dentists, physicians might practice dentistry. Doctors, dentists, and midwives were requested to register with the local governing authority within one month after establishment.

The Panhellenic Medical Society is an "entity of public law." Its purposes are to promote the public health and interrelationships and welfare of the physicians, and to act as a disciplinarian for enforcement of measures relating to medical practices. It is obligatory for all practicing physicians to be members of the Medical Society. Monthly meetings of the Nome Medical Council of seven members were held, in addition to the annual meetings of the Nome Medical

Society. Presidents of the Nome Medical Society constituted the Medical Council at Athens. It should be noted that there was no standing health committee provided to facilitate interrelationships between the Nome Medical Society and the health centers in the promotion of public health.

The organization of the Dental Society was similar to that of the Medical Society.

Pharmacists were required to be members of the Nome Pharmaceutical Society, which was a branch of the Panhellenic Pharmaceutical Society. Pharmacists dispensed drugs only on doctors' prescriptions. They were required to sell drugs to certain classes of the population at reduced rates—veterans and indigents, for example. Authorization might be given to grocery stores to sell simple medicines such as quinine, bismuth, aspirin, and castor oil. Before being offered for sale, proprietary medicines had to be approved by the Supreme Sanitary Council of the Ministry of Hygiene.

Graduation from the gymnasium and completion of a special three-year course in midwifery, followed by one year of service in the institution of training or a selected hospital, were prerequisite to a license to practice midwifery. Those who received a license were required to practice during the first three years in a rural area specified by the Ministry of Hygiene. In these assigned localities the community was compelled to pay the midwives' fees for taking care of indigent mothers delivered by them. The duties of the midwife included prenatal care, delivery of normal cases, and the education of mothers on child care. She was not allowed to prescribe drugs. She was required to keep a register of necessary information on each delivery. Registered midwives were also required to take such special courses each five years as were prescribed by the Ministry of Hygiene. There was no midwifery association. The law did not recognize untrained midwives.

In comparison with the United States, the medical services in Crete were found to be extremely limited, but in comparison with Mexico, they seemed relatively more adequate. In proportion to population, doctors were about half as numerous in Crete as in the United States but 50 per cent more plentiful than in Mexico. Particularly in the rural areas, there were few doctors, fewer dentists, and an insufficient number of trained nurses, trained midwives, and pharmacists. On the other hand, there were more so-called "bone-setters" than doctors in rural areas. Other comparisons may be made from Table 21 below.

TABLE 21. Ratio of population to professional personnel in communities, cities, and Crete, 1948

Specialists	Communities	Cities	All Crete
	(persons per specialist)		
Doctors[a]	2,750	580	1,630
Dentists[a]	10,980	2,300	6,470
Nurses-trained[b]	7,390	10,930	7,880
untrained	7,840	575	2,350
Midwives-trained[a]	6,200	5,830	6,140
untrained	540	1,560	610
Pharmacists[a]	17,470	3,120	9,460
Herb doctors	48,040	43,730	47,280
Bone-setters	2,000	29,150	2,420
Veterinarians	16,010	29,150	17,510
Priests	710	2,300	810

a Survey by Dr. W. A. McIntosh indicates about 7 per cent more doctors, one-eighth as many dentists, one-fourth as many trained midwives, and one-third as many pharmacists in rural communities as the sample survey. For the cities, the difference varied from 30 per cent more trained midwives to 10 per cent fewer dentists and pharmacists relative to the population. This was due to a difference in classification of municipalities in which data from four additional municipalities characteristically rural were included in the data by Dr. McIntosh.

b Probably refers to trained volunteer nurses, not graduate nurses.

Source: Sample Survey of Crete, Form C, Community.

Poor roads and inaccessible villages added to the difficulties in reaching persons or centers which offered medical and dental facilities. In rural communities about one-third of the families were located less than 1.5 miles from a doctor, one-third 1.5 to 7.5 miles, and one-third over 7.5 miles. For the average community household, the doctor was 6.0 miles, and the dentist and trained nurse over 13 miles away. In contrast, the midwife was less than three miles distant.

E. HOSPITAL SERVICES

Hospitals in Crete were classified as follows: (a) General Hospitals, which were owned and operated by the Ministry of Hygiene; (b) Entities of Public Law Hospitals, which were owned by the government, received funds from the Ministry, but were administered by a hospital board with minimum supervision by the Ministry; and

(c) Entities of Private Law Hospitals, which were subject to the supervision of the Ministry of Hygiene.

Private clinics and dispensaries were licensed by the Ministry of Hygiene, and legal regulations governed their establishment and maintenance. A register of patients and individual files of patients were required from each private clinic, and a record of laboratory and post-mortem examinations from clinics with more than fifteen beds.

State and municipal hospitals in Crete had about 1,000 beds, or an average of 2.1 beds per 1,000 population, in 1946-1948. About one-fifth of these beds were located in each of the surgical, leprosy, and general medical hospitals. One-sixth of the beds were in tuberculosis hospitals and one-tenth in mental. Six per cent of the beds were for obstetrical cases, 5 per cent for VD, and 2 per cent for pediatrics.

There were 23 full-time and 14 part-time medical personnel, 116 nurses, and 156 other personnel working in these hospitals. This provided 3.7 medical personnel, and 11.7 nurses, and 15.7 other personnel per 1,000 beds.

Of the total expenditures for these state and municipal hospitals in Crete in 1947, about one-fifth (18 per cent) was spent for professional personnel, one-fifth (20.8 per cent) for other personnel, and three-fifths (61.2 per cent) for operating expenses. Only 11 per cent of the income came from patients, with the general hospitals receiving about one-fifth of their total income (and expenditures) from patients. Of their total income, the tuberculosis sanitariums received one-tenth from patients, while the mental and VD hospitals received only 7 per cent from patients. The leprosy hospital had no income from patients.

Admissions to the public hospitals, exclusive of private clinics, for 1946-1948 averaged 7,132 annually, consisting of 6,601 to the general hospitals, 310 to the VD hospitals, 145 to the tuberculosis sanitariums, 66 to the mental hospital, and 10 to the leprosarium. On the average, about 15 persons per 1,000 population were admitted annually to some public hospital. In addition 15.7 persons per 1,000 population were admitted to the private hospital clinics.

On the basis of these admissions it might be assumed that the total hospital bed capacity for the island was approximately 1,400 beds, or about four beds per doctor, as compared with seven beds per doctor in the United States. There were three hospital beds per 1,000 population in Crete, as compared to ten in the United States. One-third of these beds in Crete and two-fifths of those in the United States were located in state and municipal general hospitals. The hospital admissions in Crete—at 28 per 1,000 population—were only one-fourth as many as in the United States with 108.

F. Public Health Service

The public health services of Crete were administered from three levels—the national, the nome, and the local community or municipality.

1. Central Services

The Ministry of Hygiene was the national or central administrative body; the Minister, chosen from among the members of Parliament, was customarily a physician. He was advised by a Supreme Health Council, which contained representatives of the medical faculty of the University of Athens, the Athens School of Hygiene, and the medical profession. Public health agencies and institutions for medical care were under this ministry, which also compiled statistics and carried out inspection.

The Athens School of Hygiene, established in 1929, offered training for technical personnel in public health service. Three schools educated students in nursing for hospitals, public health work, and visiting nurse service.

The two schools of midwifery in Greece, like the other schools for training medical personnel, were in Athens.

Numerous public health services were under governmental agencies other than the Ministry of Hygiene. These included health services offered by the Ministry of Education, the Prison Health Service, the state monopoly of quinine, and the like. There were also a few private health agencies.

In addition, there were a number of international health services, governmental and voluntary.

2. Regional and Local Health Services in Crete

In health matters, the Governor-General of Crete had an adviser, a Director of Hygiene, who had no subordinates. Although he might confer with other government personnel concerned with health matters, there was little active committee work. When action was required for the whole island, as in the immunization against cholera in 1947, the machinery for consultation had to be improvised.

Health centers were established in the major Cretan cities, with offices and small staffs. A jeep was provided for transportation of the nomiatros (nome doctor), but only half of the rural communities were accessible by road.

Legally there was provision for health committees in nomes, municipalities, and rural communities. These committees were inactive and purely nominal except in the nome of Rethimnon. The nomiatros normally carried out whatever health administration was done at the local or provincial level.

Municipalities usually had no medical health officer, but might employ one or more doctors on a part-time basis. Whenever such arrangements existed, the doctor's time was usually occupied in attending to the poor. Other functions, such as direction of the dispensary at the municipal hospital, examination of school children, immunization, and food inspection might or might not be assigned to such a part-time physician.

Though rural villages had the right to employ a community physician or medical health officer, either individually or in groups, they did not do so. There was no sanitary officer in the small communities. Local health committees usually existed only on paper, and there were no local expenditures for health except for occasional immunization and DDT spraying. Even the private village physicians were few and ill equipped, while the midwives were untrained.

3. The General Picture

The general picture of health services was therefore one of an ambitious central organization with many vacant positions and lacking in effective action at the island, nome, and community levels.

A list of sixteen auxiliary services in Crete which were working on health problems suggests an important task of correlation and coordination. This job could be accomplished through the nome health committees, if they were provided with general guidance, encouragement, and assistance by the Director of the Directorate of Health for Crete and his four nomiatroi. These auxiliary services may be grouped into governmental, semi-governmental, world-wide relief and health organizations, and local private societies or organizations.

Governmental organizations included: Municipal and State Hospitals, Clinics and Sanitariums; School Health Services, Ministry of Education; Statistical Services, Ministry of National Economy;

Veterinarian Services, Ministry of Agriculture; Chemical Laboratories, Ministry of Finance; Nome Technical Services for Municipalities and Communities; Municipal Public Works; and the Malaria Control Branch, Athens School of Hygiene.

The semi-governmental organizations were the Social Insurance Institute (IKA) and the Patriotic Institute of Social Welfare (PIKPA).

The world-wide health and relief organizations included the Anti-Tuberculosis Association; Hellenic Red Cross; Greek War Relief Association; Greek War Relief Fund of Canada; and the Engineering Service of the World Health Organization.

The private local societies and organizations interested in health problems included the nome Medical, Dental, and Pharmaceutical Societies.

G. VITAL STATISTICS SERVICES

The collection of statistics regarding births, deaths, marriages, and divorces was not under the supervision of the Ministry of Hygiene, which could only prescribe certain forms, but was shared by the Ministry of Justice, which was concerned with enforcing registration, the Ministry of National Economy, which was interested in the statistics, and the Ministry of Public Order, which issued burial permits and checked death registrations. It is therefore not surprising that many of the data were inaccurate and inadequate for an effective analysis of the health problems of Crete.

The war, too, interfered; the Ministry of National Economy had not published an annual report of vital statistics since 1938. Communities were expected to make reports to the nome or provincial registrar, but only three-quarters of the communities did so from 1946 to 1948. Other inaccuracies were due to lack of records or understatement.

"In summary of the situation, then," states Dr. Paul M. Densen, "we find a vital statistics system, characterized administratively by a division of responsibility among four different Ministries, and statistically by a highly centralized program with practically no analysis at the local level where the public health program is put into operation. With respect to both characteristics, we find the Ministry of Health in the role of a passive recipient of these data rather than providing the creative stimulus which will result in achieving the objectives set forth above, namely, to furnish factual data which are needed to define the nature and magnitude of the problems confronting the administrator, to suggest points of attack upon these problems, and to evaluate the success of the program. In so far as program statistics are concerned, these are to all intents and purposes non-existent, largely due to any lack of statistical direction and to the statistical naïveté of the local authorities."

H. Public Health Activities

Crete had several kinds of public health services. Some of them functioned satisfactorily; others were ineffective or lacked personnel. Among those which affected the larger share of the population were the immunization program for smallpox and the anti-malaria campaign. Services to limited numbers of individuals affected with special diseases included those for tuberculosis, venereal diseases, leprosy, and trachoma. Special services were also provided to limited numbers of women and children through the maternal and child hygiene services and by visiting nurses. Public dental services were lacking in professional personnel.

In the municipalities, community water supplies and sewage disposal were available to a portion of the population. Sanitary inspection of food-handling and other establishments was found only in the larger municipalities. Public health education was limited and uncoordinated. Laboratory and X-ray services were meager.

1. Immunization

Although immunization for smallpox was supposed to be compulsory by the time a person was through elementary school, less than half of the population indicated that they had been vaccinated for it.

According to Dr. Valaoras, about 75-80 per cent of the population had been vaccinated for smallpox some time during their lives. Memory bias showed a large understatement in this instance although the vaccination mark should have been a reminder.

One-fourth of the population stated they had been immunized for typhoid or typhus; 3 per cent for cholera after the outbreak in Egypt in 1947; 1 per cent or less indicated they had been vaccinated for diphtheria, chicken pox, measles, tetanus, scarlet fever, or tuberculosis.

The record of immunization for 1946-1948, according to the nomiatroi, indicates that about 25,000 persons were vaccinated for smallpox and 10,000 for typhoid annually. The number of people vaccinated for diphtheria depended upon the incidence of the disease. A total of 4,471 persons were immunized for diphtheria in 1946, less than half that number in 1947, and only 68 in the first half of 1948. More than 13,000 persons were immunized for cholera in 1947 during the Egyptian outbreak. Vaccine inoculations against rabies increased from none in 1946 to six in 1947, and to 808 in the first six months of 1948. Tuberculosis vaccination increased tenfold from 1947 to 1948 with a total of 2,633 immunizations in the latter year.

2. Anti-Malaria Campaign

Efforts to control malaria in Crete had been made since World War I, but its prevalence had remained high until DDT spraying for anopheles mosquitoes was successfully introduced in 1946 with funds supplied by UNRRA and later by WHO and AMAG-ECA in cooperation with the Greek Government. Crete comprised Region 10 of the eleven regions into which Greece was divided for the purpose of malaria control. In charge of the region was a medical malariologist who cooperated with the Division of Malariology and Tropical Diseases of the School of Hygiene in Athens.

Associated with the malariologist, who had headquarters in Iraklion, were a sanitary inspector, a secretary, and three other employees. Two trucks were assigned to the headquarters. Plans for the campaign were prepared every year in February and March, in cooperation with the nomiatroi of the four nomes.

Funds for carrying out the work were sent directly from Athens to the nomiatros of each prefecture. Supplies were furnished through the aid of UNRRA, Greek War Relief, American Military Government and other special agencies. The nomiatros selected the local employees and was responsible for execution of the work.

Local teams sprayed the walls and ceilings of rural homes with 1.8 grams of DDT per square meter, furnishing protection for six months. In 1947, the average cost per person protected was about 45 cents, of which the cost of material was slightly more than half.

Larva control in breeding areas was used in more thickly settled districts where house-spraying would be too costly. This spraying, done from the ground every twelve days, cost about 12 cents per person protected for the year. Airplane spraying is much quicker and cheaper, though it needs to be supplemented by ground work.

Two planes were assigned to Crete for this purpose, with excellent results.

Checks were made continuously on malaria-carrying mosquitoes and mosquito breeding during the season; blood smears were taken during the fall, and school children were examined. The campaign was one of the most successful carried on in Crete.

3. *Tuberculosis Services*

There were government sanitariums for tuberculosis in the nomes of Khania and Rethimnon, with 165 beds. There was also a private sanitarium with 24 beds at Spilia in Iraklion nome, and construction was under way for another of 21 beds. The Khania sanitarium, which had 130 beds, operated at full capacity with about 10 per cent of the patients paying. The Rethimnon sanitarium, with 35 beds, operated at about one-third capacity, but admission to it was confined to cases in the early stages.

Diagnostic services in clinics were available in the four larger cities. Patients came to these clinics on their own initiative or were referred by physicians or hospitals. There were no diagnostic clinics in the rural villages.

A mass vaccination with BCG for the benefit of children and adolescents was organized.[21] Cooperating in the anti-tuberculosis work were an anti-tuberculosis association with local branches, the Red Cross, the United Nations Children's Emergency Fund, and the Greek Government, as well as members of the medical profession.

4. *Venereal Disease*

Venereal disease was not reportable in Crete. Clinic services were provided in the nome capitals, and diagnosis was based on clinical findings. Penicillin, arsenic compounds, and bismuth compounds were used for treatment of cases. Public education on venereal disease was not well developed, though printed material was available.

Prostitution, which is often associated with the spread of venereal disease, was legalized, and prostitutes were subject to medical examination twice a week. In 1948, there were 76 licensed prostitutes in the three largest nome capitals. There was an attempt to salvage wayward girls by finding employment for them or putting them in the care of families.

[21] The vaccine is known as BCG (*Bacillus Calmette Guérin*), which is an attenuated strain of tubercle bacillus.

5. *Leprosy Services*

As early as Venetian times (A.D. 1204-1667) lepers were concentrated in hamlets, living mostly on alms of the passerby. In 1903, the leper colony was set up on the island of Spina Longa off the coast above Ay. Nikolaos. This was the second largest (300 beds) of the three leper institutions of Greece which accommodated a total of 790 beds. This small island of barren rock offered little of therapeutic value to its inmates. The hospital building in the colony had not been furnished with beds. A physician, five practical nurses, and 42 other employees made up the staff. The occupants had few diversions except conversation and games at the coffee shop. The lepers were generally dissatisfied with their bitter lot.

No special leprosy service was organized as a part of the prefectural health center of Crete, and the control of leprosy was essentially a responsibility of the Ministry of Hygiene. The nomiatroi are given special training to qualify them as diagnosticians.

6. *Trachoma Services*

Crete had seven anti-trachoma clinics—one each in Khania and Iraklion, four in Lasithi nome, and one Class A clinic in Ay. Nikolaos, the capital of Lasithi prefecture.

Older remedies for trachoma have been replaced by a new four-week course of treatment using lutazol and ophtazol. This treatment, which is reported to give great relief, is not a complete cure. This approach to the problem from the curative side evades the possibility of an attack through an integrated program of prevention. Trachoma, which is transmitted primarily from person to person under circumstances of poor sanitation and of poor diet, is susceptible to the preventive approach.

7. *Maternal and Child Hygiene*

Maternal and child hygiene services were rendered by the Patriotic Institute of Social Welfare (PIKPA). This organization stimulated teamwork with other agencies concerned, such as health centers, Red Cross, and the Anti-Tuberculosis Association. PIKPA, as a legal entity, collaborated closely with the Ministry of Hygiene and Ministry of Welfare.

Only the Khania and Iraklion branches—out of seven pre-war branches—were in operation in Crete in 1948. Branches at Ay. Nikolaos and Ierapetra were in the process of reactivation. The staff consisted of a practicing pediatrician, a part-time gynecologist, a full-time midwife, and two nurses. The cooperating organizations furnished supplementary services.

PIKPA provided four clinic services: (1) a prenatal clinic; (2) a clinic for infants under two years; (3) a well-baby clinic and (4) a clinic for sick children (2-14 years). Any expectant mother was eligible for the prenatal clinic, and all children might be brought to the well-baby clinic. This important service included instruction in child care, weighing, and immunization against typhoid, smallpox, and diphtheria. Only underprivileged children were eligible for admission to the sick children's clinic. At Khania the BCG station was operated three times a week for two-hour sessions. Home nursing visits were also made by PIKPA and the Red Cross Nurses.

8. Visiting Nurses

There were six visiting nurses in Crete. Only one of these was associated with a health center—that at Khania. One was at the BCG station in the same city. Two others were with hospitals.

In general it may be said that the nursing profession in Crete was still in a rudimentary state of development. Nurses were looked upon essentially as attendants who did menial work in caring for the ill.

Only three graduate nurses (all located in municipalities) were found in Crete. However, 60 trained nurses were indicated in the sample survey of Crete, and about 200 untrained nurses. The trained nurses probably included the "best family" volunteer nurses who were prepared for emergency nursing, such as was required during war. They secured three months' theoretical and three months' apprenticeship training in hospitals. Such a course was in progress at Iraklion in 1948 with 19 selected girls, and there was provision for a similar course in Khania.

Training for graduate nurses was found only in Athens, and, because of better opportunities in the mainland cities, few who went there from Crete ever returned to the island.

9. Dental Services

While office space and equipment were provided in the health center at Khania and the Greek War Relief Health Clinics at Kastelli-Kisamos and Ierapetra, the dental clinics were not in operation in 1948. Funds and personnel were lacking.

Consultation with a number of the practicing dentists by the public health member of the survey staff regarding the status of oral hygiene in Crete indicated "the percentage of persons in the age group 20-40 years with: (1) sound sets of permanent teeth, 10-20 per cent for municipalities and 5-25 per cent for communities; (2) extractions, 5-60 per cent for municipalities and 5-80 per cent for communities; (3) dental caries, 60-90 per cent for municipalities and 20-90 per cent for communities; (4) fillings, 30-70 per cent for municipalities and 10-70 per cent for communities; and (5) gingivitis or pyorrhoea, 20-40 per cent for municipalities and 30-90 per cent for communities. It would appear that the six-year molars are commonly lost. While there are differences of opinion, the status of oral hygiene in general is regarded as better for children than for adults. Mal-occlusion was reported as infrequent."

10. *Community Water Supplies and Sewage Disposal*

Such community facilities as water supplies and sewage disposal, commonly accepted community responsibilities in many Western countries, were not so common in Crete. A central system of water distribution to individual homes was found in only six towns and 30 villages. Thousands of wells, cisterns, and springs, supplying water for family use in villages where body wastes were disposed of indiscriminately, greatly increased certain kinds of health hazards.

Only 2 per cent of the rural households had running water in the house. Other households in the rural communities had to carry water various distances requiring from less than one to as many as 90 minutes. Forty-six per cent of city households had running water in the house, but even this percentage, which is considerably higher than in the rural communities, is much lower than might be expected on an island which provided its Queen with a flush toilet in her palace some 4,000 years ago. This low percentage in cities is partially explained by inclusion of the outlying districts where water mains were not available.

The means of drawing water from the wells were usually unsanitary—with uncovered wells. Only 2 per cent of the community wells had a pump. Nor were other facilities that we associate with health and well-being adequately supplied. Sewage disposal facilities were largely lacking, and indiscriminate pollution of the soil was common practice.

About 86 per cent of the rural communities had no provision for sewage disposal, and only one-half of the villages in the municipalities provided sewerage systems. Over one-third of the villages in the municipalities used the "pit" disposal, as may be noted in Table 22 below. (See Appendix 5, Tables A54 and A55.)

TABLE 22. Percentage of villages in communities and municipalities having certain types of sewage disposal, Crete, 1948

Type of Disposal	Communities[a]	Municipalities[a]	All Crete[a]
	(percentage)		
None	86	—	85
Pit	9	36	9
Ditch	4	—	4
Pit and septic tank	3	11	4
Absorbing tank	—	54	1
Sewerage system	1	14	1
Septic tank	3	—	3

a Totals more than 100 per cent since some villages and towns had more than one.
Source: Sample Survey of Crete, Form C, Community.

In the four seacoast municipalities, sewers opened into the sea; the waste was usually not carried far enough out to prevent pollution of coastal waters. The stench from manholes indicated improper operation of water carriage sewerage systems. Some public comfort stations of the municipalities were commendable; others were disgustingly filthy.

Garbage and refuse were hauled to dumps outside the cities. Sitia and Neapolis provided street receptacles. Part of the garbage was used by farmers as fertilizer or animal food. In small towns, villages, or outlying districts the householder usually disposed of his own garbage and household wastes.

But, according to the survey, some type of sanitary endeavor had been made during the post-war period in one-third of the communities. These improvements included construction of a public latrine, installation of a machine pump, swamp drainage, repair of a water reservoir, and the completion of a pipe line. Many of the communities had a tentative plan for improving their water supply or sanitation facilities.

Among the municipal water works, the major problems consisted of inadequate supplies during the dry season, insufficient capacity of the distributing system (Khania), broken water mains, and a lack of water meters. With water distributed intermittently during the dry season and cracked water pipes near underground sewers, the opportunity for pollution was considerable. Only in Iraklion was there adequate chlorination equipment installed and in use. Iraklion, alone, had water meters, but only to a portion of the dwellings along the major water mains was a continuous supply of water available. Yet not enough typhoid fever was found during the survey to cast suspicion on the water supply, except in one town.

The possibilities of finding added sources of water to supplement present supplies seemed promising for three of the municipalities and for many of the communities and villages. In most cases this involved the building of dams down to bedrock near springs, deepening wells, or locating additional wells in areas likely to have underground water supplies. In other areas, large underground cisterns for water storage from late winter rains seemed to be the only possibility.

Governmental organization of sanitary services was complex. At the central government in Athens, five agencies were concerned. The Ministry of Hygiene had a Sanitary Engineering Service; the Ministry of Interior a Technical Service of engineering assistance for local public works of many kinds, including sanitation; the Ministry of Public Works was concerned with drainage, flood control, large irrigation projects, and the like; the Ministry of Reconstruction had charge of housing developments and reconstruction in war damaged areas; the Ministry of Agriculture was involved in smaller irrigation projects and veterinary medicine. There was little cooperation between these engineering services and the sanitary inspectors of the local health centers.

The World Health Organization was contributing to sanitary improvements in Crete by employing a sanitarian, draftsman, and several foremen to assist with the installation of sanitary community water supplies and public latrines. In this work the Ministry of Hygiene provided funds for technical and supervisory services and materials, such as pipe and cement, which were not procurable locally. The communities provided labor and local materials. The Economic Cooperation Administration was working on a large program to improve water systems[22] in the smaller towns of 800 communities of Greece, to be carried out in 1948-1952.[23]

[22] For a more complete discussion of water supplies, see Irving B. Crosby, "Reconnaissance Report on Ground Water Resources of Crete for The Rockefeller Founda-

11. *Sanitary Inspection of Food-Handling and Other Establishments*

In the larger Cretan municipalities, restaurants, markets, bakeries, coffee shops, hotels, meat markets, candy and ice cream shops, milk distributing stations, and barber shops were licensed and inspected. The attendants were registered and given medical examinations. However, village food operators were not registered.

The dairies which distributed milk directly to consumers in Khania were not inspected. The milk consumed directly or used in ice cream mix was generally boiled. Although tested for dilution, milk was not tested for sanitary quality.

In Khania and Iraklion, slaughtered meat animals were inspected regularly; in villages, only occasionally. Echinococcus, or hydatid cysts, were found in 80 per cent of the lungs and livers of sheep over three years of age. The cows of Khania nome were recently tuberculin tested; there were few reactors. Sheep and goats were also said to be free from tuberculosis. Hogs were inoculated against cholera, and in general animals were immunized against anthrax. Malta fever was somewhat prevalent in Iraklion nome; cheese was presumed to be the chief source.

A rat eradicator made monthly rounds of the business sections of Khania and might extend his services to ships in port. Because of the use of "1080" for rats and DDT powder for delousing school children, occupants of prisons, and other institutional groups, typhus fever was rare in Crete. The advent of DDT spraying of homes in the anti-malaria control program had also helped to prevent lice. As a food conservation measure, however, a broader anti-rat program might be desirable.

12. *Public Health and Education*

Though public health education was provided for in the organization of the central government, there were few systematic or well developed programs at the local level. Talks were given in local villages during epidemics, there were occasional newspaper items on health topics, and leaflets were provided on tuberculosis and venereal diseases. Work done by the Anti-Tuberculosis Association or the Social

---

tion." Unpublished manuscript, New York, February 1949. See Appendix 4 for list of depository libraries.

[23] ECA Mission to Greece, "A Four-Year Program for Public Health in Greece." Unpublished manuscript. Athens, November 10, 1948.

Insurance Institute was not coordinated with that of health centers or local governments.

In schools, there was a plan for bringing the level of sanitation and education in hygiene up to the requirements established by law in 1939, but this plan was far from being carried out. In the primary grades, no textbook was used, and hygiene instruction depended on the initiative of the teacher. In the gymnasium or high school, hygiene was taught by the school physician or physical education professor. But only a small minority of Cretan children went to the gymnasium.

Only one-third of the primary schools in the communities in 1948 provided satisfactory sewage disposal facilities; about three-fifths of the primary schools in the cities and almost all (96 per cent) of the gymnasiums were so equipped. School bath facilities existed in only four primary schools and one gymnasium. These served only one per cent of the primary pupils and 13 per cent of the gymnasium students. They were located in Khania and Rethimnon nomes, where water supplies were relatively more abundant.

Smallpox immunizations in the schools averaged about 10,000 per year during the 1946-1948 period, about half of them in Rethimnon nome. Only Iraklion nome indicated typhoid immunizations in this three-year period, averaging 22 per year. In 1947, Khania nome immunized 250 children for diphtheria.

About one-tenth of the primary schools and two-thirds of the gymnasiums had satisfactory sources of drinking water, according to the school physician reports.

13. *Laboratory and X-ray Services*

Several medical laboratories existed in Athens, covering malaria and parasitology, bacteriological examinations of water and milk, chemical analysis of quinine and narcotics for the state monopoly, and preparation of biological products. In Crete, chemical laboratories in Khania and Iraklion, operated by the Ministry of Finance, made analyses of market milk for adulteration and fat-content and of olive oil for toxicity and acidity.

Laboratory quarters were provided in the Khania health center, but the laboratory had not recently had a director. Class B health centers did not have laboratories, and other laboratories were largely unmanned.

In Khania alone a fluoroscopic clinic was provided at the health center.

14. Public Health Costs and Financing

Funds for the state public health expenditures were provided by the Ministry of Hygiene. Salaries of regular employees were budgeted by this Ministry at the Athens office. The budgeting of other expenditures was a joint responsibility of the Ministry and of the Director of the Directorate-General of Hygiene for Crete, who also happened to be nomiatros of Khania nome. Unfortunately he did not consult with the three other nomiatroi in developing his estimates.

Health expenditures in Crete through the National Ministry of Hygiene, including the operation of the state and municipal hospitals in 1947-1948, were about one-half million dollars, or about $1.00 per inhabitant.[24] (For details see Appendix 5, Table A56.) Individual patients paid $38,000 of this sum for services rendered. Of the public health dollar, 31 cents went for the operation (including personnel) of the general hospitals, 18 cents for the leprosarium, 12 cents for the tuberculosis sanitariums, and 6 cents for the mental and venereal disease hospitals. State hospitals used two-thirds of the health dollar, leaving only 33 cents for control and preventive health programs. State and municipal health center programs spent only 10 cents of the health dollar in 1947. Malaria control required 18 cents, and other disease control programs utilized 5 cents of the government health dollar in Crete.

These data do not include the health services provided in the schools through the Ministry of Education or those provided by PIKPA, IKA, The Anti-Tuberculosis Association, and many other governmental or semi-governmental groups. But in general these services were of the relatively less expensive type in Crete and would not add more than 5 per cent to the above costs.

Capital expenditures for state hospitals and equipment during 1947-1948 were largely contributed by outside agencies such as the Canadian Greek War Relief Fund, which provided a modern fully-equipped polyclinic and two prefabricated health centers.

Total health and hospital expenditures for Crete should also include private clinics and hospitals and fees of professional personnel. Since the private clinics admitted about the same number of

[24] Ministry of Hygiene expenditures listed for Crete in the fiscal period 1947-1948 were about $308,427, as compared to a net of $458,953 for state and municipal programs. What share of this difference was paid by other ministries and by municipalities or other sources of income is not known.

cases annually as the state and municipal general hospitals, an additional estimated $150,000 was added to the total health bill in Crete. Also it is necessary to include the usual private fees for doctors, dentists, nurses, midwives, and others, which might total a half million dollars—based on a rough guess. With pharmaceutical and other health costs, the total health bill from private and public funds for Crete probably exceeded $1,175,000, or $2.50 per capita, in 1947. This does not include new capital outlays of $137,000 for the Ierapetra polyclinic and $30,000 for the two prefabricated health centers supplied by the Canadian Greek War Relief Fund in 1948. Similarly, no estimate has been made of other new construction for public or private sanitariums, hospitals, and clinics for which small sums were spent.

Two-thirds of the expenditures for control and preventive measures in Crete over a fifteen-month period in 1947-1948 were for prevention of malaria. However, with the expenditures for malaria air spray and malaria control being quite seasonal, the particular fifteen-month period covered in Table 23 probably shows a higher percentage of expenditures for these two measures than would a

TABLE 23. Total and percentage expenditures for preventive and control measures, Crete, April 1, 1947-June 30, 1948

Service	Expenditures	Percentage			
		Total	Professional	Clerical Admin.	Operating
Malaria air spray	$ 24,607	14	*	—	14
Malaria control	90,110	54	1	23	30
Health centers	27,029	16	5	7	4
Tuberculosis control	8,729	5	1	*	4
Trachoma control	4,207	3	3	—	*
Maternal and child hygiene	3,917	2	*	*	2
Vital statistics	3,837	2	—	2	*
School hygiene	2,420	2	2	—	*
Communicable diseases	2,246	1	—	*	1
V. D. control	1,647	1	1	—	*
Rabies	516	*	*	—	—
Total	$169,265	100	13	32	55

* Less than 0.5 per cent.
Source: W. A. McIntosh, "Public Health Survey in Crete, Greece." Unpublished manuscript. Rockefeller Foundation, New York, 1949, p. 89.

twelve-month period. Professional services required only one-eighth of the total, clerical and administrative work one-third, and operating expenses 55 per cent.

Municipal expenditures for health services in 1948 totalled $24,-136 in Iraklion and $2,368 in Khania, according to information supplied for the public health phase of the survey. These were the only municipalities which maintained such services in Crete in 1948.

The expenditures for health (malaria air spray omitted) by nomes for this fifteen-month period indicate that except for Rethimnon nome (36 cents per capita) each of the other nomes spent about the same per capita funds (28 to 30 cents) from the Ministry of Hygiene. But since malaria control headquarters were located in Iraklion, the expenditure of state-controlled funds for health work—other than for malaria control—was less than half as much as in the other three nomes. However, if the municipal funds for health work are included, the expenditure per capita is more nearly equalized—Khania and Iraklion at 18 and 19 cents per capita respectively and Rethimnon and Lasithi at 14 and 13 cents per capita—all malaria control omitted.

Some data are also available for costs of sanitation works carried out in Iraklion and Lasithi nomes during 1946-1947. In a sixteen-month period, aqueduct, reservoir, sewage, public latrine, and spring protection projects totalling $21,552 were constructed or were under construction. Almost one-half of the cost of these projects was borne by the local communities largely through labor and local materials. One-third of the cost was from UNRRA funds and one-sixth from the Athens government. After UNRRA funds became unavailable, the government paid three-fifths of the cost, the remaining two-fifths coming from local funds. Further details are shown in Table 24 below.

These data suggest that without foreign aid, projects costing more than $1,200 will be very infrequent, although one project of $2,457 at Neapolis was completed in late 1947. They also indicate that current projects were primarily for improved water supplies, with a few for other sanitary measures.

I. Summary

In summary, the crude death rate in Crete was found to be about the same as in the United States and lower than in most of the Eu-

TABLE 24. Cost of sanitation works by type, Iraklion and Lasithi nomes,
Crete, April 1, 1946-July 31, 1947

Type of sanitation works and nome	Total Expenditure	Source of Funds		
		Gov't	UNRRA	Local
	(dollars)	(percentage)		
Aqueduct—Iraklion	$5,520[a]	12	69	19
" "	4,690	9	43	48
" "	4,280	7	10	83
Aqueduct—Lasithi	1,173	11	34	55
Spring "	546	16	11	73
Sewage "	295	33	13	54
Pumps "	1,800	2	67	31
Sewer cover "	82	62	—	38
Public latrine "	250	100	—	—[b]
Reservoir and spring protection—Lasithi	781[c]	46	—	54
Reservoir—Iraklion	1,130	60	—	40
" "	686	60	—	40
Hand pump, etc. "	319	60	—	40
Total	$21,552	17	37	46

a To be completed by community—power pump from German war booty.

b Estimates of community costs not given.

c Incomplete; additional $700 of government funds available for cement, reinforcing materials, and internal piping.

Source: Ministry of Hygiene through Health Division, ECA, unpublished data, Athens, Greece, 1948.

ropean industrialized nations. Infant mortality rates in Crete were double those of the United States. Rural areas had lower mortality rates than cities. The average age at death in Crete increased one-fifth during the past decade. Pneumonia, influenza, and intestinal infections (infectious diseases of the intestinal tract) caused three to four times as many deaths per 100,000 population in Crete as in the United States. The rate of tuberculosis and violent and accidental deaths was 40 per cent higher in Crete. On the other hand, cancer and heart diseases caused almost three times as many deaths proportionally in the United States as in Crete. During the past decade, deaths caused by malaria, influenza, nephritis, and intestinal infections showed the greatest decline in Crete.

Compared with Mexico, where the climate and living conditions are somewhat similar to those in Crete and considerably more familiar to Americans, death rates were only three-fifths as large. Most of this difference was due to the smaller number of deaths in Crete caused by intestinal infections (one-eleventh), malaria (one-twentieth), and pneumonia and influenza (one-half).

In Crete colds, influenza, and grippe, malaria, and intestinal infection diseases were the major illnesses. Trachoma, tuberculosis, leprosy, and oriental sore were also important diseases, economically and socially. While post-war anti-malaria control programs had been successful in reducing the incidence of malaria, survey data suggested its continuing presence. Smallpox immunization was compulsory in the elementary schools. Typhus, typhoid, and cholera immunizations were next in frequency.

While doctors, dentists, nurses, pharmacists, and trained midwives received adequate training, the numbers available were limited, especially in the rural areas. Public and private hospital and clinical services provided about 1,400 beds, of which 900 were available for general surgical, obstetrical, and pediatric patients. The remainder were for tuberculosis, leprosy, mental and venereal diseases.

The public health services in Crete might be characterized as having a few understaffed health centers in the major cities. The central organization, however, despite much paper planning, failed to utilize the local lay leaders and professional personnel effectively or to coordinate the sixteen auxiliary services working on health problems in Crete.

With only two of its seven pre-war branches in operation, the Patriotic Institute of Social Welfare (PIKPA) was doing outstanding work in providing its Maternal and Child Hygiene Services. While sanitary inspection of food handling and related establishments was provided, there was no sanitary officer in the villages.

The few seacoast municipalities which had sewerage systems directed them into the coastal waters, which were thereby polluted. More than four-fifths of the rural communities had no provision for sewage disposal. But since 1945, according to the survey, one-third of the communities had made some type of sanitary improvement— public latrines, pumps, pipelines, or water reservoirs.

Public health education was not well developed. Public health expenditures in 1947-1948 averaged $1.00 per inhabitant, of which only 33 cents was available for preventive health programs, including 18 cents for malaria control.

Malaria, the most important (economically speaking) health

problem in Crete in 1946 was well on its way to solution in 1948. The major health problems remaining included: lack of sanitation, high infant mortality, trachoma, tuberculosis, and the need for a full-time competent administrator for the whole island who would devote his efforts to utilizing more effectively the funds, personnel, and facilities—public and private—currently available for health work. Included among the more important problems facing such an administrator would be the need of:

(1) An able sanitary engineer to assist in coordinating all sanitation engineering problems and to give leadership to nome and community personnel in methods of disposal of human wastes, protection of water supplies, public laundries, public baths, and sanitary food handling, with more emphasis on educational aspects than on routine enforcement.

(2) Systematic anti-typhoid immunization in communities where it is endemic.

(3) The reactivation of community and nome health committees.

(4) Accurate statistics and responsibility for selection, analysis, and interpretation of morbidity data.

(5) Public health education.

(6) Public health nursing services and training of nurses and midwives.

(7) Branch health centers in all municipalities.

(8) Integration between health centers and hospital services.

(9) Combined public health and hospital laboratory services.

(10) Modernized methods of handling leprosy.

(11) Selection of an oral hygiene committee.

(12) Organization of an island hospital committee to study problems, plan hospital administration improvements, and secure co-ordination of hospital and health services.

In addition, there was need for the organization of a medical committee to assist in the development of doctor-nurse workshops, of in-service postgraduate training programs, of methods for coordinating the various aspects of the medical services. While accomplishing these tasks through a more effective use of available funds and facilities, such an administrator would have the opportunity to plan and develop the type of public health program which would be most significant for the economic development of the island.

CHAPTER 8

COMMUNITY FACILITIES AND
LIVING LEVEL COMPARISONS

COMMUNITY FACILITIES for health and community water supplies have been discussed in the previous chapter on health. Additional important facilities in Crete include telephones, electricity, roads, business establishments, and educational institutions. In order to present a clearer understanding of the types of problems in Crete, some comparisons of living level and economic development indexes are made with a few selected countries.[1]

A. COMMUNITY FACILITIES AND SERVICES

Some of the services used by households or available for their use are what we shall call community services—defined broadly enough to include the more important ones whether they are privately or publicly provided.

1. Business Establishments

The kind of goods used by households depends in part upon the availability of those goods and upon the consumer buyer's knowledge of or interest in them.

Though size of money income is one of the most important factors limiting the quantity of goods and services purchased in the market, the variety of goods and services available is, in part at least, related to the number of business establishments and their specialization.

Crete, particularly its rural communities, seemed well supplied with coffee houses, 7.7 per 1,000 inhabitants or one for each 130 persons. Cities and villages apparently fared about equally well in numbers of taverns and barber shops. There were relatively more tailor shops in the cities, as one might expect in view of the greater production of

---

[1] The discussion on educational facilities is based on an unpublished manuscript, "Education: Formal and Informal," which utilized data from the Crete Survey, prepared for The Rockefeller Foundation in September 1949, by Dr. Ralph H. Woods, President of Murray State Teachers College, Murray, Kentucky, and adviser to AMAG-ECA in Greece on education problems in 1948. The remaining sections of the chapter, on community facilities and living level comparisons, were developed from an unpublished report on "Living Levels in Crete" prepared by Dr. E. Jean Learned Mickey for The Rockefeller Foundation in 1949.

clothing in rural households. There were relatively fewer "specialty" shops than one would find in a more highly developed market economy. The details are shown by Table 25. The omission from the questionnaire of the cobbler and leather shops was an unfortunate oversight.

TABLE 25. Business houses per 1,000 inhabitants, Crete, 1948

Types of businesses[a]	Communities	Cities	All Crete
Coffee shops	8.2	5.7	7.7
Grocery stores	2.7	5.4	3.2
Butcher shops	3.4	1.5	3.0
Tailor shops[b]	2.0	3.9	2.4
Barber shops	2.1	2.6	2.2
Taverns[c]	1.4	1.8	1.4
General stores	1.5	.7	1.3
Blacksmith shops	1.0	1.4	1.0
Restaurants	.5	1.1	.6
Bakeries	.2	1.1	.4
Pharmacies	.1	.3	.1

a Shoe and leather shops omitted.
b Tailor shops include haberdasheries.
c Taverns include restaurants when serving both purposes.
Source: Sample Survey of Crete, Form C, Community.

2. *Other Facilities and Services*

For many indigents, government contributions (particularly of food) make up a large part of their subsistence. This important responsibility has fallen to the government largely as a result of the war. Crete was not faced with a large refugee problem such as was found on the mainland. Only 581 people, about 145 families, were listed as refugees in Crete in May 1948. The small bands of guerrillas, totalling 300, raided only for food and caused few, if any, families to move out of their home villages.

Large numbers of indigent children received free school lunches which constituted an important part of their food intake in terms of nutritive value. In 1947-1948, one-third of the elementary school pupils were reported as indigents, eligible to receive free school lunches and free textbooks and school supplies. Brief mention of the matter is appropriate here in pointing out the importance of government services in the real income of some households.

Only one rural village in five had access to a telephone, about a third had bus service, a little over a fourth had radios, and very few had electricity and post offices. Comparatively, the village suburbs of the municipalities and the cities fared better—as shown in Table 26.

TABLE 26. Percentage of villages in communities and municipalities having certain communication facilities, Crete, 1948

Facilities	Communities	Municipalities	All Crete
Telephone	20	39	20
Electricity	2	46	3
Bus service	33	64	34
Radio	28	46	29
Post office	5	21	6

Source: Sample Survey of Crete, Form C, Community.

The type of road leading to approximately half the rural villages was only a mule trail. The villages in the outskirts of the municipalities fared better; over two-thirds of these villages had "improved roads" while 14 per cent had only trails (Table 27).

TABLE 27. Percentage of villages in communities and municipalities having stated types of roads, Crete, 1948

Best type of road	Communities	Municipalities	All Crete
Improved roads	22	68	24
Unimproved roads	28	18	27
Trails	50	14	49

Source: Sample Survey of Crete, Form C, Community.

A comparison of the estimated average distances of community and city households from medical and other facilities shows all facilities except elementary schools were much more accessible in the cities, according to Table 28.

The importance of the church in the lives of the Cretan people is suggested by the average distance of one mile from a priest, as compared to an average of five miles from a doctor, dentist, or others who ministered to their physical disabilities.

TABLE 28. Average distance (miles) of households from medical and
other facilities, Crete, 1948

Facilities	Communities	Cities	All Crete
Doctor	6.0	.8	5.0
Dentist	12.9	.9	10.6
Nurse	17.4	1.3	14.3
Midwife	2.9	.8	2.5
Priest	1.1	.4	.9
Elementary school	.3	.3	.3
Gymnasium	11.2	1.1	9.3

Source: Sample Survey of Crete, Form C, Community.

B. EDUCATIONAL FACILITIES

Broadly speaking, education was high in the scale of values among
the Cretan people, especially in Rethimnon nome. In nine-tenths of
the communities, officials and ordinary citizens expressed their respect for education by such phrases as: "All wish to educate their
children," or "We wish to educate our children but can't afford it."
In the other 10 per cent of the communities surveyed, however, the
response was of the sort: "Most people don't care," or "We don't
trust people who are too educated."

A common attitude toward education for women—not so different
from that in America less than a century ago—was indicated by the
statement often heard: "If money is short, boys, not girls, should be
educated." This viewpoint might partly account for girls often marrying in their teens, although marriage customs and other factors
were also present.

Men usually dominated the teaching profession, but during the
war their number was reduced. In 1948, several high government officials bewailed the high percentage of women teachers then in Crete.
Some typical remarks were: "Boys should seldom, if ever, be taught
by women or they become effeminate," and "Girls should have men as
teachers in certain subjects, in order that they learn to obey and so
make better wives." School officials seemed to prefer about two men
to each woman teacher, or almost the reverse of the ratio in 1948.
Limited economic opportunities in Crete also created political and
social pressures for using men as teachers.

The school system in Crete was found to consist of a six-year compulsory elementary school, a six-year secondary school, and limited

opportunities for two to six years of higher education. Although the first six years were compulsory and free, the law was hard to enforce. Greece, however, was one of the first nations to install free, compulsory elementary education. In 1948, there were about 62,000 pupils and 1,260 teachers in the elementary schools and 11,300 pupils and 260 teachers in the secondary schools of Crete.

1. Elementary Schools

Nearly six out of ten elementary schools in the rural communities of Crete were one-room schools; three out of ten were two-room schools; only one out of ten had three or more rooms. In Rethimnon one elementary school had 22 rooms and in Iraklion there was an elementary school with 28 rooms.

No transportation for school children was provided. Both community and city households lived close to the elementary school—an average distance of three-tenths of a mile. Hence the lack of public transportation for pupils to and from these schools was of little importance.

In 1948, there were 813 elementary schools, about one for every two rural villages and more than one per municipality. There were 10 per cent more pupils per teacher in the urban schools than in the rural. The high enrollment (51) per teacher in 1947-1948 was not solely a result of the war, but appeared to be a chronic condition, even before 1939. Village schools averaged fewer rooms than schools in the cities; also a smaller proportion had toilets and good drinking water; but relatively more of them served school lunches. The number of blackboards, desks, and chairs was inadequate since many of them had been used for firewood during the war. As a result of the war, few schools had playgrounds or playground equipment. Even before the war, the playgrounds were inadequate. One-seventh of the elementary schools were being held in churches or places other than regular school buildings. It is particularly striking that even in the municipalities less than 30 per cent of the schools had enough books to satisfy their meager needs. Additional details are shown in Table 29.

The school lunches, served by 61 per cent of all schools, consisted typically of milk (made from the dried or powdered product) with raisin bread. The nutrition survey found this mid-morning lunch to be a valuable nutritive supplement to the children's diets. This daily

Table 29. Percentage of elementary schools with certain facilities,
Crete, 1948

Facilities	Communities	Municipalities	All Crete
Stoves	22	19	22
Toilet	34	55	35
Good water	24	71	26
Playground	56	45	56
Playground equipment	10	0	9
School lunch served	63	32	61
Regular school building	86	84	86
Enough books	26	29	26

Source: Sample Survey of Crete, Form C, Community.

lunch was provided for only about 25 cents per pupil per month, and
was paid for by the pupil unless he was from an indigent family.

Numerous courses, many hours in school, and emphasis on the
classics characterized the Greek school curriculum. This generaliza-
tion holds even for the curriculum of the elementary schools, which
included Greek language, geography and history of Greece, and religious history in each of the six elementary grades. Arithmetic,
drawing, writing, and handicrafts were also taught in each of these
elementary grades. In addition, geometry, physics, chemistry, bot-
any, and zoology were taught in the fifth and sixth grades. Gymnastics was required in all grades. (See Appendix 5, Table A69.) Inasmuch as relatively few Cretans went beyond the elementary level,
such a curriculum was designed to expose them to as complete a survey of knowledge as possible.

The elementary schools were coeducational but the secondary
schools were not.

2. Secondary Schools and the University

In 1948, there were 28 public and three private high schools located in 14 towns and cities. They had an estimated enrollment of
10,321 and 431 pupils respectively—an average of about 44 pupils
per teacher. These high schools, or gymnasiums, covered the same
grades as both junior and senior high schools in the United States,
but calculus and other subjects seemed to provide the approximate
equivalent of junior college training in this country. Besides the regular high schools, offering a classical curriculum, there were three

commercial schools with an enrollment of 565 pupils in Khania, Iraklion, and Ierapetra, a pedagogical academy for elementary teachers at Iraklion, and two agricultural schools at Mesara and Asamatos. The school at Asamatos was not in operation between the end of the war and 1948.

The 28 gymnasiums or high schools of Crete were located in the larger towns and villages—an average distance of 11 miles from rural households. These gymnasiums were less than 7 miles from one-half of the households, but 15 to 40 miles from one-third of them. Children living far from a gymnasium had to board and room in the city. Parents were hesitant about having their children leave home unless they could stay with relatives. Especially was this true of their attitude where daughters were concerned. This helps to explain why the enrollment in the gymnasiums was less than one-fifth as large as in the elementary schools.

While the number of pupils in secondary schools had more than doubled since 1937-1938, only 22 per cent of the young people of high school age were enrolled in 1948. Upon passing a public examination (at about age 11) the student might enter the secondary school or gymnasium. Small entrance and tuition fees ($1 and $4, respectively) were required, though for indigents and children of war casualties and invalids, this requirement might be waived.

Even greater emphasis was placed on the classics in the gymnasiums. Over half of the six-year high school curriculum was made up of languages, including ancient Greek, 18 per cent; modern Greek, 8 per cent; French and Latin, 11 per cent; and English, 18 per cent. An additional 15 per cent of the curriculum consisted of history, religion, and geography, and 17 per cent consisted of mathematics and science. Only 13 per cent of the curriculum was left for physiology, logic, sociology, and music. Gymnastics—the Swiss System—was required of both boys and girls. Bookkeeping, manual training, stenography, and other vocational courses were taught only in the commercial schools.

Many subjects were taught in a short time. The average Greek gymnasium student carried eleven to fourteen subjects at a time, as compared with four or five in the American high school. (See Appendix 5, Table A69.) The program consisted largely of recitations without provisions for supervised study, and with little or no library or laboratory work. Extra-curricular activities were virtually unknown.

However, many Greeks maintained that the emphasis on history and the classical studies, including ancient Greek, had been the means of unifying the people on widely scattered islands and in isolated communities into a close-knit nation. This emphasis in their educational system, they suggested, had developed a pride in the past, a faith in the present, and hope for the future. Whether this was the cause or not, these were three noticeable characteristics in the culture of Greeks and Cretans.

Only about one-quarter of the schools had enough textbooks, which, though the Ministry of Education prescribed them, were not provided free. Other teaching materials were largely lacking. A limited number of free books was provided to very needy pupils by a society organized for the purpose.

Teachers in the elementary schools must have had at least two years of training in a "pedagogical academy." One of these academies was at Iraklion. Secondary school teachers were required to be graduates of one of the two universities in Greece—Athens or Salonika. In neither the teachers' college nor the university, however, did the students receive instruction in the principles of education.

In an economy where white-collar or industrial jobs are few, teachers, as employees of the state, hold a position of somewhat enviable security, even though their salaries are low. In 1948, starting salaries were $37.50 per month, and the maximum salary, with all extras allowed for years of service, number of children, etc., was $70 per month. These salary scales were the same for all types of civil servants in the professions. (See Appendix 5, Table A71.)

Requirements for university entrance included an entrance fee of about $40. After payment of the entrance fee, the prospective student was permitted to take the entrance examination. If he failed to pass the first time, he might try again in two to four months for an additional $20; a third try was permitted with payment of $10.

Usually there were more applicants for admission to the university than there were facilities and space available. If this was the case, even though the entrance fees had been paid, some students were not permitted to enter. Later they might repeat the examinations upon repayment of appropriate fees.

School libraries had been almost completely lost or destroyed during the war and occupation. The existing limited library facilities were found only in Khania, Iraklion, and Sitia. The library of the Literary Association "Chryssostomos" in Khania had been almost entirely destroyed by bombing in 1941. In Iraklion there was a municipal library, and in Sitia a very small private library of the Literary Association "Vicenzios Kornaros."[2]

Because agriculture is the vocation of the majority of Cretan workers and is the mainstay of the island's economy, the agricultural school at Mesara was of special importance. It left much to be desired, however, as vocational training. During the day, the boys had but two and three-quarter hours for practical work in field or laboratory. Too many subjects were taught, and too little time was assigned to each. The classwork was not well correlated with work on the farm. Of the 2,200 to 2,400 young men who became farmers each year, not more than fifteen had the advantage of this two-year course. It was reported that between one-fourth and one-half of those who received the training left the farm for some other occupation. Perhaps the youth of the boys, usually 10 to 16, was responsible for such indecision as to their future occupation. In any case it raised serious question as to whether government funds were being used to best advantage with boys of this age, when older boys beyond the elementary, or even gymnasium, level had no opportunity for additional vocational training except to attend the Superior School of Agriculture in Athens.

3. *Adequacy of Facilities*

The adequacy of educational facilities may be reflected, in part, by literacy rates and average level of education attained by the adult population. These are summarized in the tables which follow. Since, in the 1928 census, a literate person was defined as one "eight years old or over who can read and write," the same definition was used in the 1948 survey.[3] On this basis, 82 per cent of the males and 60 per cent of the females were literate in 1948. In the cities 86 per cent of the males and 68 per cent of the females stated they could read and write, while in the communities the percentages were 81 per cent and 58 per cent respectively (Table 30).

Another suggested measure of literacy is the percentage of persons in this same age group who have completed the fourth grade in

[2] Geo. Naxakis, and C. Markidis, "Customs in Crete." Unpublished manuscript prepared for Crete Survey. August 1949.

[3] Recently the United Nations has been using "ten years or over" in the definition; on this basis 84 per cent of the males and 59 per cent of the females were literate in Crete in 1948.

school. This measure of literacy is almost consistently 10 per cent below the percentage of those who state they can read and write.

TABLE 30. Percentage of persons 8 years old or over who are literate,[a] by sex, Crete, 1948

Literacy criteria	Communities[b]			Cities[b]			All Crete[b]		
	M	F	T	M	F	T	M	F	T
Percentage who say they can read and write	81	58	69	86	68	76	82	60	70
Percentage who have had at least 4 years of schooling	71	48	59	78	55	65	72	50	60

a Ability to read and write is most commonly accepted definition of "literate."
b M = Males, F = Females, T = both Males and Females.
Source: Sample Survey of Crete, Form A, Household.

In general, more men attained a higher level of education in Crete than women. Among both men and women, those living in the municipalities attained, on an average, a higher level of education than did those living in the rural communities, as shown in Table 31. (For further details see Appendix 5, Tables A59 to A62.)

TABLE 31. Percentage of adults[a] completing stated grades in school, by sex, Crete, 1948

Highest year completed	Communities		Cities		All Crete	
	Male	Female	Male	Female	Male	Female
6 grades or less	87	98	69	83	84	94
7 grades to 12 inclusive	11	2	24	16	13	5
12 grades to 18 inclusive	2	*	7	1	3	1
Total	100	100	100	100	100	100

* Less than 0.5 per cent.
a Adults are all persons 21 years old or over on September 1, 1948.
Source: Sample Survey of Crete, Form A, Household.

Four-fifths of the men and nine-tenths of the women in Crete had not gone beyond the sixth grade in school, and the proportion was still higher for the rural communities. A very small percentage of either men or women had completed twelve or more grades in school. But freedom from control of foreign powers had been relatively recent (1913). Though two world wars and many internal struggles had hampered the development of many desirable improvements, Crete showed real progress in increasing literacy from 57 per cent to 70 per cent during the twenty-year period since 1928, and from a reported 15 per cent during the previous seventy-year period.

4. *Administration and Control*

If anything is to be done to alter the emphasis of the Greek educational system, it must be done through the central authorities, rather than by local activity, since the school administration is highly centralized. The organization of the schools, the curriculum, the textbooks, the courses and their content are prescribed by the Higher Educational Council in Athens, which works with the Minister of Education and his staff. The eighteen members of this Council are usually eminent classical scholars who have become leaders in the educational world. Their proclivities determine the great attention to classical studies.

The Higher Educational Council not only decides, with the co-operation of the Minister, on the dates of the examinations and the questions to be asked, but in the same way appoints, transfers, or promotes teachers. Local citizens can exert influence, provided they have interest enough to do so, only by working with the centrally appointed director and inspector of the school.

There was in Crete, to be sure, an educational council for elementary education and one for secondary education, with special jurisdiction over the island. These councils, however, were made up entirely of supervisory employees of the Ministry of Education, responsible to Athens.

All the educational funds were supervised and allocated through the Ministry of Education. That part which was allocated to a specific school was expected to be supplemented by contributions from the local government in question. It was used, not for paying teachers, who were on the central government payroll, but for erecting, repairing, furnishing, maintaining, and operating the building and grounds. The fund might consist of an appropriation raised by local taxes or lotteries, legacies or donations, private gifts of land and labor, or land supplied by the community. These funds were managed by a School Fund Committee, consisting of the Director of the

School, a member of the local Council, a member of the Church Council, and two to four parents or prominent citizens. The Committee, however, was supervised by the Ministry of Education.

5. *Education Outside the Schools*

The Agricultural Extension Service and Agricultural Bank provided extension and service workers. These workers arranged meetings and conferences designed to help farmers. Their program would be more effective, however, if they could spend more time on education and relatively less on regulation and administration.

The Ministry of Agriculture operated experiment stations dealing with various phases of agriculture in an effort to provide needed information on varieties, cultural practices, etc. One of the greatest weaknesses here was failure to get experimental results to the farmers. Perhaps through simple, well-illustrated bulletins or circulars the results of scientific investigation could be presented to farmers and to those who teach farmers in such a way that practical applications could be made more effectively. But even more effective would be a concerted effort to enable agricultural experts to discuss and demonstrate new methods and techniques with individual farmers and groups of farmers.

According to the survey, one-third to two-fifths of the farmers who had heard about new varieties of wheat, barley, oats, and oranges received such information from their agriculturist or the agricultural schools. These same sources provided information on Bordeaux Mixture and other spraying materials to 61 per cent of the farmers. They were notably less effective, however, in supplying information on new varieties of olives, peanuts, and pistachio nuts.

The large number of farmers who heard about spray materials from the agriculturist was in part accounted for by the fact that they had to obtain from the agriculturist the permit to purchase spray materials. This is only one example of the many regulations to which farmers were subject. Individual efficiency and well-being await increased emphasis on education as contrasted with regulation.

Besides this education at the adult level, there was much emphasis placed on Boy Scouts, Girl Scouts, and Sea Scouts. These groups remained very popular even through the war period. Drill, so appealing to Cretan youngsters, was an important feature of their activities. First aid, local and national loyalty, manners, and many other things were taught in these organizations.

The coffee house contributed to informal education. Here everything of interest to the Greek people was discussed, including philosophy, history, economics, religion, and the current topics of the day. The coffee house was not only the social gathering place and recreational center of each village; it was an information center as well.

C. Comparison of Resource-Use, Living Levels, and Economic Development in Crete and Selected Countries

A comparison of information on living levels in Crete with a few other "underdeveloped" countries should assist in determining the relative importance of certain problems to the Cretan people. As a general background for such a comparison, brief consideration was given in Chapter 1 to the basic economic causes of low living levels existing in various parts of the world. Since both terms "low level of living" and "underdeveloped" are relative terms, suggesting that other areas have higher living levels and are more fully developed, the definition of the basic causes of low levels of living was also stated in relative terms.

Various combinations of relatively limited natural, human, capital, and entrepreneurial or management resources, as related to the quantity of man labor available, were suggested as the basic causes underlying conditions in the underdeveloped areas of the world. More specifically, the causes of low levels of living, as expressed by "output per man" were listed as:

(1) limited natural resources—quantity and/or quality,
(2) scarcity of capital—amounts and efficiency in its use,
(3) lack of skills and education of labor force—quality,[4] and
(4) limited number of entrepreneurs and lack of quality of management, both private and government.

1. Four Categories of Underdeveloped Areas

Based on these suggested causes of underdevelopment, the various areas of the world may be classified into four separate categories

---

[4] Since the *quantity* of labor is in "surplus" relative to the other factors of production, it has been omitted from this list of causes of low output per man. Others might desire to express the cause as "too much labor" in relation to all the other factors. But Western civilization has generally taken the position that any person, once born, becomes a fixed asset in terms of the labor force (except as his quality is improved by education, training, etc.) unless he elects to break certain moral codes. Consequently, measurements are usually made in terms relative to man, for instance, "output per man," leaving the factors listed above as the variables.

according to the relative scarcity of the factors of production. There are many areas of the United States which are underdeveloped relative to other parts of the country. But in the nation as a whole, mass poverty is lacking. Similarly, in comparison with the rest of the world, the peoples of Central and Northern Europe, Australia, New Zealand, Canada, and Japan (in comparison with other Far Eastern countries) have relatively high output and consumption per capita. These are generally called the "industrialized" nations.

The remainder of the world may be divided roughly into four categories, as to types of "un-industrialized" or so-called underdeveloped areas. For descriptive purposes and because each category requires a different treatment in the solution of its problems in economic development these may be designated as: (I) the "undeveloped" areas; (II) the "undeveloped-industrializing" areas; (III) the "underdeveloped-heavy population" areas; and (IV) the "underdeveloped-limited natural resources" areas.

In the first category (Category I, "undeveloped" areas) are found large sectors of the world's surface such as most of Africa, much of South America, Central America, the Middle East, and certain areas of the South Pacific. These areas have large *known*, as well as unknown, but undeveloped natural resources and have little or no industrialization. Capital formation is largely through outside sources. In general, labor is uneducated and unskilled.

Other areas with undeveloped natural resources, such as Mexico, Brazil, Venezuela, Argentina, and Russia, are industrializing. Technical skills are being developed. Educational and health facilities are being made available. Capital formation, from both internal and external sources, is taking place at an increasing tempo. These countries may be classified as Category II, "undeveloped-industrializing" areas.

The largest number of people with low output per man and consumption per person are found in the areas where the major problem is the high ratio of population to land resources—even though some industrialization and some undeveloped resources are present. Because of the relatively large number of people and their low efficiency all the causes of underdevelopment seem acute in these countries. These "underdeveloped-heavy population" areas in Category III include India, Pakistan, China, Korea, Haiti, the Philippines, and similar countries.

The "underdeveloped-limited natural resources" areas in Category IV include many of the countries in the Mediterranean Basin in which Crete and Greece are located (see Crete map). France and Italy have industrialized to such an extent that these two countries are included among the industrialized nations. In comparison with most of the world, these countries around the Mediterranean lack power, soil, and mineral resources. Capital formation has taken place over the centuries, but "venture" capital is lacking, partly due to political instability, but also due to the lack of known natural resources.

The importance of differentiating between these four categories of underdeveloped countries will become more evident as the problems of measurement are discussed and the comparative analysis with specific countries proceeds.

2. Problems of Measurement

For this comparison, some quantitative measures of resource-use, living levels, and economic development have been selected for Crete, Greece, and six other countries. Unfortunately another and perhaps even more important category of indexes has been omitted because of the difficulty of finding measurable criteria. This category includes social organization, cultural patterns, and moral codes. It would take into account such items as personal, economic, and political security; personal, economic, political, and religious freedom; spiritual development; and social adjustment of the people of a nation to the local, national, and world community; and others. Throughout this book, and others of this type, the lack of specificity and clarity on these points is evident.

Granting that there are some immeasurables and many valid objections to any selection of quantitative indexes for a comparative analysis of nations or areas, the advantage of sharpening the focus on certain measurable elements of the national segments of our world society suggests a value for their use. They should provide a more accessible factual insight into those aspects of present-day nations and their social organization which can be measured.

In addition, nations, like people, constantly make comparisons of individual progress with other nations and people having similar resources; with those less fortunately situated as to their resources; and with those having greater resources and opportunities for development. These comparisons enable the nation, and the individual, (1) to determine the degree of adjustment made to the resource, economic, and social situation; (2) to re-assess goals and social responsibility in the area-community; and (3) to provide challenges to new levels of attainment in the light of these readjusted goals.

If such comparisons are to be valid, the indexes should be relatively accurate, objective, and up-to-date, and should cover the same period of time. In the discussion to follow, emphasis has been placed on obtaining post-war information, if possible. Changes in birth rates, death rates, life expectancy, illiteracy, and many other items have been marked during the past decade, and recent data for these indexes for all countries have been used. For all other items, data during the decade prior to the last war have been used. Most of the post-war data, except for Crete and Paraguay, were obtained from the yearbooks of the United Nations: *Statistical Yearbook, 1948* and *Demographic Yearbook, 1948*. The figures for the remaining items are from a recent publication, *Point Four*, issued by the State Department of the United States, presenting the latest comparable figures during the decade of 1930-1939.

Although some of these data are lacking in accuracy, they are presented as suggested types of indexes of living levels. As other more useful measures are developed and improved data made available the comparisons between countries will be even more helpful in determining the relative importance of the problems needing solution. As suggested above, however, the relative importance of the problems to be attacked will be affected by the cultural factors as they impinge upon the goals and desires of the people, as well as by the basic economic factors.

3. Reasons for Country Selection

Greece, Italy, and Egypt were selected from the Mediterranean area for comparison with Crete. Greece is the mother country of the Island of Crete and represents an underdeveloped country in Category IV. Except for France, Italy is the most industrialized nation in the Mediterranean Basin. Egypt suffers from population pressure on the occupied portion of its vast area and is a neighboring country representative of Category III. India was chosen to represent Category III, the "underdeveloped-heavy population" area from the Far East. Mexico, with a climate somewhat similar to that of Crete, was chosen from the Western Hemisphere to represent Category II, the "undeveloped-industrializing" areas. Paraguay, in South America, was selected to represent Category I, the "undeveloped" areas.

The United States was selected primarily to provide a basis of comparison which Americans might understand, although it also represents an industrialized nation with a high level of economic development. For the latter purpose alone, however, Canada or Great Britain might have been used from the Western world, or Japan from the Far East.

4. General Analysis of the Indexes

In general, countries under population pressure, as measured by a large number of persons per square mile of land area or of agricultural land, a high annual rate of population increase, and a high percentage of population engaged in agriculture producing mostly primary food products for local consumption, will have low economic development. Such countries will have few communication and transportation facilities; a low percentage of the labor force engaged in manufacturing, construction, transportation, and communication; and a low percentage of the population in urban centers with a population of 2,500 or more. Usually such countries will have a high percentage of illiteracy, high birth and death rates, a high infant mortality rate, and a low life expectancy at birth (both of the latter two items being some indication of the lack of sanitation), and low food consumption as measured by calories, protein, and fats consumed per capita per day.

The major economic and resource-use problems in these countries will be quite different than those in countries with large undeveloped natural resources and limited human resources available. In the discussion to follow, it will become evident that one of the major analysis jobs is to find the key problems which are meaningful from both an economic and cultural viewpoint for a particular country.

5. Comparison of Crete and Selected Countries

With 148 persons per square mile, Crete had almost twenty times as many persons per square mile of land area as Paraguay, and three to five times as many as the United States and Mexico, but about half as many per square mile as India and Italy and one-ninth as many as occupied Egypt (Table 32). Crete, with 485 persons per square mile of agricultural land, was under relatively more population pressure than the total land area indicates. While the rate of

TABLE 32. Selected indexes of resource-use, living conditions, and economic development, Crete, Greece, and six other countries. Post-war or latest pre-war

Indexes	Crete	Greece	Egypt	Italy	India	Mexico	Paraguay	United States
Country category	IV	IV	III	Ind.†	III	II	I	Ind.†
Population/land ratio								
Population per square mile, '48	148	152	1,331ᵃ	393	295	32	8	49
Annual rate population increment	0.9	1.4	1.1	0.8	1.4	1.8	2.0	0.7
Health								
Crude birth rateᵇ	26.1	30.0	42.6	22.1	27.8	44.0	38.2	24.5
Crude death rateᵇ	10.6	13.5	27.7	11.3	19.2	17.3	8.9	10.0
Infant mortality rate	79	101	153	82	151	105	52	32
Av. life expectancy, males, '40	50	49	36	54	27	37	44	62
*Physicians per 100,000 pop.	65	86	21	87	12	51	28	137
Food								
*Calories per capita per day	2,547	2,323	2,469	2,636	1,976	1,855	2,813	3,098
*Animal protein per capita per day — oz.	0.6ᶜ	0.7	0.4	0.7	0.3	0.7	—	1.8
*Fats per capita per day — oz.	3.7	2.6	1.5	2.1	1.0	1.5	—	4.3
Education								
Per cent of illiteracy—pre-war	43	41	85	22	91	52	65	4
*Elementary teachers per 1,000 pop.	2.7	2.2	1.6	3.4	1.3	2.4	3.3	4.3

Economy

*Per capita income (1939)—dollar	74[d]	136	85	140	34	61	39	554
Per cent of labor force in:								
Agriculture	57	54	71	48	67	68	70	18
Manufact. and construction	14	—	10	27	10	13	—	30
Per cent of population, urban	23	36	25	45	13	35	20	57

Crop yields

*Wheat	12.8	14.0	31.3	22.1	10.7	11.5	12.1	13.2
*Potatoes	71	101	172	97	150	66	75	117

Transport & communications

Telephones per 1,000 population	1	8	5[e]	21[e]	0.2[e]	10	3	242
*Miles R.R. per 1,000 sq. miles	0	36	9	119	26	19	4	80
*Motor vehicles per 1,000 population	2	2	2	11	0.3	5	2	250

*These items are from *Point Four*, with most data from 1930-1940. Unstarred items are from U.N. *Yearbooks*, mostly 1945-1948. Some Paraguay items are from Institute of Inter-American Affairs.

† "Ind." indicates industrialized country.

a Based on inhabited and cultivated land area of 14,676 sq.mi. U.N. *Demographic Yearbook*, 1948, p. 75.

b 1946-1948 average.

c Adjusted annual estimate used as basis for this.

d 1947 cash income per capita.

e Data for telephones per 1,000 population for Egypt, Italy, India, from *World Almanac*, 1950, p. 622.

Sources: U.N. *Demographic Yearbook*, 1948, and *Statistical Yearbook*, 1948 and 1950 supplements. Department of State, *Point Four*, publication 3719, Economic Series 24, Division of Publications, 1950. Sample Survey of Crete: Forms A, B, C, Household, Farm, Community, and Form Ia, Seven-day Diet.

population increase in Crete was among the lowest of these countries, the excess of births over deaths during the post-war period for Crete indicated that higher annual rates of population increase were in prospect.

Crete, together with the United States and Italy, had the lowest crude death rate, birth rate, and infant mortality rate among these selected countries. The average life expectancy at birth in these three countries was also 5 to 25 years longer than in the remaining countries, and physicians were 2 to 10 times as numerous in proportion to the total population.

While large differences in food consumption were evident as between the United States and Paraguay in comparison with India or Mexico, the differences among the remaining countries, all in the Mediterranean Basin, were small. Crete consumed considerably more fat per capita per day than any other country except the United States.

Although the illiteracy figure given here for Crete and Greece is for 1928, the percentage of illiteracy was lower than for other countries except Italy and the United States. Except for Paraguay, a major cause for this is found in the number of teachers in the elementary schools per 1,000 population.

Income figures for Crete in 1939 are not available, but even with the inflated cash incomes in 1948 of $74 per capita, it is evident that Crete was among the lowest in annual income per capita. Although in Crete 57 per cent of the labor force was engaged in agriculture, Mexico, India, Egypt, and Paraguay had 10 to 16 per cent more of their population so engaged. While Crete had a slightly higher percentage of its labor force engaged in manufacturing and construction than Mexico, Egypt, or India, it showed only half as high a proportion as Italy and the United States. Only 23 per cent of the population in Crete lived in urban centers of more than 2,500 population, or about the same as in Egypt, but less than in Greece or any other of these countries except India and Paraguay. This suggests both a low level of capital accumulation per capita and a lack of industrial development.

Wheat and potato yields in Crete were low in comparison with all other countries except Mexico, where corn was relatively more important as the major food crop. Without railroads and with only a few telephones and motor vehicles, Crete, together with India, had the least amount of transport and communication facilities of these countries studied.[5]

Crete, except for infectious diseases of the intestinal tract, ranked "high" in health in comparison with both neighboring and other countries, including the United States. Crete was "medium" in population-land ratio, food consumption, and illiteracy in comparison with Greece and the other six countries. But Crete ranked "low" in income per capita, in economic development, crop yields, and transportation and communication facilities, in comparison with the countries studied.

D. SUMMARY

In 1948, Crete was lacking in roads, telephones, and other community facilities. Although great strides had been made in education during the past two decades, pupil-teacher ratios continued high. The school curriculum emphasized the classics. Only one-fifth of the pupils of secondary school age were in attendance. Textbooks, library facilities, and other equipment were extremely meager. Schoolhouses and school equipment were needed to replace war devastation. The agriculturist and the agricultural school were the main, but inadequate, sources of information on agriculture. The coffee house was the main place for the exchange of ideas among men and the community open-air washhouse among women. The church played an important role in the lives of the Cretan people. Because of the close church-state relationship in Greece and Crete, the bishop or priest might be as effective and in many communities more effective than the local officials in assisting with the solution of many social and economic problems.

In comparison with many other countries of the world (which include a majority of the world's population), the solution of the problems of low income, low crop yields, inadequate transportation and communication facilities, and the small amount of economic development seemed to be, at the time of this study, relatively more important in improving the living levels of the population of Crete than solution of the problems of health, food, and illiteracy. While the rate of increase in the population-land ratio in Crete was declining in the pre-war period, recent data on the excess of births over deaths suggested additional population problems in the future unless this

[5] For a more complete list of suggested indexes and comparison of Crete with some additional countries recently studied, see Appendix 5, Table A70.

should be only a temporary post-war condition or unless additional mineral or power resources should be discovered and industrialization increased.

Although incomes were low, their relationship to low productivity made them a long-run problem. The influence of government on productivity and the problems in increasing productivity in agriculture, industry, and commerce are discussed in the chapters which follow.

CHAPTER 9

GOVERNMENT ORGANIZATION
AND ITS IMPACT ON THE ECONOMY

THE GREEK GOVERNMENT is highly centralized. Its many inefficiencies, like those of other governments, might be reduced by reorganization, by clarification of functions and responsibilities, and by operational changes. During war and post-war years, it resorted to extreme deficit-spending which led to uncontrolled issuance of money. Even the local communities and municipalities lived within their budgets only by being dependent on the state and by providing a minimum of services through personal labor and gross taxes on production. National services included social insurance and supervision over banking and credit facilities. Inflation was great following the beginning of the war. The small farmers of Crete, who consume a large part of their own produce, did not benefit from a rise in price as did the commercial farming areas of the world.

A. ORGANIZATION AND ADMINISTRATION OF THE NATIONAL GOVERNMENT

Crete, once governed by Cretans (called Minoans) who dominated the commerce of the whole Aegean Sea in 1500-1100 B.C., has been ruled until recently by a succession of masters from various parts of the Mediterranean Basin. After 3,000 years of subjugation, Crete was ceded to Greece by the Treaty of London in 1913. Since then its history and government have been merged with that of the Greeks.

In a country with a highly centralized government, the pattern of governmental organization is important—particularly when limited resources make the local communities dependent upon aid from the central government or from foreign groups. This is especially true in considering any program designed to develop local resources and broaden the economic base to any considerable extent.

1. Organization of the National Government

Through popular elections held in 1946, King George II was returned to power. Upon his death in April 1947, he was succeeded by his brother, Paul, the present King. Under this monarchial system of government the King summons the leader of the party with the majority in Parliament and requests him to form a government. This party leader, together with the minority party leaders, selects ministers from Parliament to head various ministries in the government. If the coalition cabinet of ministers proves satisfactory to the various party leaders and is confirmed by the King, the full council of twenty-one ministers proceeds to carry on the government business under the successful party leader as Prime Minister. In 1948, Th. Sophoulis, head of the Liberal Party, acted as Prime Minister, although there were a half-dozen crises and reorganizations of the government during the year. Some idea of the complexity and possible duplications in the government may be gained from Figure 10, which shows the "Organization of the Greek Government."[1]

In Greece, as in the United States, there are the three branches of government: legislative, executive, and judiciary. In 1948 the legislative branch was composed of 354 members, elected by proportional representation for four-year terms. Crete had 21 members, one from each of the 20 eparchies and one elected at large. After the elections in 1950 Parliament consisted of 250 members, 16 of whom came from Crete. Parliament stays in session continuously in Athens, except for holidays and recess during the summer months.

The judiciary has one Supreme Court of fifteen and sits in Athens. There are seven Courts of Appeal, one in Crete. A Court of First Instance is located in each nome and Justices of the Peace in each eparchy capital.

The Prime Minister and Cabinet of fifteen ministers determine policies and make decisions within the framework of legislation laid down by Parliament. These legislative laws and decrees, together with the executive policies, are carried out through the twenty-one ministries and their government workers. The line of administrative authority shown in Figure 10 is frequently not observed. Many functions are performed only in Athens. The Ministries of Finance, Public Order, Communications, Education, and Reconstruction have district or regional organizations. A Council of State, consisting of 21 members, has to do with the powers of administrative bodies and has the power to draft bills. The most important special boards and committees consist of the Board of Reconstruction, Currency Committee, Communications Committee, Coordinating Committee, and Economic Committee.

[1] Outline Chart furnished by Greek Government through AMAG-ECA.

FIGURE 10. Organization of the Greek Government, 1948

LEGISLATIVE	EXECUTIVE	JUDICIARY
Parliament	King	Justice
(354 members, 4-year terms, one member per 25,000 population)	Prime Minister	Court of Cassation (Supreme Court—15)
	Cabinet (15 Ministers)	Courts of Appeal (Crete—1)
(Crete— 21 members)		Lesser Courts (King appoints judges)
	21 Ministries*	

Foreign Affairs	Agriculture
Mercantile Marine	Economic Coordination
National Economy	Labor
Public Works	Finance
Reconstruction	Supply
Transport & Communications	Navy
	Army
Interior	Education
Public Order	Welfare
Aeronautics	Health
Justice	Governor General (Northern Greece)

3 Governors-General
(Crete, Epirus, Macedonia)

47 Nomes—Administrative units similar to Central Government
(Crete—4 nomes)

150 Eparchies—Election districts, some administrative functions
(Crete—20 eparchies)

160 Demes—Approximately 160 cities   (Crete—10 demes)

5,000 Communes (under 10,000 population)   (Crete—550 communities)
(Crete—1,405 villages)

* Note groupings of 21 ministries to provide 15 Cabinet members.
Source: Greek Government through AMAG-ECA.

2. Efficiency of Administration

Highlights from the detailed studies made in 1947-1948 by the civil government division of AMAG (American Mission for Aid to Greece) point up situations and problems involved in working with the Greek Government in Crete. Government, in any country, is not immune to inefficiencies in both organization and operation, but some examples stressed by the AMAG study of the Greek Government are relevant here: "When the Mission (AMAG) came to Greece it found the Government administrative machine poorly organized, badly operated, and overcentralized in Athens. The Civil Service . . . was overstaffed and weak . . . pension rolls were badly swollen. . . ."[2]

The overstaffing of civil service and pension rolls was in part due to the serious economic crisis, as this was about the only way in which employment could be obtained by many persons. To its credit be it said that the Greek Government was aware of this situation and requested help from AMAG to reorganize, simplify, and decentralize its administration, improve its civil service, and revise the educational training methods.

a. *Overcentralization.* Previous missions to Greece had stressed the overcentralization of government in the capital. Field trips in Crete confirmed the great need for better administration and a more decentralized government.[3] Local island and nome officials as well as private citizens of Crete commented many times on the need for improved administration and more control at the local level of government.

As pointed out in the previous chapter, even the rural community elementary school teacher must be hired, fired, and replaced by the Minister of Education in Athens. Many times this meant that a position was vacant for several months. There was relatively little local autonomy or authority in the operation of the schools, except as local citizens were able to influence the school inspector and local teacher.

Government officials of all ministries at the nome level had to await decisions from the central government on many things requiring immediate action for effective solution. For example, one of the nome agriculturists needed a certain type of chemical for a newly

[2] American Mission for Aid to Greece, *A Factual Summary Concerning the American Mission for Aid to Greece,* June 15, 1948, p. 15. The accuracy of the statements quoted from AMAG reports cannot be vouched for by the members of the Survey team.

[3] *ibid.,* p. 15.

discovered tree disease. But not even limited funds could be obtained through regular channels without months of delay. Thus a whole year of experimentation was lost on what might have proved to be a very costly disease. Funds were budgeted so closely for known expenses that not even limited amounts were available for attacking unusual problems which frequently occurred.

An important procedure in securing proper organization in government is to develop an effective balance between central-staff responsibilities and field-staff responsibilities. Certainly the central staff should determine major policies and secure coordination of effort among areas and among various ministries at all levels. On the other hand, the most effective organization would seem to place in the hands of the field staff the major responsibility for determining procedures to develop understanding among the people. The field staff should then be able to adapt central-staff policies to local conditions (within limits) and determine their relative importance to the particular area and problem.

b. *Overstaffing and ineffective organization.* The need for staff reduction and reorganization was recognized by many officials throughout the Greek Government: ". . . Emergency measures were taken designed to improve the effectiveness of the government and to alleviate the undue budgetary drain caused by civil service abuses. These principally comprised (1) a reduction in force (15,000 surplus with 8,000 actually released) ; (2) an increase in the work week from 30 to 40 hours; (3) elimination of overtime pay; and (4) a reduction in extra pay for service on committees and councils."[4]

On the basis of the AMAG study and in conference with Greek authorities, suggested revisions in the organization of several ministries were also made. As an illustration of the recommendations, the suggested revisions for the Ministry of Agriculture are presented below.[5] In brief, the number of bureaus was reduced from 3 to 2; the number of sections from 55 to 40; and legal entities from 66 to 10. From a total of 2,641 positions, 309 were eliminated; functions of departments were clarified, and overlapping and duplication were reduced. "In summary, a reorganization of the Ministry of Agriculture was recommended in the following general areas: (1) the or-

[4] *ibid.,* p. 16.
[5] H. R. Gallagher, and Others, *Organizational Study of the Ministry of Agriculture,* Civil Government Division, AMAG, 1948.

ganization of the Ministry's operating program under two bureaus
—Agriculture and Conservation, reporting to a Director General
of the Ministry. The Directorate of Administration and the field
services (acting in a staff capacity) would also report to the Director
General of the Ministry; (2) abolition of the office of Secretary-General; (3) abolition of all existing special funds and the concentration of all financial responsibility in a single fiscal officer; (4) abolition of many existing legal entities and transfer of their functions
to appropriate program directorates of the Ministry; (5) placing
of additional emphasis upon programs of marketing and soil conservation; (6) regrouping, abolition and transfer of certain existing directorates and sections whose functions duplicate, overlap or
conflict with one another; (7) reorganization and simplification of
the Ministry's mail, file and messenger service; and (8) development
of an extension field service to coordinate, implement and apply the
various programs and services of the Ministry to meet farmers'
needs."[6]

A summary of the present and revised staffing of the Ministry of
Agriculture indicates the types of positions in which American observers thought efficiency could be improved by an 11 per cent reduction in staff.[7] Of the 2,641 staff positions, one-fifth were in the
Central Services at Athens; more than a fourth in the nome agricultural field service; more than a third in forestry; about one-tenth in
research and teaching; and the remainder in topography and settlements.

Of the 309 positions eliminated, 173, or almost three-fifths, were
in the Central Service and one-third were in the regional topographic
work which was to be turned over to the Ministry of Reconstruction.
The remaining positions abolished were ushers in the forestry field
service. Approximately one-third of the Central Service positions
were to be abolished. These included one-half of the section chiefs,
two-fifths of the reporters and secretaries, a third of the clerks, ushers, Director-Generals, and Directors, and one-fifth of "others."
(For further details see Appendix 5, Table A72.)

Only 102 of 300 additional employees in the legal entities (not
listed above) were to be retained under the Ministry of Agriculture.
The remaining 198 were to be released or shifted to other departments or ministries.

c. *Salary scale.* In 1948, the majority of government employees

[6] *ibid.,* p. 45.   [7] *ibid.,* pp. 49-59.

received $15 to $65 per month, depending upon the job status, length of service, and number of dependents. A few of the top government jobs paid $100 per month. These low wages for government employees, combined with rising costs-of-living, caused a large portion of them to carry on other activities in addition to their government work. With short office hours in the summer, many had outside jobs working for private business, tutoring, translating, or doing whatever they could. These outside pressures on many employees led to abuse and loss of interest in the official job. In some instances, it seemed that the government job served as a base of operations, with guaranteed minimum wage and pension privileges, from which to secure as much additional income as possible or to curry favor with those who might need outside assistance later. On the other hand, there were many conscientious and well-trained government workers in responsible positions who were putting in hours of overtime in an attempt to accomplish their tasks. (For details on salary scales for teachers and professors see Appendix 5, Table A71.)

Teachers in Crete were on civil service and held the same grades as other professional people in the government service so that the salaries stated above were representative for similar training and experience. The High Court Justices (of highest rank) received a base salary of $100 per month, while ushers and beginning clerks started with a base salary of about $15 per month. Stenographers and office secretaries (clerks) received $33 to $45 per month.

d. *Operational efficiency.* One way of measuring the efficiency of operation in government is to study the functions of the agency or organization and determine whether such groups are rendering positive and concrete service to the economy or welfare of the nation. Agencies which tend only to study conditions and past events without determining their effects and developing means to improve conditions are apt to become a hindrance to political, economic, and social development. An example of this type of operational inefficiency in one of the ministries studied by the Civil Government Division, AMAG, is suggested in the following statement from one of the reports:

"It is impossible to find a single directorate or section in the Ministry of National Economy which is actually rendering positive and concrete service to the trade and industry of the nation. Many of its functions exist only on paper and where performed are usually typified by an extreme regulatory attitude. . . . It is actually fulfilling its responsibilities with respect to only one of its many competencies —that of the processing and issuance of import and export licenses."[8]

Even in the field of licensing imports, about one-half of the applications received had to be returned to the importer for further information and completion. The average processing time for applications was from one to two months. This could be cut to two or three weeks.[9] "The most wasteful and ill-advised function observed in the survey of the Ministry of Agriculture was the Topographic Service which maintains a large number of employees both in Athens and in the field. Most field employees come to Athens during the winter months even though the engineering crews of another ministry, engaged in rebuilding villages, work on project sites throughout the winter."[10]

In the Ministry of National Economy there were also illustrations of the failure of a division of government to determine its proper function for the greatest service to the nation. For example, the prevailing emphasis on the fisheries problem was on the administrative and legal, rather than the technical and research, aspects. Yet the need for protein foods and the scarcity of fish in the local markets were well known. Likewise, the geological service was analyzing the content of water from various mineral springs with a view to the future use of these waters for uncertain resort purposes, while basic geological surveys for use in studying water and mineral resource possibilities were lacking in many areas.[11]

Similarly, "The present activities of the Commercial Treaties Section are largely confined to assimilating information on trade negotiations and commercial treaties among other countries. The emphasis is on 'following' and 'observing' rather than upon active investigation and promotion of export possibilities for the products of Greece."[12] Yet Greece was "starved" for foreign exchange and dependent on special semi-luxury product markets for exports, requiring more than normal amounts of sales promotion.

Even in the Ministry of Agriculture, the agricultural marketing section emphasized the governmental purchasing of agricultural

[8] H. R. Gallagher, and Others, *Organizational Study of the Ministry of National Economy*, Civil Government Division, AMAG, 1948, p. 8.

[9] *ibid.*

[10] H. R. Gallagher, and Others, *Organizational Study of the Ministry of Agriculture*, Civil Government Division, AMAG, 1948, p. 35.

[11] H. R. Gallagher, and Others, *Organizational Study of the Ministry of National Economy*, Civil Government Division, AMAG, 1948, pp. 22 and 30.

[12] *ibid.*, pp. 36-37.

products with a view to stabilizing prices rather than other more important aspects. "These aspects include the classification, grading, and standardization of agricultural products; new methods of preservation and processing, such as refrigeration, canning, etc.; and new methods of packing and shipping agricultural products."[13]

Duplication of services in several ministries was further evidence of improper organization in government. Such duplication was found not only in many staff functions but also in such fields as water and education. Water problems, for example, were attacked in the Ministries of Agriculture, Public Works, Reconstruction, National Economy, and Health, with little, if any, exchange of data, information, or personnel.

"Too much administrative work is being handled by committees." This is "extremely time-consuming as well as costly." These matters should be "transferred to responsible officials who should be given authority to decide the problems independently."[14]

"There is 'undue waste of money in the use of ushers' in the ministries, as most of the time they have nothing to do. This lowers the morale of other civilian employees in the Ministry. A central pool of ushers subject to call would easily reduce the number by half."[15]

"The present practice of permitting the citizens to see the top executives on personal matters or minor problems during visiting hours should be immediately discontinued."[16] This procedure of allowing contacts to be made with high officials rather than with persons responsible for the work in question tended to break down organization, destroyed responsibility, lowered morale, and wasted the time of competent personnel.

In attempting to increase the economic base and to improve living levels in Crete or any other area of Greece, the following points made by Mr. Michael Samiotakis, Director in the Khania Chamber of Commerce, and Constantine Georgakis, Vice-President of the Credit Union of Khania, in conference with William L. Tait, field representative of AMAG, are pertinent:[17] "They emphasized, however, during the interview, that in their opinion two major factors

---

[13] H. R. Gallagher, and Others, *Organizational Study of the Ministry of Agriculture*, Civil Government Division, AMAG, 1948, p. 37.

[14] H. R. Gallagher, and Others, *Organizational Study of the Greek Air Ministry*, Civil Government Division, AMAG, 1948, p. 7.

[15] *ibid.*, p. 7. [16] *ibid.*, p. 7.

[17] Wm. L. Tait, Field Report, Island of Crete, AMAG, December 1947, p. 17.

were hindering commercial enterprises: (1) the exorbitant interest charges levied on commercial credits, and (2) the restrictions particularly related to the time factor which were placed by the Government upon the notification of allocations made to this Nomos by the Ministry of National Economy. Mr. Samiotakis produced a folder of such notifications of allocations which had expired due to the short period of time allowed by the Ministry for the submission to them by the importers of the necessary application forms and the establishment of the necessary credits.

"Another difficulty faced by all importers and exporters is the fact that it is necessary for them either to go to Athens personally, or send their Representative in order to obtain import and export permits. Even when they go to Athens the fact that they are Provincials makes it more difficult for them to obtain the required papers than if they were residents in Athens. This practice entails unnecessary trouble and expense."

These are important problems requiring government study and solutions if entrepreneurs in Crete are to do their share in improving the economy and living levels of the island and the nation.

3. Budgeting Procedures

Even the process of budgeting was centralized to an unusual degree in Greece. The allocation of funds for all major items including personnel was made by the central-staff representatives of each ministry. Only small expenses, such as for day labor, supplies, electricity, telephone, bookkeeping, travel, etc., were estimated at the local, nome, or island level. Even typewriters and other such equipment were handled as special cases. Regular employee salaries were made up in the respective ministries in Athens, as they knew all the names and had a personnel section constantly checking on these matters. That little thought was given the budget at the local level was indicated by the fact that budgets were requested only one month before the new fiscal year started—and estimates were always back in Athens within 30 days.

From discussions with government officials, it was evident that the budgeting procedures in Greece were a responsibility of the General Accounting Office, with primary emphasis on the drachma estimates, without annual purging of inefficient or useless projects or inefficient personnel. There was no method (such as the budget might provide) by which departments were encouraged to bring new ideas and projects into competition with old programs and force consideration of alternatives by the Minister and Parliament.

The centralization of accounting was so great that budget estimates and statements of government receipts and expenditures in total or by sources were sent directly to Athens by the ten finance offices in Crete and were unavailable at the island office in Khania.

B. GOVERNMENT IN CRETE

The Council of Ministers nominated (and the King appointed) the Governor-General for Crete. His appointment extended for an indefinite term. He was on the payroll of the Ministry of Interior. Ministerial Directorates operated from Athens through the Governor-General on matters of administration and policy, but not always on technical matters. The Director of the Governorate-General was a career representative of the Ministry of Interior—which gave him rank over other ministry directors in Crete. For all ministries, staff members of each Directorate were employees of the corresponding ministry in Athens, whence came the funds for their salaries and expenses. Pensions on retirement were provided for career employees as civil servants.

As was true at the national level, the services of the Military Governor of Crete and of the judiciary were not regarded as a part of the executive branch represented by the Governorate-General.

The duties of the Governor-General were to act as the government's regional representative and to serve as coordinator of the island directorates of the various ministries. These included agriculture, education, finance, hygiene, justice, public works, reconstruction, social welfare, supplies, transport, and communications. The heads of these departments on the island acted as a Council of Advisers to the Governor-General. The Governor-General was also head of the nomarchs, who were over each nome. A Secretary-General, also a political appointee, worked closely with the Governor-General and assumed his duties when absent.

Crete, as one of the governmental districts in a highly centralized Greek Government, is directly affected by the organization, efficiency, and economy of the various ministries which direct the governmental work of their island representatives.

1. Organization of Ministry of Agriculture in Crete

To provide a clearer picture of how the national ministries functioned at the local level, the organization and functions of one very important ministry with representatives in Crete are described here. A Ministry of Agriculture organization chart to show the flow of administrative responsibility down to the community is presented in Figure 11. This deals with the personnel in only one (but the largest) of the four nomes in Crete. There was an additional "Practical" School of Agriculture at Asomatos in Rethimnon nome with only a director and no professors (in 1948) and a Tree Nursery near Suda Bay with a director.

In general, the agricultural employees were well trained but lacked up-to-date information, supervision, specific goals, and educational contacts with farm people. Applications for positions were made at the Ministry of Agriculture, where the Personnel Committee, the Director-General, and the Secretary-General decided as to qualifications. The Secretary-General decided where appointees would be placed. There were four civil service grades in addition to the Director. The job of the nome agriculturist (at Director grade) was somewhat comparable to that of the county agent in the United States.

Too large a share of the time of the nome agriculturist (agronome) was spent on regulatory and control measures. In Iraklion, the largest nome, the nome agriculturist estimated that 50 per cent of his time was spent on Asia Minor Refugee work, acting as judge and arbiter in disputes; 15 per cent on dacus fly control; 5 per cent in grading agricultural products; 5 per cent in the distribution of fertilizers and seeds; leaving only 25 per cent of his time for real extension education and demonstration. The attitude of farm families toward an official with regulatory powers hampered his educational work. Regulation and education do not mix in Greece, any more than they do in the United States.

2. Nome and Eparchy

Each of the four nomes was governed by a nomarch who was appointed by Athens for an indefinite period. As political head of a nome he was responsible for necessary investigations in behalf of nome citizens appearing for redress of actions of nome representatives of directorates. But the nomarch did not direct the activities of these representatives.

Fig. 11. Organization of the Ministry of Agriculture, Crete, 1948

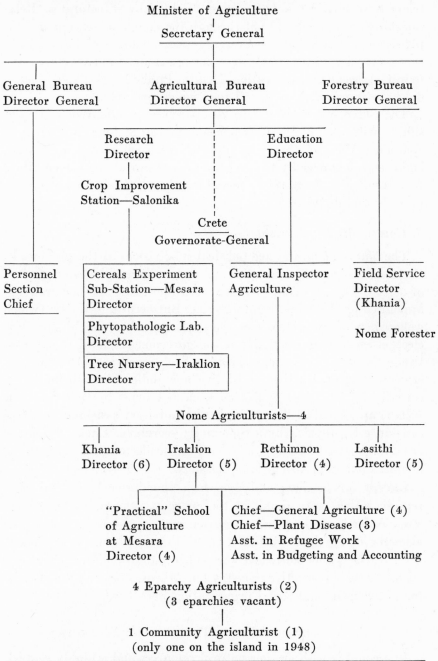

Minister of Agriculture

Secretary General

General Bureau
Director General

Agricultural Bureau
Director General

Forestry Bureau
Director General

Research
Director

Education
Director

Crop Improvement
Station—Salonika

Crete
Governorate-General

Personnel
Section
Chief

Cereals Experiment
Sub-Station—Mesara
Director

General Inspector
Agriculture

Field Service
Director
(Khania)

Phytopathologic Lab.
Director

Nome Forester

Tree Nursery—Iraklion
Director

Nome Agriculturists—4

Khania
Director (6)

Iraklion
Director (5)

Rethimnon
Director (4)

Lasithi
Director (5)

"Practical" School
of Agriculture
at Mesara
Director (4)

Chief—General Agriculture (4)
Chief—Plant Disease (3)
Asst. in Refugee Work
Asst. in Budgeting and Accounting

4 Eparchy Agriculturists (2)
(3 eparchies vacant)

1 Community Agriculturist (1)
(only one on the island in 1948)

Number in ( ) indicates civil service grade.
Source: Dr. Ayontantis, Director Phytopathology, Min. of Agric.; C. Kafatos, Nome Agricultural Director, Iraklion.

Personnel in the nome Branch Services of Directorates (ministries) were civil servants assigned to duty by directorates. Relationships were direct and not through the nomarch—except in supply services. Not all ministries were represented in each nome at any time—especially when there were personnel and fund shortages due to war. Agriculture, Education, Health, Public Works, and Finance did have representatives in all four nomes of Crete.

The island was divided into 20 eparchies or subdivisions (townships), with each of the four nomes made up of four to seven such eparchies. Many of the eparchy functions, such as gendarme post, had been taken over by the larger towns of one of the communities. As a result, the 20 eparchies served mostly as a basis for parliamentary election districts.

3. *Community Government*

The 550 communities are political subdivisions of the province of Crete, consisting of rural areas and one or more villages or clusters of houses. The president or mayor is proposed by the nomarch and appointed by the Ministry of Interior. But according to law (which was suspended by Metaxas in 1936) the president should stand for election every four years. He is the government's local representative in the community and the community's agent in matters of government. He has neither legislative nor judicial responsibility. A council of from three to five men, elected prior to 1936 but now (1948) appointed by the nomarch, gives advisory assistance. Clerical assistance is provided by a community secretary. Each community has a land guard who is paid from funds collected according to the number of trees or size of land holdings.

Except for teachers and policemen (gendarmes), few ministry representatives were found at the eparchy, community, or village level. A few eparchies had an agricultural agent representing the Ministry of Agriculture but most of these positions were vacant. Both teachers and policemen were subject to appointment and dismissal by their respective ministries in Athens. Local responsibilities for government and social organization were few.

C. Government Fiscal Policies and Finances

In a country with meager natural resources and a highly centralized government, fiscal policies and methods of taxation are especially important influences upon the general economy and the amount of national self-help which can be provided for improved living levels.

1. Fiscal Policies

The general fiscal policies in Greece are set forth in the AMAG report of June 1948:[18]

"During the German occupation and the postwar period Greece experienced two ruinous inflations. The first of these culminated at the end of 1944 and resulted in a currency conversion whereby 50 billion old drachmas were exchanged for 1 new drachma, thereby wiping out all bank deposits and drachma savings and leaving with the Greek people a lasting fear of inflation and lack of confidence in their currency.

"Owing in part to the continuing effects of the war and of the German occupation and in part to the present struggle against the bandits in Greece, government expenditures have continued greatly to exceed revenues. The government is unable to borrow money in Greece because the people who have savings are doubtful about its stability and fearful about the future. In consequence any budgetary deficit can be met only by printing new money. In addition any substantial extension of credit for essential loans must be financed by means of the printing press. In spite of careful controls, the amount of currency in circulation increased by 80 per cent during the past year.

"This increase was directly reflected in higher prices. The rate of increase in the monetary supply far exceeded the rate of domestic production and of imports of consumer goods. Because of their fear of the future, manufacturers have held back on production, farmers have hoarded their produce, merchants have avoided building up inventories, and importers have gone slow on purchases abroad.

"Greeks who have savings have hesitated to invest in productive enterprises and have preferred to use their funds for speculation and for recourse to all kinds of hedges and safeguards. The most popular of these is the gold sovereign, which has become a barometer of morale. The heavy demand for highly liquid assets has forced up the prices of those goods which are available, because almost all wholesale transactions are based on the rate at which the proceeds of sale can be converted into gold sovereigns, dollars or other foreign

[18] American Mission for Aid to Greece, *Factual Summary Concerning the American Mission for Aid to Greece.* Athens. June 15, 1948, p. 17.

exchange. Higher wages, salaries and pensions intended to offset higher living costs have only increased the inflationary pressure."

2. National Tax System, Revenues, and Disbursements

In comparison with other Balkan countries, taxes in Greece in 1931-1932 were very high, almost double those levied in neighboring countries. In 1932-1933, the national taxes were 24.4 per cent, or one-fourth of the national income. Local taxes were an additional 1.3 per cent of national income.[19]

More than half of the tax revenue in pre-war years came from indirect taxes which placed a relatively heavier burden on low-income groups than on high-income groups. The sources of these taxes were import duties, levies on tobacco and alcohol, and net profit from state monopolies on such necessities as salt and matches. Stamp duties, entertainment taxes, and transportation duties were the other sources of indirect taxes.

About one-fifth of the pre-war tax revenues were derived from direct taxes on professional income, net income, and gross income, as well as on inheritances, gifts, and dowry property transfers, turnovers, and insurance premiums.

The income tax on salaries and wages was collected annually from the employer at the source. All other income taxes were obtained through individual yearly declarations, payable quarterly. Rates on income from real estate were higher than rates on salaries. Import duties were higher on goods imported from countries without commercial treaties. Export duties were imposed on some articles. Import duties and the tax on tobacco were the two most remunerative taxes.

The net income tax was based on taxable capacity of the individual according to specified income source categories and a complementary tax of a purely personal character on income from any source. The professional tax was based on the presumed (evidential) income of the business, industry, speculative or liberal profession for presumed profits, within certain specified incomes. The gross income tax was levied on income from agriculture and animal breeding and included an acreage tax, a tax on slaughtered animals, currants, tobacco products, olive oil, etc.

[19] American Military Government, *Civil Affairs Handbook on Greece*, sec. 4, "Government Finance." Washington, Armed Forces Services, 1943. Declassified circular 20, January 1946, pp. 2-5.

During the Occupation some taxes were suspended and replaced by others. In 1941-1942 the General Consumption Tax in the form of a Sales Tax and Tax on Commercial Services was imposed. The indirect taxes were not modified much because of the lesser importance of imports, consumption, and transactions.

After liberation the sales tax was abolished, the turnover tax was reimposed with a higher percentage, and extraordinary taxes were imposed to absorb some of the extra profits during and immediately following the Occupation. Even with these increased tax coefficients the direct taxes did not yield budget estimates. Reasons for this were the low rents on buildings, falsifications on new rental rates, loans and dividends lowered by drachma inflation, government restrictions on loans to prevent inflation, fear of investing by investors, and low agricultural gross income because of devastation and lack of supplies for production. But even before the war the state was suspending the tax on agricultural incomes because of "poor" returns. At the time of the survey, commerce and manufacturing seemed to be the only possibilities of increased taxation yield.

A summary of national revenues and expenditures for four fiscal years, 1935, 1937, 1938, and 1939 (1936 not available), indicates the relative importance of the various sources of revenues and types of expenditures (Table 33). During this four-year period the average annual revenue was $126.3 million and the average annual expenditure was $118.9 million (at an exchange rate of 100 drachmas to the dollar).[20]

Almost one-third of the national expenditures was for the Ministry of Finance, one-fourth for War, Navy, and Aviation, and one-ninth for communications. The Ministries of Education, Health, and Interior spent almost equal shares of another fifth of the expenditures. Of the total budget shown for education in 1948 about one-fourth was for fine arts, 3 to 4 per cent for religion, and the remaining 70 per cent for education.

In the fiscal years 1937 and 1938 import duties accounted for one-third of the total tax revenues and one-fourth of all revenues. Consumption taxes were approximately one-fifth of the tax revenue and one-sixth of all Greek Government revenues. Income taxes were only one-tenth and one-fourteenth.

In 1948, according to Mr. Conlon, Civil Affairs Division, AMAG,

[20] American Military Government, *Civil Affairs Handbook on Greece*, sec. 4, "Government Finance," Washington, Armed Forces Services, 1943, Table II, p. 2.

"the cigarette tax is the largest revenue producer, with the customs, turnover, stamp, professional, net income tax, alcoholic, business-enterprise, and luxury taxes following in order. Port charges are terrific, including a tax for dacus-fly control funds, overtime for longshoremen, transport tax for boats and caïques, and pension funds for longshoremen, ships' crews, and claims agents."[21]

In 1948-1949, direct taxes were expected to furnish only one-sixth

TABLE 33. Percentage of revenues and expenditures of Greek Government for stated items (fiscal years of 1935, 1937, 1938, and 1939)

Revenues		Expenditures	
Direct taxes	19.3	Legislative body	0.3
Indirect	46.8	Finance	30.7
Monopolies	5.2	Foreign affairs	1.6
Stamped paper	6.0	Justice	2.9
Posts, teleg., teleph.	3.4	Interior	6.3
State domain	1.1	Communications	11.5
Recoveries, etc.	1.8	Education	7.9
Additional taxes	2.0	National economy	0.7
Sundry revenue	2.8	Agriculture	3.7
Extraordinary receipts	4.0	Public health	7.0
Capital movements	7.6	Army, navy, aviation	27.0
		Railway, labor, marine	.4[a]
Total revenues	100.0	Total expenditures	100.0

a Data for one year only.

Source: American Military Government, *Civil Affairs Handbook on Greece*, sec. 4, "Government Finance," Washington, Armed Forces Services, 1943. Data computed from Table II, p. 2.

of the Greek budget, and indirect taxes about one-third. An additional 11 per cent of the budget was expected from extraordinary taxes, 15 per cent from ECA aid, and 12 per cent from the sale of UNRRA surplus property and other supplies. National defense was allocated a third of the budget, health and social welfare one-seventh, and administration slightly more than half of the total expenditures.[22]

[21] M. Conlon, *Taxation System in Force in Greece, 1947-1948*, Civil Government Division, AMAG; Ministry of Finance ref. no. 211, and L.G.A. diary notes June 30, 1948.
[22] Ministry of Coordination. Quarterly Report of the Government of Greece on Operations under ECA Agreement. Athens, October to December 1948, Tables 3 and 4.

3. National Revenues and Disbursements in Crete[23]

Disbursements through the Public Cashier's Offices in Crete for national government services during the two fiscal years of 1948 and 1949 were twice as much as the collections, according to data secured from the Ministry of Finance in Athens.

Disbursements totalled $8.7 million in 1947-1948 and $9.4 million in 1948-1949, while collections were only $4.9 million in the first period and $3.9 million in the second fiscal year (Table 34). Average collections of approximately $4.4 million were only 49 per cent of

TABLE 34. Collections and disbursements by ministries through public cashier's offices, Crete, fiscal years 1948 and 1949

	Fiscal 1948		Fiscal 1949[a]	
TOTAL COLLECTIONS	$4,937,393	57%	$3,869,899	41%
TOTAL DISBURSEMENTS	$8,697,534	100	$9,446,358	100
Disbursements by ministry:				
Finance		55		44
Exterior (foreign affairs)		*		—
Press		*		*
Justice		4		3
Interior		1		1
Public order		2		9
Supply		1		*
Public works & reconstruction		1		1
Communications (postal, telegraph)		5		5
Transport		*		*
Education and religion		14		13
National economy		*		*
Merchant marine		*		*
Labor		*		*
Agriculture		1		1
Public welfare		3		8
Health		3		3
Army		10		12
Navy		*		*
Air forces		*		*

a Covers period July 1, 1948 to May 31, 1949, only.
* Less than 0.5 per cent.
Source: Compiled from records of General Accounts Department, Ministry of Finance, Athens. Unpublished data, July 1949.

[23] Ministry of Finance, *Expenditures on Island of Crete by Public Cashiers*. Data compiled from General Accounts Department, Athens, by C. Markidis, July 1949.

the average disbursements of $9.0 million during the two-year period.

About half of the disbursements in Crete for the past two fiscal years were spent for the Ministry of Finance, one-seventh for Education and Religion, and about one-tenth for War Services. Ministries of Public Welfare, Public Order, and Posts, Telegraph and Telephone (P.T.T.) each spent an average of 5 per cent of the disbursements. Only 3 per cent each of the disbursements were for the Health and the Justice Ministries in Crete. Although agriculture is the main source of income in Crete, the Ministry of Agriculture spent only 1 per cent of the total disbursements, according to the above figures. Inclusion of the dacus-fly control campaign might increase this expenditure to a total of 2.5 per cent.

Since the duties of the Ministry of Finance included the assessment as well as the collection and disbursement of public funds for the island, some question might be raised as to its present effectiveness and efficiency, since at the time of the survey there was a continuing deficit of more than 50 per cent between receipts and expenditures in Crete. Especially was it pertinent when the total collections of the Ministry of Finance in Crete for all ministries were insufficient to cover even its own ministerial disbursements on the island during this two-year period.

D. COMMUNITY TAX SYSTEM AND REVENUES

The Community Council, including the community president, had the right to impose a tax of not to exceed 4 per cent on all agricultural products grown or raised within the community territory. Usually the tax was 1 or 2 per cent on the principal products, such as olive oil, cereals, citrus fruit, wine, and vegetables.

A list containing all the names of persons liable to taxation, with the amounts to be paid by them, was prepared by the Community Council and sent to the nearest justice of the peace, under whose jurisdiction that particular community came. Copies of the same list were posted at the Community Office and at all the villages included in the community. Unless objections were filed within fifteen days the list became automatically enforceable through the Public Collector's office to which it was forwarded.

In some instances, where the Community Council did not want to wait for every villager's "sweet will" to pay the amount fixed for him, the collection of these taxes was "rented out" or sold at public auction. In one community the bid of 10 million drachmas ($1,000) seemed so inadequate that the community authorities collected the taxes and secured an additional 30 million drachmas ($3,000).

The Community Council also had the right to ask every male villager over eighteen years of age to devote not to exceed ten days per year to work on community projects, such as intercommunity and village streets and fountains. At the same time the Council, subject to nomarch approval, set a redeeming value, per day, of personal labor for those who preferred to pay cash. Other sources of revenue which might be tapped by the Community Council included taxes for using the communal water supply either for irrigation or drinking purposes, for stamping measures and weights used by traders, and for the use of pavements and squares by coffee houses and other business stores. In addition, voluntary contributions were sometimes made.

Additional sources of revenue included the sale of oil from community-owned olive groves, rent from community grazing land (10 to 15 cents per head), and an animal slaughter tax of 4 to 20 cents per head. In the few communities having water systems, a tax of 40 cents per family was levied on outside communal faucets and $1.40 on each faucet in the family home. For the control of the dacus fly, a 1 per cent tax on olive production was collected by the state and utilized in its annual campaign, with a cost in Crete of $80,000 to $160,000 annually. The major source of community revenue, however, was from the tax on olive oil and wheat, in some communities almost the sole source of revenue.

In four of the communities visited in the fall of 1948, budget estimates were being made for the first time since the war—most items to date having been paid for out of special assessments and voluntary contributions. The revenue expected in these communities ranged from $300 to $1,200, of which the Secretary's salary would amount to $50-$250 and representation expenses of the community president to $50-$200. No plans had been made for spending the remainder, except to indicate it would be sufficient to cover only the bare essentials, without school equipment, school repairs, water systems, and road improvements.

The budget for one of the larger communities (1,492 population in 1940, which placed it in the upper one-third in population), Alikianos in Khania nome, showed a revenue and expenditure budget of 8,500,000 drachmas, or $850, for 1947-1948 (Table 35).

About 40 per cent of the revenue of Alikianos community was derived from the tax on agricultural production and an additional 35 per cent from the counter value of personal labor. Administration expenses were more than one-fourth of the total expenditures, and community projects almost two-fifths. Health, hospital, and school expenses were about a fourth of the total expenditures.

In a smaller community (Malaxa, with a population of 426 in 1940) the budget was only $270. The tax on agricultural production provided two-thirds of the revenue, while a fourth came from a legacy and the remainder from the counter value of personal labor. In this

TABLE 35. Revenue and expenditure budget estimates, Alikianos, Crete, April 1, 1947-March 31, 1948 (1940 population: 1,492)

Source or Type	Amount approved by nomarch	Per cent of total
REVENUES		
Rent from communal fields	$ 10	1
Irrigation ditch tax (2 mills per tree)	200	24
Transfer of buildings and state contribution	10	2
Tax on value agricultural production @ 1%	330	38
Counter value of personal labor	300	35
Total revenues	850	100
EXPENDITURES		
Administrative expenses	228	27
Allocation to school subsidy—two schools	110	13
Hospital subsidy and communal doctor salary	79	9
Engineer, records and memorial service	69	8
Community projects:		
Purchase of property	50	6
Water system—new and maintenance	150	18
Sewers and W.C. places	20	2
Cemetery, wall and war dead monument	90	11
Books for communal library	10	1
Ceremony expenses	15	2
Reserve funds balance	29	3
Total expenditures	850	100

Source: C. Markidis. Compiled from typed copy of *Alikianos Community Budget*, Khania, 1948.

community, administrative expenses were a sixth of the total expenditures; community projects (including a road- and bridge-building project) were 60 per cent and health about 10 per cent of the total expenditures. A reserve of 30 per cent of the income was set up.

Unfortunately, similar information was not secured from each of the sample communities, although it was clear that the tax on agricultural production was the largest source of revenue in rural areas. All sources provided less than 70 cents per person for community expenses, of which less than 50 cents per person was available for community projects.

E. Tax System and Revenues in Municipalities

In some of the larger demes or municipalities, the responsibility for collecting the government taxes was divided between the Economic Inspector, as assessor, and the Tax Collector. They were even supplied with different offices to minimize the chance of dishonesty.

In Khania, the capital of Khania nome and the second largest city in Crete (about 34,000 population), the fiscal year began on July 1 of each year. The budget of the municipality, as well as any alteration in it, was subject to the approval of the nomarch. The municipal budget was not assisted by the state through allocations of tax money collected. However, certain municipal taxes were collected by the state services and returned by the Ministry of Interior. After 1945, certain of these municipal taxes, as for example the building tax and professional tax, which were collected together with similar state-imposed taxes, were not returned to the municipalities because certain necessary decisions by the Ministry of Finance had not been issued (as of 1949).

The total revenue budget of about $300,000 for the municipality of Khania in 1948-1949 was about $8.75 for each inhabitant (Table 36). Almost three-fifths of these municipal revenues were budgeted to come from indirect taxes on goods brought in for consumption in Khania (including fish, wheat, animals, and local or Greek merchandise) and from a municipal export tax on olive oil, olive products, and raisins. The other large sources of revenue were from the sale of landed property (10 per cent), fines and miscellaneous revenues (7 per cent), water supply (7 per cent), and outstanding revenues to be collected from past fiscal years (5 per cent). The remaining 12 per cent of the revenues was expected from various other sources.

TABLE 36. Revenues and expenditures budget, Municipality of Khania, Crete, 1948-1949 (1948 population: 35,000)

Category	Amount	Per cent of total
REVENUES		
Ordinary revenues		
Use of municipal property	$ 9,801	3
Town cleaning, water supply, slaughter	37,525	12
Indirect taxes on imports: Greek goods, wheat, etc.	128,560	43
Indirect taxes on exports: olive oil, etc.	42,000	14
Direct taxes and state-collected import taxes	5,852	2
Municipally owned enterprise operations revenue	2,500	1
Fines and outstanding revenues	13,275	5
Extraordinary revenues		
Pensions and miscellaneous interest and fines	20,061	7
Sales of landed property	30,000	10
Cash balance, carried forward	10,000	3
Total revenues	299,574	100
EXPENDITURES		
Regular personnel	24,510	8
Tax-collection expenses	34,050	11
Other administration expenses	23,460	8
Health services	24,200	8
Sewage and water supply	16,700	6
Town cleaning	31,600	11
Other city services, market, fire, slaughter, etc.	29,479	10
Social welfare	7,650	3
Education and culture	3,430	1
Boy Scouts, Girl Guides, and other societies	3,000	1
Town plans and property acquisition	11,200	4
Municipal hall and other building construction	30,000	10
Road building and maintenance	25,500	8
Other municipal projects	15,500	5
Reserve fund	19,295	6
Total expenditures	299,574	100

Source: C. Markidis. Compiled from typed copy of *Khania Municipal Budget for 1948-1949*, Khania, 1949.

More than one-fourth of the budgeted expenses for the municipality of Khania was allocated to administrative expenses, one-third to city services, and more than one-fourth to municipal projects.

Only 2 per cent of the funds was set aside for education and culture (mostly for sports) and 3 per cent for social welfare.

The largest items of expense were "expenses incurred in tax collections," 11 per cent, and town cleaning service, 11 per cent. The beginning of a new municipal hall and other municipal buildings was budgeted to take 10 per cent of the revenue, and a 6 per cent reserve fund was set aside. Other large items of expense included 8 per cent each for health, regular personnel payroll, and road and street maintenance. The water-supply service and "town plans and property acquisition" were allotted 4 per cent each.

A revenue item of considerable importance, amounting to $41,000 (second only to Athens) from road toll taxes in 1947-1948, was not included in the Khania budget statement, as AMAG personnel indicated that reports on the use of these funds by the various municipalities were not available.

F. SOCIAL INSURANCE

Social insurance included such government-guaranteed services as medical care, unemployment benefits, pensions, and limited-time benefits for accident and partial disability. Insurance was compulsory for employees working on a salary or wage basis, except for permanent civil servants, farmers, and employees affiliated with similar insurance agencies, organized prior to IKA. A résumé of past and present government deficits indicated the unlikelihood that any increase in such services—above income from employees and employers (less operating expenses)—would be paid from government surpluses or regular government appropriations in the near future.

The Social Insurance Institute (IKA) was based on a law, Act No. 6298 dated September 24, 1934. It was put into effect in 1937. There were five departments in Social Insurance: Health, Studies, Actuaries, Legal, and Finance.

IKA was relatively new before the war and had no chance to build reserves or acquire property. Consequently progress was interrupted by bankruptcy, according to one of its officials. Although there were 80 security agencies in Greece with large funds and buildings, they were unwilling to join with the Social Insurance Institute. On the other hand, those social insurance groups which went bankrupt during the war, and people with chronic diseases (5,000 tuberculosis cases), were forced on IKA. They had never paid in a cent although they collected from the organization. Likewise, the civil servants who were on a pension and other non-permanent civil servants were forced on IKA for medical care.

While IKA had repaid the early government loans, reserve funds and the capital basis of payments were still low. There were 16,310 persons on pension from Social Insurance funds in all Greece. Over 10,000 persons received a sickness allowance, of which 5,000 were tuberculosis patients. The IKA agency was insuring 750,000 for mixed and medical care only; 330,000 persons for full care, retirement, medical care, appliances (glasses and dentures), and hospital; and 420,000 for medical care only.

The employer contributed 9 per cent and the employee 4 per cent of his wages as a premium. The unemployment benefits were 40 per cent of the salary. Pensions after 65 were $12.50 per month with the same amount for a widow as long as she lived.

The main efforts at the time of the survey were to include all employed people, even to absorbing those in other insured groups. Later, rural people might be included through their agricultural cooperatives. In order to open an agency without too high a cost, 1,000 people had to be available. The Khania branch, which was established in 1910, had 2,500 people insured. Rethimnon and the recently established Ierapetra branch were connected with Iraklion.

About one-third of the cost of operating the program, $4,229,465, was paid for sickness allowances, one-fifth for hospital care, one-seventh each for medical care and administration, and 10 per cent for drugs. Other items of supplies, damages, etc., made up the remainder of the costs.

G. Credit Facilities

Since banking and credit facilities were so closely supervised by the centralized government, it seems appropriate that they be included in the discussion of government services.

The banking and credit facilities consisted of branches of the Bank of Greece, the Agricultural Bank of Greece, branches of five commercial banks in Athens, local cooperative credit associations, and private lenders. The branch banks were in the nome capitals and larger towns. The 427 credit cooperatives were found in various communities scattered over the island. These credit cooperatives were primarily local commodity loan associations.

1. *Commercial Banks*

Five commercial banking concerns—National Bank of Greece, Bank of Athens, Commercial Bank of Greece, Ionian Bank, Ltd., and Popular Bank—operated sixteen branches in Crete from their head offices in Athens. Of these branches four each were in Khania and Iraklion, three in Rethimnon, two each in Ay. Nikolaos and Ierapetra, and one in Sitia. These commercial banks served the business community and made loans to individuals.

The Bank of Greece, with a branch in each nome capital, functioned as the government control bank in issuing currency and credit and in determining controls. At one time the National Bank of Greece functioned in this capacity, but at the time of the survey it was functioning as a regular private commercial bank. As such it had six branches, in Sitia and Ierapetra in addition to the four nome capitals.

The total investments of the five branches of the National Bank of Greece in Crete on Dec. 31, 1938 were about $2,486,475 (100 drachmas to $1). This was approximately 2 per cent of the total assets of the National Bank of Greece.[24] On Dec. 31, 1948, the total investments in six branches in Crete were $2,199,660 (10,000 drachmas to $1), also 2 per cent of the total assets of the National Bank of Greece.[25] The percentage decrease in investments in Khania and Rethimnon from 1938 was made up by a doubling in Sitia and Ay. Nikolaos and the addition of the Ierapetra branch, established in 1940.

For comparison, the Khania branch of the Ionian Bank, Ltd., had one-sixth as many assets as the Khania branch of the National Bank of Greece in 1938 and one-fourth as many in 1948. Data on other banks were not made available.

Interest rates on commercial paper were 10 per cent during the first six months of 1948 but were raised to 12 per cent by government regulation in July 1948 in an attempt to control inflation. Additional rulings required that loans be repaid in full every two months, later changed to thirty days. Certain charges were involved in these renewals—similar to American short-term finance company loans—which raised the annual interest rates to a reported 40 per cent or more. This placed a heavy burden upon the business com-

[24] National Bank of Greece, *Annual Report*, 1938, Athens, p. 48 and Letter 109103.
[25] National Bank of Greece, *Annual Report*, 1948, Athens, pp. 50-51.

munity and purchasers who had to finance merchandise through bank loans. Since agricultural loans could be obtained at considerably lower interest rates through the Agricultural Bank, the commercial banks made few, if any, loans of this type. No agricultural loans were shown on the National Bank of Greece Statement for December 31, 1948, and very few for 1938.

Interest rates on long-time loans have been high in Greece for many years. For example, the Iraklion Port Fund obtained a twenty-nine-year loan of about $900,000 in 1927 from the National Bank of Greece at 9 per cent.[26]

Most transactions, including the payment of salaries to government personnel, were in cash. The time required to cash checks, the costs of cashing checks at any other than the issuing branch, the delay caused by mail delivery of customer-withdrawal notification to other branches, and the "morning only" banking hours and many holidays all put a premium on "cold cash" transactions. With inflation and the use of only 10,000-drachma ($1.00) and 20,000-drachma ($2.00) bills, satchels were needed for any sizable transaction. To add confusion, small change of 100-, 500-, and 1,000-drachma were also in bills of about the same size as the larger denominations.

Bank-book entries of deposits and withdrawals and check-book stubs were the only evidences available to the customer for record-keeping, as cancelled checks were held by the bank. Deposit slips and checks to be cashed had to be initialed by two or three bank officials before action was taken by the bank teller. This caused delay, even with the limited number of check transactions. All record-keeping was in longhand. An interest rate of 1½ per cent was paid on checking accounts semi-annually. Important decisions could rarely be made by the local bank manager but had to be referred to Athens. Over-centralization of authority reduced efficiency in the credit field, too.

2. Agricultural Credit

The Agricultural Bank of Greece was formed in 1929 (under E. Venizelos' guidance) as a public service with 2 million gold pounds to make loans to farmers through cooperatives. All this gold was lost during the war, and at the time of the survey the bank was being refinanced through the Bank of Greece.

[26] Gardner Richardson, U.S. Commercial Attaché, Athens, in letter dated Feb. 7, 1928 to Director of Bureau of Foreign and Domestic Commerce, Washington.

The Agricultural Bank of Greece had eight offices in Crete—at Khania, Vamos, Rethimnon, Iraklion, Moires, Ay. Nikolaos, Sitia, and Ierapetra. They employed 381 people, of whom 161 were permanent employees, 167 temporary employees, and 53 laborers.

The services of the Agricultural Bank in Crete were similar to the government facilities for agricultural credit to American farmers, as follows: (a) Short-term loans: for farm operations, such as seasonal loans for seed, fertilizer, spray material, etc., at 6 per cent for members of cooperatives and 7 per cent for nonmembers—repayable at harvest time (similar to Production Credit Association Loans); (b) Intermediate credit: for livestock, bees, silkworms, machinery, and small irrigation works—at 7 per cent for members and 8 per cent for nonmembers, for one to four years, and 7 per cent for Union of Cooperatives (similar to the intermediate credit loans made by the Production Credit Associations); (c) Long-term loans: for land, olive presses, buildings, and larger irrigation works, at 7 per cent to individual members or cooperatives and 8 per cent to nonmembers for longer periods of four to fifteen years (similar to Bank of Cooperatives loans); (d) Warehouse loans: for storage on farm or in warehouse of olive oil, carobs, raisins, and wine at 7 per cent to Union of Cooperatives and 8 per cent to the cooperatives (similar to Commodity Credit loans); (e) Co-op loans: to Wine Growers Association and other cooperatives needing financial credit (similar to Bank of Cooperatives credit).

Loans on houses in villages (costing $200-$1500 per room) were handled by a separate land bank similar to the Federal Housing Administration in the United States.

Fear of the future was clearly reflected in these interest rates higher on the longer time loans than on the short-term loans.

Since by law the Agricultural Bank loans were first liens, commercial bank loans were second liens, and private loans were third liens, there was little competition for the agricultural loans from private or commercial credit sources.

Seven branches of the Agricultural Bank of Greece (Iraklion data not available) made loans between September 1, 1947 and August 31, 1948, totaling about $4,500,000. About one-third of these were short-term loans and one-sixth medium- and long-term loans, leaving one-half for financing agricultural institutions, according to figures available from four of the branches. Chattel mortgages for fertilizers, sprays, and seeds were among the short-term loans.

According to the survey, 57 per cent of the farmers had chattel mortgages or unsecured loans, averaging $72. Almost half the chattel loans were under $40 each and 78 per cent were less than $120 each. Only 12 per cent of such loans were over $160 each. According to the farmers the rate of interest on these loans varied from 4 to 12 per cent, with over half (56 per cent) of the loans at 8 per cent. Almost one-fourth of the loans earned 9 to 12 per cent interest rates and only one-twentieth less than 6 per cent interest. The average rate of interest on chattel loans was 7.9 per cent. Ninety-three per cent of these chattel mortgages were secured from the Agricultural Bank, 5 per cent from Agricultural Credit Cooperatives, and 1 per cent each from banks and private individuals.

As is true in many small land-holding areas with owner operators, most of the farmers had never had a land mortgage. Eighty-eight per cent of the farmers in Crete had not had a mortgage and 96 per cent did not have one at the time of the survey. The average mortgage of those who had them was $184 at an average interest rate of 6.7 per cent. This interest rate, which averaged lower than that for chattel mortgages, probably reflected the lower pre-war interest rates. (See Appendix 5, Tables A78 and A79.)

Sometime during the past, another 8 per cent of the farmers surveyed had placed a mortgage against their land. Of these, one-third had paid off the mortgage during the war or in the post-war period, 1942-1947, one-third in 1938-1940, one-sixth in 1935-1937, and the other sixth in 1915-1920. Three-fourths of the land mortgages were with the agricultural banks and commercial banks and about one-fifth with private individuals.

Warehouse loans and cooperative association loans were available from the Agricultural Bank to the 302 cooperatives. A third of these cooperatives handled or processed the olive crop, one-fifth wine, one-sixth citron (virtually inactive in 1948), and one-twelfth raisins and cheese. Five per cent of the cooperatives obtained loans for land improvement, including irrigation and drainage, and the remainder serviced those engaged in fishing, bee raising, and undefined categories. These cooperative associations together with the 427 cooperative credit associations included as members 61,001 heads of families, 53 per cent of all household heads on the island, and about two-thirds of those classified as farm or sub-farm household heads. (See Appendix 5, Table A95.)

H. Prices and the General Economy

Some effects upon costs of living by government fiscal policies and taxing methods, discussed earlier, are reflected in the trends of prices during the pre-war and post-war periods. National income per capita in Greece indicates that the relative economic output per person is low in comparison with the peoples of other countries.

1. Price Trends

Some indication of the recent trends in prices in Greece and Crete, in comparison with those of other specified countries, is shown in the cost of living index for 1945 to 1948 in Table 37.[27]

TABLE 37. Post-war trends in cost of living index for specified countries, 1945-1948 (1937 = 100)

Country	Cost of living index			
	1945	1947	Jan. 1948	Sept. 1948
United States	125	155	164	170
United Kingdom	132	*	104	108
Sweden	145	150	157[a]	160
Switzerland	153	159	164	163
Holland	176	199	202	—
Belgium[b]	333	339	362	399
France[c]	436	1,207	1,663	2,132
Italy	—	4,575	4,842	4,910
Greece and Crete	1,896	17,463	22,807	25,130

* Since the second half year 1947, new index, basis June 17, 1947 = 100.
a March 1948.
b Retail price index.
c Price index of food articles in Paris.
Source: National Bank of Greece, *Annual Report*, 1948, Athens, 1948, p. 66.

The cost of living index has risen in all countries since 1945 and 1947, with the smallest increases in Switzerland, Sweden, Holland, United Kingdom, Belgium, and the United States. In contrast, the cost of living index has risen tremendously in France, Italy, and Greece. The largest rise since pre-war has taken place in Greece.

In Greece, however, there had been another tremendous increase (about 21 times) in the cost of living index between 1914 and December 1937, from 100 to 2,203 (Table 38).

27 National Bank of Greece, *Annual Report*, 1948, p. 66.

TABLE 38. Trends in cost of living in Greece, 1933 to 1937 and 1945 to 1948 (pre-war period, 1914 = 100 and post-war period, 1938 = 100)

Pre-war period		Post-war period		
Year	Price index	Year		Price index
1933	1,904	1945		1,896
1934	1,937	1946		14,350
1935	1,957	1947		17,463
1936	2,027	1948	(Jan.)	22,807
1937	2,185		(June)	24,347
			(Dec.)	26,560

Source: *First period*: Ministry of National Economy, *Official Statistics*, Athens, 1938. *Second period*: National Bank of Greece, *Annual Report*, 1948, Athens, p. 66.

A more concrete example of the change in prices which has taken place in Crete since pre-war days is shown in Table 39. These data show the ratio of post-war to pre-war retail prices for many items produced and/or purchased by the farmers of Crete.

Although the price of a majority of these items has increased between 300 and 400 times, there are a few, such as rice, bread, eggs, coffee, and macaroni, which have increased considerably more than the average. It will be noted that these are all imported items. On the other hand, sugar is also imported, but increased only the average amount in price. Charcoal, kerosene, beef, and milk showed the smallest increases. Most of the island-produced items, except cereals for bread, show about the average price increase. The smaller increase in milk may be due to the rationed supplies of tinned milk to babies and nursing mothers, as well as the plentiful supplies of evaporated and dried milk in the markets.

In periods of inflation, some prices rise faster than others; wages usually lag behind the rise in living costs. The lag is apt to be still greater in a country like Crete, where there was a surplus of labor, even in normal times; where factories were small and used relatively few persons, and these unskilled and unorganized; and where there was a scarcity of raw materials, fuel, and power. A high percentage of home ownership, together with rent controls, had kept shelter costs relatively stable for a large percentage of the households. However, families with war-damaged properties had found repair and replacement costs increased three-fold. Instances of "extra-charge" black market rental rates were also reported.

Table 39. Retail prices of specified items, pre-war and post-war, Crete

Items	Retail prices		Ratio, Post-war to pre-war prices 1949 to 1933-37
	Pre-war 1933-37 average	Post-war January 1949	
	(drachmas per oke)		
Rice	14.6	13,312	912
Bread	7.6	4,392	575
Coffee	76.6	36,864	481
Macaroni	15.8	6,963	441
Potatoes	6.6	2,867	431
Beans	13.3	5,632	424
Olive oil	40.0	14,336	358
Sugar	20.6	7,168	347
Eggs	4.7	2,048	431
Butter	103.8	40,960	394
Fish (good)	22.3	8,806	395
Beef	34.1	13,312	300
Lamb	48.8	18,432	378
Milk	10.4	3,123	301
Firewood	1.4	614	432
Charcoal	3.8	717	187
Kerosene	20.2	2,048	102

Source: Ministry of Supply, "Special Report to Crete Survey," Khania, 1949, private communication.

But living costs for food, clothing, and replacements for supplies and equipment had shown the greatest rise in comparison with wages. The long occupation during the war resulted in the need for replacement of many items of equipment and supplies which were lost, stolen, requisitioned, or utilized for other purposes. Under such conditions, persons working either for the government or for firms whose incomes or profits increased very little had suffered most during this period of inflation. While daily wage rates for farm laborers increased, some reduction in the number of days worked was reported. Because of lack of materials this same situation prevailed in some of the industrial plants.

By 1948, prices for industrial products for use in agriculture had risen 41 per cent more since 1939 than those for agricultural products (Table 40); and prices of agricultural consumer goods had risen 30 per cent more than agricultural prices. On the other hand, agricultural prices had risen only six per cent more than the cost of living index during this ten-year period.

After a complete collapse of prices during the war, price inflation during post-war years was large. Inflation of prices of articles consumed by farmers defeated the favorable position which the farmer might otherwise have enjoyed through higher prices of what he sold. With relatively high fixed charges in terms of fertilizers and living costs, small volume of production, reduced market outlets, and little produce actually marketed, the average farmer of Crete was not able to profit from war and post-war inflation as were farmers in areas where commercial farming was dominant.

TABLE 40. Price index of agricultural products, agricultural consumer goods, and industrial products for agricultural use, Greece, 1939, 1946-1948

Year	Cost of living	Agricultural products	Agricultural consumer goods	Industrial products used in agriculture
1939	100[a]	100	100	100
1945	1,896	—	—	—
1946	14,350[b]	15,130	19,250	28,530
1947	17,463	21,350	25,030	29,340
1948	25,156[c]	26,690	34,680	37,610

a 1938.

b Average of final month in each quarter.

c Average of 8 months March and June-December.

Source: Ministry of Coordination, *Quarterly Report of the Government of Greece on Operations under ECA Agreement*, Athens, 1949 unpublished version (October-December 1948), Table 30.

2. *The General Economy of Greece*

In an article in 1947-1948, "Greece Puts Us to the Test," George Polk, the American newspaper reporter who lost his life in line of duty, stated: "Greece and poverty have always been sisters is an old proverb. Even in 1939 Greece was near the bottom of Europe's standard of living."[28] Data from two recent publications[29] give some indication of relative per capita incomes for Greece and selected European neighbors. The figures for Crete have been estimated from survey data (Table 41). While there are some differences between

[28] George Polk, "Greece Puts Us to the Test," *Harpers Magazine*, 1948, pp. 529-536.

[29] Seymour E. Harris, *The European Recovery Program*, 1948, Table 8, p. 88. Ministry of Coordination, *Quarterly Report of the Government of Greece on Operations Under ECA Agreement*, Athens, October-December, 1948, Table 14.

TABLE 41. National income per capita in Greece and selected countries,
1939 and 1946

(dollars per capita)

Country	1939[a]	1939[b]	1946[b]
England and Wales[a]			
United Kingdom[b]	$ 481	$ 468	$ 653
Switzerland	448	445	—
Sweden	430	436	635
Norway	372	279	279
Denmark	336	338	562
Germany	328	520	—
Ireland	259	—	—
Belgium	257	261	517
Netherlands	—	338	321
Iceland	250	—	—
France	244	283	214
Finland	189	—	—
Austria	165	166	88
USSR	154	509	—
Czechoslovakia	137	134	232
Italy	132	140	94
Hungary	112	125	109
Bulgaria	110	—	—
Poland	94	95	70
Greece	79	136	—

[a] Source: Ministry of Coordination, *Quarterly Report of the Government of Greece on Operations under ECA Agreement*, Athens, October-December, 1948. From a manuscript translation. Table 14.

[b] Source: Seymour Edwin Harris, *The European Recovery Program*, Harvard University Press, 1948. Table 14, p. 88.

the pre-war estimates from these two sources, both agree that national income per capita in Greece was low in comparison with most countries in Europe. Since mainland Greece is industrialized relatively more than Crete, income per capita for all Greece would be higher than for Crete—estimated at $79 for the former and $55 for the latter in 1939. In 1948, the average cash income per capita in Crete was estimated at $74.

While national income data for the Island of Crete are not available, estimates of total income based on the household income data should be helpful. Based on the average household cash income of $300 for family use obtained in the Crete Survey, the total cash income for the estimated 115,000 households would amount to $35 mil-

lion in 1947. In view of an estimated $7 million of national, munici-
pal, and local taxes paid by the people of Crete, this estimated income
appears reasonable. Pre-war estimates for Greece showed taxes to be
about 25 per cent of national income. While post-war tax rates were
higher than pre-war, a large percentage of farmers were still ex-
empted from paying taxes in 1947. The Crete Survey indicated that
only half the farmers paid land taxes in 1947. Prices and incomes
also increased faster in the post-war period than did taxes. If the
value of home produce were included, the total island income would
approximate $55 million for 1947.

In his article, Mr. Polk pointed out some of the problems facing
the Greek economy in 1948:

"Greece's post-war problem, complicated by wartime destructions,
would be severe enough if Greece's economy would be bent dynami-
cally to the task of solving the nation's crisis. But almost the exact
opposite is true. . . . So the wealthy are concentrating on protecting
their money, and their methods happen to be those most detrimental
to the country's recovery. . . . Such methods are easy because Greek
economy for so long has been tightly controlled. . . . The only sphere
in which this two per cent is not dominant is land ownership—a result
of the Venizelos policy following the first world war. Greece became
a country of small holdings . . . distributed land plots to hundreds
of thousands of families.

". . . but Greece remains a country of big business. A person cannot just start building a factory or organizing an export-import
firm, a government permit is required . . . and has a way of getting
only to the 'right people.'

"Although Greece is poverty-stricken nationally, Athens stores
are stuffed with luxury items. Prices . . . are among the highest in
the world. . . . Shopkeepers do not want to sell. . . . Turnover is a
less enticing gamble than holding items and waiting for inevitably
higher prices . . . *portability* is a vital factor in the economy. *Con-
vertibility* is equally important. . . .

"As the American Mission headed by Paul Porter reported: 'There
exists a wide disparity in living standards and income throughout
Greece. Profiteers, traders, speculators, and black marketeers thrive
in wealth and luxury—a problem which no government has met effectively. At the same time, the masses of people live on a bare subsistence. . . .

"During the past year a currency control committee, imposed by

America and Britain, has been battling with this problem, trying to get Greek-held foreign exchange into use to improve Greece's internal situation. . . .

"The committee's effectiveness is not yet fully evident, but 1946 afforded a good indication of need for the committee. During that year Greece spent drachmae to buy $145,000,000 in foreign exchange. Of this sum $141,000,000 went into luxury items, deposits of money in foreign banks, purchase of property outside Greece, and other activities that were nonproductive so far as the internal Greek economy was concerned.

"Only $4,000,000 of the $145,000,000 went for machines, parts, and other equipment desperately needed to rebuild Greece's industrial plant. . . . Few Greeks are willing to invest in factory equipment or mining machinery because these require too long for amortization. Also such items are too heavy to be taken away physically 'when trouble begins'. . . .

"The arrival of the American Aid Mission, headed by Dwight P. Griswold, has not greatly eased the internal insecurity of the country. . . .

"Certainly such a program is necessary for achievement of the American objective of 'saving democracy' in Greece. In 'saving democracy' we must quench the fires of both the extreme right and the extreme left to give the great majority of the democratic-minded Greek population some faith in their future. . . .

"The American economic aid program can be built successfully only on a broad, moderate political foundation. However, in the time remaining between now and June 30, 1948, the Griswold Mission will be able to make no more than a start on Greece's necessary rehabilitation. In general terms the American aid program will attempt to: (1) equip the Greek army completely (almost two-thirds of our $300,000,000 will go for this purpose); (2) repair Greek roads; (3) continue wreckage-clearing projects at Piraeus, Salonika, and Volos (cargo handling costs are among the world's highest); (4) remove the landslides blocking the vital Corinth canal; (5) reconstruct factories so as to save foreign exchange, reduce prices on a few textile supplies, and obtain small shipments of materials for export; and (6) back efforts to achieve government administrative reforms. . . . No matter how great the accomplishments of the Griswold Mission, they will no more than beautify certain spots in the war-shattered, impoverished, confused country of Greece. . . . The one element necessary to real Greek recovery—the continuity of a long-term program—is missing."

These statements of George Polk may and probably do present a distorted picture, but such charges were common in the corridor chatter, the individual conference, the group discussions of the general economic problems facing Greece at the time the survey was made. They suggest that economic uncertainty and political insecurity due to the international political situation were basic causes of low capital investment by Greek businessmen, excessive liquidity, and flight of capital. It is a price which any freedom-loving people might expect to pay under similar conditions. Perhaps it would be unfair to expect any change in the Greek situation until some solution is found for the basic problems. In the meantime, these practices were retarding Crete in its attempt to reconstruct and develop itself politically and economically.

In the four years since Mr. Polk wrote his article the American aid program has proceeded. The Greek army has stopped the guerrilla warfare in Greece, the Corinth Canal has been cleared, government reforms are under way, harbor-clearing projects are making progress, roads are being repaired and reconstructed. But other basic problems are yet to be resolved.

I. Impact of Government on Economic Activity and Improvement

Certainly a government has important responsibilities which it must accept in a country distraught by civil war, political instability, inflation, reduced industrial and agricultural production, flight of capital, and high interest rates; and with part of its population refugees from their home communities.

Even in pre-war times, the Greek Government faced important economic problems as indicated by these excerpts from reports presented by local groups during the Crete Survey:

". . . commercial and industrial credit . . . is very restricted because in the allocation of the limited funds, commercial and industrial centers in Athens and Piraeus take a preponderant and privileged place."[30]

". . . a reduction of the excessive charges in both imports and ex-

[30] Iraklion Chamber of Commerce and Industry, Protocol No. I-1548, May 6, 1948.

ports, is necessary . . . so that cost of goods would be equalized to that in other districts."[31]

"In addition to the physical and basic economic factors which retard production, there are other conditions restricting output which must be eliminated. Local capital is available to industry only in limited amounts and at exorbitant rates of interest. There are restrictive laws and government regulations which discourage production. There are various taxes which have the same effect. The Mission is working with the Greek Government and Greek industrialists in a joint effort to bring about conditions in which industry can expand and make its contribution to a strong and healthy economy.

"A serious handicap to industrial rehabilitation and expansion in Greece is a shortage of technical manpower. The vocational training system in the prewar period was inadequate, and such training programs as did exist were largely stopped during the war and occupation. A sound and progressive system of vocational and industrial training is essential if Greek industry is to expand. A training program has been developed by the Mission and a proposed law providing for the necessary governmental action has been drafted and submitted to the Greek Government, with a recommendation for early enactment by the Parliament."[32]

Through precepts and political discussions the government can develop attitudes among the people either of providing self-help or of depending upon "come-and-get-it" aid from both their own government and outside agencies or governments. With years of Greek Relief, Red Cross Aid, UNRRA, AMAG, and now ECA funds, it is not surprising that Greeks and Cretans look to outside aid as a normal form of income and relief from internal economic burdens. In view of their past history and aid to their Allies in two recent wars, they feel that such aid is deserved. As a native Cretan expressed it: "The problem of reconstruction is a tremendously difficult problem and no two experts will agree on it. Greeks with their fertile imagination, instead of finding a practical solution for this vital problem, ask for the impossible with the result that nothing may be attained ultimately. Take for instance the Memorandum addressed by the Nome of Rethimnon to The Rockefeller Foundation. The whole Nome has a population of 70,000 inhabitants and they fixed

[31] *ibid.*
[32] American Mission for Aid to Greece, *A Factual Summary Concerning the American Mission for Aid to Greece.* June 14, 1948, p. 15.

the amount needed for reconstruction at 600,000,000,000 drachmae, almost 65,000,000 dollars, or nearly 1,000 dollars per person."

Granted that help must come from abroad and that Greece cannot carry her burden of reconstruction alone, the government officials have a responsibility for developing attitudes among the people about the relative importance of accepting outside aid for reconstruction jobs and the need for local initiative.

During 1948-1950, under the guidance of ECA, a new sense of responsibility for self-determination and a new conception of self-help were being fostered. Programs and plans were being developed by Greek personnel with only advisory assistance from American specialists. The effect of this method should be evident in the results to be obtained.

J. Summary

In ancient times, Greece was a leader among nations in the development of law and democratic ways. During the late medieval and much of modern times, Greece and Crete were under the yoke of foreign powers with little opportunity for developing their own political and social controls. Consequently an attitude of dependence upon others for decision-making and action in regard to community programs and projects has developed, even though the desire for freedom from foreign domination has lingered through the centuries.

While the framework for a democratic, locally-controlled government exists in Crete and Greece, a decade of dictatorship followed by war has paralyzed its use. Ways and means to provide for local elections and for more local responsibility, both inside the government, through its field staff, and outside the government among the people, constitute a major problem facing the Greek nation and the Cretan people. The Greek Government is faced with the dilemma of increased pressures for local self-government at the same time that it is receiving larger numbers of requests for central government assistance.

Short hours, low pay, large numbers of political appointees, and over-staffing to reduce unemployment—all these tend to increase inefficiency in the government and become both a cause and an effect of a dulled social conscience among many officials. Whether the handicaps of over-centralization, duplication, over-staffing, incompetence, and inefficiencies can be remedied will depend upon the ability of competent political leaders in all active parties to reorganize the government, clarify functions, assign responsibilities, and develop a core of conscientious, hard-working, competent civil servants with a desire to serve the public. Closer contact with the people by officials at all levels of government is greatly needed.

National revenues are largely from indirect taxes. One-half of the national government disbursements in recent years have been made by the Army and Finance ministries—two of the fifteen ministries in the cabinet. In Crete, the expenditures by the Finance Ministry personnel alone were equal to all tax revenues collected for the national government in 1948 and 1949, and amounted to one-half of the total national government expenditures in Crete. A high percentage of revenues has been used for administrative expenses rather than for services to the people.

Most of the community revenues for local government were derived at the time of the survey from taxes (1 to 4 per cent) on agricultural production and the counter value of personal labor on community improvements. With an annual tax of less than $0.60 per person for the local community budget, income was not sufficient to provide adequate community facilities. In the city of Khania the budget of $9 per capita in 1949 came largely from the indirect gross-income type of taxes and road tolls. Budgets at all levels needed revision to meet the financial realities in Greece.

Briefly, the major problems in government in Crete largely originate at the national level. However, there is much to be done in developing local initiative and responsibility, with less dependence upon the national government for project planning and execution. Taxing methods and credit facilities need study in order to find ways of encouraging the formation of capital and its use for the most productive purposes. To a large extent, over-all improvement in the general economic situation in Greece and Crete is dependent upon national and international political stability, which would restore the confidence of the people in their government.

CHAPTER 10

AGRICULTURE

CONSIDERATION of the agriculture of Crete during earlier civilizations indicates that relatively little change has occurred in the agricultural economy and in crop and livestock production since Minoan times.[1]

A. BRIEF RÉSUMÉ OF AGRICULTURE IN EARLIER TIMES[2]

In the mythology of Crete, the great importance of the goat and the honey bee was evident. Zeus himself was raised on goat's milk and honey—the honey to keep him from crying, so that his father, Cronus, would not hear him. Crete became known as the "land of milk and honey." This attitude of semi-reverence of the Greek people toward the goat, as well as information on climate, land, and land cover, may help to explain the relative importance of the goat in the present agricultural economy. Similarly, the story that the Hellenes sprang from the rocks thrown over the shoulders of Deucalion and Pyrrha provides the Greek people with a unique attitude of semi-reverence toward their rocky landscape. The Cretans are as proud of their rocks as any American Midwesterner is of the depth of his black soil. Land without rocks has an extra barren look to the Greek.

Recent excavations of the Minoan palaces in Crete provide concrete evidence of the agricultural production of that civilization 3500-1100 B.C. Carbonized barley, peas, and wheat have been found in these remains. Large olive oil jugs were numerous. The frescoes and art work indicate that honey, goat's milk, figs, and pomegranates were common at that time. In spite of their devotion to the sacred bull, it is believed that the indigenous short-horned ox, the swine, and the goat were the animals most commonly slaughtered. Except for the vineyards and some of the newer fruits and vegetables, the present type of agricultural production is not very different from that

[1] Because of the limited amount of information obtained, the discussion of forestry and fisheries has been, except for a few references in this chapter, limited to that contained in Chapter 4.

[2] Helen Sdrin, Professor Petrakis, and G. S. Naxakis, *Crete, A Glimpse at its Development from the Neolithic Era to the Present.* Unpublished manuscript, New York, The Rockefeller Foundation, 1949. Also miscellaneous references in Appendix 4.

of the Minoans. The long-handled sickle of that early day would seem to be even more efficient than the short-handled sickle used by Cretan women today.

During the Roman times, 67 B.C. to A.D. 330, the Mesara Plain was known as the "Granary of Rome" and 1,000 years later under the Venetians as the "Breadbasket of Venice." The importance of the island's cereal production for the eastern half of the Mediterranean seems clearly evident. During the Saracen, Egyptian, and Turkish periods little is known about the agriculture of Crete. But a study of the agriculture in Minoan, Venetian, and recent times suggests that little change has taken place. Exceptions are new products such as potatoes, tomatoes, citrus fruits, deciduous fruits (except pears, which seem more native to this area than many others), and certain vegetables. Perhaps other products developed in much the same way as the Sultana raisin, the production of which received great impetus when the Greeks, repatriated from Asia Minor in the 1920's, brought both "know how" and improved varieties to the Iraklion area.

While Cretan agriculture seems basically the same today in type of crop and livestock production and in methods of production as it was forty centuries ago, history suggests that many changes have occurred in the forests of Crete. The writings of Pliny, Homer, and others indicate that Crete may have been the home of the cypress. Some writers indicate that the island was covered with cypress. Others suggest that tall cypress trees made it possible for the Minoans to build the ships with which to develop the trade that made them known as the Cretan Sea Kings in the middle of the second millennium B.C. Most archaeologists believe that the immense beams and columns in the Minoan Palaces at Knossos and Phaestos were made of cypress.

But the wars between towns and cities during the Doric era, the hundreds of revolutions during the Roman, Saracen, Venetian, and Turkish periods all led to the use of forest fires, with which to rid an area of the enemy or of the guerrillas.

Little is known of fish production in ancient times, but there are evidences that during Minoan times this great seafaring nation was well supplied with the products of the sea. Under the Doric, Roman, and Venetian domination, however, the people of Crete became little more than serfs and agricultural workers for others. They had little reason and less opportunity to keep in contact with the sea. Consequently, the island has become known in recent centuries as a place inhabited by "agricultural people who do not know the sea." With dry stream beds in summer, only one small fresh-water lake, and rough waters for deep, off-shore fishing, conditions are not favorable for the development of amateur fishing in small boats.

B. Resources in Agriculture

The physical resources are here briefly reviewed from Chapter 4, but the human and capital resources are presented more in detail in relation to their effect upon agricultural production on the island.

1. Physical Resources

While wide variations in temperature and rainfall are found between various districts of the island, the coastal-plain areas are characterized by subtropical temperatures, heavy winter rains, and dry summers. A very limited acreage of land is irrigated.

The soils of Crete which are suitable for cultivation are limited in acreage. A large percentage of them, although "rich" in potassium, are lacking in nitrogen, available phosphorus, and the proper percentage of calcium carbonate for good crop production. Some of the best soils on the island lack water for irrigation at the present time.

2. Human Resources

In "underdeveloped" areas, a large percentage of the population is engaged in agriculture and a large proportion of such persons are underemployed.

a. *Persons engaged in agriculture.* In the rural communities of Crete, more than three-fourths of the household heads were found to be in agriculture, forestry, and fisheries or in agriculture with some other occupation as subsidiary income. But if women and children were included in the nonlabor force under their primary occupation of housework or attending school, less than one-fourth of the total population was actually occupied in agriculture as farmers, farm managers, farm laborers, unpaid farm workers, or part-time farmers.

Among the estimated 114,750 households in Crete, about 52,000 household heads stated that they were farmers and an additional 40,000 declared another occupation but raised some crops, livestock, or both. These latter households, called "sub-farms," had only 12 per cent of the total acreage in farms but had one-third of the sheep, one-fourth of the goats and donkeys, one-fifth of the poultry, one-seventh of the swine and rabbits, and nearly all the cows kept for milk only.

About half of the household heads in the sub-farm group either did their own housework, were unable to work, or were farm laborers. Another fourth of them were service workers and craftsmen. Even two-thirds of the professional workers and half of the proprietor-manager group were in this sub-farm group, carrying on some type of agricultural activity—primarily for home use—in addition to their main occupation.

In the rural communities over two-thirds of the people who worked (classified as being in the labor force) were engaged in agriculture. Almost two-fifths of the rural labor force were occupied as farmers, farm managers, or farmers with some additional occupation, and one-seventh each as farm laborers and unpaid farm workers.

b. *Utilization of labor on farms.* The average farm operator in Crete worked for some part of 201 days during the year 1947, and family members worked on 152 days. On a full eight-hour workday basis, which they considered normal, these figures would probably be reduced to about 160 and 110 days respectively. Though these figures seem high for the amount of farm land and the volume of business, they were the best estimates of the farmers themselves.

The majority of farmers (55 per cent) indicated an eight-hour workday in addition to time out for midday meal and siesta, although one-sixth of them indicated a ten-hour workday and a fifth of them stated nine hours as making up a full workday. Only 6 per cent indicated less than eight hours as a full workday.

On the other hand, with farm dwellings clustered in villages and land holdings scattered because of the inheritance system, an unusual amount of time is spent in getting to and from the fields. On the average this added 1.1 hours to the workday; the nearest lot being, on the average, about 10 minutes distant and the farthest lot 90 minutes. Time was also wasted in moving from one lot to another during the day.

About half the farms employed no nonfamily labor, about one-fifth of them employed 1 to 19 days of nonfamily labor, another fifth employed 20 to 69 days of such labor, and only 13 per cent employed more than 70 days of nonfamily labor. In an area of small farms, low crop yields, and widely scattered seasonal harvesting, even these percentages of farms employing nonfamily labor seem high.

Three-fourths of the household heads indicated that they needed between two and five workers during the busiest season. Only 4 per cent indicated their need for more than ten workers during the busiest season.

c. *Management skills and farm practices.* New varieties of various crops have been found through experiments in Crete to increase yield and quality and so bring better incomes. But even among those interviewed who had heard about these new varieties, less than a third and in most instances less than a tenth had actually planted them (Table 42).

TABLE 42. Percentage of farmers who have heard about new varieties or plant species, who planted any, and of all farmers planting, Crete, 1948

New varieties	Per cent heard about	Per cent hearing, who planted any	Per cent planting, of all farmers
Eretria wheat	47	31	14
Athenias barley	77	31	24
Calamon olives	50	14	7
Valencia oranges	2	0	0
Jaffa oranges	10	6	1
Pistachio nuts	52	6	3
Peanuts	75	12	9

Source: Sample Survey of Crete, Form B, Farm.

Since 97 per cent of the farmers had olive trees and 83 per cent raised cereals, the low percentage (7 per cent and 14-24 per cent respectively) planting these improved varieties indicates that even profitable management practices are adopted slowly in Crete.

The application of fertilizer was profitable according to general opinion (and to those who use it)—especially on olives, tree fruits, and vineyards. Of the farmers growing various crops, more than one-half used fertilizers on cereals and grapes, and about one-fourth on bananas, oranges, and olives (Table 43).

Although 83 per cent of the farmers indicated that erosion was a problem on their farms, less than half of them utilized terraces or a combination of terraces and ditch-waterways[3] to prevent erosion. A

[3] In Crete, as in most of the Mediterranean area, the "ditch-waterways" consist of a single plow-furrow made diagonally down the slope across each small cultivated field, to provide an outlet for the water and to break the momentum of the runoff of the winter rains.

TABLE 43. Percentage of farmers using fertilizers on various crops, Crete, 1948

Crops	Percentage using fertilizers
Olives	27
Oranges	25
Tangerines	*
Lemons	5
Bananas	20
Deciduous fruits	*
Grapes	60
Cereals	66

* Less than 0.5 per cent.
Source: Sample Survey of Crete, Form B, Farm.

seventh of those farmers who recognized the problem had taken no measures to prevent erosion.

In the matter of rotating crops, which would seem of first importance on land of relatively low fertility, 13 per cent of the farmers stated that they practiced no rotation. An additional 24 per cent had a rotation of cereal crops only—making a total of 37 per cent of the farms without a rotation in the usual sense of changing types of crops on their land. Only 12 per cent of the farmers included pulses in a regular rotation system and only 25 per cent included pulses and a hay crop, which is considered essential in good rotations, especially on rolling land. However, two-thirds of the farmers grew some pulses, even though in too small acreages to list as a part of the rotation.

These examples are sufficient to indicate that though the farmers of Crete recognized some of their more important problems and many knew what should be done about them, something more is necessary to stimulate action. On their small farms, intensive agriculture requires great efficiency to obtain high output per acre, but there is much to be done in developing the will to act and the skills to do an effective job.

3. Capital, Power, and Equipment Resources

In 1948 the average farm had an estimated value of $5,455 or about $590 per acre. In view of the quality of the land and its economic productivity, such estimates reflect the effects of inflation, population pressures, and few land transfers. A recent purchaser of

small plots of land in the Ano Arkhanais community paid $3,000 per
acre for 1.5 acres of "raw" land to be used for the production of
Rosaki table grapes. After preparation of the land, planting of
vines, and erection of trellises, the owner expected the vineyard to be
worth about $4,000 an acre, at the currently inflated prices. (See
also Appendix 5, Tables A74 to A77.)

Credit facilities were found to be used relatively little in Crete
for procuring capital to purchase land but were used by almost three-
fifths of the farmers to finance their crop production. A fuller discussion of credit facilities and their use by farmers will be found in
Chapter 9 under "Agricultural Credit."

In 1948, farm operators on the average used tools and equipment
—usually nothing more than a plow, a sickle, and a hoe—valued at
about $32; more than half the farms having less than $20 worth. In
addition, the average farmer had a donkey, an ox or a work cow, and
harness. The frequency of some of the larger items of equipment is
shown in Table 44. Two-thirds of the farmers had saddles, two-fifths
wooden plows, and about one-fifth had sprayers, wooden harrows,
and steel plows.

In addition, there were estimated to be 19 drills and 335 hammer-
mills on the island. There were 37 tractors on the island owned and
operated by the government for their schools or for hire to farmers
through the agricultural bank. Three tractors in Iraklion were privately owned.

TABLE 44. Percentage of farms having specified types of equipment,
Crete, 1948

Equipment	Having one	More than one
Wooden plow	42	1
Steel plow	24	3
Wooden harrow	21	1
Steel harrow	1	—
Pumps (animal driven)	4	1
Pumps (wind driven)	2	2
Pumps (engine driven)	*	*
Carts and wagons	3	—
Saddles	70	9
Sprayers[a]	22	—

* Less than 1 per cent.
a Computed from Form C, Community.
Source: Sample Survey of Crete, Form B, Farm.

The main source of farm power came from the 35,000-45,000 oxen and work cows, 4,500 horses and mares, 9,000 mules, and 45,000 donkeys on the island. The work stock on the 52,350 farms totalled 70,000 head or about 1.3 head per farm. Only 4 per cent of the farms with mules had more than one, while 11 per cent of farms with donkeys had more than one. Since oxen and cows work best in teams, 22 per cent of the farms with work cows had two on the farm.

The donkey, which seems able to live on almost anything, and limited quantities of that, has a great advantage in Crete over horses and cattle, which require both feed grains and good forage crops. The donkey was the major means of transportation. For field work, cattle, mules, and horses seemed more efficient.

Primitive methods of tillage were found to prevail in Cretan agriculture. Most of the field work, except plowing, was done with hand tools. The average farmer had little equipment, using a wooden plow and plank harrow for seedbed preparation, the hoe for cultivation, and the hand sickle for harvesting. Cereal crops were seeded by hand and threshed out by tramping of men and beasts on threshing floors. One-fifth of the farmers indicated that new and additional machinery and tools were needed to increase production. Another 7 per cent suggested the need for work animals. With an average of 13 lots of land, widely scattered over the community, hand tools or small horse-drawn equipment would appear to be the only type which might be utilized conveniently unless farm consolidation could be attained. In the Episcopi peanut area, a government-owned tractor was used to plow and prepare the ground. The steep slopes and rocky soils interplanted with trees of various types make larger-type machines impractical except for limited acreages in a few of the plains areas, such as Ierapetra, Lasithi, Mallia, Episcopi, Kastelli, Platinias, and Mesara.

4. Organization of Agricultural Resources

Centuries of political and economic instability have taught the Cretan farmer to plan and operate his farm for security and self-sufficiency. With very few exceptions the farms are small, owner-operated, and free from land mortgages. The value of home production of food and clothing equals half the total income. With small farms and limited production, a majority of the farmers belong to one or more cooperatives as a means of improving their market outlets, or of facilitating purchases of supplies and equipment.

a. *Size of farms.* The average farm in Crete, although under ten acres, was made up of 13 lots scattered over the community. Even the farms between 12.5 and 250 acres were scattered in 20 to 85 lots each. Some farms under 12.5 acres had as many as 19 separate plots of land.

Almost two-thirds of all farms and sub-farms and about two-fifths of the "farms only" were under five acres in size. Over two-thirds of the "farms only" were under 10 acres in size; only one-seventh over 15 acres. (See Figure 12 and Appendix 5, Tables A80, A81, and A82 for details.)

There has been little change in size of farms during the past twenty years, although there is a slight tendency for the percentage of farms of 12.5-49.9 acres to increase and above 50 acres to decrease. According to the 1929 census, only 1.9 per cent of the 88,000 farms were 50 acres in size or larger. Twenty years later only 1.0 per cent of the 92,250 farms and sub-farms were that large. In 1929 there were 115 farms of 250 acres each or more—with one farm containing more than 25,000 acres, and another between 6,250 and 12,500 acres. In 1948 the sample survey did not include any farm larger than 250 acres.[4] But special inquiry did reveal one private landholding containing between 6,000 and 12,000 acres and a half dozen others of more than 250 acres.

b. *Land ownership and acquisition.* Ninety-six per cent of the farmers in Crete owned all or part of their land.[5] Three-fourths of the farmers owned all the land which they operated, with an additional 20 per cent owning some and renting the remainder of the land which they operated. Ninety per cent of the renting was on a "crop-share" basis.

How were the farms acquired in an area of low production and low income? Almost half of the farmers acquired all of their land by inheritance, but these controlled only two-fifths of the land in farms. An additional seventh of the farmers acquired an additional seventh of the land by inheritance and purchase from relatives. However, one-third of the farmers owned 45 per cent of the land obtained

[4] This is entirely within the sampling probability for this scheme of sampling, since the number of such large farms is so small that a 1/150 sample would not be expected to obtain a schedule for even one such farm.

[5] The remaining 4 per cent are farming (a) lands assigned to them by the Greek Government in the 1922-1923 transfer from Turkey, (b) lands transferred by parents but not yet formally deeded, or (c) a tract owned by the occupant's relative and farmed rent free.

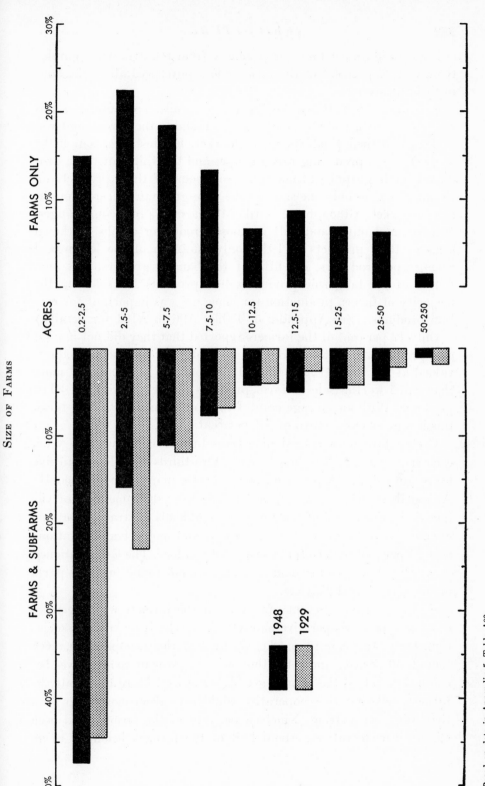

SIZE OF FARMS

FARMS & SUBFARMS | ACRES | FARMS ONLY

0.2-2.5
2.5-5
5-7.5
7.5-10
10-12.5
12.5-15
15-25
25-50
50-250

1948
1929

FIGURE 12. Size of farms in Crete, 1929 and 1948

Based on data in Appendix 5, Table A80.

either through inheritance or purchase from relatives and nonrelatives. Only 3 per cent of the farmers had purchased all of the land in their farms.

c. *Marketing methods.* Among farmers raising various tree and vine crops, a considerable variation was found in the percentage who sold some of their products on the market. For instance, four-fifths of the farmers producing raisin grapes and two-thirds of those producing table grapes and chestnuts sold some of these products on the market while only one-sixth of the wine-grape producers brought any to market. Although one-third of the farmers producing oranges, cherries, and olives and half of those producing carobs marketed some of their products in 1947, only one-sixth of the lemon and wine-grape producers, one-fifth of the banana growers, and one-fourth of the tangerine producers had products for sale. On the majority of farms, production for home use was important for certain products. (See Appendix 5, Tables A96 to A101 for details.)

Only 12 per cent of the farmers reported that they did not market any products. Slightly more than half of the farms sold products valued at less than $125 in 1947-1948; only 15 per cent sold more than $375 worth. Sale of farm products marketed averaged $170 per farm. With an average capital value of about $5,500 per farm, this is a gross cash return of 3.1 per cent.

Cretan farmers averaged nine trips to market during the year, each trip requiring two hours' time. Two-thirds went less than five times annually, but 8 per cent averaged more than two trips a month. Almost three-fifths of the farmers marketed in the same town or village every time. Half of them used pack animals for transportation; another 15 per cent used pack animals and motor transportation; only 27 per cent used motor transportation alone. The last-mentioned were located near motor roads, which were not found in many parts of the agricultural districts.

d. *Cooperatives.* Seventy per cent of the farmers were members of some type of cooperative marketing, purchase, or credit association. Only 34 per cent marketed through their cooperative, even though 59 per cent indicated they were in favor of cooperatives because they helped the farmer get higher prices. More than half the farmers felt that the cooperative could give them more help than they were then getting. Nineteen per cent of the farmers had been officers in cooperatives. About half of the farmers belonged to an agricultural credit cooperative, one-third to an agricultural commodity cooperative, and one-tenth to an olive oil cooperative.

The Agricultural Credit Cooperatives supervised the granting of loans to their members, through the Agricultural Bank, for the purchase of seeds, fertilizers, agricultural implements, and supplies. The Agricultural Bank had empowered the unions of these cooperatives to take delivery, store in the union warehouses, transport, and distribute agricultural supplies, against a commission ($\frac{1}{6}$ cent per pound) to the unions for supplies handled. The member of the cooperatives obtained needed supplies on credit, if their individual accounts at the Agricultural Bank for the previous year had been settled, otherwise on cash terms.

These credit cooperatives also collected, stored, processed, if necessary, and sold the agricultural products produced by their members, at a price fixed by a competent official body. The operations were financed by the Agricultural Bank at reasonable (7 to $8\frac{1}{2}$ per cent) interest rates. In 1948, there were cooperatives using this plan for six different types of commodities: Sultana raisins, olive oil, wine, cheese, honey, and fish. The fishing cooperatives also provided fishing boats on a cooperative basis.

The procedure followed by these commodity groups in Crete was quite similar to the National Wool Growers Association, a cooperative handling wool for producers in the United States for many years. At harvesting time, the cooperatives advised their members as to the price at which they would take the members' production, payable upon delivery of the goods to the cooperative warehouse. At a later date, any excess from the sale remaining after deduction of the association overhead and cooperative handling charges was paid the individual producer. This provided the producer with funds at harvest time, without making him subject to flooded market prices. It also allowed the cooperative to select the time for sale. Usually this resulted in more favorable prices for the producer—particularly when prices were rising due to inflation. The long-time results will be dependent upon the competence of the cooperative management to forecast supply and demand factors and the relative competition of the private trade. In a country with extremely high interest rates on commercial paper and the demand for high profits by private enterprisers, the advantages to the small producer have been greater than might seem possible to those accustomed to conditions in the United States.

As an example the wine-grape growers of Kastelli-Kisamos formed a cooperative and received an advance of about 3 cents per pound while those who sold to private wine merchants received less than 1 cent per pound. Part of the reason for this was the fact that the cooperative had the facilities and equipment to produce higher grade wine than the private merchants.

There was some complaint from private enterprise and the general public that the cooperatives did not limit themselves to servicing their members on the sale of products and to the purchase of agricultural supplies. The cooperatives were charged with taking advantage of their privileged position to import and sell all sorts of household and personal articles such as cloth, footwear, etc., which were in the field of private business. But the law enacted in 1929, which brought the cooperative movement into formal existence, clearly stated that one of its aims was to meet the needs of its members for such items. By obliging the merchant to be more moderate in his prices the cooperatives enhance the purchasing power of all farmers, according to the members.

In addition to the above there were Land Amelioration (Improvement) Cooperatives for irrigation and drainage works which would develop and enhance the value of the land through more intensive cultivation. One land-purchase-and-renting cooperative was in operation in 1948. It purchased or rented land for its members. This type of cooperative could be the means for enlarging the size of fields for mechanical cultivation in suitable areas.

The citron-cultivation-and-handling cooperatives, which had been numerous at one time in Crete, were no longer in operation. Few citron (similar to lemon) trees were found on the island at the time of the survey due to their destruction by disease. This illustrates one of the hazards of highly specialized agriculture and the need for continuing and competent research work.

All of these cooperatives came under the jurisdiction of the Ministry of Agriculture. According to a recently (1949-1950) conceived program, all farmers in a community, who might then be in three or more commodity cooperatives, would be grouped into a single cooperative. This was expected to increase the efficiency of the cooperatives and certainly should reduce overhead expenses.

C. Agricultural Production and Land Use

Land use in Crete was discussed briefly in Chapter 4. Additional

background material on the relative importance of its major products in comparison with Europe and the Near East is presented in
a series of maps prepared by the Office of Foreign Agricultural Relations in a recent publication of the United States Department of
Agriculture.[6] The significant aspects of these maps are briefly discussed below.

1. Comparison of Agricultural Production and Consumption Needs with Those of Other Countries

The production of olives, goats, and sheep was found to be heavier
in Crete than in other areas of Europe and the Near East. Since
Crete produced about 27 per cent of the olive oil in Greece and 3 per
cent of that in the Mediterranean Basin,[7] the importance of this crop
to the economy of the island is self-evident (Figure 13). For the

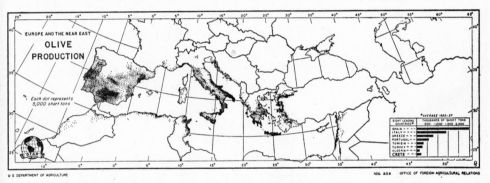

FIGURE 13. Olive production, Crete and nearby countries, pre-war

period 1930-1938, olives were about 40 per cent of the total value
of the agricultural products of Crete.[8] Only on the mainland of
Greece and on Cyprus were goats as important in the agricultural
economy as in Crete. In number of goats per 1,000 inhabitants and
per square mile, Greece (and Crete) ranked second only to French
Morocco in the Mediterranean area (Figure 14).

Grapes, mules, and asses were next in relative importance—in
comparison with neighboring countries (Figure 15). While Greece

6 Office of Foreign Agricultural Relations, *Agricultural Geography of Europe and the Near East*. Misc. Pub. 665. Maps. Washington, United States Department of Agriculture, 1948.

7 Office of Foreign Agricultural Relations, "Mediterranean Olive Oil Output." Mimeograph, FOD 1-48, February 2, 1948, p. 2.

8 Greek Ministry of National Economy, L'Annuaire Statistique de la Grèce, 1938, Athens.

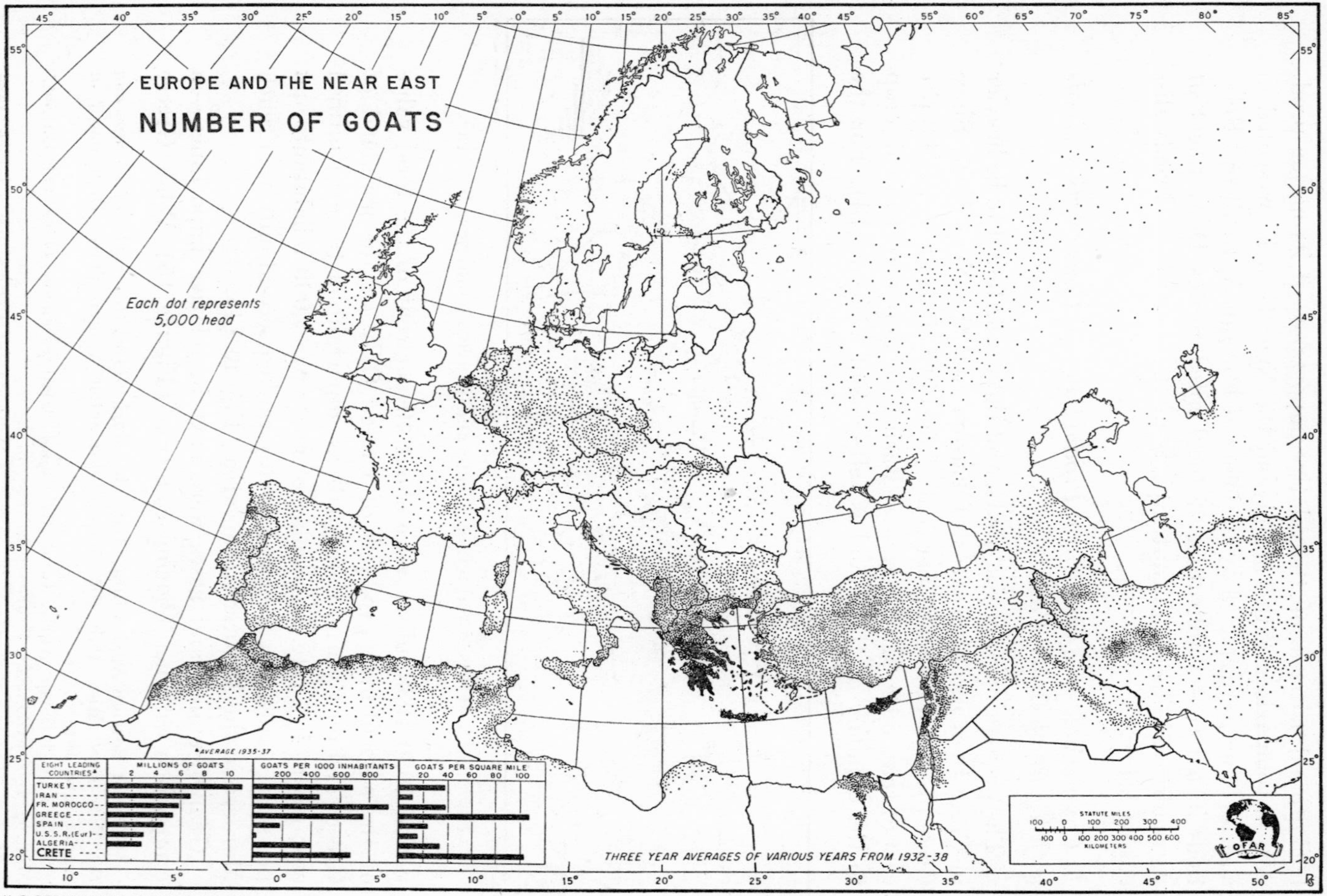
EUROPE AND THE NEAR EAST
NUMBER OF GOATS
Each dot represents 5,000 head
EIGHT LEADING COUNTRIES*
MILLIONS OF GOATS
GOATS PER 1000 INHABITANTS
GOATS PER SQUARE MILE
TURKEY
IRAN
FR. MOROCCO
GREECE
SPAIN
U.S.S.R. (Eur)
ALGERIA
CRETE
*AVERAGE 1935-37
THREE YEAR AVERAGES OF VARIOUS YEARS FROM 1932-38
STATUTE MILES
KILOMETERS
OFAR
U. S. DEPARTMENT OF AGRICULTURE
NEG. 876. OFFICE OF FOREIGN AGRICULTURAL RELATIONS

FIGURE 14. Number of goats

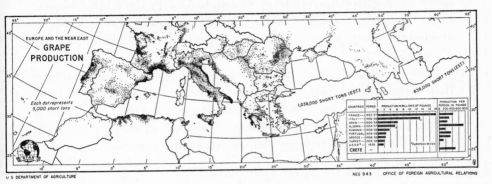

FIGURE 15. Grape production, Crete and nearby countries, pre-war

rated seventh in total grape production it raised more than twice as many raisins as its nearest competitor, Turkey. Crete produced about 62 per cent of the Sultana raisins in all Greece, and approximately three per cent of the world production.[9]

Although wheat and other cereals were grown on 35-40 per cent of the cultivated land the low yields per acre and the small percentage of total land under cultivation made Crete relatively unimportant as a wheat or cereal producer. Lack of feed grains and of root and forage crops explains Crete's low rank in production of cattle, swine, and horses.

While production of cotton and tobacco is possible in Crete, present Greek acreages in these crops were concentrated on the mainland. Potato acreage was small in Crete and Greece.

Greece has made various attempts to expand cultivated areas. From 1924 to 1939 cultivated area was expanded from 4.3 million acres to 8.0 million acres, an increase of about 85 per cent. Further expansion, however, will be limited and costly. In Crete, development of small areas by drainage and larger areas by irrigation may enable agriculture to be further intensified, as will be discussed later.

The inadequacy of the land and the low agricultural production for Crete in comparison with other countries are further shown in Table 45. Except for Italy and Egypt, Greece and Crete had one-half to two-thirds as much arable land per inhabitant and one-fourth to three-fifths as much cereal-potato production per person as was

[9] Office of Foreign Agricultural Relations, *Foreign Crops and Markets.* Mimeograph, vol. 57, no. 18, p. 338.

found in neighboring countries.[10] Compared with the United States, Crete had about two-fifths as much arable land per person and about one-fourth the grain resources per capita. For further details see Table 45.

While Crete had 20-25 per cent more arable land per inhabitant than Greece, the wheat yield was approximately the same and the wheat production per inhabitant was lower than for Greece as a whole. In a country where two-fifths to one-half of the diet was composed of cereals and potatoes, this relationship was important.

2. Irrigation and Its Effect upon Land Use

Scanty rainfall from April to November was found to reduce crop yields and limit the types of crops which can be grown. Consequently the amount of irrigation water available helped to determine the use which was made of cultivable land. Production of fresh vegetables for the family was given a high priority on irrigated land. Its use for commercial crops was affected also by its location, markets, topography, soil, and climatic factors. "When irrigation water comes in, the olive tree steps out and citrus fruits or other specialty crops take over," was a common expression. In general the irrigated land was used for vegetables, citrus and other fruits, potatoes, tomatoes, and bananas. If olive trees were interplanted with such crops they might benefit by such irrigation.

The ranking of crops on irrigated land and nonirrigated land according to gross value of products was made by three of the more experienced agriculturists on the island. For the major items, their judgments were confirmed by the data in Table 11, Chapter 6. Of the irrigated crops, bananas and early tomatoes gave the highest gross returns, with citrus fruit, potatoes, peanuts, and deciduous fruits next. Olives and cereals were seldom found on irrigated land except as interplanted. On the nonirrigated land the gross and net incomes from table grapes, raisin grapes, wine grapes or olives, and cereals were ranked in that order, if produced on suitable types of soil.

About 83 per cent of the farmers of Crete practiced irrigation on some land, even though it was only for a vegetable garden. About

---

[10] In order to include both cereals and potatoes on a comparable energy-unit basis, one-fifth of the total potato production has been added to the wheat, rye, barley, maslin, rice, and maize production. This rough approximation of the cereal-potato foods produced per person has made no allowance for seed, waste, or livestock feed. Spelts and oats were omitted, as being little used for food.

TABLE 45. Arable land per inhabitant, wheat yield, and comparative cereal resources, Crete, Greece, and specified countries, 1934-1938

Country or area	Arable land per inhabitant[a] (acres)	Average yield wheat crop (bushels per acre)	Comparative cereal-potato[b] production per inhabitant
Average 17 Mediterranean Basin countries[c]	1.02[d]	14.6	100
Crete[e]	1.0	12.8	65
Greece	.8	13.4	78
Albania	*	15.6	71
Turkey	1.3	14.7	157
Yugoslavia	1.3	16.9	218
Bulgaria	1.5	18.8	182
Rumania	1.7	14.4	217
Hungary	1.5	20.8	284
Average of 7 Balkan countries	1.4	16.4	172
Italy	.8	21.4	115
Egypt	.4	29.8	93
France	1.2	23.4	134
Spain	1.3	14.2	151
United States	2.5	12.9	257

* Not available.

a Number of inhabitants for column 2 and 4 based on 1936 population (midyear) or extrapolation of available data to that date.

b Average annual total production for 1934-1938 of wheat, rye, barley, maslin, rice, and maize plus one-fifth of potato production divided by the average number of inhabitants described in (a) above to approximate equal caloric value, 333 per 100 grams.

c For this country-to-country comparison an unweighted mean of 17 country computations was used, including all countries touching the Mediterranean, and the islands of Malta and Cyprus.

d Available for only eight countries.

e 1933-1937 data for Crete.

Source: International Institute of Agriculture, *International Yearbook of Agricultural Statistics, 1941-1945, Agricultural Production and Livestock Numbers*, FAO, United Nations, Rome, 1947. vol. I, Tables 1-9, pp. 3-47, and vol. II, selected countries. Statistical Office and Department of Social Affairs, *Demographic Yearbook*, 1948, United Nations, New York, 1949. Table 3, pp. 98-105.

three-fifths of the total land irrigated had sufficient water, according to the farmers who used it.

On farms having irrigation, an average of ¾ acre was irrigated. Fifty per cent of the farms with irrigation had less than a half acre of land irrigated and four-fifths less than an acre.

There were no large irrigation areas on individual farms such as are found in the United States and elsewhere. With only 3 per cent of the farms having more than five acres of irrigated land, there were few large fruit orchards and none such as are found in Sicily (citrus) and the Po Valley (deciduous) of Italy. Irrigated land was used largely for a mixture of various fruits and vegetables, with edges of drainage ditches having a single row of corn (maize) for feed. The fact that holdings were scattered helped to cause this hodge-podge of various crops on the individual farms.

Prevention of drainage-water wastage, control of torrents, and development of sources of irrigation water were the principal water problems in agriculture. Water wastage was evident at each of the irrigation projects visited. Flooded roadways, canal seepage, and strong currents in canals at the lower end of the project were concrete evidence of the need for education and for the advisory and supervisory assistance of a competent irrigation engineer.

Since one-fourth of the farmers reported that all of their irrigated land received insufficient water, improper planning or water wastage was reducing production on these farms. According to a Ministry of Agriculture representative, a newly constructed irrigation canal in the citrus-fruit area near Khania would provide less than half of the water needed for maximum yields.

At Stavrochori in southeastern Lasithi nome, water supplies for irrigation are available from springs. But here irrigation would be virtually pointless without a road outlet for the products of the area. At present the quickest means of transport is a 3½-hour donkey pack or a 1-hour donkey pack together with a 1-hour sea trip by caïque. On many days the weather does not permit the caïques to pick up or deposit cargo. Since this area is suitable for the production of bananas, early tomatoes, and other high-gross-income but perishable crops, quick and dependable transportation is essential.

Preliminary investigations indicated that the greatest possibilities for increasing agricultural production in Crete were in developing satisfactory irrigation projects for five plains areas. In two of these areas supplies of underground water, which the geologists believe are available, must be located.

In the *Kastelli-Kisamos area* in northwest Khania nome, the development of a project using water from the Drapania-Nopiyi springs and dug wells seemed feasible and was under consideration by ECA. Test wells for artesian supplies may be needed, also.

In the *Lake Kournas-Episcopi-Yeoryioupolis area* of north-western Rethimnon nome, water is already available from Lake Kournas and neighboring springs. This project was being planned with ECA assistance.

Irrigation of the *Lasithi Plain* is linked with its drainage problem and involves cleaning out its "sinkhole" outlets and installing concrete structures with control gates and trash racks about each sinkhole. This should reduce flooding in winter and spring and maintain the ground water level after the spring flood waters have drained out, for wells and summer irrigation.

Additional dug wells are believed capable of supplying the needs of the *Kastelli-Pedhiadhos area* in northeastern Iraklion nome. This is a large productive area with good soil types available for greater production if water is provided.

By far the most extensive area with good soil types is the *Mesara Plain* (Mesara-Monofatsi) of 90,000 acres in the southern part of Iraklion nome. Full exploitation of this area would involve drainage of 7,500 acres of rich, alluvial bottom land, and construction of a dam (near Ay. Deka or Ayios Dheka) to reduce flooding and provide power and some water for irrigation of the western third of the plain. The other two-thirds of the plain could utilize underground water (which geologists believe to be present) from small surface wells, with windmills or engine pumps for gardens and small plots, together with deep-well pumps for larger areas.

A nearby lignite mine (northeast of Ay. Deka) was used by the Germans during the war. This fuel deposit might produce enough power, at mine source, for irrigation pumping. If not, a study to determine the economic feasibility of importing fuel oil for pumping and light industries in the area should be made.

Some of the best surface-soil types in Crete are found in this valley. At present they are used largely for low-yielding dry-land wheat farming. With water available, considerably more food of a higher quality could be produced. But a detailed water and geologic survey, including test drilling and a soil-engineering-economic survey, is needed to determine costs and income possibilities.

The Mesara Plain presents an opportunity to test proposals for the agricultural adjustment of the whole island. Monasteries and the Church are reported to own large acreages in this valley, so that certain changes in production and ownership patterns through exchange or rentals might be possible more readily here than elsewhere. This is the only large level land area in Crete, where the cooperative use of tractors and large machinery might be economically feasible for the small farmer.

The use of cooperative land rental associations might be feasible in some communities, to provide large fields in which to operate mechanized equipment. One hypothesis that needs testing in Crete is that more diversified types of farming would increase efficiency. Many of the small farms on irrigated land seem to be overspecialized with seasonably idle land and labor. This suggests that marked improvement in efficiency could be achieved by more balanced farming, with supplementary and complementary enterprises to use more fully the labor and land resources. With adequate water supplies, it would be possible to test different combinations of enterprises on the Mesara Plain. In fact the siroccos in this area tend to force mixed patterns of farming, requiring olive or other trees as protection for citrus fruit and vegetable production.

New crops for the area might include rice, potatoes, corn, peanuts, soybeans, and cotton, as well as more legumes, including broad beans, alfalfa, chick peas, hubam clover, etc. Use of these legumes should increase soil fertility and the production of other crops which follow them.

This same area provides an opportunity to test other changes in land use to increase farm production, such as (1) reforesting nearby mountains; (2) increasing the feed supply for sheep and goats, supplied by legumes and grasses, in order to permit reforestation of the hillsides; and (3) combining scattered landholdings into more efficient units. Although several people proposed sites for dams for irrigation and water power, it was the conclusion of Mr. Crosby, in his report that "there are very few if any places where the conditions are suitable for a dam with a satisfactory reservoir."

After detailed geologic studies have been made to determine whether any faults (important in an area of earthquakes) cross the proposed dam site on the Lithaios River near Ay. Deka in the Mesara Plain, and after other investigations suggested in his detailed report are made, Mr. Crosby feels it might be safe to construct a moderately high dam here. Of the many proposed sites this seems to be the only one on the island capable of considerable water storage.

3. Land Use

Although Crete has only 30 per cent of its land in farms and 2 per cent in forests, another 48 per cent is estimated to be used for nomadic grazing, according to a recent estimate supplied by the Ministry of Coordination.[11] (See Figure 2 and Table 46.) The remaining 20 per cent of the land area is in mountains, unused hills, torrents, and other land not in farms. Although there are many conflicting data on land use in Crete, this table presents the best comparable estimates obtained over the past two decades. While this total area for Crete is about 77,000 stremma or 20,000 acres larger than that provided the Crete Survey by the Ministry of Reconstruction, this difference may be explained by the inclusion of a few small uninhabited nearby islands which were omitted from our investigation. A more serious error in all data obtained on land use in Crete, however, is the lack of any estimates as to the acreage which was double-cropped and interplanted. For example, an estimate of the number of olive trees (at 15 per stremma) from the acreage data in Table 46 would suggest only 6 million trees, yet government officials estimate a total of more than 13 million olive trees in Crete. Similarly there was much interplanting of cereals and other crops among the trees and vineyards in some areas. Unfortunately, sufficient data were not secured from the sample survey to make estimates of these practices.

In 1948, about 8 per cent of the total land area was in cultivated crops, 10 per cent in vine and tree crops (other than forests), 5 per cent in fallow land, and 7 per cent in grazing and meadow, probably of a permanent pasture and very rough land type. Over the past twenty years, marked increases may be noted in the acreages devoted to fruit and nut trees (a ten-fold increase), olives, cereals, raisins, forage crops, vegetables, and potatoes. A decline is noted in fallow land and other annual crops, in addition to the reduction by one-half of "other land not in farms." Most of these acreage changes took place between 1928 and 1938, the cereal and pulses acreages being considerably larger in 1938 than in 1948. It will be noted that this expansion in agriculture occurred during the period of greatest industrial expansion, and a decade after the transfer of the Asia Minor refugees. These data are also significant in relation to import-export changes which will be discussed in Chapter 11.

In addition to the general increase of 10 per cent in the total land in farms from 1928 to 1948, according to Table 46, the percentage

[11] Ministry of Coordination, *Land Use in Crete, Greece, 1928, 1938, and 1948*, Athens. Private communication, 1951.

TABLE 46. Land use in Crete, Greece, 1928, 1938, and 1948
(in stremma—approximately 1/4 acre)

Land use	1928	1938	1948
LAND IN FARMS			
Cereals	400,780	576,941	484,470
Vegetables and potatoes	48,832	65,032	70,000[a]
Pulses	61,576	128,760	70,000[a]
Forage crops	2,800	19,868	20,000[a]
Other annual crops	14,615	9,478	10,000[a]
Total rotation crops	528,603	800,079	654,470
Table and wine grapes	154,020	170,650	170,000[a]
Raisin grapes	69,359	103,675	105,000[a]
Olive trees	294,704	350,000[a]	400,000[a]
Fruit and nut trees	14,024	100,000	130,000[a]
Total rotation, tree, and vine crops	1,060,710	1,524,404	1,459,470
Fallow land	500,480	375,596	440,530
Grazing and meadow	704,331	600,000[a]	600,000
Total land in farms	2,265,521	2,500,000	2,500,000
LAND NOT IN FARMS			
Mountains—nomadic graze	4,000,000[a]	4,000,000[a]	4,000,000[a]
Forests	165,000	160,000	155,000
Total land in some productive use	*6,430,521*	*6,660,000*	*6,655,000*
Torrents	10,000[a]	10,000[a]	10,000[a]
Mountains, hills unused	1,500,000[a]	1,500,000[a]	1,500,000[a]
Other land not in farms	438,279[a]	208,800[a]	213,800[a]
Total land	*8,378,800*	*8,378,800*	*8,378,800*

[a] Estimates by C. A. Doxiadis and co-workers, Ministry of Coordination.
Source: Ministry of Coordination, *Land Use in Crete, Greece, 1928, 1938, and 1948.*
Estimates based on official Greek Agricultural Census of 1929 and other official
Greek data, except as indicated. Athens, 1951.

of this farm land in each of the major types of rotation, tree, and
vine crops also increased. (See Figure 16.) During this 20-year
period the percentage of total farm land in cereals increased from
18 to 19 per cent; in vegetables, from 2 to 3 per cent; in pulses,

LAND IN FARMS

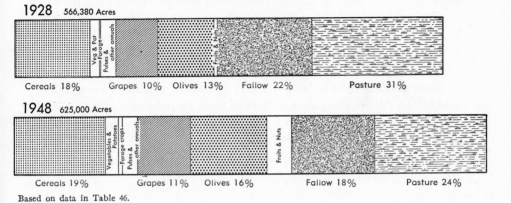

Based on data in Table 46.

FIGURE 16. Land in farms and changes in land use, 1928 to 1948, Crete

forage crops, and other annual crops, from 3 to 4 per cent; in grapes, from 10 to 11 per cent (especially in raisin grapes) ; in olives, from 13 to 16 per cent; and in fruit and nut trees, from 1 to 5 per cent. These increases were made possible by reductions in the percentage of farm land in fallow, from 22 to 18 per cent, and in pasture (grazing and meadow), from 31 to 24 per cent. In fact, the percentage increase in acreages and production of rotation, vine, and tree crops was greater than the percentage increase in population during these two decades.

D. Crops, Livestock, and Farming Systems

Crete produces a wide variety of crops with great variations in crop yields, crop rotations, and cultural practices. The lack of forage crops and feed grains limits livestock production to power replacements, nomadic sheep and goats, and relatively few poultry and hogs. The farming systems are based on intensive specialty crops (Sultana raisin grapes, Rosaki table grapes, oranges, truck crops) or more extensive acreages on which cereal, tree, and vine crops are grown, with or without some interplanting.

1. Crop Production

The Cretan farms were found to average 9.2 acres in size, with 6.6 acres under cultivation, 0.3 in forest, and 2.3 in grazing, nonfarm land, or in almonds, carobs, chestnuts, or walnuts in areas where grown. Of the land under cultivation 2.0 acres were in cereals, about equally divided among wheat, barley, and oats or maslin; 0.5 acre in vetches and pulses; 2.5 acres in 140 olive trees; 0.8 acre in 1,300 grapevines; and the remaining 0.8 acre in vegetables and hay, or fallow. In the irrigated areas citrus and deciduous fruits replaced the olives.

Most farmers (83 to 97 per cent) produced cereals, wine grapes, and olives. Approximately one-half of them raised some pulses, pears, figs, and carobs. A fourth to a third produced oranges, walnuts, and almonds. One-ninth to one-fifth grew peaches, tangerines, plums, apples, apricots, lemons, and quinces. A few produced cherries, chestnuts, and acorns, with some for sale (Table 47).

TABLE 47. Percentage of farmers growing various crops, average number of units per farm reporting, and average yields, Crete, 1947

Crop	Percentage of farms growing crop	Average number of units per farm reporting	Yield per unit per farm producing	
			1947	Normal[a]
		(no. acres)	(bushels per acre)	
Cereals	83	2.1	—	—
Wheat	(76)	(1.1)	8.6	11.6
Barley	(63)	(1.1)	13.8	15.9
Oats	(45)	(0.9)	18.0	21.3
Maslin	(23)	(1.1)	10.8	12.0
Pulses	68	0.3	11.0	14.4
Grapes		(no. vines)	(cwt. per acre)	
Table	15	774	62.4 (grapes)	—
Wine	85	1,340	26.6 (wine)	—
Raisin	29	819	15.6 (raisin)	—
Trees		(no. trees)	(pounds per tree)	
Olives[b]	97	141	7.6	—
Oranges[c]	27	42	24.8	—
Lemons[d]	16	9	36.4	—
Almonds[e]	38	19	4.8	—
Carobs[e]	48	39	38.9	—

a Normal yields are estimates by farmers of annual averages over a five-year period.

b Based on 14 trees per stremma, the yield of olive oil in 1947 was approximately 425 pounds per acre.

c Orange yields in 1947 were approximately 4,000 pounds per acre.

d Lemon yields in 1947 were approximately 5,500 pounds per acre.

e Almond and carob trees are so scattered that yields per acre are not computed.

Source: Sample Survey of Crete, Form B, Farm.

Fall-sown cereals were found to be the principal cultivated crops in Crete and were grown on about one-fifth of the farm land. Total acreages of wheat and barley were somewhat larger than of oats and maslin combined. One-fifth of the farmers grew maslin—a mixture of wheat and barley, usually in equal portions. Pulses and hay crops were produced on less than a tenth of the farm land.

Except for olives and table grapes, crop yields in Crete were exceedingly low in comparison with the yields of nearby countries. Most yields were also low in comparison with the possibilities as revealed by experimental or demonstrational results. Especially was this true of cereal crops.

a. *Cereals and pulses.* Yields of wheat and barley, the two main cereals in Crete, were lower (except barley in Rumania) than in other countries of southern and eastern Europe. Potato and bean yields in Greece were about the average of the Mediterranean countries but lower in Crete.

In Table 48 yields of these four crops in bushels per acre are shown in comparison with yields of other countries.[12]

TABLE 48. Major cultivated food crop yields, Crete, Greece, and selected countries, 1934-1938 (bushels per acre)

Country	Wheat	Barley	Potatoes	Beans
Crete	12.8	15.0	70[a]	—
Greece	13.4	17.6	99	9.6
Albania	15.6	19.3	80	—
Turkey	14.7	20.4	46	12.5
Yugoslavia	16.9	17.8	92	14.7
Bulgaria	18.8	25.0	90	8.2
Rumania	14.4	12.2	133	8.6
Italy	21.4	20.2	98	4.9
Egypt	29.8	36.7	197	—
Average 17 Mediterranean countries	14.6	18.6	105	9.2

a 1947 average for Lasithi Plain area was 127 bushels per acre.
Source: International Institute of Agriculture. *International Yearbook of Agricultural Statistics*, 1941-1945, Agricultural Production and Livestock Numbers. FAO, United Nations, Rome, 1947, volume I, Tables 1, 3, 9, 10, pp. 3-9, 14-19, 42-47, 48-53.

12 International Institute of Agriculture. *International Yearbook of Agricultural Statistics*, 1941-1945, Agricultural Production and Livestock Numbers, FAO, United Nations, Rome, 1947, volume I, Tables 1, 3, 9, 10, pp. 3-53.

The pre-war yields of 12.8 bushels of wheat and 15.0 bushels of barley for Crete were somewhat higher than the estimate derived from the survey for 1947, which showed 8.6 bushels per acre of wheat and about 13.8 bushels per acre of barley. Crop yields in 1947 were about 25 per cent below normal (past five-year average) according to reports of community and island officials.

Yields on small plots at the Mesara Experimental Station[13] were of course much higher. The margin was so great as to indicate a considerable possibility for improvement. Best varieties of wheat now used by farmers in Crete yielded 49 bushels per acre when grown at Mesara. But the new experimental varieties tested at Mesara gave the remarkably high average yield of 56 bushels per acre. If the varieties of wheat which Cretan farmers now plant were properly cultivated, a considerable increase in yields over the post-war 12-bushel average or the 13-bushel pre-war average could be expected. In fact, a fifth of the farmers on the island normally produce 19 bushels of wheat and 23 bushels of barley or more. If the better varieties developed at the station were planted, still higher yields could be obtained. One high-yielding variety of wheat at the Mesara Station produced 75 bushels per acre, as compared to one low-yielding variety at 25 bushels per acre. Of course, these plots were well fertilized and irrigated. The weeds were destroyed and the seedbeds properly prepared.

The research work done at the Mesara Experimental Station has had some effect on Cretan cereal production. Better varieties have been distributed to farmers within a 15-mile radius of the station through a government-distribution plan. It was estimated by the station workers that 90 per cent of the farmers in this area use the high-yielding Eretria variety of wheat and the other 10 per cent the second best, Minos variety. This method of distribution through farmers selected by government officials has caused some difficulty, even though it seems to have been fairly effective in getting new varieties of seed distributed. Only recently an attempt was made to intimidate the director of the station with a show of knives and guns.

The present distribution method is as follows: The best varieties tested for two years are given to farmers who have applied and whose land is inspected, whose farming methods are approved, and whose cooperative attitude is assured. One hundred okes (4.7 bushels) of

[13] Mr. Pierakeas, Director of Mesara Experiment Sub-Station in Crete. Diary L.G.A., September 25, 1948.

These Rosaki grapes—large, sweet, and juicy—are grown near Ano Arkhanais for export to London by refrigerated Swedish ships

Grapes being delivered to the press in Iraklion nome

Home-made wooden plow

Hand-sifting of wheat on a concrete threshing floor

seed for each 10 stremma (2.5 acres) are furnished to the farmer, who is to return 900 okes (43 bushels) of wheat at harvesting time. Three visits are made to the farm each year for inspection of land, seeding operations, and fields for variety and weed check, prior to harvesting time. The farmers given the new varieties are expected to produce clean seed for distribution through the station to other farmers. In return, they receive a 25 per cent margin above market price.

Previous tests have shown that outside varieties of wheat do not yield as well as native varieties in Crete. The best imported Italian variety, Senatore Capelli, yielded 30 per cent less than the Greek-developed Eretria variety. Both were irrigated, fertilized, and grown on similar soils in the same field. American and Australian varieties had also been tested during the pre-war period.

Yields of pulses in 1947 were almost one-fourth below normal yields. Pulse acreages were about 60 per cent of pre-war. The large amount of pulses in government rations to families may have reduced the necessity of growing them on many farms.

b. *Olives.* Olive oil yields per tree in Crete were higher than for all Greece, Italy, and Turkey. In pre-war years, olive trees in Crete yielded 5.0 pounds of oil per tree as compared with 3.7 pounds for all Greece and 3.1 pounds for Italy and Turkey. By applying the best practices known, average production in Crete could be raised even higher. In the "good" crop year of 1947-1948, the average production of all farms in Crete was 7.6 pounds of olive oil per tree according to the survey. But one-fifth of the farmers averaged 14.0 pounds of oil or more per tree in 1947-1948, and one-sixth of the farms reported their normal yield equally large. In the Ierapetra area where winter irrigation, fall and winter cultivation, fertilizers, pruning, and best known methods of dacus-fly control were practiced, the olive crop averaged between 7.0 and 8.0 pounds of olive oil per tree in the short-crop year of 1948-1949. The estimated yield for all areas of Crete for this year was 3.5 pounds of olive oil per tree. Of course soil fertility, age, and variety of tree, as well as cultural practices affect olive oil yields.

Farmers estimated an average reduction of 44 per cent in the olive oil yield due to the olive fruit fly (*Dacus oleae* Rossi) commonly called the dacus fly. Two-thirds of the farmers estimated the damage from the dacus fly was as much as 40 to 80 per cent of the olive crop; three-fifths, over 50 per cent. (For details see Appendix 5, Table

A90.) The nome agriculturists stated that the damage varied from 15 to 80 per cent, according to the degree of attack. In a recent bulletin of the Ministry of Hygiene, Athens, discussing control methods for the dacus fly, the following statement appears in reference to all Greece, "It is generally accepted that in this country 30 per cent of the average yearly production of olive oil and pickled olives is lost on account of this pest."[14] In any case the loss due to the dacus fly is a substantial portion of the crop in Crete.

In addition to the reduced quantity of oil (from early dropping and larvae damage to the berry), the quality of the oil is lowered considerably. Oil is graded according to its acidity, which dacus fly damage greatly increases. Without dacus attack, olive oil with 3° acidity is possible, but with dacus attack, even a 5° acidity is possible only by quick transportation to the factory. With the usual 20- to 30-day delay in getting berries to the factory the acidity is usually 10°. For every 1° over 5° acidity the price is reduced 1 per cent and above 10° the rate of reduction in price is 1½ per cent. For example, if 5°-acidity oil is worth 30 cents per pound at the factory, 15°-acidity oil would be worth about 26 cents per pound.

For control of the dacus fly the Greek Government adopted the sodium arsenite-molasses control method in 1920.[15] The cost of this annual campaign in Crete varied from $80,000 in 1948 to $160,000 in 1947. Treatment is given only in areas where 25 per cent or more of a normal crop is in prospect. Consequently the total costs are less in short-crop years, although the cost of control per pound of oil may be higher.

Unlike the Greeks, the Italians, who developed the molasses-arsenite method of control, have not been sufficiently convinced of its effectiveness to use it on any broad scale. Some dacus fly investigators favor the use of parasites for control and for this reason resist the use of DDT-control measures which would also kill the parasites. To date, DDT-control experiments for the dacus fly have met with uncertain and mixed results.[16]

[14] John Hadjinicolaou, *Comparative Effectiveness of DDT, Chlordane, Aldrin, and Dieldrin Residues against the Olive Fruit Fly (Dacus oleae Rossi)*, 1950, Athens School of Hygiene, Malaria Division, no. 351, p. 3.

[15] This arsenical bait method consists of sugar cane or beet molasses 10-15 per cent, sodium arsenite 0.25 per cent, and ammonium sulphate 0.5 per cent in water and sprayed on the olive trees every four to six weeks from May through August and occasionally later in the fall, depending upon the number of broods and severity of attack.

[16] John Hadjinicolaou, *op. cit.*, pp. 15-16.

Dr. Hertig, entomologist with the World Health Organization, and Dr. John Hadjinicolaou, entomologist with the Athens School of Hygiene, made inquiries which satisfied them that no one in charge of the dacus fly control program knew the full life cycle of the dacus fly or had either experimental or demonstrational proof of the effectiveness of the present control measures, using molasses and arsenite, or of DDT. Dr. Hadjinicolaou states, "Considering the destructive importance of the dacus fly to the national economy . . . any effort and expense leading to a satisfactory control of this insect is well worth while. . . . To this end . . . a detailed study, by a trained entomologist on the spot, of the biology of the dacus is of prime importance, since as you know there are still many unknown aspects of the life cycle of the insect."[17]

Deep cultivation of olive groves in October-November to permit absorption of fall and early winter rains was found effective in increasing olive yields. A second cultivation in February and another light one in March or April toward the end of the rainy season were also beneficial. The last cultivation tended to kill weeds and prepare the ground for summer fallow. One or more of these cultivations were in evidence in a large number of the olive groves on the better soils.

Different varieties of olives grew at the higher elevations. In general, 1,800 to 2,000 feet (600 meters) was the upper limit for olive production, but certain varieties were producing up to 2,600 feet (800 meters) or more.[18] Although these varieties were lower yielding, they did produce food and a cash crop on land which otherwise produced only a poor quality of goat feed. Officials in the Greek Recovery Program estimated that about 50,000 acres of grazing land could be planted to two or three million olive trees. They added, however, that the growth of such trees would be slow, requiring 20 years to get into production instead of the usual 12-15 years.[19]

Part of the higher olive yield in Crete was credited to more frequent pruning than in the rest of Greece. Experimental evidence on this practice was not available on the island or on the mainland. Wide differences in the frequency of pruning were apparent from the survey. (See Appendix 5, Table A91.) In 1948, one-fourth of

[17] John Hadjinicolaou, memorandum to L.G.A., November 1948, and confirmed by verbal report of Dr. Hertig, World Health Organization Entomologist.

[18] G. Kavouras and C. Kafatos, nome agriculturists in Lasithi and Iraklion nomes.

[19] Ministry of Coordination, *Land Use in Crete, Greece, 1928, 1938, and 1949.* Athens. Private communication, 1951.

the farmers stated that they had never pruned their olives and an additional fifth stated that they pruned no oftener than every ten years or more. About one-third of the farmers had pruned their olive trees annually or biennially and another sixth every three to five years.

When queried as to how often they *should* prune their olive trees, only 2 per cent said "never" and 11 per cent said every ten years or more. Eighty per cent of the farmers indicated that olive trees should be pruned one or more times during a five-year period.

There is strong disagreement among both the agricultural experts and farmers as to whether a saw can be used on the olive tree without damage. Only an axe, wielded by an expert, will satisfy some specialists and many farmers. On the other hand, Dr. Panos Anagnostopoulos of the Superior School of Agriculture in Athens has used the saw, together with wound treatment, with excellent results on his experimental olive orchard.

c. *Grapes.* Without any experiment station on the island and without supervised field research, some farmers have found ways of increasing their yields of grapes considerably above the average of all farmers. In 1947, one-seventh of the farms had table grape yields which were 50 per cent or more above the average of all farms. A fourth of the farms producing either wine grapes or raisin grapes also had yields which were 50 per cent or more above the average. Studies by extension workers and other farmers of the methods used on these higher yielding farms should point the way to increased yields on additional farms.

Grape yields in Crete were not affected by grape phylloxera since it had not reached farther south than Athens. Yields of wine were affected by the attempted production of wine grapes on a high proportion of the farms, although many had soil conditions that were none too favorable. The lack of rain during the summer months was a boon to grape production, reducing diseases and the number of chemical sprays needed. Nearly all farmers who produced grapes were using the Bordeaux mixture for spraying.

The consumption of ouzo and tsikoudia (distilled spirits), retsina (wine stored in barrels lined with resin), and other local wines in lieu of water (scarce and dangerous to health in many areas) was an important part of the diet of the Cretan people. Both natural and cultural factors gave grapes a high comparative advantage in large areas of Crete.

d. *Other crops.* Citrus fruit areas were increasing where irrigation was available. Returns from these fruits were relatively higher than from olives, cereals, and many other crops. (See Chapter 6, Table 11.) Seedlings budded from new improved varieties of proven mother trees were distributed to farmers at the Kalo Khorio station south of Ay. Nikolaos. About a fourth of the farmers had yields of oranges of 56 pounds or more per tree, which was over twice as much as the average of 25 pounds per tree for all orange producers in Crete.

The Lasithi Plain is especially adapted to summer production of potatoes and has become the center of seed-potato production. Potato yields here were 127 bushels per acre, which was almost double the island average yield. Other irrigated areas produced some potatoes also, the south coastal plains producing winter potatoes. Irrigation water in the Mesara Plain would make possible August-to-December potato production. Director Pierakeas of the Mesara Experiment Station estimated that with irrigation yields of 250-300 bushels per acre would be possible.

Peanut production was limited to two coastal plains—Episcopi and Kastelli-Kisamos and a few scattered plantings where irrigation was available. They are especially adapted to the irrigated areas along the northern coast where the strong north winds hamper tree culture. Yields were said to be relatively low because of poor varieties and poor cultural practices.

Vegetable crops, including melons, were largely grown for home use, with a few commercial vegetable areas on the plains near the larger towns where irrigation was possible. Early tomatoes were one of the most profitable crops on the island and were produced on the south coast near Ierapetra where irrigation was possible. Yields of early tomatoes in 1947 were 3.25 tons per acre, as compared to 4.1 tons for all tomatoes, but prices were considerably higher. Bananas were found also in this same area and, although of poor quality and low yields, high prices made them profitable.

e. *Crop rotations.* The small amount of crop land in hay and pulses on a mountainous island indicated that Cretan farmers were unable or unwilling to use recommended crop rotations which included one or more leguminous crops in each rotation. One-third of the farmers did not have any pulses or legumes in their crop rotations. Lack of water might have been the limiting factor in their production in some areas. On the other hand, according to the rotations reported by the farmers of Crete, about one-seventh of the cultivated land considered in rotation was left fallow each year. Greek officials estimated the total fallow land at approximately one-sixth of the land in farms or about 100,000 acres. Since this land was barren during the rainy fall and winter season, lack of moisture would not prevent the growing of vetches or other suitable legumes for forage or cover crops. While a portion of this fallow land—about one-fourth—may be located in the higher mountain areas where temperatures would prevent successful production of winter legumes, large acreages are on the plains near the seacoast. Here the growing of leguminous winter cover crops could be utilized for livestock production for the prevention of soil erosion and for the supplying of needed nitrogen for cereal crops to follow.

Three-year crop rotations[20] of various types were used by almost half the farmers. (See Table 49 and Appendix 5, Table A87.) But the most commonly used was a four-year rotation consisting of "cereals-cereals-cereals-fallow." The second most common is the three-year "cereal-cereal-cereal" or "straight cereal" rotation, with the three-year "cereal-cereal-fallow" rotation a close third. The "straight cereal" rotation, including wheat, barley, oats, or maslin, and rotations consisting of cereals with one year of fallow are all soil-depleting. None of them would benefit the land, as they make no

TABLE 49. Percentage of farmers practicing various types of crop rotations[a], Crete, 1948

Length of rotation	Farmers rotating crops	Most common rotation[a] and percentage of rotation group[b]			
	(percentage)	(percentage)			(percentage)
Two years	9	*C-C	(52)	C-F	(33)
Three years	43	*C-C-C	(43)	C-C-F	(38)
Four years	37	C-C-C-F	(52)	C-C-C-H	(8)
Five years	11	C-C-C-F-P	(32)	C-C-C-F-F	(20)

a Letters used to indicate crops: C-cereal; F-fallow; H-hay; P-pulses.

b Figures in parentheses indicate percentage of farmers in that "length of rotation" group who use the type of rotation listed.

* A combination of continuous cereals but with different crops—wheat, barley, maslin, oats—from year to year.

Source: Sample Survey of Crete, Form B, Farm.

[20] While many of these rotations would not be so classified by agronomists, they do indicate the attitude of farmers in Crete toward the changing of the cereal crop grown on a piece of land from year to year.

provision for legumes or grass crops for soil building, soil conservation, or for livestock feed.

f. *Fertilizers.* With the types of rotations used by farmers in Crete, crop yields can be maintained only by the use of commercial fertilizers in addition to the conservation and use of the limited quantities of animal manure available. But the natural fertilizers were not utilized as effectively as they might be. One-third of the farmers stated that they stored their animal manures in the stable, one-third in pits, and the remainder spread direct to fields. Of those farmers who stored animal manure, one-half stored for 6-8 months, two-fifths for 10-12 months, and the remainder for 3-4 months.

The farmers of Crete used 31.8 pounds or three times as many nutrients—nitrogen (N), phosphorus pentoxide (P_2O_5), and potassium (in terms of K_2O)—in commercial fertilizers per acre of cultivated crops as any other area of Greece and nine times the national average. Even in comparison with other European countries the Island of Crete, with 32 pounds, used more commercial-fertilizer nutrients per acre in pre-war years than Spain (18 pounds), Italy (19 pounds), and France (28 pounds). In comparison with Germany, Belgium, and the Netherlands, however, Crete used relatively small quantities of commercial fertilizers per acre.[21]

The lack of nitrogen and phosphorus in most of the soils and the high lime content in others emphasize the need for commercial fertilizers containing phosphorus as well as nitrogen. On these soils containing calcium, soluble forms of phosphate fertilizers (superphosphates) will give better results than raw rock phosphate or other relatively insoluble phosphates, which are very slowly available and of very little value on such soils.

In 1948, slightly more than half the farmers who produced cereals, table grapes, and raisin grapes used commercial fertilizers on these crops. One-fourth of the farmers raising olives, oranges, and wine grapes used commercial fertilizers to increase yields, but only one-tenth of the farmers producing pulses applied commercial fertilizers to that crop.

Mr. Pierakeas, Director of the Mesara Station, emphasized the need of additional fertilizer research to correct the present misuse of fertilizer on the island, stating that "thousands of tons go into the sea every year." The use of a 6-8-8 fertilizer containing nitrogen, phosphorus, and potassium plant food nutrients in those ratios on soils in which there were abundant supplies of potassium is a case in point. The use of nitrogen fertilizers on pulses and alfalfa and applications of fertilizers containing only phosphate to cereals were other examples of misuse of critical and costly fertilizer nutrients.

Since the more commercialized farms which produced the larger acreages of the various crops tended to use fertilizers more than the farms with smaller acreages, three-fifths to four-fifths of the cereal, table grape, and raisin grape acreages were fertilized. One-half of the orange tree acreage, about one-third of the olive and wine grape acreages, and a sixth of the acreage in pulses received commercial fertilizer applications. Specific figures were not secured for vegetable crops, but because of their importance in supplying human food, they probably received preferential treatment in the use of fertilizers, especially animal manures. In contrast to the heavily populated areas of the Far East, "night soil" was not used in Crete.

Although many factors, such as differences in soils, crop rotations, quantities of animal manure applied, crop varieties, and other management and cultural practices, affected crop yields, the differences in yields between crops grown on farms *using* commercial fertilizers and those on farms *not using* fertilizers seem worthy of note, especially for pulses and all types of grapes. Fertilized fields of pulses, wine, and raisin grapes gave yields one-third greater than unfertilized fields; while fertilized table-grape acreages produced three-fourths more. In contrast, yields on fertilized fields of oranges, olives, and cereals were less than one-sixth larger than on fields not receiving commercial fertilizer. (For further details see Table 50.) Some reduction in quality of wine was reported from grapes receiving applications of commercial fertilizers. This consideration may help to explain the small percentage of wine grape land receiving fertilizer applications.

Since many farmers used commercial fertilizer on poor land which would not produce crops without it, these comparisons do not tell the whole story of the effect of fertilizers on crop yields. This is especially true of cereals, olives, and wine grapes, which were produced on more than four-fifths of the farms, including a great area of poor land.

For these and other reasons, figures of net return above fertilizer costs cannot be computed accurately from data available. Special experimental research on similar soils, etc., where the only variable is the amount of fertilizer used, would need to be carried on for sev-

TABLE 50. Crop yields classified by use or non-use of fertilizers, Crete, 1947

Crops	Yield			Difference		Percentage of acreage fertilized
	Average	Fertilized	Not fertilized	Quantity	Percentage	
	(bu. per acre)					
All cereals	9.6	9.8	9.0	0.8	9	72
Pulses	11.0	14.3	10.3	4.0	38	16
Grapes	(cwt. per acre)					
Table (grapes)	61.6	74.8	42.3	32.5	77	60
Wine (wine)	26.3	31.6	23.5	8.1	35	35
Raisin (raisins)	15.4	16.6	12.4	4.2	34	74
	(lbs. per tree)					
Olives	7.6	8.2	7.1	1.1	16	38
Oranges	24.3	26.5	23.1	3.4	15	51

Source: Sample Survey of Crete, Form B, Farm.

eral years before an accurate measure of such returns could be secured.

Nevertheless, rough calculations based on differences in gross value of product from fertilized and unfertilized fields, with fertilizer costs deducted, indicated a wide margin in gross returns above fertilizer costs only—about $180 per acre in 1947—in favor of table grapes grown on fertilized fields. Raisin grapes also indicated a margin of $17 per acre above fertilizer cost while wine grapes showed less than $6 margin. On the other hand, wheat and olives showed little or no net returns above fertilizer costs.

These data help to explain why small percentages of farmers used commercial fertilizers on wine grapes and olives. The higher percentage of wheat growers using fertilizers indicated that much of this land might have been of the type requiring fertilizers in order to produce even a low-yielding crop. A total yield of four bushels per acre (less than half the average) from land that would not produce a crop unless fertilized would more than pay for its application in an area short of cereals, where the market price was $5.50 to $6.00 per bushel.

Despite plentiful supplies of limestone and gypsum there were evidences of soil conditions which need applications of these materials. Dr. P. Anagnostopoulos of the Superior School of Agriculture stated that both the cankerous growths on olive tree limbs and fern growth under olive trees could be corrected and prevented by applications of gypsum to such fields.

g. *Plant diseases and insects.* One-fourth to two-fifths of the farmers reported mildew as the most serious disease affecting vegetables and grapevines. Rust on grapes, vegetables, and cereal crops was also serious. Although less serious, aphis was reported for grapes, cereals, and vegetables. Anthracnose was more important than aphis for grapes. The use of the Bordeaux mixture and other insecticides was common throughout the island.

Ninety-eight per cent of the farmers stated that their olive trees were infested with the dacus fly in 1948. This problem and the control methods now in use have already been discussed.

"Branch sclerosis" (*Koryphoxira*), a parasitic and exceedingly infectious disease which attacks the lemon, citron, and bitter orange, according to P. Linardos, Director of the Phytopathological Laboratory, was becoming so serious that it seemed possible that lemons might be eliminated from the island economy, much as citrons had been eliminated during the past two decades. Research on this disease might develop satisfactory control measures.

A partially used Phytopathological Laboratory of ten rooms was available for reactivation in Iraklion. A small but ineffective staff was being maintained. A complete reorganization was in process. The Director of this work in the Ministry of Agriculture at Athens expressed his interest in having an entomologist from another country as adviser to the Laboratory to develop an effective and up-to-date research program.

2. *Livestock Production and Practices*

Livestock production in Crete was definitely limited by the few land areas suitable for feed and forage crops. The heavy human population made it necessary to get maximum food production on the small areas suitable for crop production, as was pointed out in Chapter 6.

Numbers of most kinds of livestock seemed to be somewhat less than pre-war, although estimates varied widely. Estimates by the community presidents indicated that all livestock numbers except poultry and rabbits were back to pre-war levels of 1933-1937 or above. In general it was the feeling of both farmers and agricultural scientists that except for power animals, livestock numbers were still 20 to 30 per cent below pre-war levels. It was estimated that about 2,700 cows were used for milk in Crete, and one-third of these were also used for work.

Numbers of swine and poultry were sharply reduced because of the shortage of feed grains in the immediate post-war period. These animals were largely scavengers which range about the yard and village for their feed, and receive a minimum of grains suitable for food consumption. Three-fourths of the farms reported less than 10 chickens in their poultry flocks and none over 50 chickens. Agriculturists estimated the average annual egg production per hen at the low figure of 50 to 60 eggs each. (Also see Appendix 5, Tables A93 and A94.)

About three-fifths of the sheep and goats in Crete were in nomadic herds collected from several families and placed in the care of a shepherd. These herds moved up into the mountains in early spring and returned to the coastal plains in the late fall. The principal lambing seasons were in August-September and in February-March-April. Sheep and goats furnished the principal source of meat and milk to the Cretan people. Most families kept one or more goats and sheep in the village to furnish milk for the family. An average of about 60 pounds of cheese also was produced per family, but a large share of this was produced in the mountains from the nomadic herds during the cheese-producing season in early spring and early fall. After the lambs and kids had suckled their mothers for twenty to thirty days, the mothers were placed in corrals at night and milked by the shepherds. This milk either was made into cheese on the mountains by the shepherds or itinerant cheesemakers, or was brought down to the villages for this purpose.

3. *Farming Systems*

Based on the land use, crop, and livestock data, as well as a rather complete field-reconnaissance survey of the island, the major type-of-farming areas have been outlined on the Land Use map. This map shows only the principal areas of production of the various crops, as most crops were grown throughout the island—where soil and climate permitted. This was especially true of cereals, olives, wine grapes, and vegetable crops for home use. Except for olives, which did not grow above 2,000-2,600 feet elevation, these crops were found in almost every community on the island.

The areas of heaviest olive production were located near Ierapetra and Khania. Other major olive producing areas along the northern coast were found near Kastelli-Kisamos, Kastelli-Pedhiadhos, and east of Rethimnon and Sitia. Palaiokhora and portions of the Mesara Plain also had large olive groves. The most extensive cereal (wheat and barley) production was found in the Mesara Plain, especially the eastern half. The major raisin grape areas were near Iraklion, Sitia, and Khania, while table grapes were concentrated near Ano Arkhanais, southwest of Iraklion. (See Land Use color map.)

Climatic conditions, together with the availability of irrigation water, were responsible for the concentration of the production of citrus fruits, apples, peanuts, bananas, early tomatoes, and commercial crops of potatoes and vegetables in specific regions. The citrus fruit area was south and west of Khania in some valleys protected from the northern winds. Apples and potatoes were concentrated in the Lasithi Plain and other high intermount basins of Omalos and Khandra. By improving the water resources greater seed-potato production in the Lasithi Plain and a winter-potato crop in the Mesara Plain would be possible. Peanuts were grown on the Episcopi Plain near Yeoryioupolis, where northern winds prevented tree growth and where irrigation was available. Some peanuts were also produced on the southern coast near Ierapetra, where early tomatoes and bananas were grown because of irrigation water and subtropical climate. The major commercial vegetable crops were on the coastal plains near each of the three principal cities. Nearness to the market was an additional factor in the case of the truck gardens.

Climatic and soil conditions were largely responsible for the location of the major production areas for raisin and table grapes, cherries, walnuts, almonds, and chestnuts. The walnuts and almonds were concentrated in Lasithi nome while the chestnuts were found only in western Khania nome on the noncalcareous base soils. Carobs were found mostly in Rethimnon and Lasithi nomes growing in a semi-wild condition on land unsuited for other than nomadic grazing. As would be expected, the nomadic herds of sheep and goats took over the more mountainous areas from one end of the island to the other, from early spring until late fall. This enterprise was the major source of income for the high mountain communities.

While each of these type-of-farming areas was quite distinct, there were some mixtures of farming systems within each of them, according to the availability of land and water. Probably the most specialized and most intensive farming system in Crete was in the Sultana raisin grape district near Iraklion. Except for a few olive trees and a garden, most of these farmers produced nothing but raisin grapes, using two to four workers on their small acreages. In this district, farm size was measured by the number of workers rather than by the acreage or number of vines. Much the same specialization existed on the Rosaki table grape farms in nearby Ano Arkhanais. In contrast, the vegetable crop areas tended to produce some cereals and olives as supplementary and complementary crops to their major production.

At the time of the survey the citrus fruit crop was largely a joint enterprise with other fruits, olives, or cereals. Especially was this true on farms where irrigation had been made available rather recently during the past decade. There was some evidence of a continuing complementary relationship of citrus fruit and other tree crops in the Mesara Plain where the strong sirocco winds might cause damage unless wind protection was provided.

Because of the topography of the land, its elevation and lack of irrigation water, many farmers in the high mountain sheep and goat communities produced relatively less food for household consumption. Interestingly enough, the only visible evidence to survey staff members of malnutrition in rural communities was found in one of these communities. On the other hand, most of the principal sheep and goat communities, such as Anoyia, had some land at lower elevations which was used for olives, cereals, and gardens. Under such conditions, diets were above the average in most nutrients and especially in animal proteins.

In general, the farming systems in Crete were of a subsistence type, producing largely for home use with some surplus for market. But the more commercial type of farms producing food for export— table grapes, raisin grapes, and citrus fruits—were small, highly specialized farms, utilizing large amounts of family or hired labor.

E. Farm Incomes and Prices

Because of the importance of agriculture in the total economy of Crete, some further discussion of cash and total incomes of those engaged directly in the industry and of farm prices seems warranted. (See also Chapter 5.)

282 AGRICULTURE

1. Farm Incomes

The average total income for all rural households was $453, which is about one-fifth less than for the city households. The average total income of $708 for "farmers with other occupations" was the third highest among the ten occupational groups. Farmer households averaged $582 total income, which was about $100 higher than the average for all households on the island. Rural farm laborer households averaged total incomes of $229, or less than one-half that for all households. Farm laborer households for cities and communities averaged $201 cash income and $286 total income. About one out of every 13 farm laborer households was in the city, reflecting the proximity of Iraklion to the raisin and table grape districts and Khania to the raisin grape and citrus fruit districts.

The effect of the amount of home produce on total income is suggested in Table 51, which shows the percentage distribution by income groups for total income and cash income for the three agricultural groups of households.

TABLE 51. Total incomes and cash incomes of "farmers and other," farmers, and farm laborers, by income classes, Crete, 1947

Income class	Total incomes			Cash incomes		
	Farmers and other[a]	Farmers and managers	Farm laborer	Farmers and other	Farmers	Farm laborer
(dollars)			(percentage)			
0-249	9	22	70	50	57	77
250-499	35	24	17	22	25	16
500-749	24	27	11	9	13	4
750-999	12	13	—	9	3	1
1000-1249	5	9	2	6	2	1
1250 & over	15	5	—	4	—	1

[a] "Farmers and other" refers to those household heads who stated they were farmers but also had another supplementary occupation.
Source: Sample Survey of Crete, Form A, Household.

About half of the farmers, farm managers, and farmers with a supplementary occupation received less than $500 total income in 1947. Eighty-seven per cent of the farm laborers had incomes below $500. Omitting the value of home produce, however, more than half of all three groups received less than $250 cash income in 1947. Regardless of the amount of their total income, about half the annual income of farmers came from the value of home production of clothing and food.

2. Farm Prices

While the prices of agricultural products had increased to 267 times their 1939 prices by 1948, agricultural consumer goods had increased 347 times, and industrial products used in agriculture increased 376 times. (Table 40, Chapter 9.) Consequently, inflated prices had benefited only those farmers who had a considerable surplus for sale and those whose production required the purchase of relatively few supplies. The farmers had also been under government pressure to keep agricultural prices down in order to hold food prices as low as possible. The rehabilitation of agriculture in a war-torn and occupied area, however, had necessitated the buying of many things not frequently purchased during a high-cost period—harnesses, carts, hoes, shovels, and other items lost, strayed, or stolen during occupation.

The seasonal variation in the prices of the several agricultural products differed greatly, in accordance with their perishability and competitive uses.[22] Cereals on the Iraklion market were cheaper at harvest time in June than in the winter month of December. Other products which could be stored—such as potatoes, onions, walnuts, and alfalfa—showed the same tendency though in different months of the year. On the other hand, some perishables and products to be processed, such as table grapes, raisin grapes, and wine grapes, had their highest and lowest prices during the same month. This rapid price fluctuation for grapes probably resulted from an attempt to "find" the market price for the year's crop when several types of processors, in competition with each other and exporters to off-the-island markets, were seeking to obtain their share of an output which had two or three alternative uses. For example, two of the main raisin varieties of grapes (Sultana and Rosaki) were used also as table grapes—the early harvest having a higher alternative fresh-fruit market in the Iraklion area.

Prices also varied more widely in some areas of the island than in others. Prices of most commodities varied more widely in Khania

[22] C. Kafatos, G. Kavouras, S. G. Boultadakis, "Month of Highest, Lowest, and Average Price Received by Farmers for Various Farm Products, 1947." Unpublished data, Khania, November 1948.

nome than in Iraklion or Lasithi. Unfortunately, data were not supplied from Rethimnon nome. Pork product prices varied more in Iraklion, probably because the larger city demand and distance to hinterland pork production made the supply of a perishable product —with warm temperatures and no refrigeration—subject to more price fluctuation in accordance with the current demand.

These fluctuations and differences in prices reflected both difficult transportation and communication facilities and differences in quality of products as between areas as well as within the same market. With small holdings, long-time crops (trees and vines), and lack of adult education, standardization of products and quick adoption of new improved varieties of these crops were difficult. To a degree, all of these differences were reflected in price differences.

In brief, incomes of farmers and prices of farm products varied widely, although not as much as in more commercialized agricultural areas. Post-war inflation had raised costs to farmers at a faster rate than it had the prices of his products. With relatively high fixed charges in terms of fertilizers and living costs, coupled with a small volume of marketable produce and reduced market outlets, the average farmer of Crete had not been able to profit from war and post-war inflation as much as the farmers in areas where commercial farming was dominant.

F. SUMMARY

Agriculture in Crete has changed relatively little during the past four thousand years. The survey found that primitive methods of production, marketing, and transportation were in general use. Power and machinery in agriculture were largely of the Minoan era. Half the farmers marketed by donkey-back. The hand sickle and the threshing floor were the major means of harvesting and threshing cereals.

Ninety-six per cent of the farmers owned all or part of the land which they operated, most of it secured through inheritance. Only 4 per cent of the owners had a land mortgage, averaging $184 with 8 per cent interest. About three-fifths of the farmers had a chattel mortgage, averaging $72. The farms averaged 9.2 acres in size with nine-tenths of them less than 25 acres in area. On the average these small farms consisted of 13 lots scattered throughout the community, requiring 5 to 90 minutes to reach them. These farms were valued

An olive grove in the eastern Mesara Plain

A cooperative olive oil factory in Rethimnon nome

Goats and sheep furnish most of the milk and meat in the Cretan diet

at $5,500 and had equipment consisting of small tools, plow, saddle, and harness valued at $32. Two-thirds of the farmers belonged to a cooperative purchasing or marketing association.

About two-thirds of the average farm was in crops, divided about equally among cereals, olives, and a mixture of other crops—vineyards, fruit trees, vegetables, and forage crops. Ninety-seven per cent of the farms produced olives, 85 per cent wine grapes, and 83 per cent cereals. The livestock consisted of a donkey, a couple of sheep, a goat or two, a half-dozen chickens, and less than a half-dozen sheep or goats in a nomadic herd. Livestock production was limited by the land areas suitable for feed and forage crops and the need for food crops for human consumption.

Low crop yields reflected limited natural and capital resources, in spite of abundant labor resources. Two-fifths of the farms did not practice a crop rotation. Scarcity of water during the summer months, limited or improper use of fertilizers, and damage by insect pests and plant diseases also reduced crop production. The dacus fly was estimated to reduce the olive crop by a fourth to a half. One-fourth of the farmers had never pruned their olive trees. Commercial fertilizers were used on the majority of the acreages in cereals, raisin and table grapes, and oranges; they were used on limited acreages of olive trees and wine grapes.

In brief, the major agricultural problems center on a fuller utilization of available manpower resources through increased capital outlays and improved management practices to increase output. Larger capital outlays would make possible such things as the development of the Mesara Plain, the Lasithi Plain and other areas through irrigation or water control projects, the erection of processing plants for further processing of certain agricultural products, and the necessary research work for the control of the dacus fly and other insect pests and diseases. Problems which require less capital but sounder management practices include the proper use of fertilizers, weed control in cereal crops, olive tree pruning, the use of improved crop varieties, improved grading and better market outlets, and increased legume and forage crop production to improve the crop rotation and increase feed for livestock production. The need for greater quantities of animal products to improve diets has already been mentioned in Chapter 6. Other problems involve the development of methods to reduce land fragmentation and allow the introduction of mechanization (perhaps on a cooperative basis) in the few areas where it can be used—especially in a possible Mesara Plain development project. The latter would also provide for the introduction of new crops to utilize more fully the labor and capital resources and for possible reforestation on nearby mountain slopes.

CHAPTER 11

INDUSTRY AND COMMERCE

THE LEVEL of living of the population of Crete depends not only upon the quantity and efficiency of the production factors in agriculture —but also upon the quantity and efficiency of manufacturing and trade and the development of a balanced economy which effectively utilizes all available resources.[1]

A. POWER

The survey found that animal power was used not only in agricultural production but also in industry, commerce, and trade. Mules and donkeys were the major source of power in the operation of the water-pumps, olive oil crushers and presses, and in transportation. Diesel or gas engines, windmills, charcoal, and water also were used for power in Crete.

At the time of the survey water power resources were small and scattered. The only hydroelectric plant of any importance, located at Ayia Springs, supplied the city of Khania intermittently with a third to a half of its electric current.

According to a report from the Ministry of Finance there were seven electric-power plants in Crete. Two of these, including the one at Ayia Springs, were in Khania province, one in Rethimnon, one in Iraklion, and three in Lasithi nome at Sitia, Ierapetra, and Ay. Nikolaos.[2] But the Lasithi engineer also reported electric plants in Neapolis, Máles, and Tourtoula.[3] There may have been other small plants near larger springs or operated with German diesel engines near former airfields.

In each of these communities the supply of electricity was insufficient for consumer needs and the cost was relatively high. In Khania it was 14 cents per kilowatt-hour or about double the price paid in United States cities of comparable size. In Sitia the existing requirements were almost three times the capacity of the 90 horsepower plant. The survey showed that only 2.5 per cent of rural community

---

[1] For brevity this chapter is called "Industry and Commerce," although power, internal trade, tourism, transportation, warehousing, storage, grading, and refrigeration are also included.

[2] Ministry of Finance, Khania, protocol no. 1522, May 18, 1948.

[3] Lasithi Nomarch, protocol no. 2939, May 4, 1948, Nomarch to Governor-General.

households had electricity and only 46.4 per cent of the households in the nome capitals had electric lights.

Many small gristmills were operated by water power in areas where larger springs were found, such as Drapania, Spili, Stavrochori, Zakros, and Zaros. In some places the water was used several times (4 to 7) in a succession of mills below the springs before it was used finally for irrigation purposes. Even here, there was great waste of power during the many hours when milling was not done.

Windmills with large cloth sails, set at little if any angle, were used for pumping water from shallow wells on several coastal plains and in the intermountain basins where winds were strong and frequent. In 1929, Gardner Richardson, Commercial Attaché in Greece, stated: "There are 6,000 windmills of so-called 'Aeolian' type in operation on the plains in the Province of Lasithi which embraces one-sixth of the Island. All of these have been erected in the last five years—made by farmers and local blacksmiths. . . . The total horse-power of the 6,000 mills is estimated at 4,000 h.p. . . . American mills are too high in cost.[4] Most of these mills were still in operation. In addition, there were a few thousand in the nome of Iraklion, especially on the Mallia Plain and in the plain near Arkalokhori. How efficient these windmills were in the use of available winds was questioned by both irrigation engineers and the consulting engineering geologist. Since they became completely inadequate on the Mallia Plain during the short but critical three to six weeks' period of gentle breezes in May and June some study to improve their design for efficiency was suggested.

The larger factories and newer cooperative oil presses had installed diesel engines for power. While these engines were efficient for this purpose they necessitated the import of expensive fuel oil. This required that they be used primarily for highly productive purposes. In rural areas funds for the purchase of engines and necessary equipment were lacking. The uncertainty of securing imported fuels was an added complication in their use.

However, Crete is fairly close to the great Middle East oil supplies and lies to the north of the main oil-supply line from the Middle East through the Mediterranean to the Western world. Oil pipe lines are being laid to the western Lebanon Coast. Oil tankers also come through the Suez Canal. These fuel-oil supplies for power production

---

[4] Gardner Richardson, letter of January 8, 1929 to Director, Bureau Foreign and Domestic Commerce, Washington, D.C.

may offer the best possibility for an expanded industrialization or agricultural-development program if local lignite supplies are found to be uneconomical. If the economy of the island should improve, fuel oil might well replace a portion of the wood and charcoal used for fuel.

Charcoal was used in many service industries. Brick kilns, raisin factories, soap factories, and other industries requiring heat used charcoal, wood, olive pomace or "sensa" (olive seed and pulp residue), and usually did not depend on imported fuels, which would have required additional capital outlays for financing and equipment.

Because of the timber shortage on the island, the use of charcoal burners on automobiles or trucks had not been developed, as in Italy. For autos, buses, and trucks, imported gasoline (benzine) was used. But at 54 cents a U.S. gallon, tax included, this type of fuel had limited use.

While there were additional possibilities for water power development, none of the presently known sources was large enough to assist greatly in solving the power or fuel problem of the island. Until more is known about the possibilities of the lignite mines in Crete, further development of power depends upon more efficient use of present facilities, or increased imports of fuel or fuel oil. With current exchange difficulties, these imports must be utilized only for productive purposes which can show a profit over high costs of installation and operation. Until new sources are made available, new industries requiring much power—or in many places, any at all— must provide their own source of power.

B. INDUSTRY

Industry in Crete was characterized by small plants clustered in three northern coastal cities, with a few processing industries scattered over the island in the larger villages. Industrialization in Crete was far below even the meager level of the mainland. Tremendous strides in industrial development took place in Greece during the two decades preceding World War II, the value of industrial production increasing 1,300 per cent and the volume of production 200 per cent from 1921 to 1939. The base of this development, however, was exceedingly small.[5] But that experience does suggest the neces-

[5] American Military Government, *Civil Affairs Handbook on Greece*, sec. 8, "Industry and Commerce," Armed Forces Services, Washington, 1943. Declassified circular 20, January 1946, p. 8.

sary components of any considerable expansion in industrial production in Greece or Crete. Power production was expanded greatly, capital was invested with confidence, skilled management developed new industries, competent technicians trained in other countries returned to Greece to direct and operate new enterprises, and skilled labor was available. All these were combined during the 1920's and 1930's to start Greece toward some industrial expansion.

Most of the gains were on the mainland. Greek industry was mainly concentrated in a few firms located in a few strategic mainland cities, such as Athens-Piraeus, Salonika, Volos, and Patrai. However, the town of Iraklion in Crete ranked fifth among the top ten cities in number of establishments employing five or more workmen in 1940.[6] The importance of Iraklion, Khania, and Rethimnon in the industrial production of Crete in 1940 is clearly evidenced by the length of the bars indicating the number of workmen in industries with five or more workmen for the major towns of Crete and Greece (Figure 17).

In 1928, industrial production in Crete was estimated at $2,000,-000—about 2 per cent of the estimated value of all industrial production in Greece for 1929.[7] Processing of agricultural products accounted for most of the industrial development on the island.

1. Number and Types of Factories

In Crete, according to the survey, nearly all industries and factories processed or manufactured food, clothing, or building products (brick, tile, window and door frames). Of the 243 factories listed by the Ministry of Finance and the Iraklion Chamber of Commerce, 39 per cent utilized products of the olive tree; 9 per cent processed products of the vineyards; 9 per cent processed livestock products; 18 per cent prepared cloth and leather for island use; 5 per cent milled flour; 3 per cent processed other agricultural products; 11 per cent manufactured shelter products; and the remaining 6 per cent included electricity, ice, and pottery plants and tobacco factories.[8] About two-thirds of these factories were in Khania and

[6] C. A. Doxiadis, and Others, *The Sacrifices of Greece in the Second World War,* pages unnumbered.

[7] R. B. Curren, Commercial Attaché, Athens, report no. 685 on Crete, November 26, 1929, to United States Department of Commerce.

[8] Ministry of Finance, Khania, protocol no. 1522, May 18, 1948, pp. 2-4. Chamber of Industry and Commerce of Iraklion, reference no. 3704, December 15, 1947, pp. 2-3.

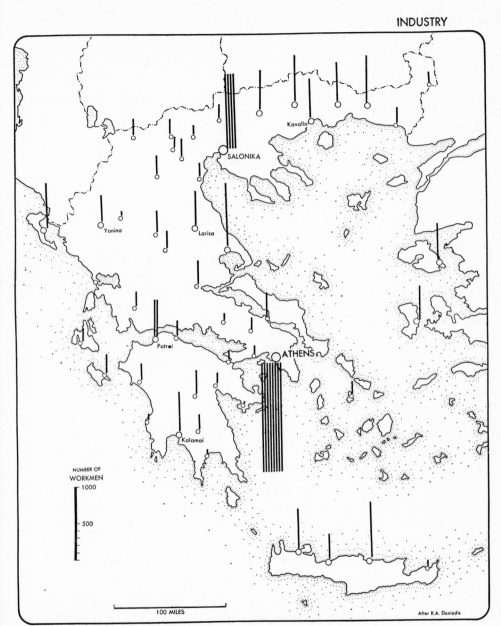

NUMBER OF
WORKMEN
— 1000

— 500

100 MILES

After K.A. Doxiadis

Based on chart in *The Sacrifices of Greece*, C. A. Doxiadis and Others, Athens.

FIGURE 17. Major industrial centers, Crete and Greece, 1940

Iraklion nomes. Further details as to numbers and location by types are shown in Table 52.

The importance of olive, grape, cereal, and livestock production in Crete for supplying raw materials for these various industries is indicated by the high proportion (80 per cent) of the factories which utilized these products. These included oil, soap, raisin, wine, and cheese factories, flour mills, carob mills, and vegetable, fruit, and essential oil plants. Many of the raw materials for the flour mills, macaroni factories, weaving factories, and woodworking industries were imported.

TABLE 52. Industrial plants, by type and location, Crete, 1948

Type of product processed or manufactured	Khania	Rethimnon	Iraklion	Lasithi	Island Total
(number of plants by nome)					
Olives	12	16	9	22[a]	96[b]
Grapes	1	—	17	2	22[b]
Flour and macaroni	3	1	4	4[a]	12
Juices (vegetable and fruit)	2	—	1	—	3
Cheese					22[b]
Carob	—	—	3	2	5
Cloth and leather	25	10	7	2	44
Building materials, etc.	7	—	19	—	26
Other (electricity, ice, pottery, tobacco)	4	1	4	4	13
Total number of plants	54	28	64	36	243[b]

[a] Eight "olive oil factories and flour mills" reported have been distributed equally between "olives" and "flour and macaroni" in this table.

[b] These figures include the following cooperative enterprises for which specific locations are not given: 37 oil crushers, 2 wine presses, and 22 cheese factories.

Source: Ministry of Finance, Khania, protocol no. 1522. May 18, 1948, pp. 2-4. Chamber of Industry and Commerce of Iraklion, reference no. 3704. December 15, 1947, pp. 2-3.

Besides the above industries and factories, the Crete Survey indicated that there were on the island 85 grape pressers, 2,400 olive crushers, 2,200 mule-driven hand-operated oil presses, 390 mechanical oil pressers, and 51 distillators. These were in the rural communities, extracted the oil for further processing in the city factories, and were seasonal in operation. They required two to five persons for operation, although some of the new power-driven oil crushers and presses were larger and used additional personnel. Undoubtedly there were additional numbers of small wine presses, flour mills, and other small plants scattered throughout the island.

There were 12 quarries, 23 kilns, and 16 pottery works employing 312 persons in the four nome capitals. Additional industries of this type were scattered over the island, bringing the total to 165 quarries and 10 gypsum mines in operation.

In Rethimnon there were 127 handicraft factories making shoes with 350 workers, 15 tanneries with 80 workers, 20 saddleries with 90, and 46 woodworking factories with 140. While similar data were not secured from other large towns, leather and woodworking were important handicraft industries in other parts of Crete.

2. Size and Efficiency

Judged by Western standards, these factories were small. They utilized small amounts of power and had few employees. About half the establishments employed 11 or fewer employees and the other half 12 to 25 persons. A few employed 50 or more people. The only factories utilizing more than 100 horsepower were a flour mill with 325 horsepower, an alcohol factory with 180 horsepower, and a raisin factory with 110 horsepower. Most of the factories used 15 to 35 horsepower developed from steam, diesel, or benzine-powered engines.

Wide variations in size and productive efficiency were found in the same industry.[9] For example, a study of eleven Sultana raisin factories in Iraklion indicated a range in daily output from 6 to 60 tons per 8-hour day. (See Appendix 5, Table A102.) The number of laborers and employees varied from 8 to 360 per factory and the horsepower from 18 to 110. Size as measured by output or input, however, is not indicative of efficiency in raisin production in Crete. One of the smaller raisin factories produced one ton of raisins with the same amount of horsepower but only one-sixth the man labor required by two of the larger factories. The most efficient third of these factories processed raisins with 30 per cent less power and one-fourth as much labor per ton as the least efficient third. An analysis of production methods in the more efficient factories of all types of industries should provide useful suggestions for increased efficiency and lowered costs in other factories.

[9] Chamber of Industry and Commerce of Iraklion, reference no. 3704, pp. 2-3. Copy of letter to Mr. William L. Tait, December 15, 1947.

3. Additional Factories Requested

Types of additional factories needed on the island were suggested by the local government representatives. According to their requests for assistance, 39 additional oil factories, 16 cheese factories, 10 canning plants, two wine factories, three carob mills, and one tannery were needed in Lasithi and Rethimnon nomes. In Khania nome the Agricultural Bank had built 11 cooperative crushing plants with hydraulic presses and planned 97 more.[10] Funds then available provided for only three each year, although eight to ten could be built annually if funds were available.

Large quantities of laurel leaves, dictame, and thyme were exported in the pre-war period, and local authorities suggested that essential oil factories be erected in Crete to process these native plants.

On the other hand, a canning plant of 700 tins (1 kilogram each) daily capacity was in storage awaiting delivery to the Credit Union of Khania. Although paid for on December 14, 1946, suitable premises for its use had not been found two years later. Similarly, factory equipment for the daily manufacture of more than 7 tons of oranges into orange juice and essential oils remained idle because the seven chief orange-growing villages could not agree upon a suitable site for the erection of the plant. Funds and encouragement had been offered by the Agricultural Bank but the machinery remained idle at Kalamata.[11]

4. Industrial Labor Force

About one-sixth of the labor force in Crete was engaged in manufacturing and handicraft industries. In the four nome capitals about two-fifths of the labor force was engaged in these industries.

This industrial labor force included the craftsmen, foremen and kindred workers (22.1 per cent of the labor force), the operatives and kindred workers (7.5 per cent), and a portion of the non-farm laborers (16.8 per cent) and proprietors, managers, and officials (8.4 per cent) (Table 53).

In addition to commercial enterprises, spinning was carried on in more than half of the households and weaving in more than a third.

[10] William L. Tait, *Field Report; Island of Crete.* December 5-23, 1947 to Herbert P. Lansdale, AMAG, Appendix VIII.
[11] *ibid.*, p. 15.

TABLE 53. Percentage of labor force in various occupations, four nome
capitals, Crete, 1948

Craftsmen, foremen, and kindred workers	22.1
Laborers (non-farm)	16.8
Service workers (not domestic)	15.0
Clerical workers and sales people	9.3
Proprietors, managers, and officials	8.4
Operatives and kindred workers	7.5
Professional workers	5.6
Farmers and farm managers	3.7
Farm laborers	2.8
Domestic servants	2.3
Farm workers unpaid	2.8
Occupation unknown	3.7
Total	100.0

Source: Sample Survey of Crete, Form A, Household.

While the majority of this production was for home use, some articles
were sold or exchanged with neighbors.

C. COMMERCE

The commerce of Crete consisted of exports of surplus processed
agricultural products and a few raw materials. Imports were mostly
food, construction materials, fuel, and fertilizers either unavailable
or in insufficient quantities on the island.

1. Exports

Some of the agricultural products processed in Cretan industrial
plants were shipped to the mainland and to foreign markets. The
main exports from Crete in 1947-1948, according to the Finance
Department Office, were "olive oil, soap, carob beans, acorns, dried
raisins, citrus fruit, wine, table grapes, mineral ores, gypsum, lignite, olive residue oil, cheese, charcoal, cattle, pigs, and potatoes."[12]

For the period April 1, 1947 to February 29, 1948, the principal
exports from Crete to the mainland and to foreign countries were
citrus fruit, carob beans, raisins, olive oil, and wine (Table 54). Of
the 95,000 metric tons of these commodities exported during this
eleven-month period, more than two-fifths were citrus fruit, a fourth
dried raisins and wine, a fifth carob beans, and one-tenth olive oil.

[12] Ministry of Finance, Khania, protocol no. 1522, May 18, 1948, p. 1.

All the citrus fruit and four-fifths of the wine and raisin shipments were sent to foreign countries. Only one-tenth of the carob bean and olive oil shipments went to foreign markets, the remainder going to mainland cities.[13]

Of these items exported, Khania nome furnished 99 per cent of the citrus fruit and one-fourth of the olive oil and wine exports, while Iraklion nome supplied nine-tenths of the raisins, three-fourths of the wine, and two-fifths of the olive oil shipments. Rethimnon nome produced more than half of the carob bean exports but only 5 per cent of the olive oil, while Lasithi nome supplied two-fifths of the carob beans, one-fourth of the olive oil, and 4 per cent of the dried raisins exported from Crete during this period.

TABLE 54. Principal products exported, sources by nomes, and percentage of shipments exported to foreign countries from Crete, April 1947-February 1948

Item	Quantity shipped	Shipments to foreign countries	Sources of shipments by nomes			
			Khania	Rethimnon	Iraklion	Lasithi
	(metric tons)		(percentage)			
Citrus fruit	40,563	100	99	—	1	—
Carob beans	20,704	10	3	53	5	39
Dried raisins	17,037	80	3	—	93	4
Olive oil	9,003	7	26	5	41	28
Wine	7,417	78	26	—	74	—

Source: Ministry of Finance, Khania, protocol no. 1522, May 18, 1948, p. 1.

Although the above figures were said to be less than normal because of post-war restrictions, they were indicative of the relative importance of the main export items, the percentage of each destined for foreign markets, and the nome from which shipment was made. The total of 26,222 metric tons of the above selected exports for eleven months from Iraklion was surprisingly close to the pre-war 1936-1940 annual average[14] of 26,066 metric tons for the same items from the same port. Some decline in olive oil, wine, and citrus fruit was offset by the increased tonnage of dried raisins.

Since pre-war export figures for all Crete were reported as de-

[13] *ibid.*

[14] Iraklion Chamber of Commerce and Industry, protocol no. L 1548, May 6, 1948 with tables attached.

stroyed during German occupation, the following table for Iraklion
only is used to indicate the proportion of exports of various products
from the island during 1936-1940 (Table 55). The Iraklion port
handled 45 to 60 per cent (in value and by weight) of all island
exports and imports.[15] Except, then, for citrus fruit and chestnuts

TABLE 55. Total quantity and percentage of principal commodity exports,
abroad and to interior ports from Iraklion, Crete (1936-1940 average)

	Exports		
Commodity	Total	Abroad	Interior
All commodities—in metric tons	38,664	29,349	9,315
		(percentage)	
Dried raisins	44.0	39.7	4.3
Wine and grape must	16.2	9.9	6.3
Table grapes	13.4	13.3	0.1
Olive oil	11.9	8.2	3.7
Other olive products	5.5	0.7	4.8
Carob beans	2.8	1.8	1.0
All fruit	1.3	1.2	0.1
Other	4.9	1.0	3.9
Total exports	100.0	75.8	24.2

Source: Iraklion Chamber of Commerce and Industry, protocol no. L 1548, May 6,
1948, compiled from detailed list of annual exports.

from Khania and carob beans from Rethimnon and Lasithi, these
data should indicate roughly the relative percentages of the various
products exported.

For the Iraklion area of Crete, grape products constituted three-
fourths and olive products one-sixth of the export tonnage in 1936-
1940. Fruits were 1.3 per cent of the exports, and shipments of
tobacco, firewood, sage augaman, and hides were over 50 tons each.
Small quantities of numerous other items made up 4 per cent of the
total exports. (For details see Appendix 5, Tables A104 and A105.)

Three-fourths of the exports from Iraklion—mostly grape products—went abroad. If Sultana raisins, which were two-fifths of all
exports from this port in the pre-war period, went to the following
countries in the same ratio as for all Greece, more than one-third

[15] United States Department of Commerce, Office of International Trade, Table
prepared in April 1949 for period December 1925 to June 1948 from Bulletin *Mensuel
du Commerce Spécial de la Grèce, avec des Pays Etrangers.*

went to Germany, one-fourth to Great Britain, one-tenth to Yugo-
slavia, and the remaining 8 per cent to Italy and Czechoslovakia.
Because of shipping facilities, Great Britain probably received a
larger share of the raisins from Crete than from all Greece, while
Yugoslavia and Czechoslovakia received theirs largely from the
Peloponnesus or mainland Greece by rail or truck transportation.
Interior markets on the Greek mainland absorbed a high percentage
of the wine and olive shipments from Crete.

In 1937-1938, one-third of all Greek exports, by volume, were sent
to Germany, one-sixth to the United States, and one-ninth to the
United Kingdom.[16] Italy, with 5 per cent, was the only other country
taking more than 3 per cent of the Greek exports. Similarly, Germany was the principal exporter to Greece with 28 per cent of the
total; United Kingdom with 12 per cent; Rumania, 11 per cent;
and the United States only 8 per cent.

Great Britain, the United States, and Central European countries
continued to receive the major share of the Greek exports in the
post-war period. But with unsettled conditions in Germany, and increased production of citrus fruits and raisins in the United States
and the British Commonwealth countries, markets for these products
were more limited than in pre-war days.

2. Imports

The major items of imports, by volume, to Iraklion in 1936-1940
may be classified as follows: food, 26 per cent; building and construction, 33 per cent; fertilizer, 10 per cent; coal, benzine, naphtha,
and kerosene, 11 per cent; insecticides and chemicals, 5 per cent;
and currants and raisins for re-export, 3 per cent. The remaining 12
per cent of the imports were made up of more than 114 items[17]
(Table 56).

Approximately half of the imports came direct from abroad and
many other items such as coal, wheat, and rice, which were listed from
interior ports, had originated in foreign countries. About 10,000
tons or 40 per cent of these interior imports bore additional port
taxes and reloading charges caused by routing through Piraeus
(the port of Athens)—charges that would have been avoided by
direct shipments from foreign ports.

[16] UNRRA, Operational Analysis Paper no. 14, Foreign Trade, December 1946,
p. 5.

[17] Iraklion Chamber of Commerce and Industry, protocol no. L 1548, May 6, 1948.

TABLE 56. Total quantity and percentage of principal commodity imports from abroad and interior ports to Iraklion, Crete (1936-1940 average)

Item	Imports		
	Total	Abroad	Interior
Total import shipments—metric tons	52,070	—	—
		(percentage)	
Food items	26.4	16.0	10.4
Building and construction	32.9	19.0	13.9
Insecticides and chemicals	4.4	3.5	0.9
Fertilizers	9.6	—	9.6
Fuel, benzine, and naphtha	11.1	2.3	8.8
Raisins and currants for re-export	3.4	—	3.4
Hides and leather	0.3	0.1	0.2
Cars, spare parts, and agric. implements	0.2	*	0.2
Tobacco and cigarettes	0.4	—	0.4
Paper ware	0.7	*	0.7
Others—114 items	10.6	unknown	unknown
Total imports	100.0		

* Less than 0.1 per cent.

Source: Iraklion Chamber of Commerce and Industry, protocol no. L 1548, May 6, 1948.

3. Import-Export Relationship

If Crete is to import capital equipment from abroad or is to obtain more petroleum for fuel and other industrial supplies, it is important to know something about how these imports are to be paid for. Does Crete have an export surplus that could yield foreign exchange for such purposes?

According to United States Department of Commerce data for the three main ports of the island, Crete exported about the same total tonnage of merchandise, actually 2 per cent less, that it imported during the period 1925 through June 1948. (This did not include imports during occupation or "gift" imports by UNRRA and ECA.) These three ports handled an estimated 80 to 90 per cent of the island shipping; these data then should be indicative of the relationship between merchandise imports and exports for the whole island.

If value, rather than tonnage, is used as a basis of comparison, then exports from these three ports were more than twice as large as imports during the 1925-1941 period. Except for a few years during the war, the export values of merchandise from the island were greater than the import values every year since 1926.

In the decade prior to 1926, the value of imports to Crete exceeded the value of exports—by as much as three to five times during 1918-1920. (See Figure 18 and Appendix 5, Table A106.) This excess of imports over exports came in the wake of World War I and continued during the transfer of Asia Minor refugees to the island. From 1925 to 1928, merchandise imports and exports were approximately in balance. The expansion in export values (a doubling of both the quantities and value per ton) and the decline in the quantity of imports during the thirteen-year period following, however, caused exports to rise to almost five times the value of im-

BALANCE OF TRADE

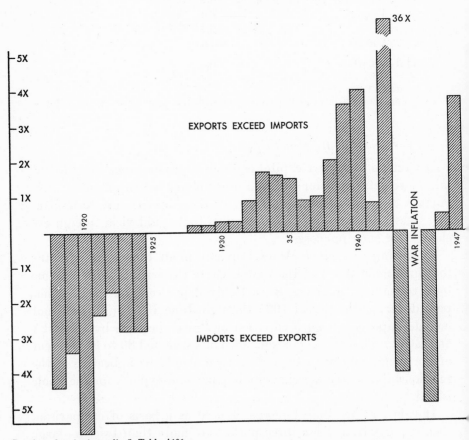

Based on data in Appendix 5, Table A106.

FIGURE 18. Balance of trade, Crete, 1918 to 1947

ports in 1939 and 1940. Again in 1947, when foreign aid supplied a large portion of food and rehabilitation items, and there was a scarcity of other desired import goods, exports were 4.7 times the value of imports for Crete.

In short, Crete shifted from the position of being a heavy net importer of goods in the early 1920's to that of being a heavy net exporter of goods in 1927 to 1948, except for three war years. Her exports were almost exclusively agricultural products with a minimum of processing. The major markets for Crete exports abroad had collapsed economically and alternative sources of supply for other countries had developed during World War II. Thus Crete may find this excess of merchandise exports diminished unless large foreign funds continue to furnish wheat and reconstruction materials or unless new markets for her products are found. Since data on the invisible items in the balance of payments for Crete are either meager or unavailable, the data for all Greece will be presented first, followed by a brief discussion of the available information for the island.

4. Balance of Payments, Greece

Greece as a whole has recently had a large deficit in her international payments, balanced by foreign aid. The balance of payments for 1948 showed a deficit in current transactions of $186.1 million, partially offset by capital imports of $77.4 million. The revised 1949 program required total aid of $224 million to cover the deficit. For 1950 the estimated deficit was $308.5 million with an additional $25 million in capital imports from revised reparations receipts, as may be noted in Table 57.

Further details available as to the make-up of certain items for 1949 and 1950 are of interest. Of the $375.7 million of imports in 1949, $83.2 million were for reconstruction and $22.7 million for invisible receipts and the United Nations Children's Fund, leaving $269.8 million for current imports. A large percentage of these current imports consisted of food needed to maintain the daily intake per capita of 2,350 calories as compared to a pre-war diet of 2,584 calories, according to the Greek Government.

Of the total expenditures of $411.9 million, $180.6 million were in currencies other than dollars, which were to be made available through $80 million of exports, $45 million of ECA drawing rights, and $55.6 million of invisibles and decreases in foreign exchange assets of the Bank of Greece in these currencies. Of the dollar funds,

TABLE 57. Balance of payments, Greece, 1948, 1949, and 1950

| | | Revised programs | |
	1948	1949	1950
		(millions of dollars)	
Imports F.O.B.	342.8	375.7	408.7
Freight	48.0	36.2	52.0
Imports C.I.F.	390.8	411.9	460.7
Exports	89.4	101.5	99.5
Net invisible receipts	115.3	56.9	27.7
Total exports	204.7	158.4	127.2
Deficit	186.1	253.5	333.5
Capital imports	77.4	29.5	25.0
Net deficit	108.7	224.0	308.5

Source: *Battle for Survival*, no. 44, July 6, 1949, p. 2, and *Quarterly Report of the Government of Greece on Operations under ECA Agreement*, October-December, 1948, Table 19.

ECA was to provide $179 million in fiscal 1949 in addition to $8.6 million carried over from April to June 1948 balances.

In 1950 the capital goods for reconstruction were estimated at $78.7 million; food and agricultural imports at $147.2 million. Net invisible receipts in 1950 showed reductions in remittances and shipping income.

Before the war, in 1938, Greece had a deficit of $5.3 million in current transactions, including both visible and invisible items. The net deficit in merchandise trade alone was $48.5 million. Among the important invisible items tending to offset this deficit were private remittances, mainly from emigrants' gifts, amounting to $23.7 million, miscellaneous items of $15.9 million, net income from tourist traffic of $3.1 million, and $9.9 million for transportation services— mainly from the Greek merchant marine. The government had a net foreign deficit.

The deficit on current transactions was offset by capital and gold movements. Notable among these was an increase of private (nonbanking) long-term investment in Greece by foreigners amounting to $9.4 million. The detailed figures are given in Table 58.

TABLE 58. Current and capital transactions, Greece, 1938 and 1947
(millions of dollars)

	1938			1947		
	Credit	Debit	Net Credit	Credit	Debit	Net Credit
CURRENT TRANSACTIONS						
1. Merchandise	93.5	142.0	−48.5	79.4	306.6	−221.2
2. Nonmonetary gold movement (net)	—	—	—	—	4.2	−4.2
3. Foreign travel	6.6	3.5	3.1	3.4	4.0	−0.6
4. Transportation	9.9	—	9.9	10.7	40.0	−29.3
5. Insurance	—	1.3	−1.3	—	—	—
6. Investment income	8.2	8.3	−0.1	0.4	0.9	−0.5
7. Government, n.i.e.	1.6	9.6	−8.0	27.1	6.2	20.9
8. Miscellaneous	15.9	—	15.9	2.2	3.2	−1.0
9. Donations	23.7	—	23.7	106.8	—	106.8
Private remittances	(23.7)	—	(23.7)	(20.0)	—	(20.0)
UNRRA	—	—	—	(28.7)	—	(28.7)
Other government grants	—	—	—	(58.1)	—	(58.1)
10. Total current transactions	159.4	164.7	−5.3	230.0	359.1	−129.1
Errors and omissions (16 minus 10)			0.1			3.5

Net Movement Increasing or Decreasing (−)

MOVEMENT OF CAPITAL AND MONETARY GOLD	Assets	Liabilities	Net Assets	Assets	Liabilities	Net Assets
Private (excluding banking institutions)						
11. Long-term capital	−9.4	—	−9.4	−21.6	—	−21.6
12. Short-term capital	—	−0.4	0.4	−18.7	3.4	−22.1
Official and banking institutions						
13. Long-term capital	−1.3	—	−1.3	—	58.1	−58.1
14. Short-term capital	1.3	−1.3	2.6	−19.0	—	−19.0
15. Monetary gold	2.5	—	2.5	−4.8	—	−4.8
16. Total movement of capital and monetary gold	−6.9	−1.7	−5.2	−64.1	61.5	−125.6

Source: International Monetary Fund, *Balance of Payments Yearbook*, 1949, Washington, p. 203.

After the war, in 1947, Greece had a deficit of $129.1 million in current transactions. The net deficit in merchandise trade alone was $221.2 million, with an even larger deficit of $305.1 million in 1946, UNRRA alone donating $210 million for that year in comparison with $28.7 million for 1947. Private remittances in 1947 were $20 million, or about the same as pre-war, while other government grants, such as American Aid to Greece, were $58.1 million. One of the outstanding differences from the pre-war period was the post-war net deficit of $29.3 million for transportation or shipping services as compared to a $9.9 million credit pre-war. This reflected a loss of ships due to the war but also some loss reportedly due to the extremely high taxes levied at Athens on the Greek Merchant Marine, resulting in some ships choosing to fly the flag of another country.

This large deficit on current transactions was offset by private long-term investments of $21.6 million and short-term investments of $22.1 million by foreigners, together with government and banking institutions' long-term capital of $58.1 million and short-term capital of $19 million.

For further details on current transactions and the movement of capital and gold to offset this deficit also see Table 58.

5. Balance of Payments for Crete

In contrast to Greece as a whole, Crete has had, in times of world peace since 1926, a considerable surplus of merchandise exports over imports. According to data supplied by the United States Department of Commerce, this excess at the three main ports in Crete was $3.75 million in 1947 and an average of about $3.90 million for the 1935-1939 period. Recent estimates, prepared for this study by the Ministry of Coordination, place the average pre-war (1936-1938) excess of merchandise exports at $1.8 million annually and the post-war (1947-1949) excess at $1.7 million—about half those suggested above.[18] However, both estimates show that the island had a surplus —13 to 30 per cent of the total balance of payments in the pre-war period and 5 to 10 per cent in the immediate post-war years. In both the pre-war and post-war periods, merchandise accounted for about 80 per cent of the receipts and slightly more than 70 per cent of the

[18] Primary interest at this point is in a comparison of the percentages in the various categories within each period or for the same category between the pre-war and post-war periods. Also wide fluctuations in the value of the drachma during 1947-1949 suggest only rough conversions be made of the drachma totals into dollars, here. For detailed data in drachmas, see Appendix 5, Table A73.

payments. Invisible accounts made up about one-sixth of both the receipts and payments, in both periods. (See Table 59 for details.)

Agricultural and forestry products made up 96 per cent of the merchandise exports. Exports of olive tree products—olive oil, olives, kernel oil, and soap—comprised almost two-fifths of all receipts in both the pre-war and post-war periods. Exports of vineyard products—raisins, table grapes, wine, and alcohol—made up one-third of the total receipts in the pre-war period but only one-fourth in the post-war years, due to the lack of any German market and a reduced British market. Exports of potatoes, vegetables, and forest products furnished about one-tenth and the products of small industries, one-twentieth of the receipts in each of the periods.

Receipts from invisible accounts included emigrants' remittances, tourism, and net surplus of state expenditures, the latter comprising about half of the total for this group. Capital movements included investments in Crete of non-Cretan funds and other transfers—including AMAG funds during the post-war period.

In both the pre-war and post-war periods, imports of direct consumption goods—food, tobacco, and fuel—were about 30 per cent of the total payments, with cloth and shoes an additional 10 per cent. The other major merchandise imports were fertilizers, chemicals, building materials, engineering products, paper, books, magazines, and other domestic and foreign items. Invisible accounts payments were mostly travel expenses of Cretans, being eight times the payments for the combined expenses of Cretan students off the island and remittances of Cretans to persons not in Crete. Capital movements were only 4 per cent of the total payments and were comprised of investments outside of Crete of funds earned in Crete and the transfer of profits and other debit transfers. Changes in liquid reserves were about twice as large as the capital movements and consisted of increases in reserves and in currency circulation. Since the war, three-fifths of this increase was in hoardings of gold sovereigns.

In comparing the percentage of receipts in various categories for the two periods, it is noted that the decrease in vineyard product exports in the post-war period was offset by a larger net surplus of state expenditures than pre-war together with AMAG funds provided. Among the payments, the decrease in percentage for food items—cereals, pulses, etc.—was offset by percentage increases in cloth, fuel, fertilizers, and chemicals. Following the war, travel ex-

Table 59. Estimated average annual balance-of-payments receipts and payments by categories, Crete, pre-war and post-war

		1936-38	1947-49
Total Balance of Payments—in millions of dollars		$12.2[a]	$31.8[b]
Receipts		(percentage of total)	
A.	Merchandise exports—F.O.B. values		
	Olive oil, olives, kernel oil, fats, & soap	37[c]	39
	Raisins, grapes, wine, & alcohol	33	25
	Potatoes, vegetables, livestock, forest products	10	10
	Others	4	4
B.	Invisible accounts		
	Emigrants' remittances and tourism	8	6
	Net surplus of state expenditures	7	11
C.	Capital movements		
	Non-Cretan funds invested in Crete & AMAG	1	5
		100	100
Payments			
A.	Merchandise imports—C.I.F. values		
	Food items—cereals, pulses, sugar, rice, coffee	27	22
	Fertilizers, medicines, and other chemicals	7	9
	Cloth, shoes, and hides	10	13
	Engineering products, cement, iron, lumber, paints, paper	7	8
	Fuel and tobacco	3	6
	Other domestic and foreign items	17	15
B.	Invisible accounts		
	Foreign travel, student expenses, and remittances from Crete	17	19
C.	Capital movements		
	Investments outside Crete	2	3
	Profit transfers and other debit payments	2	*
D.	Changes in liquid reserves		
	Increases in reserves and currency circulation	8	5
		100	100

a Computed at 100 drachmas to the dollar (1,225,000,000 drachmas).

b Computed at 15,000 drachmas to the dollar (477,000,000,000 drachmas).

c Six-year (1933-1938) average used for olive products estimate because of wide fluctuation in yearly production.

* Less than 0.5 per cent.

Source: Ministry of Coordination, Greek Recovery Program Coordinating Office. Basic estimate data provided by C. A. Doxiadis and A. Delenda, Athens, September 1950.

penses of Cretans and investments outside of Crete increased, while profit transfers and liquid reserves decreased. The character of the liquid reserves also changed—from bank and credit reserves to gold sovereign hoardings. These hoardings have averaged about $1 million annually in recent years—forming 60 per cent of the total changes in liquid reserves. In addition there has been an accumulation of stocks of olive oil, wine, and other commodities.

With a stabilized currency, a larger share of the present production or some increase in production might be available for foreign trade, making additional surpluses available to pay for added imports or to service loans from abroad. In fact this seems to be a prerequisite for any great improvement in the living levels of any large proportion of the population. Of course, any opportunity for this to occur is greatly affected by the situation in Greece as a whole, since any capital or trade transactions involving governmental sanction must be negotiated through the authorities at Athens.

D. INTERNAL TRADE

While trade throughout the island was more widely scattered than industry, the main trade centers were the three cities of Iraklion, Khania, and Rethimnon on the northern coast of Crete. Sitia, Neapolis, Ay. Nikolaos, and Ierapetra were relatively more important as trade centers than industrial centers. Crete and Iraklion held about the same importance relative to the mainland in trade as they did in industry (Figure 19). Since industrialization in agricultural Crete was primarily for the processing of food, shelter, and clothing, the business houses handled consumer goods almost exclusively. Even imports were largely for these same purposes. Few capital-equipment goods were found in the stores as there was little effective demand.

In the four nome capitals, the food stores (761) were the largest group and employed 1,183 workers. Coffee houses and taverns totaled 650 and employed 1,097 workers, while dress and sartorial shops totaled 572 and engaged 1,255 workers. Even omitting the shoe and leather workers, the clothing and sartorial group employed more people than either of the other groups. Except for the tailor shops, which averaged almost three workers each, most of the businesses employed only one or two persons each.

Because of its large hinterland area, the town of Iraklion had more business houses of all types in proportion to its city population than

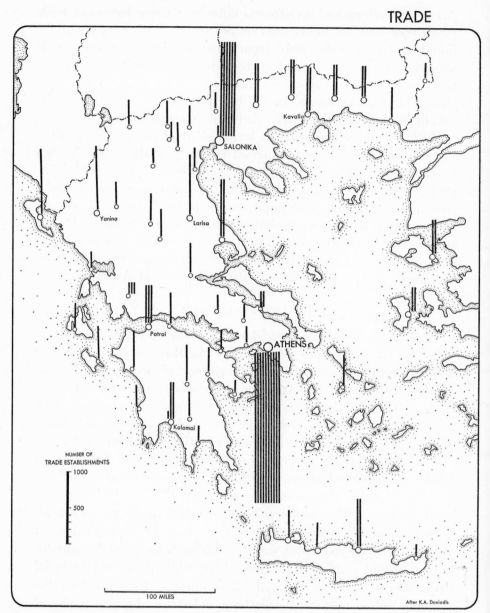

Based on chart in *The Sacrifices of Greece*, C. A. Doxiadis and Others, Athens.

FIGURE 19. Major trade centers, Crete and Greece, 1940

any of the other nome capitals. The more numerous business houses and service stores in the four nome capitals are given in Table 60. In relation to the population per business house, coffee houses were

TABLE 60. Number of service stores and workers in four nome capitals,
Crete, 1948

Type of store	Total no. stor.	Khania (34,200)		Rethimnon (12,000)		Iraklion (38,100)		Ay. Nikolaos (3,150)	
		stor.	wkrs.	stor.	wkrs.	stor.	wkrs.	stor.	wkrs.
Foods	761								
Butcher shop	133	52	82	12	30	61	130	8	12
Grocery	474	70	100	100	130	274	360	30	30
General store	60	30	70	10	15	—	—	20	25
Bakery	94	30	55	17	32	44	110	3	2
Drinks	650								
Coffee house	495	120	200	80	100	277	520	18	22
Tavern	155	67	110	30	50	53	80	5	15
Dress & sartorial	572								
Tailor shop	238	85	185	40	150	102	280	11	31
Haberdashery	104	20	40	50	50	30	60	4	4
Barber	230	80	130	35	80	106	220	9	21
Pharmacy	23	4	8	5	15	13	28	1	1
Blacksmith	117	30	50	40	100	44	160	3	12
Total	2,123	588	1,030	419	752	1,004	1,948	112	175

Population is shown in parentheses beneath name of each capital.
Source: Sample Survey of Crete, Form C, Community, 1948.

the most numerous of all businesses on the island—one for each **129**
persons. Butcher shops and grocery stores were next in frequency,
pharmacies and bakeries the least frequent. In proportion to population, tailor shops, pharmacies, and bakeries were two to four times
as frequent in the cities as in the rural communities.

E. TOURISM

Since tourism is, economically speaking, the export of food,
shelter, services, scenery, history, hospitality, and other local products, in exchange for dollars, pounds, francs, etc., it seems more fit-
ting that it be treated in this chapter than elsewhere.

310 INDUSTRY AND COMMERCE

Crete, as the home of the Minoan (Cretan or Aegean) civilization (3500-1100 B.C.), has a potentially strong appeal for tourists interested in history. For archaeologists, historians, students of language, and treasure hunters, Crete—in its Minoan ruins at Knossos, Phaestos, and Mallia—has few equals. Here palaces, frescoes, baths, sewer and water systems, water tiles, and huge vases of unequalled strength from an ancient civilization have been excavated for study and enjoyment. Carbonized oats and barley over 3,000 years old will interest the agriculturist. The artist may study the Minoan bull, the Goddess of Snakes, the double hatchet, and the long head, "wasp waists," and long black hair of the Minoans in their frescoes.

Christians will be interested in the visit of St. Paul to Crete[19] at Lasea on the southern coast and his epistle to St. Titus. St. John the Hermit came to the island to convert the Cretans. Monasteries, churches, and chapels with their many icons are found everywhere on the island.

Those interested in mythology can visit the cave in Mt. Dhikti above the Lasithi Plain, where, according to one version of early mythology, Zeus was born; Mt. Ida, where he was reared and later ruled; the White Mountains, where he was married; and Mt. Yuktas, where he was buried. The Labyrinths, the Minotaur, Theseus, and other names in mythology had their setting here.

Many travelers will be interested in the Venetian walls, moat, and harbors of Iraklion; the Venetian warehouses in Khania, intermixed with the Turkish minarets; and old forts and old cities within the present north-coast cities. The home of the Greek statesman Venizelos and his tomb at Khania, historic Suda Bay near by, and the seascapes and mountain scenes along the coastal drives provide variety and beauty.

But the Cretan dances (dating back 2,000 years), Cretan walk, and Cretan knives; striking red Cretan blankets and handbags in a relatively drab setting; and Cretan cheeses and Cretan foods, including fresh fruits in season the year round, are really distinctive. Artists may wish to see the place near Zaros where El Greco learned to paint.

Two recent excavations (1949) near Arkhanais and Mt. Yuktas ("the latter probably the town of Lycastos mentioned by Homer as

[19] Acts, 27:1-13.

having taken part in the expedition against Troy"[20]) have brought forth many new evidences of the Minoan and Roman civilizations in Crete. These ruins attract many archaeologists.

To attract many types of tourists, however, there must be good hotels, comfortable beds, clean food of wide variety, clean eating places, safe water supply, up-to-date toilet facilities, hot water for baths, freedom from dysentery, and established prices published in advance for services and goods. Much of the drabness (to some Americans) of the island could be overcome by reforestation. On these points Crete has far to go. The language difficulty is not serious for those who can speak French. An increasing number of Cretans are learning English.

While Crete has many possibilities for tourism, only the more seasoned travelers will enjoy it in its present state. Because of the torrential rains in the winter months, the more enjoyable seasons are from late spring through early fall. The summer nights are always cool in the north coastal towns and in the mountains. It is reported that before the war about 5,000 visitors came to Crete annually. A large share of these pre-war tourists were from northern and central Europe—an area now short of funds for travel. However, if a portion of this trade could be regained, together with additions from other areas, such as the Middle East and America, a considerable income would accrue with which to purchase productive capital goods.

F. TRANSPORTATION

Since Crete had no railroads, movement of goods and people depended upon road transportation and a small amount of uncertain coastwise shipping. Airplanes and ships provided off-island transportation.

1. Roads

The lack of anything but mule pack trails to about half the rural villages and the poor condition of the main highways explain why public officials indicated roads as their second most important problem—next to war. (See Crete map and Figure 20.)

a. *Condition of roads.* Bomb damage, pitted and narrow macadam resulting from heavy wear, and lack of repairs were the major evi-

[20] *Kathimerini* (Greek newspaper), Tuesday, September 27, 1949. Newspaper report of the findings of Professor Spiridon Marinatos, archaeologist at the University of Athens.

dences of poor road conditions. Preliminary estimates by the Ministry of Public Works put the cost of restoring these national roads to pre-war condition at $4 million. The provincial and community roads were also in disrepair. While estimates of the cost of repairing them were not available, the annual upkeep of national and provincial roads combined was estimated at $400,000.[21]

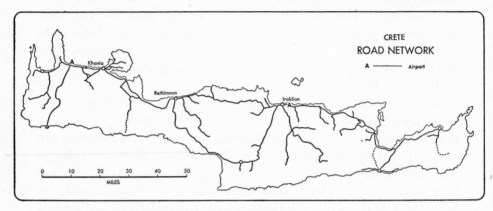

CRETE
ROAD NETWORK
A ——— Airport

Khania

Rethimnon

Iraklion

0   10   20   30   40   50
MILES

Based on *Maps of Crete*, British Army Air Forces, and 1948 Survey.

FIGURE 20. Location of roads, airports, and seaports, 1948

Of the 1,960 miles of roads planned for Crete, only 860 miles or 45 per cent were completed; 300 miles or 15 per cent were not yet finished; and 800 miles or 40 per cent were not yet begun. (See Appendix 5, Table A107.) While two-thirds of the national roads were said to be completed, they were badly in need of heavy repairs in the summer of 1948. For example, the 90-mile trip from Khania to Iraklion required five hours' steady driving in a new American car before the roads were repaired in late 1948 with ECA funds. Repairs cut driving time to four hours. And this was the best road on the island. Buses were scheduled to make the 90-mile trip in seven hours. Without some relocation and considerable widening, the traffic in donkeys, sheep, goats, and people on the highways will keep speeds extremely low and horn-honking incessant.

b. *Financing of roads.* National roads joined the capitals of the nomes as well as the historical and archaeological cities. They were financed entirely by the national government—including both construction and repairs. The provincial roads were of two types, but

21 Em. Kavgalakis, Director, Public Works Directorate, Khania, Crete, and F. E. Tutt, Transportation Division, AMAG-ECA; L.G.A. diary notes.

in either case were "foreseen by the state and approved by national law." They were either constructed by the national government and repaired by the provincial government, or built and repaired by the provincial government. Local taxes levied on rent value of town houses and property and a gross sales tax on products were sent to Athens and returned with some additions from other national tax funds for these roads. Admittedly some of the provincial roads were more important to the economy of the island for the marketing of agricultural products than certain national roads.

The community roads were only 10 per cent of the completed roads of the island and were financed entirely by local funds and donated labor. Prior to 1929, however, all roads were built by the national government.

c. *Use of roads.* The importance of local roads and transportation facilities in the health and economy of Crete was evident from sample survey data. Half the population of Crete was three miles or more from a doctor and had to reach him by donkey back or on foot. Almost half the farmers marketed their produce in a village or town different from their own. Half the farmers required two hours or more to reach the market and one-eighth of them required four to nine hours. One-third of the farmers made six or more trips to market each year and some the equivalent of once a week. (See Appendix 5, Tables A100 and A101.)

One-half of the farmers marketed their products by mule packs, about one-sixth used a combination of mule pack and motor truck, slightly more than one-fourth used motor truck only, and a few (1 per cent) used animal-drawn vehicles. The transfer of products, such as citrus fruits, grapes, raisins, oil, etc., from the local village or community center to large consuming centers or export markets involved motor-truck transportation to the ports. For this reason the type of construction and the condition of the national and major provincial roads were important.

The 953 trucks, buses, and passenger cars of all types in Crete in 1948 were about the same number (1,000) as estimated by Mr. R. B. Curren in 1929. However, this was considerably more than the 30 motor vehicles estimated to be on the island in 1921, when the road from Rethimnon to Iraklion was completed.[22] According to the

[22] Department of Overseas Trade, Great Britain, *Economic Conditions in Greece,* February 1921, H.C. 295-G7, p. 37.

Mechanological Department statement[23] for August 1948, there were 511 trucks for public use (plying for hire) and 103 privately owned trucks operating for factories, firms, or various government departments. There were 155 buses owned and operated for public use. These seemed always to be overloaded. In contrast, many trucks were busy carrying passengers or many times were almost empty during the summer season. (For details by nomes see Appendix 5, Table A108.)

The 120 taxicabs were plentiful for current needs, although most of them were American-made cars built 15 to 20 years ago. Taxi rates were 25 cents per kilometer or 40 cents per mile. High gasoline prices and high interest rates, together with high depreciation and repair costs on poor mountainous roads, made this charge seem reasonable. Taxicab operators of the pre-war period, together with doctors, were given top-priority listings for import licenses or permits to purchase cars. For local transportation about Iraklion and Khania, horse-drawn carriages were also available.

The total of only 64 privately owned passenger cars in Crete was explained by the extremely high import and special taxes levied on private cars. In late 1948 these taxes and customs duties alone amounted to the equivalent of $2,000 for lower-priced cars. The auto tax and operating fees for private cars amounted to $600-$800, and income taxes were levied in accordance with the rated wealth of the individual as an automobile owner. Custom also required the added expense of a hired chauffeur.

About two-fifths of the automotive vehicles were in Khania nome, one-third in Iraklion, one-tenth in Rethimnon, and one-sixth in Lasithi. According to the transportation division of AMAG-ECA, "competition in trucking and transportation is needed in Crete. The bus situation is bad as the present use of trucks for passengers in many areas is very inefficient. Fifty new buses are being requested and will be provided if needed."

2. Ports and Water Transportation

When good roads and vehicles are available it is more efficient to make longer hauls by truck, rather than to move goods by water through additional ports with their often expensive port-loading facilities. There was general agreement by AMAG-ECA and the Ministry of Public Works that port-rehabilitation efforts should be

[23] I. Stambouzas, Chief of Mechanological Department of Crete, 1948, by letter.

centered on Iraklion and Suda Bay, two main ports being all that the island could support. Even these two ports had only 45 to 65 miles of hinterland, whereas "efficient ports need 1,000 miles of hinterland, according to transportation experts in ECA. Since small boats are delayed by treacherous weather conditions on the south coast, no ports other than present facilities were recommended there. While some coastwise shipping of the more staple products—oil, wheat, carobs, lumber—is still a possibility for ships under 1,000 tons, the upkeep cost of harbors and breakwaters is so great that few installations are recommended."[24] (See Crete map and Figure 20.)

According to the Director of Public Works for Crete, the Iraklion port had made a rapid recovery, the tonnage of exports and imports rising from 25,000 in 1946 to 80,000 in 1947 and moving at the rate of 150,000 tons annually during the first half of 1948.[25] Of this, 40,000 tons were for relief purposes, and the remaining 110,000 tons were commercial, the same as pre-war and larger than the tonnage of Salonika or Piraeus in 1947. Of this commercial tonnage, 80,000 tons were expected to be exports and 30,000 imports. This Iraklion harbor has 500 yards of quays for caïques and small ships in addition to quays for four to five coastal ships and three to four ocean-going vessels. By salvaging two wrecks in the harbor, mooring space for two more ocean-going vessels could be provided.

Suda Bay harbor, toward the west end of the island, is important to provide competition to both the Iraklion harbor and truck transportation and thus reduce hauling costs. It also has military significance. The major problem here in 1948 was an inactive port committee.[26] Later reports indicated that necessary repairs were being made.

Regular passenger and freight service by ship from the island to

---

[24] In Iraklion, for instance, a charge of 12½ per cent tax on each import or export as a harbor-construction duty and ⅓ cent per pound on olive oil when the harbor was first constructed caused the farmers to take their olive oil and other commodities to Rethimnon 45 miles away. And currently the Iraklion harbor requires $750,000 for rehabilitation. In addition a new warehouse is needed, as the present method of transporting for uptown storage is costly.—Iraklion Port Committee, protocol no. 880/557, Iraklion, 1948.

[25] Chamber of Commerce data for 1936-1940 indicate a total of 88,000 tons with 50,000 exports and 38,000 imports. United States Department of Commerce data never exceeded 62,000 total import and export tonnage, which was highest in 1933 and 1935.

[26] Since the survey was completed, a plan for reconstruction has been developed and work started.

Athens was provided three times a week, with additional service irregularly. While the ship accommodations were adequate, they would attract only the more rugged tourists. Aside from special export ships for raisins, table grapes, or other export products carried in large quantities, no large foreign ships docked nearer than Athens or Alexandria, Egypt. From either of these ports a side-trip by plane or small ship was required to reach the island. This was a distinct handicap to tourism.

3. Airports and Air Travel

Two airports, Iraklion and Maleme (near Khania), were in use for passenger, mail, and air-express service. Iraklion had two daily round trip planes (21-passenger) while Khania provided daily afternoon service and thrice-a-week morning service. Because the airports provided adequate east-west landing strips only, flight cancellations were frequent and unpredictable. For this reason, Rethimnon had urged the building of a large airport near Latzima (Prinos) to provide an all-weather landing strip for Continental-Egyptian traffic, too. But this proposal was firmly disapproved by the Government and ECA. Plans were under consideration to lengthen the Maleme 950-meter east-west tarred strip by 100 meters and to complete the remaining 500 meters of a 1,000-meter north-south strip.

4. Communications

Since cable communications with the mainland—only via Iraklion —were also unpredictable, contacts between Crete and the outside world were uncertain. On several occasions, persons reached their destinations before cables sent 2 to 48 hours earlier, since delayed cables were frequently forwarded by air mail, without warning to the sender.

According to the Director of Posts, Telegraph, and Telephone, Crete had 60 post and telegraph offices and 960 telephones in villages and communities in the pre-war period.[27] Although there had been some reconstruction, materials were still needed to rebuild or repair telephone and telegraph lines for 740 of these telephones in the communities. Survey reports indicated that in 21.4 per cent of

27 Ministry of Posts, Telegraph and Telephone, *Director Letter* no. 48,721, May 19, 1948, and *List of Materials Needed*, May 17, 1948. Reports by Commercial Attaché, Gardner Richardson, for 1927 showed that 64 post offices, 331 telegraph stations, 655 private telephones and 100 government telephones were in operation in that year, indicating little progress on this score in the decade preceding World War II.

the villages a telephone was available and in 29.0 per cent a radio was found.

Since posts, telephones, and telegraph (and cables) were all handled by the same branch of the government, the strikes in 1948 by postal employees virtually isolated island communications on two different occasions, once for a period of ten days. A government monopoly which includes all types of communication facilities may easily become a serious handicap to business, if government employees exercise their right to strike.

G. Warehousing and Storage, Refrigeration and Grading

Some idea of the size and type of the warehousing, storage, refrigeration, and grading problem for import and export products can be gained by reviewing the list of major items imported and exported. In general the exports were olive oil and olive oil residue, raisins, table grapes, carobs, citrus and other fruits, and wine. The imports were largely non-perishable items such as cereals, lumber, coal, fuel and oil, etc.; semi-perishables such as flour, sugar, rice, coffee, fertilizers, and cement were the other main categories. But all items except coal and lumber needed adequate storage facilities.

Bomb damage to the port areas of Iraklion and Suda Bay destroyed key warehousing and storage space. While other storage space was found, the cost of moving imports to distant warehouses at Iraklion and Suda Bay was great. At Suda Bay it was seven miles to the Venetian warehouses, which served that port. With these exceptions warehouse and storage space were adequate. However, nome agriculturists suggested that large olive oil storage tanks of 1,200-2,000 tons be built near the port at Iraklion, Ay. Nikolaos, and Sitia, as a means of improving the quality of product and reducing storage costs.

The amount and type of warehousing facilities needed are dependent upon the amount of storage needed for locally produced and consumed items as well as for imports and exports. Since vegetables and fruits were produced and utilized in season throughout the whole year in the coastal areas, little canning and storage of these items took place. Storage of dried pulses and cheeses for the larger towns was required. Because of a lack of refrigeration, meat was purchased and generally consumed the day it was butchered.

The commercial food-storage problem was considerably reduced by the large amount of home storage of olive oil, wine, and cereals which made up three-fourths of the Cretan diet. Over two-thirds of the families stored olive oil for four months or longer and almost half of them for a year or longer. About two-fifths of the households stored wine and one-eleventh of the city families had special store-room space provided in their houses for these and other items. The tendency of a large percentage of the households in Crete to produce many vegetables, fruit, and milk for their own use also reduced the amount of market warehousing, transportation, and refrigeration required.

Because of a lack of refrigerated storage facilities, the season for citrus fruit on the island ended about June 10. The many other excellent-quality fresh fruits—cherries, peaches, apricots, and plums —were limited to a two- to four-week period of consumption in Crete. The need of cooling table grapes before loading on refrigerated boats was learned through costly experience. Serious damage from rotting in shipments of Rosaki table grapes was reported in 1947, indicating the necessity of a refrigeration plant with facilities for treating with sulphur-dioxide to prevent loss and maintain quality for future markets.

Whether refrigeration or a frozen-food type of industry should be developed as more fruits and vegetables are produced by increased irrigation will depend on costs and market outlets. On the island the demand for either will be extremely limited until tourism increases or higher economic levels are reached.

Virtually no homes had electric refrigerators because of the high initial cost ($750 to $1,000 for a 5 to 8 cu.ft. capacity) and an electric bill of $5 to $10 per month for operation. Daily or thrice-a-week marketing for fresh fruits and vegetables was common during the summer in households where there was no home production. This practice indicates the undesirability of planning refrigeration storage beyond the needs for export and an extremely limited amount of storage for meats, fruits, and vegetables for local consumption until the general economic level is raised.

In Iraklion there were two ice factories and cold-storage rooms which could produce 420 columns of ice in an eight-hour period with 260-horsepower equipment and 13 employees.[28] There was also an ice plant in Khania. In each city ice deliveries were made to a limited number of business houses and homes with refrigerators.

[28] Chamber of Commerce and Industry, Iraklion, reference no. 3704, p. 3. Copy of letter to Wm. L. Tait on December 15, 1947.

Grading of fruits and vegetables was not practiced in the local markets because of the large numbers of producers and small retailers at the market place. This policy also affected the grading of export products, resulting in discrimination (perhaps justified) by foreign buyers. Reports from importers via United States Department of Agriculture officials indicated that one of the real problems of developing export markets for Greek products arose from the poor quality and poor packaging of shipments received direct from Greece. Interestingly, Greek olive oil and other products had been processed in neighboring countries and sold as high-quality goods in foreign markets. Certainly the original products—olive oil, raisins, fruits—produced in Crete were of excellent quality, although much could have been done to standardize them.

The grading of fruits for export was hurriedly supervised by the nome agriculturist who had many other duties to perform during the same period of the year. Again, the mixture of regulatory and extension work was not conducive to the best efforts or results in either.

H. SUMMARY

Power resources suitable for industrial expansion on the island were meager, including only ten small diesel-engine-powered electric works. Demands were greater than facilities. Large increases in water power were not feasible, and even small increases would generally require additional detailed surveys. Wood and charcoal were found to be a constantly decreasing resource. Lignite of unknown quantity and quality was reported in nine places on the island, but it was far from the cities and water transportation. However, in one place it was conveniently located for use in pumping water for irrigation purposes. Many thousands of windmills of unknown efficiency utilized the strong north winds for pumping and milling. Donkeys were widely used for pumping water and operating oil presses and crushers. Diesel engines utilizing imported fuel oil were the major possibilities for additional power.

The industrial production of Crete was primarily for food, shelter, and clothing, with great emphasis on self-sufficiency enterprises in the homes. Data available indicated that far more people were employed in the handicraft industries than in the so-classified industrial factories. In contrast to the Greek mainland, little industrialization had occurred in Crete since liberation in 1913. The reasons for this were apparent—lack of power, minerals, and raw materials.

Exports consisted chiefly of products of the vines and trees—olive, citrus, and carob. Imports were mostly lumber, fertilizers, and fuel items not found on the island. Most of the exports went abroad, but a majority of the imports came from or through other Greek ports. In contrast to Greece, Crete had, since 1926 and except for recent war years, exported merchandise annually valued at 1.2 to 4.8 times as much as her imports. Recently many of these earnings have accumulated as gold sovereigns.

Trade was found to be closely related to the distribution of the population in Crete. More than half the business houses were engaged in providing food and drink, and another third, clothing and sartorial services. Only a few local businesses engaged in selling or servicing capital goods and equipment.

Crete has Minoan palaces, Venetian walls, ancient dances, and many other touristic attractions, but it is "off the beaten path" and lacked important tourist facilities at the time of the survey. Consequently tourism had limited possibilities of bringing any considerable income to the island in the near future.

The island had no railroads and had to depend on truck and bus transportation for efficient land travel. The primary modes of travel were by donkey or on foot, or by taxi for those who could afford it. Roads, harbors, and airports, were all in disrepair but receiving aid from ECA grants. Communication facilities were few and frequently undependable.

The need for commercial centralized storage was lessened in an economy where one-half of the households provided storage space in their houses for the more bulky items. But sufficient warehousing was essential at the major ports to reduce handling charges. Refrigeration facilities were meager in Crete. Grading of export products was carried out somewhat indifferently by officials hired for educational work.

The major problems affecting these industrial and commercial phases of the economy in Crete were the lack of power, skilled labor, and management for industrial development, uncertain fuel and mineral resources, relatively poor transportation and communication facilities at high costs, lack of port-storage and refrigeration facilities, poor tourist accommodations, together with those cited earlier such as continuing inflation, hoarding, lack of capital formation, and high interest rates.

PART III

APPENDICES

APPENDIX 1

STATISTICAL METHODOLOGY IN MULTI-PURPOSE SURVEYS OF CRETE, GREECE

CONTENTS

LIST OF METHODOLOGY TABLES FOR APPENDIX 1

APPENDIX 1. STATISTICAL METHODOLOGY IN MULTI-PURPOSE SURVEYS OF CRETE, GREECE

By Raymond J. Jessen and Norman V. Strand

The purpose of Appendix 1 is to set forth a detailed description and evaluation of the technical procedures used in carrying out the Crete investigation, particularly the procedures concerned with the obtaining and analysis of quantitative information. Although a statement of this sort should accompany any report on a study that claims use of scientific method, it is even more necessary here because of the considerable amount of stress laid on methodology and its possible use in additional foreign countries. The study was carried out with the idea that even if usable data were not obtained, something could be learned about the procedures showing some promise of providing a greater degree of success in another study of the same sort.

In order to give the general reader a quick summary of the reliability of the (seemingly small) samples used in the survey, a brief statement is given herewith of the conclusions on methodology, together with some general recommendations on the adequacy and efficiency of the methods used in the survey. The details of the statistical methodology are presented later, in lay language for the most part, in order to give the reader a better basis for understanding the procedure used in the Sample Survey of Crete and its possibilities for other areas.

A. Conclusions on Methodology and Recommendations

Much of the data used for the findings presented in this book were obtained by surveys undertaken specifically for this investigation. These surveys were planned cross-sections of the communities, households, and farms of Crete. Although these surveys were based on small samples, they were designed to be efficient so that a maximum of information was obtained for the expenditures made in time and money. Furthermore, they were designed in such manner that the precision of the estimates based on them can be assessed from an examination of only the sample itself. Details on the logical structure of these surveys are given later. (See section C. The Technical Description of the Survey.)

As stated in Chapter 1, the accuracy of data from any investigation, whether based on a sample or a complete census, depends ultimately on the accuracy of the observations themselves—which in the surveys of Crete were data obtained by questioning people about the household, farm, and community. There is evidence that data of this sort can contain errors—in some cases serious errors—attributable to such causes as misunderstanding of what is wanted, inability of the memory to recall accurately, lack of understanding of the answer required, or deliberate falsification. The possibilities of errors of this sort were recognized in the planning of the surveys and a number of measures were taken to prevent or minimize them. In some instances measures were taken to detect such errors by obtaining information on presumably the same subject in different ways either from the same source or from different sources. Unfortunately, time and resources did not permit an exhaustive investigation of these possible errors. What was actually done and the findings on these matters are discussed below.

It is hoped that the reader does not conclude that these findings show the data to be worthless. Nor should the reader believe that all the data are perfect. Rather, it would seem that the data should be studied critically with a view to insisting that all types of future investigations be made in such a manner that the quality of data can be, and is, assessed.

1. Conclusions on Methodology

In Table MS 1 are shown a selected number of estimates made from these surveys and the standard errors of these estimates arising from the fact that they are based on samples rather than complete censuses. A "standard error" is not really an "error." It is merely a yardstick by which the reliability of an estimate can be judged. It is calculated from the sample itself and can be interpreted as follows: The number of inhabitants in households in Crete as of August 1948 is estimated from the survey to be 472,800. According to Table MS 1 the standard error of this estimate is $\pm 2\%$. Thus if a complete census of the population in the households of Crete were taken in August 1948, instead of just a sample, the result would be found to be within 2% of 472,800, that is, between 463,800 and 481,800, *unless* a 1 in 3 chance has come off. To lessen chances of being wrong, the odds can be put at 1 in 20, in which case the limits are now put at 454,800 to 489,800 (that is two times ± 2, or $\pm 4\%$).

Sampling errors have been computed for a variety of items and are presented in Table MS 1 so that the reader will have a means of approximating the reliability of the estimates. Estimates are not shown in the table for a large number of other characteristics given in this book. For these it may be surmised that there is a fairly close relationship between the sampling error of an estimated figure and the magnitude of that figure. Such relationships are usual with survey data. Thus, from the magnitude of the errors listed in this table, standard errors of other characteristics may be qualitatively inferred.

2. Recommendations

Although a thoroughgoing study of adequacy, soundness, and efficiency of the survey methods used in this investigation has not been made, it is possible to arrive at some general conclusions and recommendations.

TABLE MS 1. Estimated standard errors for various characteristics

Characteristics	Estimate (number or percent)	Standard Error as percentage of estimate
Number of households[a]		
Communities	92,550	2
Municipalities	22,200	5
Total	114,750	2
Number of inhabitants[a]		
Communities	385,350	2
Municipalities	87,450	6
Total	472,800	2
Males as percent of total[a]	49.0	2
Selected age groups[a]		
0-5	51,000	7
21-25	43,800	8
41-45	27,750	7
61-65	16,200	12
Selected occupational groups[a]		
Professions	3,450	19
Farmers	46,500	6
Craftsmen	21,900	10
Number of Doctors[b]	290	16
Number of Priests[b]	581	10
Percent of households using wood for fuel[a]	78	4
Type of heating unit[a]		
Percent using fireplace	65	5
Percent using brazier	25	7
Percent of households having[a]		
One room	13	11
Three rooms	25	9
Five rooms	13	11
Number of farms[c, d]	50,700	7
Area in farms (stremma)[c, d]	1,918,950	14
Area per farm (stremma)[c, d]	37.9	12

Characteristics	Estimate (number or percent)	Standard Error as percentage of estimate
No. farms using fertilizer[c]	38,100	8
No. farmers with membership in cooperative association[c]	35,910	8
Wheat:[e]		
No. stremma	161,580	13
No. okes produced	7,234,350	13
No. okes per stremma	45	7
Pulses:[d]		
No. stremma	39,795	13
No. okes produced	2,510,250	16
No. okes per stremma	63	8
Vetch:[e]		
No. stremma	23,550	19
No. okes produced	1,061,550	25
No. okes per stremma	45	12
Olives:[e]		
No. trees	8,009,400	11
Production of oil (okes)	21,690,750	8
Okes oil per tree	2.7	8
Farm animals:[e]		
Donkeys	21,000	13
Mules	11,250	15
Goats and kids	175,500	26
Sheep and lambs	205,650	21

[a] Form A, Household [b] Form C, Community
[c] Form B, Farm [d] Excluding municipalities
[e] Forms A and B

It appears that certain improvements could be made in sampling efficiency —particularly in sampling farms and in sampling households in municipalities. The prospects for gains in sampling efficiency on estimating crops and livestock appear to be great if special attention is given to the "large" farms. The improvements in the municipal household sample would result from devoting more attention to getting better estimates of block sizes in the walled portion of the city of Iraklion.

No biases due to the sampling procedure have been detected in any of the surveys, and of course none was expected. Apparently all deviations from exact representations were attributable to the vagaries of random sampling. Because the samples were drawn in a randomized manner, it was possible to assess the magnitudes of these errors, and this proved quite helpful in evaluating the estimates.

A number of flaws have been detected in the questionnaire and a statement has been prepared on them (see section C.4h). Some of these could have been detected and eliminated before the survey if more time had been available for additional study and testing in the field.

Alternative methods of obtaining certain types of data should be seriously considered. For example, certain quantities, such as number of olive trees, might be obtained by a scheme requiring the investigator to make actual counts for the sample farms (or a subsample of them) or for certain sample areas. This would clarify our position on the accuracy of the data obtained by interview which in fact can be checked.

In general, it seems that much of the data obtained by interview are about as good as similar data obtained in this country by the more careful surveyors. But this does not mean it is necessarily satisfactory. There are many data which present a difficult problem because of their unknown quality even within reasonably wide limits. If thought is given to this problem during the design of the survey, it is possible to devise methods of assessing the quality as part of the survey.

In future work of this sort it would be helpful if funds and time would permit a thorough pilot investigation before the main investigation is launched. It is almost impossible to overestimate the importance of this feature. A considerable amount of time could be spent to good advantage in acquiring background information on the job to be done. This information makes it possible more accurately to focus attention on those problems requiring further information. Hence the survey can be designed more efficiently and the subsequent analysis can be more complete and conclusive.

In a country where customs and language are familiar, the time required for acquiring "background" for planning an investigation is usually more than expected. Where customs and language are strange, even more time is required. For example, late in this investigation, information "finds" were made—quite by accident—that would have been very useful if known earlier.

B. The Problem of Sampling, Survey Design, and Accuracy

1. *The General Problem of Obtaining Useful Information*

In general, the investigators on this project found no paucity of information in Greece. If one sought long enough he was almost sure to find information of some sort on almost anything. In fact one was likely to be overwhelmed with information, much of which was conflicting and contradictory. The job at this point was one of assessing the relevance and accuracy of the data—in most cases a very formidable job indeed.

Examination of available information for relevance and accuracy raises the question of how the information came into being. How were the data obtained, when and for what purpose? Some very disheartening revelations often take place at this point. The data may be pure guesses, or may have been obtained from sources involving a moral risk (for example, ration registrations or tax records) on accuracy.

In view of these problems it appeared that alternatives should be carefully considered—particularly those of obtaining data from new sources and of utilizing methods which would permit statistical evaluation, that is, the use of "statistical surveys."

In addition to contacts with insular authorities and personal journeys over the island to obtain an idea of its over-all characteristics, two other sources of information appeared to be particularly worthy: local officials and the individual families. By local official is meant the mayor of a municipality or the equivalent person (president) presiding over a community. (According to the 1940 Greek census of population there were 4 municipalities and 546 communities in Crete, a total of 550 such local officials. Also there were about 108,000 families on the island in 1940.)

It seemed reasonable to expect that the local officials could provide useful information on the general characteristics of their municipality or community, its industry, agriculture, schools, customs, community needs, etc.; whereas the individual families could provide useful information on the characteristics of the family—its sources and amount of income, health, material wealth, attitudes, customs, diet, farm enterprises, needs, etc.

Because of the large number of communities as well as families it would have been no small undertaking to look into each community and family for the desired information. Immediate consideration was given, therefore, to the possibilities of carrying the investigation out on a *sampling basis* so that with very little loss in useful information a great reduction in the overall number of observations could be made.

2. Some Problems of Sampling

Almost everyone is familiar with the general idea of sampling. For example, a small amount of soup is tasted in order to decide if the whole potful has the proper amount of salt; a handful of the grain in a bin is used to decide on the quality of the grain in the bin; while traveling through France a number of French people are observed—from these observations are drawn some conclusions about the "French people" in general.

In each of these cases the characteristics of a "sample" are observed and then it is inferred that all the soup in the pot, or all the grain in the bin or all persons in France have the same or similar characteristics as those revealed by the sample. Experience has shown that there is a certain amount of reasonableness in drawing inferences of this sort, particularly if it is felt that in the cases of the soup and grain the material was thoroughly mixed before the sample was taken, and in the case of France, if the tour seemed to go into many different parts of France such as city, village, and country, rich and poor, agricultural and manufacturing, etc. In other words if a person believes the sample contains the diverse elements that make up the "universe" of which it is a sample, then he is often willing to conclude implicitly, if not explicitly, that if the whole universe were examined it would be found to be similar to the sample.

Experience has taught another rule to observe in drawing inferences from samples and that is that although samples do seem to represent their universes in many respects, yet seldom are they exactly representative and in some cases they are very dissimilar. This experience is a reminder that reasoning from a sample to the universe is beset with some hazards which may lead to disappointment.

The remarks above briefly state some intuitive arguments for and against sampling. Fortunately, it is not necessary to rest the case here. The theory underlying sampling has been developed to the point where sampling is a "scientific procedure." Certain methods of selecting samples lead to predictable results. For example, if samples are selected truly at random then it can be predicted how closely *true values* can be estimated and *with what probability of error*. Thus even scientific sampling is not without its hazards— but in this case the hazards can be evaluated. It can now be determined— from the sample itself—what the chances of error are for the inferences drawn from it. Illustrations of this idea will be shown later.

A great variety of methods may be used in selecting samples, and each may be regarded as scientific in the sense that the accuracy of the results can be measured exactly. However, some methods are easier to carry out in practice, some are more accurate than others for a given size of sample (such as *amount* of soup or grain or *number* of French people observed). The essential problem of the sampler is to choose a method of selection and a size of sample such that the results are adequately accurate and yet not too costly to obtain. This is usually regarded as the problem of "sampling design."

But why sample at all? Why not take all or none? In many cases the practicability of sampling is obvious—as in the case of soup tasting. If all soup had to be tasted before the cook could be satisfied as to its flavor what would be left to serve? In other cases the answer is not so obvious. But in the case of the study of Crete, more time and a much larger budget would have been required if all samples were to be distrusted.

3. *Accuracy of Observations*

In simple random sampling, the error due to sampling can be reduced by taking an increasingly larger sample. Obviously by taking a complete census rather than a sample, the error due to sampling can be reduced to zero. The error due to sampling is not the only error to which surveys are subject. For example, in the case of surveys of persons, households or farms, the characteristics of which are given by persons, errors are likely to occur because that person does not know the correct answer or does not want to give it. These are errors of the interrogation process; they exist whether the survey be confined to a sample or extended to a complete census. These errors of interrogation may, in some cases, be so large that little, if any, use may be made of the information. Fortunately, this is not always the case, but it is the responsibility of the surveyor to provide evidence that these errors are unimportant. First let us consider some of the main reasons why errors of interrogation occur.

1. The investigator has influenced the answers knowingly or unknowingly.
2. The respondent has purposely given wrong information.
3. The respondent does not really know the answers and is merely guessing.

4. The question itself is vague or misleading and therefore fails to convey the concept desired.

In the Crete Survey a number of steps were taken to minimize the errors in the data which might come for any of these reasons. First, the investigation was confined to a small sample so that the investigators could be well trained in their job of interrogation. This training is made easier and more efficient by keeping the number of trainees small. Secondly, some time was spent in testing the questionnaire to make sure that the concepts involved were clearly stated and could be understood by all Cretans without difficulty. This required the testing of words and phrases, both Greek and English. After this was done in the office, the questionnaire was taken to randomly selected Greek communities and families near and in Khania for full unrehearsed interviews. Even with this testing it was felt that if additional time had been available it could have been used to good advantage for further testing.

In order to get the respondent's full cooperation, the investigator devoted several minutes before the questioning started in the interview to explain to him the purpose of the inquiry and its importance. Shortly before the investigators left for the field a general announcement that the Rockefeller Survey was to begin was sent to the various community presidents, the Greek Orthodox Church, and the local newspapers. Even so, it was a surprise, though a pleasant one, to find only 3 households (of 744 met) which refused to give information. This is a remarkably small number for a survey of this sort.

Having taken these precautions, how accurate are the data? The answer to this question is not as complete as desired, although some information is available. In the planning of the survey this problem was considered and an attempt was made to obtain information which would throw some light upon it. For example, questions dealing with the same concepts were put on both the farm (Form B) and the community (Form C) questionnaires. These were usually on agricultural items. The data from these two sources provide separate estimates of essentially identical quantities which can be compared for consistency. Another example of an internal check was that made possible by the questions on food consumption obtained from the seven-day diet survey and from the general household survey with questions on total consumption of foods during the year 1947. This is, incidentally, quite rough but it is still of some help. Since the estimates from the survey are not dependent on any official statistics, survey results may be compared with those official statistics. Some of these comparisons have been made, and appear in another section of this Appendix under the title "Quality Evaluation."

4. *Other Considerations Affecting the Design of the Survey*

It has been indicated in preceding sections that sampling has been regarded as a reliable means of obtaining data, if it is carried out according to certain statistical principles. It has been found to be a means of accomplishing economy and manageability in the conduct of investigations such as this one and still obtaining useful results. Some remarks have also been made on the measures taken to reduce errors of interrogation. In addition to these, there were other problems in designing (that is, giving a logical structure to) the general survey. For example, there were a number of different investigations which it was wished to group together into a single survey. Not only were the characteristics of households of interest but also those of farms and of communities. In addition, more detailed studies were desired on diets, tuberculosis affliction, etc. By setting up a design which permitted all of these and other studies to be dealt with at the same time and with the same general sampling scheme, a number of economies were made, with no sacrifice of information. In fact the value of the information so obtained was increased because the smaller studies could be strengthened with the data from the larger survey if proper statistical methods were employed. The alternative economy would have been to omit from the investigation an examination of some of these aspects of the over-all Crete problem and take an expected loss in the general usefulness of the data.

Some attention was also given to the problem of making special investigations from time to time which could be related to some base such as the general survey. The exact nature and number of these special investigations could not be anticipated, but still some preparation could be made for quite a variety of them. By taking a sub-sample of the households in the general survey for the special inquiry on the seven-day diets, it was possible to make greater use of the data in the smaller survey.

Other considerations required in making up the proper design for a survey include the costs (in time and equipment) of traveling, sampling, and interviewing, as well as a number of other operations involving expense in time or money. The number of farms and households finally decided on for each of the sample communities was determined by the time required of the investigators to travel to and from communities, to obtain the list of the households within those communities, to designate the specific households to be examined, and to carry out the interviews. It was estimated that a team of two investigators could complete this work in each community within three days. When compared with alternative assignments of work load, this allocation of our resources was regarded as about the best that could be done. Experiences gained during the survey indicated that the guesses on these matters were reasonably good, and that if this particular survey were to be done again, about the same allocation would be made.

Still another consideration was that of anticipating the kinds of comparisons that might be made between different groups on the Island of Crete. For example, a comparison between the characteristics of the households in communities versus those in municipalities should be helpful. In order to make this comparison as efficiently as possible, the sample should contain about the same number of households from each group. This would lessen the accuracy of our estimates of over-all characteristics of Crete, so it was finally decided that a proportionate sample would be the best choice. The numbers that would be obtained by this scheme of allocation would be sufficiently large to permit comparison with a degree of accuracy which seemed adequate.

5. Brief Outline of the Survey Plan

After the considerations mentioned in the preceding sections and many others were made, the final design was formulated. Eight different kinds of units were chosen for examination. These were as follows:

Schematic Summary of Units in Crete Observed and Studied by Planned Surveys

Unit observed	Form on which data were recorded
1. Community (or Municipality)	C
2. Village	C
3. Occupied dwelling unit	A
4. Household	A, I, Ia, J
5. Person, any age	A
Born during 1946, 1947, 1948	A-1
1-6 years	G
7-19 years	H
Pregnant woman	F
Lactating woman	E
6. Farm and sub-farm	A, B
7. Entries on community death catalogues	C
8. Community birth registration catalogues	C

To obtain the desired information for these eight different kinds of units (which were to be put under observation) eleven different forms were prepared on which to record the information and—where interrogation was used—the questions to be put to the respondent. These were as follows:

Schematic summary of survey forms used in the Crete Survey, their sources of information, and units under investigation

Identification Designation	Source of Information	Units under Investigation
Form A	Interview with head of household or other suitable person	Occupied dwelling unit, household, each person in household, sub-farm.
Form A-1	Interview with head of household or other suitable person	Persons born during 1946, 1947, 1948.
Form B	Interview with operator of farm or other suitable person	Farm (as determined by respondent).
Form C	Interview with community president, physician or other officials and taking information directly from the community's catalogues of births, deaths and marriages	Community, village, entries of deceased persons or community catalogues of deaths, catalogues of birth.

Form E	Interview with pregnant women	Pregnant women
Form F	Interview with lactating women	Lactating women
Form G	Interview with mother and direct measurements on child by investigator	Person 1-6 years of age
Form H	Interview with child and direct measurements	Person 7-19 years of age
Form I	Interview with housewife	Households
Form I-a	Records kept by housewife under direction of investigator	Households
Form J	Interview with housewife	Households

The sorts of things for which the eight different units under investigation were to be examined are as follows:

1. *Communities.* To obtain data on such characteristics as: composition of the community (number and size of villages), general community services and facilities, social customs, public health, food handling and customs, farm crops, farm animals, general vital statistics, general housing.

2. *Villages.* To obtain data on such characteristics as: sources, distribution and treatment of drinking water, schools and school facilities, general village services and facilities.

3. *Occupied dwelling units.* To obtain data on such characteristics as: composition of the dwelling unit (number and kinds of rooms), wartime damage, sanitary facilities, etc.

4. *Households.* To obtain data on such characteristics as: composition of the household, food consumption, food practices, a day's menu, household income, home industry, mortality, morbidity, diet over a seven-day period, equipment and supplies, etc.

5. *Persons.* To obtain data on such characteristics as: physical measurements, education, employment, health, etc.

6. *Farms and sub-farms.* To obtain data on such characteristics as: land resources, farm crops, farm animals, bio-industry, marketing of agricultural products, human resources, capital equipment, management, phytopathological problems, animal pathological problems, specific crop problems, etc.

7. *Entries* on community catalogues of deaths. To obtain data on number of deaths by cause.

8. *Catalogues* of births. To obtain data on number of births during recent years (1946, 1947, 1948).

In addition, certain sub-groups of these units were selected for special study. These were:

1. Persons born during 1946, 1947, and 1948 (information to be obtained from householders to compare with results of the birth catalogue investigation).

2. Persons 1-6 years old, for detailed study of health, nutritional state, etc.

3. Persons 7-19 years old, for detailed study of health, nutritional state, etc.

4. Pregnant women for detailed study of health, nutritional state, etc.

5. Lactating women for detailed study of health, nutritional state, etc.

The units to be examined were confined to a combined sample consisting of 40 communities, 4 municipalities, 178 villages, 772 occupied dwelling units, 772 households,[1] 3152 persons, 346 farms, 271 subfarms, 1128 entries on catalogues of deaths and 44 catalogues of births. In order to draw the sample of 40 communities, all 546 communities were grouped into strata consisting of contiguous communities, each group having about the same number of inhabitants (according to the 1940 census). Within each of these strata the communities were drawn at random. The selection of the communities was not done with the assignment of equal probability to each community, but rather with a probability based upon the number of inhabitants each had in the 1940 census. By design, then, the sample consisted of communities of larger than average size and in order to obtain unbiased estimates for all communities, it was necessary to weight the data from each community inversely to its probability of selection. (See next section for details.) All four municipalities were selected for the sample.

The sampling of farms and households in each of the sample communities and municipalities was the second operation. In each community, a fraction of all elements (households, farms, etc.) was taken such that it was inverse to the probability of selection of the sample community. By this means, each household and each farm on the Island of Crete had an equal probability of being selected.

In order to obtain estimates, for example, for the whole of Crete, all that was required was to take the sample total and multiply by 150. No other information was required to make estimates from the sample. Therefore, it was completely independent of any assumptions on the adequacy of other data. With this scheme, each sample community had about 15 households and about 8 farms in the sample. Each household in the sample was specified by rules drawn up by the sampling statistician. For example, when the investigators arrived in a sample community, they secured a listing of all the households in that sample community. Then the rules specified that, for example, the 4th house and every 10th house thereafter was to be investigated. In this example, household No. 4, household No. 14, household No. 24, et cetera through the whole list were the households designated by the sampling plan for that community. Those households which were found to be operating farms were interrogated on the characteristics of the farms.

After the basic sample for the general sample survey was completed, then another sample, or rather a sub-sample of it, was specified for the seven-day diet survey, etc. This can be simply described as follows: A random selection of one-half of the communities was made, and in those communities one-third of the households were specified for the seven-day diet inquiry. The seven-day diet sample, therefore, consisted of 1/6 of all the households in the basic sample. This sample, then, represented 1 out of 900 of all households in Crete (in the municipalities this sub-sample was made by merely taking

[1] It should be noted that throughout the text it was stated that the sample contained 765 households, whereas in this methodology section the number is given as 772. The discrepancy arises from different methods of treating results, though the methods are equivalent for all essential purposes.

a one out of six sample from the basic sample). Other sub-samples were selected in a similar manner. (See following section.)

C. A Technical Description of the Survey

1. The Sampling Plan

The purpose of this statement is to put on record the procedures followed in selecting the sample upon which this survey is based, and insofar as it is felt relevant and convenient, to provide an explanation of the rationale behind these procedures. By having this information on record, the critical reader will have a clear basis for judging the adequacy of the sample and therefore the reliability of the results.

a. *General characteristics of Crete relevant for sampling design.* By the measurements of the Ministry of Reconstruction, the land area of Crete is 8,294.32 square kilometers (about 3,202 sq.mi. or about the size of 5 1/2 Iowa counties) and, according to the 1940 census of population, contained 438,206 inhabitants.

Its political divisions consist of four nomes which are subdivided first into eparchies and then into communities and municipalities. All land in Greece is contained in some community or municipality. Table M 1 below provides a statistical summary of this political structure together with population data taken from the 1940 Greek Census of population.

Four populated centers (the capital of each nome) were regarded as municipalities (10,000 or more inhabitants, or, if less, the capital of a nome) for the sample. If the populations of municipalities are regarded as "urban" and those of communities as "rural" it can be seen from Table M 1 that Crete is essentially rural—81% of its population in 1940 being so classified.

The community consists of one or more populated clusters, or villages (Greek, Khoria) and the surrounding open country in which some families or members of the family may reside temporarily during the summer. However, the overwhelming bulk of the people live in the populated centers.

TABLE M 1. Rural and urban population, and number of political units of Crete, by nomes

	Inhabitants[a]			Number of political units		
Nome	Total	Urban[b]	Rural[b]	Eparchies	Municipalities	Communities
Iraklion	167,918	42,557	125,361	7	1	181
Lasithi	71,172	2,558	68,614	4	1	83
Rethimnon	73,026	10,972	62,054	4	1	133
Khania	126,090	28,213	97,877	5	1	149
Total	438,206	84,300	353,906	20	4	546

a 1940 census.
b "Urban" = municipalities; "Rural" = communities.

Geographically, Crete is somewhat similar to some areas in southwestern United States because of its warm dry summers and relatively barren, rugged mountains. Crete is a rather slender island lying on an east-west axis and situated almost midway from Europe to Africa. A mountain range roughly divides the island into north and south halves (the mild "European half" and the hot "African half"). It appears that from a number of viewpoints, such as agriculture, halves are more alike within than between themselves.

b. *Resources and estimates of costs.* In order to make the most efficient sampling plan, that is, to obtain the desired information with the minimum expenditure of resources such as time, labor and material, it is necessary to estimate (1) kinds and amounts of resources available and (2) the costs of carrying out all possible operations. Certainly an accurate estimate of either of these is difficult if not impossible to obtain, but fortunately even rough estimates are quite useful.

Considering the nature and amount of information desired, it appeared advisable to plan on obtaining it on several bases or units of observation, namely (1) the household, (2) the individual persons, (3) the farm, and (4) the community. By *base* is meant the unit to which the data refer; for example, the income of a family, the number of olive trees of a farm, the number of births per year in a community, the age at which a person is immunized, the number of cases of various diseases treated by a physician during a specified period of time, etc.

This being the case, it would conserve resources if a sampling scheme could be devised so that all these units could be dealt with simultaneously. It would be desirable, for example, that this scheme provide cross-sections of households, communities, individual persons, etc., of Crete, or the means by which such cross-sections can be estimated by appropriate statistical technique.

In view of this consideration, a sampling design was chosen which required a sample of communities and then within those communities sample of households, farms, and individual persons. A choice had to be made on the number of communities which should be selected and the number of households, farms, etc., which should be selected within each. The rationale for this choice depended on a number of things, the main ones being: (1) the cost of visiting a given number of communities selected at random, (2) the cost of visiting a given number of households selected at random within a given community, (3) the amount of variation among communities in the characteristics being measured, (4) the amount of variation among households and other observation units within selected communities in the characteristics being measured, (5) the resources available and (6) the accuracy desired in the final estimates to be made from the sample data.

It is estimated that a week would be required for one investigator to travel to a selected community and obtain all the necessary information. This is based in part on the experience with a somewhat similar survey made by the Allied Mission observing the election registers for the plebiscite of 1946.[2]

[2] R. J. Jessen, R. H. Blythe, O. Kempthorne, and W. E. Deming, "On a Population Sample for Greece." *Jour. Amer. Statis. Assn.*, 42:357-384. 1947.

This estimate, of course, presupposes a relatively small sample of households and farms in each sample community. A breakdown of this estimate would include:

Travel to sample place	1 day
Laying out the sample of households and farms	1 day
Obtaining information pertaining to the community	1 day
Obtaining information pertaining to farms and households	3 days
Total	6 days

c. The size and structure of the sample. Considering simultaneously the estimates of costs, the kind and amount of resources available, and the accuracy required, and other considerations of practicalities, the following scheme was adopted:

1. Select a sample of 40 communities in addition to 4 municipalities.
2. Select a sample of approximately 15 households from each of the 40 communities, a total of about 600 households for the rural zones, and a sample of about 140 households in the municipalities.
3. Administer a farm questionnaire in addition to the household questionnaire to those households in the sample which operate farms.
4. Obtain community information from all relevant respondents in the community (such as physicians, the president, the secretary, etc.).
5. Select the sample so that it would comprise a 1/150th of all households then in existence on the island. A total of about 740 households (and some smaller number of farms) will be in the sample.

The 40 communities would provide satisfactory accuracy on a large number of items, provided the appropriate methods of estimation are followed. Likewise the 740 households should give suitable accuracy for a wide range of different items.

d. Use of available information. A sampling design is inadequate or at least wasteful if it does not provide for the proper utilization of information already available to the investigator. It is indeed rare when a study is undertaken by someone who is completely ignorant of any knowledge about the universe of inquiry. However, in some cases it may be only an hypothesis or perhaps some guesses as to the general nature of the universe to be investigated.

In the present case there were a number of public sources of information such as the *Annuaire Statistique de la Grèce*, and the *Population de la Grèce* (results of the 1940 census of population), to mention only two on general population and agricultural statistics. In addition, several of the ministries had prepared bulletins, maps, etc., presenting information having some relevance to the present study, although many of these data were too general to be of much use for the purpose under consideration. In regard to agriculture, for example, there appeared to be many data in offices, and information in the minds of the agriculturists, which, until it was collected and thoroughly examined and tested, was of doubtful value.

Consequently, as one of the objectives of this study, some effort was re-

quired for the problem of studying the means of searching out, testing, and
—where feasible—of utilizing this information. The kinds may be classified
as follows: (1) Published data (usually out of date). (2) Unpublished data.
(3) Judgments of various specialists. (4) Combinations of the above.

This information may be used: (1) As a check on the accuracy of the
sample survey. (2) For selecting a more "representative" sample. (3) For
making more accurate estimates from a sample drawn without regard to the
information.

In this section the concern will be with putting some of this information
into use in the selection of the sample, i.e., the design of the sample. For
this purpose there are three phases where it might be used: (1) In stratification. (2) In assigning different probabilities for selecting the individual sampling units. (3) As a basis for differential rates of sampling.

Since phases (1) and (2) will be dealt with in the next two sections (e and
f) a remark on (3) only will be made here. As a basis for differential rates
of sampling, the utilization of prior information is limited almost solely to
cases where only one characteristic is under measurement. In this case the
interest was in a large number of characteristics for each unit of measurement (such as farm, community, household, etc.), and therefore was not
considered further.

e. *Stratification.* The arguments just presented above against the use of
differential sampling rates in general purpose samples are equally appropriate for simple stratification (actually in order to use differential sampling
rates some scheme of stratification must be decided upon). There is one important difference, however. Whereas the misapplication of differential sampling rates may cause serious losses in accuracy, the poor choice of criteria
for stratification does not result in serious losses in accuracy over that of no
stratification at all.

Again, considering the general purpose nature of the survey the most appropriate method of stratification is that which uses information on homoge-
neity which is difficult to quantify. This would include spatial contiguity,
general type-of-farming areas, broad regions of similar climate, etc. Information which is easily quantified, such as elevation, density of population, average size of family, etc., can usually be more effectively utilized in the estimation procedure. In the present case a combination of type-of-farming area,
geography, and watershed areas was used as a basis for stratification. Also,
in order to keep the calculations for the statistical analysis as simple as
possible the strata were made equal in number of sampling units. On this
basis Crete was partitioned into 20 strata from each of which two communities were selected (see Figure 21; for size and location of sample communities see also Figure 1).

f. *Equal versus variable probabilities for selecting places.* Considerable
thought was given to the idea of selecting communities from the strata with
equal probabilities, in order to facilitate the computation of estimates for
communities. If this were done there would undoubtedly be some loss in accuracy in the household and farm data. The amount of such loss would
depend considerably upon the amount of variation which exists among com-

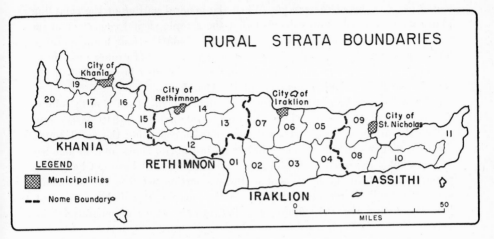

Based on map prepared by Ministry of Reconstruction for Crete Survey.

FIGURE 21. Rural strata boundaries, Crete Survey, 1948

munities in regard to numbers of farms and households. To examine this, Table M 2 was prepared. (For population distribution see Figure 3.)

Inspection of this table suggested that controlling the size variation of communities was of primary importance for an adequate household sample, and that selecting communities with probabilities based on "size" was the best solution even though it would result in a more complicated procedure of estimating characteristics of communities.

TABLE M 2. Frequency distribution of communities and municipalities by number of inhabitants in 1940

No. of inhabitants	Frequency	No. of inhabitants	Frequency	No. of inhabitants	Frequency
0- 99	0	1100-1199	4	5000-5499	—
100- 199	19	1200-1299	7	5500-5999	—
200- 299	63	1300-1399	8	6000-6499	—
300- 399	94	1400-1499	5	6500-6999	—
400- 499	71	1500-1999	13	7000-7499	—
500- 599	75	2000-2499	7	7500-7999	—
600- 699	56	2500-2999	2	8000-8499	—
700- 799	40	3000-3499	4	8500-8999	—
800- 899	35	3500-3999	1	9000-9499	—
900- 999	27	4000-4499	—	9500-9999	—
1000-1099	15	4500-4999	1	10000-and over	3

Total number of communities and municipalities: 550.

Source: Ministry of National Economy, *Population de la Grèce*, Athens, 1940.

g. The selection of the sample. When the general outline of the sampling plan was considered, it was decided that the sample should consist of about 725 households situated in the 40 communities and the four municipalities. This represented an over-all sampling rate of 1 in 150. (If proper procedures are followed 1/150th of the farmers of Crete will also be included in the sample and likewise other elements of the island.)

Two zones may be designated for convenience in the discussion to follow: (1) urban and (2) rural, where the four municipalities (1940 basis) constitute the urban zone and the 546 communities constitute the rural zones. Table M 3 shows the number of inhabitants in the two zones and the number of households expected in the sample from each (1940 basis). Changes in population both in the totals and in the proportion between the two zones since 1940 will be reflected properly in the sample. It will be convenient, however, to use the 1940 figures to illustrate the order of magnitudes involved.

TABLE M 3. Allocation of the sampling between urban and rural zones

Zone	No. of places	No. of inhabitants	No of households	"Expected" no. of households in sample
Urban (cities)	4	84,300	20,730	138.20
Rural (com- munities)	546	353,906	87,703	584.69
Total	550	438,206	108,433	722.89

Data from 1940 census. "Expected" number is number of households divided by 150.

It will be noted in Table M 3 that 138 households are "expected" in the urban portion of the sample and 585 in the rural portion. These "expectations" will be satisfied only if there is no difference in the present numbers of households from that in 1940. Of course some change is expected and it is the purpose of the sample to provide a reasonably accurate measure of that change. If the numbers found in our sample differ from these "expected" numbers, it will be a measure of that change.

The "expected" 138 households for the urban sample are to be obtained by sampling each of the 4 cities comprising the urban zone at the 1/150th rate. On this basis the number of households "expected" from each city is shown in Table M 4. Details on the sampling within the city are given in section "i."

The "expected" 585 households for the rural sample were not taken from each of the 546 communities but from only 40 of them. These 40 communities were selected from the 20 strata, 2 from each. The composition of each

TABLE M 4. Structure of the urban zone by municipality

City	No. of inhabitants	No. of households	"Expected" no. of households in sample
Khania	28,213	6,914	46.09
Rethimnon	10,972	2,780	18.53
Iraklion	42,559	10,333	68.89
Ay. Nikolaos	2,558	703	4.69
Urban zone, totals	84,300	20,730	138.20

Data from 1940 census. "Expected" number is number of households divided by 150.

of the 20 strata is given in Table M 5. Details on the sampling within a stratum is given in the following section.

TABLE M 5. Structure of the rural zone by strata

(1) Stratum Number	(2) No. of Communities	(3) No. of Inhabitants	(4) No. of Households	(5) "Expected" no. of Households in sample
1	23	17,144	4267	28.45
2	26	17,070	3985	26.57
3	23	17,059	4027	26.85
4	26	14,810	3936	26.24
5	30	19,836	5215	34.74
6	25	20,929	5042	33.61
7	28	18,513	4587	30.58
8	23	16,089	4286	28.57
9	19	18,393	5431	36.21
10	19	16,754	4373	29.15
11	22	17,378	4693	31.29
12	39	17,761	4548	30.32
13	35	18,127	4260	28.40
14	40	17,682	4284	28.56
15	32	17,868	4209	28.06
16	27	19,098	4479	29.86
17	20	17,050	3856	25.71
18	25	15,934	3590	23.93
19	31	18,007	4211	28.07
20	33	18,437	4424	29.49
Total	546	353,939	87,703	584.69

Data from 1940 census. "Expected" number is number of households divided by 150.

h. *The rural sample.* The average number of sample households "expected" from each of the 20 strata was 29. These were to be taken from two selected communities (from the total of 29 in the average stratum). By using stratum 1 as an example (see Table M6), the way by which the sample communities were selected may be described.

Each of the 20 strata was regarded as having 300 sampling units, two of which are to be selected at random (thus a sampling rate of 1/150). These 300 sampling units (s.u.) were allotted to each community within the stratum in proportion to the number of inhabitants it had according to the 1940 census. The number of inhabitants per s.u. was 57.147 (17,144 ÷ 300). (Allocation would have been based on household numbers rather than inhabitants but these were not conveniently available at the time.) In order to avoid the

TABLE M 6. Structure of Stratum 1 of the rural zone

(1)	(2)	(3)	(4)	(5)	(6)	(7)
Community		No. of Inhabitants		No. of s.u.'s[a]		
				Universe		Sample
Serial No.	Census Code	No.	Cumulative Totals	Cumulative Totals	No.	Random Nos. 7 to 201
1	12-6-1	704	704	12	12	7
2	12-6-2	433	1137	19	7	
3	12-6-3	518	1655	28	9	
4	12-6-4	602	2257	39	11	
5	12-6-5	407	2664	46	7	
6	12-6-6	136	2800	48	2	
7	12-6-7	835	3635	63	15	
8	12-6-8	769	4404	77	14	
9	12-6-9	628	5032	88	11	
10	12-6-10	2455	7487	131	43	
11	12-6-11	520	8007	140	9	
12	12-2-3	521	8528	149	9	
13	12-2-8	565	9093	159	10	
14	12-2-9	881	9974	174	15	
15	12-2-12	1956	11930	208	34	201
16	12-2-13	362	12292	215	7	
17	12-2-14	512	12804	224	9	
18	12-2-17	1250	14054	245	21	
19	12-2-21	225	14279	249	4	
20	12-2-22	594	14873	260	11	
21	12-2-23	396	15269	267	7	
22	12-2-26	1551	16820	294	27	
23	12-2-27	324	17144	300	6	
Total		17,144	—	—	300	

[a] 57.147 inhabitants = 1 s. u.

assignment of fractional sampling units and still assure that the total would be 300 for each stratum, the cumulative totals of inhabitants (column 4, Table M 6) were compiled and the corresponding cumulative totals of sampling units were computed by dividing the inhabitant numbers by 57.147 and recording the whole number only. The number of sampling units assigned to each community is given by Col. (6) which represents successive differences between the values of Col. (5). (For example, the assigned number for community number 5 is the cumulative total for No. 5 less the cumulative total for No. 4, or $46 - 39 = 7$. Actually all the values for Cols. (5) and (6) need not be computed—just those on and preceding the line in which the sample number falls. All values are shown here for illustrating the general idea.)

For selecting the sample communities two random numbers were chosen in the range 1-300 (the total number of sampling units). In this case the numbers were 7 and 201. Since these sampling units were in communities No. 1 and No. 15 these will be regarded as the sample communities.

The number of sampling units assigned these communities indicates the rate at which they are to be sampled, namely 1/12 for No. 1 and 1/34 for No. 15. This was done by requiring the investigator to make a complete list of all households in each sample place and to number them in a prescribed manner. The sample households were designated by rule. For example, see Table M 7, where a rural stratum is shown as an example. Sample communities No. 1 and No. 15 of Table M 6 are identified here by a code keyed to the published census. Code 12-6-1 means the community can be found in the census booklet as the 1st community in the 6th eparchy in the 12th nome

TABLE M 7. Specification of sample households in the sample communities, Rural Stratum 1

(1)	(2)	(3)	(4)	(5)	(6)	(7)
Stratum and s.u. no.	Sample community (Census Code)	No. of s.u.'s (col. 6, table 6)	Random start no.	Sampling interval[a]	No. of HH's[b]	Serial numbers of sample households
1-1	12-6-1	12	8	12	172	8, 20, 32, 44, 56, 68, 80, 92, 104, 116, 128, 140, 152, 164, 172, . . .
1-2	12-2-12	34	15	34	438	15, 49, 83, 117, 151, 185, 219, 253, 287, 321, 355, 389, 423, . . .

[a] i.e. "Take every — households."
[b] From 1940 census.

of Greece. A random number is drawn in the range 1 to 12 (the total number
of s.u.'s—sampling units—assigned to the community) which in this case
was 8. This household, the 8 + 12 or 20, and 20 + 12 or 32, and 32 + 12 or
44, etc. are the sample households for this community. Similarly for the
second sample community, where 15 is the random start number and 34 the
interval. Hence the sample households are 15, 49, 83, . . . Each such group
of households is regarded as a sampling unit.

   i. *The urban sample.* In section g. it was indicated that based on 1940 population figures a total of 138 households were "expected" in the sample. In
the urban zone sampling was distributed throughout all the cities rather than
just to a sample of places as was done in the rural zone. No information was
available on the distribution of the population within the cities (such as by
block) so it was decided that some quick estimates would be made by a can-
vassing of each city and by observation of the number and nature of structures
on each block to estimate quickly the number of households on each. Town
plan maps of 1:20,000 scale (one sheet) and 1:2,000 scale (four sheets) were
obtained from the Ministry of Reconstruction. These block data were referred
to as "eye" estimates (made by observers riding bicycles around each and
every block). The nature of this information is shown in Table M 8, where

TABLE M 8. Structure of the city of Khania by district

(1)	(2)	(3)	(4)	(5)	(6)	(7)	(8)
		Households		No. of s.u.'s[a]			
		(eye estimates)		Universe		Sample[b]	
Khania District	No. of blocks	No.	Cum. totals	Cum. totals[c]	No. s.u.'s	Serial no. of s.u's	No.
1	82	1,729	1,729	582	582	21, 171, 321, 471	4
2	55	1,187	2,916	982	400	621, 771, 921	3
3	72	827	3,743	1,260	278	1,071, 1,221	2
4	48	956	4,699	1,582	322	1,371, 1,521	2
5	37	671	5,370	1,808	226	1,671	1
6	61	1,092	6,462	2,176	368	1,821, 1,971, 2,121	3
7	48	666	7,128	2,400	224	2,271	1
Totals	403	7,128	—	—	2,400	—	16

[a] 2.970 households = 1 s. u.   [b] Start no. = 21. Interval = 150.
[c] Col. (4) divided by 2.970.

summaries of these eye estimates by district are given for the city of Khania.
These districts were areas of the city convenient as work areas for the several crews of observers doing the work (see Figure 22). They were also made
as "homogeneous" as conveniently possible so they could be used directly
(or with some simple modification) as strata.

   An estimated total of 7,128 households for Khania was obtained by this
procedure. A sampling unit (cluster of households and abbreviated s.u.) of

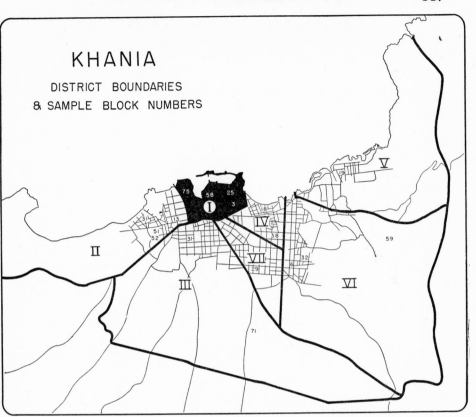

Based on map prepared by Ministry of Reconstruction for Crete Survey.

FIGURE 22. Khania: District boundaries showing location of numbered sample blocks, Crete Survey, 1948

about 3 households was regarded as a good choice for the urban sampling contrasted with 15 in the rural sampling).

Considering the over-all sampling rate of 1/150, this suggested that in Khania we should have 16 sampling units of an expected 2.970 households each; i.e. there were an estimated 7,128 households, of which 1 in 150, or 47.52, were to be selected for the sample. This exact s.u. size was determined by dividing the number of households expected in the sample, 47.52, by 16, the number of s.u.'s in the sample, giving 2.970. Of the universe of 2,400 s.u.'s from which 16 are to be selected for the sample, the number to be taken from each district was determined by selecting a random number within the range 1-150 (in this case: 21) and marking off each 150 from 21 on the cumulative total of s.u.'s shown in Col. 6 of Table M 8. In effect the districts are now strata and the numbers in Col. 8 are the numbers of s.u.'s to be drawn from each (the total being fixed at 16, this procedure avoids some problems of rounding).

Table M 9 shows the data required for the next step, that is, drawing the sample of s.u.'s within the districts. The scheme is identical to that described

TABLE M 9. Structure of District 1 of the city of Khania

(1)	(2)	(3)	(4)	(5)	(6)	(7)	(8)
	Households[a]			Sample units[b]			
Block No.	No.	Cumulative Totals	Random No.	Cumulative Total	Selected	In block	In sample
1	31	31					
2	21	52		17			
3	33	85	63	28	21	11	1
4	30	115					
5	30	145					
6	41	186					
7	10	196					
8	2	198					
9	26	224					
10	33	257					
11	16	273					
12	13	286					
13	15	301					
14	13	314					
15	6	320					
16	2	322					
17	45	367					
18	14	381					
19	10	391					
20	5	396					
21	25	421					
22	26	447					
23	41	488					
24	19	507		170			
25	14	521	513	175	172	5	1
26	2	523					
27	0	523					
28	4	527					
29	7	534					
30							
31	29	563					
32	16	579					
33	7	586					
34	26	612					
35	27	639					
36	44	683					
37	22	705					
38	16	721					
39	34	755					

40	12	767					
41	36	803					
42	9	812					
43	15	827					
44	14	841					
45	0	841					
46	8	849					
47	7	856					
48	6	862					
49	8	870					
50	22	892					
51	17	909					
52	13	922					
53	11	933					
54	10	943					
55	1	944					
56	2	946					
57	5	951		320			
58	22	973	963	327	324	7	1
59	49	1022					
60	18	1040					
61	3	1043					
62	3	1046					
63	21	1067					
64	17	1084					
65	21	1105					
66							
67	40	1145					
68							
69	33	1178					
70	25	1203					
71	36	1239					
72	23	1262					
73	47	1309					
74	69	1378		463			
75	60	1438	1413	484	475	21	1
76	31	1469					
77	70	1539					
78	41	1580					
79	64	1644					
80	64	1708					
81	10	1718					
82	11	1729		582			
Total 1729				582			4

a Eye estimates.

b 2.970 HH's = 1 s. u.

for the selection of sample communities (Table M 6) except the measure for the number of s.u.'s to be given each block is based on eye estimates rather than the number from a previous census. As in the case with Table M 6, the random numbers were actually drawn for the cumulative totals of households rather than that for s.u.'s. The conversion to the scale of s.u.'s was made by dividing the random number by the s.u. "size" (in this city: 2.970) and omitting the fraction. The random number drawn on the household scale was 63, which corresponds to the 21st unit on the s.u. scale which is found to be in Block no. 3 as one of 11 such units. The next random number is 513 (which is 63 + 450, the interval), the next, 963, 1413, etc. In District 1 the sample blocks were therefore Nos. 3, 25, 58, and 75. These were identified on the town plan maps and re-visited for "map-listings." The map designation of Block no. 3 (the first sample block of District 1, Khania) is shown in Figure 23.

A scheme of designating the sample households within the sample block was similar to that for communities (Table M7). This scheme is indicated by Table M10.

TABLE M 10. Specification of sample households in the sample blocks, District 1, city of Khania

(1)	(2)	(3)	(4)	(5)	(6)
Sample Block No.	Estimated no. of households	No. of s.u.'s (table 9, col. 7)	Random start no.	Sampling interval	Serial number of sample households
3	33	11	10	11	10, 21, 32, . . .
25	14	5	4	5	4, 9, 14, . . .
58	22	7	2	7	2, 9, 16, . . .
75	60	21	5	21	5, 26, 47, . . .

After the sample blocks have been selected and indicated on a map (for Khania, see Figure 22) the next step involves the map-listing of each, viz. obtaining an exact count of the households on the block, indicating their exact locations, and assigning a serial number to each in a prescribed manner. To carry out the operation properly it is advisable to make, in large scale, a sketch of the block on which the buildings are outlined (see Figure 24). Serial numbering should start from some convenient point and continue around the block. In this case the sample households are those numbered 10, 21, and 32. The map-list gave a final count of 34 rather than the original estimate of 33, and 3 households came into the sample. The next sample household would be 43. If 43 households had been found, household no. 43 would also have to be interviewed. Hence the number taken in the sample is determined ultimately by what is found in the survey. Similarly, every sample household for the survey was predesignated.

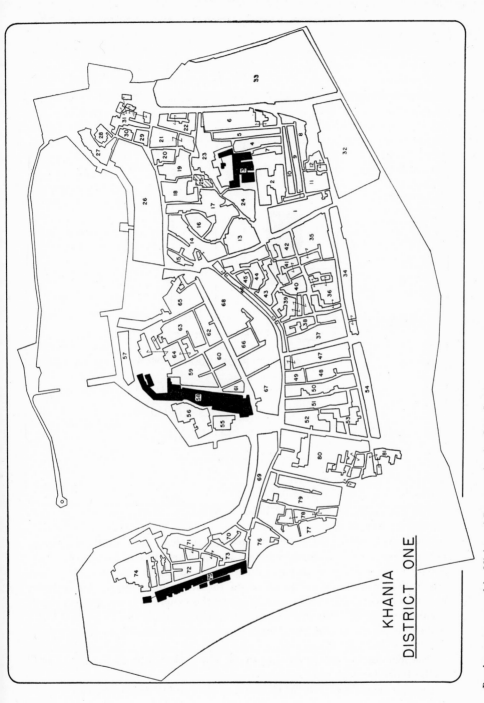

KHANIA
DISTRICT ONE

Based on map prepared by Ministry of Reconstruction for Crete Survey.

FIGURE 23. Khania: District one and sample block locations, Crete Survey, 1948

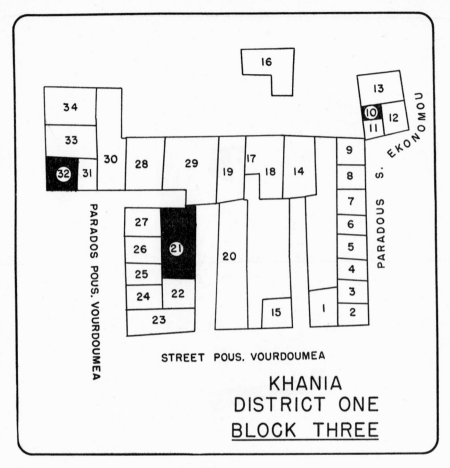

Based on map prepared by Ministry of Reconstruction for Crete Survey.

FIGURE 24. Khania: District one, block three and sample household locations, Crete Survey, 1948

j. *The sub-samples.* In addition to the household, farm, and community information which the Form A, Form B, and Form C schedules were designated to elicit, rather detailed information on certain segments of the population was desired for other aspects of the study of Crete. It was decided to obtain this information by sub-sampling the general survey sample. Three such sub-samples were drawn and they will be designated: (1) nutrition and clothing sub-sample, (2) children's sub-sample, (3) pregnant and lactating women sub-sample.

The methods used in obtaining these sub-samples will be briefly outlined in the following three sections.

(1) *Sub-sample of households for nutrition and clothing.* Considering the time and resources available and the accuracy desired, a 1/6 sample of the general survey sample, or a 1/900 sample of the households on the Island of

Crete, was considered optimum for this sub-sample. Somewhat different methods were followed in the communities and the cities in obtaining the sub-samples so each will be dealt with separately.

To obtain a 1/6 sample of the general survey sample in the rural section of Crete the following procedure was adopted. Twenty of the forty sample communities were selected by choosing at random one from each stratum. One-third of the sample households for the general survey sample were then chosen for the nutrition and clothing sample (see Table M 11).

TABLE M 11. Specification of households in the sub-samples, rural Strata 1 and 2 (part)

(1)	(2)		(3)	(4)	(5)	(6)
				Sample Household serial no.	Sub-sample of Households for	
Stratum	Sample Community					
					Nutrition and	
Code No.	Census Code	Name		(Table 7, col. 7)	Clothing	Children
1	12-6-1	Vorroi	(not in sub-samples)			
	12-2-12	Zaros		15		x
		Zaros		49	x	
		Zaros		83		x
		etc.		117		x
				151	x	
				185		x
				219		x
				253	x	
				287		x
				321		x
				355	x	
				389		x
				423		x
				457	x	
				491		x
2	12-2-6	Vasiliki	(not in sub-samples)			
	12-4-1	Varvara		5		x
		etc.		31	x	
				57		x
				etc.		

To obtain a 1/6 sample of the general survey sample in the four munici-palities, a list of all sample households was made, and 1/2 of the sample households were selected in each municipality by choosing a random start number (1 or 2) and then taking every other household included in the general survey sample. This set of households was then further sampled by designating one-third of the households in which the nutrition and clothing

questionnaire was to be used and the 2/3's in which the children's questionnaire was to be used (see Table M 12).

TABLE M 12. Specification of households in the sub-samples,
city of Khania, Districts 1 and 2

(1)	(2)	(3)	(4)	(5)	(6)
Line			Sample Household	Sub-sample of Households for	
No.	District	Block	Serial No.	Nutrition and Clothing	Children
1	1	3	10		
2			21		x
3			32		
4		25	4	x	
5			9		
6			14		x
7		58	2		
8			9		x
9			16		
10			23	x	
11		75	5		
12			26		x
13			47		
14	2	13	6		x
15			14		
16			22	x	
17		31	12		
18			26		
19		51-52	4		x
20			8		x
21			12		
22			16	x	

(2) *Sub-sample of children (ages 1-19).* For this sub-sample a sampling
rate of 1/900 of the children, ages 1-19, on the Island of Crete was considered optimum with respect to the time and resources available and the
accuracy desired. To achieve the 1/900 sampling rate, and to simplify the
field work and administration, this sub-sample was taken in the following
manner: (a) The sample of households for this investigation was selected
by the procedure described above and shown in Tables M 11 and M 12; (b)
For these households the sample of children was selected from a listing of
all the children with their identification numbers (within the household)
from the household questionnaire. This list was prepared for the households
in (1) above in each of the twenty communities and four municipalities. As
shown in Table M 13, 1/2 of the children's sample in these households was
then selected by taking every other child.

TABLE M 13. Specification of sample children in the sub-sample of
households for children, rural Stratum 1

(1)	(2)	(3)	(4)	(5)	(6)	(7)
Sample Commu- nity (Census Code)	Household Serial No.	No. of Chil- dren (age 1-19)	Serial No. of Child	Line No. of child in household (Form A)	Age & Sex of child	Child selec. for sample
12-6-1	(Community Not in Sub-samples)					
12-2-12	15	1	1	5	19-F	x
	49*					
	83	0				
	117	7	2	4	19-F	
			3	5	15-F	x
			4	6	11-F	
			5	7	9-F	x
			6	8	7-F	
			7	9	4-F	x
			8	10	2-M	
	151*					
	185	1	9	3	18-F	x
	219	2	10	3	4-M	x
			11	4	2-M	
	253*					
	287	1	12	3	3-F	x
	321	4	13	6	3-M	
			14	7	1-F	x
			15	8	17-F	
			16	9	15-M	
	355*					
	389	6	17	4	17-M	
			18	5	13-F	x
			19	6	10-M	
			20	7	7-M	x
			21	8	5-M	
			22	9	2-M	x
	423	0				
	457*					
	491	6	23	5	19-M	
			24	6	17-M	x
			25	7	15-F	
			26	8	13-F	x
			27	9	9-M	
			28	10	6-M	x

* Not in sample of households.

The procedure outlined above thus gives a 1/2 x 2/3 x 1/2 = 1/6 sample of the general survey sample children or a (1/6 x 1/150 = 1/900) sample of the children, ages 1-19 on the Island of Crete.

(3) *Sub-sample of pregnant and lactating women.* A 1/2 sample of the general survey sample was used for this sub-sample, or a 1/300 sample of the pregnant and lactating women on the Island of Crete. The 1/2 sub-sample consisted of all the pregnant and lactating women found in all the households in the Nutrition and Clothing Sub-sample and the Children's Sub-sample.

k. *Sampling materials for the investigator.* Each investigator was provided a set of materials to facilitate his carrying out of the sampling operation. Each of the 40 questionnaires for community information (Form C) was pre-posted with the name of the village in order to avoid possible errors in identification (there are many communities in Crete with the same or similar names, or with local names differing from "official" names).

A list of sampling "aids" included: (1) A general road map of Crete. (2) A tracing of an enlarged map of the sample community showing location of its boundaries and the names and location of each village in it (from the Ministry of Reconstruction). (3) A piece of a military map of the community showing topographic detail. (4) "Pre-posted" questionnaires (Form C) on which the sample start numbers and intervals were indicated; this specified the households in the sample of households. (5) A small-scale town-plan map, for municipalities and large communities. (6) Investigators assigned the work of eye estimation were provided with large-scale town-plan maps. (7) Interviewers in cities were provided with large-scale maps of the sample blocks which also indicated the start numbers and sampling intervals. (8) Instructions on field sampling procedures (included in the manual). (9) Miscellaneous Listing Forms.

2. The Field Work

a. *Selection and training of the interviewers.* Two difficulties arose in the selection and training of interviewers. First, there were no persons available who were trained and experienced in interviewing, and second, it was impossible to find enough technically competent people who could speak both English and Greek. It was decided, therefore, to lay great stress on selecting Cretans of general high quality for these positions and then, by the use of interpreters, to train them as thoroughly as possible in the time available.

Island officials were asked to submit names of young men of outstanding ability. These candidates were invited to Khania, the survey headquarters, for a two-day meeting. Lectures on surveys and sampling and trial interviews in the city constituted the main elements of this session. By means of observation and written tests, the more promising twelve of the twenty dealt with were selected. The investigators ranged in age from 21 to 43 years of age, all but one being under 30 years old.

At this point some remarks may be in order about the physical set-up of the training process. The interviewers sat around a long table, with the trainer and his interpreter at its head. The trainers (the American survey staff) directly addressed their remarks to the group in English. These were immediately restated in Greek (usually sentence by sentence) by the translator. Questions from the group and answers to them required double translation, of course. Instructions were originally prepared in English, translated into Greek and mimeographed. Each man had copies of these instructions. They covered interviewing technique, sampling instructions, remarks on the meaning of each question in the questionnaire, and some administrative matters. The questionnaires were in both English and Greek.[3]

Five full days were allocated to the training school. The sessions were principally devoted to the explanation of the three primary questionnaires (Forms A, B, and C). The men had previously, in the selection school held earlier, been trained in general interviewing techniques, so this subject was not taken up in the regular school. Because of the language difficulty, three days were required to go over the questionnaires, one day for each, probably taking about twice as much time as would have been necessary if trainer and trainee had been able to speak the same language. The fourth day was devoted to practice interviews in the city of Khania. On the evening of the same day the supervisors went over the practice questionnaires, correcting them and criticizing as necessary.

On the fifth day the kind of sampling required of the interviewer was discussed. Only the sampling procedures to be followed in the communities were presented to the whole group. Sampling procedures in the municipalities were handled directly by one of the supervisors who was assisted by a Greek adviser and two investigators specially trained for the work. Administrative details, such as assignments of communities to individuals, pay, materials, and transportation, were also treated.

The interviewers were divided into six two-man teams. Sampling and interviewing require different aptitudes that frequently do not exist in the same individual. Therefore an attempt was made to pair up persons who would complement one another. Both members did interviewing, however, since the completion of the sampling operation in each community required only a small part of the time of one man.

Two supervisors accompanied the interviewers on the first day of actual field work, each one observing three teams. As time permitted, steps were taken to get the men properly started on all phases of their job. Upon completion of the first community, each team returned to headquarters.

When they returned, at least four hours per team was given to the examination of the work done and to the answering of questions. This step in the training process was of great value because it brought out the fact that some points were being handled differently by the several interviewers. At this time such erroneous interpretations and procedures as existed were corrected. Relatively few misinterpretations occurred during the remainder of the survey. This completed the formal and supervised training, although the super-

---

[3] Since the majority of questions on the schedules required answers stated only in Arabic figures or as "yes" and "no," a minimum of translation was necessary. Consequently the use of the bilingual questionnaire was a great time saver, as well as a means of eliminating the chances for error in copy work by untrained personnel. Coding for the Hollerith machine was done directly from the field schedules.

visors remained in contact with the investigators throughout the entire interviewing phase.

The Greek Red Cross women who volunteered to obtain the records pertaining to diet and health were trained in about the same way as the men. Selection of the Red Cross workers was from the membership in local chapters of the organization.

b. *The field operation.* The field work on the main and sub-samples was carried out in two distinct but coordinate operations. The main sample work was about two-thirds completed before the sub-sample work was started.

The interviewing teams moved from west to east across the island, a team spending about three days in each community. The municipalities were dealt with directly by a special team consisting of a supervisor and two interviewers. Three sets of questionnaires were used, Forms A, B, and C. Work was begun on August 15, 1948, and was all but completed by September 20, 1948.

In the second interviewing operation, seven volunteer Greek Red Cross women visited the households in the sub-samples. Seven sets of questionnaires were used—Forms E, F, G, H, I, Ia, and J—the most important being the seven-day diet record, Form Ia. Twenty of the 40 communities and all of the 4 municipalities were included in the sub-samples. Work was begun by the Red Cross women on September 11, 1948, and largely completed on October 25, 1948.

Two automobiles were available full time to transport the workers from one community to the next. One supervisor was occupied almost wholly with the problem of movement of the crew. At the same time, he was able to advise and check constantly on each team because he saw them twice each week and had ample opportunity to go over their questionnaires and assist them in solving the problems they encountered. For the city interviewing, another automobile was available part time and it was possible to use bicycles for this work as well. The bicycles were used in "block cruising" in the cities and for reaching the designated sample households.

In a few cases it was not possible to reach a sample community by automobile. In these cases, donkeys were used, or the interviewers walked from the road end to the community. In almost all communities some of the villages had to be reached on foot—the cars were not there and could not have been used in any case because of lack of roads. One community was reached only after a five-hour donkey ride, another by sea caïque and donkey.

When checking the work of the interviewers, the supervisors were especially interested in the quality of the interviewing and the accuracy of the lists of household heads. The lists were to contain the names of all household heads in the communities and only household heads. The lists were examined in detail in each community. Certain standard queries were made in each community, the most important having to do with actual residence of ration holders.[4] The interviewers were also checked to see that they had applied

---

[4] Sometimes householders had their residence in one community but held ration cards in a different community. Since the ration holders list was an important source of names of heads of households the lists had to be carefully checked for completeness.

the proper within-community sampling rate and, finally, to see that they had filled in all the applicable questions. These steps were taken as the field work progressed when the supervisors made contact with a team. Pressure was constantly applied in an effort to do as complete and accurate a field job as possible.

The Red Cross nurses working on the sub-sample enumeration did not work as teams. Each woman went alone to a community where she stayed for seven to ten days. Transportation was by the vehicles brought to Crete for the survey. Field checking was done in about the same way as for the main survey.

3. *Treatment of the Data*

While the field work was under way, the materials and questionnaires for sample communities and municipalities regarded as completed by the investigators were given first to the supervisors for a quick check to see if rules were being properly followed, etc., and then sent on to the central office in Khania where the answers in Greek were translated to English and a number of preliminary tabulations were made. The final processing of the data was in the Statistical Laboratory of Iowa State College at Ames, Iowa, where a more detailed procedure was established.

a. *Coverage.* The first examination to which the data were put was on completeness of coverage. Were all the households, farms, etc. specified as in the sample actually accounted for in the data turned in? Could each questionnaire be identified with its proper place in the sample structure? In order to make these checks it seemed desirable to have a convenient "blueprint" of the sample structure so that its specifications could be easily seen. Table M 7 for the rural and Table M 10 for the urban zone show in part the desired information. In the case of the first sample community of Rural Stratum 1, 204 households (compared with 172 in the 1940 census) were found, which meant that households numbered 184 and 196 (the next number, 208, is too large) must also be included in the sample. In some cases fewer were found than that given by the 1940 census and therefore fewer were required in the sample (depending on whether households were fewer than the last serial number in the sample). Omissions may occur because the sample household refused to give information, or was "not-at-home." Fewer, or more than the required number, might be taken because of confusion. Whatever the cause, some adjustment was made to bring the sample into proper balance. Overtakes were removed from the finally accepted set of data. Omissions were "filled" by choosing another unit (household or farm) from the remaining units in the sampling unit and duplicating its data for the missed one. (In only 28 cases was this required for households; 3 of these refused information, 9 were not at home during the survey week, 13 were discarded for sub-sampling reasons, and 3 because of miscellaneous difficulties.) In many cases the sketches and other data turned in by the investigator had to be examined carefully to determine the situation. Since this was anticipated, the investigators were instructed to prepare these materials and to turn them in along with the interview information.

It will be noted in Tables M 14 and M 15 that the urban sample required 147 households and the rural sample 625 or a total of 772.

b. *Completeness of the questionnaires.* As with nearly all surveys dependent on interview information, there were some unanswered questions on the questionnaires. There are several reasons for these non-replies. Unwillingness to make an estimate where the respondent does not know the answer, refusal to answer certain questions, and neglect on the part of the interviewer account for most of the omissions. In this survey non-responses were few. Many questions were complete for all interviews and the maximum missed for any

TABLE M 14. "Expected" and required sample households and number properly accounted for by sampling unit, urban zone

(1)	(2)	(3)	(4)	(5)	(6)	(7)
		In Sample Block		In Sampling Unit		
Line no.	District & Block no.[a]	Estimated by eye[b]	Final count[b]	"Expected" (table 10, col. 6)	Required[c]	No. Missing[d]
KHANIA						
1	1-3	33	34	3	3	0
2	1-25	14	15	3	3	0
3	1-58	22	27	3	4	1
4	1-75	60	57	3	3	1
5	2-13	22	25	3	3	0
6	2-31	39	32	3	2	0
7	2-51 & 52	12	17	3	4	0
8	3-31	11	15	2	4	0
9	3-71	63	99	3	5	0
10	4-18	78	71	3	3	0
11	4-38	16	10	3	2	0
12	5-19	18	19	3	3	0
13	6-6	19	28	3	4	0
14	6-32	19	22	3	4	0
15	6-59	52	102	3	6	0
16	7-29	24	23	3	3	0
Total	—	—	—	47	56	2
RETHIMNON						
17	1-15	33	36	3	3	0
18	1-33	12	7	3	2	0
19	1-55	20	23	3	4	2
20	1-76	38	42	3	3	0
21	3-1	10	8	3	3	0
22	11-1	35	28	3	2	0
Total	—	—	—	18	17	2

IRAKLION

23	W-2	26	36	3	4	0
24	W-17	11	10	3	3	1
25	W-34	162	8	3	1	0
26	W-54	56	1	3	0	0
27	W-59	37	38	3	3	0
28	W-76	71(17)	(16)	3	3	1
29	W-97	36	39	3	3	0
30	W-113	38	45	3	4	0
31	W-132	85(23)	(32)	3	3	0
32	W-152	7	8	3	3	0
33	W-180	94(13)	(11)	3	2	0
34	W-198	7	9	3	4	0
35	W-218	17	5	2	0	0
36	2-3	17	16	4	4	3
37	2-21	28	32	3	3	0
38	5-5	31	34	3	3	0
39	6-1	24	21	3	3	1
40	10-1	125	119	3	2	0
41	13-7	18	14	3	2	0
42	14-3	135(21)	(18)	3	2	0
43	16-3	50	57	3	3	0
44	16-15	70(11)	(14)	3	3	0
45	18-3	46	45	3	3	0
46	19-1	22	50	3	7	1
Total	—	—	—	72	68	7

AY. NIKOLAOS

47		—	—	1	1	0
48		—	—	1	1	0
49		—	—	1	1	0
50		—	—	1	1	0
51		—	—	1	1	0
52		—	—	1	1	0
Total		—	—	6	6	0
TOTAL, URBAN ZONE		—	—	143	147[e]	11

[a] No sample of blocks taken in Ay. Nikolaos.

[b] Figures in parentheses refer to "sub-blocks." Estimates in District "W" based on water lists.

[c] The random start nos. of Col. 4 and sampling interval number of Col. 5 of Table 10 are applied to Col. 4 of this table to get required number of households in sampling unit.

[d] Of the 11 "missing": 2 were due to errors in determining sampling rate; 6 were not at home during survey week; 2 refusals; 1 unable to speak Greek (Armenian family).

[e] A number slightly different from this (148) was actually used in the analysis.

TABLE M 15. "Expected" and required sample households and number properly accounted for by sampling unit, rural zone

(1)	(2)	(3)	(4)	(5)	(6)	(7)
		In Sample Community		In Sampling Unit		
Stratum no.	Sample Com. no.	Greek Census (1940)	Crete Survey (1948)	"Expected" (table 7, col. 7)	Required[b]	No. Missing[c]
1 (1)	12-6-1	172	204	15	17	0
(2)	12-2-12	438	511	13	15	0
2 (1)	12-2-6	139	141	16	16	0
(2)	12-4-1	324	373	13	15	0
3 (1)	12-4-7	168	174	14	15	0
(2)	12-4-5	495	526	14	14	0
4 (1)	12-1-6	102	100	13	13	0
(2)	12-5-30	119	137	12	14	0
5 (1)	12-5-31	395	397	17	17	0
(2)	12-5-7	196	207	18	19	0
6 (1)	12-5-12	148	172	17	19	0
(2)	12-7-3	193	261	16	22	0
7 (1)	12-3-4	206	228	14	16	0
(2)	12-3-23	210	209	18	18	0
8 (1)	24-2-2	334	376	14	16	0
(2)	24-1-12	264	251	17	16	0
9 (1)	24-3-7	94	131	19	26	13
(2)	24-3-10	203	191	19	18	0
10 (1)	24-1-5	1252	1408	14	15	0
(2)	24-4-29	258	288	14	16	2
11 (1)	24-4-31	218	250	14	16	0
(2)	24-4-6	276	338	15	19	0
12 (1)	29-1-25	154	160	15	16	0
(2)	29-2-17	91	88	18	18	0
13 (1)	29-2-12	81	80	21	20	0
(2)	29-3-8	675	664	13	13	0
14 (1)	29-3-2	51	59	13	15	0
(2)	29-4-40	152	137	14	12	0
15 (1)	37-1-8	315	314	15	15	0
(2)	29-4-10	89	90	13	13	0
16 (1)	37-1-20	209	229	17	18	0
(2)	37-1-19	87	81	15	14	0
17 (1)	37-3-26	383	396	13	14	0
(2)	37-3-23	187	196	13	13	0
18 (1)	37-4-7	488	441	12	11	0
(2)	37-5-10	155	111	13	9	0

19	(1)	37-3-27	168	165	12	12	0
	(2)	37-2-12	224	227	15	16	2
20	(1)	37-2-34	54	56	11	11	0
	(2)	37-2-13	155	146	14	13	0
RURAL ZONE, TOTALS		—	—	593	625[a]	17	

a A number slightly different from this (617) was actually used in the analysis.

b The random start nos. of Col. 4 and sampling interval nos. of Col. 5 of Table 7 are applied to Col. 4 of this table to get required number of households in sampling unit.

c Of the 17 "missing": 3 were not at home during the survey week; 1 refused to give information; 13 were omitted by a sub-sampling scheme to save time.

question was about 10 per cent. In general, only 5 to 15 non-responses occurred with any question. Such a small number as this can cause only a negligible bias in the final product if appropriate means are followed in estimation. Such omissions can be responsible for an appreciable bias in estimating aggregates, if missing values are regarded as zeros. Also a bias in sampling error may result where the missing data are ignored (that is, if they are implied to be zeros).

Although the non-responses in questionnaires were not sufficiently numerous to have an important effect even with the simplest appropriate scheme of treatment, it was thought advisable to eliminate by certain office procedures, insofar as possible, as much influence as they might have. Two schemes were followed: (1) Items such as household income, value of farms, crop acreages and production, tenure of farm operator, occupation of inhabitants, were "edited in" on the individual questionnaires since these items were to be used in cross-classification. The "edited in" values were synthesized from other information on the records for households or farms being dealt with. (2) Most items, however, were not filled in by the editors, being marked as "non-response." On final tabulations the non-responses for any question were allocated to the classes in the tables on a proportionate basis. Thus, if there were 10 non-responses, 250 yeses and 250 noes, 5 of the non-responses would be allocated to the yes class and 5 to the no class, not changing the original ratio of yes to no answers.

(NOTE: *The following section is somewhat mathematical. A summary of several estimates of the reliability of the several samples was presented in the "Conclusions on Methodology" at the beginning of this appendix. Those not interested in the mathematical procedures for arriving at such conclusions may wish to omit the next few pages and continue with the section "Examination for Quality.")*

c. *Estimates and their measures of reliability.* For simple estimates of totals for data from the household and farm questionnaires all that was required was the sample total multiplied by the factor 150. For example the total number of households obtained in the sample (see Tables M 14 and M 15) was 772. An estimate of the total in Crete is 772 x 150 or 115,800.

Since the sample on which this estimate is based was selected by a randomization procedure, it is possible to determine a measure of its accuracy.

For this purpose the sample of households and farms will be regarded as of a stratified-random design of one stage where the sampling units consist of "clusters" of households and farms. In the rural zone there are 20 strata and in the urban zone each pair of sampling units will be regarded as having been drawn from a stratum (by appropriate partitioning of the districts) and therefore there is a total of 26 strata in the urban zone.

In general an unbiased estimate of the total of some character x, from a stratified-random sample of n units is given by the estimator,

$$\hat{T}_x = \sum_{i=1}^{P} N_i \bar{x}_i, \tag{1}$$

where: $\hat{T}_x$ is the estimate of the total x, T_x, in the universe,

P is the number of strata,

N_i is the number of sampling units in the ith stratum,

$\bar{x}_i$ is the mean of x in the sample for the ith stratum.

Formula (1) can be written,

$$\hat{T}_x = \sum_{i=1}^{P} \frac{N_i}{n_i} \sum_{j=1}^{n_i} x_{ij} \tag{2}$$

where: x_{ij} is the value of x for the jth sampling unit in the ith stratum,

n_i is the number of sampling units in the sample in the ith stratum.

In the Crete sample of households $\dfrac{N_i}{n_i}$ was made a constant, that is, 150.

$$\hat{T}_x = 150 \sum_{i=1}^{P} \sum_{j=1}^{n_i} x_{ij} \tag{3}$$

which is merely the sample total of x multiplied by the factor, 150.

The variance of $\hat{T}_x$ (3) is given by the estimator,

$$V(\hat{T}_x) = (150)^2 \left(\frac{N - n}{N} \right) \frac{\bar{\sigma}_w^2}{n} \tag{4}$$

where: $\bar{\sigma}_w^2$ is the universe average variance of x within strata,

N is ΣN_i, and

n is Σn_i.

Since $\dfrac{N-n}{N}$ is approximately 1, and since $\bar{\sigma}_w^2$ can be estimated from the sample

by

$$\bar{s}^2 = \frac{1}{P} \sum_{i=1}^{P} \sum_{j=1}^{n_i} \frac{(x_{ij} - \bar{x}_i)^2}{n_i - 1} \tag{5}$$

then the variance of $\hat{T}_x$ is estimated by

$$V(\hat{T}_x) = (150)^2 \frac{\bar{s}^2}{n}. \tag{6}$$

In order to keep the computations as simple as possible the urban sample was regarded as one comprising 26 strata of equal size and from each of which 2 sampling units were drawn at random. Therefore $\bar{s}^2$ for the urban zone is based on 26 degrees of freedom. Since the rural zone sample comprises 20 strata of 2 sampling units each, $\bar{s}^2$ here is based on 20 df. (degrees of freedom). As an illustration of the standard errors of sample estimates Table M 16 was prepared.

TABLE M 16. Estimates of total households in Crete by urban and rural zones, and their standard errors

| Zone | Estimated HH's | Standard Error | | (Df. on which based) |
		HH's	% of Estimate	
Urban	22,000	1,000	4.5	26
Rural	93,800	1,850	2.0	20
Total	115,800	2,125	1.9	46

The estimates for the farm data (Form B) were made in the same way as for household data (Form A) outlined above and likewise the method for estimating their standard errors.

The problem was somewhat different for the community data. In this case the estimates of totals are given by

$$\hat{T}_x = \sum_{i=1}^{P} \sum_{j=1}^{2} w_{ij} x_{ij} \tag{7}$$

where w_{ij} is the reciprocal of the probability with which the jth community within the ith half-stratum was chosen (see Table M 17) and x_{ij} is the observed value of some characteristic for the jth community in the ith stratum.

The variance of this estimator is given by

$$V(\hat{T}_x) = \sum_{i=1}^{P} (w_{i1} x_{i1} - w_{i2} x_{i2})^2 + (\text{bias})^2 \tag{8}$$

where w_{i1} and x_{i1} are the weights and observed value for the 1st half-stratum in the ith stratum respectively. (Note: This estimate of variance will be biased slightly because of the use of half-strata. The bias in this case appears to be small enough so the use of this variance ignoring the bias is not seriously impaired.)

TABLE M 17. The sample communities and their weight factors, rural zone, Crete

(1)	(2)	(3)		(4)	(5)	(6)

		Sample Community			Inhabitants (1940)		Community Weight Factor, w_i
Stratum	Census Code	Name	Sample Survey Number	Half-Stratum	Community	(4) ÷ (5)
1 (1)	12-6-1	Vorroi	33	8,007	704	11.373
(2)	12-2-12	Zaros	23	9,137	1,956	4.671
2 (1)	12-2-6	Vasiliki	22	9,552	537	17.787
(2)	12-4-1	Ay. Varvara	26	7,517	1,431	5.253
3 (1)	12-4-7	Akhendria	28	8,469	689	12.292
(2)	12-4-5	Arkalokhori	27	8,590	2,042	4.207
4 (1)	12-1-6	Kato Viannos	21	7,414	376	19.718
(2)	12-5-30	Kastamonitsa	31	7,396	502	14.733
5 (1)	12-5-31	Kastelli-Ped.	32	10,379	1,542	6.731
(2)	12-5-7	Apostoloi	29	9,457	716	13.208
6 (1)	12-5-12	Ay. Paraskion	30	9,944	655	15.182
(2)	12-7-3	Veneraton	34	10,985	847	12.969
7 (1)	12-3-4	Avyeniki	24	9,133	860	10.620
(2)	12-3-23	Rogdhia	25	9,380	793	11.828
8 (1)	24-2-2	Ay. Yeoryios	38	7,669	1,286	5.963
(2)	24-1-12	Mournies	37	8,420	824	10.218
9 (1)	24-3-7	Exo. Lakonia	39	8,951	324	27.626
(2)	24-3-10	Kastelli-Fourni	41	9,442	684	13.804
10 (1)	24-1-5	Ierapetra	36	8,943	4,949	1.807
(2)	24-4-29	Stavrokhori	43	7,811	1,010	7.734
11 (1)	24-4-31	Sfaka	44	8,880	871	10.195
(2)	24-4-6	Zakros	42	8,498	1,061	8.009
12 (1)	29-1-25	Sellia	13	8,318	569	14.619
(2)	29-2-17	Monastiraki	15	9,443	299	31.582
13 (1)	29-2-12	Kaloyerou	14	9,342	260	35.931
(2)	29-3-8	Anoyia	17	8,785	3,072	2.860
14 (1)	29-3-2	Ay. Ioannis	16	8,796	228	38.579
(2)	29-4-40	Khromonastiri	19	8,886	640	13.884
15 (1)	37-1-8	Yeoryioupolis	1	9,354	1,319	7.092
(2)	29-4-10	Yerani	18	8,514	401	21.232
16 (1)	37-1-20	Neon Khorion	10	9,459	816	11.592
(2)	37-1-19	Melidoni	2	9,639	381	25.299
17 (1)	37-3-26	Mournies	9	9,120	1,645	5.544
(2)	37-3-23	Meskla	8	7,930	826	9.600
18 (1)	37-4-7	Palaiokhora	11	7,991	2,130	3.752
(2)	37-5-10	Khora-Sfakion	12	7,943	600	13.238
19 (1)	37-3-27	Neon Khorion	3	9,373	786	11.925
(2)	37-2-12	Drapania	4	8,634	913	9.457
20 (1)	37-2-34	Panethimos	6	9,101	302	30.136
(2)	37-2-13	Elos	5	9,336	674	13.582

Because a randomized sample was used, an "interval of confidence" can be constructed for the estimate which can be used for determining the risks that are taken when a given estimate is used. For example if

$$d = s_E \; t \; (a; n-1) \tag{9}$$

where: s_E is the standard error of E estimated from a sample of n—1 degrees of freedom,

$t(a; n-1)$ is Student's "t" for confidence coefficient,

a and $n-1$ degrees of freedom,

then $E \pm d_a$ is the desired interval for a confidence.

To illustrate let us look at Table M 16 where we find the estimated households in rural Crete to be 93,800 and its standard error, $s_{\bar{x}}$ to be 2.0% or 1,850 households. Within what range from 93,800 can we feel confident that the true numbers must be, unless a 1/20 chance has come off? The confidence coefficient desired in this case is .95 and our estimate is based on 20 degrees of freedom. t(95;20) found in published tables is 2.086, therefore,

$$d = (1,850)(2.086)$$
$$= 3,900$$

and $\quad E - d_a = 93,800 - 3,900$
$$= 89,900$$

and $\quad E + d_a = 93,800 + 3,900$

$$= 97,700$$

Therefore we can say that the true number of households in the rural zone of Crete must be between 89,900 and 97,700 unless a one in twenty chance came off in sampling. Thus the range 89,900 to 97,700 is one in which we have 95% "confidence."

Ordinarily the range given by $E \pm$ s.e.(E) is the approximate 67% confidence interval (if degrees of freedom are say 20 or more), $E \pm 2$ s.e.(E) is the approximate 95% confidence interval and $E \pm 3$ s.e.(E) is the 99% confidence interval. The standard errors of the sample estimates are valuable guides therefore in interpreting estimates from randomized samples. (See Table MS 1 at the beginning of this appendix and Tables A 109 and A 110 in Appendix 5.)

4. Examination for Quality

The purpose of this section is to examine the intrinsic quality of the data. For example, how accurate are the data given by the various respondents? If a farmer says he has 45 olive trees, does he in fact have 45 olive trees? If the birth records contain 10 births for a given year, were there actually 10 births in that community for that year? The evaluation of quality of interrogation information is usually very difficult—even if a special investigation is undertaken for this purpose. On the other hand some approximations can be made by various devices.

Estimates from samples can be compared for quality where different methods of elicitation or sources of information were employed to learn the same facts. If differences exist among sample estimates and/or censuses which cannot be explained by sampling error, there is ground for believing that one or more is biased. This assumes that the same universe is being measured, that the definitions of the observation units are the same, that the estimates are for the same period or point in time, etc.

It is sometimes assumed that the sampling error for unbiased estimates completely describes, in the probability sense, the closeness of estimated values to true values. Sampling error describes only variability due to chance selection of the elements in the universe. There are non-sampling errors—which result from the interviewer's or respondent's misinterpretation of questions, from ignorance or dishonesty—in general, failure to elicit correct information. A census (that is, a 100% sample) is subject to errors of this type as much or more so than a sample, because the scale of operations would usually require a larger staff of interviewers leading to the possibility that the larger staff would not be as adequately trained.

The non-sampling errors in a sample survey should be evaluated by some means and it is for this reason that quality checks are made. Frequently the *causes* of differences are not disclosed by quality checks. If differences in two sources appear which are larger than sampling error, the most that can be said is that one or the other or both must deviate significantly from the true or universe figure. Further investigations would have to be made to attempt to explain the reasons for differences.

In the Crete Survey the main sources of information for comparison and the items used were:

1. The Greek Malaria Control Board. Number of inhabitants in Crete in 1948.

2. The Nome agriculturalists. Items: Land use, numbers of farm animals, acreage, and production of crops.

3. The Sample Surveys of (a) Households—items: number of inhabitants, number of farms, household characteristics; (b) Farms—items: farm characteristics; (c) Communities—items: number of households, inhabitants, agriculture, characteristics of villages, etc.; (d) Families—items: diet, clothing.

4. The Greek Census of Agriculture (1929) and current estimate of the Ministry of Coordination.

5. The Greek Census of Population (1940).

In the following pages there will be presented a number of comparisons between the values given for various items by these sources. Some remarks describing the content of the tables containing the comparisons and the qualifications necessary in their interpretation will be given.

The general plan of the survey was to obtain information from local sources—the community president, reporting for his community; the householder, reporting for his household; and the farmer, reporting for his farm. In this way, it was anticipated, each respondent would be giving information on items he knew enough about to supply answers of satisfactory validity.

However, in order to test the quality of responses for certain agricultural items—principally land area, crop production, and numbers of animals—

identical questions were put into the farm and community questionnaires. Ordinarily one would believe that farmers should know more about the areas under crops, number of animals, etc., on their own farms than community presidents know about such things in their communities, as aggregates of all farms. In the absence of complete counts conducted in each community the presidents could only estimate such matters (for example: total number of sheep in his community).

If the two sources differed more than would be expected by reason of sampling error, it could be concluded that one or both must be in error. This process is, of course, beset with hazards. Perhaps the source which should best *know* the answers to questions does not, for some reason, provide correct information. At this point the experience of the survey personnel must be drawn upon to make a judgment as to the relative quality of sources (in the absence of better, available ways to make the evaluations). The supervisors and interviewers, being closely associated with the data-collection phases, get impressions as to the quality of answers given them by the informants. While they may be fooled, it is not likely that the impressions are always in error. The general quality of the responses of the householders and farmers seemed to the investigators to be high. They frequently commented on the willing and cooperative attitude of these respondents. A space was provided on the forms used in the survey for a record of the interviewers' comments on each interview. Only a very few of these comments reflected adversely upon the honesty and integrity of the respondent. Some of the questions on the community questionnaire were, on the other hand, reported by the investigators to be poorly answered by the officials; not because of ill will, but because the facts requested were not known except within wide limits. This was particularly true of items such as numbers of trees and vines, area under specified crops, numbers of animals in the community at certain dates, etc., and in general anything which involved relatively large numbers. Unless there was evidence to the contrary, data on the characteristics of households and farms which were obtained from the heads and operators of these units were preferred to those obtained from community presidents and others. The most notable exceptions were "scarce" farm items, for example, number of tractors (which would be better obtained on the community level since the presidents would know how many of these existed, and since a small sample of farms, such as was used in Crete, must be expected to provide estimates with very large sampling errors).

What if the survey estimates differ from "official" estimates, more than would be expected from sampling variation? Which, if any, is to be accepted as having the greatest accuracy? Again, the process of evaluation is most difficult. For example, it is seldom known whether the same things are being compared, exactly how the "official" estimates were obtained, etc. Furthermore, two independent sets of official figures, purporting to measure the same things, may vary widely.

In comparing "official" figures with those of the surveys, it was found that in few cases did the time periods or dates exactly correspond with those for the survey. It was not possible to determine whether the items being measured were defined the same for all sources. In view of this, it could not be expected that estimates from the survey sources would be within sampling error of official sources. General similarity is all that could be expected. It is of considerable interest, in spite of these difficulties, to make the comparisons. Such an exercise shows that the numerous sets of information available must be carefully scrutinized before being considered acceptable as to quality. Unless there was evidence to the contrary, an estimate from the survey was generally preferred over "official" estimates. Contrary evidence would include: (1) large sampling error and (2) vague concepts.

a. *Physical characteristics.* It may be of some interest to examine the sample of communites for their representativeness in regard to two characteristics which are known for all communities in Crete, namely, elevation of the principal village (in meters above sea level) and area (in square kilometers). If the area (or elevation) of the jth village in the ith half-stratum is denoted as x_{ij} then the total area (or elevation) in communities in Crete is given by

$$T_x = \sum_{i=1}^{40} \sum_{j=1}^{N_i} x_{ij} \tag{10}$$

where N_i is the total number of communities in the ith half-stratum. Since the sample of communities consisted of a single community selected from each of the 40 half-strata with probability of selecting the jth community in the ith stratum equal to

$$p_{ij} = \frac{h_{ij}}{H_i}$$

where h_{ij} is the number of inhabitants in the jth community in the ith half-stratum and H_i is the number of inhabitants in the ith stratum as given by the Greek population census of 1940.

$$H_i = \sum_{j=1}^{N_i} h_{ij}.$$

An estimate of T_x is obtained from the sample by the estimator:

$$\hat{T}_x = \sum_{i=1}^{40} w_{ij} x_{ij} \tag{11}$$

where the weight,

$$w_{ij} = \frac{1}{P_{ij}}.$$

(These weights are given in Table M17, above.) This estimator is unbiased because the expected value of its estimate is T_x. The variance of T_x is given by

$$\sigma^2 = \sum_{i=1}^{40} \frac{1}{w_{ij}} \left(w_{ij} x_{ij} - \sum_{j=1}^{N_i} x_{ij} \right)^2 \tag{12}$$

since

$$\sum_{j=1}^{N_i} x_{ij}$$

can be computed, the variance can be estimated from the sample by

$$s^2 = \sum_{i=1}^{40} \frac{1}{w_i} (w_i x_i - T_{x_i})^2 \tag{13}$$

where T_{x_i} is

$$\sum_{j=1}^{N_i} x_{ij}$$

or the total quantity of x in the ith stratum. The subscript j can be dropped since there is only one observed value for each half-stratum.

Computations were carried out for area and elevations and the data are shown in summary form below:

Community Characteristics	True Total:	Estimated Total:	Estimated Standard Deviation of $\hat{T}_x$:	Discrepancy	Probability of Occurrence if True Difference is Zero
x	T_x	$\hat{T}_x$	s	$\hat{T}_x - T_x$	
Land Area (sq. kilometers)	8,271	7,810	160.6	—461	.01
Elevations (meters)	180,657	184,393	6,311	+3,736	.57

It will be seen that the communities in the sample are smaller in area than the over-all average and higher in elevation than the over-all average. In the case of elevations the discrepancy is easily ascribable to sampling variation, but not so with land area. However, even in this case it seems reasonable to conclude that a 1 in 100 chance of sampling variation has occurred partly because it would be very difficult to show how a bias could occur with the procedure followed.

Inasmuch as the sample communities were 5.57 per cent smaller in land area than the true and 2.07 per cent higher in elevation than the expected, it might be expected that other characteristics related to these may show a similar discrepancy. This could be partially dealt with by the adoption of certain methods of estimation which would adjust for these variations but due to the pressure of work and the smallness of the expected gain they were not investigated further.

b. *Households and persons.* The estimates of total number of households in Crete in August 1948 compared with that given by the Greek census of 1940 is given below: (Sample Estimate figures from text, not Table M 16.)

Zone	Greek Census of 1940	Sample Estimate, 1948	Standard Error of Sample Estimate	Indicated Increase	Probability of Occurrence if True Difference is Zero
Urban	20,730	22,200	± 1,000 (26 df)	1,500	.15
Rural	87,783	92,550	± 1,850 (20 df)	4,700	.02
Total	108,513	114,750	± 2,125 (46 df)	6,200	.005

It will be noticed that each zone as well as the total has an indicated increase in households from 1940. It is possible that this indicated increase is merely a discrepancy in the sample, and that the true situation is one in which the number of households is the same as 1940. The probability that this possibility is true, however, is not very great. There is a 15 in 100 chance that it could be true for the urban zone, only a 2 in 100 chance for the rural zone, and only a 1 in 200 chance for being true of the whole of Crete. We conclude that if the survey were a complete census rather than a sample the final count of households would be greater than that of the 1940 census and the amount of the increase is about 6,200 households or 5.7 per cent.

Similarly, an increase in number of inhabitants (in households) over that given by the Greek census of 1940 was indicated by the survey. Below, the sample estimates and their standard error are shown with the corresponding counts given by the Greek census:

Zone	Greek Census of 1940	Sample Estimate, 1948	Standard Error of Sample Estimate	Indicated Increase	Probability of Occurrence if True Difference is Zero
Urban	84,300	87,450	± 4,800 (26 df)	3,150	.52
Rural	353,906	385,350	± 7,600 (20 df)	31,450	.0005
Total	438,206	472,800	± 9,000 (46 df)	34,600	.0004

The situation for total inhabitants differs somewhat from that of households, particularly when the urban zone is examined. Here there is insufficient evidence that an increase has occurred in the urban zone—the indicated increase could easily be attributed to a sampling variation. In the rural zone and for Crete as a whole, however, there is a great weight of evidence that an increase has occurred. (Our chance of error in drawing this conclusion is only 1 in 2,000!) This estimated increase is 34,600 persons or 7.9 per cent.

The estimate of 472,800 inhabitants for Crete in 1948 compares very well with the Greek Malaria Board's 477,492. When the sub-totals for urban and rural are examined, some discrepancies can be seen. The data are:

Zone	Malaria Board 1948	Sample Estimate 1948	Divergence of Sample from Malaria Board
Urban	109,588	87,450	—22,100
Rural	367,904	385,350	+17,400
Total	477,492	472,800	—4,700

Since the standard error of the sample estimate for the urban zone is only 4,800, the 22,100 difference cannot be regarded as sampling variation. Although the evidence is a bit weaker for the rural zone, it is still strong enough to draw the same conclusion. The difference in the totals is easily attributed to sampling. We, therefore, disagree with the Malaria Board's zonal totals. A possible explanation of this difference is that the Board's figures are based on ration registrations. It appears that persons need not register in their community and, therefore, persons living outside the legal limits of a municipality, but who purchase their food in the city, may be on the city's ration lists (this is particularly relevant for the city of Iraklion). Also, the number of municipalities has increased from 4 in 1940 to 10 in 1948 (with a corresponding decrease in communities). The Malaria Board's figures very probably are based on 540 communities and 10 municipalities while the sample estimates are based on 546 communities and 4 municipalities, enough in itself to account for the differences in zone totals. (See Appendix 5, Table A14.)

Although there is no evidence available which indicates either under or over coverage of households in the sample, it must be noted that in regard to the coverage of persons, the survey purposely excluded persons *not* living in households. Such persons as children in orphanages, occupants of institutions (penal, asylum, etc.), monasteries, etc. were excluded. (Members of the armed forces and the merchant marine were generally included by Greek families as members of their households, and were therefore counted, except when such men in service had no families.) The number of non-household persons is believed to be small—probably of the order of 1 per cent of the total population.

c. *Farms and agriculture.* Most of the detailed information on agriculture was obtained from those households regarded as operating either a farm or a sub-farm. Agricultural activities carried out by other forms of organizations such as corporations, monasteries, churches, etc. were excluded from the general sample surveys. It was decided that if these other types of farms existed they would be small in number and could be dealt with by other schemes (such as complete coverage, for example). But due to lack of time and other demands on attention, nothing was done about the non-family production units. The consequences of this omission will be examined in part here.

(1) *Coverage of farms.* Although the survey seems to be well within sampling error on the total number of farms, there are three classes of farms which are undercounted as "farms," though some were probably counted as "sub-farms": (1) farms consisting of livestock grazing only; (2) farms on which production was by share-cropper labor; (3) farms operated by corporate or other non-family operatorships.

The estimate of total farms and sub-farms in Crete is given separately in Table M 18, together with the counts of the Greek census of agriculture in 1929. (No tabulations were available from the 1940 census. Many of the data were destroyed during the war and occupation.) Although the census data are old, they are of some help when proper allowances are made in obtaining a general picture of the situation at that time. It can be observed that the survey obtained an estimate of 51,900 ±7% "farms" in 1948 as compared with the 1929 census count of 87,954. If the "sub-farms" are added the survey estimate becomes 92,250 ± 5%, which is essentially the same as the 1929 census figure. It was not possible to determine the concept of farms used by the Greek census, so an interpretation of this comparison is very difficult to make. It is felt, however, that the concept used by the survey, namely, the acceptance of those cases where the respondent said "yes" to the question, "Is household head a farmer?", was not inclusive enough because cases where the household head grazed sheep, goats, or cattle (that is, raised livestock but did not till the soil) may have obtained "no" answers. (Some of such persons may not regard themselves as "farmers," which is similar to the western states of the U.S. where many "ranchers" or "stockmen" do not regard themselves as "farmers.") There is some evidence that this distinction also exists in Crete and, therefore, the survey's concept of farm would exclude "ranchers." These should be picked up as "sub-farms," however.

TABLE M 18. Number of agricultural production units estimated by the survey (1948) and as given by the Greek census of agriculture (1929)

Type of agriculture production unit	Greek Census of Agriculture		Sample Survey of Crete, 1948 (Estimate and its estimated standard error)
	1929	1940	
Farm	87,954	(not known)	51,900 ± 3,500 (or 7%)[a]
Sub-farm	*	*	40,350 ± 2,800 (or 7%)[b]
Total farm and sub-farm	87,954	—	92,250 ± 4,600 (or 5%)

* Greek census did not use this classification.
[a] Estimates from Form B, Farm.
[b] Estimates from Form A, Household.

When the number of farms by sizes (land area in the farm) obtained by the survey are compared with the Greek agricultural census (Table M 19), it will be seen that there were 115 farms in 1929 that contained 1,000 or more stremma—none of which (if they still exist) came into the sample (the probability of obtaining one of these is 115/150 or .77, so the failure to obtain one cannot be ascribed to biased selection). Because of the im-

TABLE M 19. Number of agricultural production units in Crete by size (total area), 1929 and 1948

(1)	(2)	(3)	(4)	(5)
Class Limits	Farms, as of 1929[a]	Agric. Production Units as of 1948[b]		
(stremma)	Farms	Farms	Sub-farms	Total
0-9	39,183	7,800	35,850	43,650
10-19	20,120	11,700	2,850	14,550
20-29	10,481	9,600	600	10,200
30-39	5,964	6,900	150	7,050
40-49	3,500	3,450	300	3,750
50-59	2,275	4,500	150	4,650
60-69	1,404	1,500	150	1,650
70-79	995	1,650	—	1,650
80-89	674	900	—	900
90-99	552	—		
100-199	1,843	3,150	150	3,300
200-299	443	600	150	750
300-399	155	—	—	—
400-499	98	—	—	—
500-599	79	—	—	—
600-699	24	—	—	—
700-799	28	—	—	—
800-899	13	—	—	—
900-999	8	150	—	150
1000-1999	68	—	—	—
2000-4999	32	—	—	—
5000-9999	7	—	—	—
10,000-14,999	4	—	—	—
15,000-24,999	2	—	—	—
25,000-49,999	1	—	—	—
50,000-99,999	0	—	—	—
100,000-299,999	1	—	—	—
Total,Crete	87,954	51,900[c]	40,350[d]	92,250[e]

a Number of farms as reported by Greek Census of Agriculture.
b Number, from estimates based on Sample Survey of Crete.
c ± 3,500 or 7%.   d ± 2,800 or 7%.   e ± 4,600 or 5%.

portance of these large farms for our study of Crete, further examination of these problems will be made in the next section on coverage of land.

The farms operated by corporations, monasteries, cooperatives, etc., that is, non-family units, were not a part of the universe sampled through the use of households as operating units. The survey procedure provided a means for obtaining only those farms "operated" by the head of a household. Although it was said that there are few if any farms operated otherwise, it was subsequently learned that there were some (see Table M 22) and that their acreages were large. However, these farms should be included in estimates of the nome agriculturalists and those of community presidents.

(2) *Coverage of land.* The land "covered" by the survey of farms and sub-farms was essentially that "covered" by the Greek census of agriculture (1928) brought up to date (1949) by estimates of the Ministry of Coordination. The estimated total land in farms (and sub-farms) for Crete (1948) was 2,179 ($\pm$ 327 or 15%) thousand stremma from the survey and 2,707 thousand stremma from the Ministry of Coordination. (The difference, 528 thousand, is greater than the sampling error by a factor of only 1.6 and therefore the difference between the two estimates could easily be ascribed to sampling variation.) (See Table M 20.)

TABLE M 20. Area of "farm" land in Crete by class of use
(in thousands of stremma)

Use Class	Census of Agric. 1928	Estimates of Ministry of Coordination[a] 1949	Estimates from Sample Survey of Farms and Sub-farms 1948
TOTAL IN FARMS	2,707	2,707	2,179($\pm$ 327 or 15%)
Under cultivation	1,561	1,900	1,547($\pm$ 140 or 9%)
Mainly for grazing	975	646	498($\pm$ 107 or 22%)
Mainly for forest	165	155	77($\pm$ 50 or 65%)
Other (barren, waste, etc.)	6	6	57($\pm$ 10 or 18%)

[a] From private correspondence.

On the other hand, a comparison of the estimates of amount of land in different "use classes" as given by the several sources: (1) the Nome Directors of Agriculture, (2) the Ministry of Coordination, and (3) the survey of communities (shown in Table M 21) indicate that the various sources hold widely differing concepts of what the land use classes mean. These concepts by their very nature are vague, so this is not surprising. Perhaps the most useful estimates on this matter are those of the Ministry of Coordination in view of the fact that its figure for area under cultivation is in agreement with that based on the farmers' own statements (the survey of farms and sub-farms).

Table M 21. Area of land in Crete by class of use, 1948
(in thousands of stremma)

Use Class	Estimates of Nome Directors of Agriculture[a]	Estimates of Ministry of Coordination[a]	Estimates from Sample Survey of Communities
TOTAL LAND IN CRETE	8,273	8,379	7,822 (± 161 or 2%)
Under cultivation	2,531	1,900	3,730 (± 336 or 9%)
Mainly for grazing	3,437	4,600	3,219 (± 579 or 18%)
Mainly for forest	50	155	396
Other (barren, etc.)	2,255	1,724	477

a From private correspondence.

Although there is no great weight of evidence for support there is reason to suspect that the survey of farms and sub-farms omitted some land because it was confined to "family farms." If farms existed which were operated by a monastery or a school, for example, they did not have a chance to come into the survey, unless the manager was a member of some "household." The number of such farms is probably small; the only evidence on their possible existence is given in Table M 22. It will be noted that ownership is given for all land in Crete and that operatorship is given for the portion "in farms." It is

Table M 22. Ownership and operatorship of land in Crete, by class

(1)	(2)	(3)	(4)
	Area owned,[a] 1948	Census of Agriculture, 1928	
		Number of operating units	Area operated[b]
Class	(thousand stremma)	(no.)	(stremma)
Private	6,806	87,642	—
State	1,027	25	—
Communities	337	74	—
Churches and Monasteries	142	158	—
Veterans organizations	80	—	—
Banks	—	21	—
Cooperatives	—	3	—
Schools	—	9	—
Other institutions	—	22	—
Totals for Crete	8,392	87,954	2,704,970

a From private correspondence with Nome directors of Agriculture.
b Not available by class.

not possible to compute the sizes of these farms by the classes—only the upper limit. It is not known how these 312 "non-private" farms in 1929 were operated, that is, whether by renting to families or by paid managers or what. In the case where these farms were operated by tenants or managers, the survey was designed to include them; if not, the result is not clear.

(3) *Field crops.* Data on the more important field crops are shown in Table M 23 and the estimates from the two sample surveys can be compared with each other and with the figures obtained by the directors of agriculture. It may be noted that relative sampling errors, which are available only for the farm based estimates, are rather large (ranging from 13 to 32%) and, therefore, obscure the comparisons somewhat. A big discrepancy appears when the nome officials' estimates of production for the barley and maslin combination is compared with that for either or both of the surveys, the official estimates being about twice those of the surveys. Also, the production and yield of maslin given by the sample of communities appears to be high and there is a statistically significant difference between the two survey estimates on yield of pulses.

(4) *Vine and tree crops.* The estimates from the farm survey (see Table M 24) are substantially below the community survey for area, number of plants, and production of grapes, olives, carobs and oranges, the only crops in this class examined. Part of this may be due to the possibility that the farm survey failed to obtain *all* classes of farms. Another part may be attributed to some possible differences in concept and in conversion coefficients (for example the conversion of table olive production into the oil equivalent).

(5) *Farm animals.* Substantial differences appear between the two surveys on estimates of numbers of different species of livestock—the farm-based estimates being lower (see Table M 25). For sheep and lambs, for example, the farm-based estimate is less than half the community estimate or the directors' estimate. Even in view of the 21% relative sampling error, the difference is statistically significant. Since all householders in the sample were asked about numbers of animals they owned, it is difficult to attribute the large differences in numbers to faulty survey methods. Possibly the Cretans, for one reason or another, did not report the correct number of animals they owned; on the other hand, estimates of the nome officials and community presidents may have been in error. Their reports are not based on actual counts but rather are in the nature of "informal guesses" in many cases.

d. *Vital characteristics.* Only a cursory examination of the quality of vital characteristics will be made. Some data are given in Table M 26 for comparing results from the community survey with those from 1938 *Population de la Grèce*, Ministry of National Economy, supplied by Dr. V. G. Valaoras, Since direct comparison is not possible due to difference in time, only general impressions can be used for an evaluation. A few persons familiar with vital statistics have examined these data and have considered they are within the realm of expected values.

In order to evaluate the completeness of the birth registers, additional information on each child picked up on the list of inhabitants (in the survey

TABLE M 23. Estimated areas harvested and production (harvested during 1947) of several field crops, Crete, by the Directors of Agriculture and by the survey of communities and farms

(1)	(2)	(3)	(4)	(5)	(6)	(7)	(8)	(9)	(10)
	Estimates of the Directors of Agriculture			Estimates from Sample Surveys					
				Data from community presidents			Data from Farmers[a]		
Species	Area harvested (thousand stremma)	Production (thousand okes)	Yield (okes per stremma)	Area harvested (thousand stremma)	Production (thousand okes)	Yield (okes per stremma)	Area harvested (thousand stremma)	Production (thousand okes)	Yield (okes per stremma)
Wheat, for grain	152b	8,089b	53.2	137 (±15 or 11%)	7,109 (±995 or 14%)	51.9 (±4.2 or 8%)	162 (±21 or 13%)	7,234 (±940 or 13%)	44.7 (±3.2 or 7%)
Barley, for grain	320b	19,039b	59.5	129 (±17 or 13%)	7,656 (±1302 or 17%)	59.3 (±5.9 or 10%)	133 (±19 or 14%)	7,665 (±1226 or 16%)	57.6 (±4.0 or 7%)
Maslin, for grain				57 (±15 or 27%)	3,960 (±1267 or 32%)	69.5 (±7.0 or 10%)	47 (±13 or 28%)	2,360 (±660 or 28%)	50.2 (±4.5 or 9%)
Oats, for grain	—	—	—	118 (±27 or 23%)	5,050 (±858 or 17%)	42.8 (±6.0 or 14%)	84 (±13 or 15%)	4,248 (±680 or 16%)	50.6 (±2.5 or 5%)
Pulses	—	—	—	47 (±1.4 or 3%)	2,137 (±43 or 2%)	45.5 (±1.4 or 3%)	40 (±13 or 15%)	2,510 (±402 or 16%)	62.8 (±5.0 or 8%)
Potatoes, Irish	27	19,161	71.0	46	18,636	40.5	36 (±5 or 13%) (±4.7 or 13%)	14,391 (±3644 or 25%)	40.0

a Includes operators of "sub-farms."
b Harvested in 1948, not available for 1947.

TABLE M 24. Estimated number of trees and vines, areas in planting, and production (harvested during 1947) of several crops, for Crete, by Directors of Agriculture and from the survey of communities and farms

(1)	(2)	(3)	(4)	(5)	(6)	(7)	(8)	(9)	(10)
	Estimates of the Directors of Agriculture			Estimates from Sample Surveys					
				Data from Community Presidents			Data from Farmers		
Species	No. of trees or vines (thousand)	Area (thousand stremma)	Production (harvested in 1947) (thousand okes)	No. of trees or vines (thousand)	Area (thousand stremma)	Production (harvested in 1947) (thousand okes)	No. of trees or vines (thousand)[a]	Area (thousand stremma)	Production (harvested in 1947) (thousand okes)
Grapes: total	—	261	—	113,586	212	—	85,074 (± 10,172 or 12%)	176 (± 20 or 11%)	—
bearing	—	—	72,572[d]	108,210	—	82,121[d]	80,185	—	66,368[d]
non-bearing	—	—	—	5,376	—	—	4,889	—	—
Olives: total	13,918	—	—	13,851	—	—	8,010 (± 881 or 11%)	—	—
bearing	—	—	29,535[b]	12,871 (± 1673 or 13%)	—	41,706[b] (± 3753 or 9%)	(± 6,735	—	21,691[b] (± 174 or 8%)
non-bearing	—	—	—	980	—	—	1,275	—	—
Carobs: total	—	—	—	3,203	—	—	1,010 (± 399 or 44%)	—	—
bearing	—	—	—	3,104 (± 1552 or 50%)	—	43,481 (± 24349 or 56%)	918	—	14,358 (± 4083 or 28%)
non-bearing	—	—	—	99	—	—	92	—	—
Oranges: total	—	—	—	950 (± 27 or 4%)	—	—	672 (± 249 or 37%)	—	—
bearing	—	—	—	665	—	11,645 (± 5007 or 43%)	480	—	5,699 (± 1825 or 32%)
non-bearing	—	—	—	285	—	—	195	—	—

a As of August-September 1948.

b Crop harvested October 1, 1947–September 30, 1948; all in terms of oil and oil equivalent; includes portion of crop harvested during early 1948.

c Includes operators of "sub-farms."

Table M 25. Estimated numbers of farm animals, in thousands, in Crete, from Directors of Agriculture (for December 31, 1948) and from the surveys of communities and farms (for August-September, 1948)

Species	Estimates Directors of Agriculture 31 Dec. '48	Estimates from Sample Surveys	
		Data from Community Presidents Aug. -Sept. '48	Data from Farmers[a] Aug.-Sept. '48
Sheep, all ages	454	522(± 115 or 22%)	206(± 43 or 21%)
Goats, all ages	280	328(± 69 or 21%)	176(± 46 or 26%)
Mules, all ages	9	12(± 1.4 or 12%)	11(± 2 or 15%)
Donkeys, all ages	45	51(± 2.6 or 5%)	48(± 4 or 9%)
Horses, all ages	4	7	4(± 1.3 or 32%)
Cows, for milk and draft	48	50(± 4.5 or 9%)	36(± 2.8 or 8%)
Swine, all ages	44	60(± 17 or 29%)	27(± 3.4 or 12%)
Poultry, all kinds, all ages	664	603(± 60 or 10%)	534(± 40 or 8%)
Rabbits, all ages	115	149(± 21 or 14%)	71(± 8.6 or 12%)

a Includes operators of "sub-farms."

of households—Form A) who was born during 1946, 1947 or 1948 was to be obtained (Form A-1) so that an examination could be made of the birth registers for the community in which he was alleged to be born. The results of this investigation are not available.

e. *Health and disease.* A comparison can be made between the two methods of eliciting information on number of cases of a disease, namely, from the observations and memory of community officials for the inhabitants of this community or from the household for the members of his (her) family. No records of numbers of cases of diseases were kept in the communities so the community presidents' estimates are necessarily rough. Data for this comparison are presented in Table M 27. It can be seen that in some cases large differences are apparent. At the present time, however, no worthwhile conclusions can be drawn and the data are presented so that comparisons of the two sources of information may be made.

f. *Food consumption.* A comparison of several different estimates of essentially the same quantity can be made from the survey of farms (for production of food products), the survey of households (for the householders' estimate of consumption of food) and the survey of households on sub-sample basis (for the 7-day records of food consumption). Data from these surveys are presented in Table M 28 for several selected food items.

If the consumption data from the two sources are examined it will be seen that the seven-day record indicated lower consumption of cereal grains, pulses, wine, raisins, and milk. It will be recalled that the sample week was

TABLE M 26. Numbers and crude rates of several vital characteristics of
the Cretan population, 1938 and 1946-48

| Characteristic | Non-survey sources[a] 1938 | Estimates from sample survey of communities (data from official registers) | | |
		1946	1947	1948[c]
Inhabitants, total,				
June 30:	—	463,432[b]	467,756[b]	472,800
				(± 9,000 or 1.9%
Marriages: number	—	3,336	3,246	2,380
		(± 200 or 6%)	(± 162 or 5%)	(± 231 or 10%)
crude rate (per				
1000 inhabitants)	6.8	7.2	6.9	5.0
Divorces: number	—	25	73	32
crude rate (per		(± 11 or 45%)	(± 32 or 44%)	(± 27 or 84%)
1000 marriages)	—	7.5	2.2	1.3
Births, live: number	—	12,225	12,037	10,175
crude rate (per				
1000 inhabitants)	24.1	26.4	25.7	21.6
Deaths, total: number	—	4,596	3,626	4,119
crude rate (per				
1000 inhabitants)	11.9	9.9	7.8	8.7
Excess of births over				
deaths: number	—	7,659	8,411	6,056
crude rate (per				
1000 inhabitants)	12.2	16.5	18.0	12.8
Deaths, infants: number	—	515	478	731
crude rate (per				
1000 live births)	91.1	42.0	39.7	71.8

[a] Ministry of National Economy, *Population de la Grèce, 1938.* Athens, 1939.
[b] Interpolations from Greek census of population (1940) and sample survey of households, 1948.
[c] Based on data from Jan.-Aug. only.

generally in October and, therefore, it is reasonable to expect consumption
of these items to be below the annual average in that season. On the other
hand consumption of fresh table grapes was high (58 okes compared with
22) for the seven-day record which was taken while grapes were being
harvested.

The production figures are based on the farm and sub-farm data and it
was concluded in the section on farms and agriculture that they appeared in
general to be low. When they are adjusted, col. 7 for exports, and imports
and non-food uses (which can be done only roughly), they should agree with
the food consumption figures of cols. 4 and 5, but it can be seen that they are

Table M 27. Estimated cases of specified diseases per 100,000 inhabitants per year, Crete, based on the two sources (i) sample survey of community officials and (ii) sample survey of householders

(Note differences in periods covered)

	Sample Survey of		
	Community officials		Householders
Diseases	For the period 1947	For the period Jan.-Sept. 1948	For the period 1946, 1947 and Jan.-Sept. 1948
Dysentery	2426	3956($\pm$ 1413 or 36%)	976($\pm$ 157 or 16%)
Kala-azar	20	29($\pm$ 17 or 59%)	12($\pm$ 12 or 100%)
Malaria	2713	2464($\pm$ 646 or 26%)	5312($\pm$ 989 or 19%)
Measles	2292	483($\pm$ 425 or 88%)	1470($\pm$ 185 or 13%)
Trachoma	961	1393($\pm$ 535 or 38%)	96($\pm$ 40 or 42%)
Tuberculosis	440	301($\pm$ 66 or 22%)	84($\pm$ 53 or 63%)
Typhoid	1407	317($\pm$ 115 or 36%)	445($\pm$ 91 or 20%)
Whooping cough	3938	3211($\pm$ 1028 or 32%)	1385($\pm$ 289 or 21%)

low in every case for the householders' estimates of consumption and in every case for the seven-day record except for olive oil and fluid milk. This is further evidence that the production figures may be low.

g. *The sampling design.* In general the sampling designs used for the surveys of Crete were satisfactory. The amount of time required to complete the household and farm inquiries for a sample community turned out to be quite close to that estimated; therefore, the setting of the number of households to be taken from each sample community at 15 was a good guess so far as time requirements were concerned. There is still a question on the allocation of time between the visiting of communities on one hand and interviewing households on the other. For example, could we have visited, say, 60 communities (rather than 40) and interviewed, say, 8 households in each (rather than 15) for the same cost in time and other resources? And would we have increased or decreased our sampling errors thereby? This is a matter which can be investigated by further examination of our data.

An examination of the estimated variances for each municipality for number of households reveals that a substantial portion of the sampling error for estimated total households in the urban zone is attributable to the city of Iraklion. In this city, lists of water users by streets were used for the first stage of sampling households within the included portion of the city. Later, in the course of the survey, these were found to include a number of non-household users and there were, therefore, considerably fewer households on a number of the sample streets than expected and a consequent large variance in the sample estimate. It appears that if we were to sample this city again

TABLE M 28. Estimates of per capita and total consumption, total production, and net available for consumption, selected farm food products from the sample surveys of Crete, 1948

Farm Product	Consumption per year per person (okes)		Consumption per year total (thousand okes)		Production 1947[f] (thousand okes)	Available for Consumption as food[g] (thousand okes)
	Source A[d]	Source IA[e]	Source A[d]	Source IA[e]		
Wheat and barley grain	129.54[a]	99.11[a]	61,247[a]	46,859[a]	17,259[p]	52,066[h]
Potatoes	49.06	46.07	23,196	21,782	14,391	12,952[i]
Pulses	18.20	12.79	8,605	6,047	2,510	2,008[j]
Olives, total	36.27[b]	23.72[b]	17,148[b]	11,215[b]	21,691	14,018[k]
Grapes, total	75.49[c]	69.69[c]	35,691[c]	32,949[c]	66,368	12,924[l]
consumed fresh	(21.68)	(57.51)	(10,250)	(27,191)	(12,160)	(8,101)
consumed as wine	(36.56)	(7.69)	(17,286)	(3,636)	(22,330)	(16,009)
consumed as raisins	(2.84)	(0.90)	(1,343)	(426)	(8,959)	(-5,560)
Milk (goat, sheep and cow)						
consumed as fluid milk	15.90[m]	6.63[m]	7,518[m]	3,135[m]	4,626	4,626
consumed as cheese	2.65[n]	2.48[n]	1,253[n]	1,173[n]	606	606

a The raw barley and wheat content of raw grain (1.0), bread (1.0), rolls (1.0), rusks (1.0), hondros (.7), and macaroni (1.0). Figures in parentheses indicate factors used for conversion of food units into grain units.

b The oil content of table olives (.2), olive oil (1.0) and margarine (1.0).

c The raw grape content of fresh grapes (1.0), wine (1.25) and raisins (2.857). Figures in parentheses indicate factors used for conversion of food units into units of fresh grapes.

d Source: Form A, household.

e Source: Form IA, seven-day diet record.

f Source: Forms A and B, household and farm.

g Production plus net imports (or minus net exports) less amount used as non-food (no allowances for inventory changes).

h Production of wheat, barley and maslin in 1947 minus 20% deduction held for seed, plus imports.

i Production of potatoes in 1947 minus 10% deduction held for seed. It is believed that potatoes are imported but data were not available.

j Production of pulses in 1947 minus 20% deduction held for seed.

k Production of olive oil equivalent in 1947-1948 less exports April 1947-March 1948.

l Production in 1947 less fresh grape equivalent of exports of fresh grapes, wine, and raisins. Exports based on April 1947-March 1948 for raisins and wine; for grapes, the annual average of exports of grapes from the port of Iraklion 1936-40.

m Includes milk for drinking and cooking.

n Includes "hard" and "soft" cheese.

p Including maslin.

we would either attempt to eliminate the effect of these non-households on the list by some means or the use of block cruising as was done in Khania and Rethimnon. This would result in an estimated 28 per cent reduction in sampling variance for the estimate of number of households in this zone. The estimate for total inhabitants in the urban zone would also have its variance reduced by about the same amount.

The sampling errors for many of the agricultural items appear to be quite large, many of them exceeding 20 per cent. These could be reduced by increasing the size of the sample, by adoption of better schemes of estimation, or by better design. As indicated in the section on farms and agriculture, it was felt that large farms existed and that none of these happened to come into the sample and, therefore, an underestimation of land in farms resulted. This is an undesirable feature of the sampling design used. In the future it is suggested that a special effort be made to obtain a complete list of these large farms and obtain interviews from all or from some fraction larger than 1/150.

No change in the sampling of communities is suggested, although it should be mentioned that this matter has not been really studied. It might be advisable to consider the drawing of the communities with replacement from the full stratum rather than individually from the half-strata in order to get a simpler means to estimate the sampling error. Perhaps other methods could be devised to accomplish this.

h. *The questionnaires.* Perhaps of all the aspects of the surveys of Crete the one which seemed to appear most frequently as a source of difficulty was the questionnaire. It is here that the essential units dealt with (such as households, farms, etc.) were to be made clear in the interviewing procedure so they would be properly identified. It was here that numerous concepts in the form of questions were put to respondents for answers. Even when the questionnaires were finally put in form for duplication we felt uneasy about certain parts of them and wished we had more time to consider and test. A number of specific flaws have been noted and are listed below.

In this section we will examine the questionnaires to see if they were phrased and formulated so as to achieve the results intended. Some of the criticisms to be given will be of elements important in their effect on the survey results, but in the usual case the suggested changes and additions would result in rather minor improvements. A large number of the comments have to do with additional information which would have been valuable in the survey but have nothing to do with the validity of the questions actually used. Others concern changes in the form of the questions which would have facilitated the processing of the data by machine methods. It should be noted that many of the faults described here were discerned prior to the interviewers' school and corrected at that stage both by verbal instruction and by inclusion in the manual for interviewers. Each questionnaire used as a source of data for this report (Forms A, B, C, Ia, and J) will be discussed. It will be necessary for the reader to refer to the appropriate questionnaire for the wording of questions not quoted here in full.

FORM A, HOUSEHOLD

The questions in this form applied to characteristics of the household and its members, and dwelling units. The information was taken from the head of the household usually. If not, it was taken from an adult member capable of supplying the information desired.

Question A-1 (Table). Certain characteristics of members of the households were to be recorded in this part of the form. One of these was age. To determine age the *year* in which such persons were born was asked, but both *month* and *year* of birth should have been asked. Because of this omission we were unable to tell the ages of persons within a year as was desired. The period of the survey field work was mid-August to mid-September 1948. Thus, a person recorded as having been born in 1947 might or might not have had his first anniversary in the period in which the survey was made, depending on the month in 1947 in which he had been born.

Since it is believed babies tend to be overlooked when respondents are reporting on household membership, we should have probed to make sure that all infants were reported.

Question B-1. This question was phrased "Is yours the only household living in this building? Yes __ No __ . (If no) How many different households live in this building? No. __ ." The first part is a leading question. In the second part the persons concerned could interpret the question either to include or exclude the respondent household.

Question B-5. This question was phrased "Of what material is the roof made?" Clay __ Tiles __ Reeds __ Other (specify) _____ . The persons concerned interpreted this question variously to mean the material of the framework, the framework and the exterior material, and the exterior material of the roof. Only the latter was desired.

Question C-1 (Table). In this table the information desired was number of units of food consumed by the households in stated periods of time. Major categories of foods were listed in the first column of the table. Several categories were omitted which should have been included in the list, principally fish, sugars and sweets and rolls and buns. This kind of questioning on food consumption may also be subject to memory bias and inaccurate knowledge on the part of the respondent. It was largely experimental and was not used in the report. The more detailed sub-sample on nutrition forms the basis of the discussion on food consumption used in this book.

Question D-4. "What is your main method of cooking meat and fish? Bake __ Boil __ Fry __ Stew __ Broil __ ." Inasmuch as the main method is likely to be different for meat and fish, two questions should have been used, one for meat and the other for fish. Actually, the interviewers were instructed to distinguish methods for the two.

Question D-6. (If water not available at a tap) "Where do you store water?" Some respondents interpreted this as the place in the house and others as the type of container used to store water.

Question F-1. "About how much money does your family earn or receive each month for the use of the family?" Drs. per month _____ . Drs. per year _____ ." Since we wanted annual income the question should have been phrased with reference to a year rather than a month. However, the interviewers were instructed to obtain the information for the 12 months previous to the survey regardless of the wording of the question. The word "family" should not have been used but, rather, "household."

Question I-1. "Is household head a farmer?" This question was very important because it determined whether a farm questionnaire (Form B) was taken. There were three main faults with it. (a) A "farmer" may have been resident in the household but not the head. (b) A reference to agricultural units carrying on the production of livestock (ranches) should have been a part of the question. (c) A person who operated a farm could have had another occupation he considered primary and hence have answered the question "no." The meaning of this question was broadened by instructions in the interviewers manual and in the sessions with the interviewers.

Question I-2. "Do you grow any crops?" The reference to "you" meant the household collectively and the question should have been phrased to convey this meaning. The same criticism applies to the two questions following (I-3 and I-4) concerning farm animals and size of the place in terms of stremma.

Questions I-4 (Table), I-5, and I-6. These questions appear also in Form B, Farm, and will be discussed later.

Question J (Table). Several personal characteristics of members of the household were to be entered in this table. Deformities was one of these. Instructions were given the interviewer to make his record on deformities from observation only; hence the answers given would be only for those apparent without questioning.

The health history part of the table had a mechanical fault which caused some trouble. Each person may have had immunizations for a number of different diseases and space was provided for only one disease. With respect to the translations of typhus and typhoid it was apparent that the translators did not properly distinguish between the very similar Greek words. Hence, we had to classify immunizations for these two diseases together.

Question K-1 (Table). In this table we wanted to obtain the age at death and cause of death of the father, mother, and brothers and sisters (if "now" dead) of the head of the household. We wanted the same information for the family of the wife of the head and also for the family being interviewed. With households in which there were two generations, or in other households in which the usual father-mother-children relationship did not prevail, the interviewers tended to become confused as to whose father or mother was appropriate for entry in the table. Also, we failed to ask the year of death so we could not place the occurrence in time. It was recognized that age at death and causes of death would necessarily be approximations, subject to memory bias and lack of knowledge on the part of the informant. This question was not summarized.

Question K-2. "How many children were born in all to the husband's parents? ____ persons; to the wife's parents? ____ persons; in your family? ____ persons?" This question was subject to misinterpretation as to which "family" was relevant in the cases of non-regular households (see K-1 above). This question was not summarized.

Question K-3. "(To the mother) Have you ever had a baby born dead?" In many households there is more than one mother. In this case the usual thing was to enter the information for the wife of the head. Even so, the answers here could not be clearly associated with a particular woman since the question did not require this association to be made. Also, many of the women in the proper age and marital classes may have had children who were "now" all dead. Since the question is addressed "to the mother" the interviewer may not have asked the question.

Question M-1. By observation the interviewer was supposed to count the number of beds, chairs, mirrors, and window drapes. This question was frequently not answered because the interviewer could not arrange to see the entire house so chose not to complete it for the part of house he did see. Note: A complete inventory of household goods and furnishings was taken on a sub-sample of the households on Form J. (See Appendix 5, Tables A36 to A40.)

FORM B, FARM

The questions in this form applied to the characteristics of the farm—its size, tenure, crop acreages and productions, income, problems of the operator, etc. Form B was taken when the answer to I-1, Form A, indicated that the "household" operated a farm. In almost all cases the information was given to the enumerator by the operator himself.

Question A-1a. "How many stremma do you operate in all your farm activities?" By "operate" we meant "have charge of." Land reported should have included that which was operated by the labor of the operator and of his household, and labor which he may have hired, either for cash or a part of the product. The word "operate" should thus convey the meaning managerial control of land, both owned and rented. Land of all types in the farm—grazing, cultivated, forest, etc.—was intended to be included.

In evaluating Question A-1a we must take account of the possible differences in Cretan ways of looking at land operatorship and ours. It is not apparent that the meaning of "managerial control" was attached to the term "operate" by the respondents. Thus, land which the respondent actually farmed but did not own may not have been reported by him in answer to Question A-1a. On the other hand, some farmers may have included land which they rented to others.

Landowners may pass the control of their land to a shepherd who grazes the flocks of all on the pooled grazing area. The landowners may not, thereafter, consider this a part of the land they operate in their own "farming activities" and hence not report it.

Another criticism of Question A-1a is that no mention of "ranches" is made, making it doubtful that so-called ranch land would be reported.

Question A-6. "Do you operate this farm alone or in partnership with others? If not alone, explain." In answer to the request for an explanation, the respondent might comment that the "partner" cultivated a certain number of stremma for half the product. The respondent may have been referring to a rental arrangement or to a method of paying laborers rather than to a partnership agreement as intended. Since few farm partnerships exist in Crete it is believed that the term was not correctly understood.

Question A-7. "At about what price would your farm sell for now if it were put up for sale?" This question should have referred to a specified number of stremma and should have stated whether the buildings—house, sheds, etc.—were to be included. However, since houses are in villages and not on the "farm" there is little chance that their value would be included in the farm figure.

Question B-1 (Table). In this table there was recorded the number of stremma, and production and amount sold of grain, vegetable, feed, seed, vine and tree crops. Number of trees and vines were also to be recorded when applicable. A line was provided in the table for each crop.

Several improvements could have been made to supply more and better information. The number of stremma of fallow land was not asked for, nor was any attempt made to learn about interplanted and succession crops. We were unable to add acreage of individual crops to get total crop acres because there were omissions of crop land (fallow in 1947) and some duplicated crop land (for example, olive orchards interplanted with wheat in 1947). Some modification of the form should have been made to supply information about the disposition of trees of various kinds—whether they occurred in orchards or scattered singly or in small groups. It is reasonable to request stremma figures for orchards but not so for scattered trees. The unit in which products were to be reported should have been specifically included on the question. The form of the product should have been specified. For example, figs were reported as both fresh and dried and the interviewers sometimes failed to note the form in which the farmer would report. For grapes the unit of production and form of product was very important and the questionnaire should have been so constructed that the figures for grapes could be given as fresh (table grapes), as wine, and as raisins. Finally, in order to be able to check the sample estimates against local Cretan estimates, it might have been desirable to obtain production figures for the same time periods used locally.

Question D-1 (Table). "Do you make or prepare at home either for home use or for sale the following? Fresh olives for home use? Yes ____ No ____ . For market? Yes ____ No ____ ." Several other items such as raisins and wine were listed for similar treatment. The quantity produced, home-used and sold should also have been asked for. The words "for market" should not have been used in the question, but rather "for sale."

Question E-1. "Considering everything that you brought to market during the year 1947, about how many drachma did it all sell for?" Total annual sales were wanted and not just the sales to organized markets. Again the word "market" should not have been used. As a memory jog the main categories of products should have been listed and repeated to the respondent one by one.

Question E-3. "Do you market your products at the same village or town?

Yes __ Where __ No __ Explain _____ ." It would have been better to provide specific places for entries by categories, such as for grain, livestock, and wine. Many of the farmers used different markets for different products and no place was provided in the form to make the entries required in such cases. Also, the question was sometimes interpreted to mean "your village or town." This, of course, was not the interpretation intended.

Question E-5. "How long does it take to reach the market? ____ minutes." Spaces should have been provided for more than one market since many farmers used several. Names of markets and distances to them would have been valuable additional information.

Question F-3. "How many man-days did non-family laborers work on your farm?" This question should have specified "in a year."

Question F-7. "What are the prevailing wages for a farm laborer?" This question should have specified "per day."

Question H-1 (Table). In this question the respondent was asked whether he had heard of or seen some rather common varieties of wheat, barley, oranges, etc. Also, if he had heard about a variety, he was asked whether he had planted any and where he had heard about it and from whom. For the latter, specific categories of sources of information should have been made and included on the questionnaire. The answers were difficult to put into a consistent classification. This problem could have been avoided had the classification been specified in advance.

Question H-4. "Do you plant a wheat-barley mixture? Yes __ No __ . If yes, how do you determine the proportions of each to sow?" Many respondents interpreted the latter question to mean how do you measure the proportions. Such answers as "with tins" were given. Actually it was desired to know why they would sow the wheat and barley half and half or in some other proportion.

Question H-10. "When did you last prune your olive trees? __ years ago." This question does not provide for the contingency that a farmer may prune some trees one year, a few more the next year, etc.

Question H-12 (Table). "Do you use fertilizer on your fields? Yes __ No __ . If yes, give name of crop, kind of fertilizer and amount used per stremma." In addition, the number of stremma fertilized and the production for the last crop year should have been asked. By suitable further questioning it would have been possible to get at the differences between yields on fertilized and unfertilized land, or perhaps adequately and inadequately fertilized land.

Question L-1. This question refers to mortgages on land and chattels. One omission in the information asked for was the length of time mortgages were to run. An improvement could be made in that part of the question concerning source of credit. The phrase "source of credit" used in the form does not elicit answers easily amenable to consistent classification. Categories of sources should have been provided in order to avoid the classification problems that arose as a result of the way this part of the question was asked.

Question L-2. "(If a member of any cooperatives) Which ones?" Again, the problem of classification of replies could have been avoided by provision of a set of categories on the questionnaire.

Question L-3. "How did you obtain your land?" The question assumes that all persons who farm *own* land. Provision should have been made for an "other" category (in addition to those provided) so that all land which may have been acquired would be reported.

Question L-4. "What was your total land tax bill in 1947?" Land taxes are not important in Crete. A question should have been asked about taxes on produce—the main type of tax assessed against farmers.

FORM C, COMMUNITY

Form C, Community, was to be taken from officials in the 40 communities and 4 municipalities of the sample. Facts concerning the community as a whole were to be gathered in this manner. When planning this questionnaire it was intended to make an internal check of certain questions. This check was to be made possible by means of identical questions on this questionnaire and those for farms and households (Forms A and B). For this reason the reader will find certain questions repeated verbatim in two forms.

Question B-1 (Table). This question concerned the drinking water supply available to residents of the communities. The main fault of this table was that it failed to provide for any information on springs, wells, cisterns, etc. not directly associated with a village or town. We thus failed to get information on drinking water for the whole of the community or municipality. The question should have been broadened to cover water for purposes other than for drinking and house use.

Question D-1 (Table). This question dealt with community facilities. In general, it was satisfactory, but in answer to the question "Bus service, no. per day?" we found that there were irregular bus schedules, the number per day varying by day of the week. In connection with method of sewage disposal it was found that villages sometimes employed several methods and there was no way provided in the table to indicate which was the characteristic method used.

Question D-2 (Table). In this question an attempt was made to learn about the various types of business in the communities—the number of each type, the number of employees, the location (that is whether the place had a regular building or whether the owner set up shop or moved his cart when he wished), and finally the number of shops operating part time. Two main problems arose in the analysis. First, it was not known whether the number of employees given included the owner and unpaid members of his family and second, whether the number of shops open part time meant those open part of all work days or all day some days of the week. The interviewers interpreted these two questions variously.

Question D-7. "Where do the people of this community usually market their farm products?" This question should have provided for answers by major products. For example, oil might be marketed in one center and wine in another.

Question F-1 (Table). In this table an attempt was made to estimate the number of cases of specified diseases "now," the number in 1947, and the number in 1948. The question was to have been asked of physicians, or mid-wives. But, many of the communities in the sample did not have physicians, and midwives proved to be uninformed on general diseases, so the information was obtained from local officials in many cases. From examination of the responses to this question, it was evident that mere guesses were made for most of the diseases. The respondent did not know the number occurring in his community. No records were kept of such occurrences.

Question F-5. "Have you noticed a marked decrease since DDT was intro-duced in: house flies? Yes __ No __ ; sandflies? Yes __ No __ ; mosquitoes? Yes __ No __ ." This is a loaded question and should have been phrased neu-trally.

Questions K-1 and K-2. "How much land in this community is owned by the community? _____ stremma." We should have asked for land owned by the state, by institutions, and by private persons as well as that of the community. Also, uses of the land should have been ascertained by type of ownership. Data concerning land operated by shepherds—its amount, own-ership, rental arrangements, etc.—could have been supplied by community officials.

Question K-3. This question is identical with question B-1, Form B, and has been commented on previously.

Question L-1 (Table). This question concerned number of head of live-stock (by types and kinds) in this community now, the number of head born in 1947 and number slaughtered each year. Livestock is mobile and can be moved easily from one community to another. This is frequently the case with sheep and goats. In order to be comparable with Question C-1, Form B, this question should have been phrased to get numbers of livestock belonging to residents of this community regardless of present location. The same applies to number born in 1947.

Question M-1 (Table). The information for this question came from the public records. It had to do with the number of deaths in the sample com-munities in 1946, 1947, and 1948 by sex, age, and cause of death. In order to be sure that all interviewers treated ages alike we should have specified how to record age. This is particularly important for infants where the question-naire should have indicated specifically to record age at death in *months.*

Question N-1. "Do any families in this community have toilets inside the house? Yes __ No __ ." The word "toilets" should be delimited to mean "flush toilets" and "chemical toilets." The wording is too broad in its present form to mean much.

FORM Ia, SEVEN-DAY FAMILY FOOD RECORD

This form is the seven-day diet record. It contained an inventory record for food on hand at the beginning and end of the seven-day period, a place to record food brought into the house during the seven-day period, a record for food eaten away from home during the period, a place to record the menus for all meals in the period and a page for favorite recipes of the housewife. No faults were observed during the analysis phase on this form.

FORM J, ADDITIONAL SCHEDULES

Form J listed items of clothing, household supplies, furniture and equipment. The clothing items were classified for men, boys, women, and girls. Also, there was a listing for infants wear and supplies. Two things were to be obtained for each item in the lists—"number on hand now" and "number acquired in 1948." As far as is known, the lists were complete, that is, no omissions of important items were noted. While the form did not appear to be at fault, it was evident from the analysis that some interviewers included items acquired in 1948 in the number on hand now while others did not.

A definite age should have been established to differentiate boys and men and girls and women. The interviewers had difficulty in classifying clothing as between men and boys and women and girls. Furthermore, it would have been desirable to associate items of clothing with particular persons in the household so that in later analysis we could classify the information in more meaningful ways than is possible under the present arrangement. For example, classification of clothing items by age groups would then have been possible.

5. Glossary of Terms and Concepts

1. *Community*—An area about the size of a survey township (may be larger or smaller, size not fixed). Head is a president. There were 546 communities in Crete in 1940. May contain one or more villages. Rural in character.

2. *Municipality* (or demos)—An area of land about the size of a township. Municipalities contain a city and, usually, several villages. Head is a mayor. There were 4 municipalities in 1940. Urban in character.

3. *Nome or nomos (plural nomes or nomoi)*—A governmental unit of the nature of a state or province. There are four in Crete. Head is the Nomarch or Governor.

4. *Household*—The unit usually thought of as the family. Broader than the family in that it includes all persons living as a group within a dwelling unit.

5. *Dwelling unit*—The place of abode of a household.

6. *Farm*—A unit carrying on agricultural activity sufficient in scale to be thought of by its operator as a farm and so stated to the interviewer.

7. *Sub-farm*—A unit carrying on agricultural activity but not sufficient in scale to be thought of by its operator as a farm. Information gathered from sub-farms was limited to stremma and production of grapes and field crops; number of trees and production of fruits and nuts; kind and number of animals; and production and use of animal products.

8. *Farm operator*—A person who directs the work and management of a farm, in most cases performing all or a part of the labor himself. An operator

may own all the land he farms, own part and rent part or rent all the land he farms. A farm laborer is not an operator.

6. Letter of Invitation from the Greek Government

(Translation)

PRIME MINISTER

Ref. No. 13   Athens, February 10, 1948

To: THE ROCKEFELLER FOUNDATION

GENTLEMEN:

The Greek Government is vitally interested in the general problem of rehabilitation of conditions due to War Damage, as well as the future economic development and improvement of social and health conditions in Crete.

The island of Crete offers itself as an ideal place for a model demonstration to serve as an example for Greece.

To implement a preliminary survey will require the active coordination and participation of a number of Ministries, i.e., the Ministry of Health, Finance, Reconstruction, Tourism, Public Works, Agriculture, Social Welfare and such others as might be involved.

In view of the broad interests of The Rockefeller Foundation, the Greek Government is turning to that organization with the hope that they might be willing to take the initiative in conducting a survey, the result of which would be to advance recommendations for a rehabilitation program and plan for future economic, health and social development.

As their contribution to such survey the Greek Government would obligate itself, within the bounds of the economic possibilities of the country, to provide facilities, materials and trained and untrained personnel from their respective organization, representing in monetary value an amount equal to any amount provided by The Rockefeller Foundation. It will be further agreed that all material and equipment brought into Greece for official use in connection with the program will be admitted duty free.

(Signed) TH. SOPHOULIS

SCHEDULES FOR SAMPLE
SURVEY OF CRETE

Form A, Household

The information contained herein will be kept strictly confidential. It will not be disclosed to any Governmental or other private agency.

ROCKEFELLER FOUNDATION
General Survey of Crete

Nomos _____   Interviewer _____

Eparchy _____   Date _____

Demos or Koinotis _____   Village _____

Household _____

A. COMPOSITION OF THE HOUSEHOLD

A1.   a. How many persons do you have in your family in all?   ____ No.

      b. In order to get an idea of the kind of family you have, I would like some information on each member, including others who are living with you.

Relationship to head	Year born	Sex	Living in the house now		Born in this Community		Occu-pation
			Yes	No	Yes	No	
1. Head							
2.							
.							
.							
.							

Note: Be sure to list all persons born since 1 January 1946 on Form A.A1

A2.   Are there any members of the household here because they have no home of their own due to the war and occupation?
      (If Yes, specify by noting here the members in table on previous page)

A3.   Is there another family sharing these living quarters with you? Yes ___ No ___ (If Yes) how many families? ___ No. How many persons in all? ___ No.

B. THE DWELLING UNIT

B1.   Is yours the only household living in this building? Yes ___ No ___ If No, how many different households live in this building? ___ No.

B2.   Do you own or rent this house? (Encircle which)
      Own, Rent, Requisitioned, Other, Describe _____

B3.   (By question and observation record the following kind of information on the rooms of the dwelling unit)

Room No.	Story	Use made of Room	Material of Floor	Floor Area	Height of Room	Kind of Windows	Orien- tation
1. etc.							
.							
.							

B4.   Of what material is the exterior wall of this house made? (Encircle which) Stone Brick Adobe Wood Concrete Boughs and Reeds If others (Specify) _____

B5.   Of what material is the roof made? (Encircle which)
      Clay Tiles Reeds Other (Specify) _____

B6.   Was this house damaged during the war? Yes ___ No ___
      (If Yes, classify the damage):
      Less than 50% destruction _____ 50 to 100% destruction _____
      (If damaged) What repairs have been made? (Describe briefly) ____
      _____

B7.   a. Is there running water in the house? Yes ___ No ___
         (If No), what is the source of the water? (Encircle which)
         Spring Well Cistern Other (Describe) _____
      b. Where do you go to get your water? _____
      c. How long does it take to fetch it? ____ Minutes

B8.   a. Do you heat your house in cold weather? Yes ___ No ___
      b. (If Yes) What kind of heating do you have? _____
      c. What kind of fuel? _____

B9.   What kind of lighting do you have? (Encircle which)
      Electricity Kerosene Lamp Oil Lamp Other (Specify) _____

B10. Do you have a telephone in the house? Yes ___ No ___

B11. How do you dispose of body wastes? (Encircle which)
      Inside Toilet Outside Toilet Common Toilet No Fixed Toilet
      (If toilet is inside) How is sewage disposed of? (Encircle which)
      Public sewerage net Cesspool Pit No provision

B12. a. Are you satisfied with your housing accommodation? Yes ___ No ___

    b. Why? _____

    c. (If not satisfied) What do you plan to do about it? _____

C. FOOD CONSUMPTION

C1. In order to get an idea of the diets of the people of Crete we would like to ask you some questions about the kinds and amounts of food eaten by your family in 1947. Include that home-produced as well as that purchased.

Kind of food	How much does your family consume. (Report in the time period most convenient to the respondent)							
	A year	Unit	A month	Unit	A week	Unit	A day	Unit
Bread								
Wheat and Barley								
(If not included in bread)								
Pulses								
Horse-beans								
Lentils								
Dried beans								
Peas								
Potatoes								
Wine (all kinds)								
Tsikoudia								
Olive oil								
Fresh pork, veal and mutton								
Cured and processed meat								
Rabbits								
Chickens and other poultry								
Macaroni								
Hondros								
Eggs								
Tinned milk								
Dried milk								
Fresh milk								
Yoghurt								
Cheese								
Butter								
Margarine								
Lard								
Table olives								
Raisins								
Currants								
Figs								
Chestnuts								
Almonds								

Other nuts
Onions
Others

C2.   What kind of fresh fruit, melons and other vegetables do you eat?

Kind of fruit or vegetable	During what period do you use it? Beginning of season End of season	Amount used per week during this period
Tomatoes		
Water melons		
Table grapes		
Oranges		
Others		

D. FOOD PRACTICES

D1.   Do you have an oven? Yes __ No__

D2.   On what do you cook your meals? _____
      Is it located outside? _____ Inside? _____

D3.   How many times a day do you cook? In summer? _____ In winter? _____

D4.   What is your main method of cooking meat and fish? (Encircle answer)
      Bake   Boil   Fry   Stew   Broil

D5.   a. Do you use fresh milk? Yes __ No __
         If yes, where do you get it? (Encircle answer)
         From own animals   Purchase from a vendor, or in market?
      b. Who in the family uses it?_____
      c. Do you boil it before serving? Yes __ No __
      d. Do you like tinned milk? Yes __ No __
      e. Do you like dried milk? Yes __ No __
         If yes, how do you use it? _____

D6.   (If water is not available at a tap) Where do you store water? _____

D7.   What food items do you store and for how long a period? _____

Item Stored	Length of time usually in storage	Months
Olive oil		
Wine		
Meat		
Wheat		
Cheese		
Vegetables		

D8.   a. Do you can or bottle as a way of preserving food? Yes __ No __
      b. Do you preserve meats by placing them in salt brine or animal fat?
         Yes __ No __
      c. Do you make hondros? Yes __ No __
      d. Do you dry fruits? Yes __ No __ If yes, what fruits? _____
      e. Do you make Tsikoudia? Yes __ No __

f. Do you make butter? Yes __ No __

g. Do you make cheese? Yes __ No __

E. YESTERDAY'S MENU

E1. How many people were present at meals yesterday?

    a. Breakfast _____ persons   c. Dinner _____ persons

    b. Supper _____ persons   d. Extra meals __ persons

E2. What kind of food did you serve your family yesterday? What amount of each kind?

Kind of food served yesterday	Amount of each food served yesterday
Breakfast _____	_____
Mid-morning _____	_____
Dinner _____	_____
Afternoon _____	_____
Supper _____	_____

F. HOUSEHOLD INCOME

F1. a. About how much does your family earn or receive each month for the use of the family?

      Drachmas per month _____ or Drachmas per year _____

    b. Does this amount include all members of the household? Yes __ No __

    c. Does this amount include money from all sources, such as earnings, profits, gifts, pensions? Yes __ No __

    (If No is answer to either F1.b, F1.c, or both, correct F1.a above accordingly)

F2. At about how much would you value your family's production of clothing and food during the year in terms of money? About _____ Drs.

F3. About what proportion of your income is spent for food? _____ %

G. COMMUNITY FACILITIES

G1. What is the distance from this household to the: Doctor __ Km. Dentist __ Km. Nurse __ Km. Midwife __ Km. Priest __ Km.

G2. How far is it to: Elementary School __ Km. Gymnasium __ Km.

H. HOME INDUSTRY

H1. What kind of handicrafts are carried on in this house? (Encircle answers) Spinning Weaving Leather work Silver smithing Wood carving Furniture making Stone sculpturing Making of finished articles of fabric or cloth such as handbags and dolls. Specify others. _____

I. AGRICULTURAL PRODUCTION

I1.   Is household head a farmer? Yes ___ No ___
      (If answer is *Yes* proceed to section J, complete questionnaire, then use Form B)
      (If answer is *No*, ask questions I2 and I3 below)

I2.   Do you grow any crops? Yes ___ No ___

I3.   Do you keep or raise any farm animals? Yes ___ No ___
      (If answer is *Yes* to either or both I2 or I3 continue with I4, next page)

I4.   (If yes, to I2 above) How much land do you have? Stremma or M2 ___
      (List the crops grown and the number of stremma or trees involved in each)

Crop	Stremma	No. of trees	Production in 1947 (Specify Unit)	Amount sold in 1947
.				
.				
. etc.				

I5.   (If *yes*, to I3 above) What kind of animals do you have? List below

Species	No. of heads or hives	No. of animals born in 1947	No. sold in 1947	No. used at home in 1947
.				
.				
. etc.				

I6.   (If *yes* to I3 above) What was your total production and disposition of the following items in 1947?

Product	Production in 1947 (Specify Unit)	Amount sold in 1947	Amount home used in 1947 (Specify Unit)
Milk (from what animals)			
Milk used fresh			
Cheese			
Butter			
Wool			
Hides			
Honey			
Raw silk			
Other			

J. INDIVIDUAL PERSON SCHEDULE

H.H. Line No.	Physical Measurements Height (cms.)	Weight (kilos)	Deformities Describe	Education Highest Grade Reached	Read and Write?
.					
.					
. etc.					

(continued)

Employment			Health History		
Employed? Yes or No	(If Yes) Occupation and Industry. List All	(If No) Seeking Work? If Not, Why Not?	Ever Immunized? For What?	At What Age?	Ever Had Malaria?
.					
.					
. etc.					

K. MORTALITY

K1. We wish to obtain by our next set of questions specific information on the cause of death of members of your family now deceased.
(If parent is still alive, write 'alive' in 'age at death' column) below.

Member (State whether Brother or Sister)	Age at Death	Cause	Remarks
Father's father			
Father's mother			
Deceased Sisters and Brothers of the Father			
Mother's father			
Mother's mother			
Deceased Sisters and Brothers of the Mother			
Father of the family			
Mother of the family			
Deceased Sons and Daughters of the Family			

K2. a. How many children, in all, were born to the husband's parents? __ persons.
b. To the wife's parents? __ persons. c. In your family? __ persons.

K3. (To the mother) Have you ever had a baby born dead? Yes __ No __
(If Yes) How many times has this happened? __ Times

L. MORBIDITY

L1.   a. Is any one ill* in the household at the present time? Yes __ No __
         If Yes, give the following information:

Number of Individuals (Form A1.)	Cause of illness	Date of Onset
.		
.		
. etc.		

    * (Illness is defined as any marked condition resulting in a person not being able to carry on his usual activity for 24 hours or longer.)

         b. During 1946, 1947 or 1948 has anyone in the household been ill?
         Yes __ No __
         If Yes, give the following information:

Disease	Who was affected	Date of Onset	Duration	Where located
Typhoid Fever				
Dysentery				
Tuberculosis				
Malaria				
Trachoma				
Whooping Cough				
Measles				
Diphtheria				
Tetanus				
Other (Specify)				

L2.   a. In your opinion, what is the cause of dysentery in children? _____
         b. What would you do for a child with this trouble? _____
L3.   Were there any cases of malaria within the last 12 months in your household? Yes __ No __ If yes, how many? __
L4.   Do you wash dishes with both hot water and soap? Yes __ No __ If No, how? __

M. MISCELLANEOUS OBSERVATIONS

(Do not ask these questions of the respondent. Obtain the required information by observation only)

M1.   Furniture: Beds __ No. Wall pictures or wall hangings __ No.
                 Chairs __ No. Windows draped __ No. Mirrors __ No.
M2.   Inside the house whitewashed or painted recently? Yes __ No __
M3.   Do the methods of disposing body wastes appear to be sanitary or insanitary? Yes __ No __ Why?
         (If more than one method specify sanitary condition for each separately.)

M4. Does source of water appear to be protected against contamination? Yes ___ No ___

M5. Does family have a yard? Yes ___ No ___ What does it appear to be used for?

M6. (If there are any animals) Where are they sheltered? (Encircle answer)

Separate shelter,   In room(s) connected with house,   Under the main room,   Co-sheltered with the family,   No shelter.

N. INTERVIEWER'S REMARKS

Write here any observations on this household, which in your opinion will be of interest to those analyzing these data.

Form A, A1, Birth Check

Confidential

ROCKEFELLER FOUNDATION
General Survey of Crete

Date _____ Interviewer _____

Note: This form is to be used to record certain information useful for checking the accuracy at birth catalogs. During the Household Interview, Section A page 1 of the questionnaire, members of the household are listed and their years of birth recorded. Whenever a child, born during 1946, 1947 or 1948, is mentioned by the respondent, obtain the information called for below. Those who are now dead are obtained from Section J of that questionnaire. One of these forms can be used for each community.

COMMUNITY   NOMOS

Designation of child			Name of Father (Obtain indirectly if advisable)			
House-hold No.	From Section A or J Form A	Date of Birth Mo. Year	Sex	Surname	Middle	First	Birth Recorded Yes—No

. etc.

.

.

Form B, Farm

Confidential

ROCKEFELLER FOUNDATION
General Survey of Crete

Nomos _____   Interviewer _____
Eparchy _____   Date _____
Demos or Koinotis _____
Village _____
Household No. _____

A. LAND RESOURCES

Stremma

A1. a. How many stremma do you operate in all your farm
        activities?   _____
     b. How many stremma do you have?
        (1) Under cultivation.   _____
        (2) Use mainly for forest.   _____
        (3) Use mainly for grazing.   _____
        (4) Not used for farming, i.e. barren, waste, etc.   _____
        (5) Any other (describe)   _____
                Sum of (1) to (5)   _____
(If the sum does not agree with the figure given in "A1.a" find
the reason why and correct accordingly).

A2. a. How many stremma do you irrigate?   _____
     b. Of these __ stremma how many get all the water the
        crops need?   _____
     c. How many stremma get less than is needed?   _____

A3. In how many separate lots is your land? No. of lots.   No. _____

A4. About how much time does it take to walk to:
        (a) the farthest lot   _____ minutes
        (b) the nearest lot   _____ minutes

A5. Do you own all the land in this farm or do you rent part or all of it
     from others?

Own   _____ stremma   Manage   _____ stremma
Rent   _____   "   Other, explain   _____   "
Cash   _____   "   Livestock-share _____   "
Crop-share   _____   "

A6. Do you operate this farm alone or in partnership with others? If not
     alone explain.

A7. At about what price would your farm sell for now if it were put up
     for sale? _____ drachmas.

B. FARM CROPS

B1. What was the area harvested and production of each of the following
crops during the calendar year 1947 and the average or normal production on your farm?

Crop	Number stremma	Av. production (specify unit)	'47 Production (specify unit)	Amt. sold '47 (specify unit)
Wheat				
Barley				
Oats				
Rye				
Maslin				
Corn				
Sorghum				
Millet				
Sesame				
Peanuts				
Alfalfa				
Vetch				
Bitter vetch				
Other feed crops				
Pulses				
Potatoes				
Tomatoes				
Other vegetables[a]				
Grapes-Table				
(vines) - Wine				
- Raisin				
Olive trees[b]				
Oranges[b]				
Tangerines[b]				
Lemons[b]				
Citrons[b]				
Figs				
Apricots				
Peaches				
Cherries				
Plums and Prunes				
Pears				
Apples				
Quinces				
Bananas				
Almonds				
Walnuts				
Pistachios[b]				
Carobs				

Acorns
Mulberries
Chestnuts
Other tree crops

a *In Other Vegetables* are included: onions, garlic, melons, fresh beans, broad beans, okra, spinach, egg-plant, etc.
b Production is for crop year 1947-48.

C. FARM ANIMALS

C1. How many farm animals do you have *now*, and how many were produced, sold, and slaughtered for home use in *1947*.

Species	Number head you have now		No. head born during 1947	No. head sold in 1947	No. slaughtered for home use in 1947
	Over 1 year	Under 1 year			
Sheep and Lambs					
Domestic					
Nomadic					
Goats and Kids					
Domestic					
Nomadic					
Mules, all ages					
Donkeys, all ages					
Horses and Mares					
Colts					
Cows for: Milk only					
Work only					
Milk and Work					
Oxen					
Calves					
Swine, all ages					
Poultry (all kinds)					
Rabbits					
Bees (No. Hives)					
Cocoons (No. okes)					

D. BIO-INDUSTRY

D1. Do you make or prepare at home either for home use or for sale the following?

Product	For Home Use		For Market	
	Yes	No	Yes	No
Table olives				
Raisins				
Wine				
Spirits				
Dried fruits				
Tomato paste				
Leather				
Meat products				

E. MARKETING

E1. Considering everything that you brought to market during the year 1947, about how many drachmas did it all sell for? _____ drachmas.

E2. About how often do you take farm products to market? ____ times per year.

E3. Do you market your products at the same village or town? Yes __ No __ Where_____ Explain _____

E4. What kind(s) of transport do you use? (circle answer), pack animal, animal drawn vehicle, motor truck, boat, other, specify.

E5. How long does it take to reach the market? __ hours.

F. HUMAN RESOURCES

F1. About how many days during the year do you work on this farm? Self? ____ days. Your family? ____ days.

F2. About how many of those are full work days? For yourself? ____ days.
For your family? ____ days.

F3. How many man days (1 laborer working one day is man day) did non-family laborers work on your farm? ____ man days.

F4. About how much time on the average is used each work day in getting to and from the fields? ____ hours.

F5. What is regarded here as a full work day?
a. Total time from start to finish for the day. ____ hours.
b. Siesta, meals, etc. ____ hours.

F6. How many workers (family and non-family laborers) are required on this farm during the busiest season? ____ persons.

F7. What are the prevailing wages for a farm laborer? Male __ Drs.
Female __ Drs.

G. CAPITAL EQUIPMENT

G1. Let us say that you decide to sell your tools, machinery, and other farm equipment used on this farm. About how much would it sell for today? ____ Drs.

G2. How many of the following do you have now?

Items	Number	Items	Number
Plows, wood		Pumps, animal drawn	
Plows, steel		Pumps, engine drawn	
Harrows, wood		Pumps, wind drawn	
Harrows, steel		Carts and wagons	
		Saddles	

H. MANAGEMENT

H1. Which of these varieties and species of field and tree crops have you ever:

	Heard of or Seen?		From whom and where?		Planted any?	
	Yes	No	Yes	No	Yes	No
(a) A variety of Wheat called "Eretria"						
(b) A variety of Barley called "Athenais"						
(c) A variety of Oats called "Athenais"						
(d) A variety of Orange called "Valencia"						
(e) A variety of Orange called "Jaffa"						
(f) A variety of Olives called "Calamon"						
(g) "Pistachio nuts"						
(h) "Peanuts"						

H2. a. Have you ever heard about Bordeaux mixture spray for downy mildew? Yes ___ No ___
b. If yes, from what source did you learn it?
c. Do you use it? Yes ___ No ___

H3. a. Is soil erosion a problem on your farm? Yes ___ No ___
b. If yes, what do you do to prevent soil erosion?

H4. a. Do you plant a wheat-barley mixture? Yes ___ No ___
b. If yes, what are proportions of each? Barley ___ Wheat ___
c. How do you determine the proportions of each to sow?

H5. a. Do you rotate crops on any fields in your farm? Yes ___ No ___
b. What is your usual rotation on such fields?

H6. a. In deciding which crops to plant or animals to produce each year, do you take into account the probable market price at harvest or sale time? Yes ___ No ___

b. If yes, where do you get information on anticipated prices for the following year?

H7. Do you interplant olive trees and grape vines with annual crops such as cereals?

a. Olive trees? Yes ___ No ___   b. Grape vines? Yes ___ No ___

H8. Let us consider for a moment all the possible things that can be done to increase the food production and income on farms. What, in your opinion, are the two things which would help you most?

a. _____

b. _____

H9. What are your most important problems in:

a. Growing of crops in general? _____ Why? _____
b. Raising animals? _____ Why? _____
c. Marketing produce? _____ Why? _____

H10. a. When did you last prune your olive trees? _____ years ago
b. How often do you think olive trees should be pruned? Every _____ years

H11. Do you think there is usually enough, too little or too much rain, for the best yields of:

	Too little	Enough	Too much
(a) grapes?			
(b) olives?			
(c) cereals?			

H12. Do you use fertilizer on your fields? Yes ___ No ___
If yes, give name of crop, kind of fertilizer and amount used per stremma.

Kind of crop	Kind of fertilizer	Amount used per stremma in 1947

I. PHYTOPATHOLOGICAL PROBLEMS

I1. Are your crops troubled with any diseases or pests? Yes ___ No ___
With what diseases or pests?   Crop affected

(If respondent does not know the diseases or pests by name, indicate symptoms below).
Give species of crops and detailed symptoms.

I2. What is done to control pests and diseases? Give crop species and control measures.

I3.   (Fill out for either dacus fly or phyloxera, if not mentioned above).
Are you troubled with the dacus fly in olive trees? Yes __ No __
If yes, what percentage does it reduce your yield? _____ percent.
Are you troubled with phyloxera? Yes __ No __
If yes, what percentage does it cut your grape yield? ____ percent.

J. ANIMAL PATHOLOGICAL PROBLEMS

J1.   Are your farm animals troubled with any diseases or pests? Yes __
No __
If yes, list below: Disease or pest _____ Animals affected _____
(If respondent does not know the disease or pest by name, ask for symptoms and write below. Give species of animal and detailed symptoms).
J2.   Control measures (If yes to J1 above).
What is done to control the diseases or pests which attack your animals?
Give species of animal and control measures.

K. PROBLEMS WITH CERTAIN CROPS

K1.   Do you have any special problems in the growing of olive trees? Yes __
No __
If yes, what are they?
K2.   Do you have any special problems in the growing of grapes? Yes __
No __
If yes, what are they?
K3.   Do you have any special problems in the growing of cereals? Yes __
No __
If yes, what are they?

L. MISCELLANEOUS

L1.   a. Do you have a mortgage on your land? Yes __ No __
If yes, amount drs.? ____ Interest Rate?____ percent per year.
or Interest Rate?____ percent per month.
b. (If there is no land mortgage now)
Did you ever have a mortgage on your land? Yes __ No __
If yes, when was it completely paid or settled? Year ____
How many years did you pay on this mortgage? ____ Years
What was your source of credit?
c. Do you have a chattel mortgage or unsecured loan? Yes __ No __
If yes, amount drs.? ____ Interest Rate?____ percent per year.
or Interest Rate?____ percent per month.
Source of credit _____
L2.   a. Are you a member of any cooperatives? Yes __ No __
If yes, which ones?
b. Do you market any farm products through a cooperative? Yes __
No __

    c. Have you ever been an officer in any cooperative? Yes __ No __

    d. In your opinion is the cooperative of help to you in getting higher prices for your products? Yes __ No __

    e. Do you think the cooperatives could give you more assistance? Yes __ No __.

L3. How did you obtain your land?   Stremma

    a. By purchase from non-relatives?   _____

    b. By purchase from relatives?   _____

    c. By inheritance?   _____

L4. Taxes

    a. What was your total land tax bill in 1947? _____ Drs.

L5. What was your total production and disposition of the following items in 1947?

Product	Production in 1947 (Specify Unit)	Amount sold in 1947 (Specify Unit)	Amount Home Used 1947 (Specify Unit)
Milk (From all animals)			
Milk used fresh			
Cheese			
Butter			
Wool			
Hides			
Honey			
Raw-silk			
Other			

M. INTERVIEWER'S REMARKS

Enter here any remarks you may have which would be of help in interpreting results.

Form C, Community

ROCKEFELLER FOUNDATION
General Survey of Crete

Nomos _____   Interviewer _____
Eparchy _____   Date_____
Deme or Koinotis _____   Sample: Start No. __ Take every_____

PART I

(Obtain information by interview from president and his associates)

A. COMPOSITION OF COMMUNITY

A1.   a. (Check following list of villages, modify if necessary).

	Village	1940 Census Data		Estimated at present	
Code No.	Name	No. of Inhabitants	No. of Families	No. of Inhabitants	No. of Families
	Total				
. . . etc.					

      b. (Land area of Community   _____Sq. Kilometers)

      c. (If there is a large population change since 1940, ask for an explanation).

      (Show the group your map of the Community).

A2.   Are the boundaries of the Community identical with those shown on map?

A3.   (If there is more than one village in the Community):

      a. Why is this particular set of villages grouped into a community?

      b. Do you think some other grouping would be better? If Yes, Why?

A4.   a. Do any families of this Community permanently or temporarily live outside of the village clusters (that is, in the open country, on farms, with herds, etc.)?

          Yes __ No __ If Yes, how many? 1. Permanent families. __ No.
                                   2. Temporary families. __ No.

      b. (If there are some families temporarily living outside of village clusters, get an explanation of the reason for this and briefly describe).

B1.   Now some questions about the drinking water supply in each village of the Community. (In the table on next page select a village and ask questions suggested by the study rather than follow the customary procedure for tabular questions, "From what Sources do families in this village obtain their drinking water?" Put a (v) in the village column opposite the appropriate source of water. Then ask questions pertaining to the specific sources and the distribution questions in table.)

Sources of Drinking Water

Item	Number or name of village									
	1	2	3	4	5	6	7	8	9	10
Springs—Number of										
Community Wells—Total Number										
No. Capped										
No. Collared										
No. with pumps										
Community Cisterns—Total Number										
No. Capped										
No. Collared										
No. with pumps										
No. treated with										
Calcium Hyperchloride										
Individual Wells—Number of										
Individual Cisterns—Number of										
Other Sources (Describe)										

Distribution of water: (Where water is brought in from outside the village)
Aqueduct or pipe
Open (V) or Closed (O)

Water distribution
to individual homes?
Yes (V) or No (O)

If Yes, give village number and indicate how below:

C. SCHOOLS

C1. We would now like to know a few things about the schools of this Community. How many Elementary Schools does Community have? In what villages are they located? (Write in, name of village. If there are two or more schools in a village, use as many spaces as there are schools).

Item; Village Code Number	School Designated by Number and Village by Code No.									Gym
School Number	1	2	3	4	5	6	7	8	9	10
Villages served, No.										
Teachers, No.										
Pupils, No.										

Rooms, No.
Chairs, No.
Pupils' Desks, No.
Teachers' Desks, No.
Stove, Yes or No
Toilets, Yes or No
Good water at school, Yes or No
Common drinking cups, Yes or No
Playground? Yes or No
Playground Equipment? Yes or No
School Lunches served, Yes or No
School building-Reg., Yes or No
    If No, where?
How many pupils are indigent?
Have pupils enough school books?

D. COMMUNITY FACILITIES

D1.   Our next questions deal with Community facilities. We would first like to know something about communications. (List villages in the order in which they appear on page 1 by code number.)

Item	Code No. and Name of Village (From Page 1)								
	1	2	3	4	5	6	7	8	9
Post Office, Yes or No									
Any Telephone? Yes or No									
Radios? No.									
Bus Service—No. per day									
Electricity, Yes or No									
Type of best road?									
(Check which)									
Improved									
Unimproved									
Trail									
Sewage Disposal:									
(Check which)									
Sewage Net									
Open Ditch									
Septic Tank									
Absorbing Tank									
Pits									
Nothing									
Doctors, No.									
Dentists, No.									

Nurses Trained, No.
Nurses Untrained, No.
Midwives Trained, No.
Midwives Untrained, No.
Pharmacist or Druggist, No.
Veterinarians, No.
Herb Doctor, No.
Bone Setter, No.
Priests, No.

D2. In this question we want to get some information on the types of businesses that are conducted in Community.
How many are there?

Type of business	No. of each Type	Employees	Location		No. Open
		All Shops	Fixed	Itinerant	Part Time
Butcher Shop					
Coffee House					
General Store					
Grocery					
Barber Shop					
Tavern					
Restaurant					
Quarry					
Kiln					
Pottery					
Pharmacy					
Tailor Shop					
Haberdashery					
Blacksmith Shop					
Bakery					

D3. a. Are there any Cooperatives in this Community? Yes __ No __
b. If Yes, what kind are they? (1) ____ (2) ____ (3) ____ (4) ____
c. What percentage of the interested families belong to each?
(1) __ percent (2) __ percent (3) __ percent (4) __ percent.
D4. a. Is a bazaar held in this Community? Yes __ No __
b. If Yes, how often per year?
D5. a. What percentage of the people in this Community habitually read newspapers?
Men _____ percent   Women _____ percent
D6. a. Are any public library facilities available to people of this Community? Yes __ No __
b. If Yes, describe the type and amount of such service rendered.
D7. Where do the people of this community usually market their farm products?
Name of place(s).

E. SOCIAL CUSTOMS

E1. a. On what occasions do people in this Community meet with each other in groups for social reasons?
     If practice is rarely done write "rarely" in place of "Yes," otherwise write "No."

Kind of Meeting	Frequency Times per Wk. Mo. Yr.	With Relatives Only Men	Only Women	Both	With Non-relatives Only Men	Only Women	Both
Dinners in home							
Village feasts							
Birthday parties							
Coffee Shop							
Dances							
Singing							
Group games							
Others							

       b. In your opinion how much time does the average man in the Community spend in the Coffee House per week?
E2. Is it a common practice here to exchange work with neighbours, or do all the people hire extra help when they need it? Exchange _____ Hire _____
E3. a. Is it usual here for the people to be members of organized societies, either fraternal or church? Yes __ No __
     b. If Yes, what are a few of such societies?
     c. About what percentage of the men belong to one or more societies? _____ percent
E4. What is the general attitude of the father toward education of the children?

F. PUBLIC HEALTH

F1. (To be obtained from physician(s) and midwives, if any, or otherwise from other informed persons).
     a. Respondent(s)
     b. Physician's name
     (To get an idea of public health we would like to get some information on diseases in this Community.) How many cases are there of:

Disease	Number of current cases	Number of cases during 1947 1948	Remarks Comments, Epidemics, etc.
Typhoid Fever			
Tuberculosis			
Malaria			

V-D
Trachoma
Whooping Cough
Measles
Gen. Ophthalmia
Tetanus
Diphtheria
Kala-Azar
Oriental Sore
Ep. Meningitis
Dysentery
Colds and Influenza
Leprosy
Brucellosis
Scarlet Fever
Cancer
Rheumatic Fever
Others, State

F2. What has been the practice of this Community in immunization against diseases?

Disease	Has anyone ever been immunized? Yes No	Is it a general practice? Yes No	At what age?	Ever happened during epidemic or threatened epidemic Yes No
a. Small Pox				
b. Typhoid				
c. Diphtheria				
d. Whooping Cough				
e. Tetanus				
f. Tuberculosis				
g. Cholera				
h. Typhus				

F3. What is the usual diet given babies in months following weaning?
    a. Milk   Yes__ No __   If Yes, how much per day? _____
    Is it boiled or heated?   Yes __ No __
    b. Eggs? Yes __ No __ If Yes, how many per week? ____
    c. Vegetables? Yes __ No __ If Yes, what kind? ____
    d. Cereals? Yes __ No __ If Yes, what kind? ____
    e. Fruit? Yes __ No __ If Yes, what kind? ____

F4. In your opinion is this a period of particular trouble with infants? Yes __ No __

F5. Have you noticed a marked decrease since DDT was introduced in:
    a. The number of house-flies?   Yes ____ No ____
    b. The number of sand-flies?   Yes ____ No ____
    c. The number of mosquitoes?   Yes ____ No ____

G. FOOD HANDLING AND CUSTOMS

G1.   How many times a week do the butchers slaughter animals?

G2.   To what extent are religious fasts carried out by the people of this community, that is, about what percent of the people abstain from meat and eggs? _____ percent.

G3.   The families in your community may have some eating customs that prevail quite generally throughout the community. If so, what would be the customary foods eaten.

	Time of Day	General Menu	Remarks
a. For Breakfast			
b. Mid-morning			
c. For Dinner			
d. Mid-afternoon			
e. Supper			
f. After Supper			

G4.   During what seasons of the year do the families of this community consume mainly the following classes of food? (Indicate if possible, main kinds.)

Class of food	Summer	Autumn	Winter	Spring
Meat				
Fish				
Green Vegetables				
Potatoes				
Other Vegetables				

G5.   What is your community's opinion on tinned foods?
      a. canned meats?
      b. canned milk?
      c. canned fish?

H. MISCELLANEOUS FORM

H1.   a. Is there any irrigation of crops in the community? Yes ___ No ___
      b. What are the possibilities for irrigation or additional irrigation? Discuss:
      c. Is there a potential supply of water which could be developed at a reasonable cost? Discuss:
      d. Would the water supply involve construction of a dam? Discuss:
      e. Would pumps on individual farms be feasible? Discuss:

H2.   a. Is commercial fertilizer used in the community? Yes ___ No ___
      b. (If yes), what is your estimate of the average amount used per stremma per year?

	Used		Amount used per	Kind of
	Yes	No	stremma in 1947	Fertilizer
Olive trees				
Citrus fruit trees				
Nut trees				
Other fruit trees				
Grape vines				
Vegetables				
Cereals				
Feed crops				

H3. a. Is animal manure generally used for fertilizer in this community?
Yes __ No __
b. On which crops do the farmers prefer to use it?
c. Is it spread on fields throughout the year or stored? Spread _____
Stored _____
d. If stored, where and for how long?

H4. What is your estimate of the numbers of the following items of farm machinery and equipment in this community now?

Item	Number	Item	Number
Tractors		Hay Balers	
Tractor Plows		Sprayers	
Drills		Hammer Mills	
Fertilizer Spreaders		Grape Pressers	
Mowers		Olive crushers	
Binders		H M Oil pressers	
Self Binders		P M Oil pressers	
Threshers		Distillators Grade A	
Winnowing Machines		Distillators Grade B	
Maize Shellers			

H5. Give your estimate of the number of the following trees and vines per stremma.

Crop	Trees per stremma	Crop	Vines per stremma
Olives		Table grapes	
Tangerines		Wine grapes	
Lemons		Sultana grapes	
Citrons			
Oranges			

I. MISCELLANEOUS OBSERVATIONS

The answers and comments in this section are to be obtained by the observations of the interviewer alone. Do not ask your respondents for this information.

I1. Give your opinion as to whether or not the water supply in this community is sanitary. Record by village. Code reply by reference to list of villages, page 1, Form C.

Sanitary _____ Unsanitary_____ .

I2. Give your general impression of the cleanliness of the streets, shops and houses in this community, or by villages by code number.

Clean? _____ Dirty? _____

I3. What sort of facilities do the people have for taking baths?

I4. Give your general impression of the personal cleanliness of the villagers.

I5. a. Are any efforts made by the people in this community to beautify their houses, streets and squares?

b. If yes, describe.

J. INTERVIEWER'S REMARKS AND COMMENTS

J. Write here any observations on the community, which, in your opinion will be of interest to those analyzing these data.

PART II

K. FARM CROPS

From page 1, total area of this community is Sq. kil. _____

K1. How much land in this community is owned by the community? ____ Stremma

(If some, how is it used):

K2. How much land in this community is:

a. under cultivation? _____ Stremma

b. Used mainly for forest? _____ "

c. Used mainly for grazing? _____, "

d. Not used for farming _____ "
   i.e. barren, waste, etc.

e. Any other (describe) _____ "

Total land of this community
(Sum of a to e) _____

(If the sum does not agree with the total area given on the top line above, find the reasons why and correct accordingly.)

K3. What was the area harvested and production of each of the following crops during the calendar year 1947 and the average or normal production in this community?

Crop	Number Stremma	Av. Production (specify unit)	1947 Production (specify unit)
Wheat			
Barley			
Oats			
Rye			
Maslin			
Corn (Maize)			
Sorghum			
Millet			
Sesame			
Peanuts			
Alfalfa			
Vetch			
Bitter vetch			
Other feed crops			
Pulses			
Potatoes			
Tomatoes			
Other vegetables[a]			
Grapes-Table			
(vines)-Wine			
-Raisin			
Olive trees[b]			
Oranges[b]			
Tangerines[b]			
Lemons[b]			
Citrons[b]			
Figs			
Apricots			
Peaches			
Cherries			
Plums and Prunes			
Pears			
Apples			
Quinces			
Bananas			
Almonds			
Walnuts			
Pistachios			
Carobs			
Acorns			
Mulberries			

Chestnuts
Other tree crops

ª *In Other Vegetables* are included: onions, garlic, melons, fresh beans, broad beans, okra, spinach, egg-plant, etc.

ᵇ Production is for crop year 1947-48.

L. FARM ANIMALS

L1. (If records are not kept, obtain best possible estimates. If data were obtained from records, state from whom.)

Species	Number of head in this community now		No. head born during 1947	No. slaughtered each year for consumption in this community. (Both home and butcher slaughtered.)
	Over 1 yr.	Under 1 yr.		
Sheep and Lambs				
Domestic				
Nomadic				
Goats and Kids				
Domestic				
Nomadic				
Mules				
Donkeys				
Horses and Mares				
Colts				
Cows for: Milk only				
Work only				
Milk and work				
Oxen				
Calves				
Swine				
Poultry, all kinds				
Rabbits, all ages				
Bees (No. Hives)				
Cocoons (No. okes)				

M. VITAL STATISTICS

M1. (From the community's catalogue of deaths obtain the information required below. For Communities list all deaths, for municipalities, list only 1 in 10).

Order	1946			1947			1948		
No.	Sex	Age	Cause	Sex	Age	Cause	Sex	Age	Cause
.									
.									
. etc.									

M2. (From the community's catalogue of births obtain the information required below).

Total number of children born
in this community during: All of 1946   All of 1947   1948 up to now

M3. (By interrogation, preferably with the physician(s) present, obtain):

In the whole Community   All of 1946   All of 1947   1948 up to now

a. Number of babies born dead
b. Number of premature births

c. Were stillbirths included in the catalogue of: (1) births? Yes __ No __
   (2) deaths? Yes __ No __

M4. a. Number of marriages   All of 1946   All of 1947   1948 up to now
     b. Number of divorces

N. HOUSING

N1. a. Do any families in this community have toilets inside their house?
       Yes __ No __
     b. (If yes), How many families? ____ No.
N2. Out of what materials are outside walls of houses in this community
     usually made?
     Roofs? Roof covering? etc.

	Walls	Roof	Roof covering	Floors	Plastering
Building Material					

N3. a. Are there any builders living in this community? Yes __ No __
     b. (If No), When building is done, where do the builders come from?
N4. a. How many families in this village are living with other families
       because they cannot get housing accommodations of their own? (Ask
       for each village; put answers in table below).
     b. Are there any villages in this community which have more housing
       accommodations than families, that is, an excess over needs? Yes __
       No __
       (If yes, find out names of such villages and note in table below.
       Then ask):
       How many excess, or unoccupied dwelling units are there in each
       village and why?

Name of each village in community (See page one)	Estimated total No. of families living in village now. (See page one)	No. families having no dwelling unit of their own. (If none, write "0")	No. of unoccupied dwelling units. (If none, write "0")	If excess why?

.
.
. etc.

(If there are entries in both cols. (3) and (4) for the same village explain below).

Form D, Supervisory Check Lists

SUPERVISOR'S CHECK LIST

NOMOS _____ EPARCHY _____ COMMUNITY _____
INTERVIEWER _____ Date Started _____ Date Completed_____

1. How was list of households obtained? Describe.
2. Did interviewer make an effort to check name lists obtained? Yes _____
   No _____
   If yes, what did he do? _____
   If no, why didn't he? _____
3. Sampling operation performed correctly? Yes _____ No _____ If no, describe _____
4. General impression of sampling and interviewing in Community

CHECK-IN LIST

Nomos _____Community name and number _____
Eparchy _____Sampling Nos: _____
Interviewers _____Start with _____ Take every _____
Date started _____ Date completed _____TOTAL Households in
                                          Community _____

Name of Family	Household No.	Form A obtained?		Form B needed?		Form B obtained?		Reasons for not obtain- ing question- naire
		Yes	No	Yes	No	Yes	No	
.								
.								
. etc.								
Total								

1.a AA I Obtained? Yes _____ No _____
  b C I Obtained? Yes _____ No _____
  c " II Obtained? Yes _____ No _____
2. Kind of list used? Name list _____ Map list _____
3. Source, if name list _____
4. Sampling performed in accordance with instructions? Yes _____ No _____
5. Proper number secured in sample? Yes _____ No _____
6. Corrected sample: (Total families on list sampling decimal) _____
7. Original maps and lists returned by interviewers? Yes _____ No _____
8. Remarks _____

BLOCK ESTIMATES OF HOUSEHOLDS

Demos _____ or Koinotis _____

Dist. and Block No.	Estim. No. Households	Cumulated No. Households	Dist. and Block No.	Estim. No. Households	Cumulated No. Households
.					
.					
. etc.					

Form I, Seven-Day Family Record

(To be filled and kept by Interviewer)

ROCKEFELLER FOUNDATION—General Survey of Crete

Confidential

Nomos ——————————— Eparchy ———————————
Town or Village ——————— Family No. ———————————
Date Beginning Food Record ——— Date Closing Food Record ———
Name of Interviewer ———————

Family No. ———————

GENERAL INFORMATION CONCERNING FAMILY

(To be filled by Interviewer the first day of food recording)

Serial No.	Members of family, help if any included	Age	Sex	Height	Weight	Occupation Type	Hours per day	Remarks
.								
.								
. etc.								

Is there a pregnant woman in the family? Yes — No —
Is there a lactating woman in the family? Yes — No —
Is there any one sick in the family? Yes — No —
If Yes, what from?
If Yes, what kind of diet?
Is there a member of the family having meals outside the house? Yes — No —
If Yes, who? ———————
How often? ——————— What meal of day? ———————
Does he buy extra food for his outside meal? Yes — No —
If Yes, what ——————————— How much does he pay for it? ——— drs.

INFORMATION ABOUT THE FAMILY'S DIET
CUSTOMS, HABITS AND MODE OF LIVING

(To be filled in by interviewer on the day of closing the 7 day record).

1. *Milk — Cheese*

Do you boil the milk for your family? Yes — No —
If Yes, how?
If No, why?

Do you sometimes buy milk, condensed, evaporated, dry skim, encircle which
If dry skim, what uses do you make of it?

Do you buy cheese? Yes ___ No ___ If No, why? _____ If Yes, how often? _____
What kind? _____ How much each time? _____

2. *Meat — Fish — Eggs*

How often do you buy meat?

What kind of meat do you usually buy?

Do you prefer: fat meat   lean meat   encircle which.

How often do you buy Cod fish?

Do you buy other kinds of preserved fish? smoked, dry, salted, in oil,
    encircle which.
How often?

How often do you eat eggs?
Who eats them?
How do you usually cook eggs for the adults?
How do you usually cook eggs for the children?
If eggs for children cooked in a way different than for the adults, why?

3. *Pulses*

What kind of pulses is liked most in the family?
How often do you eat pulses in summer? _____ in winter? _____
Does everybody in the family eat pulses? Yes ___ No ___
If No, who does not?
What is the usual way of cooking pulses?
Do you strain them? Yes ___ No ___
If Yes, do all members of the family eat them strained?

4. *Bread and Cereals*

Do you ever have any other kind of bread than the one recorded? Yes ___
    No ___
If Yes, what kind is it?

Do you make hondros? Yes ___ No ___ If Yes, how many okes per year? _____
        _____ Okes (Get recipe for Hondros)

Do you ever get macaroni? Yes ___ No ___
If No, why?
If Yes, how do you cook it?
If boiled, what do you do with the macaroni water?

Do you ever buy rice? Yes ___ No ___
If No, why? _____ If Yes, for whom? _____
How do you cook rice?
If boiled what do you do with rice water?

5. *Vegetables and Fruits*

How often do you eat vegetables in your family?
What vegetables do you eat fresh?

What is the usual way of cooking vegetables?
If boiled, do you use soda? Yes ___ No ___
If Yes, why?
If No, how do you keep them green?
Do you salt them at beginning of boiling? end of boiling? encircle which.
What do you do with the water in which vegetables are boiled?

What are the fruits usually eaten by your family in summer? _____
     In winter? _____
How often do you eat fruits?
Do you eat them usually   fresh?   cooked?   (encircle which)
Do you peel them? Yes ___ No ___
If Yes, why? _____ If you do not peel them, why? _____

6. *Sweets*

How often does your family eat sweets?
Are they home-made or bought?
If home-made, what are the ones most commonly eaten?
Who eats most of the sweets?

7. *Alcoholic Beverages*

Do the children drink wine? Yes ___ No ___ Tsikoudia? Yes ___ No ___

8. *Beverages*

Besides milk what other hot beverages are used by your family? _____
     Who drinks them? _____

Do you drink water during meals? Yes ___ No ___

9. *Customs and Habits*

Are there special dishes used on special days? Yes ___ No ___
If Yes, what are they?

What is the family favorite dish?

Any special sweets used for special days? Yes ___ No ___
If Yes, what kind?

Do you keep fasting days in your family? Yes ___ No ___
If Yes, how many times a year?
Do you usually fast on Wednesdays and Fridays? Yes ___ No ___
Do children keep fasting days? Yes ___ No ___
If No, why?
What do you eat in your family during fasting days?

How often have you guests in your family?
How long do guests stay?
Do they bring food into the family? Yes ___ No ___ ?
If Yes, what do they usually bring?
What are the days you usually have guests?

Do you sometimes engage workers to help in the fields? Yes ___ No ___
If Yes, how often?
Do they share the family's meals? Yes ___ No ___
If Yes, what meals?

Do you think your family's diet satisfactory? Yes ___ No ___
If No, why?
What do you think you ought to add to the family's diet to make it more satisfactory?
Do you think children's diet ought to be different from the adults? Yes ___ No ___ If Yes, why?
What, according to your idea, do the children need most in order to grow in a satisfactory way?
Did any of your children go to summer school camps? Yes ___ No ___
Are the children usually well? Yes ___ No ___ If No, what do they usually suffer from?
How often? _____ What is the family's usual recreation? _____
How often? _____

Form Ia, Seven-Day Family Food Record

ROCKEFELLER FOUNDATION—General Survey of Crete

Weighing Method

Confidential

To be left with housekeeper so as to be filled in by her, with the aid of interviewer.

Nomos _____   Name of Interviewer _____
Eparchy _____   Town or Village _____
Demos or Koinotis _____   Household No. _____
Date Beginning Food Record _____   Date Closing Food Record _____

A. RECORD OF FAMILY'S FOOD SUPPLIES (2 pages)

Meal After Which Inventory Was Taken: _____
DATE BEGINNING FOOD RECORD: _____ DATE CLOSING FOOD RECORD: _____

Section I				Section II			
FOODS ON HAND AT BEGINNING OF INVENTORY				FOODS ON HAND AT CLOSING OF INVENTORY			
			Cost				Cost
Food Item	Wt.	Origin	P.Unit Total	Food Item	Wt.	Origin	P.Unit Total

.
.
.
. etc.

B. FOOD BROUGHT IN DURING NON-INVENTORY DAY

(7 pages—one for each day of week)

DATE: _____   Day of the Week _____

Food Items	Weight	Origin	Cost		Outgoing Food		Remarks
			Per Unit	Total	Kind	Wt.	
Milk, cheese							
Meat, fish, eggs							
Pulses							
Bread, Cereals, Flour, Rice							
Fats and Oils							

Fruits and Veg.
Sweets, sugar, etc.
Alc. Beverage

Note: In remarks mark always where the outgoing food went, also if a food brought in is destined to feed poultry or other animals or pets.

C. RECORD OF FOOD EATEN AWAY FROM HOME BY MEMBERS OF FAMILY No. ____

				Food Eaten		
Date	Day of Week	Fam. Member	Meal of Day	School	Other	Cost

.

.

. etc.

D. SEVEN-DAY DIETARY MENU
[Four double column pages]

Date: Date:

Week _____ Day _____   Day _____

Breakfast	Ingredients Weight Waste	Ingredients Weight Waste
Adults		
Children		
Mid-morning		
Adults		
Children		
Dinner		
Adults		
Children		
Mid-afternoon		
Adults		
Children		
Supper		
Adults		
Children		
After Supper		
Adults		
Children		

E. RECIPE for: _____

Number of Servings _____ or Pieces _____

Ingredients Used	Quantity	Cost
.		
.		
.		
. etc.		

State Mode of Preparation:

Note: If the amount of ingredients is not given by weight in dramia, report it by measure using standard measures of family. Example:—Sugar 50 dramia or Sugar 10 tablespoons. 1 oke equals 400 dramia or 1,280 grams, 1 dramia equals 3.2 grams.

GENERAL REMARKS

Form Ib, Office Summary Sheet

SEVEN-DAY DIET SURVEY

Nomos ——— Community ———   No. of Meal units served during

Eparchy ——— H.H. No. ———   week ———

Food Consumption (Enter Dramia in each column 2-9)

Food Items	Beginning Inventory	Brought in during week	Eaten Away From Home	Total Available $2+3+4$	End Inventory	Outgoing Amount	Total not Consumed $(6+7)$	Weekly Total Consumed $(5-8)$
(1)	(2)	(3)	(4)	(5)	(6)	(7)	(8)	(9)
. . . . etc.								

Code No.

Form E, Pregnant Women–Two-Day Diet Survey
Form F, Lactating Women–Two-Day Diet Survey

The information contained herein will be kept strictly confidential. It will not be disclosed to any Governmental or other private agency.

ROCKEFELLER FOUNDATION

General Survey of Crete

Nomos _____ Interviewer _____
Eparchy _____ Date _____
Demos or Koinotis _____ Day of the week _____
Village _____
Household _____

Age _____ Weight (previous to pregnancy) _____
Height _____ Month of Pregnancy _____
Weight (present) _____

Are you suffering from any disease? _____ Yes __ No __
If Yes, what? _____
Since when? _____
Are your feet swollen sometimes in the morning? _____ Yes __ No __
What do you think is the cause? _____
Are you doing the house work alone? _____ Yes __ No __
If No, who helps you? _____
Are you doing the family washing yourself? _____ Yes __ No __
If Yes, how often? _____ In what way? _____
Do you bake the family bread yourself? _____ Yes __ No __
If Yes, how often? _____ How many loaves everytime? _____
What kind of bread do you eat? _____ Brown _____ White _____
If brown, from what grain? _____
Have you running water in your house? _____ Yes __ No __
If No, who carries the water from outside? _____
If you carry it, from how far? _____
In big or small containers? _____
Do you drink milk? _____ Yes __ No __
Any milk producing animals owned by the family? Yes __ No__
If no, do you buy any milk for yourself? Yes __ No __
If yes, what kind? _____ How much per day? _____
Do you get milk as a ration due to your pregnancy or lactation? Yes __ No __
If Yes, what kind? _____ How much do you pay for it? _____
Do you drink it yourself? Yes __ No __
If No, who drinks it? _____
Do you eat eggs? Yes __ No __ If Yes, how often? _____
What is the usual way you cook eggs? _____

How many times a month do you eat meat? _____

What are the kinds of meat you eat usually? _____

How often do you eat: Fish? _____ Fresh? _____ Dry cod fish? _____

Smoked herrings?   Salted sardines?   Fish in oil?   (Encircle which)

Do you like your food well salted? Yes __ No __

Do you use crude salt? Yes __ No __

If No, what kind? _____ Why? _____

How often do you eat pulses in: Winter? _____

                                                         Summer? _____

What is the kind you prefer most? _____

How do you cook them? _____

Did you ever add soda? Yes __ No __

If Yes, why? _____

Ash water? Yes __ No __

If Yes, why?

Do you ever strain pulses? Yes __ No __

If Yes, why? _____

Do you use: Olive Oil   Butter   Margarine   for cooking? (Encircle which)

Do you ever eat fresh butter? Yes __ No __

If Yes, how often? _____ How often do you eat cheese? _____

What is the kind of vegetables you mostly eat? _____

How often do you eat vegetables? _____

Do you put soda in your boiled greens? Yes __ No __

If Yes, why? _____

If No, what do you do to keep them green? _____

What is done with vegetable water? _____

Do you eat raw salad often? Yes __ No __

If Yes, what kind in summer? _____

                              in winter? _____

Do you prefer lemon or vinegar on your boiled or raw salad? _____

Do you like fruit? _____

How often do you eat fruit in: Summer? _____

                                                     Winter? _____

What are the kinds you eat most in summer? _____

                                              in winter? _____

Do you eat them raw? Yes __ No __

If No, how do you eat them? _____

Do you peel them? Yes __ No __

If Yes, why? _____

If No, why? _____

Did you fast during the 15 days of August? Yes __ No __

If Yes, what did you eat? _____

Do you usually fast on Wednesdays and Fridays? Yes __ No __

If Yes, what do you mostly eat those days? _____

Do you drink wine? Yes __ No __

Do you drink Tsikoudia? Yes __ No __

If Yes, how often? _____
Do you drink much water? Yes __ No __
Are you constipated? Yes __ No __
If Yes, what do you do to combat it? _____
_____

Do you take cod-liver oil? Yes __ No __
If Yes, when did you start taking it? _____
What dose per day? _____
Have you ever lost any teeth during pregnancy? Yes __ No __
If Yes, what do you think was the cause of it? _____
Have good appetite? Yes __ No __
How many times per day do you eat? _____
What are the dishes you prefer most? _____
Do you think you are well fed? Yes __ No __
If No, why? _____
What do you think you ought to add to your diet? _____
Do you attend a maternity station? Yes __ No __
If Yes, did the doctor or the sister advise you what to eat? Yes __ No __
If Yes, do you follow their instructions? Yes __ No __
If No, why? _____

For Pregnant Women Only

Are you happy you are going to have a baby? Yes __ No __
If Yes, why? _____
If No, why? _____

For Lactating Women Only

Have you a good flow of milk? Yes __ No __
If Yes, was it so from the beginning? Yes __ No __
If No, since when did it start to slow down? _____
What do you think is the cause of it? _____
Has the doctor or a sister given you instructions about nursing? Yes __ No __
Is baby satisfied with the amount of milk? Yes __ No __
Do you nurse baby from both breasts in every nursing? Yes __ No __
What do you do with excess of milk if any? _____
Do you weigh baby? Yes __ No __
How much has baby gained since birth? _____
How long do you intend to nurse your baby? _____
Do you enjoy nursing your baby? Yes __ No __ If No, why? _____
_____

Is the baby happy when he nurses? Yes __ No __
Do you want more children? Yes __ No __
If No, why? _____

GENERAL APPEARANCE

Excellent
Good
Fair
Poor

ANEMIC APPEARANCE

Conjunctiva pale? Yes ___ No ___
Lips pale? Yes ___ No ___

TEETH

Excellent
Good
Bad

GENERAL REMARKS

FOOD EATEN LAST TWO DAYS

DATE _____ DAY OF THE WEEK _____

Meal	Food Eaten	Way of Cooking	Principal Ingredients	Amount of Ingredients
Breakfast				
Mid-morning				
Dinner				
Mid-afternoon				
Supper				

Form G, Children from 1 to 6–Diet Survey

The information contained herein will be kept strictly confidential. It will not be disclosed to any Governmental or other private agency.

ROCKEFELLER FOUNDATION
General Survey of Crete

Nomos _____   Interviewer _____
Eparchy _____   Date _____
Demos or Koinotis _____   Day of the week _____
Town or Village _____

Information will be given by mother. If she is not available then by one responsible for child's feeding. Child must be present so the interviewer will be able to record his or her appearance.

Information About the Child

Age _____   Weight (present) _____
Sex _____   Weight (last year's) _____
Height (present) _____
Height (last year's) _____

Was the child breast fed? Yes __ No __
How much milk does the child take per day? _____
As milk _____
In other foods _____
Does he take yoghurt? Yes __ No __
If Yes, how much per day? _____
If No, why? _____
Do you get milk from ration for child? Yes __ No __
If Yes, what kind? _____ How often? _____
If No, where do you get child's milk from? _____
Do you get other food in ration, besides milk? Yes __ No __
If Yes, what? _____
How much do you pay? _____
Do you ever use dried milk? Yes __ No __
If Yes, what uses do you make of it? _____
Has the child ever taken cod-liver oil? Yes __ No __
If Yes, for how long? _____
How do you keep cod-liver oil? _____
Is the child usually well? Yes __ No __
If No, what does he suffer from? _____
Had he a tonsillectomy? Yes __ No __
If No, does he suffer from tonsillitis? Yes __ No __
Does the child eat eggs? Yes __ No __
If Yes, how many per week? _____

Does he eat the whole egg every time? Yes ___ No ___

If No, what part? _____

How do you cook the egg for the child? _____

Do you buy the eggs? Yes ___ No ___

Does the child eat meat? Yes ___ No ___

If No, why? _____

If Yes, how often? _____ What kind? _____

What amount every time? _____

How do you cook it? _____

If meat boiled, do you skim the broth? Yes ___ No ___

If Yes, what do you do with the skimmings? _____

Does the child eat fish? Yes ___ No ___

If Yes, how often? _____ What kind? _____

Does the child eat pulses? Yes ___ No ___

If Yes, how often? _____

How cooked? _____

Does the child eat cheese? Yes ___ No ___

If Yes, how often? _____

How does he eat it?   grated   in a whole piece   (Encircle which)

Do you use olive oil   butter   margarine   for cooking. (Encircle which)

Do you ever buy fresh butter for the child? Yes ___ No ___

What kind of bread does the child eat? _____

How much per day? _____

Do you ever toast it? Yes ___ No ___

Does he eat macaroni or other paste? Yes ___ No ___

If Yes, how cooked? _____

If boiled, what is done with macaroni water? _____

Do you buy rice for the child? Yes ___ No ___

If No, why? _____

If Yes, how do you cook it? _____

If boiled, what do you do with rice water? _____

Does the child eat vegetables? Yes ___ No ___

If No, why? _____

If Yes, what kind? _____

How often? _____

How do you cook vegetables for the child? _____

Do you add soda to green vegetables when boiling? Yes ___ No ___

If Yes, why? _____

If No, what do you do to keep them green? _____

Do you salt them at the beginning or end of boiling? _____

What kind of salt do you use? _____

What do you do with vegetable water? _____

How does the child eat vegetables? whole   cut   mashed   strained (En-
     circle which)

Does he eat raw salads? Yes ___ No ___

If Yes, what kind? _____

How do you prepare tomatoes for the child? _____

Do you put lemon or vinegar on vegetables and salads? _____

Does the child eat fruit? Yes __ No __

If No, why? _____

If Yes, how often does he eat fruit? _____

What kind in summer? _____

　　　　　　　　in winter? _____

Does he eat them raw? Yes __ No __

If No, how do you cook them? _____

If Yes, do you peel them for him? Yes __ No __

Does the child suffer from dysentery? Yes __ No __

If Yes, how often? _____

Do you give tea to the child? Yes __ No __

If No, why? _____

If Yes, why? _____

How often? _____

What kind of tea do you use?　　real tea　　herb tea　(Encircle which)

Do you give child wine? Yes __ No __

Does the child eat sweets? Yes __ No __

If Yes, how often? _____

What kind? _____

How much water does he drink per day? _____

Does he drink water during meal? Yes __ No __

Does he attend a well baby station? Yes __ No __

If No, why? _____

If Yes, do you follow doctor's or sister's instructions regarding the child?
　　Yes __ No __

GENERAL APPEARANCE

Excellent
Good
Fair
Poor

ANEMIC APPEARANCE

Conjunctiva pale? Yes __ No __
Lips pale? Yes __ No __

MENTALLY

Alert
Dull

TEETH

Excellent
Good
Bad

GENERAL REMARKS

FOOD EATEN LAST TWO DAYS

DATE _____ DAY OF THE WEEK _____

Meal	Food Eaten	Way of Cooking	Principal Ingredients	Amount of Ingredients
Breakfast				
Mid-morning				
Dinner				
Mid-afternoon				
Supper				

Form H, Children from 7 to 19–
Two-Day Diet Survey

The information contained herein will be kept strictly confidential. It will not be disclosed to any Governmental or other private agency.

ROCKEFELLER FOUNDATION

General Survey of Crete

Nomos _____   Interviewer _____
Eparchy _____   Date _____
Demos or Koinotis _____   Day of the week _____
Town or Village _____

For children up to 8 years of age, mother must be present to help with the diet history.

Age _____
Sex _____
Height (present) _____
Weight (present) _____

Do you go to school? Yes __ No __
If No, what kind of work do you do? _____
How long does it take to go to your school?   to your work?   (Encircle which) _____

Do you walk there?   you ride?   (Encircle which)
How many hours of sleep do you get per day? _____
What do you usually eat for breakfast? _____
Do you eat anything in between meals? Yes __ No __
If Yes, what? _____
What kind of bread do you eat?   brown   white   (Encircle which)
How much milk do you drink per day as beverage? _____
In other foods? _____
Do you eat cheese often? Yes __ No __
If Yes, how often? _____
Do you eat eggs? Yes __ No __
If Yes, how often? _____
How often do you eat meat? _____ Fish? _____
What kind? _____ Fish? _____
How cooked? _____ Fish? _____
What kind of pulses do you eat most? _____
How are they cooked? _____
Do you sometimes eat them strained? Yes __ No __
Do you eat vegetables? Yes __ No __
How often? _____
What kind? _____

Do you drink the vegetable water? Yes ___ No ___
What do you put on vegetables? butter oil (Encircle which)
Do you put lemon or vinegar on your vegetables? _____
Do you eat raw salads? Yes ___ No ___
If Yes, how often? _____
How often do you eat fruit? _____
What kind in summer? _____
                    in winter? _____
How do you eat fruit?   raw   cooked   (Encircle which)
Do you peel fruit? Yes ___ No ___
Do you drink wine? Yes ___ No ___
Tsikoudia? Yes ___ No ___
Have you ever taken cod-liver oil? Yes ___ No ___
If Yes, for how long? _____

GENERAL APPEARANCE

Excellent
Good
Fair
Poor

ANEMIC APPEARANCE

Conjunctiva pale? Yes ___ No ___
Lips pale? Yes ___ No ___

MENTALLY

Alert
Dull

TEETH

Excellent
Good
Bad

GENERAL REMARKS

FOOD EATEN LAST TWO DAYS

DATE _____ DAY OF THE WEEK _____

Meal	Food Eaten	Way of Cooking	Principal Ingredients	Amount of Ingredients
Breakfast				
Mid-morning				
Dinner				
Mid-afternoon				
Supper				

Additional Schedules

Additional forms used but not duplicated here include a pictorial food record form in Ia, and a clothing, household supplies, furniture and equipment inventory.

The pictorial food record form for the seven-day diet study was only partially used by two families among the 128 keeping food records. Those who could read and write preferred the other forms—and others were assisted by the interviewer in filling out the survey forms.

The inventory forms were used with 128 families to secure the number of items on hand at the time of the survey and the number acquired during 1948. This information was secured on 29 major items of clothing and equipment for infants; 30 major items of household furniture and equipment; 33 items of tableware; 44 items of kitchen utensils; and 30 principal items of clothing for men, boys, girls and women.

APPENDIX 3.

PERSONNEL RESPONSIBILITIES

FOR THE CRETE SURVEY

In addition to acknowledgments made in the front of the book, special mention should be made of the valuable advisory counsel provided by Dr. W. A. McIntosh in the organization and conduct of the general survey. In the development and conduct of a survey in a foreign country, the advice of Americans who have lived in the area for some years is invaluable. Clayton Whipple, Print Hudson, William L. Tait, all of the AMAG-ECA staff, and Daniel E. Wright of WHO, provided such advisory assistance for the Crete Survey. The author is especially indebted to Miss Frances Riley, a social welfare worker in New York City for her preliminary briefing on Crete and its people. Based on two years of work for UNRRA on the island, her unusually accurate judgment of possible key personnel for the conduct of the survey was found extremely helpful.

Others deserving special thanks are the Greek personnel who worked on the survey as Greek ministry advisers: namely, P. Anagnostopoulos, G. Kavouras, C. Kafatos, and S. G. Bouldathakis, Ministry of Agriculture; H. Stephopoulo and Dr. E. Papantonakis, Ministry of Hygiene; Miss Helen Sdrin, Ministry of Education; Cleon Crantonellis, Ministry of Reconstruction; Em. Kavgalakis, Ministry of Public Works; and George Aronis, Ministry of National Economy.

In conducting surveys in foreign countries, much of the success depends upon the proper translation and interpretation of both information and happenings. In this respect the Crete Survey was extremely fortunate in having a well qualified team of translators, interpreters, administrative advisers, and supervisors: George Naxakis, Constantine Markidis, E. G. Trimis, and Peter Paradomenakis. They were ably assisted by an office staff of six bilingual typist-clerk-translators. These latter were selected from a group of twenty applicants by means of short written and verbal examinations; speed and accuracy were determined in typing both Greek and English, in Greek-English and English-Greek translation.

The importance of having drivers who knew the communities and roads of the island and could keep on prearranged schedules for moving the interview teams from one community to another—sometimes two or three in a single day—is self-evident. Contrary to custom in many European areas, all staff members willingly took on extra duties, when occasion demanded.

Island and nome representatives of the various ministries—especially the Ministries of Agriculture, Coordination, Education, Finance, Hygiene, National Economy, Reconstruction, Public Works, Supplies, Air, Transport, and Communication—were called upon repeatedly for information which they willingly supplied. In addition, representatives of the Bank of Greece, the Agricultural Bank, and commercial banks supplied information in the field of credit and finance.

Other agencies particularly helpful in supplying information leading to a better understanding of the problems in Crete were the AMAG (American Mission for Aid to Greece) and its successor, ECA (Economic Cooperation Administration); FAO (United Nations Food and Agriculture Organization); WHO (World Health Organization); Near East Foundation; UNRRA (United Nations Relief and Rehabilitation Administration); Army Service Forces; OFAR (Office of Foreign Agricultural Relations, United States Department of Agriculture); Near East Division, State Department; and the United States Department of Commerce.

A list of personnel with designated responsibilities in the Crete Survey and in the preparation of this manuscript appears below:

GREEK PERSONNEL

1. *Greek Advisers* (as needed, for one week to two months each)

Dr. P. Anagnostopoulos, Ministry of Agriculture, Athens
C. M. Crantonellis, Ministry of Reconstruction, Athens
H. A. Stephopoulo, Ministry of Hygiene, Athens
Helen N. Sdrin, Ministry of Education, Athens
George Aronis, Ministry of National Economy (Geology), Athens
Em. Kavgalakis, Ministry of Public Works, Khania
George Kavouras, agricultural officer, Ay. Nikolaos
C. Kafatos, agricultural officer, Iraklion
S. G. Boultadakis, agricultural officer, Khania
I. S. Leontiadis, regional director, Ministry of Reconstruction, Khania
Dr. Evangelos Papantonakis, director for Crete, Directorate of Hygiene, Khania
E. Yerakaris, Agricultural Bank, Khania

2. *Office Staff* (three to six months)

Constantine Markidis, administrative assistant, translator, and interpreter
Epaminondas G. Trimis, office supervisor, translator, and interpreter
George Naxakis, translator, interpreter, and adviser
Peter Paradomenakis, translator and interpreter
Vasso Balolaki, typist-translator-interpreter
Chryssoula Kandanoleon, typist-translator-interpreter
Mrs. Rena Papalexakis, typist-translator-interpreter
Miss Mat-Bak, typist-translator-interpreter
Mary Papadaki, typist-translator-interpreter
Iolanthi Naxakis, typist-translator-interpreter
Michael Kardamakis, mimeo-clerk
Evangelos Papalexakis, driver
Aristotelis Lionakis, driver
Emanuel Sfakianakis, driver

3. *General Survey Interviewers* (native Cretans; six to eight weeks for household, farm, and community schedules—Forms, A, AAI, B, C)

Paul Pavlakis, age 22; speaks English; two years at Polytechnic School, Athens (civil engineering).

Spiros Gazis, age 22; two years at Polytechnic School, Athens (electrical and mechanical engineering).

Paul Kakouris, age 22; two years at Polytechnic School, Athens (architectural engineering).

Constantine Koniatakis, age 30; graduate, Salonika University (agriculture).

George Charokopos, age 29; speaks a little English; finished high school; served in army eight years; taught school previous year.

Eleftherios Tsivis, age 43; high school; army officer.

Iraklis Stavyianondakis, age 22; high school; plans to study law.

George Siphakis, age 21; speaks English; high school; plans for business administration in university.

Theodore Anagnostopoulos, age 20; three years at Polytechnic School, Athens (architectural engineering).

Anthony Kakatsakis, age 21; high school; manages vegetable farm.

Michael Chatzakis, age 20; high school; radio shop and electrical engineering.

James (Dimitrios) Kakavelakis, age 21; speaks English; high school; news reporter; plans to study law.

4. *Nutrition Survey Interviewers* (volunteer nurses from Khania; six to eight weeks for seven-day diet, children's, pregnant and lactating women's diet, household inventory. Forms E, F, G, H, I, Ia, and J)

Rotho Vranaki
Elli Kandartzoglou
Helaktra Loupi
Stella Renieri
Emily Malandraki
Chryssoula Papadaki
Afrodeti Mavrithaki

5. *Other Greek Advisers and Organizations*

Dr. Ph. Kopanaris, director-general of Hygiene, Ministry of Hygiene, Athens

Dr. Gregory A. Livadas, director, Athens School of Hygiene

Dr. S. Karabetsos, director-general of Medical Care

Dr. Karakasonis, sanitary engineer

Professor Petrakis, Iraklion

Mr. Marcopoulos, sanitarian, WHO

William Moussouros, agricultural education, Ministry of Agriculture

Dr. Ayontantis, director, phytopathology, Ministry of Agriculture

Dr. A. Pierakeas, director, Cereals Experiment Station, Mesara

A. Xanthoudidis, general inspector for Agriculture

Mr. Tsokalis, chief, personnel section, Ministry of Agriculture

Dr. John Hadjinicalaou, entomologist, Athens School of Hygiene

C. A. Doxiadis, coordinator, Greek Recovery Program, Ministry of Coordination, 1948-1949

In addition to the officials of the various ministries, special mention should also be made of the officials of the following organizations:

Athens School of Hygiene
Athens School of Public Health Nursing
Patriotic League (PIKPA)
Hellenic Red Cross
Greek War Relief Association
Anti-Tuberculosis National Hellenic Association
Social Insurance Institute (IKA)

6. *American and Outside Agency Advisers in Greece*

Clayton Whipple, Agriculture Division, AMAG-ECA
Print Hudson, Agriculture Division, AMAG-ECA
J. D. Pope, Agriculture Division, AMAG-ECA
William L. Tait, Field Services, AMAG-ECA
Walter Packard, irrigation engineer, AMAG-ECA
M. Conlon, Civil Government Division, AMAG-ECA
Dr. Oswald F. Hedley, director, Public Health Division, AMAG-ECA
Dr. Fred M. Love, tuberculosis specialist, AMAG-ECA
Daniel E. Wright, sanitation engineer, WHO
Dr. Marshall Hertig, entomologist, WHO
Mr. Bernstein, sanitation engineer, WHO
Laird Archer, director, Near East Foundation, Athens
Dr. J. M. Vine, chief medical officer, WHO
Helene Nussbaum, chief nurse, Tuberculosis BCG Team, WHO-ICG

7. *Nutrition Advisers in Crete and the United States*

Andromache Tsongas, FAO nutritionist, Greek Ministry of Coordination, Athens, Greece
Dr. J. R. Trémolières, chief of Nutrition Section, Institut National d'Hygiène, 45, Rue Cardinet, Paris, 17, France
Helen N. Sdrin, nutritionist, Ministry of Education, Athens, Greece

8. *U.S. Personnel and Their Responsibilities in Crete*

Leland G. Allbaugh, field director, resources, education, agriculture, government, and the general economy
Dr. W. A. McIntosh, public health
Dr. Paul M. Densen, health statistics
Irving B. Crosby, water geology
Dr. Raymond J. Jessen, in charge, Sample Survey of Crete, preparation of schedules, collection of data, and statistical analysis
Norman V. Strand, preparation of schedules, sampling in municipalities, and

assistance with training interviewers; also in charge of editing, summarizing, and analyzing data in the United States.

Joseph C. Dodson, selection, training, and supervision of interviewers and collection of schedules

9. *Members of the Statistical Laboratory, Iowa State College, Assisting in Tabulation and Analysis of Crete Data and Preparation of Reports*

Dr. Raymond J. Jessen, agricultural statistician, BAE, USDA, and professor, Statistical Laboratory, Iowa State College

Norman V. Strand, agricultural statistician, BAE, USDA, and associate professor, Statistical Laboratory, Iowa State College (responsible for a typed book of 369 tables developed from the Crete Survey data from which most of the tables in this book were developed)

Assistants in statistics and schedule editing: Donovan Thompson, John Monroe, John Hoffman, Mrs. Dorothy Cooke.

In charge of computing room and tabulations: Mrs. Mary Clem, Mrs. Bertha Eastman

Secretarial assistants: Mrs. Margaret Kirwin, June Duffield, Mrs. Margaret Taylor Hoffman, Mrs. Lydia White, Mrs. Margaret Willey

10. *Additional Personnel (in U.S.) Assisting with Preparation of Background Reports*

Dr. Calla Van Syckle, consumption economist: foods and nutrition

Dr. E. Jean Learned Mickey, consumption economist: levels of living

Dr. Ralph H. Woods, president, Murray State Teachers College, Murray, Kentucky: education

Thelma J. Norris, nutrition officer, FAO: foods and nutrition

Dr. V. G. Valaoras, United Nations: vital statistics

Dr. Norman S. Buchanan: associate director for the Social Sciences, The Rockefeller Foundation: assistance in reorganization of material in a 1,500-page, twelve-volume set of preliminary reports

Dr. Joseph H. Willits, director for the Social Sciences, The Rockefeller Foundation: assistance with chapter on conclusions and the general content

L. K. Soth, editorial staff, *Des Moines Register*: editorial assistance

George Soule: editorial assistance.

11. *Persons Reviewing Preliminary Drafts of Specified Portions of Manuscript*

While many helpful suggestions were received and used, the persons listed below should in no way be held responsible for errors in content or conclusions drawn:

Foods and Nutrition

Dr. Calla Van Syckle, Michigan State College, East Lansing, Michigan

Dr. J. R. Trémolières, Institut National d'Hygiène, Paris, France

Andromache Tsongas, FAO, Athens, Greece

Thelma J. Norris, FAO, Washington, D.C.

Dr. George C. Payne, International Health Division, The Rockefeller Foundation

Dr. L. A. Maynard, School of Nutrition, Cornell University, Ithaca, New York

Dr. William J. Darby, Department of Internal Medicine, Vanderbilt University, Nashville, Tennessee

Health

Dr. G. K. Strode, Director, International Health Division, The Rockefeller Foundation (retired)

Dr. A. J. Warren, Director, Division of Medicine and Public Health, The Rockefeller Foundation

Dr. Hugh H. Smith, Division of Medicine and Public Health, The Rockefeller Foundation

Dr. W. A. McIntosh, Division of Medicine and Public Health, The Rockefeller Foundation

Dr. M. C. Balfour, Division of Medicine and Public Health, The Rockefeller Foundation

Dr. Paul M. Densen, Department of Bio-Statistics, Graduate School of Public Health, University of Pittsburgh, Pennsylvania

Complete Manuscript (preliminary draft)

Dr. J. D. Black, Littauer School of Public Administration, Harvard University

Dr. T. W. Schultz, chairman, Department of Economics, University of Chicago, Chicago, Illinois

Dr. V. G. Valaoras, statistician on vital statistics, United Nations

C. S. Stephanides, agriculturist, OFAR, Washington, D.C.

George Coutsoumaris, Agricultural Bank of Greece (on leave), University of Chicago, Chicago, Illinois

Dr. E. Jean Learned Mickey, consumption economist, Iowa State College, Ames, Iowa

Carl C. Malone, agricultural economist, Iowa State College, Ames, Iowa

James J. Wallace, farm management specialist, Iowa State College, Ames, Iowa

Lauren K. Soth, editorial staff, *Des Moines Register*, Des Moines, Iowa

Robert K. Buck, farmer, Ainsworth, Iowa

Norman V. Strand, Statistical Laboratory, Iowa State College, Ames, Iowa

Dr. Raymond J. Jessen, Statistical Laboratory, Iowa State College, Ames, Iowa

Dr. Norman S. Buchanan, Associate Director for the Social Sciences, The Rockefeller Foundation

Dr. Joseph H. Willits, Director for the Social Sciences, The Rockefeller Foundation

12. *Final Draft of Manuscript*

Dr. Joseph H. Willits, Director for the Social Sciences, The Rockefeller Foundation

Mrs. Julia Carson, editorial assistance

Elizabeth Lyman, editorial and supervisory assistance

Patricia Harris, editorial assistance

Robert L. Williams, cartographic laboratory, Yale University: preparation of maps, charts, and graphs

In addition to all these there are many others—especially the island, nome, municipal, and community officials and the 765 household heads—who so generously gave of their time and thought.

Finally, only through the wholehearted cooperation of the staff of the various departments of The Rockefeller Foundation, especially the secretarial staff of the Social Sciences and the Library, Files, and Office Services under Miss Jenifer M. Hoyt and Miss Elna Campbell, was this book made possible. The tasks of proofreading and indexing were undertaken by the Office of Publications under Mr. Henry B. van Wesep.

APPENDIX 4.

SELECTED REFERENCES

AND DEPOSITORY LIBRARIES

GENERAL REFERENCES

Allen, Harold Boughton. *Come Over Into Macedonia.* New Brunswick, N.J., Rutgers University Press. 1943.

Bacon, L. B. and others. *Agricultural Geography of Europe and the Near East.* Washington, D.C., United States Department of Agriculture. Foreign Agricultural Relations Office. Miscellaneous Publication No. 665. 1948.

Benedict, Ruth. *Patterns of Culture.* New York, Penguin Books, Inc. 1946.

Black, John Donald and Kiefer, M. E. *Future Food and Agricultural Policy.* New York, McGraw-Hill. 1948.

Botsford, George Willis and Sihler, Ernst Gottlieb. *Hellenic Civilization.* New York, Columbia University Press. 1915.

Brewster, Ralph Henry. *The Island of Zeus.* London, Gerald Duckworth & Co. 1939.

Cary, Max and Haarhoff, T. J. *Life and Thought in the Greek and Roman World.* London, Methuen & Co., Ltd. 1940.

Couch, Herbert Newell. *Greece.* (Classical Civilization, Vol. 1.) New York, Prentice-Hall, Inc. 1940.

Evans, Arthur J. *Palace of Minos at Knossos.* London, Macmillan & Co., Ltd. 1921.

Firth, Raymond. "The Effects of Western Culture Upon Primitive Peoples." pp. 107-111, in: *When Peoples Meet,* edited by Locke, Alain Le R. and Stern, B. J., New York, Progressive Education Association. 1942.

Food and Agriculture Organization of the United Nations. *Report of the FAO Mission for Greece.* Washington, D.C., Food and Agriculture Organization of the United Nations. 1947.

Glover, Terrot Reaveley. *The Challenge of the Greek, and Other Essays.* Cambridge, Macmillan & Co., Ltd. 1942.

Greek Ministry of National Economy (République Ministère de l'Economie Nationale). "Recensement agricole et d'élevage de la Grèce," in: Section B, *Statistique Générale de la Gréce.* Athens, Greece, National Printing Office. 1929.

————. *L'Annuaire Statistique de la Grèce, 1938.* Vol. X. Athens, Greece, National Printing Office. 1939.

————. *Population de la Grèce, 1938.* Issue No. 1153-29. Athens, Greece, National Printing Office. 1940.

————. Department of General Statistical Services of Greece, Section of Physical Movement of Population. *Statistics of Causes of Deaths, 1936-37.* Issue No. 999-32. Athens, Greece, National Printing Office. 1938.

————. Department of General Statistical Services of Greece, Section of

Physical Movement of Population. *Statistics of the Movement of Population, 1935.* Issue 91-29. Athens, Greece, National Printing Office. 1937.

Hanson, Simon G. *Economic Development in Latin America.* Washington, D.C., Inter-American Affairs Press. 1951.

Harris, Seymour Edwin. *The European Recovery Program.* Cambridge, Mass., Harvard University Press. 1948.

Hawes, Charles Henry and Hawes, Harriett Boyd. *Crete, The Forerunner of Greece.* London, Harper Brothers. 1909.

International Monetary Fund. *Balance of Payments Yearbook.* Washington, D.C., International Monetary Fund. 1949.

International Yearbook of Agricultural Statistics, 1941-1945. Agricultural Production and Livestock Numbers. Volumes I and II. Washington, D.C., Food and Agriculture Organization of the United Nations. 1947.

Leighton, Alexander Hamilton. *The Governing of Men.* Princeton, N.J., Princeton University Press. 1945.

Lilienthal, David Elie. *The T.V.A.: Democracy on the March.* New York, Harper & Brothers. 1944.

Lynd, Robert Staughton and Lynd, Helen. *Middletown.* New York, Harcourt, Brace and Co., Inc. 1929.

Nelson, Lowry. *Rural Cuba.* Minneapolis, Minn., University of Minnesota Press. 1950.

Pendlebury, John Devitt Stringfellow. *Archaeology of Crete.* London, Methuen & Co., Ltd. 1939.

———. *Handbook to the Palace of Minos at Knossos, with Its Dependencies.* London, Macmillan & Co., Ltd. 1933.

Perloff, Harvey S. *Puerto Rico's Economic Future.* Chicago, Ill., University of Chicago Press. 1950.

Roberts, Lydia Jane and Stefani, Rosa Luisa. *Patterns of Living in Puerto Rican Families.* Chicago, Ill., Photopress, Inc. 1949.

Rose, H. T. *Primitive Culture in Greece.* New York, Doubleday Doran & Co., Inc. 1925.

Shoemaker, Sister Mary Theophane. *History of Nurse-Midwifery in the United States.* Washington, D.C., Catholic University of America. 1947.

Smith, Thomas Lynn. *Brazil: People and Institutions.* Baton Rouge, La., La. State Univ. Press. 1946.

Smith, Thomas Lynn and Marchant, Alexander. *Brazil: Portrait of Half a Continent.* New York, The Dryden Press. 1951.

Stobart, John Clarke. *Glory That Was Greece.* Philadelphia, Pa., J. B. Lippincott Co. 1922.

Taylor, Carl C. *Rural Life in Argentina.* Baton Rouge, La., La. State Univ. Press. 1948.

Thornburg, Max Weston and others. *Turkey: An Economic Appraisal.* New York, Twentieth Century Fund Inc. 1949.

United Nations, Statistical Office, in collaboration with the Dept. of Social Affairs. *Demographic Yearbook, 1948.* New York, Columbia University Press. 1949.

United Nations, Statistical Office. *Statistical Yearbook, 1948*. Lake Success, N.Y., United Nations. 1949.

United States, Bureau of Census. *Statistical Abstract of the United States: 1949*. Washington, D.C., United States, Government Printing Office. 1949.

Whetten, Nathan Laselle. *Rural Mexico*. Chicago, Ill., University of Chicago Press. 1948.

Wythe, George and others. *Brazil: An Expanding Economy*. New York, Twentieth Century Fund, Inc. 1949.

PERIODICALS AND MONOGRAPHS

Adler, S. and others. "Investigations on Mediterranean kala azar. A study of leishmaniasis in Canea, Crete." *Proceedings of Royal Society*, Series B (Biological Sciences), *125*:491-516. 1938.

Bennett, M. K. "On measurement of relative national standards of living." *Quarterly Journal of Economics*. *51*:317-336. 1937.

Brantwood, R. J., Krogman, W. M., and Tax, Sol. *Time, Space, and Man*. Chicago, Ill., University of Chicago. 1946.

Buchanan, Norman S. "Deliberate industrialisation for higher incomes." *The Economic Journal*. *26*:533-553. 1946.

Civil Affairs Handbook: Greece. Washington, D.C., Headquarters, United States Armed Forces Services. Section 4: Government Finance. 1943. Manual M 351. 1943-1944.

———. Washington, D.C., Headquarters, United States Armed Forces Services. Section 7: Agriculture. Manual M 351. 1943-1944.

———. Washington, D.C., Headquarters, United States Armed Forces Services. Section 8: Industry and Commerce. Manual M 351. 1943-1944.

Davis, J. S. "Standards and content of living." *American Economic Review*. *35*:1-5. 1945.

Doxiadis, C. A. *Destruction of Towns and Villages*. Athens, Greece, Department of Reconstruction, Bul. No. 11. 1947.

———. *Such Was the War in Greece*. Athens, Greece, Department of Reconstruction, Bul. No. 9. 1947.

———. *The Sacrifices of Greece*. Athens, Greece, Department of Reconstruction. 1947.

Food and Agriculture Organization, Committee on Calorie Requirements. *Calorie Requirements*. Washington, D.C., Food and Agriculture Organization of the United Nations. 1950.

Foster, W. G. and McGibony, J. R. "Trachoma." *American Journal of Ophthalmology*. *27*:1107-1117. 1944.

Grant, John B. "International trends in health care." *American Journal of Public Health*. *38*:381-397. 1948.

Hadjinicolaou, John. *Comparative Effectiveness of DDT, Chlordane, Aldrin, and Dieldrin Residues Against the Olive Fruit Fly (Dacus oleas Rossi)*. Athens, Greece, Athens School of Hygiene. The Malaria Division, No. 351. 1950.

Hagood, M. F. and Ducoff, L. F. "What level of living indexes measure." *American Sociological Review.* 9:78-84. 1944.

International Agricultural Collaboration. *Report of the United States-Lebanon Agricultural Mission.* Washington, D.C., United States Department of Agriculture, Foreign Agricultural Relations Office. 1948.

Lancaster, Osbert. "The Island Greeks." *Atlantic Monthly. 182*:59-64. 1948.

League of Nations, Health Organization. Malaria Commission. "Note sur le voyage d'étude de Prof. M. Ciuca en Grèce pour la lutte antipaludique." C.H. /Malaria/ 154, 1931.

Maynard, L. A. *Evaluation of Dietary Survey Methods.* Atlantic City, N.J., Federation Proceedings: Symposium on Nutritional Appraisal of Human Subjects. 1950.

———. "Soils and Health." *Journal of the American Medical Association. 143*:807-812. 1950.

National Research Council, Division of Medical Sciences. Prepared by Mackie, T. T., Hunter, G. W., and Worth, C. B. *A Manual of Tropical Medicine.* Philadelphia, Pa. W. B. Saunders Company. 1945.

National Research Council, Food and Nutrition Board. *Recommended Dietary Allowances, Revised 1948.* Washington, D.C., National Research Council Reprint and Circular Series, No. 129. 1948.

Nevros, K. and Zyorykin, I. "The Soils of the Isle of Crete." *Soil Research Bulletin*, Athens, Greece. *1*: Bd. VI. No. 4/5. 1939.

Papantonakis, E. "Observations on leishmaniasis in the district of Canea (Crete)." *Annals of Tropical Medicine and Parasitology. 29*:191-197. 1935.

Perott, Tibbitts, and Britten. "Scope and methods of the nation-wide canvass of sickness in relation to its social and economic setting." *United States Public Health Reports. 54*:1663-1687. 1939.

Roemer, Milton I. "Rural Health Programs in Different Nations." *The Milbank Memorial Fund Quarterly. 26*:58-89. 1935.

Stillwell, Agnes. "Crete, where sea kings reigned." *National Geographic. 84*:547-568. 1943.

United Nations, Department of Economic Affairs. *Measures for the Economic Development of Under-Developed Countries.* New York, United Nations Publications, Sales No.: 1951.II.B.2. 1951.

United Nations Relief and Rehabilitation Administration. *Foreign Trade in Greece.* London, European Regional Office, Operational Analysis Papers No. 14. 1946.

United Nations Relief and Rehabilitation Administration. *Industrial Rehabilitation in Greece.* London, European Regional Office, Operational Analysis Papers No. 20. 1947.

United States Department of State. *Point Four: Cooperative Program for Aid in the Development of Economically Underdeveloped Areas.* Washington, D.C., Department of State Publication 3719. 1950.

United States Public Health Service. *Illness and Medical Care among 2,500,-000 Persons in 83 Cities, with Special Reference to Socio-Economic Factors.* Washington, D.C., United States Government Printing Office. 1945.

United States War Department. *Medical and Sanitary Data on Crete.* Washington, D.C., United States War Department Technical Bulletin. No. 61. 1944.

Wilcox, Francis O. and others. *United Nations Program for Technical Assistance.* pp. 45-53, in: "Aiding underdeveloped areas abroad." *The Annals.* The American Academy of Political and Social Science. *268*:1-187. 1950.

Williams, F. M. and Zimmerman, C. C. *Studies of Family Living in the United States and Other Countries.* Washington, D.C., United States Department of Agriculture, Miscellaneous Publication No. 223. 1935.

MISCELLANEOUS

(Taken from a list of 75 books published between A.D. 1669 and 1900. Publishers not given but list available from depository libraries listed below.)

Cornelius, F. *Creta Sacra.* Two volumes, 317 and 458 pp. Venice. 1755. (Italian)

Daru, P. *Histoire de la République de Venise.* Seven volumes. Paris. 1819. Second edition of eight volumes. Paris. 1821. Third edition of eight volumes. Paris. 1826. Fourth edition of nine volumes. Paris. 1853. (All editions in French.)

Edward, Charles. *Letters from Crete.* 394 pp. London. 1887. ("A vivid description of Cretan life")

Evans, A. J. *Cretan Pictographs and Phoenician Script.* Eight volumes. London. 1895.

Freese, J. H. *A Short Popular History of Crete.* 165 pp. London. 1897.

Gerola. *Venetian and Other Monuments in Crete.* Five volumes. Rome. 1900. (Italian)

Hoeck, Karl. *Kreta.* Three volumes. Göttingen. 1823. (German) ("The opus magnus on Cretan topography, mythology, and archaeology")

Mitchell. *The Greek, The Cretan and The Turk.* London. 1897.

Pashley, Robert. *Travels in Crete.* Two volumes. 326 pp. Cambridge. 1837. ("One of the best books on Crete. Love and folk stories and gossip")

Raullin, V. *Description Physique de l'Ile de Crète.* Three volumes and atlas. Paris. 1869. (French)

Spratt, Capt. T. A. B. *Travels and Researches in Crete.* Two volumes, 387 and 435 pp. London. 1865.

Stillman, W. J. *The Cretan Insurrection, 1866-68.* 203 pp. New York. 1874. (Mr. Stillman was the American Consul in Crete, 1865-1869.)

Tournefort, J. P. *Relation d'un Voyage au Levant.* Two volumes. Paris. 1717. Several editions. English edition of two volumes, London, 1718.

DEPOSITORY LIBRARIES

Two preliminary reports were prepared in connection with the Crete Survey: *Reconnaissance Report on Ground Water Resources of Crete for The*

Rockefeller Foundation, by Irving B. Crosby, and *Preliminary Survey for Irrigation and Water Supply Projects in Crete,* by George Aronis. These reports are available at the following libraries:

Princeton University
Sterling Memorial Library, Yale University
Widener Library, Harvard University
Department of Agriculture, Washington, D.C.
The Library of Congress
Butler Library, Columbia University
Iowa State College
Massachusetts Institute of Technology
University of Chicago
University of Wisconsin

APPENDIX 5.

SUPPLEMENTARY STATISTICAL
TABLES FOR THE CRETE SURVEY[1]

[1] These tables are supplementary to the text. They have been arranged in the same order as the chapter headings.

TABLE A 1. International weights and measures equivalents, Crete Survey, 1948

Metric measure	Symbol	Ratio to basic unit	U.S. equivalent
1 centimeter	cm	.01 meter	.3937 inches
1 meter	m.	basic unit	3.2808 feet
1 kilometer	km.	1,000 meters	.62137 miles
1 square meter	m²	basic unit	.0002471 acres
1 square kilometer	km²	1,000,000 square meters	.3861 square miles
1 hectare	ha.	10,000 square meters	2.471 acres
1 liter (liquid)	l.	basic unit	.26417 gallons
1 hectoliter	hl.	100 liters	26.417 gallons
1 kilogram	kg.	basic unit	2.2046 pounds, avoir.
1 gram[a]	gm.[a]	.001 kilogram[a]	.0352736 ounces[a]
1 metric quintal	ql.	100 kilograms	220.46 pounds
1 metric ton	M.T.	1,000 kilograms	2,204.6 pounds

GREEK LOCAL TERMS

Measure	Ratio to basic unit	U.S. equivalent
1 coffin	24.064 kgs. varies with commodity weighed	53.0515 pounds
1 dramia	.0032 kilograms	.00705 pounds
1 koilon	100 liters	26.417 gallons
1 oka or oke (400 drams)[a]	1.28 kilograms	2.8219 pounds
1 pik (pic)	.68580 meters	2.25 feet
1 stremma	.10 hectares	.2471 acres
Venetian pound	.480 kilograms	1.0582 pounds
1 zygion or load (100 okes)	128 kilograms	282.1888 pounds
1 stadium milestone	1 kilometer	.62137 miles

Okes per stremma—to pounds per acre, multiply by 11.4202243.
1 ounce equals 8.859 dramia; 1 pound equals 141.748 dramia

EQUIVALENTS FOR METRIC TONS

Commodity	U.S. unit	Number of pounds in U.S. unit	Equivalents used to convert metric tons to U.S. equivalents
Wheat, potatoes, beans	bushels	60	36.743333
Corn, rye, millet	"	56	39.367857
Barley	"	48	45.929167
Oats	"	32	68.89375
Rice, cleaned	"	61	36.100984
Rice, rough	"	45	48.991111
Cotton, ginned	bale	478	4.612134
Cotton, unginned	"	478	1.537378

[a] Liquids as oil and wine sold by the oke: 1 bbl. olive oil = 51.95 okes; and 1 bbl. wine = 63 okes.

TABLE A 2. Population estimates, Crete, 3000 B.C. to A.D. 1948

3000-1100 B.C. (Ancient times)	1,200,000[a]	
	67 B.C.-A.D. 330 Population	
	estimated to be larger	
	than at present[b]	
A.D. 1204-1669 (Venetian period)	900,000[a]	
A.D. 1204-1669 " "	250,000[b]	
1821	260,000[b]	
1836	130,000[b]	(Emigration and Greek revolution)
1865	210,000[b]	Spratt
1881	279,165[b]	Greek census of 1881
1900	301,273[b]	Greek census June 1900
1913	336,151[c]	V. G. Valaoras data
1920	346,584[c]	" " " "
1928	386,427[c]	Greek census of 1929
1935	422,570[c]	Greek estimates
1940	438,239[c]	Greek census of 1940
1947	477,492[d]	
1948	*475,800[e]	

* Includes an estimated 3,000 institutional residents in addition to persons in households.

Sources: [a] *Encyclopedia Americana.* 1947 edition, Vol. 8, p. 184.
[b] *Encyclopedia Britannica.* 1946 edition, Vol. 6, pp. 676-8.
[c] Ministry of National Economy, *L'Annuaire Statistique de la Grèce*, 1938, vol. x, p. 76. Athens, Greece. 1939. Data supplied by V. G. Valaoras.
[d] Ration card estimates. Ministry of Supplies, Athens.
[e] Sample Survey of Crete, Form A, Household.

TABLE A 3. Average (mean) monthly rainfall at five stations, Crete, 1894-1929, in inches

Month	Khania	Iraklion	Anoyia	Sitia	Ierapetra
April	1.14	1.07	2.14	.60	.32
May	.60	1.08	2.46	.65	.17
June	.09	.07	.24	.07	.23
July	.02	.04	.08	.00	.00
August	.13	.28	.56	.00	.00
September	1.27	.70	.67	.35	.20
October	1.48	1.52	2.79	1.57	.56
November	4.79	3.92	6.19	3.08	1.23
December	6.64	3.62	9.15	3.67	1.56
January	5.07	3.37	8.47	3.51	2.06
February	3.96	2.82	6.80	2.69	1.13
March	2.64	1.80	4.69	1.77	.68
Dry season (April-September)	3.25	3.24	6.15	1.67	.92
Rainy season (October-March)	24.58	17.05	38.09	16.29	7.22
Annual total	27.83	20.29	44.24	17.96	8.14

Source: Ministry of Air, National Meteorological Service, Athens. Data courtesy of Russell H. Gist, Economic Cooperation Administration.

TABLE A 4. Average (mean) monthly rainfall and temperature, six stations, Crete, pre-war, in inches and degrees Fahrenheit

Month	Khania (1932-40)	Iraklion (1932-35)	Anoyia (1932-40)	Sitia (1933-40)	Ierapetra (1932-39)	Mesara (1936-40)
			RAINFALL			
April	2.01	0.58	2.06	0.98	0.57	0.91
May	0.54	0.60	1.06	0.31	0.32	0.32
June	0.24	0.06	0.82	0.43	0.05	0.19
July	0.08	0.00	0.17	0.04	0.00	0.04
August	0.01	0.00	0.13	0.00	0.05	0.00
September	0.39	0.03	0.68	0.16	0.10	0.22
October	2.77	1.91	3.40	1.89	1.28	1.93
November	2.22	3.00	6.67	3.29	3.16	4.61
December	4.38	1.68	7.18	3.66	3.51	5.58
January	4.42	3.97	8.72	3.91	5.36	4.17
February	3.14	2.83	7.22	2.66	2.43	3.42
March	2.30	0.63	3.64	1.49	1.44	4.16
Dry season (April-September)	3.27	1.27	4.92	1.92	1.09	1.68
Rainy season (October-March)	19.23	14.02	36.83	16.90	17.18	23.87
Annual total	22.50	15.29	41.75	18.82	18.27	25.55
			TEMPERATURE			
April	62.4	63.6	56.9	63.4	63.3	63.1
May	68.3	69.7	63.6	69.3	70.0	70.3
June	73.8	76.8	60.4	73.0	84.1	78.4
July	81.2	80.5	74.3	80.2	84.1	82.0
August	80.3	79.8	72.7	80.2	70.4	80.1
September	75.3	76.0	66.2	76.3	72.3	77.2
October	70.4	71.8	64.8	71.6	72.6	70.9
November	63.0	67.0	55.7	64.1	64.8	62.4
December	56.5	58.5	48.8	58.9	58.6	55.6
January	53.3	53.6	45.3	55.8	55.5	52.3
February	54.0	54.2	45.9	55.8	55.8	52.7
March	56.5	57.4	49.5	57.9	58.4	56.3

Source: Ministry of Air, Meteorological Service, Athens, Greece. Data courtesy of Russell H. Gist, Economic Cooperation Administration.

TABLE A 5. Mean temperature, precipitation, and days raining by months and seasons, Khania, 1945-1948 average

Month	Mean temperature (degrees Fahrenheit)	Precipitation (inches)	Days raining (number)
April	61	1.8	5
May	69	.1	4
June	72	.1	2
July	79	(less than .01)	1
August	81	.8	1
September	75	.4	3
October	67	2.0	10
November	62	4.1	18
December	55	5.9	22
January	53	6.4	20
February	53	4.3	17
March	55	1.8	10
Dry season	73	3.2	16
Rainy season	59	24.5	97
Annual total	66	27.7	113

Source: Computed from data supplied by Meteorological Station of Khania through Mr. Dimitris Drossoulakis. Feb. 1949.

TABLE A 6. Area of communities and municipalities, Crete, 1940

Area (square kilometers)	Communities and municipalities	
	Number	Per cent
0.0- 4.9	90	16.4
5.0- 9.9	156	28.3
10.0-14.9	105	19.0
15.0-19.9	66	11.9
20.0-24.9	47	8.6
25.0-29.9	34	6.1
30.0-34.9	13	2.4
35.0-39.9	10	1.9
40.0-44.9	4	0.7
45.0-49.9	11	2.0
50.0-54.9	2	0.4
55.0-59.9	2	0.4
60.0-64.9	2	0.4
65.0-69.9	1	0.2
70.0-74.9	1	0.2
75.0-over	6	1.1
Total	550	100.0

(Average: 15.08 sq. km.)

Source: Ministry of Reconstruction, Map measurements of Crete. Athens, 1948.

TABLE A 7. Area by nomes, Crete, 1940

Nome	Area		
	Square kilometers	Square miles	Per cent
Khania	2,471	954	30
Rethimnon	1,481	572	18
Iraklion	2,622	1,012	31
Lasithi	1,721	664	21
Total	8,295	3,202	100

Source: Ministry of Reconstruction, Map measurements of Crete. Athens, 1948.

TABLE A 8. Elevation of communities and municipalities, Crete, 1948[a]

Height		All communities and municipalities	
Meters	Approx. feet[b]	Number	Per cent
0- 99	10- 327	79	13.6
100- 199	328- 655	79	13.6
200- 299	656- 988	100	17.4
300- 399	989-1311	105	18.1
400- 499	1312-1639	68	11.7
500- 749	1640-2460	89	15.4
750- 999	2461-3280	22	3.8
1000-1249	3281-4100	1	.2
Data not given		36	6.2
Total		579	100.0

[a] Elevation is given for principal village, except for a few communities in which more than one measurement was taken, hence the total of 579 as against 550 municipalities and communities.

[b] Original data expressed in meters.

Source: Ministry of Reconstruction, *Hyposometrical Repartition Manual*, Khania, 1948.

TABLE A 9. Population, land area, elevation, and number of households in 1940, Sampl Survey communities and municipalities, Crete, 1948

Eparchy	Community	Pop. (1940)	Land Area (sq. mi.)	Elevation[a] (feet)	Number o Household (1940)
KHANIA NOME					
Apokoronos	1 Yeoryioupolis	1,319	14.9	20	315
"	2 Melidoni	381	4.7	1,440	87
"	3 Neon Khorion	786	3.2	360	168
Kisamos	4 Drapania	913	3.1	1,310	224
"	5 Elos	674	4.5	1,800	155
"	6 Panethimos	302	1.1	920	54
Kidhonia	7 Khania[b]	28,213	6.8	70	6,914
"	8 Meskla	826	19.0	1,050	187
"	9 Mournies	1,645	2.0	160	383
"	10 Neon Khorion	816	2.4	330	209
Selinon	11 Palaiokhora	2,130	24.1	70	488
Sfakia	12 Khora Sfakion	600	15.4	330	155
RETHIMNON NOME					
Ay. Vasilios	13 Sellia	569	7.7	1,280	154
Amarios	14 Kaloyerou	260	2.8	1,710	81
"	15 Monasteriki	299	1.9	1,250	91
Milopotamos	16 Ay. Ioannis	228	1.1	1,180	51
"	17 Anoyia	3,072	41.8	2,500	675
Rethimnon	18 Yerani	401	4.7	300	89
"	19 Khromonastiri	640	3.6	1,150	152
"	20 Rethimnon[b]	10,972	10.5	30	2,780
IRAKLION NOME					
Viannos	21 Kato Viannos	376	4.5	1,510	102
Kanouryion	22 Vasiliki	537	7.7	920	139
"	23 Zaros	1,956	13.8	2,030	438
Malevision	24 Avyeniki	860	3.6	980	206
"	25 Rogdhia	793	7.5	920	210
Monofatsion	26 Ay. Varvara	1,431	6.3	2,300	324
"	27 Arkalokhori	2,042	10.2	1,280	495
"	28 Akhendria	689	12.8	2,260	168
Pedhiadha	29 Apostoloi	716	4.8	1,250	196
"	30 Ay. Paraskion	655	2.3	1,150	148
"	31 Kastamonitsa	502	4.6	1,710	119
"	32 Kastelli-Pedhiadhos	1,542	6.3	1,070	395
Piryiotissa	33 Vorroi	704	4.2	130	172
Temenos	34 Veneraton	847	4.2	1,050	193
"	35 Iraklion[b]	42,557	21.9	82	10,333

TABLE A 9. (continued)

Eparchy	Community	Pop. (1940)	Land Area (sq. mi.)	Elevation[a] (feet)	Number of Households (1940)
ASITHI NOME					
Ierapetra	36 Ierapetra	4,949	10.2	20	1,252
"	37 Mournies	824	11.3	1,020	264
Lasithion	38 Ay. Yeoryios	1,286	5.4	2,690	334
Merabello	39 Exo Lakonia	324	4.4	490	94
"	40 Ay. Nikolaos[b]	2,558	7.7	20	703
"	41 Kastelli-Fourni	684	3.3	1,890	203
Sitia	42 Zakros	1,061	17.6	1,050	276
"	43 Stavrokhori	1,010	6.9	1,150	258
"	44 Sfaka	871	4.3	980	218

[a] Estimates for principal village to nearest ten feet.   [b] Municipality.
Source: Ministry of National Economy. Census of 1940. Athens, Greece.
Ministry of Reconstruction estimates for elevations and land area. Athens.

TABLE A 10. Population size groups for all Crete and Sample Survey villages, 1940 Census

Population size group	All Cretan villages		Sample villages[a]	
	Number	Per cent	Number	Per cent
0- 249	940	66.9	120	67.3
250- 499	273	19.4	22	12.3
500- 749	108	7.7	16	9.0
750- 999	40	2.8	10	5.6
1000-1249	17	1.3	1	.6
1250-1499	12	.9	3	1.7
1500-1749	0	0	0	0
1750-1999	2	.1	0	0
2000-2249	1	.1	0	0
2250-2499	2	.1	1	.6
2500-2749	2	.1	0	0
2750-2999	2	.1	1	.6
3000-3249	1	.1	0	0
3250-3499	1	.1	0	0
3500-3749	0	0	0	0
3750-3999	0	0	0	0
4000-4249	0	0	0	0
4250-4499	1	.1	1	.6
4500-4749	0	0	0	0
4750-4999	0	0	0	0
5000 and over	3	.2	3	1.7
Total	1405	100.0	178	100.0

[a] Population size groups for communities will be found in Table M 2.
Source: Ministry of Reconstruction as derived from the 1940 Census of Population and 1948 Sample Survey of Crete. Ministry of National Economy, *Population de la Grèce*, Athens, 1940. Sample Survey of Crete, Form A, Household.

TABLE A 11. Population by age and sex, Crete, 1940

Age Group	Males Absolute Numbers	% of Males	% of 438,239	Females Absolute Numbers	% of Females	% of 438,239	Total Number	%
0- 4	22,671	10.64	5.2	22,030	9.79	5.0	44,701	10.2
5- 9	24,960	11.71	5.7	23,468	10.43	5.3	48,428	11.0
10-14	24,187	11.35	5.5	23,458	10.42	5.4	47,645	10.9
15-19	19,595	9.19	4.5	20,640	9.17	4.7	40,235	9.2
20-24	13,315	6.25	3.0	18,202	8.09	4.2	31,517	7.2
25-29	17,547	8.24	4.0	19,580	8.70	4.5	37,127	8.5
30-34	16,055	7.53	3.6	17,183	7.63	3.9	33,238	7.5
35-39	14,161	6.64	3.2	13,872	6.16	3.2	28,033	6.4
40-44	10,939	5.13	2.5	12,863	5.71	2.9	23,802	5.4
45-49	7,879	3.70	1.8	9,944	4.42	2.3	17,823	4.1
50-54	8,868	4.16	2.0	11,357	5.04	2.6	20,225	4.6
55-59	8,629	4.05	2.0	8,371	3.72	1.9	17,000	3.9
60-64	7,535	3.53	1.7	8,307	3.69	1.9	15,842	3.6
65-69	5,481	2.57	1.3	4,830	2.14	1.1	10,311	2.4
70-74	5,898	2.77	1.3	5,647	2.51	1.3	11,545	2.6
75-79	2,483	1.16	0.6	2,340	1.04	0.5	4,823	1.1
80-84	1,814	0.85	0.4	1,998	0.89	0.5	3,812	0.9
85-89	721	0.34	0.2	515	0.23	0.1	1,236	0.3
90-94	337	0.16	0.1	300	0.13	0.1	637	0.2
95-99	69	0.03	*	147	0.07	*	216	*
100 +	9	0.00	*	34	0.02	*	43	*
Total	213,153	100.00	48.6	225,086	100.00	51.4	438,239	100.0

* Less than 0.1 per cent.
Source: Ministry of National Economy. *Population de la Grèce*, 1940.

TABLE A 12. Population in households by age and sex, Crete, 1948
(in percentage)

Age Group	Males		Females		Total
	Per cent of all males	Per cent of 472,800 population	Per cent of all males	Per cent of 472,800 population	Per cent of total population
0- 4	10.2	5.0	7.6	3.9	8.9
5- 9	8.7	4.3	8.2	4.2	8.5
10- 14	11.0	5.4	9.4	4.8	10.2
15- 19	9.3	4.5	8.8	4.5	9.0
20- 24	8.9	4.4	9.8	5.0	9.4
25- 29	8.7	4.3	8.5	4.3	8.6
30- 34	6.7	3.3	8.1	4.1	7.4
35- 39	5.4	2.6	7.0	3.6	6.2
40- 44	5.8	2.9	5.3	2.7	5.6
45- 49	4.6	2.3	5.5	2.8	5.1
50- 54	3.6	1.7	5.2	2.7	4.4
55- 59	3.4	1.6	3.7	1.9	3.5
60- 64	4.2	2.1	4.8	2.4	4.5
65- 69	3.9	1.9	2.4	1.2	3.1
70- 74	1.5	0.7	2.5	1.3	2.0
75- 79	1.6	0.8	1.6	0.8	1.6
80- 84	1.0	0.5	1.1	0.5	1.0
85- 89	0.8	0.4	0.4	0.2	0.6
90- 94	0.4	0.2	.0	—	0.2
95-100	0.3	0.1	0.1	0.1	0.2
Total	100.0	49.0	100.0	51.0	100.0
Number in sample	1544		1608		3152

Source: Sample Survey of Crete, Form A, Household.

TABLE A 13. Percentage of population by age and sex, Mexico and
United States, 1940, and United States, 1948

| Age Group | 1940 | | | | | | 1948 | | |
| | Mexico (19,653,552) | | | United States (131,669,275) | | | United States (146,571,000, est.) | | |
	Male	Female	Total	Male	Female	Total	Male	Female	Total
0-4	7.4	7.2	14.6	4.1	3.9	8.0	5.2	5.1	10.3
5-9	7.3	7.1	14.4	4.1	4.0	8.1	4.5	4.3	8.8
9-14	6.3	5.9	12.2	4.5	4.4	8.9	3.8	3.6	7.4
15-19	5.0	5.2	10.2	4.7	4.7	9.4	3.8	3.7	7.5
20-24	3.8	4.1	7.9	4.3	4.5	8.8	4.1	4.1	8.2
25-29	3.8	4.3	8.1	4.1	4.3	8.4	4.0	4.2	8.2
30-34	3.2	3.5	6.7	3.9	3.9	7.8	3.8	3.9	7.7
35-39	3.4	3.6	7.0	3.6	3.6	7.2	3.6	3.7	7.3
40-44	2.3	2.5	4.8	3.4	3.3	6.7	3.3	3.3	6.6
45-49	1.8	2.0	3.8	3.2	3.1	6.3	3.0	3.1	6.1
50-54	1.5	1.6	3.1	2.8	2.7	5.5	2.7	2.8	5.5
55-59	1.1	1.1	2.2	2.3	2.1	4.4	2.5	2.4	4.9
60-64	1.0	1.1	2.1	1.8	1.8	3.6	2.0	2.0	4.0
65-69	0.6	0.6	1.2	1.4	1.5	2.9	1.5	1.5	3.0
70-74	0.4	0.4	0.8	1.0	1.0	2.0	1.0	1.2	2.2
75-79	0.2	0.2	0.4	0.5	0.6	1.1	0.6	0.7	1.3
80-84	0.1	0.2	0.3	0.3	0.3	0.6	0.3	0.4	0.7
85-89	0.1	0.1a	0.1a	0.1	0.1	0.2	0.1	0.1	0.2
90 and over	*	0.1	0.1	*	0.1	0.1	*	0.1	0.1
Total	49.3	50.7	100.0	50.1	49.9	100.0	49.8	50.2	100.0

* Less than 0.05 per cent.
a Slight difference due to rounding off decimals.
Source: Dirección General de Estadística, *Sexto censo de población* (1940). Bureau of Census, Population, vol. ii, *Sixteenth Census of the United States*, 1940, Table 26, p. 56. U.S. Department of Commerce, Washington, D.C.; also Table 2, p. 9 in vol. iv. Bureau of Census, *Statistical Abstract of the United States*, 1949. Seventieth edition. U.S. Department of Commerce, Wash., D.C., Table 9, p. 9; Interpolations made for last four age groups in accordance with 1940 census.

TABLE A 14. Population in 1940 of municipalities (demes), so classified in 1948, Crete

Municipalities (demes)[a]	Organization date	Population 1940 census
Khania[b]	prior to 1940	28,213
Rethimnon[b]	" " "	10,972
Iraklion[b]	" " "	42,557
Ay. Nikolaos[b]	" " "	2,558
Sitia	1941-1944	3,207
Ano Arkhanais	1941-1944	3,361
Ierapetra	March 3, 1946	4,949
Neapolis	May 5, 1946	3,634
Kastelli-Kisamos	May 28, 1947	1,859
Anoyia	December 13, 1947	3,072
Total population in 1940 in ten municipalities of 1948		104,382
Total population, 11 towns over 2,500 population		108,457
Total population, Crete, 1940		438,239

a According to the law, municipalities or demes are: (1) nome capitals, (2) towns of 10,000 inhabitants or more and/or (3) towns in which courts of first instance are established.

b Nome capitals and municipalities in 1940; the unmarked municipalities being organized since 1940.

Source: Greek Census of 1940 and letter from C. A. Doxiadis, Ministry of Coordination, and Cleon Crantonellis, Ministry of Reconstruction, August 16, 1949.

TABLE A 15. Number of households and inhabitants, communities and municipalities, Sample Survey of Crete, 1948

Community and City	Households		Inhabitants		Average Number Inhabitants per Household
	Sample Number	Estimated Total	Sample Number	Estimated Total[a]	
COMMUNITIES					
Khania	146	21,900	669	100,350	4.59
Rethimnon	106	15,900	433	64,950	4.08
Iraklion	224	33,600	950	142,500	4.24
Lasithi	141	21,150	517	77,550	3.67
Total	617	92,550	2,569	385,350	4.17
MUNICIPALITIES					
Khania	56	8,400	228	34,200	4.07
Rethimnon	17	2,550	80	12,000	4.71
Iraklion	69	10,350	254	38,100	3.68
Ay. Nikolaos	6	900	21	3,150	3.50
Total	148	22,200	583	87,450	3.94
Communities and Municipalities	765	114,750	3,152	472,800	4.12

[a] Does not include residents of institutions, such as prisons, asylums, and orphanages, by design. These are estimated at 3,000 for the island.

Source: Sample Survey of Crete, Form A, Household.

TABLE A 16. Birth, death, and infant mortality rates, Crete and Greece, 1930-1948

Year	Birth rates		Death rates		Infant mortality	
	Crete	Greece	Crete	Greece	Crete	Greece
1930	26.5	31.4	11.8	16.4	83.5	99.7
1931	25.6	30.9	13.3	17.8	117.8	133.8
1932	24.8	28.5	12.8	18.0	100.1	128.7
1933	25.4	28.8	12.9	16.9	97.9	122.4
1934	26.3	31.2	13.7	15.0	113.1	111.7
1935	25.7	28.3	11.8	14.9	90.6	112.8
1936	26.5	28.1	11.3	15.2	82.1	114.2
1937	23.1	26.4	13.1	15.2	117.1	122.2
1938	24.1	26.1	11.9	13.3	91.1	99.4
1939	—	25.0	—	14.0	—	118.2
1940	—	24.0	—	12.7	—	100.7
1941	—	13.4	—	24.4	—	—
1942	—	14.1	—	42.3	—	—
1943	—	22.8	—	13.9	—	—
1944	—	29.5	—	18.7	—	—
1945	—	31.6	—	12.8	—	—
1946	26.0	31.0	10.0	12.3	42.0	—
1947	26.0	29.1	8.0	14.6	40.0	—
1948	22.0	—	9.0	—	72.0	—
1946-8	26.1	30.0	10.6	13.4	72-85	—

Source: Greece, 1930-31, and Crete, 1930 to 1938; data prepared by Dr. V. G. Valaoras from *Annuaire Statistique de la Grèce*, Athens, 1930-38. Greece, 1932-1948: Statistical Office of the United Nations. *Demographic Yearbook, 1948*, United Nations, New York, 1949, Tables 14, 20, 24, pp. 264-5, 314-15, 406-7. Crete, 1946, 1947, 1948; Sample Survey of Crete, Form C, Community; Crete, 1946-48, adjusted figure, estimate by Dr. V. G. Valaoras.

TABLE A 17. Average height of persons by age and sex, Sample Survey of Crete, 1948
(measurements in inches)

Age	Communities				Municipalities				Island			
	Males		Females		Males		Females		Males		Females	
	No.	Average Height	No.	Average Height	No.	Average Height	No.	Average Height	No.	Average Height	No.	Average Height
1 and under	51	18.8	48	20.3	7	18.5	5	17.7	58	18.7	53	20.1
2	24	26.7	20	27.9	7	27.3	1	29.5	31	26.8	21	28.0
3	30	31.9	23	28.6	8	30.5	3	36.7	38	31.6	26	29.5
4	27	34.5	21	32.6	4	40.9	1	31.5	31	35.3	22	32.5
5	21	36.0	27	35.0	8	36.7	4	35.9	29	36.2	31	35.1
6	21	37.0	23	36.1	4	37.9	2	37.4	25	37.2	25	36.2
7	19	43.3	19	37.7	2	43.3	2	43.3	21	43.3	21	38.2
8	26	43.1	20	43.5	3	42.6	7	45.7	29	43.0	27	44.1
9	28	46.6	18	42.1	5	46.1	10	46.7	33	46.5	28	43.7
10	34	46.0	29	46.1	7	50.2	1	51.2	41	46.7	30	46.3
11	24	50.7	26	46.8	5	51.6	6	50.9	29	50.8	32	47.5
12	27	51.6	26	52.1	6	54.5	11	61.0	33	52.1	37	53.1
13	28	50.7	22	52.4	7	54.9	6	58.7	35	51.5	28	53.8
14	30	53.2	18	56.5	1	49.2	6	59.5	31	53.1	24	57.2
15	19	56.0	17	57.4	11	58.5	8	64.5	30	56.9	25	59.7
16	31	60.4	21	59.6	5	64.2	5	59.5	36	60.9	26	59.6
17	22	61.1	15	61.0	4	60.0	9	62.6	26	60.9	24	61.6
18	19	63.9	29	62.1	5	66.9	10	62.7	24	64.5	39	62.2
over 18	788	65.4	878	62.4	176	66.5	211	61.5	964	65.6	1,089	62.6
Total	1,269	57.1	1,300	56.0	275	59.1	308	59.9	1,544	57.5	1,608	56.7

Source: Sample Survey of Crete, Form A, Household.

TABLE A 18. Average weight of persons, by age and sex, Crete, 1948

(weight in pounds)

Age	Communities				Municipalities				Island			
	Males		Females		Males		Females		Males		Females	
	No.	Average Weight	No.	Average Weight	No.	Average Weight	No.	Average Weight	No.	Average Weight	No.	Average Weight
1 and under	51	15.9	48	20.3	7	22.1	5	11.0	58	16.5	53	19.4
2	24	26.7	20	24.7	7	33.1	1	22.1	31	28.2	21	24.5
3	30	34.6	23	31.5	8	33.5	3	41.2	38	34.4	26	32.6
4	27	37.3	21	36.2	4	48.9	1	33.1	31	38.6	22	35.9
5	21	37.9	27	39.9	8	41.1	4	46.7	29	38.8	31	40.8
6	21	48.7	23	39.9	4	48.9	2	44.1	25	48.9	25	40.1
7	19	48.7	19	47.4	2	60.6	2	68.3	21	49.8	21	49.4
8	26	51.4	20	47.2	3	63.3	7	58.2	29	52.7	27	50.0
9	28	62.2	18	58.4	5	61.3	10	59.7	33	62.2	28	58.9
10	34	64.4	29	57.1	7	72.1	1	61.7	41	65.7	30	57.1
11	24	72.8	26	69.4	5	75.0	6	71.7	29	73.0	32	65.7
12	27	72.1	26	74.5	6	81.6	11	79.2	33	73.9	37	75.8
13	28	73.4	22	74.7	7	82.9	6	100.8	35	75.4	28	80.3
14	30	88.4	18	90.6	1	77.2	6	94.1	31	88.0	24	91.5
15	19	93.0	17	95.0	11	99.4	8	119.1	30	95.5	25	100.7

Age	N		N		N		N		N		N	
16	31	109.1	21	104.1	5	123.0	5	103.6	36	111.1	26	104.1
17	22	106.9	15	116.2	4	105.8	9	110.7	26	106.7	24	114.2
18	19	128.3	29	115.1	5	133.6	10	117.1	24	129.4	39	115.5
19	21	130.5	20	114.2	6	119.1	7	114.0	27	127.9	27	114.2
20	22	130.7	30	120.6	9	115.1	8	124.6	31	126.3	38	121.5
21-25	120	137.8	126	120.2	20	141.8	26	122.6	140	138.5	152	120.6
26-30	98	147.9	118	120.8	21	137.1	24	125.2	119	145.9	142	121.5
31-35	82	145.7	95	128.1	21	140.7	26	126.3	103	144.8	121	127.7
36-40	73	142.9	96	130.5	12	155.9	22	136.7	85	144.6	118	131.6
41-45	79	149.7	69	129.6	17	146.4	20	128.5	96	149.3	89	129.1
46-50	52	144.4	72	124.1	8	160.7	20	132.3	60	146.6	92	125.9
51-55	38	140.9	55	129.6	11	152.3	13	132.5	49	143.5	68	130.3
56-60	50	143.3	64	125.0	9	149.5	13	123.9	59	144.2	77	124.8
61-65	42	141.1	39	129.6	15	143.5	12	113.1	57	141.8	51	125.9
66 and over	111	135.4	94	114.4	27	129.4	20	119.7	138	112.2	114	115.3
21 and over	745	142.6	828	124.3	161	142.9	196	126.3	906	142.6	1,024	124.8
All ages	1,269	111.8	1,300	103.2	275	114.6	308	111.6	1,544	134.3	1,608	104.7

Source: Sample Survey of Crete, Form A, Household.

TABLE A 19. Buildings destroyed in heavily damaged areas of Crete, World War II

Area of Crete		Rank	Buildings destroyed (per cent)
Nome: Khania Nome		9 : 10[a]	30.3
Eparchy: Pirgiotissa		3 : 12	85.0
	Temenos	11 : 12	46.0
	Viano	12 : 12	42.9
City over 10,000:	Khania	3 : 5	35.9
	Iraklion	3 : 5	30.2
Town (2-5000):	Anoyia	1 : 2	100.0
	Tymbaki	2 : 7	100.0
Village (0-2000):	Kandanos	1 : 10	100.0
	Margarikari	4 : 10	100.0
	Neo-Chorio	5 : 10	100.0
	Skines	6 : 10	100.0

[a] 9 : 10 etc. indicates a rank of 9 out of 10 nomes, eparchies, etc., which suffered most from war damage in the whole of Greece.

Source: C. A. Doxiadis, *Such Was the War in Greece*, Department of Reconstruction Bulletin; no. 9k, pp. 31-33.

TABLE A 20. Buildings destroyed during World War II, by nomes, Crete

	Number of Settlements Affected	Bldgs. existing	Buildings Destroyed		
			Totally	Partially	Both
Khania	96	9,332	2,456	457	2,913
Rethimnon	49	4,860	1,443	212	1,655
Iraklion	71	13,019	2,089	159	2,248
Lasithi	9	794	489	3	492
Total	225	28,005	6,477	831	7,308

Source: C. A. Doxiadis, *Destruction of Towns and Villages in Greece*, Ministry of Reconstruction, Bulletin no. 11, p. 46.

TABLE A 21. Holidays in Crete, 1948

Holidays		Observed by	
		Government services and banks	Ordinary businesses
RELIGIOUS			
St. Basil's Day	January 1	x	x
Epiphany	January 6	x	x
St. John the Baptist	January 7	x	1/2
The 3 Patriarchs (St. John Chrysostome, St. Basil, St. Gregory)	January 30	(only a school holiday)	
Beginning of fasting period	March 15	x	1/2
Annunciation	March 25	x	x
St. George's Day	April 23	x	x
Good Friday	April 30	x	1/2
Monday after Easter	May 3	x	x
St. Constantine's Day	May 21	x	
Ascension Day	June 10	x	x
Holy Ghost's Day	June 21	x	
St. Peter's and St. Paul's Day	June 29	x	
Virgin Mary's Day	August 15	x	x
The Day of the Cross	September 14	x	
St. Dimitrios' Day	October 26	x	
Christmas	December 25	x	x
NATIONAL			
Declaration of the Independence of Greece in 1821	March 25	x	x
King's Name Day	June 29	x	x
OXI Day, Greek-Italian War	October 28	x	x
LOCAL*			
Virgin's Birthday (City of Khania)	September 8	x	
Anniversary of the blowing up of the Arkadi Convent by the Greeks when besieged by the Turks (City of Rethimnon)	November 8	x	
St. Mina's Day (City of Iraklion)	November 11	x	
German Parachute Landing Day (Cities of Khania, Rethimnon, and Iraklion)	May 21	x	x

* Every village in Crete also has its religious local feast once a year, when all work is suspended.

Source: C. Markidis, Khania.

TABLE A 22. Occupation of all persons, labor force or non-labor force, Crete, 1948

Occupations	Per cent of labor force and of total population					
	Community		Municipality		Island	
	Labor force	Total pop.	Labor force	Total pop.	Labor force	Total pop.
IN LABOR FORCE:						
Farmers and farm managers	34	12	4	1	28	10
Farmer and other occupations	4	1	—	—	3	1
Farm laborers	14	5	3	1	12	4
Farm workers (unpaid)	15	5	3	1	13	5
Craftsmen, foremen, etc.	11	4	22	8	13	5
Operators, etc.	2	1	7	3	3	1
Proprietors, managers, and officials	3	1	8	3	4	1
Professional workers	1	—	6	2	2	1
Clerical, sales, etc.	1	—	9	4	3	1
Service workers (not domestic)	11	4	15	6	12	4
Laborers (non-farm)	3	1	17	6	5	2
Domestic service	1	—	2	1	1	—
Unemployed	—	—	4	1	1	—
Totals	100	34	100	37	100	35

	Per cent of non-labor and of total population					
	Non-labor	Total pop.	Non-labor	Total pop.	Non-labor	Total pop.
NOT IN LABOR FORCE:						
Housework (own)	50	33	48	30	50	32
In school	23	15	28	18	24	16
Under school age	20	13	15	9	19	12
Unable to work or attend school	6	4	9	6	6	4
Others and not reported	1	1	—	—	1	1
Totals	100	66	100	63	100	65
Grand total percentage of total population		100		100		100

Source: Sample Survey of Crete, Form A, Household.

TABLE A 23. Industry of household heads and all persons in labor force, Crete, 1948 (percentages)

Industry	Household heads			All persons		
	Commu- nity	Munici- pality	Island	Commu- nity	Munici- pality	Island
Agriculture, forestry,						
and fishing	71	13	59	64	11	54
Agriculture & other	7	—	6	4	—	3
Mining	—	—	—	—	1	*
Construction	1	2	1	1	1	1
Manufacturing	6	24	9	10	28	13
Transportation	1	10	3	2	8	3
Wholesale and retail	4	13	6	3	10	5
Finance, insurance,						
repair service	*	2	1	1	2	1
Personal service	2	2	2	2	5	3
Amusement	*	—	*	*	1	*
Professional services	1	6	2	1	5	2
Government	6	16	8	11	16	12
Industry not reported	1	12	3	1	12	3
Number in sample	491	104	595	883	214	1,097

* Less than 0.5 per cent.
Source: Sample Survey of Crete, Form A, Household.

TABLE A 24. Occupations of household heads and all persons in labor force, Crete, 1948 (percentages)

Occupations	Household heads			All persons in labor force		
	Commu-nity	Munici-pality	Island	Commu-nity	Munici-pality	Island
Farmers and farm managers	57	8	49	34	4	28
Farm laborers	13	5	11	14	3	12
Unpaid farm laborers				15	3	13
Craftsmen, foremen, and kindred workers	7	18	9	11	22	13
Service workers (not domestic)	5	12	7	11	15	12
Laborers (not farm)	3	21	6	3	17	5
Proprietors, managers, and officials	4	12	5	3	8	4
Farm and other	7		6	4		3
Clerical, sales, etc.	2	9	3	1	9	3
Operatives and kindred workers	1	8	2	2	7	3
Professional	1	7	2	1	6	2
Domestic service	*	—	*	1	2	1
Unemployed but seeking work				*	4	1
Total	100	100	100	100	100	100

* Less than 0.5 per cent.
Source: Sample Survey of Crete, Form A, Household.

TABLE A 25. Occupation of household heads of farm, sub-farm, and non-farm households, Crete, 1948 (percentages)

Occupation	Farms	Sub farms			Non-farm households
		Crops only	Animals only	Crops & animals	
Farmers & farm managers	83	—	—	—	—
Farmer and other	10	—	—	—	—
Own home housework	3	12	20	24	22
Unable to work & others	4	16	18	14	13
Farm laborers	—	18	—	25	6
Laborers not farm	—	8	13	4	13
Service workers	—	12	23	9	11
Craftsmen, etc.	—	12	11	11	14
Clerical, etc.	—	8	2	3	5
Operatives	—	—	4	2	4
Proprietors	—	6	7	5	9
Professional	—	8	2	3	3
Total	100	100	100	100	100
Per cent of all household heads	45	7	6	23	19

Source: Sample Survey of Crete, Form A, Household, and Form B, Farm, combined.

TABLE A 26. Composition of households, Crete, 1948

Relation to Head	Communities		Municipalities		Island			
	% of House-holds Report-ing	% of Persons	% of House-holds Report-ing	% of Persons	% of House-holds Report-ing	% of Persons	Number of House-holds Report-ing	Number of Persons
Head	100	24	100	24	100	24	765	765
Spouse	72	17	66	17	70	17	539	539
Son or daughter	74	49	73	49	74	49	563	1,533
Mother or father	10	3	9	2	9	3	72	84
Brother or sister	6	2	6	3	6	2	44	73
Grandfather or grandmother	*	*	—	—	*	*	1	1
Grandson or granddaughter	3	1	3	1	3	1	24	34
Aunt or uncle	*	*	—	—	*	*	2	2
Nephew or niece	2	1	4	1	2	1	17	18
Cousin	*	*	1	*	1	*	4	4
Son- or daughter-in-law	4	1	1	*	4	1	27	27
Mother- or father-in-law	2	1	6	1	3	1	24	26
Brother- or sister-in-law	1	*	1	1	1	*	9	13
Grandson- or grand-daughter-in-law	1	*	—	—	*	*	3	5
Uncle- or aunt-in-law	*	*	1	*	*	*	2	2
Servants	2	1	4	1	2	1	15	16
Nuns	1	*	—	—	1	*	4	6
Others	—	—	1	*	*	*	1	1
Hired help	1	*	—	—	*	*	3	3
Total percentage	—	100	—	100	—	100	—	—
Total number of persons		2,569		583				3,152

* Less than 0.5 per cent.
Source: Sample Survey of Crete, Form A, Household.

TABLE A 27. Cash income, home produce value, and total income per household and per person classified by income groups, 765 households, Crete, 1947-48

House-hold Income Classes (dollars)	Communities			Municipalities			Island		
	Households with stated incomes % of		Average income per person (dollars)	Households with stated incomes % of		Average income per person (dollars)	Households with stated incomes % of		Average income per person (dollars)
	H.H.	persons		H.H.	persons		H.H.	persons	
CASH INCOME									
0-249	63	55	26	31	26	35	57	50	27
250-499	23	26	73	28	26	108	24	26	79
500-749	9	12	116	18	18	157	11	13	127
750-999	2	3	156	10	14	164	4	5	160
1,000-1,249	2	3	192	5	7	240	3	4	208
1,250-1,499	*	*	460	2	1	480	*	*	473
1,500-1,749	*	1	200	1	1	318	*	1	247
1,750-1,999	—	—	—	3	5	321	1	1	321
2,000-2,249	—	—	—	1	1	540	*	*	540
2,250-2,499	—	—	—	1	1	400	*	*	400
2,500 & over	*	*	360	—	—	—	*	*	360
Average	—	—	60	—	—	138	—	—	74
HOME PRODUCE VALUE									
0-249	65	58	22	96	97	5	71	65	18
250-499	25	29	71	2	3	68	21	24	71
500-749	7	10	98	1	*	167	6	8	99
750-999	1	1	129	—	—	—	1	1	130
1,000-1,249	2	2	196	1	*	333	1	2	204
2,000-2,249	*	*	286	—	—	—	*	*	259
Average			49			9			42
TOTAL INCOME (Cash and Home Produce)									
0-249	37	29	36	27	21	41	35	27	37
250-499	25	25	85	27	26	105	25	25	89
500-749	21	24	129	21	22	148	21	24	133
750-999	8	10	154	10	12	174	8	10	159
1,000-1,249	5	7	205	6	8	214	6	7	207
1,250-1,499	2	3	207	3	2	540	2	3	242
1,500-1,749	2	2	312	1	2	320	1	2	313
1,750-1,999	*	*	346	2	3	341	1	1	343
2,000-2,249	*	*	367	2	3	381	1	1	377
2,250-2,499	—	—	—	—	—	—	—	—	—
2,500-2,750	*	*	313	1	1	417	*	*	357
4,500-4,799	*	*	646	—	—	—	*	*	646
Average			109			148			116
Total no. of cases	617	2,569		148	583		765	3,152	

* Less than 0.5 per cent.
Source: Sample Survey of Crete, Form A, Household.

TABLE A 28. Average annual income per household by occupation, in dollars, Crete, 1947

Occupation	Communities			Municipalities			Island		
	Cash	Home Prod.	Total	Cash	Home Prod.	Total	Cash	Home Prod.	Total
Professional	683	175	858	1336	81	1417	1035	125	1160
Proprietors, managers and officials	407	142	549	816	18	834	584	88	672
Clerical, sales and kindred workers	361	66	427	508	9	517	439	36	475
Craftsmen, foremen and kindred workers	252	80	332	752	2	754	428	53	481
Operatives and kindred workers	760	145	905	652	0	652	694	56	750
Domestic service	20	—	20	—	—	—	20	—	*
Service workers (not domestic)	225	62	287	524	11	535	322	46	368
Farmers and farm managers	273	309	582	298	369	667	274	310	584
Farm laborers	145	84	229	910	90	1000	201	85	286
Laborers (non-farm)	232	49	281	369	17	386	316	30	346
Farmer and other	400	308	708	—	—	—	400	308	708

* Home Produce and Total Income were not estimated for Domestic Service.
Source: Sample Survey of Crete, Form A, Household.

TABLE A 29. Cash income and occupation of household head, Crete, 1947 (percentages)

Occupation	Households with cash income			
	$0-249	$250-499	$500-749	$750-2749
Farmers and farm managers	57	25	13	5
Farmer and other	50	22	9	19
Farm laborers	77	16	4	3
Professional	—	23	15	62
Proprietors, managers and officers	23	37	17	23
Craftsmen and foremen, etc.	44	24	11	21
Operatives and kindred workers	8	16	46	30
Clerical, sales, etc.	24	41	29	6
Service workers	50	25	15	10
Laborers (non-farm)	42	44	8	6
All occupations	57	24	11	8

Source: Sample Survey of Crete, Form A, Household.

TABLE A 30. Value of home produce and occupation of household head, Crete, 1947 (percentages)

Occupation	Households with income from home produce		
	$0-249	$259-499	$500-2249
Farmers and farm managers	43	41	16
Farmer and other	47	35	18
Farm laborers	90	10	—
Professional	85	15	—
Proprietors, managers & officers	87	13	—
Craftsmen and foremen	94	6	—
Operatives and kindred workers	92	8	—
Clerical sales	100	—	—
Service workers	100	—	—
Laborers (non-farm)	97	3	—
All occupations	71	21	8

Source: Sample Survey of Crete, Form A, Household.

TABLE A 31. Total income and occupation of household head, Crete, 1947 (percentages)

Occupation	Households with total income				
	$0-249	$250-499	$500-749	$750-999	$1000-4799
Farmers and farm managers	21	24	27	12	16
Farmer and other	9	35	24	12	20
Farm laborers	66	16	14	1	3
Professional	—	8	31	15	46
Proprietors and managers and office	10	28	30	13	19
Craftsmen and foremen	37	24	18	11	10
Operatives and kindred workers	8	8	52	8	24
Clerical, sales and kindred workers	18	41	29	12	—
Service workers	47	25	15	8	5
Laborers (non-farm)	31	47	18	2	2
All occupations	35	25	21	8	11

Source: Sample Survey of Crete, Form A, Household.

TABLE A 32. Total income, cash income, and value of home produce per person, 128 seven-day diet households, Crete, 1947 (average, median, and range)

	All households	Munici-palities All classes	Communities All classes	Income groups (dollars)		
				0-99	100-199	200 & over
Number of H.H.	128	25	103	50	33	20
Avg. no. persons sharing income	4.0	3.5	4.1	4.0	4.4	3.5
Total income per pers. (dollars)						
average	143	172	135	57	133	335
median	107	120	100	52	133	267
range	3-850	60-540	3-850	3-95	100-180	200-850
Cash income per pers. (dollars)						
average	91	161	73	33	70	181
median	74	120	56	26	75	158
range	0-540	60-540	0-500	0-90	0-180	60-500
Home produce per pers. (dollars)						
average	52	11	62	24	63	154
median	33	0	40	25	58	125
range	0-500	0-100	0-500	0-71	0-150	10-500

Source: Sample Survey of Crete, Form A, Household.

TABLE A 33. Type of tenure for dwellings, Crete, 1948 (percentages)

Type of tenure	Communities	Municipalities	Island
Own	89	62	84
Rent	3	32	9
Requisitioned	1	3	1
Other	1	1	1
Rent free (relatives)	6	2	5
Total	100	100	100
Number in sample	617	148	765

Source: Sample Survey of Crete, Form A, Household.

TABLE A34. Households practicing various types of handicrafts,[a] Crete, 1948

	Communities		Municipalities		Island	
Handicraft practiced	Number Household Practicing	Per cent of Total Household	Number Household Practicing	Per cent of Total Household	Number Household Practicing	Per cent of Total Household
Spinning	370	60	18	12	388	51
Weaving	266	43	14	9	280	37
Furniture Making	2	*	—	—	2	*
Others	18	3	20	14	38	5
Total Households	617	—	148	—	765	—

* Less than 0.5 per cent.

a None of the households occurring in the sample practiced leather working, silver smithing, wood carving, stone sculpturing, or making of finished products such as handbags or dolls.

Source: Sample Survey of Crete, Form A, Household.

TABLE A 35. Households having specified number of beds, mirrors, and window drapes, Crete, 1948

	Beds		Mirrors		Window Drapes	
Number	Commu-nities	Munici-palities	Commu-nities	Munici-palities	Commu-nities	Munici-palities
			(percentage)			
0	8	1	18	13	78	49
1	40	17	70	64	6	8
2	28	37	10	14	8	20
3	16	22	1	3	4	5
4	5	14	1	3	3	10
5	2	7	—	1	*	1
6	1	1	—	1	1	3
7	*	1	*	—	—	1
8	—	—	—	1	*	3
Total	100	100	100	100	100	100
Number of house-holds	617	148	617	148	617	148
Average per household	2.0		1.1		.7	
Average per household reporting	2.1		1.3		2.6	

* Less than 0.5 per cent.

Source: Sample Survey of Crete, Form A, Household.

TABLE A 36. Bedding and linen per household, Crete, 1948

Articles of bedding and linen	Communities		Municipalities	
	Per cent of total households owning	Average no. per household owning	Per cent of total households owning	Average no. per household-owning
Mattresses	86	2.3	100	2.8
Mattress cover	1	1.0	8	1.5
Sheets	81	6.2	100	6.4
Pillows	94	4.9	100	4.8
Pillow cases	79	6.6	100	9.2
Quilts	59	1.4	80	1.4
Blankets	100	5.6	100	4.7
Bed covers	32	1.7	36	1.7
Mosquito-netting	7	1.6	28	1.6
Table cloths	85	3.2	96	3.2
Table napkins	88	12.3	92	1.5
Fancy napkins	14	5.5	36	7.3
Bath towels	1	2.0	8	2.5
Hand towels	39	3.2	40	3.3
Face towels	96	5.7	100	4.5

Source: Sample Survey of Crete, Form J, Inventory.

TABLE A 37. Dishes and tableware per household, Crete, 1948

Articles of dishes and tableware	Communities		Municipalities	
	Per cent of total households owning	Average no. per house-hold owning	Per cent of total households owning	Average no. per house-hold owning
Soup plates	91	5.3	96	5.0
Plates	88	5.3	100	5.3
Salad plates	13	3.2	24	1.5
Dessert plates	20	3.3	16	3.5
Platters	31	1.6	24	1.8
Soup tureens	23	1.1	28	1.3
Tea cups	88	3.2	88	4.1
Tea saucers	37	3.4	44	5.3
Coffee cups	75	4.6	88	4.8
Coffee saucers	51	5.1	64	4.6
Jam saucers	39	5.4	56	5.3
Jam bowls	34	1.4	60	1.5
Salt and pepper shakers	58	1.0	60	1.1
Sugar bowl	10	1.0	16	1.0
Milk pitcher	3	1.3	4	1.0
Water pitcher	38	1.1	32	1.0
Wine decanter	34	1.0	28	1.0
Water glasses	86	4.2	100	4.0
Wine glasses	93	4.6	80	5.3
Ouzo glasses	85	4.7	80	6.7
Tin cups	26	1.1	60	1.3
Vinegar and oil bottle	3	1.0	12	1.0
Ladles	18	1.7	20	2.2
Trays	67	1.2	76	1.2
Bread basket	12	1.1	28	1.1
Table knives	90	3.2	100	4.6
Spread knives	21	1.3	24	1.0
Paring knives	18	2.2	24	2.0
Tea spoons	80	3.9	92	3.8
Soup spoons	99	7.5	96	6.8
Serving spoons	19	1.6	16	1.8
Dessert forks	18	4.6	32	5.6
Table forks	97	8.6	100	7.7

Source: Sample Survey of Crete, Form J, Inventory.

TABLE A 38. Kitchen utensils per household, Crete, 1948

Articles of kitchen utensils	Communities		Municipalities	
	Per cent of total households owning	Average no. per household owning	Per cent of total households owning	Average no. per household owning
Boiling pans— metal	63	1.6	76	1.9
Boiling pans— earthenware	74	1.8	72	1.7
Baking pans	27	1.3	64	1.4
Frying pans	95	1.2	96	1.2
Cookie sheets	4	2.0	—	—
Dish pans	45	1.8	60	1.5
Strainers	45	1.2	84	1.4
Sifters	83	1.8	68	1.2
Coffee pots	78	1.6	92	2.0
Tea kettles	11	1.1	36	1.2
Egg whippers	1	1.0	4	1.0
Coffee roasters	5	1.0	8	1.0
Coffee grinders	5	1.0	24	1.0
Pepper grinders	1	1.0	—	—
Meat grinders	4	1.0	16	1.0
Hand grain mills	37	1.0	16	1.0
Spits	27	1.1	12	1.0
Boiling racks	9	1.0	32	1.1
Mortar and pestles	65	1.0	84	1.0
Chopping bowls— wooden	13	1.0	20	1.0
Mixing bowls	36	1.6	44	1.4
Rolling pins	66	1.0	72	1.1
Rolling board	67	1.0	48	1.0
Bread tubs	64	1.0	64	1.0
Bread pans	13	1.0	24	1.0
Bread baking shovels	51	1.0	8	1.0

TABLE A 38. (continued)

Articles of kitchen utensils	Communities		Municipalities	
	Per cent of total households owning	Average no. per household owning	Per cent of total households owning	Average no. per household owning
Garbage pans	6	1.0	68	1.0
Water urns	88	1.6	68	1.2
Earthen containers	91	3.9	80	1.4
Salt boxes	29	1.0	60	1.0
Bread boxes	4	1.0	4	1.0
Wooden spoons	58	1.2	40	1.0
Ladles	59	1.6	52	2.0
Water cans	57	1.1	76	1.2
Spatulas	1	1.0	—	—
Coal tongs	61	1.0	88	1.0
Grater	69	1.0	84	1.0
Coal shovels	18	1.1	32	1.1
Wash tubs	55	1.0	88	1.1
Water barrels	12	1.5	48	1.1
Floor brushes	6	1.0	40	1.0
White-washing brushes	58	1.0	68	1.1
Covered ovens	18	1.0	4	1.0
Scales	34	1.1	20	1.0

Source: Sample Survey of Crete, Form J, Inventory.

TABLE A 39. Clothing for men and boys per household, Crete, 1948

Articles of clothing	Households owning (per cent)				Average no. per household owning			
	Communities		Municipalities		Communities		Municipalities	
	Men	Boys	Men	Boys	Men	Boys	Men	Boys
Undershirts	86	36	90	50	2.8	2.9	3.6	3.0
Underpants	91	76	95	75	3.8	3.8	4.9	3.9
Nightgowns	3	—	5	17	1.7	—	1.0	1.0
Pajamas	6	4	21	17	1.0	1.5	1.5	1.0
Shirts or blouses	98	96	90	67	3.6	3.6	3.6	4.0
Suits complete	41	36	74	50	1.4	1.6	1.6	1.0
Jackets	52	36	53	33	1.7	2.2	1.7	2.2
Capes-shawls	41	2	5	—	1.1	1.0	1.0	—
Sweaters	38	42	42	50	1.6	1.6	1.5	2.0
Hats	38	13	37	33	1.6	1.3	1.1	1.0
Overcoats	43	36	58	58	1.2	1.4	1.9	1.3
Raincoats	7	2	21	8	1.0	1.0	1.0	2.0
Stockings	68	29	84	58	3.3	2.7	4.4	3.4
Shoes	46	84	79	92	1.4	1.6	1.3	2.1
Boots	83	29	63	25	1.5	1.5	1.2	1.3
Rubbers	3	2	—	—	1.0	1.0	—	—
Slippers	2	—	5	—	1.0	—	1.0	—
Handkerchiefs	83	40	95	33	3.3	2.6	5.2	3.2
Kerchiefs	38	2	16	—	1.2	2.0	1.0	—
Scarves	8	—	26	—	1.0	—	1.0	—
Gloves	6	4	37	—	1.2	1.0	1.1	—
Umbrellas	18	2	42	—	1.0	1.0	1.0	—
Trousers	100	100	100	100	2.6	3.4	2.3	3.1
Vests	41	13	32	—	1.5	1.8	2.3	—
Ties	16	2	42	8	1.8	3.0	2.2	1.0
Waist belts	46	7	21	—	1.4	1.0	1.2	—
Belts, leather	71	80	84	50	1.2	1.4	1.1	1.7
Aprons	11	—	16	—	1.7	—	2.7	—
Pocketbooks	7	2	21	17	1.0	1.0	1.0	2.0

Source: Sample Survey of Crete, Form J, Inventory.

TABLE A 40. Clothing for women and girls per household, Crete, 1948

Articles of clothing	Households owning (per cent)				Average no. per household owning			
	Communities		Municipalities		Communities		Municipalities	
	Women	Girls	Women	Girls	Women	Girls	Women	Girls
Undershirts	31	13	28	—	2.2	2.4	3.4	—
Underpants	97	93	100	83	4.6	5.8	6.3	8.0
Nightgowns	31	15	64	33	1.8	2.7	2.7	1.5
Pajamas	2	—	8	17	1.0	—	1.0	2.0
Shirts or blouses	48	48	56	67	1.9	3.0	2.5	3.5
Suits complete	16	3	36	—	1.4	1.0	1.0	—
Jackets	58	43	52	—	1.4	1.4	1.6	—
Capes-shawls	15	3	28	—	1.1	1.0	1.4	—
Sweaters	41	45	52	83	1.1	1.5	1.2	1.4
Hats	2	3	—	17	2.0	1.0	—	1.0
Overcoats	46	58	80	83	1.1	1.5	2.4	1.8
Raincoats	—	—	—	17	—	—	—	1.0
Stockings	87	50	76	50	2.5	1.9	3.3	4.0
Shoes	96	100	96	100	2.0	1.9	2.0	2.2
Boots	3	3	—	—	1.0	1.0	—	—
Rubbers	—	—	—	—	—	—	—	—
Slippers	49	8	64	—	1.2	1.3	1.5	—
Handkerchiefs	75	70	92	67	3.3	3.8	4.1	3.2
Kerchiefs	81	20	68	17	1.8	1.4	1.7	1.0
Scarves	2	5	8	—	1.0	1.0	1.5	—
Gloves	4	5	36	50	1.0	1.0	1.2	2.0
Umbrellas	13	—	24	—	1.1	—	1.2	—
Vests	1	3	—	—	1.0	1.0	—	—
Waist belts	2	—	4	—	1.0	—	1.0	—
Belts, leather	11	15	32	17	1.2	1.2	1.1	1.0
Brassières	61	43	68	17	3.0	3.1	3.6	3.0
Slips	87	90	88	67	3.2	3.6	4.3	2.5
Petticoats	30	5	16	—	2.1	2.5	1.2	—
Corsets	4	3	—	17	1.0	1.0	—	1.0
Dresses	97	100	96	83	3.5	4.4	4.3	5.4
Skirts	43	18	56	67	1.5	1.9	2.7	2.0
Aprons	78	28	84	17	1.9	2.3	2.3	1.0
Fur neckpieces	1	—	—	—	1.0	—	—	—
Pocketbooks	28	10	60	17	1.4	1.0	1.7	1.0

Source: Sample Survey of Crete, Form J, Inventory.

TABLE A 41. Rooms per household for living quarters and for storage, Crete, 1948
(percentages of dwellings)

Number of Rooms	Living quarters			Storage		
	Communities	Municipalities	Island	Communities	Municipalities	Island
0	—	—	—	49	92	56
1	22	21	22	41	7	35
2	40	29	38	8	1	7
3	29	26	28	1	—	1
4	8	17	10	1	—	1
5	1	5	2	—	—	—
6	*	1	*	—	—	—
7	—	1	*	—	—	—

* Less than 0.5 per cent.
Source: Sample Survey of Crete, Form A, Household.

TABLE A 42. Kind of windows in dwellings, Crete, 1948
(percentages of dwellings)

Kind of windows	Communities	Municipalities	Island
No windows	7	6	7
Shutters only	67	34	60
Glass	6	17	8
Shutters and glass	15	41	20
Skylight and glass	3	1	3
Open windows	1	—	1
Iron bars, glass and shutters	1	1	1
Total	100	100	100

Source: Sample Survey of Crete, Form A, Household.

TABLE A 43. Kind of roof materials on dwellings, Crete, 1948
(percentages of dwellings)

Type of roof	Communities	Municipalities	Island
Clay	43	13	36
Tile	25	56	30
Concrete	4	11	5
Tile Combination	2	1	2
Clay and Tile	14	2	12
Concrete and Tile	4	6	5
Clay and Concrete	3	2	3
Clay and Wood	1	1	1
Clay and Reeds	1	1	1
Clay and Tile Comb.	1	—	1
Clay Combination	1	—	1
Others	1	7	3
Total	100	100	100

Source: Sample Survey of Crete, Form A, Household.

TABLE A 44. Kind of floor materials in dwellings, Crete, 1948
(percentages of dwellings)

Type of floor	Communities	Municipalities	Island
Earth	46	22	40
Wood	1	17	4
Concrete	7	14	8
Earth and wood	25	9	22
Stone and wood	1	1	1
Concrete and wood	2	22	8
Earth and concrete	7	4	6
Earth and stone	*	—	*
Earth, concrete, and wood	9	3	8
Earth, stone, and wood	1	1	1
Others	1	7	2
Total	100	100	100

* Less than 0.5 per cent.
Source: Sample Survey of Crete, Form A, Household.

TABLE A 45. Method of heating dwelling in cold weather, Crete, 1948
(percentages of dwellings)

Method of heating	Communities	Municipalities	Island
No heat	7	9	8
Fireplace	79	9	65
Brazier	12	79	25
Stove	1	3	1
Fireplace and brazier	1	—	1
Total	100	100	100

Source: Sample Survey of Crete, Form A, Household.

TABLE A 46. Kind of fuel used in households, Crete, 1948
(percentages of households)

Kind of fuel	Communities	Municipalities	Island
Wood	91	19	78
Charcoal	6	56	15
Olive kernels	1	18	5
Olive kernels and charcoal	—	7	1
Olive kernels and wood	1	—	*
Charcoal and wood	1	—	1
Total	100	100	100

* Less than 0.5 per cent.
Source: Sample Survey of Crete, Form A, Household.

TABLE A 47. Sources of water for households, Crete, 1948
(percentages of households)

Source of supply	Communities	Municipalities	Island
Running water in house	2	46	11
Spring	35	29	34
Well	41	13	36
Cistern	11	1	9
Reservoir	3	6	3
Well and spring	1	1	1
Community tap and fountain	6	3	5
Spring and cistern	1	1	1
Stream or river	*	—	*
Total	100	100	100

* Less than 0.5 per cent.
Source: Sample Survey of Crete, Form A, Household.

TABLE A 48. Heating apparatus for cooking meals, Crete, 1948
(percentages of households)

Cooking apparatus	Communities	Municipalities	Island
Do not cook	*	2	1
Do cook	100	98	99
Kind of apparatus used:			
Open fireplace	97	70	92
Kerosene stove	2	17	4
Brazier	*	13	3
Open-fire outside	1	—	1
Fireplace and brazier	*	—	*
Total	100	100	100

* Less than 0.5 per cent.
Source: Sample Survey of Crete, Form A, Household.

TABLE A 49. Sources of specified nutrients in the diet, Crete, 1948
(based on diets of 128 families for one week, fall season)

	Quantity per person per week (pounds)	Contribution of food groups to selected nutrients (%)									
		Ener-gy	Pro-tein	Fat	Cal-cium	Iron	Vit. A	Thia-min	Ribo-flavin	Nia-cin	Ascorbic acid
Cereals	5.4	39	47	5	17	41	*	54	35	56	—
Potatoes	2.5	4	4	*	3	5	1	10	7	8	18
Pulses & nuts	.8	7	17	2	14	22	*	17	11	5	1
Milk & cheese[a]	.7	3	5	5	27	2	4	1	10	7	*
Meat, fish, eggs	1.2	4	19	6	13	11	13	5	14	10	1
Oils & fats	1.3	29	*	79	*	*	2	—	—	—	—
Fruits & olives	4.2	8	3	3	9	11	6	5	8	5	9
Tomatoes & citrus fruits	1.8	1	2	*	2	2	36	3	5	4	33
Vegetables	2.3	2	3	*	15	6	38	5	10	5	38
Sugar	.2	2	*	*	*	—	*	—	—	*	*
Bev.-except milk	.4	1	—	—	—	—	—	—	—	—	—
Total	20.8	100	100	100	100	100	100	100	100	100	100

* Less than 0.5 per cent.
a Milk equivalent figure upon which percentage figures are computed is 17 ounces.
Source: Sample Survey of Crete, Form Ia, Seven-Day Diet.

TABLE A 50. Range, percentiles, median, and mean of daily intake per capita for calories, fats, and eight principal nutrients, 128 households, Crete, Fall 1948 (128 families, 502 people, 512.73 person equivalents—21 meals for the week)

Per-centiles	Energy	Protein	Calcium[a]	Iron	Vitamin A	Absorbic Acid	Thiamin	Niacin	Riboflavin	Fats
	calories	gms	gms	mg	I.U.	mg	mg	mg	mg	gms
Low	829	14.7	.15	5.3	172	13	.57	6.7	.24	39.7
10	2,039	54.2	.25	13.4	1,594	48	1.37	11.9	.56	67.2
20	2,360	62.2	.28	15.6	1,870	56	1.40	15.4	.75	76.8
25	2,435	65.4	.30	16.2	2,078	59	1.56	15.9	.78	81.5
30	2,497	67.4	.33	16.9	2,284	64	1.63	17.9	.87	85.1
40	2,794	71.6	.37	18.5	2,861	78	1.76	19.9	.94	94.5
50	2,954	75.3	.40	21.0	3,286	87	1.88	21.9	1.05	107.2
60	3,097	79.9	.45	21.7	3,935	99	2.03	24.6	1.16	115.6
70	3,343	83.5	.49	23.7	4,524	111	2.20	28.0	1.25	130.4
75	3,473	87.2	.54	25.3	4,815	126	2.33	29.5	1.31	135.3
80	3,661	89.9	.55	25.7	6,053	130	2.43	30.5	1.47	149.3
90	4,087	103.3	.68	30.3	7,888	161	2.82	33.8	1.68	164.5
High	5,707	159.6	1.71	44.9	10,993	320	4.41	51.7	2.75	222.0
Median	2,965	75.3	.40	21.0	3,291	88	1.88	21.9	1.05	107.4
Mean, per consumption unit	2,992	75.9	.43	20.8	4,218	95	1.95	23.0	1.08	—
Mean, per equivalent person	2,547	70.7	.46	20.1	3,853	90	1.65	19.6	.98	107.1
NRC-RDA	2,648	65.1	1.05[a]	11.6	4,564	71	1.27	12.7	1.63	—

a See text Chapter 6 for discussion of calcium content of water and other possible omissions.
Source: Sample Survey of Crete, Form Ia, Seven-Day Diet.

TABLE A 51. Foods consumed during one week, fall 1948, Crete: total quantity[1] used by 128 households; quantity[1] per person, total and from different sources: number and per cent of households using item. 512.73 equivalent persons
(21 meals = 1 person)

Food item	Total grams used by 128 households	Average grams used per equivalent person						Number of households using item	Per cent of households using item
		Total	Purchased at market prices[2]	Obtained from ration	Home produced	Received as gift[2]	Received as pay[2]		
CEREAL PRODUCTS									
Wheat, cracked or flour 95-100 extraction	31,050	60.5	10.2	24.3	16.4	3.2	6.4	36	28.1
Wheat flour, 85 extraction	2,704	5.1	0.3	1.9	2.6	0.3		11	8.6
Barley	701	1.3	*		1.3			2	1.6
Corn starch	29	*	*					1	0.8
Oats	368	0.6	0.6					2	1.6
Rice	14,848	28.8	23.0	2.9		2.6	0.3	50	39.1
Bread and rolls, 85 extraction wheat flour	185,248	361.3	47.0	188.5	108.8	17.0		33	25.8
Bread and rolls, 95-100 extraction wheat flour	482,634	941.4	120.6	188.2	543.4	81.9	7.4	79	61.7
Bread and rolls, barley	109,562	213.8	52.8	15.7	111.4	7.7	26.2	20	15.6
Bread and rolls, barley and wheat (maslin)	53,894	105.0	1.3	35.2	60.8	7.7		7	5.5
Milk buns, sweet rolls	2,384	4.5	1.3		2.9	0.3		5	3.9
Rusks, 85 extraction	10,624	20.8	4.5	8.3	7.4	0.3		6	4.7
Rusks, 95-100 extraction wheat flour	154,288	300.8	37.1	114.6	141.4	1.9	6.1	35	27.3
Rusks, barley	75,466	147.2	26.9	1.9	116.5	4.2		17	13.3
Rusks, barley and wheat (maslin)	48,688	95.0	18.2	1.9	73.9	0.6		10	7.8

Macaroni	56,829	110.7	33.6	60.5	4.2	10.9	1.3	78	60.9
Noodles	8,016	15.7		0.3	14.7	0.6		14	10.9
Hondros	19,328	37.8	2.6		22.4	12.8		33	25.8
POTATOES									
Potatoes	581,475	1,134.1	480.3		572.8	66.2	15.0	118	92.2
SWEETS									
Sugar	46,224	90.2	19.2	66.9		3.8		115	89.8
Honey	1,808	3.5	*		1.6	1.6		7	5.5
Must sirup	1,760	3.2			2.6	0.6		2	1.6
Preserves	368	0.6			*	0.6		6	4.7
Confections, except sweetened chocolate	202	0.3	*			0.3		3	2.3
Sweetened chocolate	416	1.0	1.0					2	1.6
Sweet pastries	2,880	5.4	4.2			1.3		8	6.3
Ginger ale	480	1.0	0.3			0.6		2	1.6
PULSES									
Dry beans, unspecified	44,362	86.4	60.8	0.6	18.9	5.8	0.6	61	47.7
Broad beans	75,280	146.9	41.3	1.0	87.0	14.7	2.6	81	63.3
Lentils	18,608	36.2	13.4	0.6	15.4	5.1	1.6	26	20.3
Split peas	11,904	23.4	1.6		17.9	3.2	0.3	18	14.1
Chick peas	11,216	21.8	8.6		5.1	0.6	7.4	12	9.4
Soya beans, canned	227	0.3				0.3	*	1	0.8
NUTS AND SESAME SEED									
Peanuts, shelled	1,510	2.9			2.6	0.3		4	3.1
Almonds, shelled	893	1.6	1.3		0.3			5	3.9
Chestnuts, shelled	15,456	30.1	19.2		9.9	1.0		11	8.6
Walnuts, shelled	5,142	9.9	2.9		6.4	0.6		15	11.7
Sesame seed	198	0.3	0.3		*	*		6	4.7

TABLE A 51. (Continued). Foods consumed during one week, fall 1948, 128 families, Crete

Food item	Total grams used by 128 households	Average grams used per equivalent person						Number of households using item	Per cent of households using item
		Total	Purchased at market prices[2]	Obtained from ration	Home produced	Received as gift[2]	Received as pay[2]		
DARK GREEN LEAVES									
Dark green leaves, unspecified, chicory, dandelion greens	43,504	84.8	21.4		40.6	22.7		41	32.0
Beet leaves	640	1.3				1.3		1	0.8
Chard	2,560	5.1	5.1					1	0.8
Mustard green	6,080	11.8	3.2		1.3	7.4		5	3.9
Parsley	819	1.6	0.6		0.6	0.3		10	7.8
Radish greens	11,040	21.4			20.2	1.3		5	3.9
Spinach	5,120	9.9	9.9					2	1.6
Vine leaves	64	*				*		1	0.8
Wild herbs	2,880	5.8			4.5	1.3		3	2.3
Cabbage	64,416	125.8	30.4		73.0	21.4	0.6	19	14.8
OTHER FRESH VEGETABLES EXCEPT TOMATOES									
Cauliflower	4,800	9.6	6.4			3.2		3	2.3
Celery	10,576	20.5	12.2		8.0	0.6		12	9.4
Green pepper	6,387	12.5	6.7		5.1	0.6		17	13.3
Okra	13,280	25.9	12.8		7.0	5.8	0.6	24	18.8
Garlic	570	1.3	0.3		0.6	0.3		7	5.5
Leeks	28,406	55.4	23.0		22.1	9.9	0.3	25	19.5
Onions	106,166	207.0	71.7		117.8	12.2	5.1	128	100.0
Radishes	9,094	17.6	12.2		2.6	2.9		10	7.8
Egg plant	32,464	63.4	38.4		17.3	8.0		28	21.9

Mushrooms	960	1.9			1.9	1.9		2	1.6
Vegetable marrow	59,398	115.8	25.6		53.1	35.2	2.2	50	39.1
String beans	136,586	266.2	75.2		152.3	37.8	1.3	77	60.2
FRUITS									
TOMATOES									
Tomatoes	408,909	797.4	329.9		320.0	142.7	5.1	126	98.4
Tomato paste, sun dried	1,520	2.9	1.0		1.9	1.9		8	6.2
CITRUS FRUIT									
Oranges	2,768	5.4	4.5			1.0		2	1.6
Lemons	7,485	14.7	6.1		5.8	2.9		21	16.4
OTHER FRESH FRUIT									
Apples	12,576	24.6	7.0		9.3	8.0		16	12.5
Figs, fresh	4,560	9.0	1.9		3.8	3.2		9	7.0
Grapes	725,958	1,415.7	183.4	24.3	962.2	232.6	13.1	111	86.7
Must (freshly pressed grape juice)	38,912	75.8	75.8		59.2	11.5	5.1	22	17.2
Melons	38,816	75.8	68.8		1.0	5.4		13	10.2
Peaches	15,843	31.0	2.6		15.4	12.8		13	10.2
Pears	15,952	31.0	2.6		26.6	1.9		8	6.2
Pomegranates	52,672	102.7	3.2		57.3	42.6		24	18.8
Prickly pears	4,800	9.3	9.3		9.3	9.3		1	0.8
Quinces	9,456	18.6	0.6		13.8	4.2		13	10.2
DRIED FRUIT									
Figs, dried	2,278	4.5	4.5		18.9	3.2		2	1.6
Raisins	11,382	22.1						8	6.2
MEAT									
Beef	8,160	16.0	15.4			0.6		10	7.8
Tinned meat	1,360	2.6		1.0		1.6		2	1.6

TABLE A 51. (Continued). Foods consumed during one week, fall 1948, 128 families, Crete

Food item	Total grams used by 128 households	Average grams used per equivalent person						Number of households using item	Per cent of households using item
		Total	Purchased at market prices²	Obtained from ration	Home produced	Received as gift²	Received as pay²		
MEAT (cont.)									
Goat, kid	56,528	110.1	75.5		17.6	13.8	3.5	51	39.8
Lamb, mutton	17,114	33.3	26.9			6.4		16	12.5
Pork	12,816	25.0	22.4			2.2	0.3	17	13.3
Veal	2,880	5.8	5.8					2	1.6
Bologna, sausage	1,238	2.6	2.2		0.3		*	6	4.7
Liver	5,568	10.9	7.4		1.0	2.6		9	7.0
Kidneys and other sundries except liver	3,219	6.4	5.4			1.0		6	4.7
GAME AND POULTRY									
Birds	4,032	7.7	2.2		5.8			8	6.2
Rabbit	5,856	11.5			8.0	1.6	1.6	8	6.2
Chicken	15,712	30.7	3.2		25.9	1.6		17	13.3
Turkeys	544	1.0	0.6			0.3		2	1.6
FISH									
Cod, salted & dried	32,464	63.4	55.4	1.6		6.1	0.3	56	43.8
Herring, fresh	1,280	2.6	2.6					2	1.6
Herring, dry and cured	15,744	30.7	26.9			3.5	0.3	48	37.5
Sardines, dry cured	4,918	9.6	9.3			0.3		30	23.4
Sardines, canned in oil	963	1.9		1.6		0.3		3	2.3
Mullet, fresh	2,560	5.1	5.1					3	2.3
Sea bream, fresh	2,944	5.8	3.8			1.9		6	4.7
Smelt, fresh	14,896	29.1	23.0		2.6	3.5		21	16.4

Squid, octopus, and cuttle fish, canned	15,197	29.8	5.8	22.4		1.3		28	21.9
Cuttle fish, fresh	320	0.6				0.6	0.3	1	0.8
Fish, canned, unspecified	214	0.3						1	0.8
SNAILS									
Snails	24,086	47.0	1.3		33.9	11.8		25	19.5
EGGS									
Eggs	26,285	51.2	13.4		33.6	4.2		89	69.5
MILK AND CHEESE									
Goat milk, fresh	79,264	154.6	15.7		129.0		9.9	39	30.5
Yiagourti (yoghurt or culture milk)	1,040	1.9	1.9			*		3	2.3
Sheep milk, fresh	4,480	8.6		0.3	8.6			3	2.3
Dried milk, powdered	224	0.3		40.0				1	0.8
Evaporated milk	30,355	59.2	17.6		8.6	1.6		14	10.9
Cheese, hard	21,754	42.6	31.0			2.2	0.3	54	42.2
Cheese, soft	9,542	18.6	3.8		9.6	4.2	1.3	22	17.2
OIL AND FATS									
Butter, fresh	4,080	8.0	2.9		3.8		1.3	21	16.4
Butter, cooked (ghee)	3,661	7.0	6.4		*	0.3	0.3	23	18.0
Staka (heavy cream, cooked, salted)	358	0.6		0.6	0.6			2	1.6
Margarine	1,261	2.6		0.6		1.9		2	1.6
Meat fat rendered	1,869	3.5	1.6		1.9			8	6.2
Olive oil	292,179	569.9	185.0		353.9	18.2	12.8	128	100.0
OLIVES									
Green olives	3,040	6.1			3.8	2.2	1.0	3	2.3
Ripe olives	32,198	62.7	13.1		42.9	5.8		57	44.5

TABLE A 51. (Continued). Foods consumed during one week, fall 1948, 128 families, Crete

Food item	Total grams used by 128 households	Average grams used per equivalent person						Number of households using item	Per cent of households using item
		Total	Purchased at market prices²	Obtained from ration	Home produced	Received as gift²	Received as pay²		
BEVERAGES, except milk									
Wine	97,053	189.4	47.7		117.8	19.2	4.2	50	39.1
Tsikoudia and ouzo (distilled liquor)	1,078	2.2	1.0		1.0	0.3		5	3.9
Coffee	2,618	5.1	3.2	0.6		1.3		40	31.2
Tea, real	6	*				*		1	0.8
Tea, herb	3,510	6.7	5.1	0.3	1.0	0.6		90	70.3
Cocoa, dry powdered	6	*				*		1	0.8
MISCELLANEOUS									
Seasoning, spices	413	0.6	*		0.6	*		5	3.9
Vinegar	64	*	*					1	0.8

¹ For quantities expressed in grams, 1 gram = 0.0352736 ounces; 1 gram = 0.3125 dramia. Canned items and eggs are sold by the piece; weights used per piece in this study are 1 egg = 44.8 grams or 14 dramia; 1 tin evaporated milk = 411.1 grams or 128.47 dramia (14.5 oz.); 1 tin canned squid = 425.28 grams or 132.9 dramia (15 oz.).

² As commodities or in restaurant meals.

* Food used, but less than 0.1 gram per person per week.

Source: Sample Survey of Crete, Forms I and Ia, Seven-Day Records.

TABLE A 52. Average age at death by sex, rural and urban, Crete, 1946, 1947, 1948[a]

Year	Communities			Municipalities			Total		
	Male	Female	Both	Male	Female	Both	Male	Female	Both
1946	47.6	47.4	47.5	39.3	42.4	40.5	45.4	46.3	45.8
1947	50.0	56.2	53.0	41.4	35.1	37.9	48.1	50.4	49.3
1948	52.4	50.6	51.7	49.9	45.5	47.7	52.0	49.3	50.8
Total of 32 months	49.7	51.2	50.4	42.2	40.2	41.2	48.0	48.5	48.2

[a] First 8 months of 1948.
Source: Sample Survey of Crete, Form C, Community.

TABLE A 53. Households reporting malaria during past year, Crete, September 1948

Nome and Community	Number Households	Number Households having Malaria	Per cent having Malaria	Nome and Community	Number Households	Number Households having Malaria	Per cent having Malaria
KHANIA NOME				Vasiliki	15	4	27
Khania*	56	6	11	Zaros	15	2	13
Yeoryioupolis	14	8	57	Avyeniki	16	1	6
Melidoni	14	1	7	Rogdhia	16	5	31
Neon Khorion	18	9	50	Ay. Varvara	15	5	33
Drapania	15	4	27	Arkalokhori	15	3	20
Elos	13	2	15	Akhendria	13	3	23
Panethimos	11	4	36	Apostoloi	19	1	5
Meskla	13	1	8	Ay. Paraskion	18	5	28
Mournies	14	2	14	Kastamonitsi	14	1	7
Neon Khorion	13	3	23	Kastelli-Ped.	17	5	29
Palaiokhora	11	1	9	Vorroi	17	7	41
Khora-Sfakion	10	0	0	Veneraton	21	5	24
Total	202	41	20	Total	293	63	22
RETHIMNON NOME							
Rethimnon*	17	2	12	LASITHI NOME			
Sellia	16	2	12	Ay. Nikolaos*	6	0	0
Kaloyerou	19	0	0	Ierapetra	16	3	19
Monasteriki	17	2	12	Mournies	16	14	88
Ay. Ioannos	15	4	27	Ay. Yeoryios	16	2	12
Anoyia	13	4	31	Exo Lakonia	25	14	56
Yerani	13	0	0	Kastelli-Fourni	17	0	0
Khromonastiri	13	0	0	Zakros	18	11	61
				Stavrokhori	16	6	38
Total	123	14	11	Sfaka	17	0	0
IRAKLION NOME				Total	147	50	34
Iraklion*	69	12	17				
Kato Viannos	13	4	31	Grand total	765	168	22

* Municipalities.
Source: Sample Survey of Crete, Form A, Household.

TABLE A 54. Sewage disposal methods in Crete, 1948

	Per cent in Communities	Per cent in Municipalities	Per cent in Island
Do not have inside toilet	98	70	92
Have inside toilet	2	30	8
Total	100	100	100
Sewage disposal for those with inside toilet:			
Public sewerage	—	75	56
Cesspool	27	18	20
Pit	33	5	12
No provision	40	2	12
Total	100	100	100

Source: Sample Survey of Crete, Form A, Household.

TABLE A 55. Sanitary body-waste disposal and water source protection for households, Crete, 1948

	Per cent in Communities	Per cent in Municipalities	Per cent in Island
Waste disposal sanitary?			
Yes	7	45	14
No	93	55	86
Total	100	100	100
Water protected?			
Yes	40	90	50
No	60	10	50
Total	100	100	100
Number of households in sample	617	148	765

Source: Sample Survey of Crete, Form A, Household.

TABLE A 56. State and municipal health and hospital expenditures,
Crete, 1947

	Annual Total (dollars)	Per cent of total
STATE HEALTH EXPENDITURES		
Health centers	27,029	4
Malaria control	114,718	18
Other disease control	27,518	5
Total (15 months)	169,265	
Estimate for annual basis	135,000	27
MUNICIPAL HEALTH PROGRAM		
Khania	2,367	
Iraklion	24,137	
	26,504	6
STATE AND MUNICIPAL HOSPITALS		
General hospitals	155,990	31
Leprosariums	87,731	18
Tuberculosis sanitoriums	59,584	12
Mental	26,500	5
Venereal disease	5,609	1
	335,414	67
Total annual expenditures, Ministry of Hygiene and municipalities—health and hospitals[a]	496,918	100

[a] Of this amount, $37,965 was paid from patient income.
Source: W. A. McIntosh, "Public Health Survey of Crete, Greece," The Rockefeller
Foundation, New York, 1949, Tables 4, 16, 17, pp. 89, 194, 195 (unpublished
manuscript).

TABLE A 57. Distance of community households from doctor, priest, elementary school, and gymnasium, Crete, 1948
(percentages of households)

Distance (approximate miles)	Doctor	Priest	Elementary School	Gymnasium
.0- 1.5	34	80	98	10
1.6- 3.0	9	7	2	4
3.1- 4.6	21	10	*	12
4.7- 6.1	8	2	*	8
6.2- 7.7	8	1		12
7.8- 9.2	—			1
9.3-10.8	2			6
10.9-12.3	2			5
12.4-15.4	2			14
15.5-18.5	*			2
18.6-21.6	8			13
21.7-24.8	3			9
24.9-27.9	1			1
28.0-31.0	*			1
31.1-34.1	—			*
34.2-37.2	—			—
37.3-43.4	—			2
43.5-49.7	2			
Total	100	100	100	100

* Less than 0.5 per cent.
Source: Sample Survey of Crete, Form A, Household.

TABLE A 58. Types of water facilities in Crete, 1948[a]

	Communities	Municipalities	Island
Springs	2,454	27	2,481
Common wells:	739	10	749
Capped	123	4	127
Collared	510	10	520
With pump	13	1	14
Common cisterns:	301	14	315
Capped	163	12	175
Collared	72	12	84
With pump	2	2	4
Treated with chemicals	2	6	8
Individual wells	8,882	640	9,522
Individual cisterns	4,292	100	4,392
Villages distributing water	1,430	28	1,458[b]
Villages having aqueducts or pipe	487	19	506
Villages having water distributed to individual homes	26	10	36
Villages reporting:			
Common wells	395	6	401
Common cisterns	183	4	187
Individual wells	866	14	880
Individual cisterns	326	8	334

[a] These are island estimates based on Sample Survey data.
[b] Only 1,405 villages reported in census for 1940.
Source: Sample Survey of Crete, Form C, Community.

TABLE A 59. Highest grade in school completed by adults, Crete, September 1948
(adults are those 21 years old or over)

Highest Year Completed	Communities		Municipalities		Island	
	Per cent Males	Per cent Females	Per cent Males	Per cent Females	Per cent Males	Per cent Females
No education	14.4	45.5	13.0	40.3	14.1	44.5
1	2.1	2.2	1.9	0.5	2.1	1.9
2	3.9	4.1	5.0	3.6	4.1	4.0
3	6.0	6.5	1.9	8.2	5.3	6.8
4	15.2	8.1	14.3	5.6	15.0	7.6
5	3.8	3.7	4.3	1.5	3.9	3.3
6	42.0	27.3	28.5	23.5	39.6	26.6
Total	73.0	51.9	55.9	42.9	70.0	50.2
7	2.3	0.4	3.1	1.0	2.4	0.5
8	2.9	0.5	3.7	2.0	3.1	0.8
9	1.9	0.2	5.0	1.5	2.4	0.5
10	0.7	0.2	1.9	1.5	0.9	0.5
11	0.8	0.6	1.9		1.0	0.5
12	1.9	0.2	8.7	9.8	3.1	2.0
Total	10.5	2.2*	24.3	15.8	12.9	4.8
13	0.5	0.1	1.2	0.5	0.7	0.2
14	1.2	0.2	1.9	0.5	1.2	0.3
15	0.1				0.1	
16	0.1		2.5		0.6	
17	0.1				0.1	
18	0.1		1.2		0.3	
Total	•2.1	0.4*	6.8	1.0	3.0	0.5
Grand total	100.0	100.0	100.0	100.0	100.0	100.0

* Total is correct. Apparent error due to rounding off of figures.
Source: Sample Survey of Crete, Form A, Household.

TABLE A 60. All persons classified as to literacy[a] by age, sex, and residence, Crete, 1948 (percentages)

Age	Communities		Municipalities		Island	
	Males	Females	Males	Females	Males	Females
0- 4	0	0.1	0	0	0	0.1
5- 9	4.9	2.8	2.5	5.5	4.5	3.4
10-14	10.6	7.8	9.5	9.4	10.4	8.1
15-19	7.6	6.8	9.8	11.0	8.0	7.6
20-24	7.6	8.4	9.5	8.1	7.9	8.3
25-29	8.4	6.7	6.2	6.5	8.0	6.7
30-34	6.2	5.3	7.6	6.8	6.5	5.6
35-39	5.0	4.5	4.0	3.6	4.9	4.3
40-44	5.8	2.2	3.6	4.9	5.4	2.7
45-49	4.2	1.3	4.4	2.3	4.2	1.5
50-54	2.7	1.8	4.4	1.9	3.0	1.8
55-59	2.8	1.2	1.8	1.6	2.7	1.3
60-64	2.5	0.8	4.4	1.0	2.8	0.8
65-69	1.8	0.2	3.3	0.3	2.1	0.2
70-74	0.8	0	2.2	0.6	1.0	0.1
75-79	0.9	0	0	0.3	0.7	0.1
80-84	0.1	0.2	0.7	0	0.2	0.1
85-89	0.2	0	0	0	0.2	0
90-94	0.2	0	0.4	0	0.3	0
95-100	0	0	0.4	0	0.1	0
Can read and write	72.3	50.1	74.7	63.8	72.9	52.7
Cannot read and write	27.7	49.9	25.3	36.2	27.1	47.3
Grand total	100.0	100.0	100.0	100.0	100.0	100.0
Number in sample	1,269	1,300	275	308	1,544	1,608

a Literacy defined as those able to read and write.
Source: Sample Survey of Crete, Form A, Household.

TABLE A 61. Years of school completed by heads of households, Crete, 1948
(percentages)

Years Completed	Communities	Municipalities	Island
0	25.6	24.3	25.4
1	2.6	2.0	2.5
2	4.5	5.4	4.7
3	6.2	4.7	5.9
4	15.7	13.5	15.3
5	3.6	4.1	3.7
6	32.7	20.9	30.4
7	2.3	2.0	2.2
8	2.4	4.7	2.9
9	0.8	4.1	1.4
10	0.8	1.4	0.9
11	0.6	2.0	0.9
12	1.0	6.1	2.0
13	0.3	1.4	0.5
14	0.5	0.0	0.4
15	0.0	0.0	0.0
16	0.0	2.0	0.4
17	0.2	0.0	0.1
18	0.2	1.4	0.4
Total	100.0	100.0	100.0
Average Years Completed	4	5	4
Total households	617	148	765

Source: Sample Survey of Crete, Form A, Household.

TABLE A 62. Illiteracy by sex for specified ages, Greece, 1928, and Crete, 1928 and 1948

	Per cent of illiteracy		
	Males	Females	Total
Greece, 1928—8 yrs. and over	24	58	41
Crete, 1928—8 yrs. and over	26	59	43
Crete, 1948—8 yrs. and over	18	40	30
Crete, 1948—10 yrs. and over	16	41	29
Crete, 1948—total population	27	47	37
Crete, 1948—8 yrs. or older			
not completed 4th grade	28	50	40
Crete, 1948—not one school year completed:			
6 yrs. and older	12	34	23
21 yrs. and older	14	44	30
Total population	23	41	32

Source: 1928, Greek census of 1928. 1948, Sample Survey of Crete, Form A, Household.

TABLE A 63. Elementary school enrollment, Crete, 1936 to 1948

School years	Pupils enrolled
1936-37	62,670
1937-38	61,426
1939-40	60,967
1943-44	54,663
1944-45	59,000
1945-46	61,000
1946-47	66,000
1947-48	62,093
1948-49	60,022

Source: M. Sigalis, Chief Inspector, Elementary Education in Crete.

TABLE A 64. Pupils per school and per teacher in public and private high schools, by nomes, Crete, 1936-1937

	Per School			Per Teacher		
Nome	Elem. School	Public High School	Private High School	Elem. School	Public High School	Private High School
Khania	74	201	96	48	23	13
Rethimnon	61	218	—	44	22	—
Iraklion	85	170	215	53	18	16
Lasithi	84	206	—	47	22	—
Average	76	195	155	49	21	15

Source: Ministry of Education, *State Directory for Greece, 1938*, Athens.

TABLE A 65. Elementary schools, classes, teachers, and pupils, Crete, 1936-1937

School	No. of Schools	Classes	Teaching Personnel			Pupils Registered		
			Males	Females	Total	Boys	Girls	Total
KHANIA NOME								
State primary schools	235	1,363	188	176	364	9,720	8,191	17,911
State kindergarten schools	1	1	—	1	1	16	20	36
Private primary schools	2	12	1	2	3	26	23	49
Private kindergarten schools	1	—	—	2	2	16	16	32
Sub-total	239	1,376	189	181	370	9,778	8,250	18,028
RETHIMNON NOME								
State primary schools	171	1,011	129	113	242	5,834	4,866	10,700
State kindergarten schools	1	1	—	1	1	44	40	84
Private primary schools	1	6	—	4	4	21	31	52
Private night schools	1	6	—	—	—	24	—	24
Sub-total	174	1,024	129	118	247	5,923	4,937	10,860
IRAKLION NOME								
State primary schools	265	1,553	183	253	436	11,981	11,083	23,064
State night schools	3	3	—	—	—	200	41	241
Private primary schools	4	21	6	10	16	156	104	260
Private kindergarten schools	3	—	—	5	5	41	20	61
Private night schools	1	6	—	1	1	153	—	153
Sub-total	276	1,583	189	269	458	12,531	11,248	23,779
LASITHI NOME								
State primary schools	115	680	117	92	209	5,264	4,739	10,003
TOTAL	804	4,663	624	660	1,284	33,496	29,174	62,670

Average number pupils per school	78	Per cent of pupils, male		53
Average number pupils per class	13	Per cent of teachers, male		49
Average number pupils per teacher	49			

Source: Ministry of Education, *State Directory for Greece, 1938*, Athens.

TABLE A 66. Secondary schools, classes, teachers, and pupils, Crete, 1936-1937

School	No. of Schools	Classes	Teaching Personnel			Pupils Registered		
			Males	Females	Total	Boys	Girls	Total
KHANIA NOME								
2 class gymnasiums	1	2	2	—	2	54	18	72
Gymnasiums	5	30	48	9	57	935	357	1,292
Practical schools	1	6	12	1	13	178	5	183
Girls high school	1	4	3	3	6	—	151	151
Privately owned secondary schools	4	11	12	3	15	159	53	212
Sub-total	12	53	77	16	93	1,326	584	1,910
RETHIMNON NOME								
2 class gymnasiums	1	2	2	—	2	26	9	35
Urban schools	1	2	4	—	4	29	7	36
Gymnasiums	1	6	7	4	11	—	269	269
Secondary schools	1	6	16	3	19	422	10	432
Sub-total	4	16	29	7	36	477	295	772
IRAKLION NOME								
2 class gymnasiums	1	2	3	—	3	21	5	26
Gymnasiums	5	30	42	6	48	616	314	930
Practical schools	1	6	10	1	11	153	13	166
Girls high school	1	4	2	4	6	—	67	67
Pedagogical academy	1	2	10	—	10	54	22	76
Privately owned secondary schools	2	12	13	4	17	226	84	310
Sub-total	11	56	80	15	95	1,070	505	1,575
LASITHI NOME								
2 class gymnasiums	1	2	2	—	2	42	3	45
Gymnasiums	3	18	26	1	27	450	159	609
Practical schools	1	6	9	1	10	90	33	123
Girls high school	1	4	3	3	6	—	41	41
Sub-total	6	30	40	5	45	582	236	818
TOTAL	33	155	226	43	269	3,455	1,620	5,075

Number pupils per school	154		Per cent of pupils, male	68
Number pupils per class	33		Per cent of teachers, male	84
Number pupils per teacher	19			

Source: Ministry of Education, *State Directory for Greece, 1938*, Athens.

TABLE A 67. Elementary schools, teaching positions, enrollment, and pupils per teacher, Crete, 1947-1948

Nome	No. of schools	No. of teaching positions	No. of teaching vacancies	Pupils enrolled 1947-48	Pupils per teacher on job
KHANIA NOME					
City of Khania	15	63		4,161	66
City of Kastelli-Kisamos	1	4		358	90
Communities	224	308		13,343	43
Sub-total	240	375	22	17,862	48
RETHIMNON NOME					
City of Rethimnon	12	33		1,613	49
City of Anoyia	3	9		479	55
Communities	164	200		8,295	41
Sub-total	179	242	9	10,387	45
IRAKLION NOME					
City of Iraklion	25	75		5,382	72
City of Arkhanais	3	10		504	50
Communities	248	358		18,331	51
Sub-total	276	443	4	24,217	55
LASITHI NOME					
City of Neapolis	7	12		495	41
City of Ay. Nikolaos	1	5		368	74
City of Ierapetra	3	10		812	81
City of Sitia	2	7		463	66
Communities	105	164		7,489	46
Sub-total	118	198	2	9,627	44
TOTAL	813	1,258	37	62,093	51

Source: M. Sigalis, Chief Inspector, Elementary Education in Crete.

TABLE A 68. Secondary schools, teaching positions, enrollment, and pupils per teacher, Crete, 1947-1948

Nome	Teachers needed (organic posts)	Teachers available and assigned	No. of teaching vacancies	Enrollment 1947-1948	Pupils per teacher
KHANIA NOME					
Boys Gym. of Khania	42	26		1,501	58
Girls Gym. of Khania	35	25		1,079	43
Gym. Kastelli (Kisamos)	12	6		388	65
Gym. Palaiokhora (Salinon)	11	5		424	85
Gym. Vamou (Apokoronas)	14	10		389	39
Private Gym. Voukolies (Kisamos)	3	3		89	30
Private Gym. Alikianos (Kydonias)	4	4		100	25
Commercial School of Khania	12	8		194	24
Sub-total	133	87	46	4,164	48
RETHIMNON NOME					
Boys and Girls Gym.	35	35	0	1,626	47
Sub-total	35	35	0	1,626	47
IRAKLION NOME					
Boys Gym. of Iraklion	28	23		989	43
Girls Gym. of Iraklion	27	27		859	32
Gym. of Pombias	12	7		357	51
Gym. of Kastelli Pedhiadhos	14	7		400	57
Gym. of Viannou	12	8		235	29
Private Gym. "Korgis" Sch.	10	10		242	24
Commercial School of Iraklion	13	11		242	22
Sub-total	116	93	23	3,324	36
LASITHI NOME					
Gym. of Neapolis	10	8		654	82
Gym. of Ay. Nikolaos	15	12		337	28
Gym. of Ierapetra	17	12		454	38
Gym. of Sitia	16	10		629	63
Commercial School of Ierapetra	9	3		129	43
Sub-total	67	45	22	2,203	49
TOTAL[a]	351	260	91	11,317	44

[a] A total of 28 public, 3 private, and 3 commercial schools.
Source: Ministry of Education. Mr. Papacharalambos, Chief Inspector, Secondary Education, Crete, 1948.

TABLE A 69. Curriculum in elementary and secondary schools, Crete, 1948

ELEMENTARY SCHOOLS

Studies	\multicolumn{6}{c}{Years or grades in elementary school}					
	1	2	3	4	5	6
Modern Greek	x	x	x	x	x	x
Arithmetic	x	x	x	x	(see below)	
Religious history	x	x	x	x	x	x
History—Greece	x	x	x	x	(see below)	
Geography—Greece	x	x	x	x	(see below)	
Drawing	x	x	x	x	x	x
Handicraft	x	x	x	x	x	x
Gymnastics	x	x	x	x	x	x
Calligraphy (handwriting)		x	x	x	x	x
Natural history			x	x	(see below)	
World & Greek history (see above)					x	x
World & Greek geography (see above)					x	x
Arithmetic—geometry (see above)					x	x
Natural history—zoology, plants (see above)					x	x

SECONDARY SCHOOLS

Studies	\multicolumn{7}{c}{Years or grades in secondary schools or gymnasium[a]}						
	1	2	3	4	5	6	Total
	\multicolumn{7}{c}{(hours or yearly credits)}						
Ancient Greek	7	7	7	7	7	7	42
Modern Greek	3	3	3	3	3	3	18
Latin	2	2	2	2	2	2	12
French	3	3	2	2	2	2	14
English	10	7	7	7	7	5	43
Mathematics	3	3	3	4	4	4	21[b]
Science	3	3	3	3	4	4	20
History	3	3	3	3	3	3	18
Religion	2	2	2	2	2	2	12
Geography	2	2	2	2			8
Psychology					2	2	4
Logic					2	2	4
Sociology					2	2	4
Hygiene		2	2	2	2		8
Music	2	2	2	2	2	2	12
Gymnastics	R	R	R	R	R	R	R
Total hours or credits	40	39	38	39	44	40	240

[a] Corresponding to grades 7 to 12 in the United States.

[b] The inclusion of analytical geometry and similar courses indicates a curriculum comparable to junior college courses in the United States.

Source: Ministry of Education, Khania, 1948.

TABLE A 70. Indexes of resources, living conditions, and economic developments, Crete and five other countries; post-war or late pre-war

Indexes	Crete	Turkey	Brazil	Mexico	Puerto Rico	Haiti
RESOURCES						
Land (1,000 sq.mi.)	3.2	296	3,288	760.4	3.4	10.7
Population (millions)	0.5	19.5	48.5	24.4	2.2	3.6
Per cent of population urban	23			35		
Energy consumed per day (h.p. hrs.)	—		1.9	2.2		0.4
LAND-POPULATION RATIO						
Population per sq.mi.	148	65		32	628	331
Annual rate of population increase	0.9	1.1	1.5	1.8		
Population type[a]	2-3		3	3	3	3
HEALTH						
Crude birth rate	26.1			44.4	42.2	
Crude death rate	10.6			17.3	11.9	
Infant mortality rate	79			105		
Average life expectancy (males) 1948	50-55		39	37		
Physicians per 100,000 population	65		31	51		9
T.B. death rate per 100,000 population	66		250	56		High
FOOD						
Calories per capita per day	2,550		2,173	1,855		
Animal prot. per capita per day (oz.)	0.6		1.1	0.7		
Fats per capita per day (oz.)	3.7		1.8	1.5		
Per cent calories from wheat-potato	40-50	80-90				70-80
SHELTER						
Sq.ft. floor space per capita	97					
No. persons per room	1.8			2.5		
EDUCATION						
Per cent of illiteracy, 1948	29	79	57	52	32	90
Elem. school teachers per 1,000 pop.	2.7		2.0	2.4		0.6
ECONOMY						
Per capita income (1939)	74		46	61		50
Per cent of income for food	73					
Per cent of labor force in:						
Agriculture	57	82	67	68		85
Manufacturing and construction	14	8	10	13		
Transport, commun., commerce	9	5	9	7		
Public admin. professions	14	5	11	4		
Per cent pop. in econ. activity	35	49	35	32		
YIELDS						
Wheat (bu.)	12.8		10.5	11.5		
Potatoes (bu.)	71		93	66		
Rice (bu.)	—		28.6	42.2		
TRANSPORT & COMMUNICATIONS						
Telephones per 1,000 pop.	1	2	5	10	15	0.8
Miles R.R. per 1,000 sq.mi.	0		6	19		14
Motor vehicles per 100,000 pop.	2		4	5		0.8
Annual freight (ton-mile per capita)	—		94	182		
Miles of road per 1,000 sq.mi.	260	81	62	62		96
Miles R.R. per 100,000 pop.	0	24				5

a Population classification according to degree of excess of births over deaths.

Source: Statistical Office, *Statistical Yearbook, 1948*, United Nations, New York, 1949. Department of State, Publication 3719 Economic Series 24, Division of Publications, Office of Publications, 1950. Sample Survey of Crete, Forms A, B, C, Household, Farm, Community.

TABLE A 71. Salaries of teachers and professors, Crete, 1948

ELEMENTARY SCHOOL TEACHERS

Initial (appointment) salary: Secretary B	Drs. 375,000.-
After 4 years of service, he rises to grade Secretary A	" 385,000.-
After 9 years of service (from the date of appointment) he rises to grade Reporter	" 430,000.-
After 15 years of service he gets the grade of Section Chief B, with salary	" 470,000.-
After 20 years of service he rises to grade of Section Chief A, with salary	" 500,000.-

Of this last grade, however, there are only 3,000 posts in Greece, out of 15,000 teachers' posts. Those holding this grade (Chief A) fill the posts of elementary school directors or principals, and elementary school inspectors.

These salaries are increased in accordance with (a) the number of years of service and (b) the matrimonial status of the employee.

Thus: On completion of 10 years of service the teacher gets an increase of 5% on his basic salary. On completion of 15 years he gets another 10%; after 20 years 15% and, on completion of 25 years, he gets 25%.

Also: He gets an increase of 10% on his basic salary for the wife and 5% for each child up to 3 children, and until they become of age, viz.: male children 17 years old and female 18 years old. Maximum salary possible under above grade Chief A is about 842,000 drachmas ($84.20) per month.

GYMNASIUM PROFESSORS (Middle Education)

These are divided into (a) those holding a diploma of a university in Greece or of a corresponding institution abroad, and (b) those not holding such a diploma.

Those holding a diploma begin with the grade of Secretary A' Class, basic salary Drs. 385,000.- and reach in about 20 years' time the grade of Section Chief A' with a basic salary of Drs. 500,000.- to which are added the long service increase and matrimonial increase.

Those having no diploma begin with the grade of Assistant at Drs. 360,000.- and after a lapse of about 25 years, reach the grade of Director B' with a basic salary of Drs. 550,000.- But those posts are comparatively few.

Source: Ministry of Education, Khania, private communication, 1949.

Table A 72. Staff members and recommended reductions in Ministry of Agriculture, Greece, 1948

Divisions and departments	Present number employees	Director-General or Director	Section chief	Re-porter	Secre-tary	Clerk	Usher Char-woman	Other
		Number of positions by rank						
Central service	474	39	60	107	60	104	60	44a
To be abolished	(173)	(11)	(30)	(45)	(23)	(34)	(20)	(10)
Field service								
Area-province	37	10	5	5	2	13	2	—
Nome	738	34	154	218	162	78	16	76a
Experiment station	122	14	31	31	14	3	4	25a
Other	15	5	5	5				
Schools and services								
16 practical schools	52	11	—	7	4	3	2	25a
Forestry	882	18	55	57	446	270	36	
To be abolished	(36)						(36)	
Settlements	28	2	4	6	1	12	3	
Superior School of Agricultureb	65							
Regional topography and								
Macedonian reclamationb	228							
To be abolished	(100)							
Total employees	2,641							

Total positions to be abolished (309) or approximately 12%

a Includes some well-trained technicians.

b Above headings under "positions by rank" not applicable. In the Superior School of Agriculture there are 17 professors, 11 assistant professors, 13 graduate assistants, and 24 junior assistants.

Source: "AMAG Organizational Study of the Ministry of Agriculture," Athens, 1948, pp. 49-59.

TABLE A 73. Dollar exchange rates for Greek drachma, 1915 to 1949
(cents per drachma)

Year	United Nations data[a]	U.S. Department of Commerce data[b]	Federal Reserve Bank data[c]		
			Annual Average	Monthly Daily Average	
				High	Low
1915			19.0862	19.4458	18.9609
1916			19.5296	19.5512	19.4976
1917			19.7837	20.0500	19.4792
1918		19.30	19.4195	19.4500	19.3500
1919		18.70	—	—	—
1920		11.06	—	—	—
1921		5.85	5.0261	6.0642	4.1400
1922		3.30	3.3059	4.5082	1.2337
1923		1.71	1.7141	3.0975	1.0962
1924		1.79	1.7900	2.0091	1.6297
1925			1.5614	1.7926	1.2887
1926			1.2579	1.4349	1.1160
1927			1.3173	1.3430	1.2895
1928	1.305		1.3044	1.3255	1.2924
1929	1.298		1.2934	1.2993	1.2915
1930	1.297		1.2959	1.2976	1.2944
1931	1.292		1.2926	1.2951	1.2879
1932	0.748		0.8320	1.2877	0.5418
1933	0.690		0.7233	0.9053	0.5392
1934	0.923		0.9402	0.9565	0.8949
1935	0.922		0.9386	0.9442	0.9339
1936	0.920		0.9289	0.9509	0.8935
1937	0.898		0.9055	0.9157	0.8951
1938	0.888		0.8958	0.9190	0.8559
1939	0.800		0.8153	0.8586	0.7157
1940	0.661		0.6715	0.7176	0.6270
1941	—				
1942	—				
1943	—				
1944	0.667[D]	(Stabilization Law of 1944 provided for exchange of			
1945	0.200[D]	50 billion old drachmas for one new drachma)			
1946	0.020[D]				

TABLE A 73. (continued)

Year	United Nations data[a]	U.S. Department of Commerce data[b]	Federal Reserve Bank data[c]		
			Annual Average	Monthly Daily Average	
				High	Low
1947	0.020				
	0.010	(with certificates of exchange)			
1948	0.0200				
	0.0104	(with certificates of exchange)			
1949	0.0200				
	0.0100	(with certificates of exchange—before devaluation)			
	0.0067	(with certificates of exchange—after devaluation)			
1950	0.0200				
	0.0067	(with certificates of exchange)			

p Figures relate to part of year only.

Sources: a Statistical Office of the United Nations, *Statistical Yearbook, 1948*, New York, 1949, Table 140, p. 374.

Statistical Office of the United Nations, *Monthly Bulletin of Statistics*, New York, vol. IV, no. 12, p. 166, Table 53, December 1950.

b Bureau of Domestic and Foreign Commerce, *Report for April 3, 1926*, U.S. Department of Commerce.

c Board of Governors of the Federal Reserve System, *Banking and Monetary Statistics*, Washington, 1943, Table no. 173, p. 671.

TABLE A 74. Average land value per farm and per acre, by nomes, Crete, 1948

Nome	Value of farm	Value per acre
Khania	$ 5,730	$ 615
Rethimnon	3,025	469
Iraklion	6,291	708
Lasithi	6,142	490
Island	5,455	591

Source: Sample Survey of Crete, Form B, Farm.

TABLE A 75. Estimated number of farms, sub-farms, and acreage, Crete, 1948

	Number	Total Acres	Average Acres
Farms	51,900	479,550	9.2
Sub-farms	40,350	58,530	1.5
Island	92,250	538,080	5.8

Source: Sample Survey of Crete, Form B, Farm, and Form A, Household.

TABLE A 76. Value of tools and equipment per farm, Crete, 1948

Value (dollars)	Farms with tools and equipment	
	Number	Per cent
0- 9	95	27
10- 19	94	27
20- 29	68	20
30- 39	32	9
40- 49	10	3
50- 59	18	5
60- 69	3	1
70- 79	3	1
80- 89	2	1
90- 99	0	—
100-149	7	2
150-199	1	*
200-249	4	1
250-299	1	*
300-349	3	1
350-399	2	1
400-499	2	1
1,000 and over	1	*
Total	346	100
Average per farm, dollars 32		

* Less than 0.5 per cent.
Source: Sample Survey of Crete, Form B, Farm.

TABLE A 77. Estimated number of special pieces of equipment, Crete, 1948

	Number
Tractors	17
Tractor plows	17
Drills	19
Sprayers	11,882
Hammermills	335
Grape pressers	85
Olive crushers	2,414
Oil pressers, hand machines	2,202
Oil pressers, power machines	391
Distillators, grade A	21
Distillators, grade B	30

Source: Sample Survey of Crete, Form C, Community.

TABLE A 78. Land mortgage status of farmers, Crete, 1948

Mortgage status	Number of farms	Per cent
Never owned land	11	3
Had mortgage on Sept. 1, 1948	13	4
Had mortgage previously	28	8
Never had mortgage	305	88
Total owning land	335	97
Total farms in sample	346	100

Source: Sample Survey of Crete, Form B, Farm.

TABLE A 79. Chattel loan status of farmers, Crete, 1948

Amount of loan (dollars)	Farms with chattel loans	
	Number	Per cent
0- 19	42	21
20- 39	50	24
40- 59	33	17
60- 79	9	5
80- 99	6	3
100-119	15	8
120-139	8	4
140-159	13	6
200-219	10	5
240-259	4	2
280-299	1	1
300-319	4	2
400-419	3	2
Total	198	100
Total sample	346 farms	
Average loan reported	$72	
Average for all farms	$41	

Source: Sample Survey of Crete, Form B, Farm.

TABLE A 80. Size of farms and sub-farms, Crete, 1929 and 1948
(percentages)

Size groups[a] (approximate acres)	All farms 1929	All farms and sub-farms 1948	Farms only 1948
0.2- 2.4	44.5	47.3	15.0
2.5- 4.9	22.9	15.8	22.4
5.0- 7.4	11.9	11.0	18.5
7.5- 9.9	6.8	7.6	13.3
10.0- 12.4	4.0	4.1	6.6
12.5- 14.9	2.6	5.0	8.7
15.0- 17.4	1.6	1.8	2.9
17.5- 19.9	1.1	1.8	3.2
20.0- 22.4	0.8	0.9	1.7
22.5- 24.9	0.6	—	—
25.0- 49.9	2.1	3.7	6.2
50.0-250.0	1.8	1.0	1.5
250.0 and over	0.1	*	*
Total	100.8[b]	100.0	100.0
Total number of farms	87,954	92,250	51,900

* No farms of this size were included in sample.

a Size groups for 1929 are not quite comparable as class interval upper limits were 0.25 acre higher than in 1948, but the same general distribution of size groups is indicated.

b Error of 0.8 per cent due to cumulative decimals.

Source: Ministry of National Economy (République Ministère de l'Economie Nationale) *Statistique Générale de la Grèce,* sec. B, Recensement agricole et d'élévage de la Grèce, 1929, data supplied by C. A. Doxiadis. Sample Survey of Crete, Form A, Household, and Form B, Farm, combined.

TABLE A 81. Farms with specified number of lots, Crete, 1948

Number of Lots	Number of Farms	Per cent
1- 4	54	16
5- 9	93	27
10-14	86	25
15-19	50	14
20-24	26	8
25-29	7	2
30-34	16	5
35-39	0	—
40-44	5	1
45-49	3	1
50-59	4	1
60-64	1	*
80-84	1	*
Total	346	100
Average number lots per farm	12.7	
Average number acres per lot	0.72	

* Less than 0.5 per cent.
Source: Sample Survey of Crete, Form B, Farm.

TABLE A 82. Minutes required to walk to the farthest lot and nearest lot, Crete, 1948

Minutes	Farthest Lot		Nearest Lot	
	Number of Farms	Per cent	Number of Farms	Per cent
0- 10	10	3	250	73
11- 20	27	8	72	21
21- 30	56	16	15	4
31- 40	4	1	3	1
41- 50	20	6	1	*
51- 60	75	22	4	1
61- 70	1	*	0	—
71- 80	6	2	0	—
81- 90	34	10	1	*
91-100	3	1	0	—
111-120	55	16	0	—
121-130	1	*	0	—
141-150	13	4	0	—
171-180	17	5	0	—
191-200	1	*	0	—
231-240	4	1	0	—
291-300	13	4	0	—
351-360	4	1	0	—
411-420	1	*	0	—
591-600	1	*	0	—
Total	346	100	346	100

Average number of minutes to farthest lot	89
Average number of minutes to nearest lot	10

* Less than 0.5 per cent.
Source: Sample Survey of Crete, Form B, Farm.

TABLE A 83. Days worked annually by farm operators and families, Crete, 1948 (percentages)

Number of Days	Operator		Family	
	Days worked	Full days worked	Days worked	Full days worked
		(percentages)		
1- 49	9	18	16	30
50- 99	7	16	16	24
100-149	12	15	18	20
150-199	10	24	8	13
200-249	18	15	19	7
250-299	20	7	11	4
300-349	14	4	5	—
350-399	10	1	5	1
500-549	—	—	1	1
600-649	—	—	1	—
Total	100	100	100	100
Number of cases	315	301	274	264
Average days per year per farm reporting	201	133	152	92
Average days per year all farms	183	115	121	70

Source: Sample Survey of Crete, Form B, Farm.

TABLE A 84. Percentage of land area in major soil types, Crete, 1939

Soil type	Per cent
SOILS ON LIMESTONE, CONTAINING CaCO$_3$ AND SATURATED WITH BASES	*85*
1. Light colored soils on marls	10
2. Dark grey and light colored soils mixed with red earth	11
3. Dark grey soils mixed with gravel	7
4. Red soils and pebble mixed soils, originating from erosion and decomposition of limestone rock formations	52
5. Mesozoic (secondary) red soils originating from limestones	3
6. Alluvial deposits or alluvial formations	2
7. Saline soils (less than ½ of 1 per cent located in 3 areas)	—
SOILS ON ROCK FORMATIONS NOT CONTAINING CaCO$_3$ AND NOT SATURATED WITH BASES	*15*
8. Red soils and pebble mixed soils, originating from erosion and decomposition of schist rock formations	13
9. Mesozoic (secondary) red soils	1
10. Washed, usually acid soils of the carst valleys	1

Source: "The Soils of the Isle of Crete" by K. Nevros and I. Zvorykiu, 1939. Approximate percentages computed from map.

TABLE A 85. Amounts of phosphorus and potassium in soil samples, by nomes, Crete (percentages)

Category[a]	Khania	Rethimnon	Iraklion	Lasithi
For P_2O_5				
Rich (4.5 and up)	20	15	24	19
Average (3.0-4.4)	29	19	27	27
Poor (1.5-2.9)	30	27	35	38
Very poor (0-1.4)	21	39	14	16
For K_2O				
Rich (24.1 and up)	72	79	96	88
Average (15.0-24.0)	18	15	3	7
Poor (7.0-14.9)	9	5	1	5
Very poor (0-6.9)	1	1	—	—
TOTAL NUMBER OF SAMPLES	208	233	410	95

[a] Category determined by contents in milligrams per 100 grams of soil according to Neubauer test.

Source: *Institute of Chemistry and Agriculture* by N. Kavelopoulos.

TABLE A 86. Application rates of plant nutrients in Greece and Crete, pre-war

District	Plant nutrients (pounds per acre)
Crete	31.2
Ionian Islands	11.6
Peloponnesus	11.3
Cyclades	8.3
Aegean Islands	7.2
Central Greece and Euboea	5.4
Thessaly	1.5
Macedonia, Thrace	1.3
Epirus	0.5
All Greece	3.3

Source: *Report of FAO Mission for Greece*, 1946, Appendix D, Table 3, p. 135.

TABLE A 87. Types of rotations on farms, Crete, 1948

Types of rotations				Per cent of all farms reporting rotation of any type	Per cent of all farms reporting same period of rotation
2 YEAR ROTATIONS					
Cereal	Cereal			4.9	52
Cereal	Hay			0.3	4
Cereal	Fallow			3.2	33
Pulses	Cereal			1.0	11
Total				9.4	100
3 YEAR ROTATIONS					
Cereal	Cereal	Cereal		18.2	43
Cereal	Cereal	Pulses		2.1	5
Cereal	Cereal	Hay		0.7	2
Cereal	Cereal	Fallow		16.5	38
Cereal	Hay	Cereal		1.0	2
Cereal	Pulses	Pulses		0.3	1
Cereal	Pulses	Fallow		1.4	3
Cereal	Hay	Pulses		0.7	2
Cereal	Fallow	Cereal		1.0	2
Cereal	Vegetable	Fallow		0.3	1
Pulses	Cereal	Fallow		0.3	1
Total				42.5	100
4 YEAR ROTATIONS					
Cereal	Cereal	Cereal	Cereal	1.0	3
Cereal	Cereal	Cereal	Pulses	1.4	4
Cereal	Cereal	Cereal	Hay	3.2	8
Cereal	Cereal	Cereal	Fallow	22.6	59
Cereal	Cereal	Pulses	Hay	0.3	1
Cereal	Cereal	Pulses	Fallow	1.4	4
Cereal	Cereal	Hay	Cereal	1.0	3
Cereal	Cereal	Hay	Fallow	2.8	7
Cereal	Cereal	Fallow	Pulses	0.7	2
Cereal	Cereal	Fallow	Fallow	1.4	4
Cereal	Pulses	Cereal	Fallow	0.6	2
Cereal	Hay	Fallow	Cereal	0.3	1
Cereal	Hay	Fallow	Pulses	0.3	1
Vegetable	Vegetable	Pulses	Vegetable	0.3	1
Total				37.3	100

Table A 87. (continued)

Types of rotations					Per cent of all farms report- ing rotation of any type	Per cent of all farms reporting same period of rotation
5 Year Rotations						
Cereal	Cereal	Cereal	Cereal	Fallow	1.4	13
Cereal	Cereal	Cereal	Pulses	Fallow	1.0	10
Cereal	Cereal	Cereal	Hay	Fallow	1.4	14
Cereal	Cereal	Cereal	Fallow	Pulses	0.3	3
Cereal	Cereal	Cereal	Fallow	Fallow	2.2	20
Cereal	Cereal	Hay	Pulses	Pulses	0.3	3
Cereal	Cereal	Fallow	Fallow	Fallow	0.7	6
Cereal	Hay	Cereal	Cereal	Pulses	0.3	3
Cereal	Fallow	Cereal	Hay	Pulses	0.3	3
Pulses	Cereal	Cereal	Cereal	Fallow	2.2	19
Vegetable	Cereal	Cereal	Cereal	Fallow	0.7	6
Total					10.8	100
TOTAL					100.0	

Source: Sample Survey of Crete, Form B, Farm.

TABLE A 88. Trees and vines per stremma (0.2471 acre) in sample communities, Crete, 1948 (estimates by community presidents)

Comm. No.[a]	Number of trees per stremma					Grape vines per stremma		
	Olives	Tangerines	Lemons	Citrons	Oranges	Table	Wine	Sultana
1	20				40		900	250
2	10						800	
3	11	50			50		1,000	
4	20		68		68		800	330
5	15						750	
6	15		25		25		800	400
7	14	50	35	60	40	450	800	300
8	12			100	50		800	300
9	10	50			40	550	800	550
10	30	50	40		40	300	400	300
11	10	65	65		40		1,200	
12	20							
13	15			65			2,000	
14	5						1,500	
15	7						1,000	325
16	15						650	500
17	20						600	300
18	25						600	
19	15				25		600	450
20	12	65	65	60	65	300	400	250
21	20	50	40	40	40		300	
22	10						200	170
23	12						400	350
24	10	20	20		25	350	350	240
25	15	100	100	100	100	250	450	250
26	9					480	750	300
27	8	15	15		15	400	500	400
28	—						300	
29	15					240	300	180
30	12					230	300	200
31	30						800	400
32	22					300	800	300
33	7	40	40		40		650	250
34	10	25	25		25	300	300	300
35	14	50	40	50	40	350	300	250

TABLE A 88. (continued)

Comm. No.[a]	Number of trees per stremma					Grape vines per stremma		
	Olives	Tangerines	Lemons	Citrons	Oranges	Table	Wine	Sultana
36	10	25	25		25	250		280
37	20	100	100	100	100		300	150
38	—						200	
39	12						800	
40	12					600	800	300
41	10						500	
42	20	35	35	40	30	120	250	100
43	15	100	65	50	75	500	700	200
44	20	*	*	*	*		400	300

* Negligible number of scattered fruit trees.

a Comm. No. corresponds to community number and name in Table A 9 above.

Source: Sample Survey of Crete, Form C, Community.

TABLE A 89. Percentage of farms with normal yields per tree of olive oil and oranges, Crete, 1947-1948[a]

Olive oil		Oranges	
Normal yield (okes)	% of farms	Normal yield (pounds)	% of farms
0 - .9	4	0 - 2.8	25
1.0- 1.9	15	2.8- 5.6	1
2.0- 2.9	31	5.6- 8.5	2
3.0- 3.9	21	8.5- 11.3	2
4.0- 4.9	12	11.3- 14.1	1
5.0- 5.9	12	14.1- 16.9	4
6.0- 6.9	1	16.9- 19.7	1
7.0- 7.9	1	19.7- 22.6	1
8.0- 8.9	1	22.6- 25.1	4
10.0-10.9	2	28.2- 31.0	20
11.0-19.9	*	31.0- 56.4	14
20.0-29.9	*	56.4- 84.6	14
30.0-39.9	—	84.6-112.8	6
40.0-51.0	—	112.8-143.8	5
Total	100		100
Number of cases	335		95

* Less than 0.5 per cent.
a "Normal" yields based on farmer estimates for past five years.
Source: Sample Survey of Crete, Form B, Farm.

TABLE A 90. Farmer estimates of average reduction in olive oil yields due to dacus fly infestation, Crete

Yield reduction (per cent)	Percentage of farms
none	2
1- 9	1
10-19	5
20-29	11
30-39	13
40-49	5
50-59	40
60-69	9
70-79	9
80-89	4
90-99	1
Total	100
Have dacus fly, in percentage	98
Average reduction in yield, in percentage	43.9
Total number of farms in sample reporting	335

Source: Sample Survey of Crete, Form B, Farm.

TABLE A 91. Opinion and practice of farmers in pruning olive trees, Crete, 1948 (percentage of farmers saying olive trees should be pruned at given intervals, and that they had last pruned their trees given number of years ago)

Years	Should prune	Did prune
never	2	26
1	16	19
2	16	12
3	23	6
4	12	3
5	13	8
6	5	5
7	1	—
8	1	3
9	—	—
10	8	13
12	—	1
13	—	—
15	1	2
20	2	1
25-40	—	1
Total	100	100
Number of farmers in sample reporting	335	335

Source: Sample Survey of Crete, Form B, Farm.

TABLE A 92. Table, wine, and raisin grape vines per farm, Crete, 1948

Vines (number)	Farms with grape vines (per cent)		
	Table	Wine	Raisin
0- 249	48	13	19
250- 499	26	19	22
500- 749	10	14	21
750- 999	4	6	12
1,000- 1,249	4	10	7
1,250- 1,499	—	4	3
1,500- 1,749	4	11	6
1,750- 1,999	—	2	—
2,000- 2,249	—	5	1
2,250- 2,499	2	1	2
2,500- 2,749	—	4	3
2,750- 2,999	—	1	—
3,000- 3,999	—	3	3
4,000- 4,999	—	5	—
5,000-20,000	2	2	1
Total	100	100	100
Per cent of sample farms having	15	87	30

Source: Sample Survey of Crete, Form B, Farm.

TABLE A 93. Domestic and nomadic sheep and goats per farm and sub-farm, Crete, September 1, 1948[a]

Animals (number)	Per cent of Farmers with	
	Sheep and Lambs	Goats and Kids
1	40.1	65.5
2	21.9	20.2
3	9.4	5.7
4	9.8	2.6
5	2.7	0.8
6	1.8	0.3
9	1.3	0.3
10	1.8	1.0
11	0.4	0.3
12	0.4	0.3
13	0.4	—
15	1.3	0.3
16	0.4	—
18	0.4	—
20	2.7	0.8
25	0.9	—
26	0.4	—
30	0.9	—
40	0.9	—
50	0.4	0.8
60	0.9	0.3
70	—	0.5
100	0.4	
130	—	0.3
180	0.4	
Total	100.0	100.0
Number of farms in sample reporting	176	265
Number of sub-farms in sample reporting	48	122

[a] Includes lambs and kids, for both farms and sub-farms.
Source: Sample Survey of Crete, Form A, Household, and Form B, Farm, combined.

TABLE A 94. Size of poultry flocks on farms and sub-farms, Crete, 1948

Head (number)	Per cent of Households with Poultry		
	Farms	Sub-Farms	Island
1- 5	42	66	49
6-10	35	23	31
11-15	11	7	10
16-20	10	2	8
21-25	1	—	1
26-30	1	2	1
31-35	*	—	*
36-40	*	—	*
41-45	*	—	*
46-50	*	—	*
Total	100	100	100
Number of farms and sub-farms reporting	327	130	457

* Less than 0.5 per cent.
Source: Sample Survey of Crete, Form A, Household, and Form B, Farm, combined.

TABLE A 95. Types of cooperatives by nomes, Crete, 1948

Type of cooperative	Khania	Rethimnon	Iraklion	Lasithi	Island Total
Credit	85	107	179	56	427
Sultana raisin	23	—	—	1	24
Olive	24	15	38	31	108
Wine	61	—	2	—	63
Cheese	8	4	8	2	22
Citron	14	—	36	—	50
Purchase and rent land	1	—	—	—	1
Bees	1	1	—	1	3
Fishing	4	1	2	4	11
Land amelioration	15	—	—	1	16
Not defined	4	—	—	—	4
Total	240	128	265	96	729
Number of household heads, members	17,181	10,600	25,000	8,220	61,001

Source: From information supplied by nome agriculturists and Agriculture Bank Directors by letters.

TABLE A 96. Value of farm products marketed, Crete, 1948

Value (dollars)	Farms reporting products marketed	
	Number	Per cent
1- 124	164	55
125- 249	53	17
250- 374	40	13
375- 499	13	4
500- 624	18	6
625- 749	5	2
750- 874	4	1
875- 999	4	1
1,000-1,124	2	1
1,500 or more	1	*
Total	304	100

Do not market, 42 farms
Average value per farm reporting, $194; average value for all farms, $170

Source: Sample Survey of Crete, Form B, Farm.

TABLE A 97. Number of trips made to market each year, Crete, 1948

Trips (number)	Farms reporting trips to market	
	Number	Per cent
1- 5	193	64
6-10	53	18
11-15	16	5
16-20	12	4
21-25	3	1
26-30	13	4
40-50	4	1
50-60	6	2
80	1	*
100	1	*
200 or more	2	1
Total	304	100
Do not market	42	
Average per farm reporting	10	
Average for all farms	8	

* Less than 0.5 per cent.
Source: Sample Survey of Crete, Form B, Farm.

TABLE A 98. Field crop sales by farms and sub-farms, Crete, 1947

	Farms and sub-farms		
Crop	Raising (number)	Selling (per cent)	Quantity sold per farm selling (cwt.)
Wheat	263	5	4.1
Barley	217	9	6.4
Oats	161	10	4.0
Maslin	79	1	1.4
Sesame	5	40	1.2
Peanuts	19	74	2.7
Alfalfa	3	33	84.7
Pulses	237	2	4.2
Vetch	85	6	2.9
Bitter vetch	57	1	2.0
Other feed crops	10	10	2.8
Cereals (unspecified)	16	6	2.7
Total households in sample	346		

Source: Sample Survey of Crete, Form A, Household, and Form B, Farm.

TABLE A 99. Tree crop sales by farms and sub-farms, Crete, 1947

Crop	Farms and sub-farms		
	Raising (number)	Selling (per cent)	Quantity sold per household and farm selling (cwt.)
Olives	504	33	6.9
Oranges	100	37	18.8
Tangerines	45	27	9.2
Lemons	57	16	13.8
Citrons	2	50	1.6
Figs	166	36	1.0
Apricots	56	14	1.4
Peaches	35	6	1.6
Cherries	11	36	1.8
Plums	45	4	1.7
Pears	189	2	3.2
Apples	42	2	0.7
Quinces	66	3	1.4
Bananas	15	20	11.7
Almonds	131	7	4.4
Walnuts	79	5	0.5
Pistachios	2	50	4.2
Carobs	173	51	21.0
Acorns	11	9	11.3
Mulberries	41	—	—
Chestnuts	15	66	15.5
Others	8	50	9.5
Total households in sample	765		

Source: Sample Survey of Crete, Form A, Household, and Form B, Farm, combined.

TABLE A 100. Transportation used by farmers on market trips, Crete, 1948

Mode of Transportation	Farms reporting trips to market	
	Number	Per cent
Pack animal	152	50
Animal drawn vehicle	4	1
Motor truck	81	27
Pack animal and boat	7	2
Pack animal and motor truck	46	15
Pack man	1	1
Pack animal, animal drawn vehicle, and motor truck	3	1
Animal drawn vehicle and motor truck	10	3
Total	304	100
Do not market	42	

Source: Sample Survey of Crete, Form B, Farm.

TABLE A 101. Hours required by farmers to reach market, Crete, 1948

Hours	Farms reporting time required to reach market	
	Number	Per cent
0 - .9	56	18
1.0- 1.9	99	33
2.0- 2.9	76	25
3.0- 3.9	34	11
4.0- 4.9	9	3
5.0- 5.9	11	4
6.0- 6.9	9	3
7.0- 7.9	6	2
8.0- 8.9	3	1
9.0- 9.9	0	—
10.0-10.9	1	*
Total	304	100
Do not market	42	
Average hours for all farms	1.8	
Average hours per farm reporting	2.0	

* Less than 0.5 per cent.
Source: Sample Survey of Crete, Form B, Farm.

TABLE A 102. Labor, power, and daily production for eleven raisin factories, Iraklion, Crete, 1948

Raisin factory	Daily production, tons per 8 hrs.	Horse-power	Laborers and employees	Horse-power per ton	Employees per ton
A	60	110	360	1.8	6.0
B	30	70	180	2.3	6.0
C	20	65	13	3.2	0.6
D	16	60	15	3.8	0.9
E	15	60	50	4.0	3.3
F	6	47	8	7.8	1.3
G	15	45	82	3.0	5.5
H	6	25	10	4.2	1.7
I	10	25	53	2.5	5.3
J	6	20	8	3.3	1.3
K	9	18	8	2.0	0.9
Total	193	545	787	2.8[a]	4.1
Average	17.5	49.6	72	3.4	3.0

[a] Weighted average.

Source: Chamber of Industry and Commerce of Iraklion, ref. no. 3704, pp. 2-3.

TABLE A 103. Daily output, power, and labor for selected industries, Iraklion, Crete, 1947

Industry	Plant	Output, tons per 8 hrs.	Input	
			Horse-power	No. employees
Pyrini oil factory	A	25	25	20
Olive oil refinery	A	5	65	5
	B	4	35	5
Soap factory	A	2	30	13
	B	1	2	4
	C	3.8	2	4
Carob mills	A	7	20	5
(tons ground carobs)	B	6.4	12	2
	C	5	6	3
	D	7	25	4
Flour mills	A	16	325	21
	B	5.5	95	11
Macaroni	A	3	20	10
	B	4.2	66	16
Alcohol	A	1	180	20
Tanneries	A	.3	35	20
	B	.3	45	15
Woodworking	A		25	15
	B		35	15
	C		33	8
	D		15	10
	E		25	24
	F		15	24

Source: Chamber of Industry and Commerce of Iraklion, ref. no. 3704, pp. 2-3.

TABLE A 104. Quantity and percentage of principal exports, Iraklion
(1936-1940 average)

	Abroad		Interior		Total	
	Quantity (metric tons)	% Total exports	Quantity (metric tons)	% Total exports	Quantity (metric tons)	% Total exports
GRAPES-RAISINS, WINE						
Sultana raisins	13,080		753		13,833	
Tochta "	2,280		880		3,160	
Total	15,360	39.7	1,633	4.3	16,993	44.0
Wine	3,816		2,334		6,150	
Grape must	7		117		124	
Total	3,823	9.9	2,451	6.3	6,274	16.2
Table grapes	5,146	13.3	49	0.1	5,195	13.4
Total vineyards	24,329	62.9	4,133	10.7	28,462	73.6
OLIVE OIL						
Olive oil	3,204		1,412		4,616	
Olive residue oil	239		225		464	
Soap	34		620		654	
Olive residue			1,011		1,011	
Total	3,477	9.0	3,268	8.4	6,745	17.4
CAROB BEANS	691	1.8	374	1.0	1,065	2.8
OTHER FRUIT						
Fresh fruit	74		19		93	
Citrus fruit in brine	389		13		402	
Total	463	1.2	32	0.1	495	1.3
TOBACCO LEAF	—	0.0	162	0.4	162	0.4
FIREWOOD	27	0.1	48	0.1	75	0.2
SAGE ARIGAMAN	58		6		64	
HIDES	31		20		51	
Total	89	0.2	26	0.1	115	0.3
OTHER	273	0.7	1,272	3.3	1,545	4.0
TOTAL EXPORTS	29,349	75.9	9,315	24.1	38,664	100.0

Source: Iraklion Chamber of Commerce and Industry, protocol no. I-1548, May 6, 1948.

TABLE A 105. Quantity and percentage of principal imports, Iraklion, 1936-1940 average

	Abroad		Interior		Total	
	Quantity (metric tons)	% Total imports	Quantity (metric tons)	% Total imports	Quantity (metric tons)	% Total imports
FOOD ITEMS						
Wheat	6,480		2,720		9,200	
Sugar	977		80		1,057	
Rice	737		222		959	
Coffee	134		10		144	
Salt	0		533		533	
Dried codfish	4		291		295	
Olive oil	0		145		145	
Tomato paste	0		271		271	
Olives	0		31		31	
Macaroni	0		42		42	
Flours	1		1,081		1,082	
Total	8,333	16.0	5,426	10.4	13,759	26.4
BUILDING AND CONSTRUCTION MATERIALS						
Gypsum			798		798	
Iron	462		453		915	
Lumber	9,151		0		9,151	
Timber	143		423		566	
Asphalt	139		13		152	
Cement	0		4,081		4,081	
Tiles	0		1,453		1,453	
Total	9,895	19.0	7,221	13.9	17,116	32.9
INSECTICIDES AND CHEMICALS						
Sulphur	1,244		184		1,428	
Molasses	383		0		383	
Chemical products	41		228		269	
Sulphate or copper	148		74		222	
Total	1,816	3.5	486	0.9	2,302	4.4
FERTILIZERS			4,995	9.6	4,995	9.6

TABLE A 105. (continued)

	Abroad		Interior		Total	
	Quantity (metric tons)	% Total imports	Quantity (metric tons)	% Total imports	Quantity (metric tons)	% Total imports
FUEL, BENZINE, AND NAPHTHA						
Coal	793		1,887		2,680	
Lighting kerosene	124		362		486	
Benzine	272		654		926	
Naphtha	0		1,695		1,695	
Total	1,189	2.3	4,598	8.8	5,787	11.1
RAISINS AND CURRANTS FOR RE-EXPORT						
Korynthos raisins	—		508		508	
Sultana raisins of Crete	—		599		599	
Currants	—		646		646	
Total	—	0.0	1,753	3.4	1,753	3.4
HIDES AND LEATHER						
Hides	32		0		32	
Leather	0		126		126	
Total	32	0.1	126	0.2	158	0.3
CARS, SPARE PARTS, AND AGR. IMPL.						
Cars and spare parts	23		83		106	
Agr. implements	1		28		29	
Total	24	0.0	111	0.2	135	0.2
TOBACCO AND CIGARETTES	—	0.0	191	0.4	191	0.4
PAPER WARE	6	0.0	347	0.7	353	0.7
Total above imports	21,295	40.9	25,254	48.5	46,549	89.4
Others (114 items)					5,521	10.6
GRAND TOTAL					52,070	100.0

Source: Iraklion Chamber of Commerce and Industry, protocol no. I-1548, May 6, 1948.

TABLE A 106. Quantity and value of imports and exports, Crete, 1918-1948; all ports, 1918-1924; and three major ports, 1925-1948

Year	Quantity (metric tons)		Value[a] (dollars)	
	Imports	Exports	Imports	Exports
1918			2,959,888	680,583
1919			3,192,593	932,992
1920			2,544,383	448,908
1921			1,160,965	491,798
1922			1,049,599	620,981
1923			1,018,482	364,621
1924			1,216,782	441,632
1925	58,775	35,385	4,754,229	4,543,736
1926	33,514	27,654	2,544,216	2,421,747
1927	34,689	30,104	2,845,012	2,972,026
1928	35,457	34,065	2,526,336	2,954,779
1929	48,882	42,006	3,338,408	4,043,634
1930	54,332	31,593	2,678,172	3,636,127
1931	52,566	28,478	2,145,832	2,949,338
1932	42,602	36,371	1,209,736	3,123,786
1933	40,452	55,499	1,261,869	3,343,266
1934	33,245	57,682	1,534,764	3,946,828
1935	44,762	47,424	1,863,421	4,614,693
1936	39,330	32,682	1,816,603	3,541,506
1937	41,738	40,126	2,310,673	4,531,303
1938	43,638	49,655	2,143,802	6,757,960
1939	36,049	55,168	1,433,395	6,689,773
1940	19,666	30,997	819,921	3,939,973
1941	5,901	4,533	—	—
1942	44	345	—	—
1943	1,667	144	—	—
1944	77	—	—	—
1945	1,024	247	178,556	29,474
1946	9,951	4,147	1,208,015	1,838,585
1947	9,999	26,550	1,009,931	4,786,798
1948 (6 mo.)	610	2,380	57,019	534,293

[a] Value computed on basis of exchange rates used by U.S. Department of Commerce, 1918-1924, and Federal Reserve Bank data, 1925-1948. See Appendix 5, Table 73.
Source: For 1918-1924 data: Bureau of Domestic and Foreign Commerce, *Report for April 3, 1926.* For 1925-1948 data: Office of International Trade, European Branch, U.S. Department of Commerce, compiled from *Bulletin mensuel du commerce spécial de la Grèce avec les pays étrangers,* December 1925-1947, June 1948.

TABLE A 107. Surfacing and construction of roads by types by nomes, Crete, 1948

	Miles of roads and proposed roads				
	Khania	Rethimnon	Iraklion	Lasithi	Total Crete
COMPLETED ROADS					
National	155	119	190	95	559
Provincial	114	28	52	17	211
Community	56	12	17	3	88
Total completed roads	325	159	259	115	858
SURFACING (completed roads)					
Asphalted					
National	38	34	54	23	149
Provincial	17	6	17	5	45
Community	—	—	1	—	1
Total asphalted	55	40	72	28	195
Macadamized					
National	117	85	131	72	405
Provincial	97	22	33	12	164
Community	44	12	13	3	72
Total macadamized	258	119	177	87	641
Covered with stone layer					
National	—	—	5	—	5
Provincial	—	—	2	—	2
Community	12	—	3	—	15
Total stone layer	12	—	10	—	22
Total surfacing	325	159	259	115	858
UNFINISHED ROADS					
National	13	14	32	29	88
Provincial	50	33	26	23	132
Community	14	35	18	11	78
Total unfinished roads	77	82	76	63	298
ROADS NOT YET BUILT					
National	49	33	42	68	192
Provincial	234	101	135	140	610
Community	—	—	—	—	—
Total roads not yet built	283	134	177	208	802

564   *APPENDIX 5*

TABLE A 107. (continued)

	Miles of roads and proposed roads				
	Khania	Rethimnon	Iraklion	Lasithi	Total Crete
PROJECTED ROADS					
National	217	166	264	192	839
Provincial	398	162	213	180	953
Community	70	47	35	14	166
TOTAL PROJECTED ROADS	685	375	512	386	1,958
Area in square miles	929	546	1,059	666	3,200

Source: Em. Kavgalakis, Inspector of Public Works, Khania, June 3, 1948.

TABLE A 108. Types of automotive vehicles by nomes, Crete, August 1948

Categories	Khania	Rethimnon	Iraklion	Lasithi	Total Crete
Trucks of public use (i.e. trucks owned by individuals or firms and plying for hire)	178	55	200	78	511
Buses of public use (i.e. buses owned and operated by individuals or firms for public use)	96	13	24	22	155
Passenger cars of public use (taxicabs)	56	8	43	13	120
Trucks of private use (i.e. trucks owned by various public departments or by factories, firms, etc. which serve exclusively the transportation needs of their owners)	46	8	28	21	103
Motorcycles	*	*	*	*	*
Passenger cars of private use (same as trucks of private use)	36	4	18	6	64
	412	88	313	140	953

* Motorcycles not given.
Source: I. Stambouzos, chief, Mechanological Dept., Crete, 1948.

TABLE A 109. Relative standard errors on estimated number of persons classified by age, Crete, 1948

Age Group	Communities		Municipalities		Island			
	Estimated Number of Persons	Relative Standard Error (per cent)	Estimated Number of Persons	Relative Standard Error (per cent)	Estimated Number of Persons	Relative Standard Error (per cent)	Per cent in age group	Relative Standard Error (per cent)
0-5	43,800	7	7,200	18	51,000	7	11	6
6-10	35,250	6	6,450	18	41,700	6	9	*
11-15	35,700	9	10,050	15	45,750	7	10	*
16-20	34,650	9	10,200	14	44,850	7	9	*
21-25	36,900	9	6,900	18	43,800	8	9	7
26-30	32,400	7	6,750	18	39,150	6	8	*
31-35	26,550	8	7,050	15	33,600	7	7	*
36-40	25,350	8	5,100	18	30,450	7	6	*
41-45	22,200	6	5,550	24	27,750	7	6	6
46-50	18,600	9	4,200	16	22,800	8	5	*
51-55	13,950	9	3,600	18	17,550	8	4	*
56-60	17,100	11	3,300	24	20,400	10	4	*
61-65	12,150	15	4,050	15	16,200	12	3	12
66-70	10,950	17	4,050	21	15,000	14	3	*
71-75	6,450	15	1,350	37	7,800	14	2	*
76-80	6,750	14	450	58	7,200	14	2	*
81-85	3,450	23	600	35	4,050	20	1	*
86-90	2,100	45	150	*	2,250	22	1	20
91-95	750	23	450	*	1,200	35	*	*
96-100	300	71	0	—	300	*	*	*
Total	385,350	1.96	87,450	5.69	472,800	1.91	—	—

* Not computed.
Source: Sample Survey of Crete, Form A, Household.

TABLE A 110. Relative standard errors of the estimated number of households and inhabitants, Crete, 1948

	Estimated Total Number of Households	Relative Standard Error (per cent)	Estimated Total Number of Inhabitants	Relative Standard Error (per cent)	Average No. Inhabitants per Household	Relative Standard Error (per cent)
COMMUNITIES						
Khania	21,900	3.56	100,350	3.68	4.59	3.45
Rethimnon	15,900	6.11	64,950	4.21	4.08	7.25
Iraklion	33,600	2.09	142,500	3.69	4.24	4.68
Lasithi	21,150	5.72	77,550	3.89	3.67	4.52
Total	92,550	2.02	385,350	1.96	4.17	2.51
MUNICIPALITIES						
Khania	8,400	7.14	34,200	11.55	4.07	6.36
Rethimnon	2,550	10.19	12,000	5.00	4.71	13.69
Iraklion	10,350	7.25	38,100	7.36	3.68	3.47
Ay. Nikolaos	900	0	3,150	30.20	3.50	30.18
Total	22,200	4.48	87,450	5.69	3.94	3.58
Total, Municipalities and Communities	114,750	1.85	472,800	1.91	4.12	2.14

Source: Sample Survey of Crete, Form A, Household.

INDEX